T0188965

Lecture Notes in Computer Science　　13362

More information about this series at https://link.springer.com/bookseries/558

Tommaso Di Noia · In-Young Ko ·
Markus Schedl · Carmelo Ardito (Eds.)

Web Engineering

22nd International Conference, ICWE 2022
Bari, Italy, July 5–8, 2022
Proceedings

 Springer

Editors
Tommaso Di Noia (iD)
Polytechnic University of Bari
Bari, Italy

Markus Schedl (iD)
Johannes Kepler University Linz
Linz, Austria

In-Young Ko (iD)
Korea Advanced Institute of Science
and Technology (KAIST)
Daejeon, Korea (Republic of)

Carmelo Ardito (iD)
Polytechnic University of Bari
Bari, Italy

ISSN 0302-9743   ISSN 1611-3349 (electronic)
Lecture Notes in Computer Science
ISBN 978-3-031-09916-8   ISBN 978-3-031-09917-5 (eBook)
https://doi.org/10.1007/978-3-031-09917-5

This Springer imprint is published by the registered company Springer Nature Switzerland AG
The registered company address is: Gewerbestrasse 11, 6330 Cham, Switzerland

Preface

The Web is a digital organism in constant evolution over the years and, in fact, is the largest living laboratory of new technologies and digital solutions. It is a pervasive place where most information flows through many different media on a global scale, and new ways of digital interaction are proposed and tested every day. The International Conference on Web Engineering (ICWE) aims to capture all the scientific aspects that revolve around these activities by bringing together researchers and professionals from various disciplines in the academic and industrial world.

The International Society of Web Engineering (ISWE) has been promoting ICWE since its inception and has contributed greatly to making it the flagship conference for web engineering.

Previous editions of ICWE took place in Biarritz, France (2021) [virtually], Helsinki, Finland (2020) [virtually], Daejeon, South Korea (2019), Cáceres, Spain (2018), Rome, Italy (2017), Lugano, Switzerland (2016), Rotterdam, The Netherlands (2015), Toulouse, France (2014), Aalborg, Denmark (2013), Berlin, Germany (2012), Paphos, Cyprus (2011), Vienna, Austria (2010), San Sebastian, Spain (2009), Yorktown Heights, USA (2008), Como, Italy (2007), Palo Alto, USA (2006), Sydney, Australia (2005), Munich, Germany (2004), Oviedo, Spain (2003), Santa Fe, Argentina (2002), and Cáceres, Spain (2001).

This volume contains the full research papers, short research papers, posters, demonstrations, PhD symposium papers, and tutorials of the 22nd International Conference on Web Engineering (ICWE 2022), held during July 5–8, 2022, in Bari, Italy.

ICWE 2022 focused on seven main research themes, namely, web big data and web data analytics, web application modeling and engineering, web security and privacy, web mining and knowledge extraction, recommender systems based on web technology, social web applications, and web user interfaces.

The ICWE 2022 edition received 81 submissions, out of which the Program Committee selected 23 full research papers (28% acceptance rate among papers submitted to the research track) and five short research papers (35% acceptance rate among papers submitted to the research track). Additionally, the Program Committee accepted six demonstrations and posters, and seven contributions to the PhD symposium. Also accepted were five tutorials: (1) Web Engineering with Human-in-the-Loop; (2) A Guide for Quantum Web Services Deployment; (3) SPARQL Endpoints and Web API (SWApi); (4) About Lightweight Code Generation; and (5) A for Advanced: Becoming An Aspect-Oriented Software Developer In A Day, along with three workshops: the 2nd International Workshop on Big data driven Edge Cloud Services (BEC 2022); the 1st International Workshop on the Semantic WEb of EveryThing (SWEET 2022); the 1st International Workshop on Web Applications for Life Sciences (WALS 2022).

The comprehensive program would not have been possible without the support of the many people that contributed to the successful organization of this event. We would like to thank all the chairs for their dedication and hard work, and the keynote speakers for enriching our program. Tommaso Di Noia wishes to warmly thank Carmelo Ardito,

In-Young Ko, and Markus Schedl for having gone beyond their duties as Proceedings and Program Chairs and having helped him in taking care of Maria Sole.

We are grateful to Springer for making possible the publication of this volume. Last but not least, we thank the reviewers for their hard work that allowed us to select the best papers to be presented at ICWE 2022, the authors that sent their work to ICWE 2022, and all the participants that contributed to the success of this conference.

July 2022

Tommaso Di Noia
In-Young Ko
Markus Schedl
Carmelo Ardito

Organization

Technical Committee

General Chair

Tommaso Di Noia   Polytechnic University of Bari, Italy

Program Chairs

In-Young Ko   Korea Advanced Institute of Science and Technology, South Korea

Markus Schedl   Johannes Kepler University and Linz Institute of Technology, Austria

Tutorials Chairs

Vito Walter Anelli   Polytechnic University of Bari, Italy

Alejandro Bellogin   Universidad Autónoma de Madrid, Spain

Workshops Chairs

Cinzia Cappiello   Politecnico di Milano, Italy

Azzurra Ragone   University of Bari, Italy

Demonstrations and Posters Chairs

Yashar Deldjoo   Polytechnic University of Bari, Italy

Irene Garrigos   University of Alicante, Spain

Marko Tkalcic   University of Primorska, Slovenia

PhD Symposium Chairs

Alessandro Bozzon   Delft University of Technology, The Netherlands

Fedelucio Narducci   Polytechnic University of Bari, Italy

Proceedings Chair

Carmelo Ardito   Polytechnic University of Bari, Italy

Publicity Chairs

Antonio Ferrara   Polytechnic University of Bari, Italy
Francesco Osborne   Open University, UK

Local Chairs

Domenico Lofù   Polytechnic University of Bari, Italy
Daniele Malitesta   Polytechnic University of Bari, Italy
Claudio Pomo   Polytechnic University of Bari, Italy

Program Committee

Ioannis Anagnostopoulos, Greece
Vito Walter Anelli, Italy
Carmelo Ardito, Italy
Myriam Arrue, Spain
Mohamed-Amine Baazizi, France
Marcos Baez, Italy
Maxim Bakaev, Russia
Luciano Baresi, Italy
Peter Bednar, Czech Republic
Alejandro Bellogin, Spain
Devis Bianchini, Italy
Matthias Book, Iceland
Gabriela Bosetti, UK
Alessandro Bozzon, The Netherlands
Marco Brambilla, Italy
Maxime Buron, France
Christoph Bussler, USA
Carlos Canal, Spain
Javier Luis Canovas Izquierdo, Spain
Cinzia Cappiello, Italy
Sven Casteleyn, Spain
Stefano Cereda, Italy
Richard Chbeir, France
Dickson K. W. Chiu, Hong Kong
Pieter Colpaert, Belgium
Oscar Corcho, Spain
Alexandra Cristea, UK
Yashar Deldjoo, Italy
Shridhar Devamane, India
Tommaso Di Noia, Italy
Oscar Diaz, Spain
Francisco Jose Dominguez Mayo, Spain
Tim Draws, The Netherlands

Schahram Dustdar, Austria
Jutta Eckstein, Germany
Antonio Ferrara, Italy
Maurizio Ferrari Dacrema, Italy
Sergio Firmenich, Argentina
Flavius Frasincar, The Netherlands
Piero Fraternali, Italy
Irene Garrigós, Spain
Cristina Gena, Italy
Daniela Godoy, Argentina
Hao Han, Japan
Jan Hidders, UK
Radu Tudor Ionescu, Romania
Epaminondas Kapetanios, UK
Tomi Kauppinen, Finland
Ralf Klamma, Germany
Alexander Knapp, Germany
In-Young Ko, South Korea
Nora Koch, Spain
Dominik Kowald, Austria
Maurizio Leotta, Italy
Elisabeth Lex, Austria
Faiza Loukil, France
Zakaria Maamar, United Arab Emirates
Yannis Manolopoulos, Greece
Maristella Matera, Italy
Santiago Melia, Spain
Tommi Mikkonen, Finland
Nathalie Moreno, Spain
Lourdes Moreno, Spain
Michael Mrissa, Slovenia
Juan Manuel Murillo Rodríguez, Spain
Martin Musicante, Brazil

Fedelucio Narducci, Italy
Jose Ignacio Panach Navarrete, Spain
Oscar Pastor, Spain
Cesare Pautasso, Switzerland
Vicente Pelechano, Spain
Alfonso Pierantonio, Italy
Marco Polignano, Italy
Nicoleta Preda, France
Azzurra Ragone, Italy
I. V. Ramakrishnan, USA
Raphael M. Reischuk, Switzerland
Werner Retschitzegger, Austria
Filippo Ricca, Italy
Thomas Richter, Germany
Tarmo Robal, Estonia
Gustavo Rossi, Argentina

Carmen Santoro, Italy
Markus Schedl, Austria
Abhishek Srivastava, India
Andrea Stocco, Switzerland
Zhu Sun, Australia
Kari Systä, Finland
Marko Tkalcic, Slovenia
Maria Trusca, Romania
William Van Woensel, Canada
Markel Vigo, UK
Erik Wilde, Switzerland
Manuel Wimmer, Austria
Marco Winckler, France
Yeliz Yesilada, Turkey
Nicola Zannone, The Netherlands
Gefei Zhang, Germany

ICWE 2022 Partners and Sponsors

Partners

Sponsors

Platinum

Gold

Contents

Recommender Systems Based on Web Technology

MARF: User-Item Mutual Aware Representation with Feedback 3
Qinqin Wang, Khalil Muhammad, Diarmuid O' Reilly-Morgan,
Barry Smyth, Elias Tragos, Aonghus Lawlor, Neil Hurley,
and Ruihai Dong

MRVAE: Variational Autoencoder with Multiple Relationships
for Collaborative Filtering 16
Zhou Pan, Wei Liu, and Jian Yin

Multilevel Feature Interaction Learning for Session-Based
Recommendation via Graph Neural Networks 31
Ming He, Tianshuo Han, and Tianyu Ding

Social Web Applications

A Real-Time System for Detecting Landslide Reports on Social Media
Using Artificial Intelligence 49
Ferda Ofli, Umair Qazi, Muhammad Imran, Julien Roch,
Catherine Pennington, Vanessa Banks, and Remy Bossu

Online Social Event Detection via Filtering Strategy Graph Neural Network ... 66
Lifu Chen, Junhua Fang, Pingfu Chao, An Liu, and Pengpeng Zhao

Similarity Search with Graph Index on Directed Social Network Embedding ... 82
Zhiwei Qi, Kun Yue, Liang Duan, and Zhihong Liang

Web Application Modelling and Engineering

An In-Depth Analysis of Web Page Structure and Efficiency with Focus
on Optimization Potential for Initial Page Load 101
Lucas Vogel and Thomas Springer

Automatic Web Data API Creation via Cross-Lingual Neural Pagination
Recognition 117
Chia-Hui Chang, Cheng-Ju Wu, and Tzu-Ping Lin

Disclosure: Efficient Instrumentation-Based Web App Migration
for Liquid Computing 132
    Jae-Yun Kim and Soo-Mook Moon

Enriching Scholarly Knowledge with Context 148
    Muhammad Haris, Markus Stocker, and Sören Auer

FAIRification of Citizen Science Data Through Metadata-Driven Web
API Development 162
    *Reynaldo Alvarez, César González-Mora, José Zubcoff, Irene Garrigós,
    Jose-Norberto Mazón, and Hector Raúl González Diez*

The Case for Cross-Entity Delta Encoding in Web Compression 177
    *Benjamin Wollmer, Wolfram Wingerath, Sophie Ferrlein, Fabian Panse,
    Felix Gessert, and Norbert Ritter*

Web Big Data and Web Data Analytics

Dynamic Network Embedding in Hyperbolic Space via Self-attention 189
    Dingyang Duan, Daren Zha, Xiao Yang, Nan Mu, and Jiahui Shen

Engineering Annotations to Support Analytical Provenance in Visual
Exploration Processes 204
    Maroua Tikat, Aline Menin, Michel Buffa, and Marco Winckler

Lunatory: A Real-Time Distributed Trajectory Clustering Framework
for Web Big Data 219
    *Yang Wu, Zhicheng Pan, Pingfu Chao, Junhua Fang, Wei Chen,
    and Lei Zhao*

Web Mining and Knowledge Extraction

Building Knowledge Subgraphs in Question Answering over Knowledge
Graphs 237
    Sareh Aghaei, Kevin Angele, and Anna Fensel

Dual-Attention Based Joint Aspect Sentiment Classification Model 252
    Ping Gu and Zhipeng Zhang

Explaining a Deep Neural Model with Hierarchical Attention
for Aspect-Based Sentiment Classification Using Diagnostic Classifiers 268
    Kunal Geed, Flavius Frasincar, and Maria Mihaela Truşcă

A Model for Meteorological Knowledge Graphs: Application
to Météo-France Data 283
Nadia Yacoubi Ayadi, Catherine Faron, Franck Michel, Fabien Gandon,
and Olivier Corby

An Ontological Approach for Recommending a Feature Selection
Algorithm 300
Aparna Nayak, Bojan Božić, and Luca Longo

Towards Bridging the Gap Between Knowledge Graphs and Chatbots 315
Annemarie Wittig, Aleksandr Perevalov, and Andreas Both

Web Security and Privacy

Configurable Per-Query Data Minimization for Privacy-Compliant Web
APIs 325
Frank Pallas, David Hartmann, Paul Heinrich, Josefine Kipke,
and Elias Grünewald

Effective Malicious URL Detection by Using Generative Adversarial
Networks 341
Jinbu Geng, Shuhao Li, Zhicheng Liu, Zhenyu Cheng, and Li Fan

MEMTD: Encrypted Malware Traffic Detection Using Multimodal Deep
Learning 357
Xiaotian Zhang, Jintian Lu, Jiakun Sun, Ruizhi Xiao, and Shuyuan Jin

Web User Interfaces

A Web Crowdsourcing Platform for Territorial Control in Smart Cities 375
Andrea Pazienza, Domenico Lofù, Giampaolo Flace, Marco Salzedo,
Pietro Noviello, Eugenio Di Sciascio, and Felice Vitulano

Supporting Natural Language Interaction with the Web 383
Marcos Baez, Cinzia Cappiello, Claudia M. Cutrupi,
Maristella Matera, Isabella Possaghi, Emanuele Pucci,
Gianluca Spadone, and Antonella Pasquale

User Acceptance of Modified Web Page Loading Based on Progressive
Streaming 391
Lucas Vogel and Thomas Springer

We Don't Need No Real Users?! Surveying the Adoption of User-less
Automation Tools by UI Design Practitioners 406
*Maxim Bakaev, Maximilian Speicher, Johanna Jagow, Sebastian Heil,
and Martin Gaedke*

Ph.D. Symposium

Achieving Corruption-Transparency in Service Governance Processes
with Blockchain-Technology Based e-Participation 417
Mohammad Mustafa Ibrahimy, Alex Norta, and Peeter Normak

Applying a Healthcare Web of Things Framework for Infertility Treatments ... 426
Anastasiia Gorelova and Santiago Meliá

Blockchain and AI to Build an Alzheimer's Risk Calculator 432
Paolo Sorino

Bridging Static Site Generation with the Dynamic Web 437
Juho Vepsäläinen and Petri Vuorimaa

Enhance Web-Components in Order to Increase Security
and Maintainability 443
Tobias Münch and Rainer Roosmann

FAIRification of Citizen Science Data 450
Reynaldo Alvarez Luna, José Zubcoff, Irene Garrigós, and Hector Gonz

Towards Differentially Private Machine Learning Models and Their
Robustness to Adversaries 455
Alberto Carlo Maria Mancino and Tommaso Di Noia

Posters and Demonstrations

A Metadata-Driven Tool for FAIR Data Production in Citizen Science
Platforms 465
*Reynaldo Alvarez, César González-Mora, Irene Garrigós,
and Jose Zubcoff*

A New Compatibility Measure for Harmonic EDM Mixing 469
Gabriel Bibbó Frau and Angel Faraldo

Compaz: Exploring the Potentials of Shared Dictionary Compression
on the Web 473
*Benjamin Wollmer, Wolfram Wingerath, Sophie Ferrlein, Felix Gessert,
and Norbert Ritter*

Social Events Analyzer (SEA): A Toolkit for Mining Social Workflows
by Means of Federated Process Mining 477
  Javier Rojo, José García-Alonso, Javier Berrocal, Juan Hernández,
  Juan M. Murillo, and Carlos Canal

Solid Web Monetization 481
  Merlijn Sebrechts, Tom Goethals, Thomas Dupont, Wannes Kerckhove,
  Ruben Taelman, Filip De Turck, and Bruno Volckaert

Web Push Notifications from Solid Pods 487
  Christoph H.-J. Braun and Tobias Käfer

Tutorials

A Guide for Quantum Web Services Deployment 493
  Jaime Alvarado-Valiente, Javier Romero-Álvarez, Jose Garcia-Alonso,
  and Juan M. Murillo

About Lightweight Code Generation 497
  Andreas Schmidt

SPARQL Endpoints and Web API (SWApi) 501
  Pasquale Lisena and Albert Meroño-Peñuela

Web Engineering with Human-in-the-Loop 505
  Dmitry Ustalov, Nikita Pavlichenko, Boris Tseytlin, Daria Baidakova,
  and Alexey Drutsa

Author Index 509

Recommender Systems Based on Web Technology

MARF: User-Item Mutual Aware Representation with Feedback

Qinqin Wang[✉], Khalil Muhammad, Diarmuid O' Reilly-Morgan,
Barry Smyth, Elias Tragos, Aonghus Lawlor, Neil Hurley, and Ruihai Dong

Insight Centre for Data Analytics, University College Dublin, Dublin, Ireland
{qinqin.wang,khalil.muhammad,diarmuid.oreillymorgan,barry.smyth,
elias.tragos,aonghus.lawlor,neil.hurley,ruihai.dong}@insight-centre.org

Abstract. As deep learning (DL) technologies have developed rapidly, many new techniques have become available for recommender systems. Yet, there is very little research addressing how users' feedback for particular items (such as ratings) can affect recommendations. This feedback can assist in building more fine-grained user profiles, as not all raw clicks will truly reflect a user's preference. The challenge of encoding such records, which are typically prohibitively long, also prevents research from considering using the whole click history to learn representations. To address these challenges, we propose MARF, a novel model for click prediction. Specifically, we construct fine-grained user representations (by considering both the multiple items browsed, and user's feedback on them) and item representations (by considering browsing histories from multiple users, and their feedback). Moreover, the flexible up-down strategy is designed to avoid loading incomplete or overloaded historical information by selecting representative users/items based on their feedback records. A comprehensive evaluation on three large scale real-world benchmark datasets, showing that MARF significantly outperforms a variety of state-of-the-art solutions. Furthermore, MARF model is evaluated through an ablation study that validates the contribution of each component. As a final demonstration, we show how MARF can be used for cross-domain recommendation.

Keywords: Click-through rate prediction · Deep learning · Cross domain recommendation

1 Introduction

Predicting whether users will click on ads or items is a crucial problem in online advertising and recommender systems, where accurate predictions drive increased customer satisfaction and ultimately improve revenues [2,16,21,22]. Interestingly, the trend is that most recent solutions adopt deep learning techniques for click prediction.

Capturing user interests and constructing user profiles is an essential recommendation task. Normally, user interests are encoded into user embeddings,

© Springer Nature Switzerland AG 2022
T. Di Noia et al. (Eds.): ICWE 2022, LNCS 13362, pp. 3–15, 2022.
https://doi.org/10.1007/978-3-031-09917-5_1

which are randomly initialised at first and then optimised against records of user click behaviour. This conventional approach, while simple, does not improve recommendation quality as much as more recent sophisticated methods that either employ a sequence-based neural network with attention mechanism [5,21,22] to capture deep user interests through their behaviour history, or Graph Neural Networks [15,17] to generate richer user representations that capture both general and current interests.

Scope. We are interested in recommendation models to maximise CTR where the primary input is a dataset of implicit feedback from interactions [4] (e.g. dwelling time, number of views), while also leveraging available user and item metadata.

Problem Statement. We believe that relying strictly on user behaviour or click sequences from implicit feedback may not fully represent user interests. Besides, people are normally "cheated" to click an item by the attractive title/cover of the item and end up being dissatisfied [19]. In the movie domain, for instance, a user might watch several films of a particular genre but like a few of them; see Fig 1. Some of the clicking (e.g. 98 out of 337 drama movies) does not match users' favourites. So there is an opportunity to mine click histories for additional input signals that can complement the default implicit feedback used for click prediction. Such signals could be item ratings (explicit). For the sake of simplicity, we will henceforth refer to such complementary signals as **feedback**.

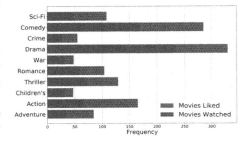

Fig. 1. Distribution of user preference cross different genres

In addition, much of the work in click-through rate (CTR) maximisation focuses on enriching user profiles to improve performance. So far, there is hardly any work that considers the whole click histories as a means of representing items. This is probably because it is more challenging to simultaneously encode long, dense histories for popular items and short click histories for fresh items in the long tail. This challenge also exists when building user profiles from click histories.

Therefore, to address these issues, we propose MARF, a new recommender for CTR maximisation that incorporates feedback when encoding user profiles. Through a novel flexible up-down sampling strategy, MARF is able to focus on representative interactions that produce richer representations to improve recommendation performance.

Contributions. The main contributions of this paper are:

- We introduce the feedback as an important feature that captures user and item properties from their interaction history.
- We propose MARF, a new recommender model for CTR maximisation that leverages feedback not only to produce richer user and item representations, but also to improve recommendation quality.
- Flexible up-down sampling strategy is proposed to choose representative users and items so that the computational costs and the impact of the long-tail problem are reduced.
- We conduct empirical tests to demonstrate the superiority of MARF over state-of-the-art models across multiple public datasets. We also present an ablation study to validate the utility of the various components in MARF.
- Finally, we show that MARF could potentially transfer knowledge across different domains with overlapping users or items.

2   The MARF Model

Our proposed, MARF model (depicted in Fig. 2) is split into three main components. Briefly, the modelling process starts from a set of inputs derived from user/item metadata and interactions. These inputs are used both to learn embeddings for users and items and as their feedback. Each user and item embedding

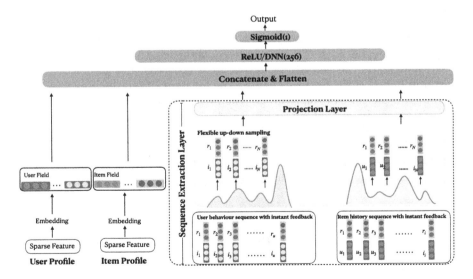

Fig. 2. The overall architecture of the proposed MARF model. The flexible up-down sampling strategy selects representative users/items with feedback to avoid loading incomplete/overloaded historical information. Projection Layer aims at projecting two different embedding into the same space and output the user/item representations

is concatenated with its matching feedback embedding. Separately, the *Sequence Extraction Layer* with our novel *flexible up-down sampling* strategy generates fine-grained representations from both user and item sequences. Finally, the outputs from the sequence extraction layer are merged with the embeddings learned from user/item side features and fed into a prediction output layer. In the rest of this section, we will describe these components in detail.

2.1 Model Inputs and Feature Representation

Overall, we use four forms of input for MARF, each composed from several sparse features. For any (u, i) interaction between user u and item i, we have these inputs: *UserProfile* provides a list of user attributes (e.g. gender, age, occupation) for the user u, whereas *ItemProfile* represents the features or metadata (e.g. color and category) of the item i. The *UserBehavior* is a sequence of (i_u, r_{ui}) tuples, where i_u is an item interacted with by the user u and r_{ui} is a feedback score (e.g. rating) assigned by the user u to item i. Similarly, *ItemHistory* is a sequence of (u_i, r_{iu}) pairs.

2.2 Embedding for User and Item Profiles

This component of MARF maps large sparse categorical features into low dense representations. In *UserProfile*, the k-th group of features such as occupation can be represented by $P_k \in \mathcal{R}^{V_k \times d_s}$, where V_k is the size of the sparse feature in *UserProfile* and d_s is the size of the sparse embedding. Similarly, in *ItemProfile*, the j-th group of features such as genres can be represented by $Q_j \in \mathcal{R}^{M_j \times d_s}$, where M_j is the size of the sparse features in *ItemProfile*.

At the same time, *UserBehavior* can be represented by $S_u = [i_1 : r_1; \ldots; i_{u_k} : r_{ui_k}; \ldots; i_{N_u} : r_{N_u}] \in \mathcal{R}^{N_u \times (d_i + d_r)}$, where N_u is the length of the user's behavior history, and i_{u_k} is the embedding of the item that the user interacts with at timestamp k, r_{ui_k} is the feedback embedding for item i from the user u, whereas d_i and d_r are the sizes of the item and the rating embedding respectively. Then we concatenate the embeddings of i_{u_k} and r_{ui_k} to construct user behavior at timestamp k. Similar to the *UserBehavior*, the *ItemHistory* is represented by $S_v = [u_1 : r_1; \ldots; u_k : r_{u_k i}; \ldots; u_{N_v} : r_{N_v}] \in \mathcal{R}^{N_v \times (d_u + d_r)}$, where N_v is the length of the item's history, u_k is the embedding of the user, and $r_{u_k i}$ is the feedback embedding for items i from the user u.

2.3 Flexible Up-Down Sampling

Most CTR models, including MARF, are characterised by a large number of parameters and are easily affected by the long-tail problem—80% of the data is comprised of information from only 20% of the users. For this reason, a large amount of the computational cost and the user and item historical sequence are significantly unbalanced. To tackle this problem, and improve memory consistency and computational efficiency, we propose the *flexible up-down sampling strategy*.

This flexible up-down sampling strategy is applied before each training step to reconstruct varying user and item historical sequences into a constant sequence. For instance, consider the example user profile in Fig. 1: a user is likely to have a propensity for certain kinds of items, thus we need not incorporate all items seen by the user into their behavior sequence. As such, for each user behavior sequence, we categorise items by their feedback (rating) and only sample a fraction of them per category as representative items. This operation is similar to the *stratified random sampling* [1] or *cluster-based sample* [20] that is commonly used to obtain representative samples from a set of entities. As a result, for any given entity (i.e. user or item) e, the size of their sequence—*UserBehavior* or *ItemHistory*—will be reconstructed to that of a constant sequence N. The number of samples we need to sample from each category is based on the portion of total number of interactions, such as $(N \times n_e^{(c)})/N_e$, where $n_e^{(c)}$ is the number of elements in category c and N_e is the total number of elements in the input sequence of the entity (i.e. user or item), whereas $N \in \mathbb{Z}^+$ is a hyper-parameter referring to the expected sequence length for the user or item that we need to reconstruct. It is important to note that the input sequence (user behaviour or item history) is concatenated with its respective feedback before the flexible up-down sampling strategy. Since different entities have different sequence lengths, the N hyper-parameter decides whether we perform an up-sampling or a down-sampling operation. If $N \geq N_e$, we up-sample, and if $N < N_u$ we down-sample.

Another noteworthy point is that not all users and items in datasets participate in the training process. This is because the flexible up-down sampler prioritises only representative users and items chosen from each category when reconstructing user and item sequence histories. For instance, Table 1 shows the percentage of users/items involved during the training process in three different datasets when the constant sequence length $N = 25$.

2.4   The Sequence Extraction Layer

To extract user interests, we begin from a set of item sequences with corresponding feedback, i.e. $S_u = [i_1 : r_1; \ldots ; i_{u_k} : r_{u_{i_k}}; \ldots ; i_{N_u} : r_{N_u}]$. After flexible up-down sampling to get the reconstructed sequence indicated as S_{un}, we pass this input through an MLP fusion layer to project the item and the feedback embeddings into the same space to get $SE_u = [e_1; \ldots ; e_i; \ldots ; e_N] \in \mathcal{R}^{N \times d_e}$, where d_e is the fusion embedding size and N is the constant sequence length. Then we sum pooling the produced embeddings, SE_u, as the output for the user u's behavior representations SE'_u. We adopt a similar workflow to generate item history representations SE'_v.

2.5   The Prediction Layer

In previous sections we described how MARF learns embeddings from user and item features where a feature (e.g. genre) has multiple values (e.g. crime, fiction), the embedding process (described in Sect. 2.2) learns separate embeddings for each feature value, and then the feature's embeddings are computed as the average of all the embeddings of its feature values. These transformed *profile embeddings* along with those learned by the Sequence Extraction Layer are then concatenated and fed into an MLP, with a final sigmoid function to predict the probability of the user liking an item.

We adopt the most widely used loss function in CTR prediction, the negative log-likelihood function defined as:

$$L = -\frac{1}{N} \sum_{(x,y) \in \mathcal{D}} (y \log p(x) + (1-y) \log(1-p(x))) \tag{1}$$

where $\mathcal{D}$ is the training set of size N, with x as input of the network, $y \in \{0,1\}$ represents if the user liked the item and $p(.)$ is the final output of the network representing the prediction probability that the user likes the item.

3   Experiments

In this section, we compare the performance of MARF against that of several *state-of-the-art* models on three public datasets. We conduct an ablation study to verify the efficacy of each MARF model component.

3.1   Datasets

For the purpose of availability, we select datasets containing explicit ratings as an feedback feature. Table 2 summarises the key statistics of the datasets.

The **Amazon dataset** [14] contains ratings, product reviews and metadata from Amazon, and is used as a benchmark dataset in [9]. We use a subset named *musical instrument* which contains 903,330 users and 112,222 items, 1,512,530 samples and 505 categories. Due to sparsity, we adopt the k-core pruning method [6] to filter short profiles and only keep users with at least 20 ratings. We include *item style*, *category*, and *price* as features during training.

We selected **ML1M** and **ML20M** due to their familiarity to recommender systems researchers. **ML1M** contains 6,040 unique users, 3,706 unique items and 1,000,209 samples. We use *genre*, *zipcode*, *gender*, *age*, and *occupation* as side

Table 1. Percentage of user/ item involved in training

Datasets	Involved users(%)	Involved items(%)
Amazon Music Instr.	98.39%	79.58%
ML1M	89.64%	89.43%
ML20M	38.16%	58.16%

Table 2. Statistics of datasets

Dataset	Users	Items	Features	Samples
Amazon Music Instr.	903,330	112,222	510	1,512,530
ML1M	6,040	3,706	26	1,000,209
ML20M	138,493	26,744	23	20,000,263

features. **ML20M** is composed of 138,493 users, 26,744 items and 20,000,263 samples. The *genre* attribute is used as a side feature.

The statistics of the above datasets are summarized in Table 2. For all datasets, we train test split based on [12,16] where we randomly select 80% of samples for training and split the rest into validation and test datasets with equal size. We use the validation dataset for hyper parameter tuning. Each experiment is repeated 5 times, and the average performance with standard deviation is reported on the hold out test dataset. For all datasets, we treat samples with a rating less than 3 as negative samples, taking the lower score to indicate user dislike. Similarly, we treat ratings greater than 3 as positive samples. Samples with a rating of 3 are treated as neutral and removed from all datasets.

3.2 Baselines

In this section, we introduce the *state-of-the-art* baseline models chosen for comparison with MARF:

- **CCPM** [13] uses convolutional layers to capture partial dependencies between input features. It also turns the pooling layer into flexible p-max pooling to deal with flexible length of input.
- **NFM** [10] uses a second-order interaction layer called bi-interaction and a sum pooling layer to capture high-order feature interactions.
- **Wide&Deep** [2] is popular in production, and uses a wide network for cross product features while learning feature dependencies in its deep network.
- **DeepFM** [8] is an enhanced version of Wide&Deep where the wide part is replaced by a factorization machine.
- **AutoInt** [16] employs a self-attention mechanism to learn higher-order feature interactions.
- **FiBiNet** [12] learns feature importances using a Squeeze-Excitation Network (SENET), and feature interactions using inner product and hadamard product.
- **DIN** [22] uses local activation units to learn user interest representations from click histories.
- **DIEN** [21] employs an interest extractor (GRU) layer to capture users' temporal interests and an interest evolving layer (attention mechanism) to capture the change in interest that is relative to the target item.
- **AFN** [3] propose a new framework to learn arbitrary-order cross features adaptively from data so as to learn useful cross features from data adaptively, and the maximum order can be delivered on the fly.

3.3 Evaluation Metrics

We use two metrics in our evaluation: *AUC* and *Log Loss*.

- **AUC**: is a widely accepted metric for CTR tasks. It measures the probability that a random positive sample is ranked ahead of a random negative one [7]. A higher score denotes better performance.

- **Log loss**: is widely used in machine learning for binary classification tasks. It measures the difference between two distributions. The lower bound of log loss is 0, which indicates that there is no difference between two distributions. The lower value indicates better performance.

It is noteworthy that, in CTR prediction tasks, a slightly higher AUC or a lower log loss results in a significant boost for production systems [8,18].

3.4   Hyperparameters

In all embedding layers, regardless of the evaluation dataset, the dimension of the *feedback, user ID* and *item ID* is fixed at 200. We apply a one layer MLP for both user and item sequence extraction layer where the size is 256. The dimension of other sparse features is 56. For ML1M datasets, the model converges around 100 epochs, while the other datasets are run for 130 epochs.

Hyperparameter Search. We conducted a grid search on the ML1M dataset to find the constant sequence length value N. Figure 3 shows the AUC score and log loss on the validation split. Clearly, for ML1M, $N = 25$ has the highest AUC score, and its log loss is within bounds of the lowest log loss observed during the grid search. We keep the same constant length value for other the two datasets. For the optimization method, we use Adam with a mini-batch size of 1024 for both ML1M and ml20m, and 256 for amazon musical instrument dataset. The learning rate is set to 0.0001. The DNN layers are set to 2 with the size of the middle layer set as 256. The hidden layer activation function is ReLU and sigmoid is used for the output. For all baseline models, we apply Adam learning algorithm with the learning rate $\lambda = 0.001$. In the output layer of all baselines models, we apply two layers of DNN hidden units with sizes of 256 and 128 respectively. With the AutoInt, we apply a 3 layer attention structure with two heads for training to achieve the best results. We fine-tuning all baseline models with sparse feature dimension at parameters [4, 6, 8, 10, 15] and report the best results in validation set with dimension setting (after each result of the

Table 3. Performance comparison between MARF and eight baselines, showing MARF's superiority across three datasets.

Model	ML1M		Amazon review		ML20 M	
	AUC	Log loss	AUC	Log loss	AUC	Log loss
CCPM	0.8657 ± 0.002 (15)	0.4058 ± 0.0058	0.8029 ± 0.0117 (15)	0.2882 ± 0.037	0.8825 ± 0.0008 (10)	0.3491 ± 0.001
NFM	0.8843 ± 0.0008 (4)	0.3436 ± 0.0034	0.8239 ± 0.0115 (4)	0.2717 ± 0.0134	0.886 ± 0.0011 (4)	0.3481 ± 0.0038
WideDeep	0.8864 ± 0.0007 (4)	0.3339 ± 0.0023	0.8424 ± 0.0086 (8)	0.234 ± 0.0159	0.8875 ± 0.0003 (8)	0.3395 ± 0.0011
DeepFM	0.8854 ± 0.0012 (4)	0.3343 ± 0.0026	0.8297 ± 0.0083 (4)	0.312 ± 0.0343	0.8878 ± 0.0006 (4)	0.3426 ± 0.0009
DIN	0.8625 ± 0.0011 (8)	0.3343 ± 0.0017	0.8219 ± 0.0093 (8)	0.2650 ± 0.0137	0.8762 ± 0.0013 (8)	0.3432 ± 0.0003
DIEN	0.8723 ± 0.0039 (8)	0.3371 ± 0.0003	0.8135 ± 0.0086 (8)	0.3019 ± 0.0235	0.8804 ± 0.0002 (8)	0.3522 ± 0.0028
AutoInt	0.8863 ± 0.001 (4)	0.3355 ± 0.0022	0.8279 ± 0.0064 (10)	0.3051 ± 0.0327	0.8867 ± 0.0004 (10)	0.3444 ± 0.002
FiBiNet	0.8821 ± 0.0009 (10)	0.3852 ± 0.0033	0.8244 ± 0.0099 (10)	0.3486 ± 0.0205	0.8855 ± 0.0005 (10)	0.357 ± 0.0034
AFN	0.8884 ± 0.0008 (10)	0.3264 ± 0.0015	0.8206 ± 0.0049 (10)	0.1972 ± 0.0072	0.8871 ± 0.0003 (15)	0.3307 ± 0.0007
MARF (our)	$\mathbf{0.8968 \pm 0.0007}$	$\mathbf{0.3193 \pm 0.0005}$	$\mathbf{0.8462 \pm 0.0137}$	$\mathbf{0.1682 \pm 0.0113}$	$\mathbf{0.8958 \pm 0.0021}$	$\mathbf{0.3242 \pm 0.0003}$

AUC score), are shown in Table 3. The code used for this work is available on github.com[1]

3.5 Performance Comparison

In this section, we summarize the hold-out test performance of the selected algorithms on the ML1M, ML20M and Amazon datasets. For all baselines, we use the validation dataset for hyper parameter tuning, and report results on the hold out test dataset. From the results, shown in Table 3, it is clear that MARF significantly outperforms the baseline models on both the ML1M and Amazon datasets. For the ML20M dataset, all baseline models achieve similar performance, but MARF outperforms them marginally.

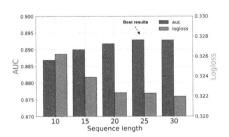

Fig. 3. Grid search sequence length for sampling

3.6 Ablation Study

Despite demonstrating strong empirical results, so far we have not isolated the specific contribution of each component of MARF. In this section we conduct an ablation study with the ML1M dataset. Table 4 shows the results of testing different components in MARF. Firstly, we seek to evaluate the impact of the up-down flexible sampling strategy. We only utilize each user and item rating sequence, sorted by their timestamps to construct $UserBehavior$ and $ItemHistory$. Rather than using the whole user and item sequence profile, we choose the latest session and a random session of each user/item profile where we keep session length $N = 25$ as the input for the sequence extractor layer. Then we put the generated representations into a 2 layer MLP after concatenation. In Table 4, the RS indicates that the model only uses rating feature sequences as input. Compared to using either the latest, or a random sequence, the up-down flexible strategy outperforms the baselines significantly.

To explore the impact of the feedback feature, we choose the popular neural collaborative filtering model [11] as a base model. It uses trained user/item embedding pairs as the input to an MLP prediction layer, and achieves 0.8649 AUC score and 0.3589 log loss on our test set. Then we average each user/item rating in their profile as the overall feedback feature and concatenate them with their embedding as the MLP prediction input, and the performance improves slightly. After changing to our proposed sequence extraction layer with up-down flexible sample strategy to generate user and item embeddings, the performance substantially improves. With additional side features, we get our final reported

---

[1] https://github.com/doubleblind3372857384/MARF.

Table 4. The performance of different components in MARF

Model	AUC	Log loss
RS-Last Sequence	0.827	0.3924
RS-Random Sequence	0.827	0.3931
RS-up-down flexible sampling	**0.8546**	**0.3649**
Base Model	0.8649	0.3585
Base Model with Feedback	0.8694	0.3523
MARF without Side Features	0.8814	0.3379
MARF	**0.8961**	**0.3158**

results using the MARF model. We can take the following observations from the results in Table 4:

- Flexible up-down sample strategy is necessary for MARF: we can see that the performance drops significantly when it is replaced with the other two methods.
- MARF's user and item representations are superior to randomly initialized embeddings from the NCF model.

3.7   Potential Transferability Analysis

So far, we have described MARF and demonstrated its ability to learn more informative user and item representations. The user representations are learned by combining user features, implicit interaction data from item and feedback signals. Item representations are learned in a similar manner but from item metadata, interaction histories from user, and feedback signals. These rich representations present an opportunity to apply MARF in a transfer learning scenario where two domain datasets have overlapping users or items. For example, commodities could appear in two different platforms, while the *ItemHistories* vary cross different platforms. One platform has a lot of interactions on items called luxury platform while the other has few called sparse platform. Because items in sparse platform have less user interactions which is hard for model to generate informative information, we use the luxury platform datasets to train MARF to get the item representations apply on sparse platform datasets. On the user representations, we can utilise pre-trained item embeddings from luxury platform and user *UserBehavior* from sparse platform to generate user embeddings.

Table 5. The analysis of transferability of the MARIF without side features

Datasets	AUC score	Log loss
ML100 K	0.8585	0.3759
ML1M	0.8869	0.3159
ML1M to ML100 K	0.7934	0.4409

Accordingly, we conduct the following experiments on ML100 K and ML1 M, which share 1,236 overlapping items—while excluding item metadata and features—to test the transferability of the model. We use ML1M dataset to pretrain the MARF model and then use the ML100 K dataset for evaluation. Without training the model using the ML100 K dataset, we get an AUC score of **0.7934** and a log loss of **0.4409** on the ML100 K test set. Table 5 shows a comparison of the performance between the MARF models trained with and without transferability on two datasets ML100 K, ML1M. It also demonstrates the performance of applying pre-trained embedding from ML1M to ML100 K. Although directly applying pre-trained embeddings from ML1M to ML100 K compromises the performance, it is acceptable compared to the cost of re-training the model.

4   Conclusion and Future Work

In this paper, we proposed a novel deep network method, namely MARF, to model user and item representations. MARF not only enhances the resulting user and item representations, but also leads to a significant improvement on the CTR task. To that end, we designed a flexible up-down sample strategy to sample both representative user and item sequences with feedback, while maintaining the original distribution of user/item rating habits, and also keeps the implicit properties of items/users in different rating categories. Using the projection layer to project the embeddings into the same space and utilizing average sum method to get the final representation of users and items. Their representation becomes more informative than random initialized and easier for CTR prediction task. Last but not least, we show a potential application to transfer learning, if cross domain datasets have either overlapping users or items. In future work, we will try to integrate implicit data which can reflect both user attitudes and item properties.

Acknowledgements. This research is supported by Science Foundation Ireland through the Insight Centre for Data Analytics.

References

1. Aoyama, H.: A study of stratified random sampling. Ann. Inst. Stat. Math. **6**(1), 1–36 (1954)
2. Cheng, H., et al.: Wide & deep learning for recommender systems. In: Karatzoglou, A., et al. (eds.) Proceedings of the 1st Workshop on Deep Learning for Recommender Systems, DLRS@RecSys 2016, Boston, MA, USA, 15 September 2016, pp. 7–10. ACM (2016)
3. Cheng, W., Shen, Y., Huang, L.: Adaptive factorization network: learning adaptive-order feature interactions. In: The Thirty-Fourth AAAI Conference on Artificial Intelligence, AAAI 2020, The Thirty-Second Innovative Applications of Artificial Intelligence Conference, IAAI 2020, The Tenth AAAI Symposium on Educational Advances in Artificial Intelligence, EAAI 2020, New York, NY, USA, 7–12 February 2020, pp. 3609–3616. AAAI Press (2020)

4. Covington, P., Adams, J., Sargin, E.: Deep neural networks for youtube recommendations. In: Sen, S., Geyer, W., Freyne, J., Castells, P. (eds.) Proceedings of the 10th ACM Conference on Recommender Systems, Boston, MA, USA, 15–19 September 2016, pp. 191–198. ACM (2016)
5. Feng, Y., et al.: Deep session interest network for click-through rate prediction. In: Kraus, S. (ed.) Proceedings of the Twenty-Eighth International Joint Conference on Artificial Intelligence, IJCAI 2019, Macao, China, 10–16 August 2019, pp. 2301–2307 (2019). ijcai.org
6. Fu, W., Peng, Z., Wang, S., Xu, Y., Li, J.: Deeply fusing reviews and contents for cold start users in cross-domain recommendation systems. In: The Thirty-Third AAAI Conference on Artificial Intelligence, AAAI 2019, Honolulu, Hawaii, USA, 27 January - 1 February 2019, pp. 94–101. AAAI Press (2019)
7. Graepel, T., Candela, J.Q., Borchert, T., Herbrich, R.: Web-scale bayesian click-through rate prediction for sponsored search advertising in microsoft's bing search engine. In: Fürnkranz, J., Joachims, T. (eds.) Proceedings of the 27th International Conference on Machine Learning, ICML 2010, Haifa, Israel, 21–24 June 2010, pp. 13–20. Omnipress (2010)
8. Guo, H., Tang, R., Ye, Y., Li, Z., He, X.: Deepfm: a factorization-machine based neural network for CTR prediction. In: Sierra, C. (ed.) Proceedings of the Twenty-Sixth International Joint Conference on Artificial Intelligence, IJCAI 2017, Melbourne, Australia, 19–25 August 2017, pp. 1725–1731 (2017). ijcai.org
9. He, R., McAuley, J.J.: Ups and downs: modeling the visual evolution of fashion trends with one-class collaborative filtering. In: Bourdeau, J., Hendler, J., Nkambou, R., Horrocks, I., Zhao, B.Y. (eds.) Proceedings of the 25th International Conference on World Wide Web, WWW 2016, Montreal, Canada, 11–15 April 2016, pp. 507–517. ACM (2016)
10. He, X., Chua, T.: Neural factorization machines for sparse predictive analytics. In: Kando, N., Sakai, T., Joho, H., Li, H., de Vries, A.P., White, R.W. (eds.) Proceedings of the 40th International ACM SIGIR Conference on Research and Development in Information Retrieval, Shinjuku, Tokyo, Japan, 7–11 August 2017, pp. 355–364. ACM (2017)
11. He, X., Liao, L., Zhang, H., Nie, L., Hu, X., Chua, T.: Neural collaborative filtering. In: Barrett, R., Cummings, R., Agichtein, E., Gabrilovich, E. (eds.) Proceedings of the 26th International Conference on World Wide Web, WWW 2017, Perth, Australia, 3–7 April 2017, pp. 173–182. ACM (2017)
12. Huang, T., Zhang, Z., Zhang, J.: Fibinet: combining feature importance and bilinear feature interaction for click-through rate prediction. In: Bogers, T., Said, A., Brusilovsky, P., Tikk, D. (eds.) Proceedings of the 13th ACM Conference on Recommender Systems, RecSys 2019, Copenhagen, Denmark, 16–20 September 2019, pp. 169–177. ACM (2019)
13. Liu, Q., Yu, F., Wu, S., Wang, L.: A convolutional click prediction model. In: Bailey, J., et al. (eds.) Proceedings of the 24th ACM International Conference on Information and Knowledge Management, CIKM 2015, Melbourne, VIC, Australia, 19–23 October 2015, pp. 1743–1746. ACM (2015)
14. Ni, J., Li, J., McAuley, J.J.: Justifying recommendations using distantly-labeled reviews and fine-grained aspects. In: Inui, K., Jiang, J., Ng, V., Wan, X. (eds.) Proceedings of the 2019 Conference on Empirical Methods in Natural Language Processing and the 9th International Joint Conference on Natural Language Processing, EMNLP-IJCNLP 2019, Hong Kong, China, 3–7 November 2019, pp. 188–197. Association for Computational Linguistics (2019)

15. Scarselli, F., Gori, M., Tsoi, A.C., Hagenbuchner, M., Monfardini, G.: The graph neural network model. IEEE Trans. Neural Netw. **20**(1), 61–80 (2009)
16. Song, W., et al.: Autoint: automatic feature interaction learning via self-attentive neural networks. In: Zhu, W., et al. (eds.) Proceedings of the 28th ACM International Conference on Information and Knowledge Management, CIKM 2019, Beijing, China, 3–7 November 2019, pp. 1161–1170. ACM (2019)
17. Wang, H., Zhang, F., Zhao, M., Li, W., Xie, X., Guo, M.: Multi-task feature learning for knowledge graph enhanced recommendation. In: Liu, L., et al. (eds.) The World Wide Web Conference, WWW 2019, San Francisco, CA, USA, 13–17 May 2019, pp. 2000–2010. ACM (2019)
18. Wang, R., Fu, B., Fu, G., Wang, M.: Deep & cross network for ad click predictions. CoRR abs/1708.05123 (2017)
19. Wang, W., Feng, F., He, X., Zhang, H., Chua, T.: "Click" is not equal to "like": Counterfactual recommendation for mitigating clickbait issue. CoRR abs/2009.09945 (2020)
20. Yen, S.J., Lee, Y.S.: Cluster-based under-sampling approaches for imbalanced data distributions. Expert Syst. Appl. **36**(3), 5718–5727 (2009)
21. Zhou, G., et al.: Deep interest evolution network for click-through rate prediction. In: The Thirty-Third AAAI Conference on Artificial Intelligence, AAAI 2019, Honolulu, Hawaii, USA, 27 January - 1 February 2019, pp. 5941–5948. AAAI Press (2019)
22. Zhou, G., et al.: Deep interest network for click-through rate prediction. CoRR abs/1706.06978 (2017)

MRVAE: Variational Autoencoder with Multiple Relationships for Collaborative Filtering

Zhou Pan[1,2], Wei Liu[1,2(✉)], and Jian Yin[1,2]

[1] School of Computer Science and Engineering, Sun Yat-sen University, Guangzhou, China
panzh8@mail2.sysu.edu.cn, {liuw259,issjyin}@mail.sysu.edu.cn
[2] Guangdong Key Laboratory of Big Data Analysis and Processing, Guangzhou 510006, People's Republic of China

Abstract. Variational Autoencoder (VAE)-based collaborative filtering (VAE-based CF) methods have shown their effectiveness in top-N recommendation. Mult-VAE is one of them that achieves state-of-the-art performance. Multinomial likelihood and additional hyperparameter β on the KL divergence term controlling the strength of regularization make Mult-VAE a strong baseline. However, Mult-VAE uses non-linear MLPs as its encoder and decoder, which will boost the performance on the dense datasets but degrade the performance on the sparse datasets in our experiments. While recent studies shed light on the non-linearity for modeling the relationships between users and items, they ignore the importance of linearity between users and items, especially on the sparse datasets. To bridge the gap and consider both the *linearity and non-linearity user-item relationships*, we design a hybrid encoder that incorporates both linearity and non-linearity, and use a linear decoder for VAE-based CF, which can achieve competitive performance on both sparse and dense datasets. Moreover, most VAE-based CF methods only consider the relationships between users and items but ignore the relationships between items for improving the performance in collaborative filtering. To overcome this limitation, we try to incorporate *item-item relationships* into VAE-based CF with the help of cosine similarity between items. Unifying these relationships into VAE-based CF forms our proposed method, Variational Autoencoder with Multiple Relationships (MRVAE) for collaborative filtering. Extensive experiments on several dense and sparse datasets show the effectiveness of MRVAE.

Keywords: Recommendation · Variational Autoencoders · Collaborative filtering

This work is supported by the National Natural Science Foundation of China (U1911203, 61902439, 61902438, U1811264, U1811262), Guangdong Basic and Applied Basic Research Foundation (2021A1515011902, 2019A1515011159, 2019A1515011704), National Science Foundation for Post-Doctoral Scientists of China underGrant (2019M663237), Macao Young Scholars Program (UMMTP2020-MYSP-016), the Key-Area Research and Development Program of Guangdong Province (2020B0101100001).

T. Di Noia et al. (Eds.): ICWE 2022, LNCS 13362, pp. 16–30, 2022.
https://doi.org/10.1007/978-3-031-09917-5_2

1   Introduction

Recommender Systems (RSs) are widely used in many platforms, such as e-commerce, music apps, short videos platform and so on. RSs can help recommend items to users according to their personalized preferences. Collaborative filtering (CF) is an effective recommendation method for mining users' personalized preferences [15], given the implicit feedback data of user, e.g., click and purchase. CF methods mainly use the similarity pattern (relationships) across users and items for recommendations [10]. Recently, top-N recommendation with CF has become prevalent in current researches [5,19].

Among the top-N recommendation CF methods, Variational Autoencoder (VAE)-based methods, such as Mult-VAE [10], have achieved state-of-the-art performance. Mult-VAE resembles the structure of common VAE but with some changes: (1) additional hyperparameter β is introduced to the Kullback-Leibler (KL) divergence term for controlling the regularization; (2) multinomial likelihood is used for model training. While these changes are helpful in boosting the recommendation performance in dense datasets, where each user has multiple interactions on average, Mult-VAE achieves a poor performance in relatively sparse datasets [4]. We attribute the performance degradation in sparse datasets to the improper design of model structure: non-linear encoder and decoder with neural networks. The non-linear structure makes Mult-VAE capture *only* the non-linearity relationships between users and items, but ignore the linearity relationships between users and items, which are important when the data is sparse [11]. Recent study [13] shows that it is not wise to adopt non-linear MLPs as the interaction function between users and items, compared with the dot product, which indicates that the non-linear decoder used in Mult-VAE may be burdensome and unnecessary and a linear decoder is desired.

While Mult-VAE considers only the relationships between users and items, other relationships are lack of mining, e.g., item-item relationships. Item-item relationships are proved significant for performance improvement in some neighbor-based CF methods [1,15,16]. For instance, item-based CF is effective in early rating prediction task [16]. They use the cosine similarity, the Pearson correlation coefficient, or the ajusted cosine similarity to compute the similarity between items. The calculated item-item similarity is used to select the most similar items for rating prediction of the target item. We argue that such item-item similarity can also be used in VAE-based CF to boost the recommendation performance.

To combine the linearity and non-linearity user-item relationships, and item-item relationships into a unified VAE-based framework, we propose a VAE-based CF model called Variational Autoencoder with Multiple Relationships (MRVAE) for CF. Firstly, we design a hybrid encoder that combines linear structure and non-linear structure in parallel with self-attention. Then we simplify the non-linear MLPs of the decoder in Mult-VAE into a linear single-layer neural network that contains merely the weight and bias. Finally, we use the cosine similarity to calculate the item-item similarity and select the top-M most similar items of each interacted item for model training. To the best of our knowledge, MRVAE is the first VAE-based CF that considers these three relationships at a unified model.

To sum up, the main contributions of this paper are summarized as follows:

– We propose a model termed MRVAE to incorporate the linearity and non-linearity user-item relationships, and item-item relationships in a unified model.
– We design an asymmetric model structure, including a hybrid encoder and a linear decoder.
– We try to incorporate item-item relationships into MRVAE through calculating the item-item similarity with the cosine similarity, and selecting the top-M most similar items of each interacted item for model training.
– We perform extensive experiments to show the effectiveness of MRVAE, compared to other variants of VAE-based CF methods and other state-of-the-art recommendation methods.

2 Preliminary

In this section, we will first introduce the notations used in this paper. Then, the problem definition is presented. Finally, the basics of Mult-VAE will be introduced.

2.1 Notations

Notations used in this paper are summarized in Table 1. We will use bold lower-case letter to denote the vector, and bold upper-case letter to denote the matrix by default. Further notations will be introduced when necessary in the later section.

2.2 Problem Definition

We consider the implicit feedback setting as in many other literatures for top-N recommendation. Our problem of top-N recommendation can be formulated as follows: given a user $u \in \mathcal{U}$ and u's interacted items, denoted by N_u, the goal is to design a personalized recommendation method that can recommend the top-N items user u most probably prefers among items user u has not interacted with, i.e., $\mathcal{I} \backslash N_u$. For the binary matrix $\boldsymbol{X} \in \mathbb{R}^{|\mathcal{U}| \times |\mathcal{I}|}$, a positive value (i.e., 1) of its entry indicates that there is an interaction between the user and the item, while a value 0 indicates the opposite.

2.3 Basics of Mult-VAE

Model Description. Mult-VAE is originally a generative model, which models the generative process of user's interaction data. As a latent factor model, Mult-VAE assumes that the user's interaction data is generated from a latent variable. Figure 1 shows the graphical model of Mult-VAE. Taking user u as an example, the generative process of u's interaction data can be described as follows:

Table 1. Notations.

Symbols	Explanation
$\mathcal{U}$	The set of users
$\mathcal{I}$	The set of items
X	User-item interaction matrix, a sparse binary matrix
$\mathbf{x}_u$	Interaction vector of user u, $\mathbf{x}_u \in \mathbb{R}^{|\mathcal{I}|}$
$\mathbf{z}_u$	Latent vector of user u

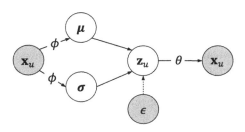

Fig. 1. Graphical model of Mult-VAE [10]. The shaded nodes are observed variables while the transparent nodes are latent.

(1) The model samples a latent representation of user u, $\mathbf{z}_u$, from a Gaussian prior;
(2) A *non-linear* function $f_\theta(\cdot)$ (usually MLPs), with $\mathbf{z}_u$ as input, is used to produce a probability $\boldsymbol{\pi}_u$ over $|\mathcal{I}|$ items;
(3) The user u's interaction vector, $\mathbf{x}_u$, is drawn from the multinomial distribution parameterized by $\boldsymbol{\pi}_u$.

Specifically, the generative process $\mathbf{x}_u$ can be formulated as follows:

$$\mathbf{z}_u \sim \mathcal{N}(\mathbf{0}, \boldsymbol{I}), \quad \boldsymbol{\pi}_u = \text{softmax}(f_\theta(\mathbf{z}_u)), \quad \mathbf{x}_u \sim \text{Mult}(n_u, \boldsymbol{\pi}_u). \tag{1}$$

n_u denotes the number of interacted items of user u. $\text{Mult}(n_u, \boldsymbol{\pi}_u)$ represents the multinomial distribution parameterized by n_u and $\boldsymbol{\pi}_u$. The multinomial likelihood for user u is:

$$\log p_\theta(\mathbf{x}_u \mid \mathbf{z}_u) \overset{c}{=} \sum_i \mathbf{x}_{ui} \log \boldsymbol{\pi}_{ui}. \tag{2}$$

$\mathbf{x}_{ui}$ and $\boldsymbol{\pi}_{ui}$ are the i's element in $\mathbf{x}_u$ and $\boldsymbol{\pi}_u$, respectively.

Variational Inference. According to the Variational Inference [6], Mult-VAE introduces a variational distribution $q_\phi(\mathbf{z}_u \mid \mathbf{x}_u)$ with parameter ϕ to help learn the model parameters $\boldsymbol{\theta}$ in Eq. (1). Specifically, $q_\phi(\mathbf{z}_u \mid \mathbf{x}_u)$ is used to approximate the intractable posterior distribution $p_\theta(\mathbf{z}_u \mid \mathbf{x}_u)$, and the Evidence Lower BOund (ELBO) can be derived as follows:

$$\mathcal{L}(\boldsymbol{\theta}, \boldsymbol{\phi}; \mathbf{x}_u) = \mathbb{E}_{q_\phi(\mathbf{z}_u|\mathbf{x}_u)}[\log p_\theta(\mathbf{x}_u \mid \mathbf{z}_u)] - \beta \cdot D_{KL}(q_\phi(\mathbf{z}_u \mid \mathbf{x}_u) \| p_\theta(\mathbf{z}_u)), \tag{3}$$

where $\log p_\theta(\mathbf{x}_u \mid \mathbf{z}_u)$ refers to the negative reconstruction error, $D_{KL}(\cdot \| \cdot)$ refers to the KL divergence between two distributions, $p_\theta(\mathbf{z}_u)$ refers to the prior distribution, and β is introduced to control the strength of the regularization, i.e., the KL divergence term $D_{KL}(q_\phi(\mathbf{z}_u \mid \mathbf{x}_u) \| p_\theta(\mathbf{z}_u))$. To calculate Eq. (3) analytically, we need to calculate $D_{KL}(q_\phi(\mathbf{z}_u \mid \mathbf{x}_u) \| p_\theta(\mathbf{z}_u))$ and $\mathbb{E}_{q_\phi(\mathbf{z}_u \mid \mathbf{x}_u)}[\log p_\theta(\mathbf{x}_u \mid \mathbf{z}_u)]$, respectively. When the prior $p_\theta(\mathbf{z}_u)$ is a standard Gaussian distribution, the KL divergence term $D_{KL}(q_\phi(\mathbf{z}_u \mid \mathbf{x}_u) \| p_\theta(\mathbf{z}_u))$ can be calculated analytically. $\mathbb{E}_{q_\phi(\mathbf{z}_u \mid \mathbf{x}_u)}[\log p_\theta(\mathbf{x}_u \mid \mathbf{z}_u)]$ can be calculated with Eq. (2). However, $\mathbf{z}_u$ needs to be sampled from the variational distribution $q_\phi(\mathbf{z}_u \mid \mathbf{x}_u)$ and the sampling process is non-differentiable, which blocks the backpropagation with gradient descent. To solve the problem, the *reparameterization trick* [9,14] is introduced: $\mathbf{z}_u = \mu_\phi(\mathbf{x}_u) + \boldsymbol{\epsilon} \odot \Sigma_\phi(\mathbf{x}_u)$. $\mu_\phi(\mathbf{x}_u)$ and $\Sigma_\phi(\mathbf{x}_u)$ together are the encoder of VAE, implemented by non-linear MLPs. They produce the mean vector and variance vector (diagonal elements of the covariance matrix) of $q_\phi(\mathbf{z}_u \mid \mathbf{x}_u)$. $\boldsymbol{\epsilon}$ is sampled from standard Gaussian $\mathcal{N}(\mathbf{0} \mid \boldsymbol{I})$. The reparameterization trick samples $\mathbf{z}_u$ in a novel way and the gradient with respect to ϕ can be taken since $\boldsymbol{\epsilon}$ is not required to be optimized. So far, stochastic gradient descent can be applied to Eq. (3) to learn model parameters ϕ and $\boldsymbol{\theta}$. After the parameters ϕ and $\boldsymbol{\theta}$ are learned, given a user interaction vector $\mathbf{x}_u$, we can reconstruct it with Mult-VAE, and items in $\mathcal{I} \backslash N_u$ with the top-N highest scores are recommended to the user.

3   MRVAE

In this section, we will firstly introduce the hybrid encoder and linear decoder. We then detail how to incorporate item-item relationships into our model.

3.1   Hybrid Encoder and Linear Decoder

While Mult-VAE uses a non-linear encoder and a non-linear decoder that consider the non-linearity between users and items, we instead design a model structure that considers both the linearity and non-linearity relationships between users and items, so that our model can adapt to both sparse and dense datasets.

As mentioned in Sect. 2.3, the encoder of Mult-VAE consists of a mean network and a variance network that output the mean and the diagonal elements of the covariance matrix of the variational distribution, respectively. In MRVAE, we use a single-layer neural network to serve as the variance network:

$$\log \Sigma_\phi(\mathbf{x}_u) = \mathbf{W}_\Sigma^T \mathbf{x}_u + \mathbf{b}_\Sigma. \tag{4}$$

$\mathbf{W}_\Sigma \in \mathbb{R}^{|\mathcal{I}| \times K}$ and $\mathbf{b}_\Sigma \in \mathbb{R}^K$ are weight and bias of the variance network, where K is the latent dimension.

The mean network consists of two parallel networks, i.e., the linear network and the non-linear network. The linear network has the same structure as the variance network, described as follows:

$$\mu_\phi^l(\mathbf{x}_u) = \mathbf{W}_\mu^{l\,T} \mathbf{x}_u + \mathbf{b}_\mu^l. \tag{5}$$

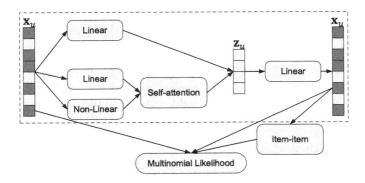

Fig. 2. The model structure of MRVAE. Inside the dotted rectangle is the backbone of MRVAE that incorporates the linearity and non-linearity user-item relationships. The 'item-item' module introduces item-item relationships.

$\mathbf{W}_\mu^l \in \mathbb{R}^{|\mathcal{I}| \times K}$ and $\mathbf{b}_\mu^l \in \mathbb{R}^K$ are weight and bias of the linear network. The non-linear network is a two-layer MLPs with one hidden layer and the network structure is: $|\mathcal{I}| \rightarrow K_h \rightarrow K$, where K_h denotes the hidden dimension of the hidden layer, described as follows:

$$\mu_\phi^n(\mathbf{x}_u) = \mathbf{W}_\mu^{n_2 T}(\sigma(\mathbf{W}_\mu^{n_1 T} \mathbf{x}_u + \mathbf{b}_\mu^{n_1})) + \mathbf{b}_\mu^{n_2}. \tag{6}$$

$\mathbf{W}_\mu^{n_2} \in \mathbb{R}^{K_h \times K}$ and $\mathbf{W}_\mu^{n_1} \in \mathbb{R}^{|\mathcal{I}| \times K_h}$ refer to the weights of the non-linear network, $\mathbf{b}_\mu^{n_2} \in \mathbb{R}^K$ and $\mathbf{b}_\mu^{n_1} \in \mathbb{R}^{K_h}$ are the biases. σ refers to the non-linear activation function, e.g., tanh. To combine the linear network and the non-linear network into a unified mean network, we resort to the self-attention mechanism. Specifically, the final mean vector of user u is obtained by the weighted sum of $\mu_\phi^l(\mathbf{x}_u) \in \mathbb{R}^K$ and $\mu_\phi^n(\mathbf{x}_u) \in \mathbb{R}^K$:

$$\boldsymbol{\mu}_u = \alpha_l \cdot \mu_\phi^l(\mathbf{x}_u) + \alpha_n \cdot \mu_\phi^n(\mathbf{x}_u), \tag{7}$$

where α_l and α_n can be calculated as follows:

$$\begin{aligned} \alpha_l &= \frac{\exp(\gamma_l)}{\exp(\gamma_l) + \exp(\gamma_n)}, \\ \alpha_n &= \frac{\exp(\gamma_n)}{\exp(\gamma_l) + \exp(\gamma_n)}. \end{aligned} \tag{8}$$

According to the self-attention mechanism, γ_l and γ_n are expressed as follows:

$$\begin{aligned} \gamma_l &= q^T \tanh(\mathbf{W}_{att}\mu_\phi^l(\mathbf{x}_u) + \mathbf{b}_{att}), \\ \gamma_n &= q^T \tanh(\mathbf{W}_{att}\mu_\phi^n(\mathbf{x}_u) + \mathbf{b}_{att}). \end{aligned} \tag{9}$$

$q^T \in \mathbb{R}^{K \times 1}$ is a learnable global query vector for self-attention. $\mathbf{W}_{att} \in \mathbb{R}^{K \times K}$ and $\mathbf{b}_{att} \in \mathbb{R}^K$ are weight and bias of the self-attention network, respectively.

After obtaining the mean vector and the variance vector, we can adopt reparameterization trick to calculate $\mathbf{z}_u$. Then $\mathbf{z}_u$ is fed into a linear decoder, which can be expressed as follows:

$$f_\theta(\mathbf{z}_u) = \mathbf{W}_\theta^T \mathbf{z}_u + \mathbf{b}_\theta. \tag{10}$$

$\mathbf{W}_\theta \in \mathbb{R}^{K \times |\mathcal{I}|}$ and $\mathbf{b}_\theta \in \mathbb{R}^{|\mathcal{I}|}$ are the weight and bias of the decoder, respectively. The decoder is a simple single-layer MLP and is equivalent to dot product with an additional bias.

The model structure of MRVAE is not a symmetric one as in Mult-VAE. Instead, we incorporate linearity user-item relationships in both the encoder and the decoder, and incorporate non-linearity user-item relationships in the encoder only. In the experiments, we show that such a model structure can achieve superior performance. Figure 2 shows the model structure of MRVAE.

3.2   Incorporating Item-Item Relationships

In this subsection, we detail the process of incorporating the item-item relationships into our model.

Some early works [16] use cosine similarity to calculate the item-item similarity between the target item and the rated items by the user for rating prediction. To predict the rating of a target item of the user, the ratings of the rated items of the user and their similarities are combined through weighted sum. However, in MRVAE, which is a latent factor model for top-N recommendation, we take a different strategy: we select the top-M most similar items to each interacted item of the user to help model training. During training, for each interacted item of the user, the selected top-M most similar items together with their similarities to the interacted item are used to more accurately reconstruct the preference score of each interacted item. To clearly show our strategy, we adapt Eq. (2) to our strategy as follows:

$$\log p_\theta(\mathbf{x}_u \mid \mathbf{z}_u) \overset{c}{=} \sum_i \mathbf{x}_{ui} \left(\log \boldsymbol{\pi}_{ui} + \eta \sum_{j \in \mathcal{N}_i} s_{ij} \log \boldsymbol{\pi}_{uj} \right). \tag{11}$$

η is a hyperparameter used to control the strength of item-item relationships and s_{ij} denotes the cosine similarity between item i and item j. Specifically, s_{ij} is expressed as follows:

$$s_{ij} = \frac{\mathbf{X}_{*,i} \cdot \mathbf{X}_{*,j}}{|\mathbf{X}_{*,i}| \cdot |\mathbf{X}_{*,j}|}, \tag{12}$$

where $\mathbf{X}_{*,i}$ and $\mathbf{X}_{*,j}$ denote the interaction vectors of item i and item j, respectively.

3.3   Discussion

Firstly, the linearity user-item relationships are reflected by both the encoder and the decoder, especially by the decoder since the decoder directly reconstructs the user's interaction vector. If we regard the weights $\mathbf{W}_\theta$ as the item embeddings with each column representing an item's embedding, the decoder is equivalent to the dot product between the user embedding and item embedding, with an additional bias term. This is in line with the finding in [13] that dot product is a better approximation of the interaction function. As for the encoder, we integrate the linear structure and the non-linear structure to let the model itself learn when to focus on the linearity relationships more and when to concentrate more on the non-linearity relationships, between users and items.

Secondly, while the design of encoder and decoder considers the linearity and non-linearity user-item relationships, we incorporate item-item relationships by means of the multinomial likelihood. The top-M most similar items measured by cosine similarity of each interacted item of the user can provide more information about the preferences of the user, thus can filter out the less preferred items and give more attention to the preferred items. In the experiments, we empirically choose a small value for M because a larger M will introduce some 'negative' items that the user dislikes.

4   Experiments

In this section, we empirically evaluate our method on four datasets in Top-N recommendation task. We firstly show the experimental settings, followed by the performance comparison of MRVAE with other competing methods. Ablation study and hyperparameter analysis are also conducted.

4.1   Experimental Settings

Datasets and Evaluation Metrics. We use four public datasets that are commonly used in the CF methods for implicit feedback: ML-1M [2], Yelp2018[1], Amazon-Book and Video-Games. ML-1M, which contains one million explicit ratings, is one of the version of MovieLens datasets[2]. We binarize the explicit ratings by regarding ratings of four or higher as implicit feedback. Yelp2018 is adopted from the 2018 edition of the Yelp challenge, where the local businesses are viewed as items [19]. Amazon-Book and Video-Games are collected from the Amazon-review datasets [3]. Yelp2018 and Video-Games are sparse datasets since they have a small average number of user's interactions, while Amazon-Book and Ml-1M are relatively dense datasets. Table 2 shows the statistics of the datasets. For each user, 80% of the interactions are used for training and the remaining 20% of interactions are used for testing. From the training set, we can select 10% of interactions as validation set to tune hyperparameters. We use recall@20 and ndcg@20 computed by the all-rank protocol, i.e., all items that are not interacted by a user are candidates, as the evaluation metrics.

---

[1] https://www.yelp.com/dataset.
[2] http://grouplens.org/datasets/movielens/1m/.

Table 2. Statistics of the experimented datasets.

Dataset	#Users	#Items	#Int.	Avg. #Int. per user	Density
ML-1M	6, 027	3, 525	574, 155	95	0.02703
Yelp2018	31, 668	38, 048	1, 561, 406	49	0.00130
Amazon-Book	52, 643	91, 599	2, 984, 108	57	0.00062
Video-Games	24, 072	10, 622	174, 989	7	0.00068

Baseline Methods. Since MRVAE is a VAE-based CF method, we compare MRVAE with several VAE-based CF variants. Moreover, we also compare MRVAE with matrix factorization and graph-based CF methods. We choose the MF-BPR [12] as the representative of matrix factorization method and Light-GCN [4] as the representative of the graph-based CF method. We also additionally include a popularity-based, non-personalized method ItemPop. They are introduced as follows:

- **ItemPop** This is a non-personalized recommendation method that recommends items based on how many users have interacted with the item.
- **MF-BPR** [12] This is a matrix factorization method that resorts to the Bayesian personalized ranking loss for model learning.
- **LightGCN** [4] This is a state-of-the-art graph convolutional network (GCN)-based CF method. It is the lighter version of NGCF [19]. By propagating the embeddings of users and items on the user-item bipartite graph through graph convolution, multiple relationships are implicitly captured in LightGCN.
- **Mult-VAE** [10] This is the base model of our proposed method. It uses non-linear encoder and decoder. Only user-item relationships are considered in Mult-VAE.
- **EVCF** [7] This is an enhancing VAE model for CF. It adopts flexible prior and gating mechanism, to enhance the Gaussian prior and encoder in the original Mult-VAE, respectively.
- **RecVAE** [17] This is an improved model of Mult-VAE. It adds multiple novelties to Mult-VAE and improves the recommendation performance significantly compared with Mult-VAE.
- **BiVAE** [18] This is a VAE-based CF method that uses two encoders to encode user and item interaction vectors, respectively, and uses a simple decoder to reconstruct the user interaction vectors for recommendations.

Hyperparameter Settings. For fair comparison, the embedding size or latent dimension of MRVAE and all the latent factor models of the competing methods are set to 64. For the VAE-based variants, we set the hidden dimension to 128 if a hidden layer exists. We tune the number of hidden layers among [0, 1, 2], except for RecVAE that has a complicated encoder. For example, we adopt the model architecture: $128 \rightarrow 64 \rightarrow 128$, for Mult-VAE. All the models are trained with Adam [8]. The learning rates of all the methods are tuned among [1e-3, 5e-4, 1e-4]. The number of graph convolution layers of LightGCN is tuned among [2, 3, 4]. For MRVAE, we use MLPs with structure $64 \rightarrow 64$ for the non-linear mean network to make MRVAE be in the same magnitude of parameters as Mult-VAE. For simplicity, we set β to 0.8 without KL annealing for MRVAE. The hyperparameter η is tuned among 0–100 and M is tuned among 5–100.

4.2 Performance Comparison

The experiment results of MRVAE and all other competing methods are shown in Table 3. The results show that MRVAE surpasses all the competing methods in terms of the two evaluation metrics, on sparse and relatively dense datasets. Firstly, MRVAE outperforms the traditional methods ItemPop and MF-BPR. Secondly, MRVAE outperforms VAE-based variants, in particular, by a large margin over Mult-VAE on four datasets (31.98% on recall@20 and 35.01% on ndcg@20, on average). EVCF, RecVAE and BiVAE achieve a better performance than Mult-VAE, but by a relatively smaller margin, compared with MRVAE's performance, which indicates the significance of mining more relationships among different entities in CF. Thirdly, MRVAE outperforms the strong baseline LightGCN on four datasets, which shows that MRVAE can capture more important relationships for recommendations.

4.3 Ablation Study

We conduct some experiments on the experimented datasets to justify the effectiveness of the components of MRVAE, which include the hybrid encoder, the integration of the linearity and non-linearity user-item relationships, the incorporation of item-item relationships. Five variants of MRVAE are considered, specifically, variant (i) is generated by removing the linear mean network; variant (ii)

Table 3. The comparison of over performance of MRVAE and competing methods. The best results are highlighted in bold. The second best ones are underlined. "%Improve" denotes the performance improvement of MRVAE over Mult-VAE.

Dataset	ML-1M		Yelp2018		Amazon-Book		Video-Games	
Method	Recall	ndcg	Recall	ndcg	Recall	ndcg	Recall	ndcg
ItemPop	0.0196	0.0219	0.0125	0.0101	0.0051	0.0044	0.0403	0.0188
MF-BPR	0.0588	0.0527	0.0485	0.0392	0.0351	0.0267	0.1120	0.0492
LightGCN	0.0571	0.0528	0.0649	0.0530	0.0411	0.0315	0.1362	0.0596
Mult-VAE	0.0553	0.0532	0.0577	0.0465	0.0387	0.0297	0.1193	0.0516
EVCF	0.0564	0.0492	0.0586	0.0472	0.0403	0.0312	0.1352	0.0584
RecVAE	0.0575	0.0526	0.0557	0.0462	0.0424	0.0332	0.1271	0.0561
BiVAE	0.0445	0.0432	0.0621	0.0504	0.0401	0.0313	0.1290	0.0574
MRVAE	**0.0595**	**0.0553**	**0.0704**	**0.0580**	**0.0644**	**0.0527**	**0.1526**	**0.0691**
%Improve	7.59%	3.95%	22.01%	24.73%	66.41%	77.44%	27.91%	33.91%

Table 4. Experiment results of ablation study. Variant (i) denotes MRVAE with non-linear encoder and linear decoder; Variant (ii) denotes MRVAE with linear encoder and linear decoder; Variant (iii) denotes MRVAE with non-linear encoder and non-linear decoder; Variant (iv) denotes MRVAE without incorporating item-item relationships. Variant (v) denotes MRVAE with self-attention in the hybrid encoder replaced by average pooling. See the text for more details.

Dataset	ML-1M		Yelp2018		Amazon-Book		Video-Games	
Variants	Recall	ndcg	Recall	ndcg	Recall	ndcg	Recall	ndcg
MRVAE	0.0595	0.0553	0.0704	0.0580	0.0644	0.0527	0.1526	0.0691
Variant (i)	0.0573	0.0532	0.0692	0.0573	0.0626	0.0508	0.1473	0.0665
Variant (ii)	0.0535	0.0525	0.0698	0.0580	0.0619	0.0503	0.1445	0.0659
Variant (iii)	0.0575	0.0521	0.0619	0.0496	0.0617	0.0509	0.1351	0.0589
Variant (iv)	0.0594	0.0549	0.0692	0.0571	0.0492	0.0379	0.1516	0.0681
Variant (v)	0.0581	0.0551	0.0691	0.0573	0.0638	0.0520	0.1481	0.0672

is generated by removing the non-linear mean network; variant (iii) is generated by removing the linear mean network and transforming the linear decoder into a non-linear decoder with network structure: $64 \rightarrow 128 \rightarrow |\mathcal{I}|$; variant (iv) is generated by removing the item-item relationships; variant (v) is generated by replacing self-attention in the hybrid encoder with average pooling. Variant (i) verifies the hybrid encoder of MRVAE, variant (ii) and variant (iii) verify the importance of integrating the linearity and non-linearity user-item relationships. Variant (iv) verifies the effectiveness of item-item relationships. Variant (v) verifies the effectiveness of self-attention in the hybrid encoder. Experiment results are shown in Table 4.

We have the following observations: (1) MRVAE outperforms all the variants on four datasets, which indicates the necessity of fusing the linearity and non-linearity user-item relationships, and item-item relationships; (2) the outperformance of MRVAE over variant (i) and variant (v) verifies the effectiveness of the proposed hybrid encoder and the self-attention used in it; (3) in most cases, variant (i) achieves better performance than variant (ii) and (iii), verifying our idea of integrating the linearity and non-linearity user-item relationships; (4) the importances of item-item relationships on different datasets vary, specifically, item-item relationships play an important role in Amazon-Book dataset but contribute less to the performance improvement on other three datasets, by comparing MRVAE with variant (iv); (5) comparing variant (ii) and variant (iii) shows that linearity user-item relationships contribute more to the superiority of MRVAE on Yelp2018 and Video-Games (sparse user interactions), but non-linearity user-item relationships play a more important role on ML-1M and Amazon-Books (relatively dense user interactions), which corresponds to the average number of interactions of users in Table 2, i.e., dataset with relatively dense user interactions favors non-linearity and dataset with sparse user interactions favors linearity. We argue that dense dataset with more ID features needs more powerful non-linear networks to learn while the sparse dataset is the opposite.

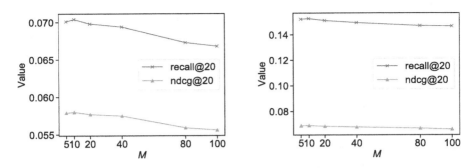

Fig. 3. The impact of M on the performance on Yelp2018 (left) and Video-Games (right).

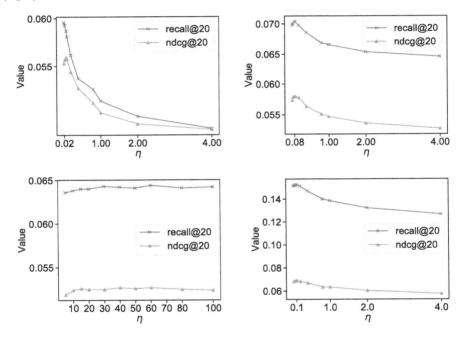

Fig. 4. The impact of η on the performance on four datasets. From left to right and from top to bottom: ML-1M, Yelp2018, Amazon-Book and Video-Games.

4.4 Hyperparameter Analysis

In this subsection, we conduct experiments to explore the impact of the hyperparameters M and η on the recommendation performance in terms of recall@20 and ndcg@20.

Impact of M. Figure 3 shows the experiment results of MRVAE with different M on Yelp2018 and Video-Games. We set M among [5, 10, 20, 40, 80, 100]. Usually, a small M can achieve the best performance, since a larger M will introduce some irrelevant item-item relationships which will hurt the performance instead, e.g., we set M to 10 for Yelp2018 and Video-Games. Similar observations can be found on ML-1M and Amazon-Book. Specifically, we set M to 5 for ML-1M and Amazon-Book and omit their illustrations due to the page limit.

Impact of η. Figure 4 shows the experiment results on four datasets. The scales of η on different datasets vary. On ML-1M, Yelp2018 and Video-Games, a small value of η can achieve the best performance and a large η will degrade the performance, especially on the ML-1M dataset. On the contrary, a relatively larger value of η is favored on Amazon-Book. Specifically, the best η on ML-1M, Yelp2018, Amazon-Book and Video-Games are 0.02, 0.08, 60 and 0.1, respectively. These show that the contributions of item-item relationships to the performance on different datasets vary. We conjecture that the linearity and non-linearity user-item relationships are more important than item-item relationships in ML-1M, Yelp2018 and Video-Games, for boosting the performance. Increasing the influence of item-item relationships will instead make the linearity and non-linearity user-item relationships fade away on these three datasets. While we get the opposite conclusion on Amazon-Book, in which item-item relationships dominate.

5   Related Works

5.1   VAE-Based CF Methods

In this subsection, we present some relevant VAE-based CF methods that make top-N recommendation under the implicit feedback setting [7,10,17,18]. Mult-VAE is the pioneer work that extends VAE to CF for implicit feedback. The multinomial likelihood and hyperparameter β on the KL divergence term are two novel contributions of Mult-VAE, which are adopted by later VAE-based CF methods [17], including our proposed MRVAE. The work proposed by [7] uses a more flexible prior to replace the original standard Gaussian distribution, and uses gated linear units to deepen the neural networks of encoder and decoder. RecVAE [17] proposes several novelties for improving Mult-VAE, including a sophisticated encoder, a novel composite prior distribution, a new approach to setting the hyperparameter β and a novel approach for training the model. Note that RecVAE also proposes to use a linear encoder, but it does not consider the linearity in the encoder and does not incorporate item-item relationships into the model, compared with MRVAE. In [18], the authors propose to use two encoders, user- and item-based, parameterized by neural networks and the decoder can take any differentiable function, e.g., inner product. While two encoders are used, they do not consider the combination of the linearity and non-linearity user-item relationships as MRVAE. Our proposed MRVAE differs from these VAE-based CF methods in that we focus on mining more relationships across users and items, to further improve the recommendation performance.

5.2 Other CF Methods

Latent factor models still dominate the CF methods family [4,11,12,19]. They can roughly divided into the matrix factorization (MF) models [11,12] and models with more powerful encoder, e.g., graph-based CF methods [4,19]. MF models project the user/item IDs into embeddings, then use dot product to calculate the preference score on item for user. Point-wise loss [11] or pair-wise loss [12] are widely used in these methods. While MF models only consider the pattern between users and items, graph-based CF methods implicitly incorporate the user-user, item-item and user-item relationships into the model, by conducting multi-layer graph convolution on the user-item bipartite graph [4,19]. Though multiple types of relationships are considered in the graph-based CF methods, some relationships between entities may be harmful for model learning since these relationships are incorporated in an implicit manner, without carefully distinguishing the helpful ones from all the relationships. Instead, our proposed MRVAE explicitly incorporates the linearity and non-linearity user-item relationships, and item-item relationships. Especially for item-item relationships, we use cosine similarity to measure the relative importance of item-item relationships and selectively incorporate them to the model.

6 Conclusion

In this paper, we propose a model called MRVAE, aiming at incorporating more relationships between entities (i.e., users or items), to boost the top-N recommendation performance. Firstly, we carefully design a hybrid encoder and a linear decoder as a backbone of our model, in which the linearity and non-linearity user-item relationships are considered. Secondly, we selectively incorporate item-item relationships into the models further through adding additional term to the multinomial likelihood. We use cosine similarity to calculate the similarity between items. Extensive experiments demonstrate the effectiveness of MRVAE, compared to other SOTAs. Future work could be exploring other similarity measures between items and attempting to incorporate user-user relationships into the VAE-based CF methods. Mining more accurate relationships by incorporating side information into MRVAE can also be a possible direction in the future.

References

1. Deshpande, M., Karypis, G.: Item-based top-n recommendation algorithms. TOIS **22**(1), 143–177 (2004)
2. Harper, F.M., Konstan, J.A.: The movielens datasets: history and context. TIIS **5**(4), 1–19 (2015)
3. He, R., McAuley, J.: Ups and downs: modeling the visual evolution of fashion trends with one-class collaborative filtering. In: WWW, pp. 507–517 (2016)
4. He, X., Deng, K., Wang, X., Li, Y., Zhang, Y., Wang, M.: Lightgcn: simplifying and powering graph convolution network for recommendation. In: SIGIR, pp. 639–648 (2020)

5. Hu, Y., Koren, Y., Volinsky, C.: Collaborative filtering for implicit feedback datasets. In: ICDM, pp. 263–272. IEEE (2008)

6. Jordan, M.I., Ghahramani, Z., Jaakkola, T.S., Saul, L.K.: An introduction to variational methods for graphical models. Mach. Learn. **37**(2), 183–233 (1999)

7. Kim, D., Suh, B.: Enhancing vaes for collaborative filtering: flexible priors & gating mechanisms. In: RecSys, pp. 403–407 (2019)

8. Kingma, D.P., Ba, J.: Adam: A method for stochastic optimization (2014). arXiv preprint, arXiv:1412.6980

9. Kingma, D.P., Welling, M.: Auto-encoding variational bayes (2013). arXiv preprint, arXiv:1312.6114

10. Liang, D., Krishnan, R.G., Hoffman, M.D., Jebara, T.: Variational autoencoders for collaborative filtering. In: WWW, pp. 689–698 (2018)

11. Mnih, A., Salakhutdinov, R.R.: Probabilistic matrix factorization. In: NeurIPS, pp. 1257–1264 (2008)

12. Rendle, S., Freudenthaler, C., Gantner, Z., Schmidt-Thieme, L.: Bpr: bayesian personalized ranking from implicit feedback. In: UAI, pp. 452–461. AUAI Press (2009)

13. Rendle, S., Krichene, W., Zhang, L., Anderson, J.: Neural collaborative filtering vs. matrix factorization revisited. In: RecSys, pp. 240–248 (2020)

14. Rezende, D.J., Mohamed, S., Wierstra, D.: Stochastic backpropagation and approximate inference in deep generative models. In: ICML, pp. 1278–1286. PMLR (2014)

15. Ricci, F., Rokach, L., Shapira, B.: Introduction to recommender systems handbook. In: Ricci, F., Rokach, L., Shapira, B., Kantor, P.B. (eds.) Recommender Systems Handbook, pp. 1–35. Springer, Boston (2011). https://doi.org/10.1007/978-0-387-85820-3_1

16. Sarwar, B., Karypis, G., Konstan, J., Riedl, J.: Item-based collaborative filtering recommendation algorithms. In: WWW, pp. 285–295 (2001)

17. Shenbin, I., Alekseev, A., Tutubalina, E., Malykh, V., Nikolenko, S.I.: Recvae: a new variational autoencoder for top-n recommendations with implicit feedback. In: WSDM, pp. 528–536 (2020)

18. Truong, Q.T., Salah, A., Lauw, H.W.: Bilateral variational autoencoder for collaborative filtering. In: WSDM, pp. 292–300 (2021)

19. Wang, X., He, X., Wang, M., Feng, F., Chua, T.S.: Neural graph collaborative filtering. In: SIGIR, pp. 165–174 (2019)

Multilevel Feature Interaction Learning for Session-Based Recommendation via Graph Neural Networks

Ming He$^{(\boxtimes)}$, Tianshuo Han, and Tianyu Ding

Beijing University of Technology, Beijing, China
heming@bjut.edu.cn, {hants,dingtianyu}@emails.bjut.edu.cn

Abstract. Predicting users' actions based on anonymous sessions is a challenging problem due to the uncertainty of user behavior and limited information. Recent advances in graph neural networks (GNN) have led to a promising approach for addressing this problem. However, existing methods have three major issues. First, they are incapable of modeling the transitions between inconsecutive items. Second, they are infeasible for learning the cross-feature interactions when learning the item relationships. Third, very few models can adapt to the improvement of embedding quality to help improve recommendation performance. Therefore, to address these issues, we propose a novel model named *Multilevel Feature Interactions Learning* (MFIL) that effectively learns item and session representation using GNN. By leveraging item side information, e.g., brands and categories, MFIL can model transitions between inconsecutive items in the session graph (session-level). We further design hierarchical structures to learn the feature interactions, which is effective to estimate the importance weights of different neighboring items in the global graph (global-level). In addition, an effective learning strategy is employed to enhance MFIL's capability, and it performs better than the classic regularization methods. Extensive experiments conducted on real-world datasets demonstrate that MFIL, significantly outperforms existing state-of-the-art graph-based methods.

Keywords: Graph neural networks · Recommender systems · Session-based recommendation

1 Introduction

The recommender systems play a crucial role in helping users target their interests. Conventional recommendation approaches usually rely on clicks feedback and may perform poorly in real-world scenarios. Consequently, session-based recommendation has attracted considerable interest recently, which predicts the next interacting item based on users' behaviors. Recently, the graph-based approaches [13,30] use graph neural networks (GNN) to capture the higher-order interaction and get the item representations. However, these methods can not effectively address the following issues in a session-based recommendation.

© Springer Nature Switzerland AG 2022
T. Di Noia et al. (Eds.): ICWE 2022, LNCS 13362, pp. 31–46, 2022.
https://doi.org/10.1007/978-3-031-09917-5_3

The first issue is the insufficient modeling of item transitions in the session.
Previous works are based only on the pairwise item-transitions [22,23,31], and
do not fully model the transitions between inconsecutive items. The idea of these
works is to calculate how consecutive items communicate with each other. Some
recent attempts have employed multilayer structures [9,17], but they only use
the direct connections between consecutive items. Hence, there is a need for more
effective exploration to learn the transitions of inconsecutive items.

*Second, current recommendation methods ignore feature interactions, and
this may affect recommendation performance in two aspects:* 1) these methods
may not be expressive enough to capture complex patterns of feature interactions. For example, the element-wise product [11,14,16] and nonlinear transformation [20,24] operations lack the ability of learning feature interactions [5]; 2)
these models do not make full use of co-occurrence information [15,26]. Thus,
exploring more effective structures and using the co-occurrence information when
learning the feature interactions will be helpful.

*The third is that they fail to adapt themselves to the embedding quality
improvement,* which may limit the further optimization of weight parameters and
decrease model-learning capability. In the literature, some methods [8] have proposed employing regularization techniques (e.g., *learning rate decay and dropout*)
to enhance performance. However, these strategies prevent the further improvement of model performance when embedding quality is improved to a certain
extent. Hence, a more effective learning strategy to enhance the model's learning
capability rather than merely prevent overfitting is required.

The main contributions of this work are summarized as follows:

- We leverage side information (e.g., *brands or categories*, as we mentioned in
  the Abstract) to learn the transitions of items within a session graph. An
  adjacent matrix is constructed, and it is capable of propagating information
  between relevant items, even if they are inconsecutive.
- We propose a hierarchical graph model to learn feature interactions and use
  the co-occurrence information, which can estimate the importance weights of
  different items in the global graph.
- A more effective learning strategy is employed, which can adapt the model to
  the improvement of embedding by adjusting internal structures, and performs
  better than the classical regularization methods, e.g., *learning rate decay*.
- Extensive experiments show that MFIL achieves significant improvements
  over state-of-the-art graph-based baseline models.

2 Related Work

2.1 Graph Neural Networks (GNN)

The most critical aspect of the aforementioned methods is the network structures
because it directly decides the recommendation performance [31]. So, we mainly
introduce the GNN techniques here. Among various GNN architectures [21],
gated GNN (GGNN), graph attention network (GAT), and graph convolutional

network (GCN) are widely used. GGNN-based methods [8, 9, 25] adopt long short-term memory (LSTM) in the update step. GAT-based methods [10, 16] update the vector of node by a weighted summation of its neighboring items. GCN-based methods [6, 28] generally aggregate feature information using convolutional neural networks. The other methods [7, 15, 31] usually adopt mean/pooling for aggregation and concatenation/nonlinear transformation for update. *Different from these works, we employ hierarchical structures for information propagation, which effectively estimate the importance weights between items.*

2.2 GNN for Session-Based Recommendation

The use of GNN techniques in session-based recommender systems is attracting increasing attention recently. The core idea of these works is to capture transition patterns in sessions. For example, SR-GNN [22] considers the transitions between items, and combines long-term preferences with current interests. FGNN [10] captures item transitions and employs the readout function to learn the session embedding. DGTN [31] and GCE-GNN [16] model item transitions in not only the current session and but also the neighboring sessions. TAGNN [25] designs a target-aware attention module to learn interest representations with different target items. MA-GNN [7] integrates the static, dynamic, and long-term user preferences with item co-occurrence patterns. *Compared to previous works that construct the session graph using edges between two consecutive items, we propose building a graph with side information and capture transition patterns between inconsecutive items.*

2.3 Regularization Techniques

Regularization techniques have been investigated extensively because of their capability to avoid overfitting; a widely used approach is l_p regularization [10]. Moreover, item sharing, dropout, layer normalization [4], gradient clipping, max norm regularization [19], and the learning rate decay [16] are effective in practice. Many new regularization techniques have been developed recently. Stochastic shared embedding [18, 19], stochastically replaces embeddings with another embedding with some pre-defined probability. A graph-based regularization approach that serves as a counterpart of the l_2 regularization has been proposed in [29]. In addition, a regularization-based approach that optimizes for robustness on rule-based (a set of expert-defined categorical rules) input perturbations has been proposed in [1]. *In this paper, we apply a more effective learning strategy to enhance MFIL's capability instead of simply using classic regularization techniques, such as learning rate decay and dropout.*

3 Methodology

3.1 Problem Definition

Let $V = \{v_1, v_2, ..., v_m\}$ be the item set, where m denotes the number of items. A session is defined as an interaction list $S = \{v_1^s, v_2^s, ..., v_l^s\}$ in chronological order, where v_i^s denotes the i-th item within session S, and l denotes the length of S, and we use $I = \{i_1^s, i_2^s, ..., i_l^s\}$ to represent the corresponding side information. The co-occurrence information of each item can be denoted as $N = \{N_\varepsilon(v_1^s), N_\varepsilon(v_2^s), ..., N_\varepsilon(v_l^s)\}$, where $N_\varepsilon(v_i^s)$ represents the co-occurrence items of v_i^s in neighbor sessions. The details of $N_\varepsilon(\cdot)$ will be described in Subsect. 3.4. Formally, the task is to predict the top-N items that the user is likely to interact with at $(l+1)$-th step.

3.2   Model Overview

We illustrate MFIL in Fig. 1, which contains three main components: a *session-level* item representation learning module, a *global-level* item representation learning module, and a *session representation* learning module. The *session-level* module learns item embeddings with the *side information I* in the session graph, and the *global-level* module incorporates information from neighboring items in the global graph based on the *co-occurrence information N*. The *session representation* learning module generates a representation of the session by aggregating the representations from the two *learning modules*.

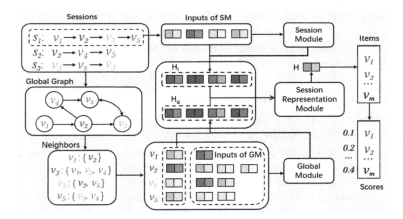

Fig. 1. Overall framework of MFIL. At first, the *global graph* and *neighbors* of session s_1 are extracted from the given *sessions* simultaneously and then fed into the *session module* and *global module* to learn item embeddings H_l and H_g. Then, they are fed into the *session represent module* to assemble the representation of session s_1, which is denoted as H.

3.3   Session-Level Item Representation Learning Module

In this subsection, we introduce how to obtain the representation $H_l \in \mathbb{R}^{L \times d}$ of items from *session-level*, and different from Subsect. 3.1, we use l to represent session-level. First, we extract the latest L items in s in chronological order, which is abbreviated as $S = \{v_1^s, v_2^s, ..., v_L^s\}$. Let $M \in \mathbb{R}^{m \times d}$ denotes the learnable item embedding matrix with d as the latent dimensionality. The session S is represented as $E_l = \left\{ m_{v_1}^s, m_{v_2}^s, ..., m_{v_L}^s \right\} \in \mathbb{R}^{L \times d}$. We also employ the corresponding side information $I = \{i_1^s, i_2^s, ..., i_L^s\} \in \mathbb{R}^L$.

We build the adjacent matrices to model the item transitions leveraging item side information, as we mentioned in the first issue in the introduction. For example, consider a session $S = \{v_1, v_2, v_3, v_4, v_5, v_4, v_6\}$ and the corresponding side information (e.g., *brands or categories*) $I = \{i_1, i_2, i_1, i_1, i_2, i_1, i_2\}$, the session graph, and adjacent matrices are shown in Fig. 2. In the left matrix A^1, for simplicity, we use symbols like *1, 2, 3, and 4* to represent the *self-loop, in-come, out-come, and in-out* relationships between two consecutive items [16], respectively. In the right matrix A^2, we set $A_{ij}^2 = 1$, if v_i and v_j belong to the same *brand* or *category*. If we consider only the relationships in matrix A^1, we will be incapable of capturing the transitions between v_1 and $v_3(v_4)$, as well as v_2 and $v_5(v_6)$, v_* represents the item in the sequence. With the help of different matrices, we can learn the transitions of consecutive and inconsecutive items.

Information Propagation: We use the attention mechanism to learn the weights of different items $\alpha \in \mathbb{R}^{L \times L}$ in the session graph. To model the feature interactions, we repeat E_l in the first and second dimensions L times to obtain $E_l^1 \in \mathbb{R}^{(L \times L) \times d}$ and $E_l^2 \in \mathbb{R}^{L \times (L \times d)}$, respectively, and then model the feature interactions by concatenation operation and multilayer perception (MLP):

$$
\begin{aligned}
a_1 &= (E_l^1 \times E_l^2) \,\|\, E_l^1, \\
a_2 &= LeakyReLU(a_1 W_1 + b_1) W_2 + b_2, \\
a_3 &= LeakyReLU(a_2 W_3 + b_3) W_4 + b_4,
\end{aligned}
\tag{1}
$$

where $\|$ denotes the vector concatenation operation, $\times$ denotes the element-wise multiplication operation, $W_1 \in \mathbb{R}^{2d \times 2d}$, $W_2, W_4 \in \mathbb{R}^{2d \times d}$, $W_3 \in \mathbb{R}^{d \times 2d}$ and b_* are weight matrices and biases for the two layers, $a_1 \in \mathbb{R}^{L \times L \times 2d}$, a_2 and $a_3 \in \mathbb{R}^{L \times L \times d}$, **only a_3 will be used in subsequent stages**, and it is calculated by a_1 and a_2.

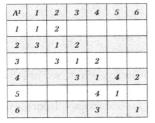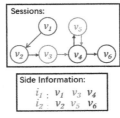

Fig. 2. Session graph of s and its adjacent matrices. In the left matrix (any two directly adjacent items) A^1, for simplicity, we use *1, 2, 3, and 4* to represent the *self-loop, in-come, out-come, and in-out* relationship, and the matrix shows the adjacency of items in the sequence. In the right matrix A^2, $A_{ij}^2 = 1$ represents that v_i and v_j belong to the same brand or category.

In the following, we will use the a_3 to get different α_*, and then get the final weight matrix $\alpha \in \mathbb{R}^{L \times L}$. For each relationship (e.g., *in-out or 'adjacent'*, as shown in Fig. 2) in the session graph, MFIL calculates and gets the corresponding matrix α_* similarly:

$$\alpha_* = a_3 W_*^\alpha, \tag{2}$$

where $W_*^\alpha \in \mathbb{R}^{d \times 1}$ and $\alpha_* \in \mathbb{R}^{L \times L}$. We use $*$ to represent the *self-loop, income, out-come, in-out, and 'adjacent'* relationship, respectively, and **please note that each relationship has a corresponding weight matrix W_* and** α_*. We only keep the items in α_* if $A_{ij}^1 = 1$ (when $*$ represents self-loop, etc.) or $A_{ij}^2 = 1$ (for the 'adjacent' relationship).

We stack different α_* in the order of *self-loop, in-come, out-come, in-out, and 'adjacent'* to obtain the final weight matrix $\alpha \in \mathbb{R}^{L \times L}$, we believe that the 'adjacent' relationship is more important than the others, and the in-out relationship is different from the in-come (or out-come) relationship. The first L represents the length of the session, and the second represents the relationships between a specific item and other L items in the session. We use a toy example to explain the stack operation. For vectors $v_1 = [1, 1, 0, 0]$ and $v_2 = [0, 2, 2, 0]$, if we stack them in the order of v_1 and v_2, we could obtain $v_{stack} = [1, 2, 2, 0]$.

Information Aggregation: the representation of items in the session graph $H_l \in \mathbb{R}^{L \times d}$ is defined with $\beta \in \mathbb{R}^1$ as follows:

$$H_l = \beta(softmax(\alpha)E_l) + E_l. \tag{3}$$

As we mentioned in the introduction, to adapt the model to the embedding quality improvement, we will update β. When the embedding quality is improved to a certain extent, the input E_l already contains explicit semantic information, and we should focus more on E_l for the follow-up tasks, especially in the later stage of training, so we adjust β during training to ensure that the model can be further optimized. It performs better than some classic regularization, and we will discuss it in Subsect. 4.4. We update β with initial value β_0 at fixed *rate* when the training *epoch* is larger than *epoch_l*:

$$\beta = \beta_0 - (epoch - epoch_l) \times rate, \quad epoch \geq epoch_l. \tag{4}$$

3.4   Global-Level Item Representation Learning Module

In this subsection, we introduce how to incorporate information from the global-level [16] and obtain the representation $H_g \in \mathbb{R}^{L \times d}$ of items. First, we use $E_l = \{m_{v_1}^s, m_{v_2}^s, ..., m_{v_L}^s\} \in \mathbb{R}^{L \times d}$ to denote items in the current session, and $N = \{N_\varepsilon(v_1^s), N_\varepsilon(v_2^s), ..., N_\varepsilon(v_L^s)\} \in \mathbb{R}^{L \times n \times d}$ to denote the co-occurrence information in the global session, where $N_\varepsilon(v_i^s) \in \mathbb{R}^{n \times d}$ represents the n ε-neighbor items of v_i^s with d as the latent dimensionality [16]. We also employ the co-occurrence information which can be represented as $w = \{w_1^s, w_2^s, ..., w_L^s\}$, where $w_i^s \in \mathbb{R}^1$ represents the co-occurrence times of v_i's n neighbor items in the global graph. For example, consider the sessions $s_1 = \{v_1, v_2, v_3, v_5\}$ and its neighbor sessions (which also contains v_2) $s_2 = \{v_3, v_5, v_2, v_6\}$ and $s_3 = \{v_4, v_2, v_6\}$, as shown in the center of Fig. 3, for the target item v_2, we can obtain $N_2(v_2) = \{v_3, v_5, v_6, v_1, v_4\}$ and the corresponding $w = \{2, 2, 2, 1, 1\}$, as shown on the left of Fig. 3. The 1-neighbors of v_2 are $\{v_6, v_1, v_3, v_4, v_5\}$ with co-occurrence times $\{2, 1, 1, 1, 1\}$. We also show the global graph of v_2 on the right of Fig. 3.

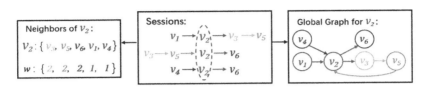

Fig. 3. Sessions that contain v_2. The 2-neighbors of v_2 are $\{v_3, v_5, v_6, v_1, v_4\}$ with co-occurrence times $\{2, 2, 2, 1, 1\}$. The global graph of v_2 is also shown on the right.

Information Propagation: We learn the weights of items in $N_2(v_2)$ for each item v_i in the session. First, we can obtain the representation of current session $s \in \mathbb{R}^d$, which is obtained by computing the average of E_l:

$$s = \frac{1}{|E_l|} \sum_{m_i \in E_l} m_i. \tag{5}$$

To model the feature interactions, we repeat s in the first dimension L times to obtain $s' \in \mathbb{R}^{L \times d}$, and then repeat s' n times in the second dimension to obtain $s'' \in \mathbb{R}^{L \times n \times d}$, and model the feature interactions between each item with co-occurrence information w as follows:

$$
\begin{aligned}
a_4 &= [(s'' \times N) \,||\, sigmoid(w)]W_5, \\
a_5 &= mean(a_4 N, -2), \\
a_6 &= \gamma a_5 + E_l,
\end{aligned} \tag{6}
$$

where $W_5 \in \mathbb{R}^{(d+1) \times 1}$, $a_4 \in \mathbb{R}^{L \times n \times 1}$ models the attention scores of the items in N, $a_4 N \in \mathbb{R}^{L \times n \times d}$, $a_5 \in \mathbb{R}^{L \times d}$ represents the average of N, and $a_6 \in \mathbb{R}^{L \times d}$ is the information propagated from N (a set of neighbours), please note that only a_6 will be used in subsequent stages, and it is calculated by a_4 and a_5. γ is a hyperparameter to be tuned. Notably, for matrix $X \in \mathbb{R}^{a \times b \times c}$, $mean(X, -2) \in \mathbb{R}^{a \times c}$.

As we mentioned in the introduction, in order to adapt the model to the embedding quality improvement, we only reserve the top-k scores in a_4 in the second dimension for the same purpose in the previous section, and we calculate k when the training *epoch* is larger than $epoch_g$ as follows:

$$k = n - epoch//rate, \quad epoch \geq epoch_g, \tag{7}$$

where $//$ is the division operation, for example, $5//2 = 2$ and $7//2 = 3$.

Information Aggregation: We aggregate E_l and a_6 with $W_6 \in \mathbb{R}^{2d \times d}$ to obtain the representation $H_g \in \mathbb{R}^{L \times d}$ of items in the current session graph:

$$H_g = dropout([a_6 \| E_l]W_6). \tag{8}$$

3.5   Session Representation Learning and Training

With $W_7 \in \mathbb{R}^{2d \times d}$, we can obtain a representation $H \in \mathbb{R}^{L \times d}$ by aggregating $H_l \in \mathbb{R}^{L \times d}$ and $H_g \in \mathbb{R}^{L \times d}$, and we also add a learnable position embedding matrix $P = [p_1, p_2, ..., p_L] \in \mathbb{R}^{L \times d}$ to suggest the importance of each item:

$$H = tanh([(H_l + H_g) \| P]W_7). \tag{9}$$

Following previous works [8,16], we use a soft-attention mechanism and multi-head attention [10] to learn the corresponding weights $\omega^* \in \mathbb{R}^{L \times 1}$ of each item in H, and obtain the final session representation $E \in \mathbb{R}^{1 \times d}$ as follows:

$$\omega^k = sigmoid(HW_8^k + s'W_9^k + b^k)q^k,$$
$$E = \frac{1}{K}\sum_{k=1}^{K}(\sum_{i=1}^{L}\omega_i^{k\top}H_i), \tag{10}$$

where K is the number of heads, $W_8^*, W_9^* \in \mathbb{R}^{d \times d}$, and $q^* \in \mathbb{R}^{d \times 1}$, b^* is the bias and $\top$ denotes the transpose of the vector or the matrix.

We obtain the interaction probability $\hat{y} \in \mathbb{R}^m$ of each item in M, and adopt binary cross-entropy loss function with one-hot ground truth $y \in \mathbb{R}^m$ as follows:

$$\hat{y} = softmax(EM^\top),$$
$$\mathcal{L}(\hat{y}) = -\sum_{i=1}^{m} y_i log(\hat{y}_i) + (1 - y_i)log(1 - \hat{y}_i). \tag{11}$$

4   Experiments

We have conducted experiments to answer the following questions:

- RQ1: How well does MFIL outperform state-of-the-art models?
- RQ2: Do the transitions between inconsecutive items improve the performance?
- RQ3: What is the role of each structure in the proposed model?
- RQ4: Can the proposed learning strategy enhance the performance?

Datasets. We conduct experiments using two million-scale datasets, Diginetica[1] and JDATA[2], for the category information in these two datasets is more diverse, compared with *Yoochoose*, and we abandoned it for the same reason. Please note that JDATA is also a large-scale session-based recommendation dataset.

---

[1] https://competitions.codalab.org/competitions/11161.
[2] https://jdata.jd.com/html/detail.html?id=8.

The average number of brands in the interaction sequence is 1.95 for Diginetica and 2.54 for JDATA; each training sample is truncated at length 20. We retain the first one million records in JDATA to generate JD-1 m dataset due to computing power limitations. Following previous works [22], we also simulate a sparse dataset JD-100 k through retaining the first 100 k records in the origin JDATA dataset. We took the earlier 90% and subsequent (most recent) 10% user behaviors as the training and test set, respectively. We search the parameters on a validation set which is a random 10% subset of the training set. Statistical details are shown in Table 1.

Table 1. Dataset statistics (after preprocessing)

Dataset	Train sessions	Test sessions	Items	Avg. length
Diginetica	167,506	18,842	33,444	4.36
JD-1m	533,981	60,484	66,976	4.96
JD-100k	43,411	5126	12,346	4.62

Baselines. Due to the space limitation, we ignore the classic models like RNN or KNN, which had been fully explored in [16,31]. We compare our method with classic method SR-GNN and three latest state-of-the-art models:

- **SR-GNN** [22]: It applies a gated graph convolutional layer to obtain item embeddings, followed by a self-attention of the last item to combine long-term and current preferences of sessions to predict users' next actions.
- **FGNN** [10]: It models the item transitions via a weighted attention graph layer, propose a readout function to learn the embedding of the whole session, and incorporates the edge weight of neighboring items.
- **DGTN** [31]: It models item transitions within not only the current session but also the neighbor sessions. They are integrated into a graph, and then the embeddings are fed into the fusion function to obtain the final embedding.
- **GCE-GNN** [16]: Similar to **DGTN**, it exploits item transitions over all sessions in a more subtle manner for inferring the preference of the current session and aggregates the representations with a soft-attention mechanism.

Evaluation Metrics and Parameter Settings. By following previous baselines, we adopt the same widely used metrics P@N and M@N [22]. For our model, we use the Adam optimizer with the initial learning rate of 10^{-3} and the linear schedule decay rate of 0.1 for every 3 epochs. The dimension of the latent vectors is set to 64, and the batch size is set to 128. We set the number of neighbors and the maximum distance of adjacent items ϵ to 12 and 2, respectively. The $epoch_l$ and $epoch_g$ are set to 4. The *rate* used in Eq. (4) is set to 0.01, and the β_0 is set to 0.2, γ is set to 0.2. The dropout ratio is set to 0.2 for Diginetica and 0.5 for JDATA, respectively. For the other baselines, to make a fair comparison, we adjust the hyperparameters (e.g., *learning rate, dropout ratio, and numbers of attention heads*) to obtain a better result.

4.1   Performance Comparisons (RQ1)

In Table 2, the best result in each column is marked in bold, and the second-best one is 'underlined'. 'Impro.(%)' denotes the percentage improvement of MFIL with respect to the best performing value in the baselines.

Table 2. Recommendation performance. All numbers are in percentage

	Diginetica				JD-1 m				JD-100 k			
	$P@10$	$M@10$	$P@20$	$M@20$	$P@10$	$M@10$	$P@20$	$M@20$	$P@10$	$M@10$	$P@20$	$M@20$
SR-GNN	41.24	14.77	54.64	16.15	28.82	13.00	37.41	14.09	18.83	5.69	21.48	9.07
FGNN	40.58	13.62	53.18	16.03	26.66	10.04	34.24	11.63	22.27	8.98	27.63	11.70
DGTN	46.21	15.89	61.21	16.54	30.28	10.41	41.17	11.72	24.80	10.08	31.16	12.31
GCE-GNN	45.71	16.37	61.84	17.38	32.78	11.35	43.32	12.70	25.63	11.61	32.85	12.01
MFIL	**51.44**	**19.88**	**69.91**	**21.09**	**35.53**	**15.67**	**45.27**	**16.73**	**29.75**	**13.83**	**37.69**	**14.39**
Impro.(%)	11.3	21.4	13.0	21.3	8.4	20.5	4.5	18.7	16.1	19.1	14.7	16.9

MFIL achieved the best performance on all the datasets compared with baselines, which demonstrates its superiority. On average, MFIL improved GCE-GNN by 11.9% (10.73%) in terms of P@10(20), and 19.3% (18.9%) in terms of M@10(20). We observe that out MFIL surpasses the classic method SR and FGNN, which means only modeling the current session are inadequate to obtain a desirable result. Moreover, we notice that though considering the neighbor sessions, DGTN and GCE-GNN are still challenged by MFIL in all cases, which actually justifies our motivations mentioned in the contribution.

We have stated the disadvantages of the four baseline models in the introduction and Subsect. 2.2, and the experiment results can validate our analysis. GCE-GNN exhibited the second-best performances more than others, probably because it did not consider the transitions of inconsecutive items and fail to model the feature interactions, which has been explored in MFIL. The DGTN slightly performed worse than GCE-GNN, except on two metrics, but still significantly outperformed SR-GNN and FGNN in most cases. Different from our model, it did not learn the transitions of inconsecutive items in the target session.

Different from MFIL, FGNN did not consider the items in the neighbor session and did not beat SR-GNN in the first two datasets, but performed better than SR-GNN in the sparse datasets JD-100k. For SR-GNN, it only obtained the second-best performance on JD-1m in terms of M@10(20). Different from these methods, our approach learns the transitions of inconsecutive items, and explores more effective structures with the help of a different learning strategy, leading to better performance.

4.2   Impact of Side Information (RQ2)

Next, we conduct experiments on the first two large datasets, Diginetica and JD-1m, to evaluate the effectiveness of learning the transitions of inconsecutive items by leveraging item side information. We design four contrast models:

- **MFIL** w/o side information: It does not use the right matrix in Fig. 2 and only considers the *self-loop*, *in-come*, *out-come*, and *in-out* relationship.
- **MFIL** summation: It only utilizes the right matrix in Fig. 2 by summation and does not consider the feature interaction in Eq. (1).
- **MFIL** w/o share: The *in-out* and *'adjacent'* relationship do not share the same weight matrix in Eq. (2), so there will be five W_*^α matrices for the *self-loop*, *in-come*, *out-come*, *in-out*, and *'adjacent'* relationship.
- **MFIL** interaction: It uses both the two matrices in Fig. 2, and when modeling the feature interactions in Eq. (1), it combines the item embedding E_l and side information embedding I to obtain a_1 used in Eq. (1).

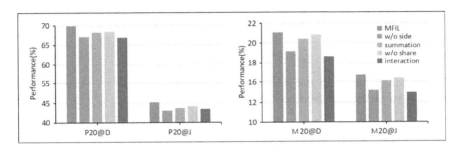

Fig. 4. Recommendation performance of MFIL with different structural designs in RQ2. All the numbers are percentage numbers with % omitted

Figure 4 shows the comparison of performance between different contrast models. The original MFIL achieves better performance. Comparing with MFIL w/o side information and MFIL summation, the original MFIL performs better on two datasets, which demonstrates the importance of side information and the 'adjacent' relationship shown in Fig. 2. The original MFIL also outperforms the last two models, MFIL w/o share and MFIL interaction. Therefore, it is less effective to introduce more parameters to describe the relationship between items, or combine the side information and learn the transitions of inconsecutive items. These results show that the original MFIL that considered about both the two kinds of relationships is more effective in balancing them.

Some possible reasons are as follows: 1) MFIL w/o side information performed worse than MFIL summation in all cases, so the 'adjacent' relationship was important for information propagation; 2) For MFIL interaction and MFIL w/o share, MFIL w/o share performed worse performance than the original MFIL. MFIL interaction's performance was even worse than that of MFIL w/o side information. So, integrating the side information into the interaction may be less efficient.

4.3   Impact of Structures (RQ3)

Then, we conduct experiments on the first two datasets, to evaluate the effectiveness of the proposed hierarchical structures in two learning modules. Specifically, we design three contrast models:

- **MFIL** w/o session: In the session learning module, it considers two kinds of relationships in Fig. 2 but does not use the MLP or concatenation operations in Eq. (1), which is similar to [16,31]. It only obtains $a_1 \in \mathbb{R}^{L \times L \times d}$:

$$a_1 = (E_l^1 \times E_l^2) \tag{12}$$

- **MFIL** w/o global: In the global learning module, it connects the embedding of items, with $W_5' \in \mathbb{R}^{(2d+1) \times 1}$, the average of neighbor embedding and the co-occurrence information to obtain the a_4 used in Eq. (6) as follows:

$$a_4 = [s'' \,\|\, N \,\|\, sigmoid(w)]W_5' \tag{13}$$

- **MFIL** single head: In the session representation module, we do not use the multi-head attention mechanism in (10).

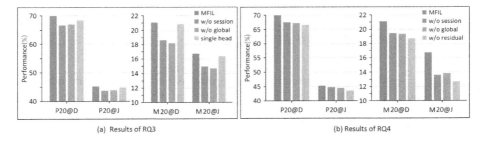

(a) Results of RQ3   (b) Results of RQ4

Fig. 5. Recommendation performance of MFIL with different structural designs in RQ3 and RQ4. All the numbers are percentage numbers with % omitted

Figure 5 (a) shows the comparison of performance between different contrast models. The original MFIL achieved better performance and demonstrated the superiority of learning feature interactions with hierarchical structures. The core idea of the two learning modules is to obtain better weight scores of the neighbor items in the current session (or neighbor sessions), and we introduced the feature interactions to model the weight scores more precisely. Compared with the first two methods, MFIL single head usually had better performance for session-based recommendation. This result demonstrated the effectiveness of aggregating different representations from different levels. The first two methods obtained similar performance, indicating that they were equally important.

4.4   Impact of Learning Strategy (RQ4)

We conducted experiments on two large datasets and reported the evaluation score at the end of each epoch to evaluate the effectiveness of the proposed learning strategy:

- **Learning** w/o session: In the session learning module, it ignored embedding quality and did not calculate the β in (3).
- **Learning** w/o global: In the global learning module, it simply reserved all scores in a_4 and ignored the k in Eq. (7).
- **MFIL** w/o residual: It ignored the residual connection operation in Eq. (3) and E_l when computing a_6 in (6).

Figure 5 (b) shows the comparison between different contrast models. Compared with the first two methods, the proposed learning strategies can improve the capability of MFIL. This actually justified our motivation to adopt the model to the embedding quality improvement. We also found that even in the later stage of training (16th epoch or later in JD-1m), the original MFIL could still optimize parameters and achieved better performance, whereas the third model began to overfit in the 10th epoch and stopped in the 13th epoch, as shown in Fig. 6. For MFIL w/o residual, we found that it is reasonable to introduce the proposed learning strategy.

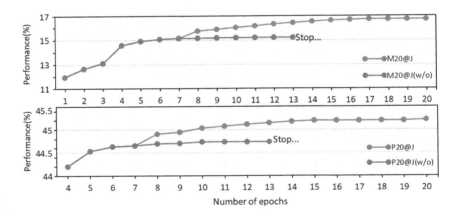

Fig. 6. Recommendation performance of MFIL with different learning strategies. All the numbers are percentage numbers with % omitted

5   Conclusion

In this paper, we propose a novel model, termed as MFIL, which learns the transitions of inconsecutive items and models feature interactions when propagating information. The experimental results show that it is reasonable to build adjacent matrices via item side information, and the hierarchical structure is able to learn the feature interactions. We also adopt a learning strategy to enhance the model capability, which can enhance the learning capability of out model. Extensive experiments demonstrate the superiority of MFIL.

In the future, we plan to find more methods to fuse different representations [2,12]. We also try to use multiple attributes, such as price or creation time. We will also explore knowledge graphs [8] and transformers [3,24] to improve the performance and efficiency of the proposed model, as well as use the items attribute [27,32] to better propagate information.

References

1. Balashankar, A., Beutel, A., Subramanian, L.: Enhancing neural recommender models through domain-specific concordance. In: Proceedings of the 14th ACM International Conference on Web Search and Data Mining, pp. 1002–1010 (2021)
2. Cen, Y., Zhang, J., Zou, X., Zhou, C., Yang, H., Tang, J.: Controllable multi-interest framework for recommendation. In: Proceedings of the 26th ACM SIGKDD International Conference on Knowledge Discovery & Data Mining, pp. 2942–2951 (2020)
3. Cho, S.M., Park, E., Yoo, S.: Meantime: mixture of attention mechanisms with multi-temporal embeddings for sequential recommendation. In: Fourteenth ACM Conference on Recommender Systems, pp. 515–520 (2020)
4. Kang, W.C., McAuley, J.: Self-attentive sequential recommendation. In: 2018 IEEE International Conference on Data Mining, ICDM, pp. 197–206. IEEE (2018)
5. Lian, J., Zhou, X., Zhang, F., Chen, Z., Xie, X., Sun, G.: xdeepfm: combining explicit and implicit feature interactions for recommender systems. In: Proceedings of the 24th ACM SIGKDD International Conference on Knowledge Discovery & Data Mining, pp. 1754–1763 (2018)
6. Liu, Y., et al.: Decoupled graph convolution network for inferring substitutable and complementary items. In: Proceedings of the 29th ACM International Conference on Information & Knowledge Management, pp. 2621–2628 (2020)
7. Ma, C., Ma, L., Zhang, Y., Sun, J., Liu, X., Coates, M.: Memory augmented graph neural networks for sequential recommendation. In: Proceedings of the AAAI Conference on Artificial Intelligence, vol. 34, pp. 5045–5052 (2020)
8. Meng, W., Yang, D., Xiao, Y.: Incorporating user micro-behaviors and item knowledge into multi-task learning for session-based recommendation. In: Proceedings of the 43rd International ACM SIGIR Conference on Research and Development in Information Retrieval, pp. 1091–1100 (2020)
9. Pan, Z., Cai, F., Chen, W., Chen, H., de Rijke, M.: Star graph neural networks for session-based recommendation. In: Proceedings of the 29th ACM International Conference on Information & Knowledge Management, pp. 1195–1204 (2020)
10. Qiu, R., Li, J., Huang, Y.: Rethinking the item order in session-based recommendation with graph neural networks. In: Proceedings of the 28th ACM International Conference on Information and Knowledge Management, pp. 579–588 (2019)
11. Song, W., Xiao, Z., Wang, Y., Charlin, L., Zhang, J.: Session-based social recommendation via dynamic graph attention networks. In: Proceedings of the Twelfth ACM International Conference on Web Search and Data Mining, pp. 555–563 (2019)

12. Tan, Q., et al.: Sparse-interest network for sequential recommendation. In: Proceedings of the 14th ACM International Conference on Web Search and Data Mining, pp. 598–606 (2021)
13. Tanjim, M.M., Ayyubi, H.A., Cottrell, G.W.: Dynamicrec: a dynamic convolutional network for next item recommendation. In: Proceedings of the 29th ACM International Conference on Information, pp. 2237–2240 (2020)
14. Wang, J., Ding, K., Hong, L., Liu, H.: Next-item recommendation with sequential hypergraphs. In: Proceedings of the 43rd International ACM SIGIR Conference on Research and Development in Information Retrieval, pp. 1101–1110 (2020)
15. Wang, X., He, X., Wang, M., Feng, F., Chua, T.S.: Neural graph collaborative filtering. In: Proceedings of the 42nd international ACM SIGIR Conference on Research and Development in Information Retrieval, pp. 165–174 (2019)
16. Wang, Z., Wei, W., Cong, G., Li, X.L., Mao, X.L., Qiu, M.: Global context enhanced graph neural networks for session-based recommendation. In: Proceedings of the 43rd International ACM SIGIR Conference on Research and Development in Information Retrieval, pp. 169–178 (2020)
17. Wu, L., Sun, P., Fu, Y., Hong, R., Wang, M.: A neural influence diffusion model for social recommendation. In: Proceedings of the 42nd international ACM SIGIR conference on research and development, pp. 235–244 (2019)
18. Wu, L., Li, S., Hsieh, C.J., Sharpnack, J.: Stochastic shared embeddings: datadriven regularization of embedding layers (2019). arXiv preprint, arXiv:1905.10630
19. Wu, L., Li, S., Hsieh, C.J., Sharpnack, J.: Sse-pt: sequential recommendation via personalized transformer. In: Fourteenth ACM Conference on Recommender Systems, pp. 328–337 (2020)
20. Wu, Q., et al.: Dual graph attention networks for deep latent representation of multifaceted social effects in recommender systems. In: The World Wide Web Conference, pp. 2091–2102 (2019)
21. Wu, S., Zhang, W., Sun, F., Cui, B.: Graph neural networks in recommender systems: a survey (2020). arXiv preprint, arXiv:2011.02260
22. Wu, S., Tang, Y., Zhu, Y., Wang, L., Xie, X., Tan, T.: Session-based recommendation with graph neural networks. In: Proceedings of the AAAI Conference on Artificial Intelligence, vol. 33, pp. 346–353 (2019)
23. Wu, S., Zhang, M., Jiang, X., Xu, K., Wang, L.: Personalized graph neural networks with attention mechanism for session-aware recommendation (2019). arXiv preprint arXiv:1910.08887
24. Xu, C., et al.: Graph contextualized self-attention network for session-based recommendation. In: IJCAI, vol. 19, pp. 3940–3946 (2019)
25. Yu, F., Zhu, Y., Liu, Q., Wu, S., Wang, L., Tan, T.: Tagnn: target attentive graph neural networks for session-based recommendation. In: Proceedings of the 43rd International ACM SIGIR Conference on Research and Development in Information Retrieval, pp. 1921–1924 (2020)
26. Zhang, J., Shi, X., Zhao, S.: Star-gcn: stacked and reconstructed graph convolutional networks for recommender systems (2019). arXiv preprint, arXiv:1905.13129
27. Zhang, T., Zhao, P., Liu, Y., Sheng, V.S., Xu, J.: Feature-level deeper self-attention network for sequential recommendation. In: IJCAI, pp. 4320–4326 (2019)
28. Zhang, W., Mao, J., Cao, Y., Xu, C.: Multiplex graph neural networks for multibehavior recommendation. In: Proceedings of the 29th ACM International Conference on Information & Knowledge Management, pp. 2313–2316 (2020)
29. Zhang, Y., Sun, F., Yang, X., Xu, C.: Graph-based regularization on embedding layers for recommendation. ACM Trans. Inf. Syst. **39**(1), 1–27 (2020)

30. Zheng, Y., Liu, S., Li, Z., Wu, S.: Cold-start sequential recommendation via meta learner (2020). arXiv preprint, arXiv:2012.05462
31. Zheng, Y., Liu, S., Li, Z., Wu, S.: Dgtn: dual-channel graph transition network for session-based recommendation (2020). arXiv preprint, arXiv:2009.10002
32. Zhou, K., Wang, H., Zhao, W.X., Zhu, Y., Wang, S., Zhang, F., Wang: S3-rec: Self-supervised learning for sequential recommendation with mutual information maximization. In: Proceedings of the 29th ACM International Conference on Information Knowledge Management, pp. 1893–1902 (2020)

Social Web Applications

A Real-Time System for Detecting Landslide Reports on Social Media Using Artificial Intelligence

Ferda Ofli[1(✉)] ⓘ, Umair Qazi[1] ⓘ, Muhammad Imran[1] ⓘ, Julien Roch[2],
Catherine Pennington[3] ⓘ, Vanessa Banks[3] ⓘ, and Remy Bossu[2,4] ⓘ

[1] Qatar Computing Research Institute, Hamad Bin Khalifa University, Doha, Qatar
{fofli,uqazi,mimran}@hbku.edu.qa
[2] European-Mediterranean Seismological Centre, Arpajon, France
{julien.roch,bossu}@emsc-csem.org
[3] British Geological Survey, Keyworth, Nottinghamshire, UK
{cpoulton,vbanks}@bgs.ac.uk
[4] CEA, DAM, DIF, 91297 Arpajon, France

Abstract. This paper presents an online system that leverages social media data in real time to identify landslide-related information automatically using state-of-the-art artificial intelligence techniques. The designed system can (i) reduce the information overload by eliminating duplicate and irrelevant content, (ii) identify landslide images, (iii) infer geolocation of the images, and (iv) categorize the user type (organization or person) of the account sharing the information. The system was deployed in February 2020 online at https://landslide-aidr.qcri.org/landslide_system.php to monitor live Twitter data stream and has been running continuously since then to provide time-critical information to partners such as British Geological Survey and European Mediterranean Seismological Centre. We trust this system can both contribute to harvesting of global landslide data for further research and support global landslide maps to facilitate emergency response and decision making.

Keywords: Landslide detection · Social media · Online system · Real time · Image classification · Computer vision · Artificial intelligence

1 Introduction

Landslides cause thousands of deaths and billions of dollars in infrastructural damage worldwide every year [16]. However, landslide events are often underreported and insufficiently documented due to their complex natural phenomena oftentimes triggered by earthquakes and tropical storms, which are more conspicuous, and hence, more widely reported [18]. Therefore, any attempt to quantify global landslide hazards and the associated impacts remains an underestimation due to this oversight and lack of global data inventories [8].

© Springer Nature Switzerland AG 2022
T. Di Noia et al. (Eds.): ICWE 2022, LNCS 13362, pp. 49–65, 2022.
https://doi.org/10.1007/978-3-031-09917-5_4

Undertaking the challenge of building a global landslide inventory, NASA launched a website[1] in 2018 to allow citizens to report about the regional landslides they see in-person or online [14]. Following a similar Volunteered Geographical Information (VGI) approach, researchers further developed other means such as mobile or web applications to collect citizen-provided data [6,17]. While VGI-based solutions prove helpful, they are not easily scalable as they require active participation of volunteers that opt-in to use a particular application to collect and share landslide-related data. Furthermore, this means the bulk of data collection and interpretation still involves time consuming work by specialists searching the Internet for news and reports, or directly engaging in communications with those submitting information [14,17,28,36].

To alleviate the need for opt-in participation and manual processing, we developed an online system equipped with state-of-the-art AI models to automatically detect landslide reports posted on social media image streams in real time. The system was developed through an interdisciplinary collaboration between the computer scientists at the Qatar Computing Research Institute (QCRI) and the earthquake and landslide specialists from the European-Mediterranean Seismological Centre (EMSC) and the British Geological Survey (BGS), respectively. The developed system employs several supervised machine learning models to (i) deal with the noisy nature of the social media data by filtering out duplicate and irrelevant images, (ii) detect landslide reports by interpreting the retained images, (iii) infer the location information of the detected landslide reports from the available metadata, and (iv) identify the type of users that have shared the landslide reports. We deployed the system online in February 2020 to monitor live Twitter data stream and it has collected more than 54 million tweets and 15 million image URLs. Only about 2.5 million of these image URLs were deemed unique and downloaded for further analysis. Eventually, the system identified about 38,000 landslide reports worldwide, which corresponds to less than 1% of the collected image URLs and highlights the challenging nature of the problem. Despite this, quantitative verification of the system's performance during a real-world deployment shows that our system can detect landslide reports with Precision = 76% and Recall = 74% (i.e., F1 = 75%).

2   Related Work

The literature on landslide detection and mapping approaches mainly uses four types of data sources: (i) physical sensors, (ii) remote sensing, (iii) volunteers, and (iv) social networks. Sensor-based approaches rely on land characteristics such as rainfall, altitude, soil type, and slope to detect landslides and develop models to predict future events [19,31]. While these approaches can be highly accurate at sub-catchment levels, their large-scale deployment is extremely costly.

Earth observation data from high-resolution satellite imagery has been widely used for landslide detection, mapping, and monitoring [37]. Remote sensing techniques either use Synthetic Aperture Radar (SAR) or optical imagery to perform

---

[1] https://gpm.nasa.gov/landslides/index.html (accessed on 12 February 2022).

landslide detection in various formulations including classification, segmentation, object detection, and change detection [4,13,20,29,30,35]. While remote sensing through satellites can be useful to monitor landslides globally, their deployment can prove costly and time-consuming.

A few studies demonstrated the use of Volunteered Geographical Information (VGI) as an alternative method to detect landslides [2,3,6,17]. These studies assume active participation of volunteers to collect landslide data where the volunteers opt-in to use a mobile or web application to provide information such as photos, time of occurrence, damage description, and other observations about a landslide event. On the contrary, our work capitalizes on massive social media data without any active participation requirement and with better scalability.

Social media data has been used in many humanitarian contexts ranging from general social analytics [32] and geospatial sentiment analysis [1] to incident detection [38] and rapid damage assessment [10], including multimodal approaches [25]. However, its use for landslide detection has not been explored extensively. The most relevant work by Musaev et al. [21,23] combines social media text data and physical sensors to detect landslides. In contrast, we focus on analyzing social media images which provide more detailed information about the impact of the landslide event. Therefore, our work complements prior art.

3   System Design

The system is designed to ingest data from an online social media platform (i.e., Twitter), analyze the incoming data, and process relevant information under the condition that all tasks must be performed in a time-sensitive manner. Figure 1 shows a high-level architecture of the system and its various critical components. Data flows from left to right through two types of connections between components. The red lines indicate streaming connections whereas the black lines represent on-demand connections. A streaming connection can be of two types (i) a publisher-subscriber channel, and (ii) a push-pop queue.

3.1   Data Collectors

We have two types of collectors. One collects data (i.e., tweets) directly from Twitter. The other one then downloads images corresponding to collected tweets.

Tweet Collector. This module uses the Twitter Streaming API[2] to collect live tweets. The Streaming API can provide data in various ways based on (i) a list of keywords, (ii) geographical bounding boxes, or (iii) both. The bounding box approach provides geo-tagged tweets which can be about any topic, thus we use the keyword-based approach through the AIDR system [11]. The keywords are related to multilingual landslide terminology and nomenclature such as landslide,

---

[2] https://developer.twitter.com/en/docs/twitter-api/v1/tweets/filter-realtime/ guides/connecting (accessed on 24 March 2022).

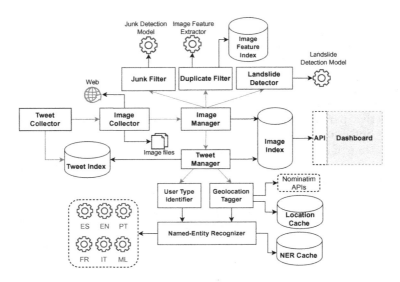

Fig. 1. System architecture with important components and communication flows

landslip, earth slip, mudslide, rockslide, and rock fall (Table 3). Tweets matching with at least one of the pre-specified keywords are acquired from Twitter in the JSON format and persisted into the Tweet Index, which is an Elasticsearch database. If a tweet contains one or more images, its *id* and *URLs* of all images are pushed to the Image Collector through a Redis[3] queue.

Image Collector. This module parses image-related attributes dispatched by the Tweet Collector module and extracts image URLs and downloads corresponding images. Due to re-tweets, same image URLs may appear multiple times during the data collection. To avoid redundant downloads, the system keeps track of previously seen image URLs in an in-memory *linked hash map* which has O(1) time complexity for adding and searching an element and O(n) space complexity. The downloaded images are saved on the file system and their paths and tweet ids are pushed to the Image Manager queue for further processing.

3.2   Image Manager

The system has multiple modules that analyze images for different purposes. Two of these modules, namely Duplicate Filter and Junk Filter, are tasked to reduce the data noise by eliminating images that are (i) near-or-exact duplicate and (ii) irrelevant for general disaster response, respectively. The third module, Landslide Detector, is the core module that interprets each image as landslide or not-landslide. All image processor modules are managed by the Image Manager,

---

[3] https://redis.io/ (accessed on 24 March 2022).

which pops items from its queue and immediately dispatches to the three image processors (i.e., Junk Filter, Duplicate Filter, and Landslide Detector) through their respective queues. The Image Manager also monitors the output of all image processors to persist them into the main Image Index.

Duplicate Filter. Image-level deduplication is important to discard near-or-exact duplicate images that are often due to high retweeting activity. This module identifies duplicate images to prevent further processing as well as information overload on end users. The module acquires images from its input queue and checks whether a given image is near-or-exact duplicate of previously seen images. To this end, it first extracts features from each image using a deep learning model and then compares these features against an Image Feature Index to detect near-or-exact duplicate cases based on a distance threshold. The image feature index keeps a record of all unique image features. If the module identifies a near-or-exact duplicate, it returns the reference image's id and the computed distance. Otherwise, it tags the image as "not-duplicate". If the image is "not-duplicate", then it is also inserted into the Image Feature Index. Section 4.1 presents details of the feature extracting model.

Junk Filter. Even though filtered through landslide-related keywords, the Twitter image stream carries images not pertaining to landslide incidents. Identifying these junk content is important to reduce information overload on end users. To this end, the Junk Filter module pops images from the input queue and processes them through the junk detection model, which outputs a class label ("relevant" or "not-relevant") and a confidence score. More detailed information about the junk detection model is presented in Sect. 4.2. The processed images are pushed into the output queue of the module.

Landslide Detector. As the main objective of the system is to identify images showing landslide incidents, in this module we perform this task using a deep learning computer vision model. The module first acquires images from its input queue and passes them through the landslide classifier, which outputs a class label ("landslide" or "not-landslide") and a confidence score. The landslide classifier is a deep learning image classification model that is presented in detail in Sect. 4.3. The classified images are pushed into the module's output queue.

3.3   Tweet Manager

The system contains three modules, namely Geolocation Tagger, User Type Identifier, and Named-Entity Recognizer, that process textual content for different purposes. Specifically, Geolocation Tagger analyzes various tweet metadata fields to infer geolocation information while User Type Identifier focuses on identifying the type of Twitter account. Both modules use Named-Entity Recognizer to tag text tokens with named-entities.

Geolocation Tagger. Identifying the location of landslide incidents reported on Twitter is an important task. A tweet reporting a landslide with some image content may or may not have an explicit mention of the location in the text where the incident took place. In that case, other meta-data fields are examined to find location cues. These fields include, *GPS-coordinates, place, user location*, and *user profile description*. To this end, we use our geolocation tagging approach presented in [12] with a different field priority order. We observed that most tweets with landslide reporting images contain location cues in their text content. Therefore, if a tweet does not contain GPS-coordinates, we give high priority to the location names mentioned in the text. Place, user location, and user profile description come later in the order, respectively. The geolocation tagger uses the named-entity recognizer to get named-entities for tweet text and user profile description fields. The geolocation tagger uses Nominatim geocoding and reverse geocoding APIs and tags each tweet with country, state, county, and city information, when possible. More details of the geotagging approach can be found in [12]. The module maintains a cache of processed locations to increase its efficiency for recurring requests.

User Type Identifier. This module uses the name of the tweet author to determine whether the account is of type person or organization. Landslide incidents reported by personal accounts are more important for our end users than those reported by organizational accounts. For this purpose, we use the English NER model through the Named-Entity Recognizer module, which tags name tokens with one of the several predefined named-entities, including PERSON.

Named-Entity Recognizer. As described above, both Geolocation Tagger and User Type Identifier modules use Named-Entity Recognizer to perform their operation. To support these operations for multilingual tweets, we use five NER models representing five international languages, including English, French, Spanish, Portuguese, and Italian. Additionally, we use a multilingual NER model (denoted as ML) for all other languages. All of these multilingual models and their performance scores are publicly available at spaCy website.[4] This module also maintains a cache of processed NER requests to increase its efficiency for recurring requests.

4   Experiments

In this section, we first describe the design and development of our image models and present experimental results. Then, we present performance evaluation and benchmarking results for the most critical components of the system. For image models, we follow the popular transfer learning approach based on convolutional neural networks (CNNs) as many studies have shown that features learned by CNNs are effectively transferable between different visual recognition tasks [7, 27,34], particularly when training samples are limited.

---

[4] https://spacy.io/usage/models (accessed on 24 March 2022).

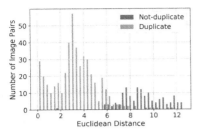

(a) Histogram of pairwise distances

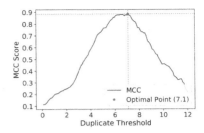

(b) MCC vs. duplicate threshold

Fig. 2. Optimal duplicate distance threshold determination: (a) Distribution of the Euclidean distances between the image pairs in the duplicate test set. (b) MCC performance as a function of distance threshold.

4.1 Duplicate Filtering

The Duplicate Filter is responsible for extracting a feature vector from a given image using a state-of-the-art deep learning model and comparing this feature vector with the feature vectors of previously seen images based on a pre-defined distance threshold d. For this purpose, we extract deep features from the penultimate layer of a ResNet-50 model [9] pre-trained on the Places data set [39], which comprises 10 million images collected for scene recognition.[5] Each feature vector has a size of 2,048. To determine the optimal distance threshold d, we performed experiments on a manually annotated set of 600 image pairs including 460 duplicate and 140 non-duplicate cases with varying pairwise distances (Fig. 2a). We used Euclidean distance metric (i.e., L2 norm) to measure the distance between two image feature vectors. Note that image pairs with a distance greater than 12.5 looked trivially distinct, and hence, we did not include them in our experiments. We then performed a grid search over a range of threshold values from 0 to 12 with a step size of 0.1 and measured the performance of each threshold value by computing the Matthew's Correlation Coefficient (MCC), which is regarded as a balanced measure for imbalanced classification problems [5]. As depicted in Fig. 2b, the optimal performance is achieved when the duplicate distance threshold is $d = 7.1$.

4.2 Junk Classification

The Junk Filter employs a CNN model to determine whether an image is relevant or not for general emergency management and response. To this end, we took a ResNet-50 model [9] pre-trained on ImageNet [33], adopted its final layer to binary classification task, and fine-tuned it on a custom data set introduced by Nguyen et al. [24]. We merged the validation set with the training set, and used the test set to evaluate the performance of the model as summarized in

---

[5] The pre-trained model is available at http://places2.csail.mit.edu/models_places365/resnet50_places365.pth.tar (accessed on Jan 23, 2022).

Table 1a. We used Adam optimizer [15] with an initial learning rate of 10^{-6} and configured the `ReduceLROnPlateau` scheduler to decay the learning rate by 0.1 with a patience of 50 epochs. We trained the model for a total of 200 epochs. The training process of the junk classification model is plotted in Fig. 3a and its performance evaluation is presented in Table 1b. The model achieves almost perfect performance in all measures due to the distinct features between relevant and not-relevant images in the training data set. We note that early stopping the model training after 100 epochs would yield the same model performance.

Table 1. Details of the data set used for training the junk classification model and the performance of the trained model on the test set.

(a) Training data set

Class	Train	Test	Total
Relevant	2,814	704	3,518
Not-relevant	2,814	704	3,518
Total	5,628	1,408	7,036

(b) Model performance (Acc: 98.79)

Class	Precision	Recall	F1
Relevant	98.31	99.29	98.80
Not-relevant	99.28	98.30	98.79
Macro avg.	98.80	98.79	98.79

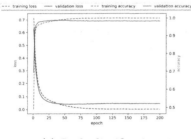

(a) Junk classification

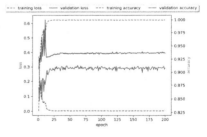

(b) Landslide classification

Fig. 3. Model training progress in terms of accuracy and loss achieved on the training and validation sets

4.3 Landslide Classification

The Landslide Detector is the most important component of the proposed system. Therefore, we performed a separate, comprehensive study to identify the optimal configuration for the landslide classification model [26]. To recap, we first created a large landslide image data set labeled by landslide specialists, who are also co-authors of this paper. The data set contains 11,737 images, which are split into training, validation, and test sets as shown in Table 2a. Then, adopting a transfer learning approach, we conducted an extensive set of experiments using various CNN architectures with different optimizers, learning rates, weight decays, and class balancing strategies. The winning model configuration is a ResNet-50 architecture trained using Adam optimizer with an initial learning rate of 10^{-4}, a weight decay of 10^{-3}, and without a class balancing strategy. Figure 3b displays the training progress of the best performing landslide classification model, which is also integrated into our system, whereas Table 2b summarizes the performance of the model on the test set. As with the junk classification model, the plot indicates that the model training process could be early stopped after 100 epochs without affecting the model performance.

Table 2. Details of the data set used for training the landslide classification model and the performance of the trained model on the test set.

(a) Training data set

Class	Train	Val	Test	Total
Landslide	1,883	271	536	2,690
Not-landslide	6,332	902	1,813	9,047
Total	8,215	1,173	2,349	11,737

(b) Model performance (Acc: 86.97)

Class	Precision	Recall	F1
Landslide	73.66	66.79	70.06
Not-landslide	90.45	92.94	91.68
Macro avg.	82.05	79.87	80.87

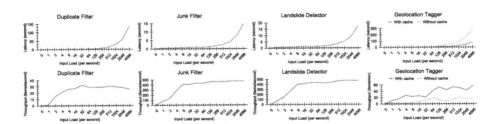

Fig. 4. Latency (top) and throughput (bottom) of the Junk Filter, Duplicate Filter, Landslide Detector, and Geolocation Tagger (left to right).

4.4 Performance Evaluation and Benchmarking

To stress-test the system and understand its scalability, we conducted performance experiments on four critical modules, i.e., Duplicate Filter, Junk Filter, Landslide Detector, and Geolocation Tagger. We use latency and throughput, as they are considered reliable measures to test a system's performance. In our case, the latency is the time taken by a module to process a given input load consisting of images. Whereas, the throughput is the number of images processed in a unit time (one second) given an input load. The experiments were conducted using a pool of 50,000 images. We developed a simulator to mimic the functionality of the Image Collector. The simulator pushed varying amounts of input loads to Redis channels, which were then consumed by modules. Based on the real-world deployment, we observed that the input load reaches a maximum of 0.08 images per second (on average). Therefore, we tested a range of input loads defined as $2^n, n \in \{0, 1, ..., 12\}$. We performed the tests on a Linux server with 256GB RAM, 2.2 GHz processor with 32 cores and two Tesla V100 GPUs with 16 GB.

Figure 4 shows the performance results. The latency for all modules follows the same pattern, i.e., as the input load (per second) increases, the latency also increases. However, as the computational responsibilities of each module differ, so do their latencies at different input loads. For instance, both Relevancy Filter and Landslide Detector show a decent latency of around five seconds even at 1024 input load. The Duplicate Filter, however, exhibits high latency (i.e., 29 s) at the same load. The latency for Geolocation Tagger is measured with and without cache, which makes a significant difference. The cache keeps a record of all existing unique requests and hence, on average, the latency of the cached version is about four times less.

In terms of throughput, Relevancy Filter and Landslide Detector maintain a high throughput of more than 400 images/second, even at the maximum input load. Throughput for Junk Filter reaches module capacity at 467 images/second on average and for Landslide Detector it goes up to 457 images/second on average. For Duplicate Filter, the throughput initially increases but then starts decreasing as the size of Image Feature Index grows. The throughput is also about 4 times higher on average with cache compared to without cache. Geolocation Tagger reaches its capacity at about 50 images per second with cache. With an empty cache, it goes as high as 21 images per second on average with cache and is expected to increase as the cache grows in size.

5   Real-World Deployment

Here we present details about our real-world deployment including data collection and statistics, quantitative verification of the detected landslide reports, and a comparison with a text-based approach.

5.1   Data Collection and Statistics

In February 2020, we launched the system online at https://landslide-aidr.qcri. org/landslide_system.php to monitor live Twitter stream for landslide-related reports. Figure 5 shows a snapshot of the system dashboard. We note that, by landslide, we refer to all downward and outward movement of loosened slope materials such as landslip, debris flows, mudslides, rockfalls, earthflows, and other mass movements. As mentioned in Sect. 3.1, the system follows a keyword-based data collection strategy. Hence, we curated a list of 339 multilingual keywords covering all types of landslides in 32 languages including English, Albanian, Arabic, Basque, Bengali, Bosnian, Catalan, Chinese, Croatian, Dutch,

AIDR Twitter Image Analysis: Detecting Landslides, Mudslides, Rockslides.

Total images collected: 2,527,175

Data available from 2020-02-04 to 2021-12-29
Start date: 12/29/2021, 12:00:00 AM 🗓 End date: 12/29/2021, 11:59:59 PM 🗓 Apply
Remove duplicates: ❷ ⦿ YES ○ NO
Remove irrelevant: ❷ ⦿ YES ○ NO
Show landslide images: ❷ ⦿ YES ○ NO
User type: ❷ ○ Person ○ Organization ⦿ All
Location filter: ❷

Country	State	City
----- All -----	----- Not available -----	----- Not available -----

Include non-geotagged images: ❷ ⦿ YES ○ NO

Total images: 1,886
Filtered images: 7
All times are shown in UTC.

Images Layout | Map Layout

(≈) : Inferred location ❷
(⦿) : Exact location ❷
Page 1 of 1   prev   next

LANDSLIDE	LANDSLIDE	LANDSLIDE	LANDSLIDE	LANDSLIDE
Time: 29-Dec-2021 13:04:34 **From:** Servicio de Información Pública **Text:** □2 Un deslizamiento de tierra a causa de las lluvias mantiene cerrada parte de la calzada en la carretera local 004, específicamente en la quebrada La Boba en Campo Elías, #Mérida. Autoridades atienden la situación para despejar la vía. 'DC @ivanrive3 **Location (≈):** Kinshasa, Capital District, Congo Tweet link	**Time:** 29-Dec-2021 13:04:34 **From:** Servicio de Información Pública **Text:** □ Un deslizamiento de tierra a causa de las lluvias mantiene cerrada parte de la calzada en la carretera local 004, específicamente en la quebrada La Boba en Campo Elías, #Mérida. Autoridades atienden la situación para despejar la vía. 'DC @ivanrive3 **Location (≈):** Kinshasa, Capital District, Congo Tweet link	**Time:** 29-Dec-2021 11:00:25 **From:** penerangan 071/WK **Text:** Hujan Deras,Dua Rumah Warga Rusak Terkena Tanah Longsor **Location:** N/A Tweet link	**Time:** 29-Dec-2021 05:56:14 **From:** Ingeniería en la Red **Text:** (vía @arriskeus + @pantoja_nilza) ₅5ᴹℂ×1×2ᴹªℰ ₂2ᴺB ₄0×2ᴺB/E, un tIpo de deslizamiento traslacional que está controlado por dos o más discontinuidades (estratificación, esquistosidad, diaclasas, fallas) **Location (≈):** Andalusia, Spain Tweet link	**Time:** 29-Dec-2021 01:15:16 **From:** Obras Quito **Text:** 59 Trabajamos en la limpieza de tierra y escombros por deslizamiento de talud sobre la vía en la av. Simón Bolívar, en el sector del Mirador de Cumbayá. #PorUnQuitoDigno **Location (≈):** Pichincha, Ecuador Tweet link

Fig. 5. Snapshot of the online system dashboard

French, Georgian, German, Greek, Hindi, Hungarian, Indonesia, Iranian, Italian, Japanese, Korean, Malaysia, Philippines, Polish, Portuguese, Romanian, Russian, Sesotho, Slovenian, Spanish, Swedish, and Turkish (Table 3).

Since its deployment until December 31, 2021, the system has collected more than 54 million tweets and 15 million image URLs, out of which about 2.5 million were deemed unique and downloaded for further analysis. Figure 6 depicts the weekly volume of raw tweets and images collected during this time period as well as the distributions of images filtered by the Junk Filter, Duplicate Filter, and Landslide Detector. The data do not show any gaps, which is an important factor for robust monitoring of real-world events continuously. On average, the Junk Filter eliminates around 76% of the collected images, the Duplicate Filter further reduces the redundancy by an additional 9%, and finally, the Landslide Detector classifies only 0.84% of the remaining 15% images as landslides. This corresponds to a significant (i.e., more than 99%) reduction of information overload for our end users. 6,523 of all the detected landslide reports were shared by personal accounts and 4,553 by organizational accounts. Figure 7 shows the worldwide

Table 3. List of all keywords in 32 languages used for data collection.

landslide, landslides, rockfall, rock-fall, rockslide, rockslides, mudslide, mudslides, mudflow, mudflows, landslip, earthslip, Sturzstrom, avalanche, glissement de terrain, glissements de terrain, chute de pierres, coulée de boue, effondrement, avalanche, frana, frane, crollo di roccia, crolli di roccia, caduta massi, cadute massi, smottamento, smottamenti, slavina, slavine, lliscament de terra, esllavissada de terra, Despreniments de roques, colada de terra, corriment de terra, allau, Esllavissaments superficials, Deslizamiento, deslizamiento de tierra, caída de roca, desprendimientos de rocas, deslizamiento de rocas, avalancha de barro, deslizamiento de barro, deslizamiento de lodo, Colapso, tanah runtuh, kejatuhan batu, tanah runtuh, lumpur, tanah longsor, batu jatuh, guguran, lahar, longsoran besar, انهيار صخري, سقوط صخري, انزلاق أرضي, انزلاق أرضي, انهيار أرضي, الانهيار الجليدي, الانهيار الأرضي, انزلاق الأرض, الانهيارات الطينية, الانزلاق الطيني, الانزلاق الأرضي, الانهيارات الصخرية, оползень, оползни, зсув, зсув ґрунту, зсув ґрунту, обвал, обвал скель, падіння скель, каменопад, грязьовий потік, селеві потоки, обрушение, лавина, 산사태, 낙석, 암반사태, 진흙사태, 이류, 사태, 눈사태, heyelan, toprak kayması, heyelanlar, toprak kaymaları, kaya düşmesi, kaya kayması, kaya göçmesi, kaya akıntısı, moloz akıntısı, moloz akışı, moloz akması, moloz kayması, kaya düşmeleri, kaya kaymaları, kaya göçmeleri, kaya akıntıları, moloz akıntıları, moloz kaymaları, çamur akıntısı, çamur akışı, çamur kayması, çamur akması, tortu akıntısı, tortu akışı, tortu akması, tortu kayması, döküntü akıntısı, döküntü akışı, döküntü akması, döküntü kayması, lahar, çamur akıntıları, çamur kaymaları, tortu akıntıları, tortu kaymaları, döküntü akıntıları, döküntü kaymaları, laharlar, çığ, çığlar, Erdrutsch, Erdrutsche, Bergrutsch, Bergrutsche, Hangrutsch, Hangrutsche, Hangrutschung, Hangrutschungen, Abrutschung, Abrutschungen, Steinrutschung, Steinrutschung, Hangmure, Hangmuren, Steinschlag, Steinschläge, Murgang, Murgänge, Mure, Muren, Schlammlawine, Schlammlawinen, Murenabgang, Murenabgänge, Bergsturz, Bergstürze, Lawine, Lawinen, Schneelawine, Schneelawinen, Eislawine, Eislawinen, Staublawine, Staublawinen, ভূমিধ্বস, ভূমিধস, 地すべり, 土砂災害, 土砂崩れ, 山津波, 地滑り, 山崩れ, 山, 坍, 土石流, 雪崩, 表層雪崩, 滑り, κατολίσθηση, καθίζηση εδάφους, πτώση βράχου, βραχοκατολίσθηση, ολίσθηση λάσπης, λασπολίσθηση, καθίζηση εδάφους, χιονοστιβάδα, pagguho ng lupa, pagkahulog ng bato, putik sa lupa, 滑坡, 山体滑坡, 岩崩, 岩滑, 泥石流, 山体坍方, 地崩, 雪崩, deslizamento de terras, Queda de rochas, deslizamento de rochas, Queda de blocos, deslizamento de lamas, lamas, Movimentos de massa, Avalanche, lur-irristatzea, harri-jausia , harri erorketa, arroka-irristatzea, Lur-kolada, azal-irristatzea , gainazaleko-irristatzea, higakin-korrontea, alunecare de teren, alunecare de teren cu caderi de roci, caderi de roci, alunecare de noroi, alunecare de pamant, avalansa, Rrëshqitje toke, Rrëshqitje shkëmbore, Rrëshqitjet shkëmbore, Rrëshqitje e tipit rënie e coprave dhe blloqeve shkembore, Rrjedhje balte, Rrjedhjet balte, Rrëshqitje dheu, Rrëshqitje toke, Rrëshqitje e tipit ortekë, zemeljski plaz, skalni podor, skalni zdrs, skalni zdrsi, blatni tok, blatni tokovi, zdrs pobočja, zdrs zemljine, plaz, skred, skreden, jordskred, jordskreden, bergskred, ierskred, slåntstabilitet, kvicklera, snöskred, lavin, odron, kliziste, lavina, kôlavina, hólavina, földcsuszamlás, talajcsúszás, talajcsuszamlás, sárfolyás, talajfolyás, iszapfolyás, sárlavina, talajkúszás, suvadás, kôomlás, hegyomlás, hegyomlások, iszapár, földcsuszamlás, földcsuszamlások, sárlavina, sárlavinák, törmeléklavina, lavina, lavinák, alunecare de teren, alunecare de teren, alunecari de stânci , alunecari de stânci, alunecare de noroi , alunecări de noroi, deplasări de teren, alunecare de pământ, avalanşă, Aardverschuiving, aardverschuivingen, Bergstorting , Rotslawine, steenlawine, puinlawine, Modderlawine, Modderstroom, modderstromen, Lawine, kliziste, klizista, odron, odroni, blatni tok, blatni tokovi, zemljani tok, zemljani tokovi, lavina, lavine, osuwisko, osuwiska, obryw skalny, obrywy skale, osuwisko skalne, osuwiska skalne, lawina błotna, lawiny błotne, osuwisko, lawina, lawiny, راش زمین, رانش زمین لغزه, ریزش سنگ, سنگ ریزش , سنگ لغزه, گل لغزه , بهمن, Ho heleha hoa mobu, Ho theteha hoa mafika, Seretse se phallang, Ho hlefoha hoa lefats'e, Ho heleha, le ho phalla hoa lehloa, მეწყერი, ქვათაცვენა, კლდეზვავი, კლდეზვავები, ტალახოვანი, ღვარცოფები, ზვავი , maanvyöry, putoavia kiviä, kivivyöry, kivivyöryt, mutavyöry, mutavyöryt, sortuma, lumivyöry, snowmelt, snow melt, debris flow, cliff fall, cliff collapse, landslips

distribution of the detected landslide reports while Fig. 8 highlights the top-10 countries with the highest number of landslide reports in each quarter. We see that US, Ecuador, Colombia, and India experience significant landslide numbers all year round. For India, landslides become even more prevalent in Q3. Likewise, Mexico experiences a significant increase in Q3. In contrast, prominent landslide numbers in Indonesia and Malaysia happen in Q1 and Q4 whereas in the UK they occur more in Q1 and Q2. Turkey experiences most landslides in Q1 through Q3.

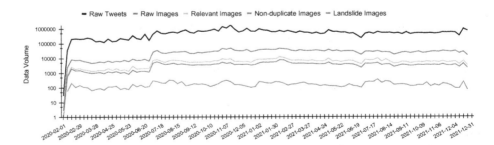

Fig. 6. Weekly distributions of raw tweets and images as well as the relevant, non-duplicate, and landslide images (y-axis is in log scale).

Fig. 7. Worldwide distribution of the collected landslide reports

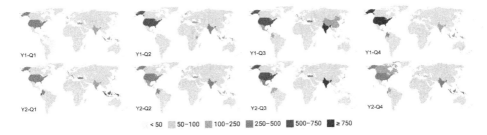

Fig. 8. Top-10 countries with the highest landslide reports in each quarter

5.2 Validation of the Landslide Model Predictions

Although the system has collected more than 2.5 million images since its deployment in February 2020, there are only about 17,000 images labeled as landslide (or 38,000 images including near-and-exact duplicates), which corresponds to less than 1% of the total volume. This highlights the difficulty of the task even though a carefully curated set of landslide-related keywords has been used to collect data from Twitter. To validate the performance of the landslide model in the real-world deployment, we sampled $N = 3,600$ tweets with images collected by our system. To avoid overburdening our landslide specialists with noisy data as well as to warrant robust statistics, we sampled only from the subset of tweets with images labeled as non-duplicate and relevant. Our landslide specialists then reviewed these images and annotated them with ground-truth landslide/not-landslide labels. Eventually, we compared the machine-predicted labels with expert annotations to evaluate the performance of the landslide model in a real-world scenario. Table 4 summarizes the number of correct (i.e., True Positive (TP) and True Negative (TN)) and incorrect (i.e., False Positive (FP) and False Negative (FN)) predictions as well as the performance scores such as accuracy, precision, recall, F1, and MCC. Overall, we see that the performance of the model in a real-world scenario is comparable to the experimental results (Sect. 4.3).

Table 4. Validation of landslide model predictions

TP	FP	FN	TN	Total
123	39	43	3,395	3,600
Accuracy	Precision	Recall	F1	MCC
97.72	75.93	74.10	75.00	73.81

5.3   Comparison with a Text-Based Approach

Text-based landslide detection is a nascent problem that only a couple of studies have addressed so far [22,23]. Since these studies did not share their data sets and models, we do not have any off-the-shelf text-based landslide classification model to use as a baseline in our study. Therefore, we consider an alternative scenario with a *proxy* text classification model based on lexicon (i.e., keyword) matching, which is already implemented in our system. That is, we assume all the retrieved tweets are already labeled as landslide by a hypothetical model. We then use the previously sampled set of tweets with their expert annotations to compute the precision of a lexicon-based text model. Unsurprisingly, we found that the lexicon-based text model achieved only about 5% precision (i.e., only about 5% of the tweets retrieved were indeed related to landslides) while the image classification model achieved 76% precision as reported before.

6   Conclusion

In this paper, we presented a system that was developed through an interdisciplinary collaboration between the computer scientists at the Qatar Computing Research Institute (QCRI) and the earthquake and landslide specialists from the European-Mediterranean Seismological Centre (EMSC) and the British Geological Survey (BGS), respectively. The developed system leverages online social media data in real time to identify landslide-related information automatically using state-of-the-art artificial intelligence techniques. The designed system (i) reduces the information overload by eliminating duplicate and irrelevant content, (ii) identifies landslide images, (iii) infers their geolocation, and (iv) categorizes the user type (organization or person) of the account sharing the information. We presented results of our model development as well as system performance evaluation and benchmarking experiments. We demonstrated the system's success with a real-world deployment. We note that some of the system components, such as the Geolocation Tagger, can be further improved for better efficiency. Online dashboard can also be enriched with a mechanism to collect user feedback. Besides, the landslide reports detected by the system can be verified against "ground truth" from official reports (when/if available), which we plan as future work. Consequently, we believe that our system can contribute to harvesting of global landslide data and facilitate further landslide research. Furthermore, it can support global landslide susceptibility maps to provide situational awareness and improve emergency response and decision making.

Acknowledgments. The British Geological Survey (UK Research and Innovation) granted supporting research funding through National Capability (Shallow Geohazards) and Innovation funding streams. European-Mediterranean Seismological Centre was partially funded by the European Union's (EU) Horizon 2020 Research and Innovation Program under Grant Agreement RISE Number 821115. Opinions expressed in this article solely reflect the authors' views; the EU is not responsible for any use that may be made of information it contains.

References

1. Alfarrarjeh, A., Agrawal, S., Kim, S.H., Shahabi, C.: Geo-spatial multimedia sentiment analysis in disasters. In: DSAA, pp. 193–202 (2017)
2. Can, R., Kocaman, S., Gokceoglu, C.: A convolutional neural network architecture for auto-detection of landslide photographs to assess citizen science and volunteered geographic information data quality. ISPRS Int. J. Geo-Inf. **8**(7), 300 (2019)
3. Can, R., Kocaman, S., Gokceoglu, C.: Development of a CitSci and artificial intelligence supported GIS platform for landslide data collection. Int. Arch. Photogramm. **43**, 43–50 (2020)
4. Cheng, G., Guo, L., Zhao, T., Han, J., Li, H., Fang, J.: Automatic landslide detection from remote-sensing imagery using a scene classification method based on BoVW and pLSA. Int. J. Remote Sens. **34**(1), 45–59 (2013)
5. Chicco, D., Jurman, G.: The advantages of the Matthews correlation coefficient (MCC) over F1 score and accuracy in binary classification evaluation. BMC Genom. **21**(1), 1–13 (2020)
6. Choi, C.E., Cui, Y., Zhou, G.G.: Utilizing crowdsourcing to enhance the mitigation and management of landslides. Landslides **15**(9), 1889–1899 (2018)
7. Donahue, J., et al.: DeCAF: a deep convolutional activation feature for generic visual recognition. In: ICML, pp. 647–655 (2014)
8. Froude, M.J., Petley, D.N.: Global fatal landslide occurrence from 2004 to 2016. Nat. Hazard Earth Syst. **18**(8), 2161–2181 (2018)
9. He, K., Zhang, X., Ren, S., Sun, J.: Deep residual learning for image recognition. In: CVPR, pp. 770–778 (2016)
10. Imran, M., Alam, F., Qazi, U., Peterson, S., Ofli, F.: Rapid damage assessment using social media images by combining human and machine intelligence. In: ISCRAM, pp. 1–13, May 2020
11. Imran, M., Castillo, C., Lucas, J., Meier, P., Vieweg, S.: AIDR: artificial intelligence for disaster response. In: WWW, pp. 159–162 (2014)
12. Imran, M., Qazi, U., Ofli, F.: TBCOV: two billion multilingual COVID-19 tweets with sentiment, entity, geo, and gender labels. Data **7**(1), 8 (2022)
13. Ji, S., Yu, D., Shen, C., Li, W., Xu, Q.: Landslide detection from an open satellite imagery and digital elevation model dataset using attention boosted convolutional neural networks. Landslides **17**(6), 1337–1352 (2020). https://doi.org/10.1007/s10346-020-01353-2
14. Juang, C.S., Stanley, T.A., Kirschbaum, D.B.: Using citizen science to expand the global map of landslides: introducing the Cooperative Open Online Landslide Repository (COOLR). PLoS ONE **14**(7), e0218657 (2019)
15. Kingma, D.P., Ba, J.: Adam: a method for stochastic optimization. In: ICLR (2015)
16. Kjekstad, O., Highland, L.: Economic and social impacts of landslides. In: Sassa, K., Canuti, P. (eds.) Landslides – Disaster Risk Reduction. Springer, Heidelberg (2009). https://doi.org/10.1007/978-3-540-69970-5_30

17. Kocaman, S., Gokceoglu, C.: A CitSci app for landslide data collection. Landslides **16**(3), 611–615 (2018). https://doi.org/10.1007/s10346-018-1101-2
18. Lee, E.M., Jones, D.K.: Landslide Risk Assessment, vol. 10. Thomas Telford, London (2004)
19. Merghadi, A., et al.: Machine learning methods for landslide susceptibility studies: a comparative overview of algorithm performance. Earth-Sci. Rev. **207**, 103225 (2020)
20. Mohan, A., Singh, A.K., Kumar, B., Dwivedi, R.: Review on remote sensing methods for landslide detection using machine and deep learning. Trans. Emerg. Telecommun. Technol. **32**(7), e3998 (2021)
21. Musaev, A., Wang, D., Pu, C.: LITMUS: landslide detection by integrating multiple sources. In: ISCRAM (2014)
22. Musaev, A., Wang, D., Shridhar, S., Pu, C.: Fast text classification using randomized explicit semantic analysis. In: IRI, pp. 364–371. IEEE (2015)
23. Musaev, A., Wang, D., Xie, J., Pu, C.: REX: rapid ensemble classification system for landslide detection using social media. In: ICDCS, pp. 1240–1249. IEEE (2017)
24. Nguyen, D.T., Alam, F., Ofli, F., Imran, M.: Automatic image filtering on social networks using deep learning and perceptual hashing during crises. In: ISCRAM, pp. 499–511, May 2017
25. Ofli, F., Alam, F., Imran, M.: Analysis of social media data using multimodal deep learning for disaster response. In: ISCRAM, pp. 1–10, May 2020
26. Ofli, F., et al.: Landslide detection in real-time social media image streams. arXiv preprint arXiv:2110.04080 (2021)
27. Oquab, M., Bottou, L., Laptev, I., Sivic, J.: Learning and transferring mid-level image representations using convolutional neural networks. In: CVPR, pp. 1717–1724 (2014)
28. Pennington, C., Freeborough, K., Dashwood, C., Dijkstra, T., Lawrie, K.: The national landslide database of great Britain: acquisition, communication and the role of social media. Geomorphology **249**, 44–51 (2015)
29. Prakash, N., Manconi, A., Loew, S.: Mapping landslides on EO data: performance of deep learning models vs. traditional machine learning models. Remote Sens. **12**(3), 346 (2020)
30. Prakash, N., Manconi, A., Loew, S.: A new strategy to map landslides with a generalized convolutional neural network. Sci. Rep. **11**(1), 1–15 (2021)
31. Ramesh, M.V., Kumar, S., Rangan, P.V.: Wireless sensor network for landslide detection. In: ICWN, pp. 89–95 (2009)
32. Razis, G., Theofilou, G., Anagnostopoulos, I.: Latent twitter image information for social analytics. Information **12**(2), 49 (2021)
33. Russakovsky, O., et al.: ImageNet large scale visual recognition challenge. Int. J. Comput. Vis. **115**(3), 211–252 (2015). https://doi.org/10.1007/s11263-015-0816-y
34. Sermanet, P., Eigen, D., Zhang, X., Mathieu, M., Fergus, R., LeCun, Y.: OverFeat: integrated recognition, localization and detection using convolutional networks. In: ICLR, April 2014
35. Tavakkoli Piralilou, S., et al.: Landslide detection using multi-scale image segmentation and different machine learning models in the higher Himalayas. Remote Sens. **11**(21), 2575 (2019)
36. Taylor, F.E., Malamud, B.D., Freeborough, K., Demeritt, D.: Enriching great Britain's national landslide database by searching newspaper archives. Geomorphology **249**, 52–68 (2015)
37. Tofani, V., Segoni, S., Agostini, A., Catani, F., Casagli, N.: Use of remote sensing for landslide studies in Europe. Nat. Hazard Earth Syst. **13**(2), 299–309 (2013)

38. Weber, E., et al.: Detecting natural disasters, damage, and incidents in the wild. In: Vedaldi, A., Bischof, H., Brox, T., Frahm, J.-M. (eds.) ECCV 2020. LNCS, vol. 12364, pp. 331–350. Springer, Cham (2020). https://doi.org/10.1007/978-3-030-58529-7_20
39. Zhou, B., Lapedriza, A., Khosla, A., Oliva, A., Torralba, A.: Places: a 10 million image database for scene recognition. PAMI **40**(6), 1452–1464 (2017)

Online Social Event Detection via Filtering Strategy Graph Neural Network

Lifu Chen, Junhua Fang$^{(\boxtimes)}$, Pingfu Chao, An Liu, and Pengpeng Zhao

School of Computer Science and Technology, Soochow University, Suzhou, China
20204227034@stu.suda.edu.cn, {jhfang,pfchao,anliu,ppzhao}@suda.edu.cn

Abstract. Nowadays, as a strongly time-dependent data type, the ubiquity of social media messages enables the detection and analysis of real-time events. Through the clustering of online posts concerning their topics, existing methods can quickly identify the current trends on social media, which helps discover marketing opportunities, prevent potential crises, etc. However, due to the diversity of social network users, the performance of current approaches is significantly affected by the long tail of random topics, which should be regarded as outliers in a clustering problem. Besides, current models are weak in detecting events that last for multiple days, which is common in real-world scenarios. Therefore, we propose the FS-GNN, a graph neural network based on a filtering strategy, for incremental social event detection in data streams. Our method uses heterogeneous information networks (HINs) to construct a social message graph, and we propose a centrality-based scoring mechanism to grade and filter noisy data before clustering. In addition, a message complement window is introduced to connect the same topic mentioned across multiple days for better clustering accuracy. Extensive experimental results demonstrate the superiority of FS-GNN over multiple baselines in both offline and online scenarios.

Keywords: Social event detection · Online clustering · Graph neural network

1 Introduction

The recent surge of social media platforms, like Twitter, Facebook and Weibo, encourages more users to share their daily lives publicly, which also causes an explosive increase of social messaging data. Such User-Generated Content (UGC) can be utilized in various data mining tasks. As one of its major applications, in recent years, researchers start to analyse online social media posts to detect real-time events [11,20].

Existing works represent a social message by the keywords it mentions, so the task of detecting events in a social message stream can be described as finding clusters of messages mentioning the same set of topics. As the traditional

© Springer Nature Switzerland AG 2022
T. Di Noia et al. (Eds.): ICWE 2022, LNCS 13362, pp. 66–81, 2022.
https://doi.org/10.1007/978-3-031-09917-5_5

clustering algorithms only extract topics from formally-written articles and news, there is a strong need for a new method to detect events from highly-diversified social message streams. Recent research shows that the Graph Neural Network (GNN) has strong capabilities in aggregating the structure and semantics of data, and the GNN-based social message analytic framework has shown its good performance in event detection [13]. However, two issues remain unsolved for event detection: 1) as the social media users are highly-diversified, most of their posts focus on random topics that are irrelevant to major ongoing events, so these 'noisy' posts will reduce the accuracy of our event detection task; 2) the influence of an event to the social media is usually long-lasting and scattered sometimes. For example, before a contagious disease outbreak is identified, multiple scattered posts mentioning related symptoms have appeared on social media. Due to the lack of long-term incremental clustering, the existing method cannot detect such signs before the outbreak spike kicks in, making the event detection less effective.

In this paper, we propose the FS-GNN, a model for incremental social event detection in social message streams. In our model, we use heterogeneous information networks (HINs) to map social communication elements to a unified heterogeneous graph, then we leverage GNNs to extract knowledge from the semantic and structural information contained in the social graph. Besides, we provide an effective solution to the aforementioned issues: 1) To solve the data noise problem, we propose a centrality-based scoring mechanism to score the nodes in the social graph based on their density. We then retain the nodes with higher scores, which imply high relevance to the event clustering problem. 2) To achieve better performance in long-term event detection, we design a message complement window in the incremental clustering phase to capture the correlation of messages across days. Overall, the life cycle of our model consists of an initial phase detecting new message events, and an incremental phase, which extends the knowledge of the model by resuming the training process. In the incremental phase, we employ a triplet loss set that contrasts positive message pairs with corresponding negative pairs. Meanwhile, we introduce an additional global-local pairs [1, 7, 15] loss function to fit the incremental context and incorporate graph structure information.

We conduct extensive experiments on the large-scale Twitter corpus [12] and the event detection corpus [17] which are publicly available. The empirical results show that FS-GNN achieves better performance over multiple baselines. Overall, we summarize our main contributions as follows:

- We design a new incremental social event detection model based on filtering strategies. Our proposed model can effectively filter data noise, and enhance the accuracy of the model for social event detection.
- We define an information complement window to capture the long-term correlation of message flows. Experiments demonstrate that our proposed information-completion scheme has higher clustering accuracy in incremental scenarios.
- Extensive experimental results on large-scale real-world datasets show that our proposed model is effective and stable in an incremental environment while guaranteeing clustering effectiveness.

2 Related Work

The social events discussed in this paper are coarse-grained, which include general events and emergent events. As a social message detection problem, existing solutions mainly fall into the following three categories:

Textual Information Extraction. As social messages are purely text messages, it is natural and common to detect social events through textual information extraction. For example, Liu et al. [10] use Word2Vec to merge identical entities and similar phrases to automatically detect events in multilingual-mixed long text streams. To further investigate deeper semantic meanings, Liu et al. [9] extract textual information into a more fine-grained representation and used this to construct story trees to represent the categories of subsequent events. However, on bigger social media platforms (such as Twitter), the detection of multilingual mixed social events becomes a major challenge. To solve this question, Hu et al. [8] use a probability distribution to represent semantic categories of multilingual mixed text divided into a fixed time slice window to detect events online. These methods focus on how to represent textual semantic information quantitatively using data structures, models or mathematical methods, but they rarely consider the data noise involved, which can strongly affect the performance of social event detection [14].

Structural Information Extraction. In addition to text content, the diversity of social connections between users and their non-textual properties have become a new source for social event detection. Specifically, some existing works focus on location, Zhang et al. [19] capture a novel authority metric of geo-thematic correlation between messages to extract high-quality events. Xing et al. [18] further consider the tags in the messages, they use probabilistic models to generate distributions of tags and topic text and propose the MGe-LDA model for discovering and representing sub-events. Chen et al. [3] utilize the message forwarding information (like the retweet in Twitter) to model the flow of information propagation, and they propose an RL-LDA model to discover the correlation between forwarding behaviour and events. Considering that the mentions among social messages speed up the spread of information, Adrien et al. [6] use the frequency of mentions to detect important events and estimate their level of impact on the population. Structural information can be seen as an additional attribute in social networks, but they also suffer from data noise. At the same time, the time-sensitive nature of structural information poses a greater challenge for the online detection of social events.

Hybrid Information Extraction. Some recent works consider both the textual and structural information in feature extraction and utilize deep learning models, like graph neural networks, to mine the social data. It aggregates information from the input graph data and acquires a vectorized representation of the nodes. Cao et al. [2] is selective in retaining old knowledge in GNN to achieve online clustering. Qiu et al. [14] define a comprehensive similarity index to filter the noisy node in the social network. Cui et al. [4] use the subject labels of events to construct multi-view text messages and design an attention neural network-based model to fuse event features between multiple views. Graves et al. [5] use BiLSTM to capture the relationship between messages better. GNNs are good at aggregating semantic information in social messages, but they can not satisfy the online detection of social events.

Overall, none of the three categories we have mentioned takes into account both the data noise and the real-time nature of social messaging, which are the main focus of our paper.

3   Preliminaries

In this section, we will introduce the problem definition and the framework overview.

3.1   Problem Definition

Definition 3.1 (Social Message Stream). A social message stream S_m is a series of social messages arriving continuously and chronologically, defined as $S_m = \{m_1, m_2, ..., m_i\}$, where m_i represents a social message arriving at time i.

Definition 3.2 (Social Events). A social event set E is a set containing all social events mentioned in a social message stream, which is defined as $E = e_1, e_2, ..., e_k$ where e_k represents a social event.

Here, we specify that each social message m_a is only associated with no more than one social event e_b through mentioning.

Definition 3.3 (Representation Learning Model). Given a social message m_i, the representation learning converts each social message into a vector representing the semantic information about itself and its neighbours, depicted as $f_v(m_i, \sigma) = r_i$, where r_i denotes the vector representation of message m_i, and σ represents the set of parameters of the model f_v.

Definition 3.4 (Social Event Detection). The social event detection problem aims to identify social events mentioned by messages in a social message stream via a representation learning model. The problem can be formalised as $f_s(f_v, \theta) = E$, where f_v denotes representation learning model, θ is the parameters of f_s and E represents the detected social event set.

According to Definition 3.4, to design a better representation learning model $f_v(m_i, \sigma) = r_i$ for event detection, the main objectives of this paper are to improve the quality of m_i, i.e. social message data, as well as optimizing parameter σ to get correct results through complete information. Therefore, we propose a model named FS-GNN to address them, respectively, which will be introduced in the next section.

3.2 Framework Overview

According to Algorithm 1, our framework is divided into two parts. In part of the initial phase, we use a social message stream to construct a social graph and then clean them with our filtering strategy. And next, we use the purified graph data to train an initial model. In part of the incremental phase, we use the remaining data to construct the message blocks for model retraining. Specifically, we use the information complement window to supplement the link between cross-days. Finally, we use the vectorized representation of the model output to cluster the social events.

Algorithm 1. FS-GNN

Input: A social stream $S_m = m_0, m_1, m_2, ..., m_i$,
the number of layers L, window size w, the number of mini-batches B.

Output: Sets of social events: $e_0, e_1, e_2, ...$

1:   /* **Start the initial phase** */
2:   $m_{in} = 0$
3:   **for** $j = 0, 1, 2, ..., 6$ **do**
4:     $m_{in} + = j$
5:   **end for**
6:   $G_{in} \leftarrow$ Create pure initial social message graph(m_{in})
7:   $G_f \leftarrow Flitering(G_{in})$
8:   **for** $L = 1, 2, ...$ **do**
9:     $h_{m_i}^{(l)} = concat(h_{m_i}^{(l)} \bigoplus Aggregator_{\forall m_j \in N_{ei}(m_i)}(Extractor(h_{m_i}^{(l-1)})))$
10:     $e_j \leftarrow$ Clustering by h_{m_i}
11:   **end for**
12:   /* **Start the incremental phase** */
13:   $k = 0$
14:   **for** $i = 7, 8, 9, ...$ **do**
15:     $G_i \leftarrow$ Create incremental social message graph(m_i)
16:     $k + = 1$
17:     **if** $i \geq 7$ **then**
18:       $G_i \leftarrow$ Delete obsolete nodes
19:       save the obsolete nodes n_i from G_i
20:     **end if**
21:     **if** $k\%w == 0 \& k! = 0$ **then**
22:       Completes the information of n_i to G_{i+2}
23:       **for** $L = 1, 2, ...$ **do**
24:         $h_{m_i}^{(l)} = concat(h_{m_i}^{(l)} \bigoplus Aggregator_{\forall m_j \in N_{ei}(m_i)}(Extractor(h_{m_i}^{(l-1)})))$
25:       **end for**
26:       $L_t = \sum_{t \in T} \max \left\{ \|V(m_i) - V(m_i+)\|_2^2 - \|V(m_i) - V(m_i-)\|_2^2 + a, 0 \right\}$
27:       $L_p = \frac{1}{N} \sum_i^N \left(\log P(h_{m_i}, s) + \log \left(1 - P\left(\widetilde{h}_{m_l}, s\right)\right) \right)$
28:       $e_i \leftarrow$ Clustering by h_{m_i}
29:     **end if**
30:   **end for**
31:   **return** the social event sets E

4   Methodology

As mentioned in Sect. 3.2, our FS-GNN method aims at improving the accuracy of event detection by (1) proposing the centrality-based filtering strategy in the initial phase and (2) introducing the information complement window to maintain the long-term message links in the incremental phase. In this section, we elaborate on the details of the two phases, respectively.

4.1   The Initial Phase

Figure 1 demonstrates the workflow of the initial phase. According to the figure, this phase consists of four steps: **Step 1.** A homogeneous message graph is first constructed from input social messages by modelling and extracting the correlations between them. (As shown in Fig. 1, circles represent messages, squares represent common words between message streams, diamonds represent common locations, triangles represent common friends, etc.) **Step 2.** A node filtering process is applied to the constructed graph to remove nodes that are noisy to the clustering task. **Step 3.** The filtered graph is used as input to a L-layer neural network to learn the representations. **Step 4.** The representations are finally grouped into multiple clusters representing the detected social events. Facing massive social message streams with complex attributes, our method is expected to 1) make full use of the social message data features to precisely model the correlation between messages via the message graph (Step 1), and 2) further improve the quality of the message graph by removing messages that are

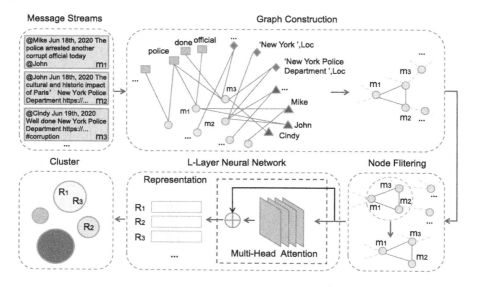

Fig. 1. Workflow of the initial phase

irrelevant to the event detection task (Step 2). To this end, we leverage the Heterogeneous Information Network (HIN) to construct the initial message graph and then filter the constructed graph by our proposed centrality-based filtering strategy.

4.1.1 Heterogeneous Social Message Modeling

The HIN is a graph that contains multiple types of nodes, which help us to represent the properties and structure of the message data better. Figure 1 shows an example, different elements in a message, such as words, locations and users, are represented as different types of nodes in the graph. And an edge between two message nodes is added when they share any element. Here, we label the node messages, words, entities and users as m, w, e, u, respectively.

Different from previous heterogeneous GNNs, FS-GNN focuses on learning correlations between messages. We use a specific method to map the original graph to a homogeneous message graph to retain only the message nodes. The mapping process is expressed as follows:

$$A_{i,j} = \min \left\{ \left[\sum_k W_{mk} \cdot W_{mk}^T \right]_{i,j}, 1 \right\}, k \in \{w, e, u\}, \tag{1}$$

where $A \in \{0,1\}^{N \times N}$ is the adjacency matrix of the homogeneous message graph, N is the total number of messages in the graph. i, j denotes the matrix element in row i column j and k denotes the node type. W_{mk} is a submatrix of the adjacency matrix of the heterogeneous message graph containing rows of type m and columns of type k. In general, if messages m_i and m_j both connect to some nodes of type k, $\left[W_{mk} \cdot W_{mk}^T \right]_{i,j}$ will be no less than 1 and the $A_{i,j}$ will be equal to 1.

4.1.2 Filtering Strategy

The research on network centrality originates from the study of social networks and is described as the degree to which a node is central to the network. In our task, as an event is usually followed by an extensive number of social messages discussing relevant topics, whereas other random posts are less likely to form dense social connections, we use the concept of centrality to describe the density of nodes for node filtering. Hence, we define I as the lower bound within the interval where the degree of the dense node lies. Based on this, the filtering strategy can be defined as follows:

$$I = K \cdot \frac{D_{\text{all}}}{N_{\text{node}}}, \tag{2}$$

where K represents the density factor, D_{all} denotes the total number of node degrees in the social message graph, and N_{node} represents the total number of nodes during a week. To decide an appropriate density factor K, we introduce the three most common types of centrality measures, shown in Table 1:

Table 1. Three types of centrality.

Centrality	Degree centrality	Closeness centrality	Betweenness centrality
Formulas	$D\left(N_i\right) = \frac{\sum x_{ij}}{D-1}$	$C\left(n_i\right) = \frac{1}{\sum d\left(n_i, n_j\right)}$	$B\left(n_i\right) = \sum_{s \neq t \in N} \frac{\sigma_{st}(n_i)}{\sigma_{st}}$

Degree Centrality: The degree of the node as a proportion of the total degree of all points. In the equation, D denotes the degree of all nodes in the network, x_{ij} indicates of connections of the node i to other nodes j, i.e. the number of degrees. **Closeness Centrality:** the inverse of the average of the distances from the node to all other nodes; In the equation, $d\left(n_i, n_j\right)$ denotes the shortest path of node n_i to node n_j. **Betweenness Centrality:** the ratio of the shortest path through a node and connecting two other nodes to the total number of shortest paths between those two nodes. In the equation, $\sigma_{st}\left(n_i\right)$ denotes the total number of paths passing through the node n_i in the shortest path between node s and node t, and σ_{st} denotes the total number of shortest paths between node s and node t.

4.2   The Incremental Phase

Figure 2 illustrates the procedure in the incremental phase. This phase can be divided into three steps: **Step 1.** as time goes, new messages (m_4 in the figure) are updated to the message graph as well as obsoleted messages (m_2) to be removed. **Step 2.** An information complement window is designed to aggregate the obsoleted node m_{i-2} at t_{i-2} time with message graph. **Step 3.** The new graph is input into the model for retraining and add a new event independently represented by R_4. Facing missing information between cross-day messages, our method is expected to: 1) capture information across days to complete the new messages (Step 2), and 2) learn to detect unknown events more accurately. To this end, we design an information complement window to supplement the message correlations across days, and then add two loss functions to detect events more precisely.

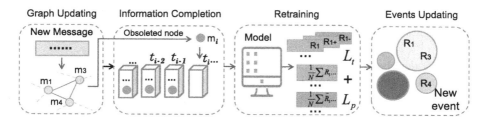

Fig. 2. Workflow of the incremental phase

4.2.1 Representation Learning

To observe the interaction between the preserved nodes and new message nodes, we use GNN to learn the message representation: $E_G : \mathbb{R}^{N \times d} \times \{0,1\}^{N \times N} \rightarrow \mathbb{R}^{N \times d'}$ and $E_G(X, A) = \{h_{m_i} \in \mathbb{R}^{d'} | 1 \leq i \leq N\}$ (Line 23–25 in Alg. 1). It is formalized as:

$$h_{m_i}^{(l)} = \text{concat}\left(h_{m_i}^{(l)} \oplus \text{Aggregator}_{\forall m_j \in \text{Nei}(m_i)}\left(\text{Extractor}\left(h_{m_i}^{(l-1)}\right)\right)\right), \quad (3)$$

where $h_{m_i}^l$ is the representation of m_i at the l-th level in the GNN. $Nei(m_i)$ represents the set of neighbours of m_i obtained from the adjacency matrix A, and $\oplus$ represents the aggregation of the information contained in its two operands. $Concat(\cdot)$ represents a multi-headed cascade. $Extractor(\cdot)$ and $Aggregator(\cdot)$ denote the extraction of useful information from the representation of adjacent messages and the summarization of adjacent information, respectively. We use $h_{m_i}^l$ as the final representation of $h_{m_i}^l$, i.e. h_{m_i}. In order to incrementally perform embedding operations on message blocks, we use the graph attention mechanism [16] for neighbourhood information extraction and aggregation.

In order to complement the message correlations across days, we design a message complement window to hold the correlations between nodes joined on the day $i + 2$ and nodes on the day i, which is formalized as:

$$A'_{i,j} = \min\left\{\left[\sum_k W_k^i \cdot (W_k^{i+2})^T\right]_{i,j}, 1\right\}, k \in \{w, e, u\} \quad (4)$$

Similar to the mapping process of homogeneous message graph, W_k^i denote the submatrix of an adjacency matrix of node type k that was deleted at time i, W_k^{i+2} denote the submatrix of an adjacency matrix of node type k at time $i+2$. T represents the matrix transpose.

4.2.2 Contrastive Learning

To handle the raw messages, we use a triplet loss function to enable FS-GNN to learn new event categories without limiting the total number of events (Line 26 in Algorithm 1). The function can be expressed as:

$$L_t = \sum_{t \in T} \max\left\{\left\|V(m_i) - V(m_i^+)\right\|_2^2 - \left\|V(m_i) - V(m_i^-)\right\|_2^2 + a, 0\right\}, \quad (5)$$

where V denotes the vector representation of the message stream m_i and $\|\cdot\|_2^2$ denotes the Euclidean distance between the two vectors calculated. The triplet satisfies $\left\|V(m_i) - V(m_i^+)\right\|_2^2 > \left\|V(m_i) - V(m_i^-)\right\|_2^2$. t denotes a triplet as (m_i, m_i^+, m_i^-), m_i^+ is a positive message (a message stream from the same category), m_i^- is a negative message (a message stream from a different category) and T denotes the set of triplets drawn in the incremental scene.

To address the problem of updating structural information in message graphs, we construct a global-local pair loss function that enables FS-GNN to discover and preserve features of similar local structures (Line 27 in Algorithm 1). The function can be expressed as:

$$L_p = \frac{1}{N} \sum_{i=1}^{N} \left(\log P \left(h_{m'_i} s \right) + \log \left(1 - P \left(\widetilde{h}_{m_i}, s \right) \right) \right), \tag{6}$$

where L_p represents the global-local pair loss function and $s \in \mathbb{R}^{d'}$ is the average of all message representations. P represents a bi-linear scoring function that outputs the probability of its two operands coming from the joint distribution. L_t and L_p represents the overall loss of the FS-GNN.

5 Experiments

5.1 Datasets

We use two large-scale, publicly available datasets, namely Twitter and MAVEN, for our experiments. Both datasets are preprocessed by the providers to remove duplicate and invalid data for better data quality. Table 2 shows the statistics of datasets.

Twitter [12]: the Twitter dataset contains 68,841 manually tagged tweets associated with 503 event classes, distributed over four weeks.

MAVEN [17]: the MAVEN dataset is a generic domain event detection dataset constructed from Wikipedia documents with no sentence (i.e. messages) associated with multiple event types. The dataset contains 10,242 messages with 154 associated event categories.

Table 2. Statistics of datasets.

Datasets	Nodes	Edges	Event categories
Twitter	68,841	16,358,812	503
MAVEN	10,242	24,238,110	154

5.2 Baselines and Metrics

We compare FS-GNN with general similarity metrics, offline social event detection methods, and incremental methods.

BiLSTM [5]: a model for learning bidirectional, long-term dependencies between words of a message. However, as it only focuses on words, the model does not utilize other attributes in social messages.

EventX [9]: this is a method for online event detection based on text after fine-grained text segmentation. Same as BiLSTM, it also ignores other attributes in social messages.

KPGNN [2]: it is an incremental learning approach based on knowledge preservation and shows good performance in an incremental environment, but it ignores the data noise and the information that exists between a span of days in data.

We also set up comparison experiments under different filtering strategies. To evaluate the performance of all models, we compare the similarity between the message clusters detected by the models and the ground-truth clusters using the following metrics:

NMI (Normalized Mutual Information): it measures the amount of information extracted from the distribution of ground truth labels.

$$NMI(U, V) = \frac{MI(U, V)}{F\{H(U), H(V)\}} \tag{7}$$

AMI (Adjusted Mutual Information): it is similar to NMI that measures the mutual information between two clusters.

$$AMI(U, V) = \frac{MI(U, V) - E\{MI(U, V)\}}{F\{H(U), H(V)\} - E\{MI(U, V)\}} \tag{8}$$

In the two formulas above, U denotes ground-truth vectors, V denotes predicted label vectors. H denotes information entropy. MI represents mutual information of U and V. Generally, F denotes arithmetic mean. E represents the expected value. Both two metrics are based on a mutual information approach to measuring the fit of the data distribution between the clustering results and the actual category information. NMI takes values in the range [0,1] and AMI takes values in the range $[-1, 1]$. A larger value means that the clustering result matches the real situation more closely.

5.3 Experimental Settings

We set the hyperparameters in EventX to their default values mentioned in the original paper [9]. For BiLSTM and FS-GNN, the Table 3 shows our parameters setting. In the initial phase, we use the K-Means clustering to set the total number of classes to the number of true classes after getting the message representation. And in the incremental phase, we use DBSCAN to fit the scenario that a total number of classes is unknown.

Table 3. Parameter settings.

Methods	Layer	Optimizer	Embedding dimension	Retraining window size	Small batch training size	a of the triplet loss function	# of neighbours sampled per message
FS-GNN	2	Adam	32	3	2000	3	800
BiLSTM	2	Adam	32	–	–	–	–

All experiments are conducted on a 12 cores Intel(R) Xeon(R) CPU E5-2650 v4 @ 2.20 GHz and 1×NVIDIA GeForce GTX 1080 Ti GPU.

5.4   Experimental Results

5.4.1   The Initial Phase

Without loss of generality, we partitioned 70%, 20% and 10% of the two datasets for training, testing and validation respectively. Figure 3 shows the result of the experiments conducted by FS-GNN with baselines on both datasets.

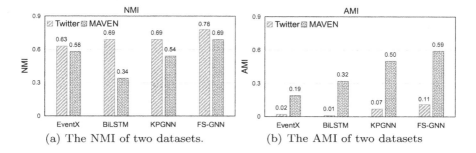

(a) The NMI of two datasets.   (b) The AMI of two datasets

Fig. 3. The results of initial phase.

Our proposed FS-GNN method has a significant advantage over all types of baselines. Based on the Twitter and MAVEN datasets, FS-GNN outperforms all types of baselines by 13%–102.9% (NMI) and 18%–210.5% (AMI), respectively. However, it is worth noting that the NMI value of BiLSTM is unusually low for the MAVEN dataset. This is because BiLSTM is a text-semantic information-based method and the dimensionality of the MAVEN dataset is only 8 while the Twitter is 16. Low experimental results of BiLSTM on MAVEN dataset due to the sparsity of data in the dataset. EventX and BiLSTM rely on message embedding and focus excessively on the interaction between text messages, thus ignoring the structural information in the social message stream. KPGNN and FS-GNN use a small batch training approach to partition the huge dataset, while the GNN-based approach can better aggregate semantic and structural information in social networks and abstract them into vectorized representations, which gives them an excellent performance on both datasets. Nonetheless, our proposed model FS-GNN employs a filtering strategy to deal with data noise and complements message associations across days, which allowing to achieve better results than any other baselines in the experiments.

We also compare the speed of the four methods during the training phase. In Fig. 4, we can see that EventX has a much larger time overhead than the other methods, as EventX uses a tree structure to divide the hierarchy of events. Each merge, expansion, insertion, etc. of the tree diagram requires a significant time overhead. In contrast, our FS-GNN model uses a filtering strategy to clean the data, and the time overhead in the training phase is smaller than that of the same KPGNN method. In terms of accuracy and time overhead, our proposed model FS-GNN has a very strong performance advantage.

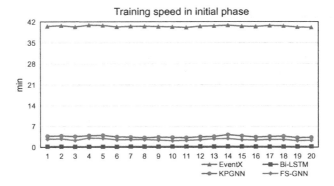

Fig. 4. The speed of 20 epochs in training.

Regarding the effectiveness of filtering strategy, Table 4 shows the improvement when applying different filtering strategies. In particular, "Degree Max" is an extra filtering strategy that indicates the proportion of the maximum degree in datasets to all degrees. Due to the negative result of the experiment with "Closeness Centrality", we also add an experiment with it removed to illustrate the effect of it on filtering strategy. The reason is that this strategy filters almost half of the nodes, including the high-density ones. In the end, the best result of these experiments will be chosen and act on the next stage.

Table 4. Results for different filtering strategies.

Metrics	Degree Max	Degree centrality	Closeness centrality	Betweenness centrality	Average of four strategies	Average of three strategies (without closeness centrality)
Value	0.02	0.12	0.45	0.01	0.15	0.05
NMI	0.73	0.73	0.68	0.75	0.77	**0.78**
AMI	0.62	0.62	0.54	0.65	0.68	**0.69**

To further prove that the performance advantage of our solution does not only come from the filtering, we apply the filtering strategy to the EventX (as other baseline methods are not applicable due to the lack of homogeneous graph structure) Fig. 5 shows the result of the experiments. We can see that the filtering strategies does not improve the performance of EventX consistently, especially in the Maven dataset, as the dataset has less semantic information when the EventX is a text-based semantic information approach. The addition of the filtering strategy filters out the noise in the MAVEN dataset and also reduces the textual semantic information needed for EventX, leading to a decrease in the experimental results. This batch of experiments demonstrates that our proposed FS-GNN still outperforms the other methods even in the same data set. The performance gains of other methods with filtering are not significant, indicating that other parts of FS-GNN also have performance advantages.

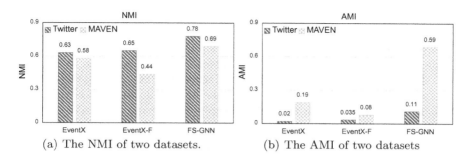

(a) The NMI of two datasets.   (b) The AMI of two datasets

Fig. 5. The filtering strategy in different methods.

5.4.2   The Incremental Phase

The number of message blocks should be consistent across each baseline. First, we note the message blocks used for initial model training and exclude them. Then, we divide the remaining message streams into a total of 21 blocks to simulate the incremental scenes. Finally, we use diverse methods to detect events in different message blocks and then obtain their results separately for comparison.

Table 5. The NMI of incremental scenarios.

Blocks	M_1	M_2	M_3	M_4	M_5	M_6	M_7
EventX	0.36	0.67	0.66	0.63	0.56	0.69	0.51
BiLSTM	0.24	0.48	0.38	0.40	0.40	0.49	0.32
KPGNN	0.38	**0.78**	0.76	0.67	0.73	0.82	**0.53**
FS-GNN	**0.76**	0.65	**0.80**	**0.75**	**0.74**	**0.85**	0.22
Blocks	M_8	M_9	M_{10}	M_{11}	M_{12}	M_{13}	M_{14}
EventX	0.71	0.66	0.68	0.64	0.60	0.56	0.57
BiLSTM	0.49	0.43	0.51	0.48	0.38	0.44	0.40
KPGNN	**0.77**	0.72	**0.79**	0.73	0.68	0.68	0.67
FS-GNN	0.49	**0.79**	0.76	**0.78**	**0.71**	**0.80**	**0.80**
Blocks	M_{15}	M_{16}	M_{17}	M_{18}	M_{19}	M_{20}	M_{21}
EventX	0.48	0.61	0.58	0.57	0.60	0.67	0.53
BiLSTM	0.38	0.50	0.48	0.46	0.48	0.44	0.38
KPGNN	0.58	0.78	0.70	0.71	0.72	0.71	0.58
FS-GNN	**0.69**	**0.79**	**0.73**	**0.78**	**0.74**	**0.73**	**0.64**

Table 5 and Table 6 show that our proposed FS-GNN performs better and more consistently in the incremental scenario than the various types of baselines which completes the missing information across days. The experimental results of BiLSTM are very poor. Due to the fact that when we divide the datasets by days, we reduce the density of semantic information, which leads to poor experimental results. However, as we can see in the two tables, the blocks M_7 and M_8 exhibit very low precision in two evaluation metrics. The reason is explained as: when the information complement window is working in the incremental phase, there is less information across days between the two message blocks. But our information complement window mistakenly added the unnecessary nodes as missing information into the message graph, which causes a loss of accuracy.

Table 6. The AMI of incremental scenarios

Blocks	M_1	M_2	M_3	M_4	M_5	M_6	M_7
EventX	0.06	0.28	0.17	0.18	0.13	0.27	0.13
BiLSTM	0.12	0.40	0.31	0.30	0.32	0.36	0.20
KPGNN	0.36	**0.74**	0.73	0.64	0.70	0.78	**0.52**
FS-GNN	**0.76**	0.63	**0.76**	**0.72**	**0.71**	**0.79**	0.17
Blocks	M_8	M_9	M_{10}	M_{11}	M_{12}	M_{13}	M_{14}
EventX	0.20	0.18	0.24	0.23	0.15	0.16	0.13
BiLSTM	0.34	0.32	0.38	0.36	0.30	0.31	0.34
KPGNN	**0.75**	0.71	**0.77**	0.71	0.65	0.65	0.67
FS-GNN	0.43	**0.74**	0.74	**0.77**	**0.66**	**0.76**	**0.79**
Blocks	M_{15}	M_{16}	M_{17}	M_{18}	M_{19}	M_{20}	M_{21}
EventX	0.06	0.19	0.18	0.16	0.16	0.17	0.09
BiLSTM	0.26	0.40	0.34	0.34	0.35	0.33	0.31
KPGNN	0.54	0.72	0.70	0.69	0.72	0.67	0.54
FS-GNN	**0.66**	**0.75**	**0.73**	**0.75**	**0.74**	**0.71**	**0.61**

6   Conclusions

In this paper, we proposed a new model named FS-GNN which combines a filtering strategy with GNN that incorporates the rich semantic and structural information in social message streams and filters harmful noise nodes. In incremental scenarios, the introduction of the information complement window can more effectively compensate for the lack of information between them, achieving good detection results while ensuring the stability of event detection. With the filtering strategy and information completion window in different stages, our proposed model FS-GNN achieved better performance over multiple baselines. The better values shown in metrics NMI and AMI at different stages demonstrated the superiority of FS-GNN compared to baseline.

Acknowledgments. This work was supported by the National Natural Science Foundation of China under the grant (No. 61802273, 62102277), Postdoctoral Science

Foundation of China (No. 2020M681529), Natural Science Foundation of Jiangsu Province (BK20210703), China Science and Technology Plan Project of Suzhou (No. SYG202139), Postgraduate Research & Practice Innovation Program of Jiangsu Province (SJCX2_11342).

References

1. Belghazi, M.I., Baratin, A.: MINE: mutual information neural estimation. CoRR (2018)
2. Cao, Y., Peng, H., Wu, J.: Knowledge-preserving incremental social event detection via heterogeneous GNNs. In: WWW, pp. 3383–3395 (2021)
3. Chen, X., Zhou, X., Sellis, T., Li, X.: Social event detection with retweeting behavior correlation. Expert Syst. Appl. **114**, 516–523 (2018)
4. Cui, W., Du, J., Wang, D., Kou, F., Xue, Z.: MVGAN: multi-view graph attention network for social event detection. ACM Trans. Intell. Syst. Technol. (TIST) **12**(3), 1–24 (2021)
5. Graves, A., Schmidhuber, J.: Framewise phoneme classification with bidirectional LSTM and other neural network architectures. Neural Netw. **18**(5–6), 602–610 (2005)
6. Guille, A., Favre, C.: Event detection, tracking, and visualization in twitter: a mention-anomaly-based approach. CoRR (2015)
7. Hjelm, R.D., Fedorov, A., Lavoie-Marchildon, S.: Learning deep representations by mutual information estimation and maximization. In: ICLR (2019)
8. Hu, L., Zhang, B., Hou, L., Li, J.: Adaptive online event detection in news streams. Knowl.-Based Syst. **138**, 105–112 (2017)
9. Liu, B., Han, F.X., Niu, D.: Story forest: extracting events and telling stories from breaking news. ACM (TKDD) **14**(3), 1–28 (2020)
10. Liu, Y., Peng, H., Li, J., Song, Y., Li, X.: Event detection and evolution in multilingual social streams. Front. Comput. Sci. **14**(5), 1–15 (2020). https://doi.org/10.1007/s11704-019-8201-6
11. Liu, Z., Yang, Y., Huang, Z., Shen, F., Zhang, D., Shen, H.T.: Event early embedding: predicting event volume dynamics at early stage, pp. 997–1000 (2017)
12. McMinn, A.J., Moshfeghi, Y., Jose, J.M.: Building a large-scale corpus for evaluating event detection on Twitter. In: ACM CIKM, pp. 409–418 (2013)
13. Peng, H., Li, J., Gong, Q.: Fine-grained event categorization with heterogeneous graph convolutional networks. In: IJCAI, pp. 3238–3245 (2019)
14. Qiu, Z., Hu, W., Wu, J., Tang, Z., Jia, X.: Noise-resilient similarity preserving network embedding for social networks. In: IJCAI, pp. 3282–3288 (2019)
15. Velickovic, P., Fedus, W., Hamilton, W.L., Liò, P., Bengio, Y., Hjelm, R.D.: Deep graph infomax. ICLR (Poster) **2**(3), 4 (2019)
16. Vinh, N.X., Epps, J., Bailey, J.: Information theoretic measures for clusterings comparison: variants, properties, normalization and correction for chance. J. Mach. Learn. Res. **11**, 2837–2854 (2010)
17. Wang, X., Wang, Z., Han, X.: MAVEN: a massive general domain event detection dataset. In: EMNLP, pp. 1652–1671 (2020)
18. Xing, C., Wang, Y., Liu, J., Huang, Y., Ma, W.: Hashtag-based sub-event discovery using mutually generative LDA in Twitter. In: AAAI, pp. 2666–2672 (2016)
19. Zhang, C., Zhou, G., Yuan, Q.: GeoBurst: real-time local event detection in geo-tagged tweet streams. In: SIGIR, pp. 513–522 (2016)
20. Zhou, X., Chen, L.: Event detection over twitter social media streams. VLDB J. **23**(3), 381–400 (2013). https://doi.org/10.1007/s00778-013-0320-3

Similarity Search with Graph Index on Directed Social Network Embedding

Zhiwei Qi[1,2], Kun Yue[1,2(✉)] (ID), Liang Duan[1,2], and Zhihong Liang[3]

[1] School of Information Science and Engineering, Yunnan University,
Kunming, China
{maryqizhiwei,kyue,duanl}@ynu.edu.cn
[2] Key Lab of Intelligent Systems and Computing of Yunnan Province,
Yunnan University, Kunming, China
[3] School of Big Data and Intelligence Engineering, Southwest Forestry University,
Kunming, China
zhliang@swfu.edu.cn

Abstract. Similarity search on directed social networks (DSNs) could help users find the K nearest neighbors (KNNs). The graph index based similarity search does not have to compare query node against every node in DSNs, since the neighbor relationship of the nodes is captured by the edges. Nevertheless, the performance of similarity search is still unsatisfactory, such as not supporting the end-to-end search or taking unnecessary detours, etc. In this paper, we propose the method of Graph Index on Directed Social Network Embedding (GI-DSNE) to facilitate the approximate KNN search on DSNs. First, the DSNE is proposed to embed the DSN into a low-dimensional vector space to achieve the embeddings for efficient calculation of similarities on the search path. Then, the nearest neighbor descent algorithm is adopted to calculate the KNN graph. Subsequently, to construct the graph index efficiently, the direction guided strategy for edge selection, maximum out-degree of GI-DSNE and the depth-first-search tree for guaranteeing the connectivity of GI-DSNE are proposed. Experimental results show that our proposed method outperforms the state-of-the-art competitors on both execution time and precision.

Keywords: Social network · Similarity search · Graph index · Network embedding

1 Introduction

Similarity search in metric space is based on retrieving similar data to the query points by incorporating a similarity function on feature vectors, which represent the complex data, such as images, video, geographic data [14,15,17], etc. Thus, the complex data in d-dimensional space could be indexed and compared. Recently, the rapid technological development has enabled users to produce complex social relationships, such as user's friendships in Twitter and author's

© Springer Nature Switzerland AG 2022
T. Di Noia et al. (Eds.): ICWE 2022, LNCS 13362, pp. 82–97, 2022.
https://doi.org/10.1007/978-3-031-09917-5_6

partnerships in published papers. Essentially, user's complex social relationships could be abstracted by a large-scale directed network with millions of nodes. Similarity search on directed social networks (DSNs) could help users find the K nearest neighbors (KNNs), such as a user's direct or indirect neighbors. Nevertheless, the state-of-the-art methods for similarity search on large-scale DSNs will require a long search path or tend to retrieve inaccurate results [13,18]. Thus, it is worthwhile to establish the method for similarity search on DSNs.

The approximate K nearest neighbor search (AKNNS), trading a small loss in accuracy for much shorter search time, is to return K ($K > 1$) points given the query points in the feature vector space $\mathbb{R}^d$. Obviously, AKNNS cannot be directly fulfilled on DSN, a network rather than feature vectors. By network embedding techniques, the large-scale networks could be mapped as dense, unique and low-dimensional feature vectors, also named embeddings, while preserving the network structure and attribute information. Thus, the AKNNS on DSN could be transformed to the AKNNS on network embeddings.

To perform AKNNS on network embeddings, non-graph indexing methods and graph indexing methods have been proposed [14,17]. The former includes tree-based, permutation-based and hashing-based methods, which cannot express the neighbor relationship and tend to check much more points in neighbor sub-spaces than the latter to reach the same accuracy, shown as Fig. 1. Meanwhile, the graph indexing methods only compare the query nodes with their nearest neighbors, and achieve much better search performance than non-graph indexing methods, verified by experimental results [14]. Therefore, we adopt the graph indexing method to perform AKNNS.

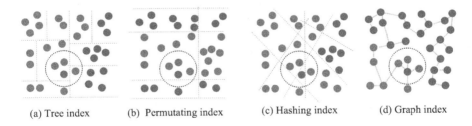

(a) Tree index   (b) Permutating index   (c) Hashing index   (d) Graph index

Fig. 1. Comparison of non-graph indexing and graph indexing methods. The red, dark green, light green and blue circles represent the query, nearest neighbor, checked and unchecked nodes, respectively. (Color figure online)

At present, almost all graph indexing methods share the same greedy best-first search algorithm [17] to perform AKNNS, which is to minimize the distance between the chosen node and query node, starting from the chosen node in the new iteration. Actually, the critical step is to construct an efficient and accurate graph index on embeddings. To this end, the KNN graph [11], relative neighborhood graph [16], navigable small world graph [8] and minimum spanning tree [10] are available. Nevertheless, these graph indexing methods generally have two limitations: (1) the performance of similarity search is unsatisfactory, since the end-to-end similarity search on DSNs could not be implemented and many unnecessary detours are doomed to obtain the search results; (2) the graph index is constructed inaccurately and inefficiently. For example, these methods suffer the curse of high dimension of feature vectors to make the distance calculation inefficient and take up lots of storage space. Moreover, the expensive edge selection strategy leads to the large average out-degree, and cannot guarantee the connectivity of graph index such that the KNN query could not be reachable.

To tackle the aforementioned problems and perform AKNNS on DSN efficiently, we propose the method of Graph Index on Directed Social Network Embedding (GI-DSNE). To fulfill the end-to-end similarity search on DSN, the query node of DSN is proposed as input and KNN as output rather than the embeddings. To avoid the curse of high dimension of embeddings, we propose the Directed Social Network Embedding (DSNE) to map the DSN into the low-dimensional vector space, while preserving the direction of each edge and node similarity in a DSN. Then, we calculate the distance similarity between low-dimensional embeddings efficiently. To improve the efficiency of edge selection, lower the average out-degree, and avoid detours on the search path, we propose the strategy of direction guided edge selection to construct the GI-DSNE, while trying to guarantee a monotonic path between any two nodes in GI-DSNE. To guarantee the connectivity of GI-DSNE, we span a depth-first-search (DFS) tree on GI-DSNE by using the navigating node as the root.

Our contributions are summarized as follows:

- We propose the end-to-end Graph Index on Directed Social Network Embedding (GI-DSNE) for efficient and precise similarity search on DSN.
- We propose DSNE to generate low-dimensional embeddings. To construct GI-DSNE, we adopt the direction guided strategy for edge selection, and a DFS tree on the GI-DSNE is spanned to guarantee the global connectivity.
- We evaluate the performance of AKNNS with GI-DSNE on DSN, and experimental results show that our method outperforms the state-of-the-art competitors.

2   Related Work

Network Embedding. The skip-gram negative sampling (SGNS) based network embedding could be fulfilled by non-linear (e.g., deep neural network based) methods, and linear (e.g., matrix factorization based) methods. The matrix factorization based SGNS is proposed for network embedding due to its interpretability and high efficiency. It is concluded that SGNS based DeepWalk, LINE, node2vec and GraRep models could be unified into the matrix factorization framework [7]. Further, SGNS is proved to factorize a shifted PMI matrix [12]. However, these matrix factorization based methods cannot be directly used for DSN, since the adjacency matrix obtained from DSN, has no negative elements. To map DSN in the low-dimensional vector space while preserving the embedding similarity and edge direction, the PMI matrix factorization is worthwhile to be improved w.r.t. DSN.

Similarity Search with Graph Index. The base graph index consists of navigable small world graph (NSW) [8], relative neighborhood graph (RNG) [16], K nearest neighbor graph (KNNG) [11] and minimum spanning tree (MST) [10], which are the subgraphs of the delaunay graph (DG) [14]. The DG in Fig. 2(a) constructed on dataset $\mathbf{Y}$ selects the edge if and only if there is no other node in the circumcircle of the triangle composed of three nodes (i.e., v_1^I, v_2^I, v_3^I). The NSW in Fig. 2(b) adopts the similar strategy of edge selection with DG, and includes short-range and long-range links [8]. The RNG in Fig. 2(c) selects the edge if and only if there is no other node in the lune region [16]. The KNNG in Fig. 2(d) selects the edge if the distance δ_{ij} between v_i^I and v_j^I is less than the given threshold [11]. The MST in Fig. 2(e) uses the least edges to guarantee the graph's global connectivity and the smallest edge's weights [10]. Overall, these methods adopt different strategies of edge selection to build the graph index, but suffer high out-degree or long detours or low precision of search. To overcome these limitations and make AKNNS on large-scale DSNs feasible, a graph index on DSNE is indispensable.

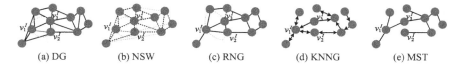

(a) DG   (b) NSW   (c) RNG   (d) KNNG   (e) MST

Fig. 2. Different base graph indexes on the same dataset with dimension $d = 2$.

3   Methodology

In this section, the definitions of directed social network, directed social network embedding, graph index and approximate K nearest neighbor search (AKNNS) are given at first. As shown in Fig. 3, the DSN is first embedded into the low-dimensional vector space. Then, to construct the GI-DSNE, the distances among embeddings are calculated to build the KNNG. Following, the edges are selected on KNNG, and the DFS tree is spanned on the previous process. At last, we perform the AKNNS on GI-DSNE to retrieve the KNNs of query nodes.

3.1   Definitions

Definition 1. *A directed social network (DSN) $G = (V, E)$ is a collection of nodes $V = \{v_i\}_{i=1}^n$ and edges $E = \{e_{ij}\}_{i,j=1}^n$. Let $\overrightarrow{e_{ij}}$ denote a directed edge from v_i to v_j. The adjacency matrix $A = \{a_{ij}\}_{i,j=1}^n$ of network G contains non-negative weights associated with each edge: $a_{ij} \geq 0$. If v_i is connected to v_j, then $a_{ij} = 1 (\overrightarrow{e_{ij}} = 1)$, and otherwise, $a_{ij} = 0 (\overrightarrow{e_{ij}} = 0)$.*

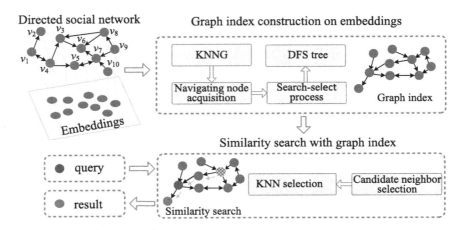

Fig. 3. Similarity search with graph index.

For a DSN G, each node v_i in G is represented by an embedding (also named feature vector) $\mathbf{y}_i = \left(y_{i0}, y_{i1}, \ldots, y_{i(d-1)}\right)$ with dimension $d\,(d \ll n)$.

Definition 2. *Given a DSN $G = (V, E)$, the directed social network embedding (DSNE) $\mathbf{Y} = \{\mathbf{y}_i\}_{i=1}^n$ is a mapping $f : v_i \to \mathbf{y}_i \in \mathbb{R}^d$ such that $d \ll n$ and the mapping function f preserves the similarity measure defined on G.*

Definition 3. *Given the DSNE $\mathbf{Y}$, a graph index $G^I = \left(V^I, E^I, \delta\right)$ denotes the graph-based index I constructed on $\mathbf{Y}$, where G^I is a directed weighted graph, v_i^I represents an embedding $\mathbf{y}_i$ in $\mathbf{Y}$, a directed edge $\overrightarrow{e_{ij}}^I \in E^I\,(0 \le i, j \le n,\ i \ne j)$ represents the neighbor relationship between v_i^I and v_j^I, $\delta_{i,j} \in \delta$ between v_i^I and v_j^I represents their Euclidean distance (l_2 norm) in Eq. 1, and smaller distance means higher similarity.*

$$\delta_{i,j} = \delta\left(v_i^I, v_j^I\right) = \sqrt{\sum_{l=0}^{d-1}\left(v_{il}^I - v_{jl}^I\right)^2} \tag{1}$$

Given a graph index G^I, query node v_q^I, routing strategy, and termination condition, the AKNNS retrieves KNN R of v_q^I, and then continue to conduct the search and update of R via the routing strategy, where the routing strategy represents the strategy of greedy best-first search or its variants. Finally, AKNNS returns the query result R once the termination condition is satisfied.

3.2 Directed Social Network Embedding

By using the non-negative matrix factorization (NMF) based SGNS, we propose DSNE to generate embeddings. The embedding input in Fig. 3 is the DSN G with dimension n, and the embedding out is the embedding matrix $\mathbf{Y}$ with dimension d, $d \ll n$. To preserve the direction of the edges in the DSN, DSNE makes the connected node-context pairs have similar embeddings, while scatting unconnected node pairs by optimizing the following objective

$$\mathcal{L} = \sum_{v_i \in V} \sum_{v_j \in V_c} \# \left(v_i, v_j \right) \left(\log \sigma \left(\mathbf{y}_i \cdot \mathbf{y}_j \right) + \beta \cdot \mathbb{E}_{v_j^N \sim P_D} \left[\log \sigma \left(-\mathbf{y}_i \cdot \mathbf{y}_j^N \right) \right] \right) \quad (2)$$

where V_c denotes the set of contexts of node v_i, $\# \left(v_i, v_j \right)$ denotes the number of directed edges between node pair $\left(v_i, v_j \right)$ in G. The default value of $\# \left(v_i, v_j \right)$ is 1, since there exists a directed edge between v_i and v_j in G. $\sigma \left(\cdot \right)$ denotes the sigmoid function. $\mathbf{y}_i$, $\mathbf{y}_j$ and $\mathbf{y}_j^N$ denote the embeddings corresponding to v_i, v_j and v_j^N, respectively. β is the number of negative node-contexts. v_j^N denotes the negative context (unconnected context of node) obeying the empirical unigram $P_D = \# \left(v_j \right) / |D|$, where $|D|$ represents the sum of frequencies of each node and $\# \left(v_j \right)$ represents the frequencies of context node v_j appearing in the edges of G.

The above objective function has been proved to factorize a shift PMI matrix $\mathbf{M}$ [6] as follows

$$\mathbf{M} = \mathbf{U} \cdot \mathbf{H} = \log \left(\frac{\# \left(v_i, v_j \right) \cdot |D|}{\# \left(v_i \right) \cdot \# \left(v_j \right)} \right) - \log \beta = PMI \left(v_i, v_j \right) - \log \beta \quad (3)$$

where $PMI \left(v_i, v_j \right)$, representing the point mutual information (PMI) between v_i and v_j, is adopted to measure the strength of dependency between v_i and v_j with the directed edge $\overrightarrow{e_{ij}}$ $\left(v_i \rightarrow v_j \right)$. To preserve the directed edge, we set $PMI \left(v_i, v_j \right) = \log \left(\frac{\# \left(v_i, v_j \right) \cdot |D|}{\# \left(v_i \right) \cdot \# \left(v_j \right)} \right)$ if $\overrightarrow{e_{ij}} = 1$, and $PMI \left(v_i, v_j \right) = 0$ if $\overrightarrow{e_{ij}} = 0$.

Let $\mathbf{W}$ represent the PMI matrix, $\mathbf{W} = \{ W_{ij} \}_{i,j=1}^n$ and $W_{ij} = PMI \left(v_i, v_j \right)$. For convenience, Eq. 3 is rewritten as

$$\mathbf{M} = \mathbf{W} - \log \beta \approx \mathbf{U} \cdot \mathbf{H}^T \quad (4)$$

To make DSNE interpretable, simple and efficient, the asymmetric NMF based on Frobenius norm (i.e., Euclidean norm) [1] is proposed to factorize $\mathbf{M}$ to obtain the low-dimensional embeddings, since the elements in $\mathbf{M}$ are nonnegative. Specifically, the asymmetric NMF is used to find the low rank decomposition of $\mathbf{M}$ by minimizing the following loss function

$$\mathcal{J} = \min \left\| \mathbf{M} - \mathbf{U} \cdot \mathbf{H}^T \right\|_F^2 = \sum_{ij} \left(M_{ij} - \left(\mathbf{U} \cdot \mathbf{H}^T \right)_{ij} \right)^2 \quad (5)$$

where $\mathbf{M} = \{ M_{ij} \}_{i,j=1}^n$ denotes the shifted PMI matrix. $\mathbf{U} \in \mathbb{R}^{n \times d}$ and $\mathbf{H} \in \mathbb{R}^{n \times d}$ denote the base matrix and coefficient matrix, respectively, $\mathbf{U} = \{ U_{ik} \}_{i,k=1}^{n,d}$ ($\mathbf{U} \geq 0$), $\mathbf{H} = \{ H_{kj} \}_{k,j=1}^{d,n}$ ($\mathbf{H} \geq 0$). Moreover, the embeddings $\mathbf{Y}$ are represented by the coeffient matrix $\mathbf{H}$ in terms of the definition of NMF [1]. $\| \cdot \|_F^2$ denotes the Frobenius norm by adopting the square Euclidean distance to measure the similarity between $\mathbf{M}$ and $\mathbf{U} \cdot \mathbf{H}^T$.

To accelerate the convergence of $\mathbf{U}$ and $\mathbf{H}$, we use the multiplicative update rules based on the gradient descent algorithm [1] to optimize the loss function $\mathcal{J}$. In all iterations, $\mathbf{U}$ and $\mathbf{H}$ are updated with the value of loss function $\mathcal{J}$ decreased monotonically by the following update rules

$$U_{i(k+1)} \leftarrow U_{ik} \frac{\left(\mathbf{M} \cdot \mathbf{H}^T\right)_{ik}}{\left(\mathbf{U} \cdot \mathbf{H} \cdot \mathbf{H}^T\right)_{ik}} \tag{6}$$

$$H_{k(j+1)} \leftarrow H_{kj} \frac{\left(\mathbf{U}^T \cdot \mathbf{M}\right)_{kj}}{\left(\mathbf{U}^T \cdot \mathbf{U} \cdot \mathbf{H}\right)_{kj}} \tag{7}$$

Now, the general framework for DSNE is presented in Algorithm 1. The total time is $O\left(n_E + N_{iter} \cdot n \cdot d\right)$, where n and n_E denote the number of nodes and edges in the DSN, respectively.

Algorithm 1. DSNE$(G, \beta, d, \epsilon, N_{iter})$

Input: G, the DSN; β, the number of negative neighbors; d, the dimension of embed-
    dings; ϵ, the error threshold; N_{iter}, the maximum number of iterations.
Output: $\mathbf{Y}$, embeddings.
1: Initialize the PMI matrix $\mathbf{W}$, base matrix $\mathbf{U}$ and coefficient matrix $\mathbf{H}$
2: Calculate $\#\left(v_i, v_j\right)$, $\#\left(v_i\right)$ and $\#\left(v_j\right)$
3: Compute the PMI $W_{ij} = \log\left(\frac{\#\left(v_i, v_j\right) \cdot |D|}{\#(v_i) \cdot \#(v_j)}\right)$ and construct $\mathbf{W}$
4: Obtain the shifted PMI matrix $\mathbf{M}$ by $\mathbf{M} = \mathbf{W} - \log(\beta)$
5: **for** $t = 1$ **to** N_{iter} **do**
6:     Update $\mathbf{U}$ by Eq. 6
7:     Update $\mathbf{H}$ by Eq. 7
8:     Update $\hat{\mathbf{M}} = \mathbf{U} \cdot \mathbf{H}^T$ by Eq. 4
9:     **if** $\left\|\mathbf{M} - \hat{\mathbf{M}}\right\|_F^2 < \epsilon$ or $t > N_{iter}$ **then**
10:        **return** $\mathbf{H}$
11:    **end if**
12: **end for**

3.3 Similarity Search with Graph Index

The construction of GI-DSNE includes the construction of initial KNNG, "search-select" process and spanning of the DFS tree.

To construct the initial KNNG efficiently, we propose the improved nearest neighbor descent (NN-Descent) method. Let $B\left(v_i^I, r\right)$ denote an open sphere with radius r such that $B\left(v_i^I, r\right) = \{v_j^I | \delta(v_i^I, v_j^I) < r\}$ $(i \neq j)$. Suppose that the neighbors' neighbors of v_i^I are also regarded as its neighbors, defined as $R_K\left(v_i^I\right) = \bigcup_{v_p^I \in B(v_i^I, r)} B\left(v_p^I, r\right)$. For each v_i^I, the sampled neighbors $\rho \cdot R_K\left(v_i^I\right)$ are selected in terms of the sample rate $\rho \in (0, 1]$. In each iteration, only the similarity of $v_p^I \to v_1^I$ and $v_1^I \to v_2^I$ are updated if v_p^I, v_1^I and v_2^I have the relationship $v_p^I \to v_1^I \to v_2^I$, which could update the distance similarity among the nodes in G^I efficiently. Meanwhile, the radius r is initialized with a large value, and gradually shrunken through iterations, until the number of nodes within the radius r will not be changed.

Nevertheless, the similarity search on KNNG tends to take long detours, since KNNG does not preserve the monotonic path and the global connectivity. To address the former problem, GI-DSNE is proposed by extending the monotonic relative neighborhood graph (MRNG) [3,4], which could guarantee a monotonic path between any two nodes in G^I to reduce the length of search path.

Definition 4. *Given the DSNE* **Y**, *KNNG* G^I, *query node* $v_q^I = v_k^I$ *and path* $v_1^I, v_2^I, \ldots, v_k^I$ *from* v_1^I *to* v_k^I *in* G^I, *the path is monotonic if and only if* $\forall i = 1, 2, \ldots, k-1$, $\delta\left(v_i^I, v_q^I\right) > \delta\left(v_{i+1}^I, v_q^I\right)$.

To build the GI-DSNE on KNNG efficiently, we first search a candidate neighbor set and further select the neighbors for each node. Given the query node v_q^I $\left(v_q^I \in V^I\right)$, the greedy best-first search (GBFS) algorithm [17] is adopted to search the candidate neighbor on KNNG from the start node v_p^I $\left(v_p^I \in V^I\right)$, also named navigating node, obtained by approximating the nearest neighbor of the centroid of the embeddings. To select the neighbors more efficiently, we propose GI-DSNE for edge selection by the direction guided strategy, which tries to guarantee a monotonic path from the navigating node to all the others.

Definition 5. *Given the DSN* G, *DSNE* **Y** *and KNNG* G^I, *the GI-DSNE is a directed graph index with the set of edges satisfying the following property: for any edge* $\overrightarrow{e_{ij}}^I$, $\overrightarrow{e_{ij}}^I \in G^I$ *if and only if* $lune_{ij} \cap \mathbf{Y} = \emptyset$ *and* $v_i \to v_j \in G$ *or* $\forall s \in (lune_{ij} \cap \mathbf{Y})$, $\overrightarrow{e_{is}}^I \notin G^I$ *and* $v_i \to v_j \in G$, *where* $lune_{ij}$ *denotes a region such that* $lune_{ij} = B\left(v_i^I, \delta_{v_i^I, v_j^I}\right) \cap B\left(v_j^I, \delta_{v_j^I, v_i^I}\right)$, $v_i \to v_j \in G$ *denotes the path from* v_i *to* v_j *in* G.

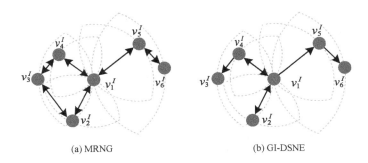

(a) MRNG   (b) GI-DSNE

Fig. 4. Edge selection strategy of MRNG (a) and that of GI-DSNE (b).

Following, the edge selection strategy of GI-DSNE is compared with that of MRNG in Fig. 4. For MRNG G_{MR}^I in Fig. 4 (a), the edge $\overrightarrow{e_{12}}^I$ of v_1^I and v_2^I is added to G_{MR}^I, since there are no nodes in $lune_{12}$. The edge $\overrightarrow{e_{13}}^I$ of v_1^I and v_3^I cannot be added to G_{MR}^I, since $v_4^I \in lune_{13}$ and $\overrightarrow{e_{14}}^I \in G_{MR}^I$. For GI-DSNE G^I in Fig. 4 (b), the edge $\overrightarrow{e_{12}}^I$ of v_1^I and v_2^I is added to G^I, since there are no nodes in $lune_{12}$ and exists the path $v_1 \rightarrow v_2$ in G as shown in Fig. 3. The edge $\overrightarrow{e_{13}}^I$ of v_1^I and v_3^I cannot be added to G^I, since $v_4^I \in lune_{13}$ and $\overrightarrow{e_{14}}^I \in G^I$. The edge $\overrightarrow{e_{51}}^I$ of v_5^I and v_1^I cannot be added to G^I, since there not exists the path $v_5 \rightarrow v_1$ in G as shown in Fig. 3. Overall, we could find that GI-DSNE has less out-edges than MRNG while guaranteeing a monotonic path between any two nodes in G^I, such as the path $v_1^I \rightarrow v_3^I$.

It is concluded that the GI-DSNE like NSG [4] and HNSW [9] tend to have high out-degree that is easily trapped in the "traffic hub". The maximum out-degrees m of all the nodes V^I is adopted to eliminate the long edges, which cannot guarantee the connectivity of G^I. To make G^I fully connectivity, a DFS tree based on GI-DSNE is spanned, where the navigating node is regarded as the root and the other nodes are linked to their nearest neighbors. Though the spanning of DFS tree will sacrifice some performance in the worse case [4], the GI-DSNE could be built efficiently.

Algorithm 2. GI-DSNE$(G, \mathbf{Y}, l, m)$

Input: G, the DSN; $\mathbf{Y}$, the embeddings; l, the candidate set size; m, the maximum out-degree.

Output: G^I, GI-DSNE.

1: $G^I \leftarrow$ build the KNNG
2: $v_c^I \leftarrow$ calculate the centroid of $\mathbf{Y}$
3: $v_r^I \leftarrow$ random node
4: $v_{na}^I \leftarrow$ GBFS(G^I, v_r^I, v_c^I, l) // navigating node
5: **for** each node v_i^I in G^I **do**
6:     $S(v_i^I) \leftarrow$ set of candidate neighbors retrieved by GBFS$(G^I, v_{na}^I, v_i^I, l)$ and sorted in ascending order of the distance to v_i^I
7:     $G^I \leftarrow$ edges between v_i^I and its neighbors selected by using direction guided strategy, where the number of edges is less than m
8: **end for**
9: $\overline{G}^I \leftarrow$ a DFS tree from root v_{na}^I being spanned on G^I
10: **return** $\overline{G}^I$

Overall, the framework for GI-DSNE is presented in Algorithm 2. First, the calculation of centroid in $\mathbf{Y}$ and the navigating node in G^I takes $O(n)$ time. Then, the KNNG is constructed by our NN-Descent in $O(n)$ time. Furthermore, the retrieved process of candidate neighbors by GBFS takes $O(K \cdot d \cdot n^{1/d} \cdot \log n^{1/d}/\triangle r)$ time, where $\triangle r$ is a constant denoting the minimum edge distance in the non-isosceles triangle v_i^I, v_j^I, v_q^I. Edge selection and spanning of the DFS tree take $O(n)$ time. Therefore, the total time of Algorithm 2 is about $O(n + K \cdot d \cdot n^{1/d} \cdot \log n^{1/d}/\triangle r)$.

Finally, the AKNNS with GI-DSNE is performed by the GBFS Algorithm, and thus the AKNNS could be fulfilled in $O\left(K \cdot d \cdot n^{1/d} \cdot \log n^{1/d}/\triangle r\right)$ time.

4 Experiments

In this section, we present the experimental study of our proposed GI-DSNE. On the datasets of DSNs, two sets of experiments are conducted to evaluate: (1) efficiency and effectiveness of DSNE, (2) efficiency and effectiveness of AKNNS with GI-DSNE.

4.1 Experimental Setting

Datasets. The DSNs[1] include soc-sign-bitcoin-alpha (Alpha), soc-sign-bitcoin-otc (Otc), wiki-Vote (Vote) and soc-Epinions1 (Soc). All datasets were divided into training DSNs, validation DSNs and query nodes. The parameters of each method on the validation datasets were tuned to make the search precision reach the optimal value as the ground-truth on the training datasets. The statistics of these DSNs are shown in Table 1, where $\#(\cdot)$ and n_E denote the number of nodes in the DSNs and the number of edges in the training DSNs respectively.

Table 1. Statistics of social networks.

Dataset	Edge direction	n_E	#(Training)	#(Validation)	#(Query)
Alpha	Directed	24186	3783	756	80
Otc	Directed	35592	5881	980	100
Vote	Directed	103689	7102	1420	150
Soc	Directed	1768149	14478	2895	300

Comparison Methods. The state-of-the-art graph indexing methods, such as NN-Descent, FANNG, NSG, and NSSG, were chosen to compare with our method GI-DSNE in Table 2, implemented in C++14 and compiled by g++9.3.0. The experiments were conducted on the machine with a 3.7 GHz ten-core Intel Core i9-10900X CPU, 128GB main memory, running Ubuntu operation system. For DSNE, the algorithm was implemented in Python 3.9 and a python library of scikit-learn was adopted for NMF.

- **NN-Descent**[2] [2] picked the K nearest neighbors to construct KNNG by shrinking the search radius between the current node and its neighbors' neighbors.

---

[1] http://snap.stanford.edu/data/.
[2] https://github.com/lmcinnes/pynndescent.

Table 2. Comparison methods.

Methods	Base graph index	Construction complexity	Search complexity
NN-Descent	KNNG	$O\left(n^{1.14}\right)$	$O\left(n^{0.54}\right)$
FANNG	KNNG+RNG	$O\left(n^{1.14} + dn^2 \log n\right)$	$O\left(n^{0.2}\right)$
NSG	KNNG+RNG	$O\left(n^{1.14} + Kdn^{1/d} \log n^{1/d}\right)$	$O\left(Kdn^{1/d} \log n^{1/d}\right)$
NSSG	KNNG+RNG	$O\left(n^{1.14} + K^2 dn\right)$	$O\left(Kdn^{1/d} \log n\right)$
GI-DSNE	KNNG+RNG	$O\left(n + Kdn^{1/d} \log n^{1/d}\right)$	$O\left(Kdn^{1/d} \log n^{1/d}\right)$

- **FANNG**[3] [5] adopted the modified occlusion rule and the optimal truncation to select the edges to build the graph index.
- **NSG**[4] [4] used the edge selection strategy of MRNG to construct the graph index and tried to guarantee the existence of monotonic paths from the navigating node to all the others.
- **NSSG**[5] [3] pruned the edges by involving both "angle" and "distance" to construct the graph index under the MSNET framework.

Evaluation Metrics. For DSNE, d was adopted to evaluate the execution time of DSNE, and $\mathcal{J}$ was adopted to test the effectiveness of DSNE. For GI-DSNE, the parameters K, d, l and m were considered to test on the execution time of GI-DSNE construction. For AKNNS, the queries per second and search precision were adopted to evaluate the efficiency and effectiveness of AKNNS, respectively. The search precision is the percentage of correct query nodes V_c in the retrieved nodes V_r, defined as $Precision = \frac{|V_c \cap V_r|}{|V_r|} = \frac{|V_c \cap V_r|}{K}$.

4.2   Experimental Results

Each experiment was repeated for 5 times, and the average evaluations of DSNE and AKNNS with GI-DSNE are reported here.

Evaluation of DSNE. To evaluate the efficiency of DSNE, the execution time of DSNE was recorded on different datasets by varying the dimension d of embeddings. To evaluate the effectiveness of DSNE, the reconstruction loss $\mathcal{J}$ of DSNE was recorded by varying the parameters β, d, N_{iter}, respectively.

Exp-1.1 Impacts of d on the Execution Time of DSNE. To evaluate the execution time of DSNE on different datasets in Table 1, d was varied from 100 to 400 when β and N_{iter} were set to 1 and 200 respectively. The execution time of DSNE is reported in Table 3. The results tell us that the execution time of our method DSNE increases by varying d from 100 to 400 on each dataset, such

---

[3] https://github.com/ZJULearning/efanna_graph.
[4] https://github.com/ZJULearning/nsg.
[5] https://github.com/ZJULearning/ssg.

as DSNE with $d = 400$ taking about 4 times more time than that with $d = 100$ on Alpha. This is because the more the dimension of embeddings, the longer the time the DSNE takes to factorize the PMI matrix. Moreover, the DSNE with $d = 400$ on Soc takes about 11 times more time than that on Alpha, since the number of nodes in Soc is far more than that in Alpha.

Table 3. Impacts of d on the execution time of DSNE.

Dataset	Execution time (s) of DSNE			
	$d = 100$	$d = 200$	$d = 300$	$d = 400$
Alpha	43	117	165	173
Otc	89	201	334	364
Vote	93	208	473	772
Soc	343	593	1025	2001

Exp-1.2 Impacts of Parameters β, d, N_{iter} on the Reconstruction Loss of DSNE. To better understand the impacts of parameters β, d, N_{iter} on the reconstruction loss $\mathcal{J}$ (in Eq. 5) on all datasets, the number β of negative neighbors was set to $\{1, 2, 4, 8, 16, 32\}$ when $d = 200$ and $N_{iter} = 100$. Moreover, the dimension d was set to $\{50, 100, 150, 200, 250, 300\}$ when $\beta = 4$ and $N_{iter} = 80$, and the maximum number N_{iter} of iterations was set to $\{40, 80, 120, 160, 200\}$ when $\beta = 4$ and $d = 200$, respectively. The reconstruction loss $\mathcal{J}$ is reported in Fig. 5. The results demonstrate that, on the whole, $\mathcal{J}$ is reduced gradually with the increase of β, d and N_{iter}, respectively. Meanwhile, β and d have significant impacts on the reconstruction loss of DSNE in Fig. 5 (a) and (b), respectively, such that $\mathcal{J}$ has reduced 63% by varying β from 1 to 32 on Soc.

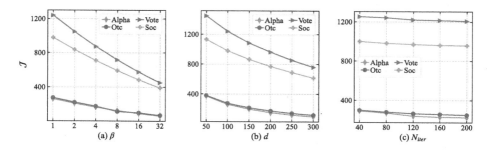

Fig. 5. Impacts of parameters β, d, N_{iter} on the reconstruction loss of DSNE.

Evaluation of AKNNS with GI-DSNE. To evaluate the efficiency of graph indexing construction on all datasets, the execution time of our proposed GI-DSNE was compared with that of NN-Descent, FANNG, NSG and NSSG, and recorded by varying the parameters K, d, l, m. To evaluate the efficiency and effectiveness of AKNNS with GI-DSNE on all datasets simultaneously, the queries per second (QPS) and search precision were compared with NN-Descent, FANNG, NSG and NSSG.

Table 4. Impacts of data size on the construction time of graph indexing methods.

Dataset	Construction time (s)				
	NN-Descent	FANNG	NSG	NSSG	GI-DSNE
Alpha	1.1	1.1+0.8	1.1+0.3	1.1+0.5	**0.8+0.3**
Otc	1.5	1.5+2	1.5+0.8	1.5+1.2	**1.0+0.7**
Vote	1.8	1.8+2.9	1.8+4.1	1.8+7.8	**1.2+1.9**
Soc	2.8	2.8+11.2	2.8+2.8	2.8+4.2	**1.8+1.8**

Exp-2.1 Impacts of Data Size on the Construction Time of Graph Indexing Methods. To evaluate the construction time of graph indexing methods on different datasets, our method GI-DSNE was compared with NN-Descent, FANNG, NSG and NSSG. For NN-Descent and FANNG, d, K, L, $iter\,(iter < 30)$, S and R were set to 100, 200, 200, 10, 100 and 100, respectively. For NSG and GI-DSNE, d, L, m and l were set to 100, 40, 50 and 500, respectively. For NSSG, d, L, $m\,(m < L)$ and angle between two edges were set to 100, 100, 50 and 60, respectively. The construction time of each graph indexing method is reported in Table 4. For FANNG, NSG, NSSG and GI-DSNE, the construction time $t_1 + t_2$ of graph index includes the construction time t_1 of the KNNG induced by NN-Descent and "search-select" time t_2 on KNNG induced by each method. The results tell us that:

- Our method GI-DSNE takes less time than FANNG, NSG and NSSG on each dataset. For example, the GI-DSNE takes 36% less time than NSG on Soc, since our method adopts the more efficient NN-Descent method for KNNG construction, and the direction guided strategy for edge selection to construct the graph index.
- Overall, our NN-Descent method is 33% faster than original NN-Descent, since our method only updates the similarity between the query node v_q^I and its neighbor v_i^I in $R_K\left(v_q^I\right)$ that exists a path from v_i^I to v_q^I.

Exp-2.2 Impacts of Parameters K, d, l, m on the Execution Time of GI-DSNE Construction. To better understand the impacts of parameters K, d, l, m on the execution time of our method GI-DSNE construction, K was set {50, 100, 150, 200, 250, 300} when $d = 100$, $l = 500$ and $m = 50$, and d was set to {50, 100, 150, 200, 250, 300} when $K = 200$, $l = 500$ and $m = 50$. Furthermore, l was set to {100, 200, 300, 400, 500, 600} when $K = 200$, $d = 100$ and $m = 50$, and m was set to {10, 20, 30, 40, 50, 60} when $K = 200$, $d = 100$

and $l = 500$. The execution time of GI-DSNE construction is reported in Fig. 6. The results tell us that, overall, the execution time of GI-DSNE construction gradually increases, which is consistent with our time complexity of Algorithm 2, by varying K from 50 to 300, d from 50 to 300 and l from 100 to 600, and m from 10 to 60, respectively. In addition, the number of nodes in different datasets has great impact on the execution time of GI-DSNE, such that GI-DSNE on Soc takes about 3.8 times more time than that on Alpha when $K = 300$ in Fig. 6 (a).

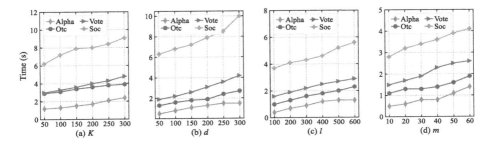

Fig. 6. Impacts of K, d, l, m on the execution time of GI-DSNE construction.

Exp-2.3 Search Precision vs Queries per Second. To evaluate the efficiency and effectiveness of AKNNS with GI-DSNE, the search precision vs QPS of our method was compared with that of NN-Descent, FANNG, NSG and NSSG. For NN-Descent and FANNG, d, K, L, $iter$, S and R were set to 100, 200, 200, 10, 100 and 100, respectively. For GI-DSNE and NSG, d, L, m and l were set to 100, 100, 50 and 100, respectively. For NSSG, d, L, m and angle between two edges were set to 100, 100, 50 and 100, respectively. The search precision vs QPS of each graph indexing method is reported in Fig. 7. The results demonstrate that:

- For each dataset, the more precise the search results, the longer the search time, such as the QPS of GI-DSNE on Alpha dropping from 1150 to 700 by varying the search precision from 0.6 to 1.
- As a comparison, the QPS of our method GI-DSNE outperforms that of NN-Descent, FANNG, NSG and NSSG on each dataset by fixing the precision, such as the QPS of GI-DSNE being about 20% more than that of NN-Descent by fixing the search precision as 0.7. This implies that the monotonic path and maximum candidate set size could improve the search efficiency.
- When the search precision of GI-DSNE attains 0.94, the QPS of our method also is larger than that of other methods on Alpha. This is most likely attributable to the GI-DSNE expressing the neighbor relationship precisely and only comparing query nodes with their nearest neighbors.

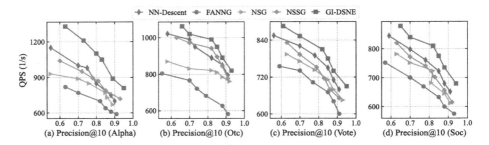

Fig. 7. Search precision vs QPS.

5 Conclusion and Future Work

In this paper, we propose a novel method of similarity search with graph index on directed social network embedding named as GI-DSNE, which could support end-to-end search on directed social network by varying the dimension of embeddings, maximum out-degree, etc. Theoretical analysis and extensive experiments have verified that our method outperforms the other graph indexing methods. In the future, to make both indexed and unindexed queries on graph index feasible, we will generate incremental embeddings and reconstruct the graph index for unindexed queries. To further improve the efficiency of graph indexing construction on the large-scale datasets, a parallel GI-DSNE is worthwhile for further study.

Acknowledgments. This paper was supported by the National Natural Science Foundation of China (U1802271, 62002311), Program of Key Lab of Intelligent Systems and Computing of Yunnan Province, Yunnan University, Science Foundation for Distinguished Young Scholars of Yunnan Province (2019FJ011), Major Project of Science and Technology of Yunnan Province (202002AD080002-1-B), Fundamental Research Project of Yunnan Province (202001BB050052).

References

1. Chen, G., Xu, C., Wang, J., Feng, J., Feng, J.: Nonnegative matrix factorization for link prediction in directed complex networks using PageRank and asymmetric link clustering information. Expert Syst. Appl. **148**, 113290 (2020)
2. Dong, W., Charikar, M., Li, K.: Efficient k-nearest neighbor graph construction for generic similarity measures. In: Proceedings of the 20th International Conference on World Wide Web, pp. 577–586 (2011)
3. Fu, C., Wang, C., Cai, D.: High dimensional similarity search with satellite system graph: efficiency, scalability, and unindexed query compatibility. IEEE Trans. Pattern Anal. Mach. Intell., 1 (2021)
4. Fu, C., Xiang, C., Wang, C., Cai, D.: Fast approximate nearest neighbor search with the navigating spreading-out graphs. PVLDB **12**(5), 461–474 (2019)

5. Harwood, B., Drummond, T.: FANNG: fast approximate nearest neighbour graphs. In: Proceedings of the IEEE Conference on Computer Vision and Pattern Recognition, pp. 5713–5722 (2016)
6. Levy, O., Goldberg, Y.: Neural word embedding as implicit matrix factorization. In: Advances in Neural Information Processing Systems, vol. 27, pp. 2177–2185 (2014)
7. Liu, X., Murata, T., Kim, K.S., Kotarasu, C., Zhuang, C.: A general view for network embedding as matrix factorization. In: Proceedings of the Twelfth ACM International Conference on Web Search and Data Mining, pp. 375–383 (2019)
8. Malkov, Y., Ponomarenko, A., Logvinov, A., Krylov, V.: Approximate nearest neighbor algorithm based on navigable small world graphs. Inf. Syst. **45**, 61–68 (2014)
9. Malkov, Y.A., Yashunin, D.A.: Efficient and robust approximate nearest neighbor search using hierarchical navigable small world graphs. IEEE Trans. Pattern Anal. Mach. Intell. **42**(4), 824–836 (2020)
10. Naidan, B., Boytsov, L., Nyberg, E.: Permutation search methods are efficient, yet faster search is possible. PVLDB **8**(12), 1618–1629 (2015)
11. Paredes, R., Chávez, E.: Using the k-nearest neighbor graph for proximity searching in metric spaces. In: Consens, M., Navarro, G. (eds.) SPIRE 2005. LNCS, vol. 3772, pp. 127–138. Springer, Heidelberg (2005). https://doi.org/10.1007/11575832_14
12. Qi, Z., Yue, K., Duan, L., Wang, J., Qiao, S., Fu, X.: Matrix factorization based Bayesian network embedding for efficient probabilistic inferences. Expert Syst. Appl. **169**, 114294 (2021)
13. Shim, C., Kim, W., Heo, W., Yi, S., Chung, Y.D.: Nearest close friend search in geo-social networks. Inf. Sci. **423**, 235–256 (2018)
14. Shimomura, L.C., Oyamada, R.S., Vieira, M.R., Kaster, D.S.: A survey on graph-based methods for similarity searches in metric spaces. Inf. Syst. **95**, 101507 (2021)
15. Symeonidis, P.: Similarity search, recommendation and explainability over graphs in different domains: social media, news, and health industry. In: Brambilla, M., Chbeir, R., Frasincar, F., Manolescu, I. (eds.) ICWE 2021. LNCS, vol. 12706, pp. 537–541. Springer, Cham (2021). https://doi.org/10.1007/978-3-030-74296-6_46
16. Toussaint, G.T.: The relative neighbourhood graph of a finite planar set. Pattern Recogn. **12**(4), 261–268 (1980)
17. Wang, M., Xu, X., Yue, Q., Wang, Y.: A comprehensive survey and experimental comparison of graph-based approximate nearest neighbor search. PVLDB **14**(11), 1964–1978 (2021)
18. Zheng, B., et al.: Towards a distributed local-search approach for partitioning large-scale social networks. Inf. Sci. **508**, 200–213 (2020)

Web Application Modelling
and Engineering

An In-Depth Analysis of Web Page Structure and Efficiency with Focus on Optimization Potential for Initial Page Load

Lucas Vogel[(✉)] and Thomas Springer

TU Dresden, 01069 Dresden, Germany
`lucas.vogel2@tu-dresden.de`

Abstract. Web pages are nowadays usually built with a variety of different tools, frameworks, and generated code. The structure and size of the resulting HTML, CSS, and JavaScript code highly influence the time for page load, and related energy consumption. However, no large-scale baseline data exists about the efficiency of the resulting page code, e.g., what amount of the code is actually used, or if code parts must be render-blocking. Furthermore, existing examinations analyze page code structure but do not investigate the potential impact on code efficiency if parts of the code would be optimized. In this paper, the top 10,000 web pages worldwide using the Tranco list were analyzed in-depth. Aspects with the highest impact on structure or performance are evaluated in detail and set into context regarding used techniques, frameworks, code efficiency, and differences in the delivered desktop- and mobile versions. The results showed that the vast majority (over 70% for JavaScript and ≈90% CSS) of externally loaded resources (both JavaScript and CSS) are loaded as render-blocking code. On average, only ≈40% of render-blocking JavaScript and ≈15% of CSS are used until page render, which unveils a significant potential for performance improvements for most analyzed websites.

Keywords: Progressive page loading · Initial page load · Page streaming · User experience · User acceptance

1 Introduction

Motivation. As continuously measured by the HTTP Archive, websites keep getting larger and more complex [2]. Still, there are many areas where no sufficient bandwidth is available to load a web page in a user acceptable time span. Especially on mobile devices, this holds true even in developed countries like Germany.[1] For web pages, various optimizations exist to speed up the loading

---

[1] https://www.breitband-monitor.de/funkloch/karte.

© Springer Nature Switzerland AG 2022
T. Di Noia et al. (Eds.): ICWE 2022, LNCS 13362, pp. 101–116, 2022.
https://doi.org/10.1007/978-3-031-09917-5_7

time. However, large-scale baseline data is missing on the efficiency and structure of the loaded data in the real world and how much potential is still left. More efficient web pages would reach a wider audience and load even quicker on fast network connections. By gathering and analyzing said data, further performance improvements can be implemented that target a specific part of a website's structure or loading behavior. This paper aims to highlight specific areas of optimization potential that is measurable by the code structure and efficiency. As this is highly dependant on code context, multiple factors of every measured aspect are compared. These include differences between the desktop and mobile versions of a website and the frameworks and libraries a website is built with. This structural analysis differs from a performance-measuring approach, as a reduction in the amount of transferred data will indirectly result in faster loading websites. For example, techniques that implement code-splitting do not provide sufficient information on the current efficiency of web pages. This paper aims to provide this missing data.

The main contribution of the paper is a in-depth large-scale code structure and efficiency analysis of the top 10,000 web pages worldwide using the Tranco list. The evaluated factors include web page structure and content, renderblocking and non-blocking resources and their locations on a page, as well as the percentages of used CSS and JavaScript until page render. All factors are compared to each other and set into relation with further gathered data, like the usage of frameworks. The impact of the four most popular JavaScript frameworks were given special consideration at each step. By analyzing code structure in this way, the optimization potential of code restructuring is elaborated.

The rest of the paper is organized as follows. In Sect. 2 we introduce key terms and concepts related to website structure. In Sect. 3 related work is discussed, followed by an explanation of measured aspects in Sect. 4.

2   Background

In this section, the structure of a website will be explained as well as common variations, starting with the loading behaviour of websites. Modern browsers like Firefox or Chrome often needs to load a set of additional external resources before rendering a web page. After a user requests a standard HTML-based web page from a server, the main HTML of the website will be sent by the server to the client. It is possible to link further resources like CSS and JavaScript within this file. The parsing halts when a browser parses the main HTML and a non-asynchronous link to an external resource is found. At this point, a further request for the external file will be sent. The file is fetched and then parsed. Afterward, parsing of the main HTML file continues. When a file pauses the rendering process, it is called *render-blocking*. External resources that can be renderblocking, like CSS and JavaScript, can be inserted in multiple ways. Both can be linked as external files (with the respective `link` and `script`-tags) and internally (with `style` and `script`-tags). In addition, CSS can be applied as inline-styles with the `style`-attribute. Typically, external links are render-blocking, however with JavaScript, the `async` and `defer`-attributes can be used to change the default behavior. In contrast, no such attributes can be applied for CSS, except for a workaround using the `media`-attribute or with JavaScript. Ideally, included render-blocking CSS styles and JavaScript code should be used to 100% in the initial page. Until now, no measurements exist on how efficient both factors are in the real world. As part of the CSS efficiency tests, the CSS-selectors are analyzed. These selectors can be described in multiple ways to access different parts of the HTML DOM. These include classes, ids, but also pseudo- and attribute-selectors. By analyzing the matches per selector, their efficiency can be measured. Ideally, one selector will style multiple elements in the HTML-Document. If a selector matches zero elements on a HTML-page, it means that the selector is 100% ineffective. In this paper, the efficiency will be described by evaluating the percentage of selectors with zero matches. For building websites and web applications, numerous frameworks exist to aid the development process. These range from CSS-Frameworks that are linked directly to a CDN that hosts the framework externally to more sophisticated technologies like React or Angular.[2] Both examples of the second category will, by default, generate the main HTML-File and, in doing so, will handle the insertion of external resources. However, it is unclear which impact those current implementations of frameworks have on the number of inserted files, their size, and their efficiency. Mobile clients are commonly less powerful due to their battery, so the delivered data on a smartphone or tablet can vary from the desktop version as an optimization step. One possible indicator is the screen size. Using the `media`-attribute, it is possible to activate certain CSS-code only at specific screen sizes. A further indicator for detecting a mobile client is the user agent of the device. When requesting a resource, a string is sent in the request header, which contains information about the device itself. With this data, the server may decide which version to send. As a result, the server might deliver a completely different 'mobile' version of a page [4]. In this paper, the factors mentioned above will be investigated. More precisely, the location and type of code import, the efficiency of the transferred code until page render, the distribution of JavaScript, CSS, HTML, and the influence of frameworks. These aspects can lead to a negative user experience as the loading times are affected if they are not optimized correctly.

3   Related Work

In this section, we explore related work for page structure and efficiency analysis. On the one hand, we discuss analysis work concerning the various ways of structuring a web page. On the other hand, we analyze optimization techniques for page code with a focus on the structural elements and inefficiencies they try to reduce. **Structural Profiling of Web Sites in the Wild** analyzes the DOM structure of the top 500 pages on the internet (filtered, from moz.com) [3]. The analyzed aspects were tag names, node depth, visibility based on the view-port, location, and CSS-selectors attributed to the element. They used the browser

---

[2] reactjs.org, angular.io.

extension TamperMonkey to inject custom JavaScript in order to analyze a web page. The main results showed that more than half of the elements of a web page are invisible. The majority of pages have less than 2000 nodes and a maximum DOM depth of 22. However, it lacks context, which links the measured data to performance impact in the real world, as its primary goal was to be a reference for future research. **Wappalyzer** is a service that analyzes websites in order to extract the technologies the website is built with. This includes frameworks, analytics, CMS, and page builders. All categories are listed on their website.[3] The detection works by testing regular expression patterns on various aspects of the page, like the HTML and JavaScript variables for indications of said technologies [1]. Wappalyzer can be used with a provided paid API. However, an open-source implementation is available on GitHub [1]. As it is expected that the technologies have a significant impact on page code structure, Wappalyzer will be used as part of this analysis to give context to the gathered structure data of websites, as the necessary data-set is not provided publicly. The **HTTP Archive** is one of the most powerful structure analysis platforms of the modern web. As described on their website, by crawling a large set of websites each month, the HTTP Archive can track how websites are built [2]. They use the URLs of the Chrome User Experience Report and analyze the websites by hosting an instance of Web Page Test.[4] Their reports cover various aspects of websites, like the total page size, the total amount of JavaScript and CSS, accessibility, speed, performance, and more. However, some factors are missing, like code efficiency until render, import location, etc. The analyzed factors are also not compared to each other and lack context of the real-world performance. The HTTP Archive provides all gathered Data with Google BigQuery, but as it is a paid service, a large-scale, in-depth analysis using the provided data is not possible due to cost. Therefore, a more in-depth analysis is needed for the missing factors and, more crucially, giving context to the gathered data. **Google Pagespeed, Minification** and bundler like **Webpack** are further technologies aiming to improve the structure of a web page. Minification and code bundler like Webpack aim to reduce the amount of requests and transferred code. By minifying the delivered code first, all unnecessary characters will be removed, like for example renaming long variables to shorter alternatives or removing unnecessary spaces. The efficiency of the delivered code will increase, and this technique is therefore commonly used. Webpack can furthermore combine all JavaScript files into a single file, and remove non-essential code by including a tree-shaking algorithm. Both methods are done while building a web application. In contrast, Pagespeed can be applied to a already built web page, as it is a module for `Apache` and `Nginx` based servers. The core idea consists of automatically improving initial page loading speeds by enforcing best practices. These include structural changes, like combining resource files of the same type or removing comments. The result is a smaller, structurally optimized web page. As a result, the delivered data should have higher efficiency. There is, however, no existing comparison on the

---

[3] wappalyzer.com/technologies.

[4] webpagetest.org.

real-life structure and efficiency impact. Wappalyzer can also detect the usage of Pagespeed, and this technique will therefore be analyzed as part of this paper. All described techniques and analysis methods either lack the necessary level of detail or do not provide comparable, real-world data to evaluate code efficiency and resulting page structure. In this paper, a large set of websites will be crawled and analyzed, focusing on code efficiency and structure as well as code distribution.

4   Structure Analysis

This section describes all considered elements, why and how it impacts the web page, and what we expect from the analysis. For analyzing the structure of a website in a way that is comparable between web pages of different sizes, most of the following measurements in percent are viewed relative to the length of the entire document in characters, if not stated otherwise. This also applies to the location of elements. For a complete structural inspection, the HTML of a website and all JavaScript and CSS (including dynamically imported resources) are loaded and analyzed.

1) **Number of external and internal JavaScript-blocks:** JavaScript can be directly embedded inside the HTML using the <script>-block or linked to an external file. This measurement will compare the percentage of the respective loading method relative to all detected imports. We argue that a higher number of files will result in a lower percentage of overall used JavaScript code and longer loading times. Loading multiple files also decreases a website's performance, as the bandwidth has to be shared, and browsers have a limit on the maximum number of parallel connections. The reason is that front-end frameworks often are linked as separate files if no optimization like **webpack** is used. If more external files are loaded, more requests have to be made to load said files.

2) **Efficiency of JavaScript:** This measurement compares the percentage of used JavaScript relative to the total amount of Java-Script code until render. Furthermore, our analysis includes the percentage of JavaScript characters used originate from render-blocking code. In an optimal scenario, all render-blocking JavaScript is used to 100% until the page loads. All other JavaScript could be loaded asynchronously. We hypothesize that this optimization is rarely implemented.

3) **Efficiency of CSS:** As described in Sect. 2, CSS might be widely unoptimized due to a lack of easy debugging options and asynchronous loading options. Currently, there is no easy or native way to load external CSS asynchronously, apart from using the **media**-attribute in certain scenarios. Therefore, we guess that, on average, used CSS is mostly not split in render-critical and non-render-critical CSS, and as a result, might result in a lower CSS code usage. Like with JavaScript, optimally render-blocking CSS should be used to 100% until the page loads. CSS frameworks bring a significant convenience at the

development stage, as usually all pre-defined elements like input-boxes and dropdowns are already styled. However, this includes elements that are not used in the page itself, but the styling information is still transferred as part of the framework's CSS file. Like with JavaScript, the percentage of used CSS and used CSS from render-blocking files is compared to the total amount of transferred CSS.

4) **CSS locations:** As part of the CSS analysis, the import locations and methods will be evaluated. CSS can be embedded externally, internally in a <style>-tag or inline with an element itself. There is no current data on what method is used the most and if the most popular websites prefer one placement over the other or if they are used interchangeably. If large amounts of external CSS are used, we hypothesize that this indicates the usage of multiple frameworks, resulting in a less efficient or less optimized website. The measurement consists of the percentage of used import methods relative to all import methods.

5) **Render-blocking and non-render-blocking CSS:** Performance wise, internal and inline-styles are the same, as both are purely render-blocking by default. Only the efficiency will change, as inline styles only apply to one element. There is no easy native way to mark CSS as asynchronous. Therefore, it is expected that most websites will use render-blocking CSS only. However, non-render-blocking CSS could significantly improve the First Contentful Paint, as the render process can be executed while displaying a page. Therefore, the percentage of render-blocking versus non-render-blocking CSS is compared.

6) **Matches of CSS selectors:** To apply styles to an element, CSS uses selectors. Most notably, they use tags, classes, and IDs. These correspond to the tag, `class`- and `id`-Attributes of a HTML-Element. These selectors can also match with multiple HTML-Elements, improving the efficiency of a CSS class. As described before, classes of frameworks might not have any matches if the corresponding classes are not used. Therefore, the number of matches per class will be evaluated. We hypothesize that the top web pages worldwide will include highly optimized CSS with a large number of matches per class, as this directly corresponds to less traffic and faster loading times.

7) **Resource distribution and element positions:** Similar to JavaScript, CSS can be included externally and internally. As described by MDN, external CSS should be linked in the <head>-Element [5]. This might be due to older HTML versions that were not compatible with link tags in the body. Now, in HTML5, some link types are `body-ok`.[5] Therefore, we guess that still most CSS is positioned near the start of a document. As described in Sect. 2, this is not the case with <script>-Elements. This metric does not have a direct impact on performance. However, it shows development habits and potentially the compatibility status of general clients. If clear patterns are visible, it might lead to possible future optimizations of the render process in modern browsers.

---

[5] https://html.spec.whatwg.org/multipage/links.html.

4.1   Website Selection

For the analysis, the "Tranco" website list will be used (downloaded April 29, 2021), as it is research-oriented and specifically hardened against manipulation [6]. The top 10.000 most popular websites on this list will be analyzed due to space and time constraints. For every website, the structure and efficiency will be investigated. While crawling the web pages of the Tranco list, not every website could be fetched and analyzed. This might be because some pages did not load until the timeout of 60 s ran out, which prevents the crawler from getting stuck loading a page. Other pages might have gone offline or unavailable from Germany, where the test was carried out. Thus, the number of readable websites for every analysis method will be named individually with n_d for desktop and n_m for mobile data sets.

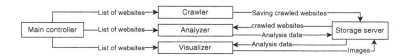

Fig. 1. Structure of the analysis software

4.2   Analysis Software

To enable repeatability of every test, the crawling and analysis steps are separated as much as possible. As seen in Fig. 1, the phases are orchestrated by the main controller. As there will be significant amounts of data, a file server is used to store all documents. This also enables the usage of multiple crawlers and analyzers, which can work in parallel. First, the controller starts the crawling process by distributing a section of the Tranco list to a crawler. This crawler will then use a remote-controlled, headless browser to fully load the website and all external resources in standard desktop mode. While loading, the JavaScript and CSS usage, CSS efficiency, and page metrics are being tested for the analysis. After saving all data to the file server, the same website is crawled again in the same way (without caching). However, this time, a phone is emulated inside the browser. The emulation changes the user agent and the screen size to the exact dimensions of a defined device.

After crawling is done, the primary analysis starts, using the same list of websites and their desktop and mobile versions. There, the main HTML will be parsed and structurally analyzed. With a framework, the technologies used to build the website are also gathered. To compare the data of different HTML-file-lengths later, the software converts all location data into percentages relative to the length of the own website. For each website, the analysis data is then saved on the file server for later use. As the last step, all individual analysis data are combined into one large analysis file to speed up the global evaluation. There, the averages of all analyzed data points are then calculated and saved. To enable the search for relations, all data is then visualized as graphs via the visualizer component.

4.3   Technical Implementation

For the crawling process, the `puppeteer`-Framework is used to load a website. As it consists of a headless Chromium Browser, the website's HTML can be extracted even after executing JavaScript that adds or modifies the page's content. In order to achieve this, the browser will wait until `networkidle0`. According to the official API, `networkidle0` considers the navigation only to be finished when zero network connections are active for at least 500 ms.[6] Furthermore, `puppeteer` is used to access JavaScript and CSS coverage of executed code. This functionality is provided as part of puppeteer and will be used to calculate efficiency by dividing the used JavaScript ranges by the total amount of JavaScript. The HTML of the page is analyzed by utilizing the `htmlparser2`-library.

4.4   Page Code Analysis

The results will be analyzed in the same groups as described at the beginning of Sect. 4. When JavaScript frameworks are analyzed, the top 4 front-end frameworks used by developers in 2021 will be mainly described in detail to compare their implementation to the total average. Those frameworks are `React.js`, `jQuery`, `Angular` and `Vue.js` according to Statista [7]. As described before, timing data will not be part of this evaluation as it is strictly a structure-focused analysis approach.

1) Number of external and internal JavaScript-blocks: On average, 68.41% of all embedded JavaScript Blocks are external files on desktop, and 70.17 on mobile ($n_d = 8417$, $n_m = 8468$). The desktop distribution is visible in Fig. 2. The graphic shows that 25.48% of the JavaScript blocks are internal scripts, with a nearly identical distribution on mobile (25.41%). However, comparing the two pairs of graphs in the figure, it is visible that the external files are responsible for over 90% of all JavaScript on a page (92.58% on mobile). As a result, even a smaller amount of externally linked files might contain the majority of JavaScript code.

With a large amount of JavaScript embedded in a page, the loading times can be improved by loading the resources asynchronously. However, 73.74% of all external JavaScript-files are render-blocking on desktop and 76.25% on mobile ($n_d = 8417$, $n_m = 8468$), which leaves significant optimization potential. Mapping the distribution to JavaScript frameworks, a trend is visible. For all websites that used one or more of the detected technologies, 74.74% of them used at least 95% render-blocking JavaScript on desktop and 87.37% on mobile. Pages with frameworks like AlloyUI or BEM used 100% render-blocking JavaScript on both

---

[6] github.com/puppeteer.

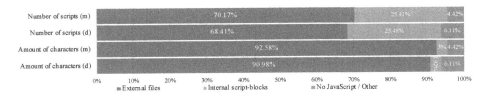

Fig. 2. The average percentage of JavaScript locations in number of files/blocks and characters on desktop (d) and mobile (m)

desktop and mobile. On the other hand, pages with the Twitter Flight framework only declared 73.42% of JavaScript as render-blocking, and even less on mobile (51.69%).

Table 1. Comparing values in percent of the most popular JavaScript-frameworks. d = desktop, m = mobile

Framework	Number of websites detected	Percentage of external files (in characters)	Percentage of renderblocking scripts (in characters)
React.js	n_d: 1413 n_m: 1457	d: 95.51% m: 97.68%	d: 94.56% m: 96.65%
jQuery	n_d: 5140 n_m: 5222	d: 97.16% m: 98.24%	d: 96.46% m: 97.39%
Angular	n_d: 378 n_m: 373	d: 94.24% m: 98.65%	d: 91.46% m: 95.53%
Vue.js	n_d: 418 n_m: 432	d: 97.47% m: 98.36%	d: 96.59% m: 97.29%

The values of the four most popular frameworks are visible in Table 1. Presented in the table is also the number of web pages in which those technologies were detected. By usage, jQuery is by far the most used technology. Websites with jQuery, Angular, or Vue.js have, on average, similar amounts of external JavaScript. Only React.js is lower by 1%–2%. The average percentages of render-blocking scripts are similar, except that Angular imports the least amount of render-blocking JavaScript code. However, in both scenarios, all values are above 90% for every technology.

2) Efficiency of JavaScript: While rendering, 40.81% of all loaded JavaScript will be executed on desktop and 40.61% on mobile. This includes render-blocking and non-render-blocking JavaScript. The amount of render-blocking JavaScript code used until `networkidle0` does not change significantly in comparison, with 40.94% on desktop and 40.65% on mobile ($n_d = 7741$, $n_m = 7741$).

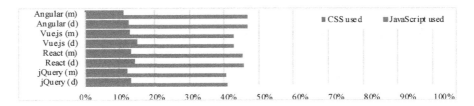

Fig. 3. The average percentage of CSS and JavaScript used until `networkidle0` on desktop (d) and mobile (m)

Considering the four major JavaScript frameworks, a minimal improvement is visible for Angular and React, as seen in Fig. 3. Both Frameworks improve JavaScript usage by 3–5%, with Angular having the most significant improvement. As jQuery is mainly used to simplify DOM manipulation and DOM traversal, it provides a significant feature-set. However, if not all functions are used, the efficiency will be lower. This might explain the slightly under-average JavaScript usage of jQuery, visible in Fig. 3.

3) Efficiency of CSS: On average, 15.86% of all loaded CSS is used until `networkidle0` on desktop and 14.84% on mobile. If only the render-blocking CSS is viewed, the loaded CSS is used near identically with 15.87% on desktop and 15.01% on mobile ($n_d = 7739$, $n_m = 7739$). Comparing the four major front-end frameworks displayed in Fig. 3, the usage is generally lower than the average of all websites together. This includes jQuery, which is a pure JavaScript framework that, in general, does not interfere with CSS. One possible explanation might be that other factors like inefficient CSS frameworks are more commonly used in unison with said frameworks to build a website.

4) CSS locations: Comparing the CSS import locations in Fig. 4 to JavaScript in Fig. 2, the ratio of internal and external blocks or scripts with the corresponding amount of characters is similar.

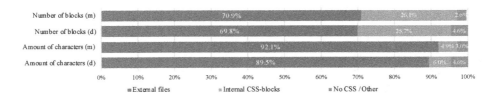

Fig. 4. The average percentage of CSS locations in number of files and blocks and characters on desktop (d) and mobile (m)

Around 90% of the CSS is linked externally (in the number of characters). On average, 8.50 external CSS documents are loaded on a page on desktop (8.74 files on mobile). As internal CSS is always render-blocking, it might seem to be an optimization step to load the CSS asynchronously with external links. However, generally, this is not the case, as described in the next section.

5) Render-blocking and non-render-blocking CSS: On desktop, an average of 89.47% of all CSS is render-blocking (in number of characters, 92.09% on mobile). Only 5.96% of pages on desktop and 4.92% on mobile use techniques to load CSS asynchronously, for example by using media queries. The remaining pages do not use externally linked CSS or could not be measured (4.57% on desktop and 2.99% on mobile). Comparing the most popular frameworks in Fig. 5, no significant difference is visible. The data for jQuery is expected to be approximately the same as the average of all websites. It does not render HTML like the other frameworks and therefore does not create or link CSS files by default. In reality, web pages built with jQuery used slightly more non-render-blocking CSS. React, Angular and Vue are all using over 90% of render-blocking CSS, which is more than average. However, Vue also uses more than average non-render-blocking CSS both on desktop and mobile. Those frameworks all have methods of creating and linking CSS, and using render-blocking CSS is, therefore, a conscious choice made by the developers of the web page or the creators of the framework. A possible explanation might be backward compatibility or ensuring that all styles are present when displaying the web page. It has to be noted that this does not directly correlate to 100% with page performance, as the amount of transferred CSS is the major performance impact. As this is highly dependant on specific page implementations, a generalization might be misleading.

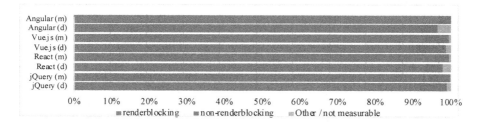

Fig. 5. Average percentage of renderblocking and non-renderblocking CSS per most popular framework on desktop (d) and mobile (m)

6) Matches of CSS selectors: Testing all CSS-selectors, 24.64% of them are pseudo-selectors on desktop (25.04% on mobile). Those include keywords like `:hover` or `:focus` resulting in a selection when a user interacts with an element, but also `:root` or `:first-child`, which work input-independently. In the following evaluation of selector-matches, only selectors that work independently of any user interaction can be tested. On average, a CSS-selector will have 3.07 matches in the HTML-Document on desktop (2.98 matches on mobile, $n_d = 8417$, $n_m = 8468$). This means that every class styles on average three elements when measured without user input after `networkidle0`. However, this is not an even distribution. 74.79% of selectors on desktop and 77.26% of classes on mobile have zero matches for their selector in the HTML document after `networkidle0`. These represent 73.57% of all CSS code on desktop and 75.87% on mobile. While there was no clear relation found between CSS usage and percentage of external or internal CSS, there is a significant correlation between the percentage of used CSS classes and the total number of CSS characters from externally loaded files. Pages with a high percentage of used CSS classes until render use a smaller amount of external CSS. Generally, the more external CSS is loaded, the fewer CSS classes are used.

7) Resource distribution and element positions: JavaScript can be linked to external Script-files in the head or body, according to the HTML specification[7]. On average, 60.55% of script-links were present in the `<head>` on desktop (61.58% on mobile), and 31.95% in the `<body>` (32.73% on mobile). The other links are outside of the `<head>` and `<body>` ($n_d = 8417$, $n_m = 8468$). As expected by the change in the specification, external CSS is linked mainly in the `<head>` with 81.75% on desktop and 82.51% on mobile ($n_d = 8417$, $n_m = 8468$). However, 5.06% of external CSS-Links are present in the body on desktop, and only 0.41% on mobile. This might be a conscious change made for compatibility reasons. The remaining pages do not use CSS or utilize other locations for inserting CSS (13.19% on desktop, 38.51% on mobile). Similarly, further investigation is needed explaining the significantly higher values on mobile. Comparing the averages node sizes of the `<head>` and `<body>`, the `<body>` is responsible for 73.28% of the complete document on desktop, and 72.75% on mobile. On desktop, the `<body>` accounts for 24.91% of the document, and 25.67% on mobile. The other data is therefore outside both elements (1.80% on desktop and 15.8% on mobile). When setting the average amount of all loaded HTML, JavaScript, and CSS in relation to each other, on desktop, 13.29% of all code is HTML, 70.07% is JavaScript and 16.64% is CSS. On mobile, 11.54% of all code is HTML, 75.51% is JavaScript and 16.95% is CSS. Both JavaScript and CSS represent significantly larger portions of the code than HTML does, with JavaScript being the large majority of data in the crawled websites. Analyzing the distribution of links to external JavaScript files shows a clear trend towards the start of a document, with an additional smaller spike at the end of the page. The data for desktop and mobile versions of the analyzed pages do not differ significantly. JavaScript files linked at the end of a page ensure that all DOM elements are loaded when the code is executed. The same can be done with JavaScript files linked at the start. However, a listener is needed to wait until the whole document is parsed if DOM-manipulation or -traversal is the goal of the executed code. We argue that the code at the start of a page will likely load asynchronously or is not necessary for the render process itself. For example, if a framework like jQuery is linked, the contained code will not manipulate the document itself. Instead, it is needed for later JavaScript code

---

[7] html.spec.whatwg.org.

that depends on jQuery functionality, and therefore it is not strictly necessary to load the framework at the beginning of a page or in a render-blocking way.

4.5 Desktop vs. Mobile

As visible in Sect. 4.4, the mobile data set was larger than the desktop data set. This is partially due to pages refusing the native puppeteer user agent, as it might indicate a crawler, which would be correct. Therefore, some pages did not load on desktop. We argue that this does not matter at the scale of the crawled data-set, as the averages of all data points are calculated. However, this margin of error is inevitable and is considered while analyzing the data. That said, mobile versions of websites performed on average slightly worse than their desktop counterparts, even with the browser and test setup hardware being the same. One explanation might be that a common modification to mobile and responsive versions is the reduction of displayed data to use the provided screen space more efficiently. By doing so, selectors like CSS media queries might only match on larger screens, as the targeted data is purposefully hidden on mobile clients, and the corresponding JavaScript functions are intentionally not called. Furthermore, most developers create websites on a desktop setup, as popular IDEs are traditionally exclusively available or usable on said setups. When developing locally, the delay of network setups and data transfer usually does not apply. Therefore, it is easy to overlook the performance impact of imported resources, even though analysis tools exist, such as the developer tools provided by most browsers.

Table 2. Average values of the page optimization framework Google PageSpeed for desktop and mobile in comparison to the average of all analyzed pages (reference) with p = PageSpeed, r = reference average, JS = JavaScript, idle = `networkidle0`, iaoc = in amount of characters

	Desktop	Mobile
% of used JavaScript until idle	p: 39.05% r: 40.81%	p: 39.93% r: 40.61%
% of used CSS until idle	p: 10.84% r: 15.86%	p: 11.10% r: 14.81%
% of renderblocking JavaScript (iaoc)	p: 90.04% r: 91.78%	p: 98.07% r: 93.36%
% of non-renderblocking JavaScript (iaoc)	p: 1.96% r: 2.11%	p: 1.93% r: 2.22%
% of unused CSS classes	p: 79.25% r: 74.79%	p: 84.21% r: 77.26%
% of CSS from selectors with 0 matches	p: 77.54% r: 73.57%	p: 82.39% r: 75.87%

4.6   Frameworks

The difference between the analyzed frameworks was often small, but existent. One factor is the combined usage of frameworks and libraries. Using Wappalyzer, a combined average of 2.12 JavaScript Frameworks and libraries were detected on every page on desktop, with the same number on mobile. Frameworks like React, Angular or Vue, will provide the functionality to build and bundle all developed resources into a deployable form. This bundling process often includes optimizations like Webpack to improve the loading performance. One optimization framework described in Sect. 3 is Google PageSpeed. While crawling all pages, 46 websites on desktop and 49 pages on mobile used Google PageSpeed to improve their performance. Comparing the CSS and JavaScript usage until page render, one JavaScript result was similar to the average results as described in Table 2. There it is visible that ≈40% of JavaScript is used until render. In most Scenarios, pages using PageSpeed fare worse than average. On desktop, pages use on average ≈5% less of the transferred CSS and have ≈4% more CSS-code with zero HTML matches. On mobile, pages using PageSpeed have ≈5% more render-blocking JavaScript code (98.07%) and ≈6.5% more CSS code with zero matches in the HTML code. One possible explanation might be that developers expect PageSpeed to correct these performance deficiencies automatically, which it does not sufficiently. Therefore, it is apparent that optimizing JavaScript and CSS until page render still yields a significant potential that PageSpeed could not solve.

4.7   Validity of Results

One of the main drawbacks of the automated crawling method is its limitation to the main page of a website. Therefore, websites behind a paywall, a login mask, or a cookie consent page do not represent the website entirely. However, filtering those websites is impossible on this scale and would skew the analysis and are therefore included in the analyzed data set. Furthermore, the mobile version is only simulated. Even though the main differentiation factors like user agent and screen size were changed for browsers, there might still be other ways of detecting mobile hardware. As a result, the validity of the retrieved mobile web pages cannot be assured to 100%. If websites use A/B testing, different web page versions might be retrieved. The measured CSS and JavaScript efficiency is only able to retrieve execution data until `networkidle0`. The actual usage is expected to be higher if a user utilizes the actual functionality of a web page. However, the captured results are valid if only the structural performance of transferred data until `networkidle0` is evaluated.

4.8   Major Insights and Possible Improvements

Lack of performance was mainly found in the efficiency of JavaScript and CSS, independently of frameworks used. In general, the goal of optimization is to utilize all of the render-blocking JavaScript and CSS until page render. All other code can be loaded asynchronously. Techniques already exist to split CSS into render-critical and non-critical files, like `critical`.[8] This is different with JavaScript, as functions might depend on each other, and an error is thrown if an asynchronously loaded function is not available in time. A possible solution is a framework that utilizes promises. Using a strict promise-based syntax, a function of asynchronously loaded JavaScript files can be called through a promise-based proxy, which waits until a function is loaded to call a function. However, this requires a deep analysis of the written code and might not be a drop-in solution. Further research is needed. Secondly, we hypothesize that current solutions for optimizing the efficiency of render-blocking resources might be too difficult to integrate into existing workflows. Therefore, easy and universally applicable solutions are needed for widespread adaptation.

5   Challenges and Research Roadmap

As described in Sect. 4.7, the validity of gathered data can only be tested to a certain degree and not on a per-page basis due to the size of the gathered data set. Furthermore, complex software had to be written to crawl and analyze said number of web pages. It depends on various tools like the code coverage information provided by `puppeteer`, which could not be evaluated independently due to time constraints. Next, further analysis of the data is planned, as the gathered information exceeds the scope of this paper significantly. Crawling websites in the future will also include other resources like fonts, and use the puppeteer stealth plugin to reduce the chance of being blocked by websites.

6   Conclusion

In this paper, the structure and efficiency of websites were analyzed. As a data-set, the top 10,000 websites of the Tranco list were crawled by a custom distributed analysis software. Apart from the main page itself, metadata like JavaScript and CSS usage and used frameworks and libraries were collected. Then, various aspects regarding positioning of code and data as well as efficiency were extracted. The results showed that the vast majority (over 70% for JavaScript and ≈90% CSS) of externally loaded resources, both JavaScript and CSS, are loaded as render-blocking code. This reduces the maximum achievable loading performance. Furthermore, on average, only ≈40% of render-blocking JavaScript and ≈15% of CSS are used until page render, which unveils a significant potential for performance improvements for most analyzed websites. Testing the CSS itself, ≈75% of the loaded CSS selectors do not have a single match in the final HTML page. As part of the test, desktop and mobile versions of web pages were gathered. In general, the efficiency of mobile versions was lower than their desktop counterparts. Evaluating the most popular frameworks in more detail, in most instances, the respective values did not change significantly compared

---

[8] npmjs.com/package/critical.

to the global average. Therefore, significant structural performance improvement potential was found in various aspects of web pages. We highlighted existing solutions for solving CSS efficiency problems and proposed a method for splitting JavaScript into render-critical and non-critical parts.

References

1. AliasIO: Github - Wappalyzer, October 2021. https://github.com/AliasIO/Wappalyzer. Accessed 14 Oct 2021
2. Archive, H.: HTTP Archive, July 2021. https://httparchive.org/reports/state-of-the-web. Accessed 5 Oct 2021
3. Chamberland-Thibeault, X., Hallé, S.: Structural profiling of web sites in the wild. In: Bielikova, M., Mikkonen, T., Pautasso, C. (eds.) ICWE 2020. LNCS, vol. 12128, pp. 27–34. Springer, Cham (2020). https://doi.org/10.1007/978-3-030-50578-3_3
4. Maurer, M.E., Hausen, D., De Luca, A., Hussmann, H.: Mobile or desktop websites? Website usage on multitouch devices. In: Proceedings of the 6th Nordic Conference on Human-Computer Interaction: Extending Boundaries, pp. 739–742 (2010)
5. MDN: The External Resource Link element - HTML: HyperText Markup Language | MDN, October 2021. https://developer.mozilla.org/en-US/docs/Web/HTML/Element/link. Accessed 16 Oct 2021
6. Pochat, V.L., Van Goethem, T., Tajalizadehkhoob, S., Korczyński, M., Joosen, W.: Tranco: a research-oriented top sites ranking hardened against manipulation. arXiv preprint arXiv:1806.01156 (2018)
7. Statista: Most used web frameworks among developers 2021 | Statista, October 2021. https://www.statista.com/statistics/1124699/worldwide-developer-survey-most-used-frameworks-web. Accessed 15 Oct 2021

Automatic Web Data API Creation via Cross-Lingual Neural Pagination Recognition

Chia-Hui Chang$^{(\boxtimes)}$ ⓘ, Cheng-Ju Wu, and Tzu-Ping Lin

National Central University, Taoyuan, Taiwan
chia@csie.ncu.edu.tw

Abstract. Information extraction, transformation and loading (abbreviated as ETL) tools are important for big data analysis and value-added applications on the Web. Typical Web scraping systems such as "Dexi.io" or "Import.io" allow users to specify where to fetch the page and what information or data to be extracted from the page. Although these commercial services already provide a graphical user interface to guide the system to the target pages for each data source, such systems are not scalable because users have to create crawlers one by one. In this paper we consider the problem of pagination recognition, which aims to automate the process of finding similar pages by locating the next page link and the list of page links from any starting URL. We propose a neural sequence model that will label each clickable link in a page as either "NEXT", "PAGE" or "Other", where the first two could guide the system to find similar pages of the seed URL. To have multilingual support, we have exploited the attribute contents in the links as well as Language-Agnostic SEntence Representations (LASER) for anchor text embedding. The experimental results show that the proposed model, achieves an average of micro 0.834 and macro 0.818 F1 score on pagination recognition. In terms of practical deployment, we are able to automatically create 1,060 (MDR) and 153 (DCADE) data APIs from 392 event source pages within 62 min.

Keywords: Web Data ETL scalability · Pagination recognition · Neural sequence labeling · Announcement extraction

1 Introduction

Web scraping is the process of using bots to download HTML pages and extract content and data from web pages. Web scraping is used in a variety of applications that rely on data harvesting such as comparison shopping agents, weather data monitoring, website change detection, and online reputation tracking from forums and social media, etc. Web scraping includes two tasks: Web page fetching and web data extraction. Because each website has its own style of information presentation, it is usually necessary to build a robot for each website.

ⓒ Springer Nature Switzerland AG 2022
T. Di Noia et al. (Eds.): ICWE 2022, LNCS 13362, pp. 117–131, 2022.
https://doi.org/10.1007/978-3-031-09917-5_8

For the past two decades, the techniques of web data extraction have evolved from supervised approaches to unsupervised approaches [4, 7]. Supervised web data extraction systems (e.g., Lixto [9], DIADEM [8], etc.) require annotated input and data schema to tell the system what to extract and how the extracted data should be organized for output. Unsupervised web data extraction (e.g., MDR [14], DEPTA [19], EXALG [1], DCADE [18], etc.) accepts annotation-free input pages with common templates to derive the schema and template for each website automatically.

On the other hand, web page fetching still relies on users' involvement to tell the system what pages to download and script. For example, existing tools such as Import.io [10] and Dexi.io [6] allow users to define the processes and rules for constructing Web robots, specify what data to be extracted from targeted websites/data sources, and designate where the data is pushed to and from.

Imagine the case when we need to monitor the latest announcements from more than 500 websites. Manually defining the processes of web page fetching for each website is time consuming and not effective. Is it possible to automate the page fetching procedure by simply giving the starting URLs as seeds without requiring additional rule settings? The answer is positive because the latest news or announcements are usually displayed in a list with a pagination design. As shown in Fig. 1, many websites contain a latest news page and provide an interactive interface (called pagination element) for transitioning from one page to another.

Fig. 1. Two news pages with page transition interfaces at the bottom.

Since there is no universal or uniform page indicator for page transition interfaces, automatic detection of the pagination links in each seed URL is a key issue for automatic page fetching and downloading. Wu and Sgro [17] filed a US patent US20160103799A1 that adopts a supervised model for automated detection of pagination. The claims include identifying characteristics of pagination elements, recording data for recognizing the pagination element, and generating the automated replay agent to recreate the identified interaction.

AutoPager [11], on the other hand, is a Python package that detects and classifies pagination elements by MIT. Autopager uses a sequence labeling model based on linear-chained CRF (Conditional Random Fields) to label each **clickable link** as either PAGE, or NEXT link or NONE. Linear-chained CRF can capture context information of all links for page indicator or page transition interface detection. The features used here include link pattern, query pattern, class pattern, and anchor text. Link pattern and query pattern refer to the host and query value pairs used in the URL link, while class pattern and anchor text refer to class attribute and text content of the HTML "<a>" tags, respectively.

Although the first three features can be extracted entirely from HTML, the anchor text is language dependent. Thus, the text features might not work well for web pages written in a language different from the training pages. In this paper, we propose a neural sequence labeling model to detect pagination elements. Through multi-lingual sentence embedding, we are able to train the model with labeled data written in English and apply the model to other languages. Meanwhile, we use n-gram to extend the attribute information of anchor tags and train custom attribute embedding for pagination recognition.

The contributions of this work are summarized below.

- To the best of our knowledge, this is the first work to achieve automatic data extraction by cascading supervised pagination recognition and unsupervised web data extraction.
- We introduce and compare a set of methods to split HTML tag into useful features embedding.
- We derived a language-agnostic model to improve the micro/macro F1 by 5% compared with AugoPager.

The rest of our paper is structured as follows. Section 2 will describe related works. Section 3 discusses the method that we proposed for pagination recognition. Experimental results and automatic data API creation are provided in Sects. 4 and 5, respectively. Finally we conclude with summary in Sect. 6.

2   Related Work

There are several web data extraction services on the market that provide users with convenient and fast extraction of data. For example, Import.io [10], which advertises full automation, is a relatively well-known service provider on the market. An user specifies the URL of the target website, and the system can analyze the possible data fields behind it automatically. If the extraction results are not well, the user can also manually label the correct data; so it can be regarded as a semi-supervised data extraction system. To deal with the multi-page input, import.io will detect possible combinations of URL parameters of the current web page, and users can also generate multiple URLs through the URL Generator.

Another data extraction service, Dexi.io [6], follows the idea of programming by demonstration to construct web robots. The user needs to predefine the entire extraction process, including how to redirect to the target page, how to extract the desired data, and click the next page. Unlike Import.io, Dexi.io can also handle the tricky problems that crawlers often encounter now, including tedious steps such as proxy server and CAPTCHA, filling in forms, and login verification.

The existing automatic page redirection programs on the market such as Import.io use a rule-based method to detect whether a URL can be adjusted to achieve page redirection. In addition to the rule-based method, the CONNO-TATE patent [17] detects whether the class name of the HTML <a> tag has a keyword similar to "pagination". While such methods can effectively detect the position of the pagination element in the traditional webpages, many mechanisms have been developed to prevent automatic detection of these pagination elements, e.g. auto-hashing of class names and URL parameters.

According to our survey, Autopager [11] is the first work to use sequence labeling for pagination recognition. They retain all HTML anchor tags (<a>) and define features based on the tag attributes (e.g. the class names of the parent and child tags), the queries in the link (e.g. whether the query contains keywords related to "pagignation"), and the anchor text content of the current, previous, and following anchor node to predict four kinds of labels including "PREV", "PAGE", "NEXT", and "Other". Based on the designed features, the linear chain CRF (Conditional Random Field) model can solve the auto-hash issue mentioned earlier. However, because CRF still relies on the features and vocabulary that the model has read before, such a model could not be applied directly to web pages written in different languages or development technologies.

In this paper, we try to explore neural tag embedding to better represent HTML tags and paths. Although there are some methods using neural embedding to represent HTML tags and paths, e.g.[12,16], most of the researches often simplify tags and ignore attributes and styles. For example, Web2Text [16] and BoilerPlate [12] use the first 50 frequent tags to construct a tag vector for HTML tag path representation.

3   Pagination Recognition Neural Sequence Model

In this section, we will introduce the pagination recognition neural sequence model and how we effectively represent the clickable links or buttons from HTML page. We start with the problem definition.

3.1   Problem Definition

For each input page, we first parse it as a DOM tree and keep only the "<a>" tags that contain the *href* attribute as well as potentially clickable "<button>"

tags. This would allow us to deal with web pages that use buttons and anchors for redirecting pages. In other words, each web page is represented by a sequence of L clickable nodes, $x = [x_1, x_2, \ldots, x_L]$, where each anchor or button node x_i is composed of three parts for processing:

- $ParentTag_i$: Parent tag of the anchor or button node,
- $AttCont_i$: Attribute content of the anchor or button node,
- $AnchText_i$: Text content of the anchor or button node.

The goal is to predict a label $y_i \in \{PAGE, NEXT, OTHER\}$ for each anchor or button node.

As mentioned above, previous works mainly rely on manually identified features extracted from the anchor node, especially the query key in the *href* link and the value in the *class* attribute. For example, for the following anchor tag, the query key "page" in the *href* link and the value "pagination" of the *class* attribute are good indicators of pagination elements.

<a class="pagination" href="/News.aspx?page=2&Size=20">NEXT</a>

Therefore, in addition to the word features from text contents of the current, the previous and the following node as well as query words and class attribute, we also consider 8 heuristic features used by Autopager in our paper, where most of them are binary features such as "Is there a disabled class in the class attribute?" Does the *href* link contain "page" or "pages"? Does the *href* link contain "number" or "year"? Whether the number of query keys in the *href* link equals 0, 1, or 2? Is the text alpha or digit? Does the node before or after the current node have a *href* link?

However, more and more web pages use non-traditional page redirection methods. Three typical approaches include replacing all page URLs with hash values, using JavaScript functions for page transition interface (instead of changing URL parameters), or using dynamic rendering methods to replace the page content (this method is used in single-page applications, especially common in programming websites). In addition, focusing only on the two attributes *href* and *class* is not comprehensive enough, because button tags (as shown below) may contain no *href* attribute at all.

<button type="button" ng-click="$ctrl.gotoPage(page)" class="ng-binding ng-scope">2</button>

Therefore, traditional machine learning that relies on manually predefined features is not enough, because there are still too many changes. Meanwhile, if the CRF model is built from mono language training pages with limited features, it may result in a significant decrease in the accuracy when processing cross-language websites.

3.2 Proposed Method

To overcome such issues, we propose a pagination recognition neural sequence model (Fig. 2), which consists of four components to represent each anchor/button node: parent tag embedding, attribute embedding, text content embedding, and heuristic features.

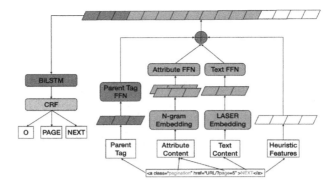

Fig. 2. Pagination recognition neural sequence model

Parent Tag Embedding. To represent parent tag, we use a vector of $d+1$ elements to encode the $d(=30)$ most common HTML tags in the parent tag, where each element is associated with a specific HTML tag. An additional dimension is added to the vector in order to handle unknown HTML tags. The tag vector $\mathbf{v_i}$ is then projected to m dimensional dense vector using a fully-connected layer $D \in R^{m \times d}$ for tag embedding.

$$TP_i = D * \mathbf{v_i} \tag{1}$$

N-Gram Attribute Embedding. Most neural sequence labeling models that accept web pages as input consider only tag paths and text contents but ignore their attribute contents. However, query keys in the *href* link and class names are two key features for the success of traditional pagination recognition methods. In the neural sequence labeling model we proposed, we examine whether proper network layers could extract important features from the class names and the query keys in the *href* link. We do not take query values in consideration because every website has it own pagination value.

As mentioned above, the attribute content of each anchor node $AttrCont_i$ can be split into two parts, one for *class* attribute and the other for the *href* link, i.e. $AttrCont_i = [CN_i, QK_i]$. For both cases, we might have multiple class names or query keys. Let CN_i denote the union of the class names from the anchor tags as well as its parent and child tag. We apply n-gram embedding for each class name $c_j^i \in CN_i$ through an embedding lookup table of 21,097 n-grams. With the n-gram embedding for each class name, we take the average pooling of all class names $Ngram_C(c_j^i)$ to get the class attribute embedding:

$$ClassEmb(CN_i) = AvgPooling(Ngram_C(c_1^i), Ngram_C(c_2^i), ...), \tag{2}$$

Similary, we apply N-gram embedding to the query keys and obtain the query embedding as follows:

$$QueryEmb(QK_i) = AvgPooling(Ngram_Q(q_1^i), Ngram_Q(q_2^i), ...), \tag{3}$$

where QK_i denotes the union of the query keys from the *href* link, and $Ngram_Q(q_j^i)$ returns the embedding of $q_j^i \in QK_i$ through the query key embedding lookup table of 2,896 n-grams.

The idea of N-gram embedding is to decompose each class name or query key into 2-gram, 3-gram, and 4-gram to capture the meaning of the value. For example, the class name "pagination" is split into 2-gram (e.g. PA, AG, GI, etc.), 3-gram (e.g. PAG, AGI, etc.), and 4-gram (e.g. PAGI, AGIN, etc.). The embeddings of all n-grams are averaged to represent the class name. Finally, we concatenate the average class embedding and average query embedding as the N-gram attribute representation:

$$AC_i = ClassEmb(CN_i) \oplus QueryEmb(QK_i) \tag{4}$$

Text Content Embedding. There are several multi-lingual embedding methods proposed in the last few years. In our proposed method, we conducted a zero-shot experiment to test BERT [5] and LASER [2], and chose to use pre-trained LASER for text content embedding. LASER allows the text content of different languages to be mapped into a single vector space, which greatly increases our accuracy in multi-lingual zero-shot tasks. We use $LASER(AnchText_i)$ to denote an embedding vector of the i-th node.

$$TC_i = LASER(AnchText_i) \tag{5}$$

Sequence Representation Layer. For each anchor node x_i, we concatenate its tag path embedding, attribute content coding, text content representation, and heuristic feature vector to obtain a representation $Rep(x_i)$:

$$Rep(x_i) = TP_i \oplus AC_i \oplus TC_i \oplus HC_i \tag{6}$$

The node representations are then fed into a bidirectional LSTM (Long Short-Term Memory) layer to capture the contextual relationship the nodes. Given a sequence of node representation $Rep(x_1), Rep(x_2), ..., Rep(x_n)$, the forward LSTM and backward LSTM yield the following outputs:

$$\begin{aligned} \overrightarrow{h}_i &= \overrightarrow{LSTM}(\overrightarrow{h}_{i-1}, Rep(x_i)) \\ \overleftarrow{h}_i &= \overleftarrow{LSTM}(\overleftarrow{h}_{i+1}, Rep(x_i)) \\ h_i &= \overrightarrow{h}_i \oplus \overleftarrow{h}_i \end{aligned} \tag{7}$$

Let d_h be the number of hidden cells for LSTM, $h_t \in R^{2*d_h}$.

Prediction Layer. After the encoding layer, a CRF layer is used on top of the BiLSTM output $H(x) = \{h_1, h_2...h_L\}$. Suppose the corresponding labels are $y = (y_1, y_2..., y_L)$, where $y_i \in \{OTHER|PAGE|NEXT\}$, the CRF inference layer predicts the label sequence $\hat{y}$ by

$$p(y|x) = \frac{1}{Z(H(x))} exp\{\sum_{t=1}^{L} T[y_{t-1}, y_t] + \sum_{t=1}^{L} U(h_t, y_t)\} \tag{8}$$

where T is a 3×3 state transition matrix and U is a function that computes the inner product of the input vector h_t with the weight vector corresponding to label y_t.

Training Objective. Finally, the training algorithm finds the best parameters by minimizing the Negative Log Likelihood as defined in Eq. (9).

$$- \log p(y|x) = Z_{log}(H(x)) - (\sum_{t=1}^{L} T[y_{t-1}, y_t] + \sum_{t=1}^{L} U[h_t, y_t]) \qquad (9)$$

4   Experiments

This section introduces the experimental evaluation of the proposed method and the baseline method, as well as the dataset and analysis report we collected. Our code can be found on GitHub[1].

4.1   Dataset

Since there is no public dataset for pagination recognition, we manually collect the training data from the Amazon global top website. We first apply Selector Gadget [3] to speed up the annotation process by locating anchor tags with the text content "PAGE" and "NEXT" to give the corresponding labels. Note that pages that do not contain any pagination links are also included in the dataset. Overall, we collected 164 training pages and 49 test pages from top US websites. As shown in Table 1, 65.20% of the training pages contain pagination elements, while 59.76% training pages contain "NEXT".

In addition to the English dataset, we also collected a total of 132 test pages from the most popular global websites in Germany, Russia, China, Japan, and South Korea for zero-shot (i.e. no training example) experiments. Table 1 shows the statistics of our datasets for each language and their respective PAGE and NEXT ratios. The PAGE/NEXT columns show the percentages of the pages containing the PAGE/NEXT labels, while the nonLabel column indicates the percentages of the pages that contain neither PAGE or NEXT labels.

Evaluation Metrics. We use micro and macro F1-score for model evaluation. Micro-F1 calculates the F1-score of each label from all testing pages globally, while macro-F1 computes the F1-score of each label locally for each page and then takes the average for each label. Since macro F1 reflects the average prediction performance of pagination recognition on a page, we use the average macro F1 as the basis when selecting the best model.

---

[1] https://github.com/UnderSam/pagination-prediction.

Table 1. Dataset collected from Amazon Global Top Sites.

Dataset	Type	Pages	Label ratio			#Labels per Page		
			PAGE	NEXT	nonLabel	# PAGE	& NEXT	# Nodes
EN	Dev	164	65.20%	59.75%	26.82%	10.0	1.4	242.7
	Test	49	34.69%	46.94%	53.06%	7.4	1.3	459.7
DE	Test	20	60.00%	55.00%	30.00%	11.6	2.0	237.6
RU	Test	21	38.10%	33.33%	61.90%	4.6	1.0	484.4
ZH	Test	44	54.55%	45.45%	45.45%	11.5	1.2	180.3
JA	Test	23	26.09%	34.78%	34.78%	8.2	1.4	401.6
KO	Test	24	25.00%	20.83%	75.00%	10.0	1.0	484.4

4.2   Results

We use Autopager as our baseline model, which adopts CRFSuite from 8 heuristic features. In addition to the 8 heuristic features mentioned before, the vocabulary size from the five feature set, i.e. the class attribute, query words, and text contents of the current, previous, and following nodes are 299, 3823, 9791, 5684, and 5153 word features, respectively.

For the proposed neural sequence labeling model, we use 32 dimensions for both the class attribute and query key Ngram embedding, and 1024 dimensions for pre-trained LASER embedding. For ParentTag encoding, we consider only the top 30 frequent tags. The number of the training epochs is fixed at 25. For each setting, we conducted the experiment five times and averaged it to obtain the performance.

Performance on EN Dataset. First, we train on the EN development set and evaluate on the EN test set. As shown in Table 2, our proposed model improves 3% F1 on PAGE, 3.6% F1 on NEXT, and increases the average F1 score by 3.3% in terms of micro evaluation. This does not seem to be a big improvement. However, the difference is significant when the evaluation method is changed from the node level to the page level. As we can see, the macro F1 of AutoPager on PAGE prediction was only 0.646, while the macro F1 of PRNSM on PAGE prediction reached 0.861.

In order to demonstrate the effectiveness of each input feature, we conducted ablation experiments on parent tag, n-gram attribute embedding, text content embedding, and heuristic features. The experimental results are shown in Fig. 3. First, removing the parent tag feature and text content embedding, the performance dropped by 3.6% and 4.4% macro F1, respectively. For attribute representation, class embedding plays a more important role than query embedding: the average macro F1 performance dropped by 4.4% (from 0.818 to 0.774) without class embedding. Finally on the effect of removing the heuristic features, the prediction of the PAGE label decreased about 10%, but the Next label was improved by 3%. Overall, the performance dropped by 1.8% macro F1.

Table 2. Performance evaluation on English dataset: Average from 5 runs

Metric	Model	Page			Next			Avg.
	(25 epochs)	P	R	F1	P	R	F1	F1
Micro	AutoPager	0.822	0.877	0.844	0.757	0.788	0.758	0.801
	PRNSM	0.824	0.932	**0.874**	0.733	0.869	**0.794**	**0.834**
Macro	AutoPager	0.645	0.663	0.646	0.683	0.778	0.727	0.687
	PRNSM	0.808	0.922	**0.861**	0.737	0.815	**0.770**	**0.818**

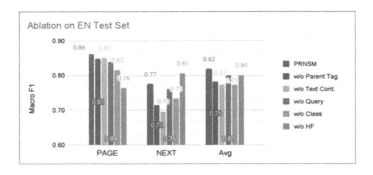

Fig. 3. Ablation test on En test set

Zeroshot Experiments. Next, we conducted zero-shot experiments on the five languages (DE, RU, ZH, JA, KO) other than EN to test how the model performs in cross-lingual dataset. Figures 4(a) and 4(b) show that the proposed method has a significant improvement on most languages except for JA and KO test sets in terms of PAGE prediction, especially on the DE set. The performance has the largest increase (from 0.634 to 0.913). Overall, the average F1 has increased by 6.6% (from 0.663 to 0.729). The improvement on the NEXT prediction is even more remarkable. The average macro F1 over five datasets differs by more than 13.1% (from 0.687 to 0.818).

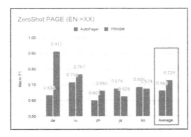

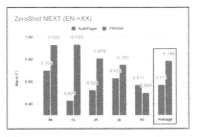

(a) Macro F1 on PAGE prediction   (b) Macro F1 on NEXT prediction

Fig. 4. Zeroshot experiments of pagination recognition

Effects of Various Embedding Methods. We experimented with two different multi-lingual text embedding methods, namely BERT and LASER, and used three different attribute embedding: (a) Char Embedding, (b) Char-CNN Embedding (c) N-gram embedding. We tried a variety of configurations for attribute embedding size and the number of filters for Char-CNN. We report the best performing configuration for each combination and omit the remaining results due to space limitations.

- **Text Content Embedding.** Figure 5a shows the zero-shot experiment on different pre-trained multi-lingual sentence embedding methods. LASER embedding beat BERT by 1.5% in average F1 score, so we chose LASER as our text embedding method.
- **Char-CNN Attribute Embedding.** We followed [20] to convert the whole Attribute value into a character level CNN layer to obtain Char-CNN attribute embedding. As shown in Fig. 5b, the N-gram attribute embedding outperforms direct character embedding with or without Char-CNN.

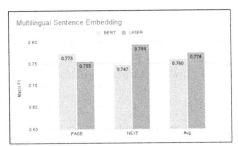

(a) Multi-Lingual Embedding

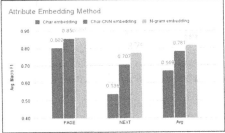

(b) Attribute Embedding

Fig. 5. Comparison of various embedding methods

5   Case Study: Automatic Data API Constructions

As mentioned in the introduction, web scraping tools usually provide users with an interface to specify where to fetch web pages. When we need to monitor a large number of data sources, it is impractical to create a data API one by one. This section demonstrates how to combine the pagination recognition model with Web data extraction technology to automatically create data APIs for these data-rich web sources.

As shown in Fig. 6, given a data source output from Anthelion [15] (a focused crawler for collecting data-rich pages) or a website's latest news announcement page from websites through data source discovery [13], we first apply the pagination recognition model to detect if the given page contains pagination elements. For each anchor or button node that are labeled as PAGE or NEXT, we will automatically download them and use multi-page web data extraction such as EXALG [1] or DCADE [18] for structured data extraction. If no PAGE or NEXT nodes are found, single-page web data extraction model such as MDR [14] is used for record set extraction. With these unsupervised wrapper induction techniques, we can automatically create application interfaces (APIs) for these web sources containing structured data.

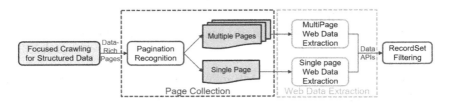

Fig. 6. Automatically data API creation via pagination recognition and unsupervised web data extraction

Because a data-rich page usually contains multiple messages as depicted in Fig. 1, we only focus on record sets that have anchors linked to some detail information. Therefore, we use a simple filtering mechanism to keep the largest record set with valid URLs as shown in the last step of Fig. 6. This design can extract the main structured data that focused crawlers target even if there are other record sets in the data-rich pages.

Dataset. As a demonstration, we collected 392 seed pages to demonstrate the possibility of large-scale website scraping. We manually labeled each anchor and button node as PAGE, NEXT, or NONE in 100 pages for pagination recognition. The ratios of these pages containing the PAGE and NEXT labels are 43% and 38%, respectively. Overall, there are 44% pages containing pagination elements.

5.1   Pagination Recognition

We show in Table 3 the performance of the pagination recognition model in the labeled 100 data-rich pages. The performance is similar to the results reported before, i.e. 0.857 and 0.773 micro F1 for PAGE and NEXT, respectively. In terms of page-level evaluation, the performance for pagination detection achieves 0.882 F1.

5.2   Data API Creation via Unsupervised Data Extraction

Next, we show the performance of data API creation and the number of message links extracted from 100 data-rich pages. As shown in Table 4, for 51 pages without pagination elements, MDR successfully generates 51 APIs, where each contains a record set. However, only 40 record sets contain anchor links, resulting

Table 3. Performance of pagination recognition on 100 structured pages

Unit	Class	Detected	Correct	Golden	Precision	Recall	F1-measure
Node	PAGE	259	213	238	0.822	0.895	0.857
	NEXT	50	34	38	0.680	0.895	0.773
Page	w. pagination	49	41	44	0.837	0.932	0.882
	w/o Pagination	51	49	56	0.961	0.875	0.916

Table 4. Results of web data extraction on 100 data-rich pages

Page type	Ext. Alg.	# Source	# API	# RecordSet	# Linked Sets	# Post
w/o Pagination	MDR	51	51	51	40	509
w. Pagination	DCADE	49	37	15	14	1,120

509 URLs in total. For 49 pages with pagination elements, we apply multi-page data extraction algorithm DCADE to generate 37 APIs. However, only 15 of them contain record sets and a total of 1,120 URLs (excluding one recordset without anchor links). The overall creation process only took 20 min to obtain 1,629 message URLs.

One reason that multi-page extraction algorithm has only 75.5% success rate may be due to the false positive anchor nodes. Since multi-page extraction algorithm assumes the input pages are of the same template, the algorithm could not generate a consistent output when input pages are inconsistent PAGE and NEXT links for multi-page extraction algorithms. This presents a new challenge for multi-page extraction algorithm to detect whether the input pages are consistent before data extraction.

Finally, we compare the number of data APIs and message URLs extraction with or without pagination recognition on 392 structured data sources. We consider three settings: (1) Apply MDR for API creation on each original input page without pagination recognition. (2) Apply MDR for API creation on original input pages and each anchor node detected by the pagination recognition model. (3) As described above, apply DCADE and MDR respectively for pages with and without pagination elements.

As shown in Table 5, we can build 392 data APIs using MDR to obtain the largest record set in each data source, but only 166 record sets contain links to 1,581 detailed posts. With the pagination recognition model, we can extract 1,176 additional PAGE/NEXT anchor nodes (from 179 data sources) and filter 377 extra record sets with links to 4,363 more posts. In total for the second setting, we can build 1,568 data APIs using MDR to obtain 549 record sets with links to 6,174 posts, 3.4 times of the original output. The third setting uses both single-page and multi-page data extraction algorithms, where MDR can build 213 APIs and filter 103 record sets with links to 1,091 posts, while DCADE can build 170 APIs and filter 56 record sets with links to 2,122 posts. In this setting, we can obtain 3,213 posts in 63 min, 1.7 times of the original.

Table 5. Results of data API creation on 392 data-rich pages

Round	Page type	Ext. Alg.	Sources	# URLs	# APIs	RecSets	LinkedSet	Posts
(1)	Original	MDR	392	392	392	392	172	1,811
(2)	w. Pagination	MDR	179	1,176	1,176	1,176	377	4,363
	(1)+(2)	MDR	392	1,568	1,568	1,568	549	6,174
(3)	w/o Pagination	MDR	213	213	213	213	103	1,091
	w. Pagination	DCADE	170	1,271	170	56	27	2,122
	Total	Both	383[a]	1,484	383	269	130	3,213

[a] Note that the numbers of data sources are not the same in the third setting because some data sources have no response.

6 Conclusions and Future Work

In this paper, we addressed the problem of automatic API creation for data-rich web sources by proposing a neural sequence labeling model PRNSM for Pagination Recognition. We constructed a data set of 345 multi-lingual training/test data from Alexa Top Sites. The model features multi-lingual sentence representation and N-gram attribute embedding. The experimental results show that our model has 11% macro F1 improvement over Autopager. Finally, pagination recognition solves the problem of multiple page collection such that multiple-page unsupervised data extraction approaches can be applied to create data APIs without human intervention. For future work, we plan to improve the precision of pagination recognition investigate to avoid the extraction of anchor nodes with inconsistent templates.

Acknowledgement. This paper is partially sponsored by Ministry of Science and Technology, Taiwan under grant MOST-109-2221-E-008-060-MY3.

References

1. Arasu, A., Garcia-Molina, H.: Extracting structured data from web pages. In: Proceedings of the 2003 ACM SIGMOD International Conference on Management of Data, pp. 337–348. ACM, New York (2003). https://doi.org/10.1145/872757. 872799
2. Artetxe, M., Schwenk, H.: Massively multilingual sentence embeddings for zero-shot cross-lingual transfer and beyond. Trans. Assoc. Comput. Linguist. TACL **7**, 597–610 (2018)
3. Cantino, A.: Selector gadget. https://github.com/cantino/selectorgadget
4. Chang, C.H., Kayed, M., Girgis, M.R., Shaalan, K.F.: A survey of web information extraction systems. IEEE Trans. Knowl. Data Eng. **18**(10), 1411–1428 (2006). https://doi.org/10.1109/TKDE.2006.152
5. Devlin, J., Chang, M.W., Lee, K., Toutanova, K.: BERT: pre-training of deep bidirectional transformers for language understanding. In: Proceedings of the 2019 Conference of the North American Chapter of the Association for Computational Linguistics: Human Language Technologies, Volume 1 (Long and Short Papers), pp. 4171–4186. NAACL, Association for Computational Linguistics, Minneapolis, Minnesota (2019)

6. Dexi.io: Dexi.io (2015). https://www.dexi.io/
7. Ferrara, E., Meo, P.D., Fiumara, G., Baumgartner, R.: Web data extraction, applications and techniques: a survey. Knowl.-Based Syst. **70**, 301–323 (2014)
8. Furche, T., et al.: Diadem: thousands of websites to a single database. Proc. VLDB Endow. **7**(14), 1845–1856 (2014). https://doi.org/10.14778/2733085.2733091
9. Gottlob, G., Koch, C., Baumgartner, R., Herzog, M., Flesca, S.: The Lixto data extraction project: back and forth between theory and practice. In: Proceedings of the Twenty-Third ACM SIGMOD-SIGACT-SIGART Symposium on Principles of Database Systems, PODS 2004, pp. 1–12. ACM, New York (2004). https://doi.org/10.1145/1055558.1055560
10. Import.io: Import.io (2012). https://www.import.io/product/
11. Korobov, M., de Prado, I., Haase, M.E.: AutoPager: Detect and classify pagination links (2020). https://github.com/TeamHG-Memex/autopager
12. Leonhardt, J., Anand, A., Khosla, M.: Boilerplate removal using a neural sequence labeling model. Association for Computing Machinery, New York, NY, USA (2020)
13. Liao, Y.C.: Event Source Page Discovery via Reinforcement Learning. Master's thesis, National Central University, Taoyuan, Taiwan (2021)
14. Liu, B., Grossman, R., Zhai, Y.: Mining data records in web pages. In: Proceedings of the Ninth ACM SIGKDD International Conference on Knowledge Discovery and Data Mining, pp. 601–606. ACM, New York (2003). https://doi.org/10.1145/956750.956826
15. Meusel, R., Mika, P., Blanco, R.: Focused crawling for structured data. Association for Computing Machinery, New York, NY, USA (2014)
16. Vogels, T., Ganea, O.-E., Eickhoff, C.: Web2Text: deep structured boilerplate removal. In: Pasi, G., Piwowarski, B., Azzopardi, L., Hanbury, A. (eds.) ECIR 2018. LNCS, vol. 10772, pp. 167–179. Springer, Cham (2018). https://doi.org/10.1007/978-3-319-76941-7_13
17. Wu, T., Sgro, V.: Methods and systems for automated detection of pagination (2016). uS20160103799A1
18. Yuliana, O.Y., Chang, C.-H.: DCADE: divide and conquer alignment with dynamic encoding for full page data extraction. Appl. Intell. **50**(2), 271–295 (2019). https://doi.org/10.1007/s10489-019-01499-0
19. Zhai, Y., Liu, B.: Structured data extraction from the web based on partial tree alignment. IEEE Trans. Knowl. Data Eng. **18**(12), 1614–1628 (2006). https://doi.org/10.1109/TKDE.2006.197
20. Zhang, X., Zhao, J., LeCun, Y.: Character-level convolutional networks for text classification. In: Proceedings of the 28th International Conference on Neural Information Processing Systems, NIPS 2015, vol. 1, pp. 649–657. MIT Press, Cambridge, MA, USA (2015)

Disclosure: Efficient Instrumentation-Based Web App Migration for Liquid Computing

Jae-Yun Kim and Soo-Mook Moon$^{(\boxtimes)}$

Seoul National University, Seoul, Republic of Korea
{jaeyun.kim,smoon}@snu.ac.kr

Abstract. *Web App migration* means capturing a snapshot of the execution state of an web app on a device, and restoring it on another device to continue its execution, for cross-device *liquid computing*. Although web apps are relatively easy to migrate due to its high portability, there is a JavaScript language feature called *closure*, which complicates migration since it requires migrating the variable states of already-finished outer functions. One approach of web app migration is to instrument the source code to trace the closure variables, yet it often suffers from performance slowdown, especially for multiple migrations. In this paper, we propose a new instrumentation-based technique called *Disclosure*, which moves the declarations of closure variables to a managed data structure and replaces closure variables by the corresponding references to the data structure. This can improve the runtime performance while enhancing security. We evaluated our work with eight *Octane* benchmarks and four real web apps. The runtime performance penalty due to Disclosure is 0%–15%, which is much better than the result of the latest instrumentation-based work that supports deep closures and multiple migrations, as Disclosure. Real web apps are also shown to migrate seamlessly, even multiple times.

Keywords: Web app migration · Closure · Code instrumentation · Liquid computing · Multiple migration

1 Introduction

Following a wide advancement of web technology, *JavaScript* has become one of the most popular programming languages used today [1]. Also, the web browser has grown into the dominant platform for various technological environments such as PCs, smartphones, smart TVs, and IoT devices. Since web applications can run anywhere regardless of CPU or operating system, *app migration* has emerged readily. It captures a snapshot of an application state in the middle of execution, and restores it to another device in order to continue the execution [2–6]. App migration can offer a novel user experience; for example, a game application running on a smartphone could be handed over to a smart TV for continued execution on a larger screen, then to another device as the user is moving. It is a form of *liquid*

© Springer Nature Switzerland AG 2022
T. Di Noia et al. (Eds.): ICWE 2022, LNCS 13362, pp. 132–147, 2022.
https://doi.org/10.1007/978-3-031-09917-5_9

computing [7]. For a manufacturer who can provide a uniform web platform for its diverse smart device products (e.g., Samsung Tizen or LG WebOS), the difficulty of liquid computing caused by the differences of the device specification or the web browser context is better surmountable, making liquid computing more feasible.

A snapshot captures the state of the objects in the heap memory along with other states in the *JavaScript Runtime* (JR). There are some challenges in capturing them. *Closure*, a language feature inherent to JavaScript, is a function with *free variables*, which are used inside the function but declared outside of the function scope. If a free variable is still alive (referenced) after the outer function is terminated, it becomes a closure variable and is stored as a closure object in the heap memory. Closure variables are inaccessible from the *execution context* (stack frame in JavaScript) or from the global *window* object, thus demanding a new strategy to capture them. Besides, JR includes *Document Object Model (DOM)*, *XMLHttpRequest (AJAX)*, and *Timeout methods*. *DOM objects* are stored in a tree structure and are accessible through Web APIs provided by the browser, so we can capture the DOM state by traversing the *DOM tree*. Timeout methods use JR's timer objects for scheduling the execution of callback functions. However, it is impossible to access the registered timer's state since there are no Web APIs. XMLHttpRequest is used to interact with servers, and it is not usually within the scope of app migration since app migration only targets applications that can run standalone. Thus, app migration technique has focused on capturing closures and timers, and two approaches have been proposed.

One is to instrument the source code of a web application in order to trace the closures within the hierarchy of the *scope tree*, a combination of scope chains, by inserting a *mirroring statement* [3,6] underneath any statement that includes the closure variables. Those mirroring statements can trace the closure variables with their position in the scope tree, but it increases the program size, hence the running time. Timers are handled by the *wrapper functions*, which wrap timeout methods so as to record the arguments passed when an event is registered, to reschedule them from the moment of migration. Overall, this approach successfully captures the snapshot but suffers from serious performance degradation due to the overhead of the mirroring statements. A recent work improved the performance by taking a snapshot lazily [8], yet it does not allow multiple migration, thus limiting the liquidity of cross-device user experience.

The other is to add new APIs to JR, which is a way of directly accessing the closures and timers via modifying web browsers [2,4,5]. This approach leaves the source code intact, so it does not affect runtime performance. However, it weakens the security of applications since JavaScript developers typically implement data encapsulation by means of closures. Such APIs, therefore, are not generally welcomed by the browser vendors, and users need to use a custom browser for migration, which hurts portability.

This paper proposes a new instrumentation-based technique called *Disclosure*, which moves declarations of the closure variables to a managed data structure named *disclosure table*, and replaces closure variables by the references to the corresponding elements within the table. In this way, Disclosure obviates mirroring statements and significantly reduces runtime overhead, maintaining almost the same performance as the original program. Moreover, we can implement the disclosure table itself *as a closure*, which can keep closure variables from being revealed, enhancing security further than previous works. For the timers, we capture them using the wrapper functions as previously, yet store them also in the disclosure table. Disclosure can fully capture the DOM tree unlike previous instrumentation-based works. Consequently, a user can take a snapshot by copying the DOM tree, the objects in the heap memory, and the disclosure table. The snapshot, written in JavaScript, is a full-fledged web application by itself, so we can simply run it on the browser of the target device to continue execution with its current display. We made the following contributions:

- We propose a novel instrumentation-based migration technique for closures that can keep the instrumented program and the snapshot program from being slowed down seriously, while allowing multiple migrations.
- Our snapshot can preserve security for closure variables, possibly enhanced with cryptographic methods.
- Disclosure can migrate a whole execution state of a web app including JavaScript and DOM tree, unlike most previous instrumentation-based works.
- Our evaluation with Octane benchmarks shows a tangible performance benefit, while real web apps are shown to migrate seamlessly, multiple times.

2   Background on JavaScript Runtime

The JavaScript Runtime is composed of a JavaScript engine and other runtime components. The JavaScript engine is composed of *call stack* (execution context stack) and *heap memory*, and other components are event queue, web APIs, and event loop. When a JavaScript application is loaded, a global execution context is first pushed to the call stack. If a new function is invoked, a new execution context is generated, referencing the global context at the top of the stack. This process is repeated so that each execution context references the outer (previous) execution context, and the chain-structured execution contexts are called *scope chain*. During this process, developers register *event handlers* by using *event listeners* to handle asynchronous events triggered by a button click, timers, etc. A triggered event is pushed to the event queue with the registered event handler. When a function is terminated, conversely, its execution context is removed from the top of the stack. Eventually, the call stack becomes empty after all functions and the code in the global scope have been executed. Then, the event loop fetches an event and the event handler from the event queue, to execute it on a new execution context assigned to the call stack. This is the way JavaScript handles asynchronous tasks. Since the JavaScript engine is single-threaded, it runs only one event at a time and cannot execute another event until the current event is terminated. Considering how the browser works, the simplest way to implement app migration is to make it as an event, since the call stack would be empty when the migration event is fetched from the event queue. This strategy has an advantage of not having to capture the state of the call stack. So, we implemented the migration task as an event so that a developer or user can call it asynchronously through a console or a browser extension.

3   Challenges for Web App Migration

JavaScript functions are objects (first-class functions), which allows defining a function within another function scope, thereby making a nested function structure. JavaScript allows for an inner function to access the *free variables* defined at one of the outer functions. Those free variables are accessible even after the lifecycle of the outer function is terminated, since the inner function is established as a closure containing the lexical environment of the outer function with the free (closure) variables. However, the environment of the terminated function is not accessible from the outside, so developers use this feature to implement data encapsulation in JavaScript. The environment is the variable-value mapping of the current scope chain, and each execution context has an internal property called *scope* to reference the previous execution context. Listing 1 provides a code example for scope chain and closures. The variable *count* (lines 2) is used in the inner function (lines 3–6). Since it is a local variable of the outer function *CreateCounter()*, it is removed from the stack once the outer function terminates. However, it is not eliminated, but saved as a closure variable in the JavaScript heap since it is still used by the returned inner function.

Listing 1. An example JavaScript code with a closure variable.

```
1  function CreateCounter () {
2      var count = 0;
3      return function () {
4          count += 1;
5          console.log(count);
6      };
7  }
8  var myCounter = CreateCounter ();
9
10 setInterval(function () {
11     myCounter ();
12 }, 1000);
```

Timeout methods utilize JR's timer to schedule the execution of event handlers which are pushed to the event queue when the timer expires. However, since web browsers do not provide Web APIs for accessing the timer, capturing their states is a challenge for app migration. Listing 1 describes an example of a timeout method, *setInterval* (line 10). It repeatedly registers a new timer event, which has an anonymous callback function (event handler, lines 10–12) that calls *myCounter* (line 11). So the event will be pushed to the event queue every second (line 12). When a migration event is pulled from the event queue and executed, the migration process must capture the state of the timer, to register any pending event and repeated ones thereafter, after migration.

4   Previous Approaches

There are two different approaches to web app migration for handling closures and timers. One is to instrument the source code of the target application statically, and the other is to modify the web browser to provide new APIs.

Imagen [3] and *ThingsMigrate* [6] instrument the source code by inserting mirroring statements as depicted in Listing 2. Since they are similar, we explain based on ThingsMigrate, which can migrate deep closures unlike Imagen. ThingsMigrate makes scope objects (line 1,3) for every execution context, including the relevant hierarchical information of each scope chain to establish a scope tree. It allocates all variables as inherent properties of the corresponding scope objects (line 5,12,15). If there is a statement affecting any of the variables, a mirroring statement is inserted below (line 8,17) to copy the updated value. Also, it wraps each timeout method to trace an event handler and a timer argument (line 19–21). So, it replaces *setInterval()* by a wrapper function *ThingsMigrate.setInterval()* to record the event handler *myCounter*, the time interval (1,000ms), and the remaining time before registering the next event.

The migration process produces a snapshot which captures all objects in the heap memory and the timers. The snapshot is generated in the form of JavaScript code so that it can be executed on any device with any web browser, as depicted in Listing 3. If a migration event occurs 3.75 s after app loading, the value of the closure variable *count* will be 3, and the remaining system time for the next event will be 0.25 s. ThingsMigrate generates a snapshot in the form of *immediately-invoked function* to restore the closures without any side effect (lines 2–9). Subsequently, the timers are restored with the wrapper function again, to allow capturing them for multiple migrations (lines 11–13).

The other approach is adding new APIs to web browsers with the aim of retrieving information on closures and timers [2,4,5]. This strategy leaves the source code intact, allowing users to capture and migrate any applications to other devices without any need for instrumentation. Also, the runtime performance of the application is identical to that of the original.

Both approaches have successfully implemented app migration technology; however, we found some issues in both methods. The former approach, which utilizes code instrumentation, results in a serious performance slowdown at runtime due to the mirroring statements to trace the scope tree (line 8, 17 in Listing 2). Although *FlashFreeze* [8] solved this problem by ignoring scope objects and tracing only the closures, it cannot support multiple migrations required for liquid computing (its performance is similar to our previous version's, presented in a work-in-progress report). Also, the former approaches support only the migration of the JavaScript state, not the DOM tree (only Imagen partially migrates the DOM objects), thus not suitable for migrating web applications. On the other hand, the latter approach cannot conceal private information since anyone can look into closure variables and timer states using the new APIs. Also, users should use a customized web browser for migration, which reduces portability.

Listing 2. The instrumented code generated by *ThingsMigrate* for Listing 1.

```
1   var global = new Scope("global")
2   function CreateCounter() {
3       var createcounter = new Scope(global, "CreateCounter");
4       var count = 0;
5       createcounter.addVar("count", count)
6       var anon1 = function() {
7           count += 1;
```

```
 8        createcounter.setVar("count", count);
 9            console.log(count);
10            return count;
11        };
12        createcounter.addFunction("anon1", anon1);
13        return anon1;
14    }
15   global.addFunction("CreateCounter", CreateCounter);
16   var myCounter = CreateCounter();
17   CreateCounter.setVar("myCounter", myCounter);
18
19   ThingsMigrate.setInterval(function() {
20        myCounter();
21   }, 1000);
```

Listing 3. Snapshot code serialized by *ThingsMigrate*, 3.75 seconds after app loading of Listing 2.

```
 1  /* The instrumented code (Listing 2) comes here */
 2  (function() {
 3      function CreateCounter() {
 4          var count = 3;
 5          var anon1 = function() { ... }
 6          ThingsMigrate.addFunction("Global/CreateCounter/anon1", anon1)
      ;
 7          return anon1;
 8      }
 9  })();
10
11  ThingsMigrate.setInterval(ThingsMigrate.
12      findFunction("Global/CreateCounter/anon1"),
13      1000, 250);
```

5   The Disclosure Approach

Disclosure is a new approach to solve the issues of the previous ones. It extends the code instrumentation scheme, yet obviates the mirroring statements to improve performance. We capture an application's scope tree by traversing from the *window* object instead of using mirroring statement. Since a closure cannot be accessed from the *window* object, the instrumented code moves the declarations of closure variables to a managed data structure called *disclosure table*, and replaces the variables with the references to the corresponding elements within the table. Serializing the timers or generating a snapshot file works similarly as in the previous works, but handling the DOM tree works differently.

Disclosure consists of three phases: instrumentation phase, execution phase, and migration phase. The instrumentation phase transform the source code by changing the closure variables using the disclosure table, wrapping the timeout methods, and generating the conversion code for the DOM objects. The execution phase utilizes a runtime library with the disclosure table, to store structures and values of the closures. The migration phase captures the DOM tree, the heap objects, the timers, and the disclosure table to produce a snapshot file.

5.1   Instrumentation Phase

The instrumentation phase finds free variables and determines those likely to become closure variables at runtime. It utilizes a *Abstract Syntax Tree* (AST) to emulate scope chains for discerning closure variables, generates the code to move their definitions to the disclosure table, and replaces them by the corresponding references to the elements in the disclosure table. Also, this phase converts each timeout method into the a wrapper function for the purpose of copying the arguments to trace the timers, to re-register them after migration. This phase consists of three phases: *AST Generation*, *AST Traversal*, and *Code Generation*.

AST is a fundamental data structure for code analysis, and we use it to determine whether a free variable is a closure variable or not. Since the AST's hierarchical structure represents function inclusion orders, each path is likely to be instantiated to a scope chain at runtime. Figure 1(a) is the AST-like representation of Listing 1, and we can observe a scope chain on the left composed of *Global*, *CreateCounter function*, and *anonymous function* scopes. On the right, we can see the timeout method, *setInterval*, defined in the global scope. It shows the event handler that will be pushed to the event queue every 1,000 ms.

As mentioned before, we can infer a scope chain by using a path in the AST. So, we traverse the AST in a Depth First Search (DFS) order to identify closure variables with a virtual stack to emulate the scope chain. Our *traverser* begins from the root node, the *window* object, and when it encounters *VariableDeclaration*, an AST node, it pushes the declared variable to the virtual stack with its expected execution context. If the traverser encounters *ExpressionStatement*, it determines whether the variable is a closure variable or not using the virtual stack. For example, in Fig. 1(a), if the traverser encounters *FunctionExpression* that includes the *count += 1* statement (red box), it can identify that variable *count* is a closure variable because it is not declared within the anonymous function scope. Then, it explores the virtual stack to find in which function scope the variable count is defined. In this case, it finds out that the variable *count* is declared in the *CreateCounter* function scope, meaning that it would be a closure variable at runtime. However, JavaScript allows assigning a value to an undeclared variable, which is regarded as being declared in the global scope, so Disclosure does not treat those undeclared variables as closure variables, but inserts them into the global scope for further analysis. Since those global variables would be accessible from the *window* object, we can infer that they are not closure variables. Finding the timeout methods is simpler because they are predefined at the global scope (e.g., we can identify *setInterval*, as illustrated in Fig. 1(a) (green box), singling out the character string "setInterval").

When the traverser encounters a closure variable, it inserts a *declaration statement* generating a scope object into the disclosure table at the top of the function scope where the closure variable is declared. Simultaneously, it replaces each closure variable by a property of the scope object in the disclosure table. For example, the instrumented version of the original source code in Listing 1 can be depicted in Listing 4. Since the variable *count* is a closure variable (line 6), the traverser inserts a statement that produces a scope object $disc0 at the top of the function scope (line 2). The expression $disc.create() creates a scope object within the disclosure table and returns the reference. Subsequently, the traverser inserts a statement to record the index of the scope object $disc0 using

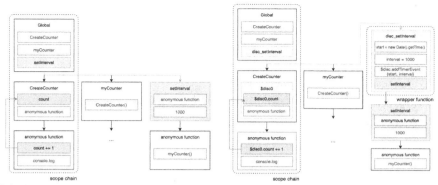

(a) AST-like representation of scope (b) Updated representation to save chains for identifying closure variables. closure variables and event handlers.

Fig. 1. Scope chains with closure variables. (Color figure online)

the global reference counter $ref\_counter$. Then, each closure variable is converted into a property of the new scope object (line 4, 6, 7). The inner function that is to be returned and served as the closure is declared as the property of the scope object for later closure reconstruction (line 9). When a timer method *setInterval* is met, it is replaced by a predefined wrapper function *disc_setInterval* (line 13) to copy the argument and the system time. The AST is updated as in Fig. 1(b).

5.2 Execution Phase

The execution phase uses a runtime library maintaining the disclosure table. It declares wrapper functions for timeout methods within the global scope. The runtime library is allocated to the global scope, accessible with $disc$, which has the *create* function as shown in Listing 5. The function generates a new scope object (line 2), and records the index of the scope object to the property named ref_index (line 3). Also, it has the $scopes$ object that maps each scope object to the corresponding index (line 4). Finally, it pushes the new scope object to the disclosure table and returns it (line 5–6).

If 3.75 s have passed since the code in Listing 4 was loaded and executed, the first scope object in the disclosure table can be depicted as in Listing 6. It maintains the closure variable *count* whose value is 3 (line 3) and the index of itself with the variable name {$disc0: 0$} (line 4). Finally, it records the object literal that will be a closure for later closure reconstruction (line 5–8). The state of the AST is depicted in Fig. 2, where the variable *count* is referred to as a property of the scope object $disc[0]$ in the disclosure table.

Listing 4. The instrumented code generated by Disclosure for Listing 1.

```
1  function CreateCounter() {
2      var $disc0 = $disc.create();
3      $disc0.$scopes.$disc0 = $disc0.$ref_index;
```

```
4       $disc0.count = 0;
5       $anon0 = function () {
6           $disc0.count += 1;
7           console.log($disc0.count);
8       };
9       return $disc0.$ret_func = $anon0;
10  }
11  var myCounter = CreateCounter();
12
13  disc_setInterval(function () {
14      myCounter();
15  }, 1000);
```

Listing 5. How *create* function works.

```
1  create: function () {
2      var obj = new Object();
3      obj.$ref_index = disc_table.length;
4      obj.$scopes = {};
5      disc_table.push(obj);
6      return obj;
7  }
```

Listing 6. An element state of the disclosure table.

```
1  /* $reference_table[0] */
2  {
3      count: 3,
4      $scopes: {$disc0: 0},
5      $ret_func: "function () {
6          $disc0[\"count\"] += 1;
7          console.log($disc0[\"count\"]);
8      }"
9  }
```

5.3 Migration Phase

The runtime library has a *serialize* function, which pushes an event handler to save the DOM objects, the heap objects, and the disclosure table. Users can transfer the snapshot to another device to restore and continue its execution. Since the snapshot code runs similarly to the instrumented code, users can again capture a snapshot during the execution of the snapshot code.

User interactions in a web application are usually conducted via DOM objects such as buttons after the global context is terminated and the call stack becomes empty. Therefore, the serialization event does not have to capture the call stack. It first generates a snapshot file with DOM objects and the instrumented code, then traverses the heap memory to capture the global variables. Subsequently, it serializes the disclosure table in order to append the reconstruction code for the closures and the timers. Listing 7 depicts the generated snapshot code. Closures are restored by an immediately-invoked function to eliminate the possibility of side effect since the execution context of the function should not be referenced by another context (lines 8–15). They are restored by $disc.create function again to generate the scope objects in the order they were created (line 9), then other properties are restored next (line 10–15). Following that, the closure is assigned to the global variable *myCounter* with the index from the disclosure table (line

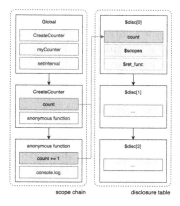

Fig. 2. Scope chain and transferred closure of Listing 4.

17). Lastly, the timers are registered with the wrapper functions (lines 20–22). If the serialization event occurs 3.75 s after the app is loaded, the *setInterval* method must be triggered 0.25 s after the snapshot is loaded and executed, and repeatedly triggered every 1,000 *ms* thereafter. Thus, the serialization method utilizes the *disc_setTimeout* method, which is fired only once to make up 0.25 s.

Listing 7. The snapshot code serialized by Disclosure, 3.75 s after app loading of Listing 4.

```
1  /*   DOM  objects   */
2  ...
3  /*   The  instrumented  code  (Listing  4)  comes  here  */
4  ...
5  /*   Restore  global  variables  */
6  ...
7  /*   Restore  the  disclosure  table   */
8  (function (){
9     var $disc0 = $disc.create();
10     $disc0.$scopes.$disc0 = $disc0.$ref_index;
11     $disc0["count"] = 3;
12     $disc0["$ret_func"] = function () {
13        $disc0["count"] += 1;
14        console.log($disc0["count"]);
15     };
16  })();
17  var myCounter = ($disc.get_ref(0))["$ret_func"];
18
19  /*   Restore  the  wrapped  timer  methods  */
20  disc_setTimeout(disc_setInterval(function() {
21      myCounter();
22  }, 1000), 250);
```

Restoration is simply achieved by transferring the snapshot file to the target device, then executing it on any web browser with the runtime library. For example, consider a scenario with four agents: web server, proxy server, smartphone, and PC. If users want to run a web application migratable later, they can use the proxy server to download the application from the web server. Then, the proxy server instruments the downloaded application and deliver it to users with the runtime library (which can be omitted if users already possess the library). Users run the instrumented application on the smartphone for a while, and at some point, they want to enjoy it on a larger screen. Then, they press the migration button to capture and transfer the snapshot to the proxy server, and then relay to a desktop PC, where they can run it continuously.

As to the DOM tree, Disclosure makes all DOM objects as JavaScript objects, by creating them as a result of executing the instrumented code. So, we can capture the DOM objects as regular JavaScript objects, even for multiple migrations. Even for those DOM objects created dynamically, we can know the execution context where they are created, so if they are included in the closures or web API states, we can add them in the disclosure table with the scope object, allowing their restoration. This works differently from Imagen [3] which uses the JsonML library to save the DOM tree [9]; it is not clearly described how to recover the link between JavaScript variables and the DOM objects referenced by them, after restoring the DOM tree, or how to handle dynamic DOM objects. ThingsMigrate and FlashFreeze do not support DOM migration.

5.4   Security and WeakMap

In JavaScript, closures are mainly used to encapsulate variables. However, the snapshot file can reveal the value of the closure variables as in Listing 3 or Listing 7, affecting security. Fortunately, Disclosure can enhance security by implementing the disclosure table itself as a closure. That is, when we initialize the $disc library, we declare the disclosure table and make the inner function create() add a new element (for a closure variable of the original code) to the table as depicted in Listing 5. Also, we can encrypt the disclosure table by passing an encryption key to the serialize() function, and decrypt it by passing a decryption key to the restore() function. This would make the snapshot file not expose any sensitive data while restoring the original disclosure table wrapped by a closure, enhancing security further.

Currently, there is a memory leakage issue in Disclosure. Since Disclosure should maintain the value and the scope chain of the free variables in the disclosure table, it currently prevents garbage collection from automatically releasing the closures variables even after they are not referenced by any variables. We can solve this problem using a feature named *WeakMap* [10] in the JavaScript specification, which enables garbage collection for the elements of a WeakMap object which are not accessed for a long time (i.e., *weak references*). Unfortunately, WeakMap is not yet supporting the iteration for the elements, so we cannot make the disclosure table as a WeakMap object since we should iterate over the elements of the table to make a snapshot file. Iterable WeakMaps are under development [11], so we leave the solution as a future work item.

6   Evaluation

We evaluate Disclosure using eight Octane benchmarks [12] and four real web applications. The eight benchmarks are *Richards*, *Deltablue*, *Crypto*, *Raytrace*,

Table 1. Instrumentation data for eight Octane benchmarks and four web apps

Benchmarks		Original code (bytes)	Instrumented code (bytes)	Increase (%)	Instrumentation time (ms)	Scope objects	Closure variables	Timeout methods
Octane	Richards	9076	9076	0	85.2	0	0	0
	Deltablue	15478	15715	1.53	110.3	1	2	0
	Crypto	45519	45519	0	236.5	0	0	0
	Raytrace	22248	22248	0	147.1	0	0	0
	Regexp	132929	146215	9.99	464.9	1	312	0
	Splay	6599	6599	0	82.3	0	0	0
	SplayLatency	6599	6599	0	82.3	0	0	0
	NavierStokes	11542	13813	19.68	109.8	2	32	0
Web apps	Maze	7226	7501	3.81	162.3	1	1	4
	Tetris	25038	26317	5.11	121.1	4	2	8
	Emoticolor	16872	17203	1.96	88.2	1	16	9
	Sokoban	59121	59144	0.04	128.3	0	0	2

Regexp, Splay, SplayLatency, and *NaiverStokes.* The web applications are *Tetris, Sokoban, Maze,* and *Emoticolor.* For benchmarks we measure the runtime performance, and for web applications we examine the overhead of multiple migrations in capturing DOM objects and timer methods. Closures are used by three web applications and three benchmarks. We also experimented with those benchmarks with no closures to confirm that Disclosure has no side effect. Timeout methods and DOM objects only exist in the web applications. We conducted the experiments on the Google Chrome browser version 64, running on the Ubuntu 16.04 LTS with an Intel i7-2600 CPU 3.40 GHz and 16 GB RAM.

6.1   Instrumented Code Size

Code instrumentation increased the code size by 0% to 20%, as depicted in Table 1. The result shows that the increase is proportional to the number of scope objects with closures and timeout methods. If there are no closures or timeout methods, code instrumentation leaves the code intact, implying that our work had no side effect in the instrumentation phase. Therefore, the instrumented codes of *Richards, Crypto, Raytrace* and *Splay (SplayLatency)* are identical to the original ones. Conversely, other benchmarks like *Deltablue, RegExp,* and *NavierStokes* have closures, thus code sizes were increased up to 20%. In particular, the code size of *RegExp* was highly increased due to the numerous closure variables. Among the real applications, the code sizes of *Maze* and *Tetris* were increased by 3.81% and 5.11% each because both had closures and timeout methods. *Emoticolor* had a few closures but numerous timeout methods, so the instrumentation increased code size by about 2%. However, the code size of *Sokoban* was hardly increased since it has only a few timeout methods. Meanwhile, the size of the runtime library is only about 50 KB, which contains code that allocates the *$disc* object including the disclosure table and serialization method, and defines wrapping functions for timer methods. The instrumentation time takes about 82.3 to 464.9 ms, proportional to the original code size and the number of closures and timer methods. Since it is tiny enough, instrumenting on a proxy server before loading an application would not affect user experience.

Fig. 3. Performance of the original, instrumented, and snapshot code.

6.2 Execution Performance and Runtime Memory Usage

We used the Octane benchmark suite to evaluate the execution performance of the original, instrumented, and snapshot code. Figure 3 is the result of the benchmark scores with the original as a basis of 100% (higher is better). We measured the benchmark scores 2,000 times and obtained an average and standard deviation, and checked the correctness of the result through its checksum. For web applications we did not measure the performance because they are executed in an event-driven manner via asynchronous events.

The experimental result shows that the average benchmark score of the instrumented codes is 2% lower than the original, and the benchmarks without closures were hardly affected. However, the benchmarks that have closures such as *Deltablue*, *Regexp*, and *NavierStokes* show a performance decrease of 1%, 15%, and 0%, respectively. *Deltablue* and *NavierStokes* show little performance loss, compared to the number of closure variables, because they use closure variables only during initialization, while mostly using the global objects thereafter. On the other hand, *Regexp* instantiates many string objects defined as closure variables and accesses them frequently during execution, showing a higher loss.

We took a snapshot right after the initialization process, and the execution performance of snapshot is usually similar to that of the instrumented code. However, unexpectedly, the snapshot performance of *Raytrace* and *NavierStokes* is slightly higher than that of the instrumented code and the original code. We found that this is when the snapshot includes the execution result of a non-trivial initialization process, so bypassing initialization shows some benefit. Also, the snapshot performance of *RegExp* is higher than that of the instrumented code, but lowers than that of the original code due to many closure variables to recover.

The memory usage of each benchmarks is depicted in Fig. 4. The memory usage of instrumented code is larger than the original one by about 14% due to the newly generated scope objects and increased code with the runtime library. *Regexp* and *NavierStokes*, which have many closure variables, use much more memory than the original. Especially, the memory usage of *Regexp* increased almost two-fold compared to the original. This is due to the lack of garbage collection for the disclosure table, as mentioned in Sect. 5.4.

One thing to note is that the memory usage of the snapshot is always smaller than the instrumented code, and in some cases, even smaller than the originals. This is also due to the elimination of the initialization process.

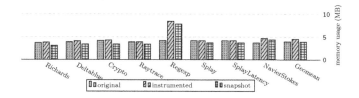

Fig. 4. Memory usage of the original, instrumented, and snapshot code.

6.3   Multiple Migrations

We migrated our web applications multiple times in the middle of execution, and confirmed that we can restore and continue execution. We also checked if Disclosure itself causes any side effect on runtime memory usage or the snapshot size. They are executed by the events, after the initialization process is over with the global context being terminated. The events are issued by the timers or user interactions such as button clicks. For example, *Maze* repeatedly generates random walls to complete a Maze, and *Tetris* periodically generates blocks. So, both increase the memory usage continuously until some point, which is when the maze is completed or when the game is over, and we migrate at this point. On the other hand, *Emoticolor* generates buttons with the RGB color codes randomly during app loading, and *Sokoban* generates a map and waits for the keyboard signal, so we migrate right after app loading without having to wait.

We performed five migrations for each app by iterating (1) take a snapshot, (2) migrate, and (3) restore execution five times. When we measured the snapshot code size during each of five migrations, we found that it is the same for all apps. We also observed that there were no differences on the runtime memory usage during five migrations. So these imply that Disclosure has no side effect.

6.4   Comparison with ThingsMigrate

We measured the runtime performance of the instrumented code generated by Disclosure and ThingsMigrate, using the Octane benchmarks except for *Reg-Exp* because ThingsMigrate did not cover it [6]. Instead, ThingsMigrate included *Factorial* to evaluate computation-intensive algorithms, so we also included it. The experiment was conducted on Node.js v10.15.3 and the performance scores were measured 100 times. Figure 5 shows the result, where Disclosure significantly improves the performance, around 30 times faster than ThingsMigrate. ThingsMigrate's low performance is mainly due to mirroring statements. The performance of *Raytrace, NavierStokes*, and *Factorial* is not lower much since they do not have many mirroring statements. So, it is clear that the mirroring statements is a serious performance bottleneck, which Disclosure can decently alleviate.

Fig. 5. Performance of original, disclosure, and ThingsMigrate code.

7   Summary

In this paper, we proposed Disclosure, a new instrumentation-based migration technique for web applications. We proposed a solution based on a disclosure table, which keeps the instrumented code from being slowed down seriously, while allowing multiple migrations. Additionally, Disclosure can enhance security of the snapshot file and fully migrate the DOM tree, unlike in the previous works.

Acknowledgement. This work was supported by Institute of Information & communications Technology Planning & Evaluation (IITP) grant funded by the Korea government (MSIT) (No. 2021-0-00180, 50%) and (No. 2021-0-00136, 50%).

References

1. Sroczkowski, P.: 100 most popular languages on github in 2019 (2020). https://brainhub.eu/blog/most-popular-languages-on-github
2. Bellucci, F., Ghiani, G., Paternò, F., Santoro C,: Engineering javascript state persistence of web applications migrating across multiple devices. In Proceedings of the 3rd ACM SIGCHI symposium on Engineering interactive computing systems, pages 105–110. ACM, 2011
3. Lo, J.T.K., Wohlstadter, E., Mesbah, A.: Imagen: runtime migration of browser sessions for JavaScript web applications. In: Proceedings of the 22nd international conference on World Wide Web (WWW), pp. 815–826. ACM (2013)
4. Oh, J., Kwon, J., Park, H., Moon, S.-M.: Migration of web applications with seamless execution. In: 2015 ACM SIGPLAN/SIGOPS International Conference on Virtual Execution Environments (VEE). ACM (2015)
5. Kwon, J.-W., Moon, S.-M.: Web application migration with closure reconstruction. In: Proceedings of the 26th International Conference on World Wide Web (WWW), pp. 133–142 (2017)
6. Gascon-Samson, J., Jung, K., Goyal, S., Rezaiean-Asel, A., Pattabiraman, K.: ThingsMigrate: platform-independent migration of stateful JavaScript IoT applications. In: 32nd European Conference on Object-Oriented Programming. Schloss Dagstuhl-Leibniz-Zentrum fuer Informatik (2018)
7. Mikkonen, T., Systä, K., Pautasso, C.: Towards liquid web applications. In: Cimiano, P., Frasincar, F., Houben, G.-J., Schwabe, D. (eds.) ICWE 2015. LNCS, vol. 9114, pp. 134–143. Springer, Cham (2015). https://doi.org/10.1007/978-3-319-19890-3_10

8. Van der Cruysse, J., Hoste, L., Van Raemdonck, W.: FlashFreeze: low-overhead JavaScript instrumentation for function serialization. In: Proceedings of the 4th ACM SIGPLAN International Workshop on Meta-Programming Techniques and Reflection, pp. 31–39 (2019)
9. JsonML. http://www.jsonml.org/
10. MDN web docs: WeakMap. https://developer.mozilla.org/en-US/docs/Web/JavaScript/Reference/Global_Objects/WeakMap
11. Iterable maps. https://github.com/tc39/proposal-weakrefs#iterable-weakmaps
12. Octane Javascript benchmark. http://chromium.github.io/octane

Enriching Scholarly Knowledge
with Context

Muhammad Haris[1]([✉]) [iD], Markus Stocker[2] [iD], and Sören Auer[1,2] [iD]

[1] L3S Research Center, Leibniz University Hannover, 30167 Hannover, Germany
haris@l3s.de
[2] TIB—Leibniz Information Centre for Science and Technology, Hannover, Germany
{markus.stocker,auer}@tib.eu

Abstract. Leveraging a GraphQL-based federated query service that integrates multiple scholarly communication infrastructures (specifically, DataCite, ORCID, ROR, OpenAIRE, Semantic Scholar, Wikidata and Altmetric), we develop a novel web widget based approach for the presentation of scholarly knowledge with rich contextual information. We implement the proposed approach in the Open Research Knowledge Graph (ORKG) and showcase it on three kinds of widgets. First, we devise a widget for the ORKG paper view that presents contextual information about related datasets, software, project information, topics, and metrics. Second, we extend the ORKG contributor profile view with contextual information including authored articles, developed software, linked projects, and research interests. Third, we advance ORKG comparison faceted search by introducing contextual facets (e.g. citations). As a result, the devised approach enables presenting ORKG scholarly knowledge flexibly enriched with contextual information sourced in a federated manner from numerous technologically heterogeneous scholarly communication infrastructures.

Keywords: Information enrichment · Scholarly knowledge · Scholarly communication infrastructures · Federated querying · Knowledge graphs

1 Introduction

Massive (meta)data about digital and physical scholarly artefacts including articles, datasets, software, instruments, and samples are made available through various scholarly communication infrastructures [12,23,24]. Individually, current infrastructures focus on finding a certain kind of artefact. Lacking the ability to present information about related artefacts, they are unable to meet complex user information needs [21]. For instance, if a researcher searches for scholarly articles she may want information about related datasets, software, projects and organizations. Obtaining such diverse information with a single request is not obvious because the information resides with distributed and technologically heterogeneous infrastructures. Separate search on infrastructures is, however, time

© Springer Nature Switzerland AG 2022
T. Di Noia et al. (Eds.): ICWE 2022, LNCS 13362, pp. 148–161, 2022.
https://doi.org/10.1007/978-3-031-09917-5_10

consuming and laborious [22,26]. Therefore, federated search is necessary for efficient and comprehensive content exploration.

For this purpose, we developed a GraphQL-based federated system [5] that integrates multiple scholarly communication infrastructures, namely, the Open Research Knowledge Graph (ORKG)[1] [11], DataCite[2], and GeoNames[3]. It supports executing queries in a federated manner and enables the integrated retrieval of scholarly information. The main purpose of the federated system is to enable cross-walking scholarly knowledge and contextual information as well as filtering at (meta)data granularity. However, the federated system currently has some limitations: 1) The scope of contextual information is limited to three scholarly infrastructures; and 2) the system requires queries to be written in GraphQL, which is untenable in practice.

As the main contribution of the work presented here, we devise a web widget based approach that retrieves rich contextual information for scholarly knowledge from distributed scholarly communication infrastructures and presents scholarly knowledge with rich context in an integrated manner. We demonstrate the integration of these widgets in ORKG to enrich its various views thus enabling rapid, comprehensive exploration of scholarly content. The proposed approach involves the following two main aspects:

1. Extend the GraphQL-based federated system[4] to include the DataCite PID Graph and REST APIs of OpenAIRE[5], Semantic Scholar[6], Wikidata[7] and Altmetric[8] and enable retrieving comprehensive contextual information for ORKG scholarly knowledge in a federated and integrated manner.
2. Building on the extended federated system, develop different web widgets to enrich scholarly knowledge viewed in ORKG with rich contextual information.

We address the following research question: How can we flexibly enrich the presentation of scholarly knowledge in web based user interfaces with comprehensive contextual information published by numerous heterogeneous scholarly communication infrastructures?

2   Related Work

Scholia [19] is a dynamic user interface that operates on Wikidata's SPARQL endpoint and supports users in searching for articles, researcher profiles, organizations and publishers. Similarly, BioCarian [25] is a SPARQL endpoint powered user-friendly interface enabling exploring biological databases. The interface is

---

[1] https://www.orkg.org/orkg/.
[2] https://datacite.org/.
[3] https://www.geonames.org/.
[4] https://www.orkg.org/orkg/graphql-federated.
[5] https://graph.openaire.eu/develop/api.html.
[6] https://www.semanticscholar.org/product/api.
[7] https://www.wikidata.org/w/api.php.
[8] https://api.altmetric.com/.

enriched with facets that enable better query construction, thus making it easier for users to filter data. OSCAR [8] is a platform for searching RDF triples using a SPARQL endpoint while hiding the complexity of SPARQL, thus making the search operations easier for users who are not aware of web technologies. Similarly, Elda[9] was proposed to access data served via a Linked Data API[10]. Elda is a Java implementation of the Linked Data API that allows customization of API requests for accessing RDF datasets.

Following the Scholix [2] framework, ScholeXplorer[11] aggregates metadata harvested from different data sources (in particular, DataCite, Crossref, OpenAIRE) and creates a graph of scholarly entities. As such, the framework supports users in discovering research articles and related datasets.

Kurteva and Ribaupierre [13] present a user interface that allows casual users to find specific types of data in the DBpedia knowledge base. The interface also provides a graphical visualization of retrieved results. Morton et al. [17] present a framework for querying biomedical knowledge graphs, ranking, and conveniently exploring the queried results. Several other systems for research data discovery exist including BioGraph [14], Het.io [10], Wikidata[12], Open Knowledge Maps[13], Unpaywall[14], Zenodo[15], Figshare[16], re3data[17].

FedX [22] was proposed to execute SPARQL queries on virtually integrated heterogeneous data sources. The practicability of the proposed framework was demonstrated by executing some real-world queries on the Linked Open Data Cloud. BioFed [7] is another federated query processing system that supports executing queries on a variety of SPARQL endpoints to retrieve life sciences data. The system integrates 130 SPARQL endpoints and supports retrieving the provenance information along with the data. The efficiency of the system was demonstrated by executing 10 complex and 10 simple queries, and the results were compared with FedX in terms of optimization. Another SPARQL-based federated system was proposed [18], whose main purpose was to retrieve Open Educational Resources (OERs) published on disparate web platforms. Federated systems also support searching for personalized information, such as retrieving information about user profiles from diverse sources [1].

The structured comparison of different scholarly communication infrastructures can be found in Haris et al. [6]. As the amount of data on these infrastructures is increasing rapidly, it is of utmost importance to enrich scholarly artefacts with their contextual information. The infrastructures reviewed here individually provide information about a particular kind of scholarly artefact, but rarely present the artefacts with rich contextual information. For ORKG

---

[9] http://www.epimorphics.com/web/tools/elda.html.
[10] https://code.google.com/p/linkeddata-api.
[11] https://scholexplorer.openaire.eu/.
[12] https://www.wikidata.org/wiki/Wikidata:Main_Page.
[13] https://openknowledgemaps.org/about.
[14] https://unpaywall.org/.
[15] https://zenodo.org/.
[16] https://figshare.com/.
[17] https://www.re3data.org/.

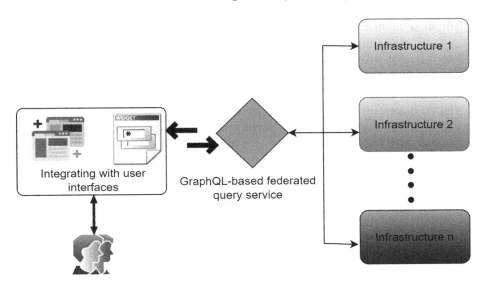

Fig. 1. Conceptual model for virtually integrating numerous infrastructures to facilitate the construction of user interface widgets that enrich displayed information with context.

scholarly knowledge as the core artefact, we propose an approach that queries a range of scholarly communication infrastructures to retrieve and present rich contextual information.

3 Conceptual Model and Its Application

Figure 1 illustrates the conceptual model underpinning our work. In this model, a federated query service abstracts and unifies access to and retrieval of data served by arbitrary scholarly communication infrastructures. Here the purpose of the service is to facilitate the efficient construction of user interface widgets that enrich the presented information with contextual information. The conceptual model comprises the following two key aspects:

1. Flexible, on-demand, virtual and federated integration of scholarly communication infrastructures and straightforward extension of the GraphQL-based federated query service to serve contextual information required by user interface widgets.
2. Uniform access by means of a single query and data exchange interface to comprehensive contextual information required to enrich with context arbitrary information presented in a user interface.

We apply this conceptual model for scholarly communication infrastructures, specifically in developing widgets that enrich scholarly knowledge presented in the ORKG with comprehensive contextual information sourced in a federated manner from numerous scholarly communication infrastructures serving metadata about articles (Crossref and Semantic Scholar), datasets and software (DataCite), projects (OpenAIRE), organizations (ROR), contributors (ORCID). Specifically, we develop widgets to enrich scholarly knowledge presented in ORKG with rich contextual information, in particular for:

1. *ORKG paper view*: Display contextual information about related datasets, projects, topics and Altmetrics for the viewed paper.
2. *ORKG contributor profile*: Display employment history, published artefacts other than those published on ORKG including articles, datasets, software, projects in which the contributor was involved, and research topics of interest to the contributor.
3. *ORKG comparisons*: Extend the faceted search in ORKG comparisons with the possibility to filter the compared studies based on rich contextual metadata, e.g., filter compared studies to include those which are cited more than a given threshold.

4 The Federated Infrastructures

This section provides a brief introduction to the scholarly communication infrastructures currently included for federated data access and presents the federated query service.

DataCite is a DOI registration service for the persistent identification of scholarly artefacts, in particular datasets and software with a common metadata schema. The published content can be discovered in global scholarly infrastructures. DataCite also provides the PID Graph [3,4], which implements the federated retrieval of metadata about and the relationships among numerous scholarly artefacts, specifically articles, datasets, software, and other entities, including organizations, projects and funders at global large-scale served by a host of scholarly communication infrastructures. The PID Graph is accessible via the DataCite GraphQL API[18]. DataCite Commons[19] is a web based user interface for content served by the PID Graph.

OpenAIRE [15,16] enables finding and accessing scholarly articles, datasets, software, researcher profiles and information about related organization. OpenAIRE harvests metadata from multiple data providers, curates and deduplicates the metadata to provide an integrated community service. **Semantic Scholar**[20] is an AI-based web tool for searching scientific literature. Its rich REST API allows DOI-based and keyword-based queries for searching scholarly articles. **Wikidata** is a knowledge graph hosted by the Wikimedia Foundation that enables searching research articles and information about related entities (e.g. organization, people, etc.). Data available in Wikidata is accessible via REST API and SPARQL endpoint. **Altmetric**[21] tracks mentions of scholarly

---

[18] https://api.datacite.org/graphql.
[19] https://commons.datacite.org/.
[20] https://www.semanticscholar.org/.
[21] https://www.altmetric.com/.

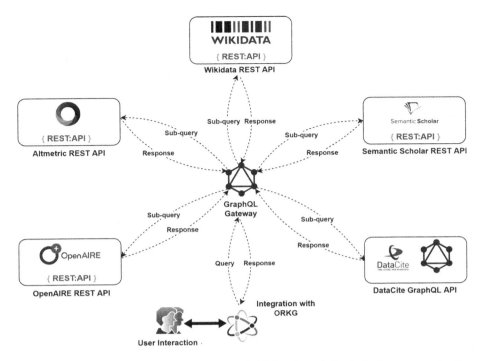

Fig. 2. Overview of the virtually integrated APIs of several scholarly communication infrastructures (DataCite, OpenAIRE, Semantic Scholar, Wikidata, and Altmetric) at a GraphQL gateway, illustrating the execution of sub-queries in the respective infrastructures, and integration of the federated query service in ORKG via web widgets to retrieve and display the contextual information. Finally, the rich scholarly information is presented to the user in an aggregated form.

artefacts across multiple platforms, including social media. It provides a visually informative and aggregated overview of the attention research work receives online. Altmetric provides access to its data via REST API.

We integrate these scholarly communication infrastructures in a federated query service that virtually connects them at a single endpoint and enables the efficient retrieval of scholarly information in an integrated manner. The main purpose of this federation is to abstract from their heterogeneous APIs and enable virtualized, integrated access to the published content through a common unified GraphQL-based interface.

Figure 2 illustrates the architecture of the federated query service. This service does not contain the data itself, but implements an integrated schema for the various sources and enables the execution of queries in a federated manner. We leverage persistent identifiers for linking data served by the various infrastructures.

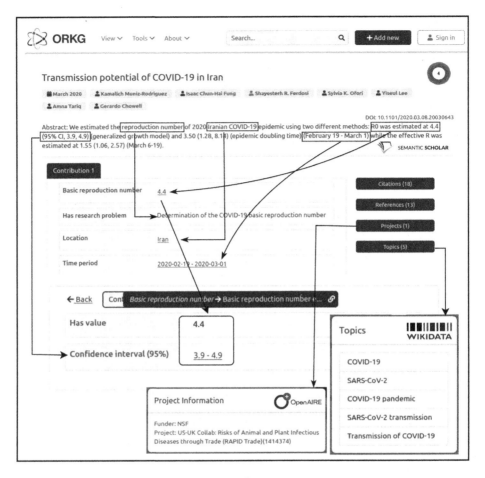

Fig. 3. ORKG paper view: Fetching abstract, citations and references from Semantic Scholar; metrics data from Altmetric; project information from OpenAIRE, and related topics from Wikidata. The view also highlights how information in the article abstract is represented in a structured manner in ORKG.

5   Web Widgets to Enrich Knowledge with Context

This section presents the integration of web widgets in ORKG to enrich its curated scholarly knowledge with contextual information sourced from the various scholarly communication infrastructures (see Sect. 4). We showcase the web widget functionality for the ORKG paper view, contributor profiles, and comparison faceted search.

Listing 1.1. Searching contextual information for the article with DOI 10.1101/2020.03.08.20030643; Semantic Scholar provides basic metadata; OpenAIRE provides the project details; related topics are fetched from Wikidata and metrics are retrieved by querying Altmetric.

```
 1 { # Semantic Scholar query
 2   paper(doi: "10.1101/2020.03.08.20030643") {
 3     doi title abstract
 4     citations { title doi }
 5     references { title doi }
 6
 7     #OpenAIRE query
 8     project {
 9       funder project
10     }
11
12     #Wikidata query
13     topicDetails { topic }
14
15     #Altmetric query
16     metricsInformation {
17       url
18       image
19 } } }
```

5.1 Visualizing ORKG Scholarly Knowledge with Context

In its paper view, the ORKG presents the content of articles, i.e. the essential information contained in articles, in a structured, machine-readable form. We enrich the ORKG paper view by displaying contextual information about related datasets, projects, topics and Altmetric for the displayed article, retrieved via the described federated query service. Figure 3 illustrates the ORKG paper view for an article. Upon viewing an article, the federated query service is automatically invoked through the integrated widget and requests the contextual information with a single query (see Listing 1.1) in a federated manner. The article's meta(data) (abstract, citations, and references) is retrieved from Semantic Scholar; related projects are retrieved from OpenAIRE; Wikidata provides information about related topics; and Altmetric provides the related metrics data. The figure also highlights that the essential content published in an article is available as ORKG research contributions in structured and machine-readable form. Specifically, we highlight how some of the information contained in the article abstract obtained from Semantic Scholar (for instance, basic reproduction number and confidence interval) is represented in structured form in the ORKG. By enriching the ORKG scholarly knowledge with comprehensive contextual information we ensure that users are presented rich information thus avoiding having to explore each infrastructure individually.

5.2 Enriching ORKG Contributor Profiles

Contributor profiles provide an overview of their work, such as published articles, datasets, software, and research topics of interest. We enrich the profile view of

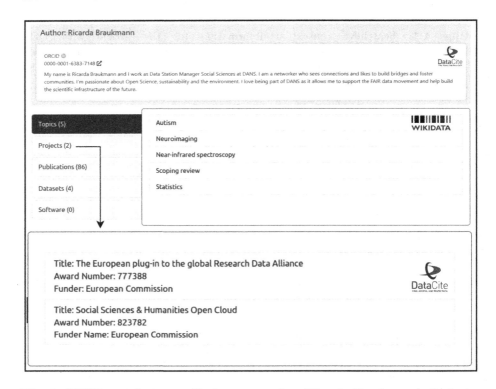

Fig. 4. ORKG contributor profile for a researcher (Ricarda Braukmann) displaying employment history, projects information, research topics and other contextual information.

ORKG contributors by displaying additional contextual information along with the contributor information already available in ORKG, specifically: career history, published artefacts including articles, datasets, software as well as project involvement and research topics of interest.

Figure 4 shows the contextual information retrieved by ORCID of an ORKG contributor. The interface displays the employment history, published research articles, datasets, and software as well as the projects the contributor has been involved. Again, we use the federated query service to retrieve this contextual information (Listing 1.2). The contributor's ORCID is used to retrieve publications, datasets, and software from ORCID via the PID Graph, project information from OpenAIRE, and research interests from Wikidata.

5.3   Advanced Faceted Search for ORKG Comparisons

ORKG comparisons are machine-readable tabular overviews of the essential content published in scholarly articles on a particular research problem [20]. These comparisons can be saved in the ORKG by specifying metadata, title, description, research field, and authors. ORKG also supports DOI-based persistent

Listing 1.2. Federated query for retrieving a person's employment history; published scholarly artefacts; projects in which the contributor was involved in; and topics of interest.

```
1  { person(id: "https://orcid.org/0000-0001-6383-7148") {
2      id name
3      employment {
4        organizationName
5        organizationId
6        startDate endDate
7      }
8      publications {
9        nodes { id type
10         titles { title }
11         fundingReferences { awardTitle awardNumber }
12         creators { givenName familyName id }
13     } }
14     datasets {
15       totalCount
16       nodes { id type
17         titles { title }
18         creators { givenName familyName id }
19     } }
20     softwares {
21       totalCount
22       nodes { id type
23         titles { title }
24         creators { givenName familyName id }
25     } }
26     topics
27 } }
```

identification of comparisons to ensure their discoverability in global scholarly communication infrastructures and enable their citability.

We integrate the federated query service in the ORKG comparison view to advance its faceted search functionality. Figure 5 shows a comparison of earth system models and a faceted search on citations to filter the comparison by articles with citations smaller or larger than given thresholds. We retrieve the number of citations for all articles included in the comparison from Semantic Scholar and refine the comparison according to the specified conditions.

6 Discussion

To answer our research question, we virtually integrated the DataCite PID Graph and the REST APIs of OpenAIRE, Semantic Scholar, Wikidata, and Altmetric to retrieve rich contextual information for ORKG scholarly knowledge in a federated manner, thus enabling the execution of complex distributed queries via a single gateway. The resulting data source abstraction facilitates the efficient development of web widgets that retrieve and display rich contextual information in different ORKG views for papers, contributors and comparisons.

Fig. 5. ORKG comparison of earth system models showing the faceted search enabling refining the compared articles by number of citations.

ORKG already supported faceted search for comparisons at content-level [9]. The work proposed here extends this functionality with facets for contextual information and thus enables more complex (meta)data-driven filtering. For example, it is now possible to not only filter articles reporting a (COVID-19) basic reproductive number $(R0) > X$ but also having a minimum number of citations N. Hence, the faceted search supports filtering for specific research results that also have high impact. The integration of the proposed widgets in ORKG supports users in obtaining an integrated overview of scholarly knowledge and rich contextual information in a single view.

We compared the user interfaces of ORKG, DataCite, OpenAIRE, Semantic Scholar, and Wikidata for information richness. Table 1 shows article contextual information presented by each infrastructure. We observe that DataCite Commons and OpenAIRE present related datasets, software, and projects whereas Semantic Scholar provides information about citations and references. In contrast, ORKG presents comprehensive contextual information from these distributed scholarly infrastructures. Moreover, ORKG enables faceted search at the level of both data (i.e. article contents) and metadata (including contextual information). Lacking structured data, the other scholarly communication infrastructures are unable to provide such functionality.

Table 2 provides an overview of contributor contextual information presented by each infrastructure. DataCite Commons and OpenAIRE present published articles, datasets, and software, while Semantic Scholar only provides information about published articles. Wikidata also provides information about articles, including topics of interest. Compared to these infrastructures, ORKG presents a more comprehensive overview of contributor contextual information.

Currently, our widgets implementation focuses on articles, contributor profiles, and comparison faceted search. As the federated query service can also retrieve contextual information about organizations, we can furthermore enrich the ORKG organization view with linked projects, papers and other contextual

Table 1. Overview of article contextual information presented by each scholarly communication infrastructure.

	DataCite	OpenAIRE	Sem. Scholar	Wikidata	ORKG
Datasets	✓	✓	✗	✗	✓
Software	✓	✓	✗	✗	✓
Topics	✗	✗	✗	✓	✓
Project	✗	✓	✗	✗	✓
Altmetric	✗	✓	✗	✓	✓
Citations	Partial	Partial	Complete	Partial	Complete
References	Partial	Partial	Complete	Partial	Complete
Facets	Metadata	Metadata	Metadata	Metadata	Meta/Data

Table 2. Overview of contributor contextual information presented by each scholarly communication infrastructure.

	DataCite	OpenAIRE	Sem. Scholar	Wikidata	ORKG
Articles	✓	✓	✓	✓	✓
Datasets	✓	✓	✗	✗	✓
Software	✓	✓	✗	✗	✓
Topics	✗	✗	✗	✓	✓
Project	Partial	✓	✗	✗	✓
Reviews	✗	✗	✗	✗	✓

information. This will assist users in exploring what is known about organizations, their activities, outputs, and impact.

As a further direction for future work, we will consider advancing the ORKG search with facets at both data and metadata granularity. In addition to facets for article contents, the federated query service can power facets on contextual information (primarily metadata about contextual entities). This enables users to formulate more complex requests with constraints on data and metadata. A concrete example is a search for the 10 most cited articles addressing the research problem of estimating the COVID-19 basic reproduction number that have reported a confidence interval for the estimated number less than some threshold T, and retrieve their citation count and the reported estimate for basic reproduction number of the virus.

7   Conclusions

We have proposed a web widget based approach for dynamic retrieval and display of comprehensive contextual information for scholarly knowledge. The approach enables rich information presentation and is powered by a GraphQL-based federated query service that virtually integrates and abstracts the technological heterogeneity of numerous scholarly communication infrastructures, in particular DataCite, OpenAIRE, Semantic Scholar, Wikidata, and Altmetric. The approach can be extended to other scholarly communication infrastructures and data sources more generally. To the best of our knowledge, no scholarly knowledge graph shows such diverse information.

As the amount of content published by scholarly communication infrastructures continues to accelerate, rich contextual information can increase research efficiency. The approach proposed and implemented in the work presented here is an important contribution towards this aim that underscores feasibility, broad applicability, and potential impact.

Acknowledgment. This work was co-funded by the European Research Council for the project ScienceGRAPH (Grant agreement ID: 819536) and TIB–Leibniz Information Centre for Science and Technology.

References

1. Arya, D., Ha-Thuc, V., Sinha, S.: Personalized federated search at Linkedin. In: Proceedings of the 24th ACM International on Conference on Information and Knowledge Management, CIKM 2015, pp. 1699–1702. Association for Computing Machinery, New York, NY, USA (2015). https://doi.org/10.1145/2806416.2806615
2. Burton, A., et al.: The scholix framework for interoperability in data-literature information exchange. D-Lib Mag. **23**(1/2) (2017). Corporation for National Research Initiatives https://doi.org/10.1045/january2017-burton
3. Cousijn, H., et al.: Connected research: the potential of the PID graph. Patterns **2**(1), 100180 (2021)
4. Fenner, M., Aryani, A.: Introducing the PID Graph (2019)
5. Haris, M., Farfar, K.E., Stocker, M., Auer, S.: Federating scholarly infrastructures with GraphQL. In: Ke, H.R., Lee, C.S., Sugiyama, K. (eds.) Towards Open and Trustworthy Digital Societies, pp. 308–324. Springer, Cham (2021). https://doi.org/10.1007/978-3-030-91669-5_24
6. Haris, M., Stocker, M.: Comparison of different scholarly communication infrastructures (2022). https://doi.org/10.48366/R165794, https://www.orkg.org/orkg/comparison/R165794
7. Hasnain, A., et al.: BioFed: federated query processing over life sciences linked open data. J. Biomed. Semant. **8**, 13 (2017). https://doi.org/10.1186/s13326-017-0118-0
8. Heibi, I., Peroni, S., Shotton, D.: Enabling text search on SparQL endpoints through Oscar. Data Sci. **2**, 205–227 (2019). https://doi.org/10.3233/DS-190016
9. Heidari, G., Ramadan, A., Stocker, M., Auer, S.: Leveraging a federation of knowledge graphs to improve faceted search in digital libraries (2021). https://doi.org/10.1007/978-3-030-86324-1_18
10. Himmelstein, D.S., et al.: Systematic integration of biomedical knowledge prioritizes drugs for repurposing. Elife **6**, e26726 (2017)
11. Jaradeh, M.Y., et al.: Open research knowledge graph: next generation infrastructure for semantic scholarly knowledge. In: 10th International Conference on Knowledge Capture, K-CAP 2019. ACM (2019). https://doi.org/10.1145/3360901.3364435

12. Khan, S., Liu, X., Shakil, K.A., Alam, M.: A survey on scholarly data: from big data perspective. Inf. Process. Manag. **53**(4), 923–944 (2017)
13. Kurteva, A., De Ribaupierre, H.: Interface to query and visualise definitions from a knowledge base. In: Brambilla, M., Chbeir, R., Frasincar, F., Manolescu, I. (eds.) ICWE 2021. LNCS, vol. 12706, pp. 3–10. Springer, Cham (2021). https://doi.org/10.1007/978-3-030-74296-6_1
14. Liekens, A.M., De Knijf, J., Daelemans, W., Goethals, B., De Rijk, P., Del-Favero, J.: Biograph: unsupervised biomedical knowledge discovery via automated hypothesis generation. Genome Biol. **12**(6), 1–12 (2011)
15. Manghi, P., Bolikowski, L., Manola, N., Schirrwagen, J., Smith, T.: OpenAIREplus: the European scholarly communication data infrastructure. D-Lib Mag. **18** (2012). https://doi.org/10.1045/september2012-manghi
16. Manghi, P., Houssos, N., Mikulicic, M., Jörg, B.: The data model of the OpenAIRE scientific communication e-Infrastructure. In: Dodero, J.M., Palomo-Duarte, M., Karampiperis, P. (eds.) MTSR 2012. CCIS, vol. 343, pp. 168–180. Springer, Heidelberg (2012). https://doi.org/10.1007/978-3-642-35233-1_18
17. Morton, K., et al.: ROBOKOP: an abstraction layer and user interface for knowledge graphs to support question answering. Bioinformatics **35**(24), 5382–5384 (2019). https://doi.org/10.1093/bioinformatics/btz604
18. Mosharraf, M., Taghiyareh, F.: Federated search engine for open educational linked data. Bull. IEEE Tech. Comm. Learn. Technol. **18**(6), 6–9 (2016)
19. Nielsen, F.Å., Mietchen, D., Willighagen, E.: Scholia, Scientometrics and Wikidata. In: Blomqvist, E., Hose, K., Paulheim, H., Ławrynowicz, A., Ciravegna, F., Hartig, O. (eds.) ESWC 2017. LNCS, vol. 10577, pp. 237–259. Springer, Cham (2017). https://doi.org/10.1007/978-3-319-70407-4_36
20. Oelen, A., Jaradeh, M.Y., Stocker, M., Auer, S.: Generate fair literature surveys with scholarly knowledge graphs. In: Proceedings of the ACM/IEEE Joint Conference on Digital Libraries in 2020, JCDL 2020, pp. 97–106. Association for Computing Machinery, New York, NY, USA (2020). https://doi.org/10.1145/3383583.3398520
21. Safder, I., Hassan, S.U., Aljohani, N.R.: AI cognition in searching for relevant knowledge from scholarly big data, using a multi-layer perceptron and recurrent convolutional neural network model. In: Companion Proceedings of the the Web Conference 2018, pp. 251–258 (2018)
22. Schwarte, A., Haase, P., Hose, K., Schenkel, R., Schmidt, M.: FedX: Optimization techniques for federated query processing on linked data. In: International Semantic Web Conference (2011)
23. Stocker, M., et al.: Persistent identification of instruments. Data Sci. J. **19**, 1–12 (2020). https://doi.org/10.5334/dsj-2020-018
24. Xia, F., Wang, W., Bekele, T.M., Liu, H.: Big scholarly data: a survey. IEEE Trans. Big Data **3**(1), 18–35 (2017)
25. Zaki, N., Tennakoon, C.: BioCarian: search engine for exploratory searches in heterogeneous biological databases. BMC Bioinform. **18**, 435 (2017). https://doi.org/10.1186/s12859-017-1840-4
26. Zhou, Y., De, S., Moessner, K.: Implementation of federated query processing on linked data. In: 2013 IEEE 24th Annual International Symposium on Personal, Indoor, and Mobile Radio Communications (PIMRC), pp. 3553–3557 (2013). https://doi.org/10.1109/PIMRC.2013.6666765

FAIRification of Citizen Science Data Through Metadata-Driven Web API Development

Reynaldo Alvarez[1]([✉]) [ID], César González-Mora[2] [ID], José Zubcoff[2] [ID],
Irene Garrigós[2] [ID], Jose-Norberto Mazón[2] [ID], and Hector Raúl González Diez[1] [ID]

[1] University of Informatics Sciences, Havana, Cuba
{rluna,hglez}@uci.cu
[2] Department of Languages and Computing Systems, University of Alicante,
Alicante, Spain
{cgmora,jose.zubcoff,igarrigos,jnmazon}@ua.es

Abstract. Citizen Science (CS) implies a collaborative process to encourage citizens to collect data in CS projects and platforms. Unfortunately, these CS initiatives do not follow metadata nor data-sharing standards, which hampers their discoverability and reusability. To improve this scenario in CS is crucial to consider FAIR (Findability, Accessibility, Interoperability and Reusability) guidelines. Therefore, this paper defines a FAIRification process (i.e. make CS initiatives more FAIR compliant) which maps metadata of CS platforms' catalogues to DCAT and generates Web Application Programming Interfaces (APIs) for improving CS data discoverability and reusability in an integrated approach. An experiment in a CS platform with different CS projects shows the performance and suitability of our FAIRification process. Specifically, the validation of the DCAT metadata generated by our FAIRification process was conducted through a SHACL standard validator, which emphasises how the process could boost CS projects to become more FAIR compliant.

Keywords: Citizen science · FAIR · DCAT metadata · Web APIs · Open data

1 Introduction

Nowadays, there is an emerging trend of democratising science, characterised as Citizen Science (CS) [19]. This term has different definitions depending on the scope, but it is mainly considered as a collaborative process to generate knowledge [15]. Interestingly, as stated in [7], CS is crucial in the production of relevant data to analyse and monitor certain natural, economic or social processes. Therefore, CS initiatives support the growth of research data, with millions of volunteers generating data from observations and sensors [2].

Data generated by CS is generally hosted by CS platforms, i.e., Web based portals which contain data from several CS projects obtained by volunteers. Those platforms, and their available projects, must follow the Ten Principles of

© Springer Nature Switzerland AG 2022
T. Di Noia et al. (Eds.): ICWE 2022, LNCS 13362, pp. 162–176, 2022.
https://doi.org/10.1007/978-3-031-09917-5_11

CS [22], which are an agreement to provide a common framework to evaluate and set up CS initiatives. Among of these principles, the importance of data is highlighted, since it is stated that "Citizen science project data and metadata are made publicly available and where possible, results are published in an open-access format". Consequently, CS data should follow the FAIR guidelines [32], aiming at making data Findable, Accessible, Interoperable and Reusable.

However, most CS platforms such as Scistarter[1] or Zooniverse[2] do not generally follow these FAIR guidelines [33]: regarding findability ("F" from FAIR), it is difficult to discover CS projects that already include CS data; considering accessibility ("A"), existing CS data is difficult to be accessed by data consumers, as they must download it as entire datasets (when available); then, the interoperability ("I") is really limited as CS metadadata is generally published in customised formats; and finally, the reusability ("R") is hampered, as CS platforms do not generally offer solutions such as Web APIs to facilitate the reuse of data. Although many CS platforms consider the Public Participation in Scientific Research (PPSR-Core) metadata standards to model CS projects, datasets and observations [9], FAIR guidelines are not considered.

To enforce FAIR, the W3C Data Catalog Vocabulary (DCAT[3]) is widely used in open data projects [29]. If DCAT is properly implemented, it facilitates the interoperability of dataset metadata and its consumption by using different applications [11]. However, DCAT is not generally adopted by CS platforms [14]. Indeed, a recent study [24] exposes the lack of metadata completeness as a general problem in CS field, describing in detail the behaviour in SciStarter as reference. Moreover, an assessment of current data practices in 36 CS projects highlights the lack of open access to data, metadata and documentation [5].

Consequently, our hypothesis is that the adoption of metadata standards like DCAT allows CS initiatives to become FAIR compliant, but the adoption of DCAT is not sufficient for this purpose. Therefore, in addition to adopting DCAT standard, more efforts are required to really achieve FAIR data by allowing also the data reuse and sharing by structures such as Web APIs [12,28]. In this sense, our paper aims to develop this FAIRfication –process of making data FAIR– by (i) mapping metadata from CS platforms and from DCAT, and (ii) providing access to CS data through Web APIs.

Adhering to the FAIR guidelines in CS initiatives will enhance contextualisation and data quality [24], as high data quality increases the value and reuse of the data. Therefore, FAIR adoption enables CS projects to be more successful and well recognised, which leads to the empowerment of the citizen scientists.

Therefore, the main contributions of this paper are:

– Review of existing CS platforms regarding FAIR guidelines' compliance.
– Development of a FAIRfication process for the enrichment of CS platforms by using DCAT as metadata standard for enabling Findability, Accesibility, Interoperability and Reusability of CS data.

---

[1] https://scistarter.org/.
[2] https://www.zooniverse.org/.
[3] https://www.w3.org/TR/vocab-dcat-3/.

– Integration of Web APIs as data services for CS platforms.
– Evaluation of our proposed approach for FAIRfication in a CS platform.

This article is structured as follows. In Sect. 2, the related work is described in detail. Then, in Sect. 3, a running example is presented in order to illustrate the process. After that, the full FAIRfication process definition is presented in Sect. 4. An evaluation of the approach is explained in Sect. 5, and finally, conclusions and future work are presented in Sect. 6.

2 Related Work

In this section, the most important related work is briefly described, highlighting existing CS platforms and solutions that support accessing CS data and metadata.

Table 1. Main CS platforms

Platform	Region	Projects	Metadata management	API for data
European Citizen Science Portal [30]	Europa	206	PPSR-Core	No
citizenscience.gov Portal	EEUU	493	PPSR-Core	No
SciStarter global citizen science hub [16]	Global	1591	PPSR-Core	No
Zooniverse [25]	Global	104	Own	No
CitSci [31]	Global	1040	PPSR-Core	Yes

CS platforms are recognised for serving as a discover point for CS projects. There are 5 types of CS platforms according to Liu et al. [18]: commercial platforms for CS initiatives, CS platforms for specific projects, CS platforms for specific scientific topics, national CS platforms and EU CS platforms. The most representative sample of CS projects are those non-commercial platforms with national and global scope, such as Scistarter. Table 1 summarises those target platform, and as can be seen, CS platforms generally adopt the PPSR-Core metadata model as practice in the CS field, although it is an ongoing work by the Data and Metadata Working Group[4] of The Citizen Science Association (CSA). Moreover, CS platforms hardly ever include an API, and it is even less frequent that a CS platform provides an API with query-level access to data, that is, a fine-grain API that allows to access not only to metadata, but also the dataset itself. Although there is a consensus about the adoption of PPSR-Core, in practice the platforms use different terms, structures, so that is not easy to harvest data from those different catalogues.

---

[4] https://citizenscience.org/get-involved/working-groups/data-and-metadata-working-group/.

In order to improve data sharing and adopt FAIR guidelines there are different related works: METAFair [28] consists of a metadata profile based on DCAT 2, a potential source schema due to the range of properties for describing different components of datasets, data services and their related resources. This metadata application profile is implemented for GenBank Metadata Analytics, not for general use or in CS as standard. Moreover, they do not approach the definition of data services in DCAT 2 as enabler of FAIR, particularly in the reuse feature. Another work includes FAIRification of the involved datasets in a research workflow [6], as well as applying semantic technologies to represent and store data about the detailed versions of the general protocol, of the concrete workflow instructions, and of their execution traces. They aim to establish a common framework between teams and experts. This approach shows good practices regarding DCAT for data sharing, but it is only developed in a closed environment and they do not address CS platforms and projects.

Also, when datasets are discoverable, the interoperability relies on the exposure of data through standard Application Programming Interfaces (APIs), improving the level of data sharing. Reviews of CS status identify as key aspect API developments to increase the capacity of the data generators apps and to help in the phase of analysis and visualization [10,17,23,27]. The previous work from the authors of this paper define an APIfication model-driven process for the automatic generation of a Web API from tabular data [13]. This process transforms a tabular dataset file to an standard Web API, allowing the reuse of dataset fields at query level. This approach is a first step in order to achieve the FAIRfication of data, but more efforts are required for improving metadata and APIs in the field of CS.

As pointed out, there is still a gap in terms of becoming FAIR, as there is a diversity of metadata types exposed in CS platforms, limiting the discoverability and reusability of CS projects out of their scope. Related research proposes different approaches, ones for specific domain solutions, others as IT solutions or models enablers for FAIR guidelines. Regarding generic solutions, they aim to create terms, processes or workflows to adopt FAIR capacities. The improvement of data repositories as FAIR is approached by different works, offering good practices, workflows and tools that try to become FAIR compliant (serving as proved good practices in their scenarios). Regarding standard adoption, different related research aim to use DCAT to increase the metadata discoverability. DCAT has created the path to do it through data services specifications, but they are not used in the main schemes reviewed, as far as the authors are concerned. Moreover, DCAT is yet not commonly used in CS projects and platforms. Therefore, these are the main reasons to contribute with our work to empower the use DCAT, APIs and data services as metadata, particularly in the field of CS.

3   Running Example

In order to illustrate the process, a sample project from SciStarter[5] is selected. SciStarter is one of the most recognised CS platform that currently includes more than 1500 CS projects [3]. Specifically, the project selected is "Street Story: Give Your Input on Safe Streets"[6], which offers public access to data about transportation collisions and other travel information since 2018, collected by non-scientist members [21]

Table 2. Fragment of "Street Story" dataset

Type	Crash/Near-miss	Involved	Was anyone injured?	Report date
incident	bike	driver	minor	2018/10/01
incident	bike	driver	none	2018/10/01
nearMiss	walk	driver	none	2020/08/02
nearMiss	ride	driver	none	2020/08/02
nearMiss	walk	ped	none	2021/10/17
incident	wheelchair	driver	sev	2021/10/25
nearMiss	walk	driver	none	2021/10/30
nearMiss	bike	ped	none	2021/10/30

The data generated in the Street Story project is public, and the dataset is accessible in tabular format, particularly in CSV, a non-proprietary format commonly used to publish and share data [12]. It contains 28 columns with different data types and more than 3500 records collected by CS volunteers. A fragment of those records is shown in Table 2. It includes information about the type of report (incident or near miss), the vehicle or activity involved in the incident (such as bike, walk or ride), who was involved (driver or pedestrian), the injured provoked (sever, minor or none) and the reporting date, among other fields.

As an example situation, a data engineer wants to perform an analysis of transportation incidents. First, the data engineer performs an exploration of the available data about the issue, using for example the search keywords "street story" or "street incidents" in the European Data Portal[7], a commonly used portal for open data. The search results obtained consists of 2893 datasets accessible in CSV format. The metadata catalogue of this open data portal is based on DCAT, including an API to harvest available metadata. However, when searching for this data in CS platforms such as SciStarter, or CS projects related to the same topic, it is hardly impossible to find, access and reuse CS data. In

---

[5] https://scistarter.org/.

[6] https://scistarter.org/street-story-give-your-input-on-safe-streets.

[7] https://data.europa.eu/.

order to integrate and analyse data from CS projects, specific procedures must be developed to harvest each platform metadata catalogue. This is the barrier about discovery approached in this work. Although DCAT adoption increase discovery, to become more FAIR compliant it is necessary to address reusability. Indeed, when the data engineer searches certain information in the data portals and CS platforms, the results indicate that none of the datasets are accessible via API services. Then, it requires an effort to develop those APIs. For this reason, approaching API generation and the annotation of data services as metadata is a higher desirable level in a FAIRification process.

As the impact of CS data in scientific and other communities has been proven, the launch in more spaces could gain attention from government or policies agencies. CS projects should be as much discoverable as possible. In this case, SciStarter and their projects should be aware of their potential and increase their discoverability, facilitating the access to their data sources and providing structures to obtain their metadata. With this running example we are approaching FAIR guidelines through an integrated process that enhances the growing and acknowledgement of CS projects out of this scope.

Therefore, this running example exposes the approach to become more FAIR, from the point of view of the data consumers and publishers. In fact, a recent study of 1020 projects from SciStarter shows an analysis of metadata completeness [24], exposing the number of projects that do no fully offer metadata. They also highlight that it is necessary for CS projects to include suitable data documentation to be able to produce scientific data [24]. Thus, CS platforms could be more integrated, sharing the same structure and metadata formats with other data repositories, supporting the harvesting of DCAT metadata, and allowing data consumers or developers to create value from CS data by facilitating the access to data through query-level Web APIs.

4   FAIRification of CS Platforms

Data publishers aim to become FAIR compliant by improving the discoverability and interoperability of CS data to enhance the engagement of new members and the recognition in open and formal sciences communities. In this sense, an important requisites for FAIRification are the adoption of established metadata standards and the inclusion of structures to access data. Therefore, standards as DCAT enable the capacity to link data services, increasing the capacity of generating value and applications; and providing Web APIs facilitate the easy access by consumers to the published data. Indeed, this integrated approach supports the use of *dcat:Dataservice*, a class included in the last DCAT version to easily provide access to data through the generated Web APIs [1].

In order to become FAIR compliant in the scope of CS initiatives, this research addresses the accomplishment of most relevant guidelines. The main goal is accordingly to contribute to the FAIRification of CS data, by a process that provides more accessible and standardised technologies and applications for improving data sharing in CS.

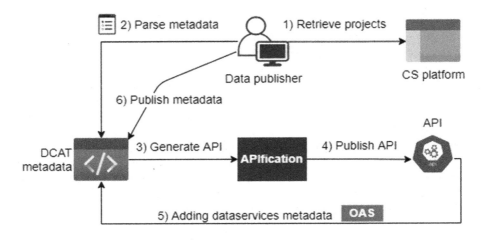

Fig. 1. General process for improving FAIR

This process for becoming FAIR in CS platforms is approached through metadata parsing and API generation. The whole process is represented by the schema in Fig. 1, and the corresponding programming code developed in Python is available in a Github repository[8].

The process begins when a data publisher or a platform manager retrieves the metadata of a CS platform (step 1 in Fig. 1). Then, the second step consists of parsing the relevant metadata fields and mapping them to the DCAT vocabulary, thus generating a DCAT metadata specification.

Once the DCAT specification is generated, the dataset distribution URL is accessible through the project metadata specification. This step aims to increase accessibility and interoperability of CS data by adopting standards and exposing data resources. Regarding reuse, the process continues with the step 3 from Fig. 1, which consists of an APIfication process to offer easy access to data at query level. This Web API generated is a desirable capacity to easily explore, reuse and access available datasets [23]. This part of the process comes from our previous work [13], which is now improved and integrated to work on CS platforms. Then, steps 4 and 5 are closely related. When the Web API is published, the specification of data services is thus added to the DCAT metadata. Finally, the process ends with the publication of the complete metadata defined as step 6.

A complete explanation of these steps to become FAIR compliant in the scope of CS, including relevant details and the inputs and outputs of each step, is described in the following subsections.

---

[8] https://github.com/ralvarezluna/csdatalab-apigen.

4.1   Retrieving the Projects

The SciStarter API[9] enables searching for CS projects within the platform. The metadata associated to the published projects is returned in a JSON file through the corresponding API call (e.g. Scistarter projects API finder). It includes a collection of objects corresponding to the existing projects that fulfil a matching condition. In order to retrieve those projects, our implementation will support JSON local files as input or API URLs.

Before the parser step, the general metadata of the catalogue must be available in a properties file. The mandatory fields for a DCAT catalogue are: identifier, language and homepage [1]. Also, for adding semantics, the catalogue "dcat:themeTaxonomy" attribute is defined by default as **citizen science**[10] from a public knowledge base, which allows to be denoted by a concept and published as Linked Data. The outputs of this step are the JSON file with the metadata retrieved and the initial configuration of the metadata catalogue.

4.2   Parsing the Metadata

The metadata retrieved in JSON format contains the attributes for projects defined in PPSR-Core [4]. PPSR-Core has four metadata components: (i) Core Attributes (Core Metadata Model - CMM), (ii) Projects (Project Metadata Model - PMM), (iii) Datasets (Dataset Metadata Model - DMM) and (iv) Observations (Observation Metadata Model - OMM).

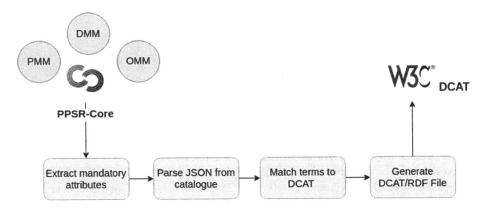

Fig. 2. Parsing metadata

The Fig. 2 shows the procedure to parse the metadata from the JSON to a DCAT compatible file. An analysis of the attributes from PPSR Core was conducted for extracting mandatory attributes to discover projects out of the

---

[9] https://scistarter.org/api.
[10] https://www.wikidata.org/wiki/Q1093434.

scope of CS. The second procedure defines how to parse the retrieved data catalogue in JSON format, how to read the objects and set up metadata for the
catalogue in general. During the procedure for matching terms to DCAT each
project entity will be mapped as a DCAT Resource, specifically as instances of
the Dataset class. This class supports 23 of 36 attributes defined in PPSR-Core,
which are enough to discovery purposes. In fact, 8 of the not supported attributes
from PPSR-Core are optional, and the others 5 mandatory attributes not parsed
are very specific domain attributes from projects, not relevant for discovering
purposes.

Table 3. Abstract of the metadata attributes

PPSR	JSON	DCAT
projectId	guid	identifier
projectDateCreated	created	release date
projectLastUpdatedDate	Date Time	update/modification date
projectName	name	title
projectDescription	text	description
hasTag	search terms	keyword
keyword	keyword	keyword
projectStartDate	begin	release date
projectScienceType	fields_of_science	theme
projectUrl	signup_url	landing_page
projectResponsiblePartyName	presenter	publisher
contactPoint	url	contactpoint
projectGeographicCoverage	geographic_scope	spatial_coverage
Not defined	sust_dev_goals	theme/category

A subset of the attributes parsed are showed in Table 3, including information
about the original attribute defined in PPSR-Core, how it is described in the
JSON, and finally, how will be expressed in DCAT.

Additionally, the metadata retrieved of the projects includes references
to Sustainable Development Goals (SDG) related to the project activities.
Those references are mapped with the definition of the corresponding terms
of the United Nations SDG Taxonomy[11]. During the mapping process, those
terms enriched with semantics are included as themes (referring to attribute
dcat:theme). After the matching of terms, the attributes of the entities from
the JSON are annotated and converted in valid vocabulary terms of the DCAT
standard. Finally, for the generation of the DCAT Resource Description Framework (RDF) catalogue the auxiliary library **datacatalogtordf**[12] is used, as

---

[11] http://metadata.un.org/sdg.
[12] https://github.com/Informasjonsforvaltning/datacatalogtordf.

it supports the DCAT specification classes and graph conversion to RDF. The resulting metadata is exported as RDF format ready to be shared as linked data.

4.3   Generating the API

In this step, the process continues generating the API, which is based in our previous work [13], a complete automatic process to generate an API from CSV datasets. In order to improve and extend the functionality of this API generator, in this work a feature to convert JSON files to CSV is included in order to consider more common formats of CS projects. Therefore, the APIfication process will be able to generate the code and documentation of an API for almost any dataset with resources (in both CSV and JSON formats). Then, data consumers only have to use these endpoints in their applications to allow users to collect and visualise data.

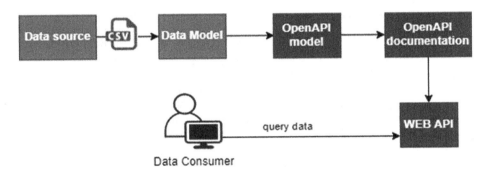

Fig. 3. APIfication process

Figure 3 shows the steps of this automatic generation process from the data source to the Web API. A data model is constructed from the data source, following this data model an OpenAPI model is generated. The OpenAPI documentation is built from the model following OpenAPI 3.0, the most common open standard regarding documentation and specification of APIs [12]. The output is a complete and running Web API accessible at localhost for development and test, which can be easily published online.

4.4   Publishing the Web API

This step depends on the infrastructure to publish data services, because OD portals do not generally cover this part itself as the growing number of requests could not be supported. Due to the existing freedom to manage their infrastructure for projects or catalogues, the API generated should be published by the owners. Therefore, the output of this step consists of a Web API with the Open

API Specification (OAS) for further addition of metadata for this endpoint as DCAT Dataservice Resource[13].

4.5 Updating Data Services Metadata

Once the API generation phase is completed and the Web API is published, the specification of data services as resources must be performed to extend the DCAT specification. Using a DCAT class for this type of resource, an instance of the class *dcat:DataService* will be created with reference to services endpoints (e.g. a URL of the published service). A feature to read the OpenAPI file or URL is developed within the process. The library Oastodcat[14] helps us with the creation of the Dataservice class from the OpenAPI specification file of the published Web API. Then, the object constructed will be able to be appended as data service in the CS metadata catalogue.

4.6 Publishing Metadata

To increase the discoverability of the projects, the DCAT catalogue obtained must be published in the CS platform. This step must be done by platforms' owners, as the open source code of the implemented process could be extended or integrated in automatic pipelines to keep this metadata catalogue updated. The way for publishing the graph database of the catalogue based in DCAT depends on the owner, but in any case, publishing it as a raw file enables the feature to be harvested or downloaded by third parties, achieving the desired discoverability. Open data portals, search engines and developers could access then the metadata and generate value, integrating data from similar projects.

The goal of FAIRification was approached by performing a parsing procedure to generate a DCAT compliant metadata catalogue, improving the interoperability of the CS metadata catalogue out of this environment. At project level the API generation enable the Reuse and integration features. Being Findable and Accessible depends of the implementation of the process for the CS platforms.

5 Evaluation

In order to perform an evaluation of our approach, we analysed the FAIRfication process for CS platforms. The evaluation aims to prove the performance of the process with different entries, and also, the compliance of the DCAT standard for metadata in RDF format. For this validation of DCAT the Shapes Constraint Language (SHACL)[15] is used, as W3C recommendation language for validating RDF data. Specifically, SHACL documents consists of constraints collections that enforce particular shapes on an RDF graph. SHACL is used in this research

---

[13] https://www.w3.org/TR/vocab-dcat-2/#Class:Data_Service.
[14] https://pypi.org/project/oastodcat/.
[15] https://www.w3.org/TR/shacl/.

for validating purposes as it is currently used for validating RDF files in recent related works [8, 20, 26].

The experiment was carried out in an Ubuntu 20.04 computer with an Intel i7 processor and 8 GB of RAM memory. The performance of the approach has been evaluated by analysing the parser time for different projects. The project metadata is the unit of information of the experiment, including 141 attributes for describing the project, related to: activities, resources, contacts, data, locations, topics and identification. Then, the entries are formed by different number of project metadata, which is remotely accessed from SciStarter. In this evaluation, the time measured does not include the time for the remote calls in order to avoid network issues.

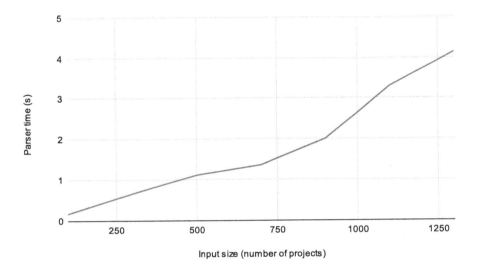

Fig. 4. Performance of the parser for diverse inputs

The results of the measurements with different size of projects are showed in Fig. 4. Beginning with 100 projects until 1300 in the X axis and from 0 to 5 s in the axis Y. The graphics shows a linear behaviour in the generation of DCAT metadata depending on the number of projects. The process with more than 300 projects takes less than 1 s and with 1300 projects takes around 5 s.

The generated DCAT file within the process is validated with a SHACL online validator[16], using the generic profile of DCAT. The validation report returns a positive conform result for the RDF file, generated using different random subsets of projects due to performance issues of the validator. The file conformity implies that the implemented parser generates DCAT complaints outputs ready to share as data catalogues.

---

[16] https://data.vlaanderen.be/shacl-validator/.

Moreover, the APIfication process was proved as part of the process, in a integration approach, because full validation of this step was exposed in our previous work [12]. The experiment exposed in this work concludes that the automatic generation process successfully achieves the objective of functionally and efficiently performing the APIfication process in an average time of 16 s using sample datasets from different sources and sizes.

Therefore, the evaluation results show that our FAIRfication process is functional and compliant with the DCAT standard, thus becoming FAIR through the adoption of established metadata standards and facilitating interoperability and access to the data. Indeed, according to the results of the experiment, a complete DCAT metadata catalogue from SciStarter is generated and made accessible in few seconds, providing also API access to the available data enforcing reuse capabilities.

6   Conclusions

The analysis of data repositories of CS projects shows the lack of metadata and sharing standards adoption, hampering the fulfilment of FAIR guidelines. Indeed, our running example shows, in a real scenario, the lack of discoverability regarding CS data, which is caused by the implementation of customised metadata solutions by CS initiatives. To overcome this pitfall, in this paper, we propose a FAIRification process to (i) enrich CS platforms by means of mapping elements from the PPSR-Core metadata (profusely used in CS projects) to their counterparts from the W3C standard DCAT metadata, as well as (ii) generating Web APIs to facilitate the access to the corresponding CS data. We argue in the paper that both mechanisms separately are not sufficient: just adopting DCAT is not enough, nor is it sufficient to provide Web API services for querying data. Consequently both mechanisms (metadata mapping and Web API generation) must be used together to make CS portals more FAIR-compliant.

In order to show the benefits of our approach, we have conducted an experiment to evaluate our FAIRfication process through performance and correctness tests. Results show that it performs efficiently and produces correct metadata in DCAT format, including suitable query-level Web APIs. Therefore, this proposal serves as driver to follow the path of the FAIRfication improvement in the field of CS.

As future work, the process will address the issue of missing metadata in most CS platforms and approaching FAIRfication from the early project set up phase, contributing from its inception in the compliance of FAIR guidelines. Also, the parser will be extended to support other CS platforms and further evaluation with user studies will be carried out.

Acknowledgement. This research work has been partially funded by the Proyecto Habana 2021 and by project GVA-COVID19/2021/103 funded by Conselleria de Innovación, Universidades, Ciencia y Sociedad Digital de la Generalitat Valenciana.

References

1. Albertoni, R., et al.: Data catalog vocabulary (DCAT)-version 2. World Wide Web Consortium (2020)
2. Baker, B.: Frontiers of Citizen Science: explosive growth in low-cost technologies engage the public in research. Bioscience **66**(11), 921–927 (2016)
3. Ben Zaken, D., Gal, K., Shani, G., Segal, A., Cavalier, D.: Intelligent recommendations for citizen science. Proc. AAAI Conf. Artif. Intell. **35**(17), 14693–14701 (2021)
4. Bowser, A.: Standardizing citizen science? Biodivers. Inf. Sci. Stand. **1**, e21123 (2017)
5. Bowser, A., et al.: Still in need of norms: the state of the data in citizen science. Citizen Sci. Theory Pract. **5**(1) (2020)
6. Celebi, R., et al.: Towards fair protocols and workflows: the OpenPredict use case. Peer J. Comput. Sci. **6**, e281 (2020)
7. Cooper, C.B., Rasmussen, L.M., Jones, E.D.: Perspective: the power (dynamics) of open data in citizen science. Front. Climate **3**, 57 (2021)
8. Corman, J., Reutter, J.L., Savković, O.: Semantics and validation of recursive SHACL. In: Vrandečić, D., et al. (eds.) ISWC 2018. LNCS, vol. 11136, pp. 318–336. Springer, Cham (2018). https://doi.org/10.1007/978-3-030-00671-6_19
9. Data, U.: Metadata WG. 2019. PPSR core data & metadata standards repository. Github (2019)
10. Ed-douibi, H., Cánovas Izquierdo, J.L., Daniel, G., Cabot, J.: A model-based Chatbot generation approach to converse with open data sources. In: Brambilla, M., Chbeir, R., Frasincar, F., Manolescu, I. (eds.) ICWE 2021. LNCS, vol. 12706, pp. 440–455. Springer, Cham (2021). https://doi.org/10.1007/978-3-030-74296-6_33
11. Färber, M., Lamprecht, D.: The data set knowledge graph: creating a linked open data source for data sets. Quant. Sci. Stud. **2**(4), 1–30 (2021)
12. González-Mora, C., Garrigós, I., Zubcoff, J., Mazón, J.N.: Model-based generation of web application programming interfaces to access open data. J. Web Eng. **19**, 194–217 (2020)
13. González-Mora, C., Garrigós, I., Zubcoff, J.: An APIfication approach to facilitate the access and reuse of open data. In: Bielikova, M., Mikkonen, T., Pautasso, C. (eds.) ICWE 2020. LNCS, vol. 12128, pp. 512–518. Springer, Cham (2020). https://doi.org/10.1007/978-3-030-50578-3_36
14. Hahnel, M., Valen, D.: How to (Easily) extend the FAIRness of existing repositories. Data Intell. **2**(1–2), 192–198 (2020)
15. Haklay, M.M., Dörler, D., Heigl, F., Manzoni, M., Hecker, S., Vohland, K.: What is citizen science? The challenges of definition. In: Vohland, K., et al. (eds.) The Science of Citizen Science, pp. 13–33. Springer, Cham (2021). https://doi.org/10.1007/978-3-030-58278-4_2
16. Hoffman, C., Cooper, C.B., Kennedy, E.B., Farooque, M., Cavalier, D.: SciStarter 2.0: a digital platform to foster and study sustained engagement in citizen science. In: Analyzing the Role of Citizen Science in Modern Research, pp. 50–61 (2017)
17. Lemmens, R., Antoniou, V., Hummer, P., Potsiou, C.: Citizen science in the digital world of apps. In: Vohland, K., et al. (eds.) The Science of Citizen Science, pp. 461–474. Springer, Cham (2021). https://doi.org/10.1007/978-3-030-58278-4_23
18. Liu, H.-Y., Dörler, D., Heigl, F., Grossberndt, S.: Citizen science platforms. In: Vohland, K., et al. (eds.) The Science of Citizen Science, pp. 439–459. Springer, Cham (2021). https://doi.org/10.1007/978-3-030-58278-4_22

19. Mueller, M.P., Tippins, D., Bryan, L.A.: The future of citizen science. Democracy Educ. **20**(1), 2 (2011)

20. Pareti, P., Konstantinidis, G., Mogavero, F., Norman, T.J.: SHACL satisfiability and containment. In: Pan, J.Z., et al. (eds.) ISWC 2020. LNCS, vol. 12506, pp. 474–493. Springer, Cham (2020). https://doi.org/10.1007/978-3-030-62419-4_27

21. Rebentisch, H., Wasfi, R., Piatkowski, D.P., Manaugh, K.: Safe streets for all? Analyzing infrastructural response to pedestrian and cyclist crashes in New York City, 2009–2018. Transp. Res. Rec. **2673**(2), 672–685 (2019)

22. Robinson, L.D., Cawthray, J.L., West, S.E., Bonn, A., Ansine, J.: Ten principles of citizen science. In: Citizen Science: Innovation in Open Science, Society and Policy, pp. 27–40 (2018)

23. de Sherbinin, A., et al.: The critical importance of citizen science data. Front. Climate **3**, 20 (2021)

24. Shwe, K.M.: Study on the data management of citizen science: from the data life cycle perspective. Data Inf. Manage. **4**(4), 279–296 (2020)

25. Simpson, R., Page, K.R., De Roure, D.: Zooniverse: observing the world's largest citizen science platform. In: Proceedings of the 23rd International Conference on World Wide Web, pp. 1049–1054 (2014)

26. Stani, E.: Metadata quality: generating SHACL rules from UML class diagrams. In: Proceedings of the 2018 International Conference on Dublin Core and Metadata Applications, pp. 63–64 (2018)

27. Sturm, U., et al.: Defining principles for mobile apps and platforms development in citizen science (2018)

28. Tompkins, V.T., Honick, B.J., Polley, K.L., Qin, J.: MetaFair: a metadata application profile for managing research data. Proc. Assoc. Inf. Sci. Technol. **58**(1), 337–345 (2021)

29. Vander Sande, M., Verborgh, R., Dimou, A., Colpaert, P., Mannens, E.: Hypermedia-based discovery for source selection using low-cost linked data interfaces. In: Information Retrieval and Management: Concepts, Methodologies, Tools, and Applications, pp. 502–537 (2018)

30. Wagenknecht, K., et al.: EU-citizen. Science: a platform for mainstreaming citizen science and open science in Europe. Data Intell. **3**(1), 136–149 (2021)

31. Wang, Y., Kaplan, N., Newman, G., Scarpino, R.: CitSci.org: a new model for managing, documenting, and sharing citizen science data. PLoS Biol. **13**(10), e1002280 (2015)

32. Wilkinson, M.D., et al.: The fair guiding principles for scientific data management and stewardship. Sci. Data **3**(1), 1–9 (2016)

33. Williams, J., et al.: Maximising the impact and reuse of citizen science data (2018)

The Case for Cross-Entity Delta Encoding in Web Compression

Benjamin Wollmer[1,3](✉) , Wolfram Wingerath[2,3] , Sophie Ferrlein[3] ,
Fabian Panse[1] , Felix Gessert[3] , and Norbert Ritter[1]

[1] University of Hamburg, Hamburg, Germany
dbis-research@uni-hamburg.de
[2] University of Oldenburg, Oldenburg, Germany
data-science@uni-oldenburg.de
[3] Baqend, Hamburg, Germany
research@baqend.com

Abstract. Delta encoding and shared dictionary compression (SDC) for accelerating Web content have been studied extensively in research over the last two decades, but have only found limited adoption in the industry so far: Compression approaches that use a custom-tailored dictionary per website have all failed in practice due to lacking browser support and high overall complexity. General-purpose SDC approaches such as Brotli reduce complexity by shipping the same dictionary for all use cases, while most delta encoding approaches just consider similarities between versions of the same entity (but not between different entities). In this study, we investigate how much of the potential benefits of SDC and delta encoding are left on the table by these two simplifications. As our first contribution, we describe the idea of cross-entity delta encoding that uses cached assets from the immediate browser history for content encoding instead of a precompiled shared dictionary: This avoids the need to create a custom dictionary, but enables highly customized and efficient compression. Second, we present an experimental evaluation of compression efficiency to hold cross-entity delta encoding against state-of-the-art Web compression algorithms. We consciously compare algorithms some of which are not yet available in browsers to understand their potential value before investing resources to build them. Our results indicate that cross-entity delta encoding is over 50% more efficient for text-based resources than compression industry standards. We hope our findings motivate further research and development on this topic.

Keywords: Delta encoding · Caching · Dictionary compression

1 Introduction

Every Web browser utilizes a local cache to reduce the payload of a website. But since cache entries are limited in their lifetime, they become useless in current schemes once they are stale. However, stale resources can still contain information that is useful for encoding related files efficiently. Delta encoding is

© Springer Nature Switzerland AG 2022
T. Di Noia et al. (Eds.): ICWE 2022, LNCS 13362, pp. 177–185, 2022.
https://doi.org/10.1007/978-3-031-09917-5_12

an example of such an approach, which is generally used to update one entity to its newest version by sending a diff rather than the whole asset. Most proposals revolving around this mechanism focus on the similarities between versions of the same entity (single-entity data encoding).

In this work, we argue that modern websites comprise many pages that are very similar among one another (e.g. different product pages) and therefore lend themselves to *cross-entity delta encoding* as well [10]. We use Compaz [9] to evaluate the concept of cross-entity delta encoding and provide evidence on its potential benefits for payload savings to motivate further research on the topic. Sections 2 and 3 discuss and distinguish cross-entity delta encoding from existing work. In Sect. 4, we present quantitative results for the potential of cross-entity delta encoding to improve compression efficiency based on real-world high traffic website traces. We discuss open challenges and conclude in Sect. 5.

2   Related Work

Delta Encoding. Mogul et al. proposed to use delta encoding in HTTP to update stale content [6], which is not implemented by any major browser. How well this scales depends on how much of the content changes between the two versions. They evaluated the delta calculation purely for updates of returning users, but did not consider deltas between different pages. Korn et al. proposed VCDIFF, a differencing algorithm [4]. They evaluated it similar to Mogul et al. by considering deltas between updates of the same file. Cloudflare's Railgun uses delta encoding to update the CDN content [3]. This approach is limited between server and CDN and also only considers updates between different versions.

Shared Dictionary Compression (SDC). In a standard compression approach, like with deflate, the encoder reads the file and tries to find repeating strings from the previously read content. The previously read content is also referred to as the dictionary. Instead of just using the previously seen content, the dictionary could also be an external file. In SDC, the same dictionary is shared between multiple compression processes and can therefore improve the overall compression ratio further. Chan et al. suggest that Web pages with a similar URL path also may have similar content and Web pages may therefore be transmitted more efficiently as a differentials to previously visited Web pages [2]. They only consider HTML files and assume them to be uniquely identifiable by URL. While the approach is similar to ours, the presented results are not applicable to modern websites. First, today's HTML files are often personalized and thus not uniquely identifiable by URL. Second, some assets are static and uniquely identifiable by URL (e.g. JavaScript or CSS), but they are not considered. Butler et al. proposed Shared Dictionary Compression over HTTP (SDCH), where the server can actively push dictionaries to the client [5]. One of the key challenges here is to find the best dictionary, since the server has to predict which dictionary would be of use for the client. This dictionary may increase the payload for the first page, since it is pushed, but maybe only used later. LinkedIn reported that generating the dictionaries took them about 7 h per deployment and could easily take days [7]. Therefore, they were forced to delay the generation of new dictionaries to every other week. This may be one of the reasons why SDCH was not widely adopted and removed from Chrome[1]. However, the key idea of sharing a dictionary led to Brotli, which was later developed at Google [1]. For Brotli, the shared dictionary is static and already part of the library and never has to be generated or transferred over the network. Most browsers support Brotli, but without the custom dictionary functionality which could be used for cross-entity delta encoding. Zstandard would allow the same, but has no browser support at all.

3   Cross-Entity Delta Encoding

As shown in the previous section, delta encoding has so far mostly been evaluated to compute deltas between different versions of the same file or with a shared dictionary. Calculating deltas between files that share similar data could provide similar advantages. In contrast to SDCH, this would remove the need to create and maintain dictionaries as we use the raw files as dictionaries. This has some implications. First, the compression for one asset may deliver different results for different users, since the result depends on the dictionaries available in the client cache. Second, using client cache entries requires a cache state synchronization as the server needs to know which resources can be used for content encoding.

Dictionary Scope Strategies. As a basic rule, only those assets can be used for encoding, which have already been loaded by the client. We therefore consider three different strategies for our evaluation. As the most powerful strategy, one could consider every previous asset (PA) as a potential dictionary, which was seen until the currently requested asset. This includes previously visited pages (page impressions, PIs) as well as assets from the currently requested PI. This strategy is difficult to implement in practice, because assets are typically not downloaded in sequence. We exclude the currently processed PI assets as another more practical strategy and only consider fully downloaded assets up to the previous PI (PP). As a third strategy, we exclusively consider assets of the entry page as dictionaries (EE). Due to a similar overall layout (e.g. same header), this could be a reasonable alternative with a fixed set of dictionaries.

4   Compression Efficiency on Real-World Traces

In this Section, we examine how cross-entity delta encoding could affect the transferred size within a user journey. We start by creating a dataset collected from real websites and used them to compare different compression approaches.

Creating a Dataset. The potential of cross-entity delta encoding relies on the journey taken by a user, since it defines which dictionaries are in the cache. We created artificial ones, since we have no access to real user journeys. We

---

[1] groups.google.com/a/chromium.org/d/msg/blink-dev/nQl0ORHy7sw/HNpR96sq AgAJ.

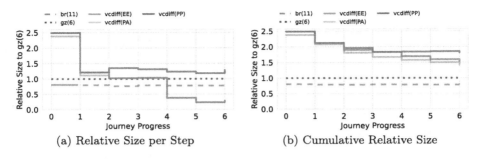

(a) Relative Size per Step   (b) Cumulative Relative Size

Fig. 1. The left chart shows the compression size relative to gzip (6), while the right chart shows the cumulative size up until each step to account for different page sizes. Replacing every compression with VCDIFF only pays off in the hot phase (>3), but is on average still worse than the default gzip compression.

assume that every website offers different kind of page types of which one is the main page type (e.g. a product in a shop or an article of a news/blog site). The other types could be types like a category site or the homepage. We further assume the users ultimate goal to be the content of this main page type. We start the navigation at the homepage and from there we try to hit different page types for Step 1 and 2. Step 3 then navigates to the main content. We name this part of the journey from now on the *cold phase*, since we hit distinct page types and the cache is cold in terms of available dictionaries. Step 4–6 are only recommendations from the previous main content and therefore navigate over potentially similar pages. In contrast, this path is from now on referred to as the *hot phase*, since it contains possible dictionary matches. We make sure that every step in the whole journey is unique. We used 40 of the traffic-heaviest websites according to SimilarWeb[2], providing the recommendation functionality.

Data Cleaning. This work focuses on text based content, therefore, we excluded every non-text asset, identified by the content-type header. We removed trivial cases, like the delta between two identical assets, since this is entirely preventable and would skew the results in favor of cross-entity delta encoding. Finally, we removed every third-party asset (other domain), since the provider would not have the possibility to change the compression for these kind of assets.

Calculating Deltas. The compression for the delta was done with open-VCDIFF to which we from now on will refer to as VCDIFF. We just brute-force every possible delta for a given asset and chose the smallest one. We only considered dictionaries which had at least the same type[3], e.g. text.

---

[2] https://www.similarweb.com/de/top-websites/.
[3] Still, the best dictionary was almost every time of the same subtype, e.g. text/html.

Comparing the Results. The data we collected was compressed by either Brotli, gzip, or no compression. To create a baseline against which we can compare, we uncompressed every asset and compressed it with the default gzip compression level (6), which on average is slightly higher than the results we got from the server. We also compare against Brotli (11), which may be impractical due to performance reasons, but represents the currently best compression ratio.

4.1 Enforcing VCDIFF

In our first experiment, we forced VCDIFF with the different strategies on every asset. It shows that regardless of the current step within our journey, just using the entry site will be outperformed in every step by gzip (see Fig. 1a). The results for PP and PE are similar in the cold phase and on par with gzip after leaving the entry page, but significantly improve and surpass even Brotli when entering the hot phase, with as low as 28% of gzip's size. This was expected, since we only look at previously visited page types. Still, due to the negative impact at the beginning, they cannot compete over the whole journey (see Fig. 1b).

4.2 Case-Specific VCDIFF

The previous experiment has shown that the results highly depend on the client cache. Therefore, we repeated the experiment but decided per asset to either use VCDIFF if it yields an improvement or stick with gzip (6) otherwise. Since the first PI still cannot leverage any dictionary, it mainly falls back to gzip (see Fig. 2a). Just using the entry page as the dictionary source can slightly improve the compression ratio overall (~5%), but as Fig. 2a indicates, this is mainly driven by similarities within the cold phase. Again, choosing the dictionary from previous assets provides the biggest impact within the hot phase and vastly outperforms Brotli. Stepping back to PP only slightly decreases the impact and can be an alternative to PA. Overall, using VCDIFF on specific assets scales well with the length of the journey, as soon as similar pages are visited. As Fig. 2a and 2b show, this will converge against 25% of the payload for longer journeys.

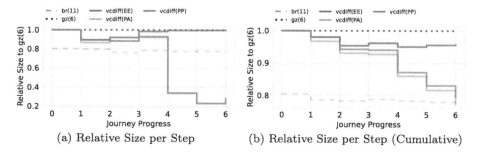

(a) Relative Size per Step   (b) Relative Size per Step (Cumulative)

Fig. 2. Using VCDIFF only when it actually provides an uplift yields small results in the cold phase (<4), but can even further improve the hot phase and overall eventually leads to results comparable with the maximum Brotli compression.

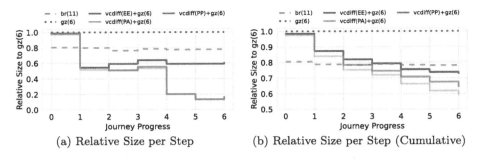

(a) Relative Size per Step   (b) Relative Size per Step (Cumulative)

Fig. 3. While VCDIFF is still not competitive on the first page load, combining it with secondary compression outperforms Brotli on every following page load.

4.3   VCDIFF with Secondary Compression

VCDIFF files can still contain many common strings and could therefore benefit from secondary compression, which is currently not implemented in open-VCDIFF. This motivated our next experiment. We used VCDIFF as an Opt-in on every text asset, but piped the VCDIFF output through gzip on level 6. Figure 3a shows that this approach drastically improves the results, as we now outperform Brotli even before entering the hot phase. Within the hot phase, we can compress the assets as low as 14% of gzip (6). Overall the cumulative size can be reduced to 58% of our baseline (see Fig. 3b).

4.4   Impact on Different MIME-Types

We expected the HTML to gain the most benefit of cross-entity delta encoding and compared them with the other types. We grouped them by the step, as well as the subtype to make sure that the actual weight of the single assets were reflected. For the cold phase, we exclude the entry pages (step 0), since the previous experiments have already shown that cross-entity encoding is no real alternative in that step. HTML benefits the most from cross-delta entity encoding (see Fig. 4) and is a safe alternative in the hot phase. We excluded

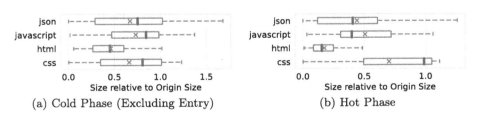

(a) Cold Phase (Excluding Entry)   (b) Hot Phase

Fig. 4. Compression efficiency by MIME type: Using HTML for cross-entity delta encoding works well in almost all cases. Using other MIME types leads to mixed results in the cold phase (a), but yields high efficiency in the hot phase (b).

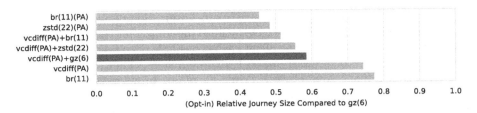

Fig. 5. Replacing the secondary compression yields even better results. Alternatively, Brotli and zstandard also allow a more efficient use of custom dictionaries.

XML and plain text responses, since we had too few samples. SVGs could in some cases further reduced by 10% compared to gz (6). While the other types on average can still greatly benefit, they are site-specific cases and need further investigation. Note that the hot phase had only a few CSS samples and may not be representative, since most sites do not load additional CSS files at this point.

4.5   Using Algorithms Beyond VCDIFF

Combining gzip (6) with VCDIFF already could on average reduce the journey size to 58%. But compression efficiency could be further improved by increasing the compression level and/or using different algorithms. We are aware that a higher compression level may be impractical in an actual deployment, but should act as an upper limit. While increasing gzip to level 9 had almost the same result, replacing gzip (6) with Brotli (11) reduces the cumulative journey size to 51% (see Fig. 5). As mentioned earlier, one could also directly use a custom dictionary with Brotli or zstandard (which is not supported by any browser). This reached the highest compression ratio and could reduce the result to 45% for Brotli (11) and 48% for zstandard (22), compared to gzip (6)[4]

5   Conclusion

Our results show that reusing cached assets for delta encoding can significantly reduce transferred bytes in the Web, even though we simulate new users who start with cold caches. This approach should thus be seen as a complement to existing compressions rather than a replacement. But it should be noted that potential uplift is even more significant for returning user who start their journeys in the hot phase and thus directly benefit from cross-entity delta encoding.

Open Challenges. In our experiments, we made several simplifying assumptions that do not hold in a real-world setting. First, we employ the perfect dictionary selection via a brute-force approach, but a more efficient heuristic would be

---

[4] Due to limited space, we only present a few selected alternatives here and refer to https://icwe.compaz.info for an extensive overview.

required for practical use. Also, cache state synchronization remains challenging: The server does not only have to select the ideal dictionary for encoding, but also one that is already present in the client cache to enable decoding. Another open challenge is the lack of browser support for different aspects of delta encoding and shared dictionary compression. While all major browsers support generic Brotli and gzip, VCDIFF and Brotli with a custom dictionary are currently not supported by any of them. While using HTML files as dictionaries was most effective in our evaluation, content that is generated per user makes it infeasible to keep all dictionaries (HTMLs) in the server. Reducing this complexity would require some kind of normalization to strip personlized content for encoding and decoding (cf. Dynamic Blocks [8]), akin to app shells in single-page applications.

Closing Thoughts. Despite a host of literature on delta encoding and shared dictionary compression from more than two decades of research, there is still a lot of untapped potential in existing compression technologies. Our results indicate that using the client cache as a dictionary for delta encoding can reduce the text payload by up to 86% for single pages and by 55–80% for user journeys over recommended content. But there is still further research needed in areas like dictionary selection and cache state synchronization. Lacking browser support for cross-entity delta encoding algorithms is another practical barrier, but could be added in platform-independent fashion with a service worker implementation. However, performance depends on the client device and is likely not comparable with native compression algorithms. Without native browser support, delta encoding only seems viable for scenarios where network efficiency is critical (e.g. for mobile users in data saving mode).

References

1. Alakuijala, J., et al.: Brotli: a general-purpose data compressor. ACM TOI **37**(1), 1–30 (2019)
2. Chan, M.C., Woo, T.: Cache-based compaction: a new technique for optimizing web transfer. In: IEEE INFOCOM 1999. Conference on Computer Communications (1999)
3. Knecht, D.O., Graham-Cumming, J., Prince, M.B.: Method and apparatus for reducing network resource transmission size using delta compression (2019)
4. Korn, D.G., Vo, K.P.: Engineering a differencing and compression data format. In: USENIX Annual Technical Conference, General Track, pp. 219–228 (2002)
5. McQuade, B., Mixter, K., Lee, W.H., Butler, J.: A proposal for shared dictionary compression over HTTP (2016)
6. Mogul, J.C., Douglis, F., Feldmann, A., Krishnamurthy, B.: Potential benefits of delta encoding and data compression for HTTP. SIGCOMM CCR **27**, 181–194 (1997)
7. Shapira, O.: SDCH at LinkedIn (2015). https://engineering.linkedin.com/shared-dictionary-compression-http-linkedin. Accessed 20 Jan 2022
8. Wingerath, W., et al.: Speed Kit: a polyglot & GDPR-compliant approach for caching personalized content. In: ICDE, Dallas, Texas (2020)

9. Wollmer, B., Wingerath, W., Ferrlein, S., Gessert, F., Ritter, N.: Compaz: exploring the potentials of shared dictionary compression on the web. In: 22th International Conference on Web Engineering, ICWE (2022)
10. Wollmer, B., Wingerath, W., Ritter, N.: Context-aware encoding & delivery in the web. In: 20th International Conference on Web Engineering, ICWE (2020)

Web Big Data and Web Data Analytics

Dynamic Network Embedding in Hyperbolic Space via Self-attention

Dingyang Duan[1,2] (ID), Daren Zha[1,2], Xiao Yang[3,4], Nan Mu[1,2(✉)], and Jiahui Shen[1,2]

[1] Institute of Information Engineering, Chinese Academy of Sciences, Beijing, China
{duandingyang,zhadaren,munan,shenjiahui}@iie.ac.cn
[2] School of Cyber Security, University of Chinese Academy of Sciences, Beijing, China
[3] Aerospace Internet of Things Technology Co., Ltd., Beijing, China
yangxiao@casciot.com
[4] China Aerospace Times Electronics Co., Ltd., Beijing, China

Abstract. Graph Neural Networks (GNNs) have recently become increasingly popular due to their ability to learn node representations in complex graphs. Existing graph representation learning methods primarily target static graphs in Euclidean space, while many graphs in practical applications are dynamic and evolve constantly over time. Besides, most of these methods underestimate the inherent complex and hierarchical properties in real-world graphs, leading to sub-optimal embeddings. In this work, we propose a **D**ynamic **N**etwork in **H**yperbolic space via Self-**At**tention, referred to as DynHAT, a novel neural architecture that computes node representations through joint two dimensions of hyperbolic structural graph and temporal attention graph. More specifically, DynHAT maps the structural graph into hyperbolic space to capture the hierarchical information, then temporal graph captures time-varying dynamic evolution over multiple time steps by flexibly weighting historical representations. Experimental results on three real-world datasets demonstrate the superiority of DynHAT for dynamic graph embedding, as it consistently outperforms competing methods in link prediction tasks.

Keywords: Dynamic graphs · Hyperbolic space · Self-attention · Representation learning

1 Introduction

Graph Neural Networks (GNNs) are widely used to model the complex graphs due to their ability to learn node representations. Its basic idea is to map each node to a vector in a low-dimensional representation space. By learning graph representations, classical machine learning algorithms can be applied to solve various task, such as link prediction and node classification. However, many real-world graphs, such as social networks where graph structures constantly evolve

© Springer Nature Switzerland AG 2022
T. Di Noia et al. (Eds.): ICWE 2022, LNCS 13362, pp. 189–203, 2022.
https://doi.org/10.1007/978-3-031-09917-5_13

over time, often exhibit scale-free or hierarchical structure [4], and Euclidean embeddings, used by existing GCNs, have a high distortion when embedding such graphs [24]. Learning representations of dynamic structures is challenging but of high importance since it describes how the network interacts and evolves, which will help to understand and predict the behavior of the system [26]. This requires the learned node representations to not only preserve structural proximity but also jointly capture their temporal evolution.

Most of these existing studies model to dynamic graphs can be divided into two different approaches: discrete-time approaches where the evolution of a dynamic graph can be described by a sequence of static graphs, with a fixed timestamp; and continuous-time approaches where the evolution is modeled at a finer temporal granularity to encompass different events in real time [21]. Essentially, these two approaches both are primarily designed for the graphs in Euclidean spaces. However, many real-world graphs, such as protein interaction networks and social networks, often exhibit scale-free or hierarchical structure [2]. In particular, the scale-free graphs have tree-like structure and in such graphs the graph volume, defined as the number of nodes within some radius to a center node, grows exponentially as a function of radius. In such cases, the polynomial expansion Euclidean space can neither capture the exponential complexity nor provide the most powerful or meaningful geometry for graph representation learning. So, the volume of balls in Euclidean space only grows polynomial with respect to the radius, which leads to high distortion embeddings [19], while in hyperbolic space, this volume grows exponentially. Therefore, Hyperbolic geometry offers an exciting alternative as it enables embeddings with much smaller distortion when embedding scale-free and hierarchical graphs.

Learning dynamic node representations is challenging due to the complex time-varying graph structures. This requires the learned node representations to not only preserve structural proximity but also jointly capture their temporal evolution. For instance, in email communication networks whose interaction structures may change dramatically due to sudden events, users will join or quit a network at any time, and also they may develop new relationships or break up with others over time. More information could be captured when we consider the dynamic features of a graph. In this case, it is common practice to build a recurrent neural networks (RNN) that summarize historical snapshots via hidden state, for example [7,8] which mainly focus on mining the pattern of graph evolvement. However, the disadvantage of RNN is also obvious, which requires amounts of data and scale poorly with an increase in number of time steps. Attention mechanisms have recently achieved great success in many sequential learning tasks. The idea behind the attention mechanism was to permit the decoder to utilize the most relevant parts of the input sequence in a flexible manner, by a weighted combination of all of the encoded input vectors, with the most relevant vectors being attributed the highest weights. When a single sequence is used as both the input and context, it is called self-attention, which are initially designed to facilitate RNNs to capture long-range dependencies. This paper [22] demonstrates the efficiency of a pure self-attentional network in achieving state-of-the-art performance in machine translation. As the change on graphs may be periodical and frequent, self-attention is able to draw context from all past graph snapshots to adaptively assign interpretable weights for previous time steps.

Inspired by the aforementioned insight, we present a novel neural architecture named Dynamic Network in Hyperbolic Space via Self-Attention, referred to as DynHAT, to learn latent node representations on dynamic graphs. DynHAT fully leverages the implicit hierarchical information to capture the spatial dependency and graph evolution over multiple time steps by flexibly weighting historical representations. In summary, the main contributions are stated as follows:

- We propose a novel hyperbolic temporal graph embedding model, named DynHAT, to learn temporal regularities, topological dependencies, and implicitly hierarchical organization.
- We devise a modular temporal self-attention layer, which captures the most relevant historical contexts through efficient self-attentions. To the best of our knowledge, this is the first study on dynamic graph embedding that utilizes joint hyperbolic structural and temporal self-attention.
- Experimental results on three real-world datasets demonstrate the superiority of DynHAT for dynamic graph embedding, as it consistently outperforms competing methods in link prediction tasks. The ablation study further gives insights into how each proposed component contributes to the success of the model.

2   Related Works

Our work mainly relates to representation learning on structure graph embeddings and temporal graph embeddings.

Structure Graph Embeddings. Static network embedding methods can be classified into two categories: one for plain networks, another one for complex information networks. The first type of approaches only utilizes the topological structure information for embedding. DeepWalk [18] transforms graph structure information into sequences by random walk. Node2vec [9] improves the random walk strategies of DeepWalk by a controllable deep or wide walking possibility. Instead of shallow embeddings, several graph neural network architectures have achieved tremendous success. GCN [13] performs graph convolutions for aggregation and update motivated by spectral convolution. GAT [23] incorporates the attention mechanism into the aggregation step. GraphSAGE [11] considers from the spatial perspective and introduces an inductive learning method. All these methods assume the representation space to be Euclidean.

Hyperbolic Graph Embeddings. Hyperbolic space provides an exciting alternative. An increasing number of studies generalize the graph convolution into hyperbolic space, recent works including HGNN [15], HGCN [3] and HGAT [27]. HGCN is a generalization of inductive GCNs in hyperbolic geometry that benefits from the expressiveness of both graph neural networks and hyperbolic embeddings. HGAT employs the framework of gyrovector spaces to implement the graph processing in hyperbolic spaces and design an attention mechanism based on hyperbolic proximity. The superior performance brought by hyperbolic geometry on static graphs motivates us to explore it on temporal graphs.

Dynamic Graph Embeddings. Recently, several solutions for dynamic graph are proposed. As discussed earlier, Temporal graphs are mainly defined in two ways: discrete-time approaches, where its life span is a discrete set, hence the evolution of a dynamic graph can be described by a sequence of static graphs, with a fixed timestamp; and continuous-time approach, where its life span is a continuous set, therefore the evolution is modeled at a finer temporal granularity to encompass different events in real time [25]. We here mainly focus on representation learning over discrete temporal graphs. DynamicTriad [28] constraints the representation in each time step, by the formulation that triadic closure process is more frequent along graph evolving. Dyngraph2vec [7] and Dyngem [8] use Auto-Encoder to learn the graph and use the Recurrent Neural Network (RNN) to model the relations over time. DySAT [20] applies attention mechanism in it, learning structural and temporal attention to adaptively obtain useful information for embedding. Most of the prevalent methods are built-in Euclidean space which leads to high distortion embeddings.

3   Preliminary

In this section, we first present the problem formulation of temporal graph embedding. Then, we introduce some fundamentals of hyperbolic geometry.

3.1   Problem Formulation

In this work, we formally define the problem of dynamic graph representation learning. A dynamic graph is defined as a series of observed static graph snapshots, $\mathbb{G} = \{\mathcal{G}_1, ..., \mathcal{G}_T\}$ where T is the number of time steps. Each snapshot $\mathcal{G}_t = (V_t, A_t) \in \mathcal{G}$ is a weighted and undirected network snapshot recorded at time t, where V_t is the set of vertices and A_t is the corresponding adjacency matrix at time step t. Unlike some previous methods that assume links can only be added in dynamic graphs, we also support removal of links over time. Dynamic graph representation learning aims to learn a mapping function that obtains a low-dimensional representation for each node at time steps $t = \{1, 2, ..., T\}$. Each node embedding h_v^t preserves both local graph structures centered at v and its temporal evolutionary behaviors such as link connection and removal up to time step t.

3.2   Hyperbolic Geometry

A Riemannian manifold $\mathcal{M}$ is a space that generalizes the notion of a 2D surface to higher dimensions [5]. For each point $\mathbf{x} \in \mathcal{M}$, it associates with a (Euclidean)

tangent space $\mathcal{T}_{\mathbf{x}}\mathcal{M}$ of the same dimensionality as $\mathcal{M}$. Intuitively, $\mathcal{T}_{\mathbf{x}}\mathcal{M}$ contains all possible directions in which one can pass through $\mathbf{x}$ tangentially (see Fig. 1).

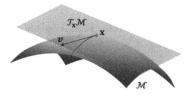

Fig. 1. The tangent space $\mathcal{T}_{\mathbf{x}}\mathcal{M}$ and a tangent vector v, along the given point $\mathbf{x}$ of a curve traveling through the manifold $\mathcal{M}$.

There are multiple equivalent models for hyperbolic space, with each representation conserving some geometric properties, but distorting others. In this paper, we adopt the Poincare ball model which is a compact representative providing visualizing and interpreting hyperbolic embeddings.

The Poincare ball model with negative curvature $-c(c \geq 0)$ corresponds to the Riemannian manifold $(\mathbb{H}^{n,c}, g_{\mathbb{H}})$, where $\mathbb{H}^{n,c} = \{\mathbf{x} \in \mathbb{R}^n : c||\mathbf{x}||^2 \leq 1\}$ is an open n-dimensional ball. If $c = 0$, it degrades to Euclidean space, i.e., $\mathbb{H}^{n,c} = \mathbb{R}^n$. In addition, [5] shows how Euclidean and hyperbolic spaces can be continuously deformed into each other and provides a principled manner for basic operations (e.g., addition and multiplication) as well as essential functions (e.g., linear maps and softmax layer) in the context of neural networks and deep learning.

4 Proposed Model

The overall framework of the proposed model (DynHAT) is illustrated in Fig. 2. DynHAT has two primary modules: **Hyperbolic structure attention**; **Euclidean temporal attention**, which benefits from the expressiveness of both hyperbolic embeddings and temporal evolutionary embeddings. More specifically, our model can be summarized as two procedures: (1) Given the original input node feature, this procedure projects it into hyperbolic space, and aggregates the latent node embeddings via attention mechanism based on the hyperbolic proximity. This procedure concerns topological embedding in hyperbolic space, which is similar to the model HGAT that designs an attention-based graph convolution in hyperbolic space. (2) These sequences of node representations then feed as input to the temporal attention, which are performed in Euclidean space due to its computational efficiency. Owing to the superiorities of self-attention, this unit fuses the final embedding by figuring out the importance of each time step graph snapshots. The outputs of temporal module comprise the set of final dynamic node representations. Furthermore, we endow our model with expressivity to capture dynamic graph evolution from different latent perspectives through multi-head attentions [22]. Finally, we feed the aggregated representations to a loss function for downstream task. We elaborate on the details of each respective module in the following paragraphs.

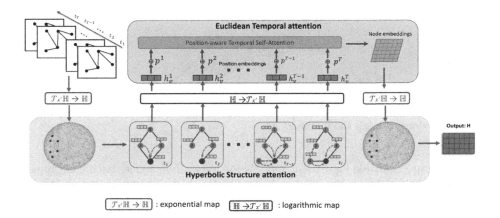

Fig. 2. Neural architecture of DynHAT: we employ structural attention layer in Hyperbolic space followed by temporal attention layers in Euclidean space.

4.1 Feature Map

Before going into the details of each module, we introduce two bijection operations, the exponential map and the logarithmic map, for mapping between hyperbolic space and tangent space with a local reference point [3,15], as presented below.

Proposition 1. *For* $\mathbf{x}' \in \mathbb{H}^{d,c}$, $a \in \mathcal{T}_{\mathbf{x}'}\mathbb{H}^{d,c}$, $b \in \mathbb{H}^{d,c}$, *and* $a \neq 0$, $b \neq \mathbf{x}'$, *then the exponential map is formulate as:*

$$\exp_{\mathbf{x}'}^{c}(a) = \mathbf{x}' \oplus^{c} (\tanh(\frac{\sqrt{c}\lambda_{\mathbf{x}'}^{c}||a||}{2})\frac{a}{\sqrt{c}||a||}), \tag{1}$$

where $\lambda_{\mathbf{x}'}^{c} := \frac{2}{1-c||x'||^2}$ *is conformal factor and* $\oplus$ *is Mobius addition, for any* $u, v \in \mathbb{H}^{d,c}$:

$$u \oplus v := \frac{(1 + 2c\langle u, v\rangle + c||v||^2)u + (1 - c||u||^2)v}{1 + 2c\langle u, v\rangle + c^2||u||^2||v||^2}. \tag{2}$$

The logarithmic map is given by:

$$\log_{\mathbf{x}'}^{c}(b) := \frac{2}{\sqrt{c}\lambda_{\mathbf{x}'}^{c}} \operatorname{artanh}(\sqrt{c}|| - \mathbf{x}' \oplus^{c} b||)\frac{-\mathbf{x}' \oplus^{c} b}{|| - \mathbf{x}' \oplus^{c} b||}. \tag{3}$$

Note that x' is a local reference point, we use the origin point 0 in our work.

4.2 Hyperbolic Structure Attention (HSA)

HSA is employed to extracts features from higher-order local neighborhoods of each node through a self-attention aggregation and stacking, to compute intermediate node representations for each snapshot, which leveraging promising properties of hyperbolic geometry. The input of HSA is the node feature, whose norm could be out of the Poincare ball defined in hyperbolic space. To make the node feature available in hyperbolic space, we use the exponential map to project the feature into the hyperbolic space, shown in proposition 1. Specifically, let a Euclidean space vector $\mathbf{x}_i^E \in \mathbb{R}^d$ be the feature of node i, and then we regard it as the point in the tangent space $\mathcal{T}_{\mathbf{x}'}\mathbb{H}^{d,c}$ with reference point $\mathbf{x}' \in \mathbb{H}^{d,c}$, using the exponential map to project it into hyperbolic space, obtaining $\mathbf{x}^{\mathcal{H}} \in \mathbb{H}^{d,c}$, which is defined as:

$$\mathbf{x}_i^{\mathcal{H}} = \exp_{x'}^c(\mathbf{x}_i^E). \tag{4}$$

We then transform $\mathbf{x}_i^{\mathcal{H}}$ into a higher-level latent representation $m_i^{\mathcal{H}}$ to obtain sufficient representation power, which is formulated as:

$$m_i^{\mathcal{H}} = W \otimes^c \mathbf{x}_i^{\mathcal{H}} \oplus^c b. \tag{5}$$

Considering vector multiplication and bias addition can not be directly applied since the operations in hyperbolic space fail to meet the permutation invariant requirement, for vector multiplication, we first project the hyperbolic vector to the tangent space, which is given by:

$$W \otimes^c \mathbf{x}_i^{\mathcal{H}} := \exp_{\mathbf{x}'}^c(W \log_{\mathbf{x}'}^c(\mathbf{x}_i^{\mathcal{H}})). \tag{6}$$

For bias addition, we transport the bias located at $\mathcal{T}_o\mathbb{H}$ to the position $\mathcal{T}_{\mathbf{x}}\mathbb{H}$ in parallel. Then we use $\exp_{\mathbf{x}}^c$ to map it back to hyperbolic space and Mobius addition to compute the bias addition: $\mathbf{x}^{\mathcal{H}} \oplus^c b := \exp_{\mathbf{x}}^c(P_{o \to x}(b))$.

The Hyperbolic Attention Mechanism. We perform a self-attention mechanism on the nodes. Aggregation is to calculate a weighted midpoint in Euclidean space [10], however, it is difficult to apply as it lacks a closed form to compute the derivative easily [1]. Similar to [3,15,27], we address this issue by applying the aggregation computation in the tangent space. The attention coefficient α_{ij}, which indicates the importance of node j to node i, can be computed as:

$$\alpha_{ij} = softmax_{(j \in \mathcal{N}(i))}(s_{ij}) = \frac{\exp(s_{ij})}{\sum_{j' \in \mathcal{N}_i} \exp(s_{ij'})}, \tag{7}$$

$$s_{ij} = \sigma(a^T[\log_0^c(m_i^l)||\log_0^c(m_j^l)]), \forall(i,j) \in \mathcal{E}. \tag{8}$$

Thus, a hyperbolic structural attention layer applies on a snapshot $\mathcal{G}$ outputs node embeddings, through a self-attentional aggregation of neighboring node embeddings, which can be viewed as a single message passing round among immediate neighbors.

4.3   Euclidean Temporal Attention (ETA)

The embeddings input to a layer can potentially vary across different snapshots. We denote the node representations output by the HSA block, as $h_v^1, h_v^2, ..., h_v^T$, which feed as input to the temporal attention block. To further capture temporal evolutionary patterns in a dynamic graph, we design a temporal self-attention layer. Note that, this layer is performed in the tangent space due to its computational efficiency. The h_v^t is expressed as:

$$h_v^t = X_t^E = \log_{\mathbf{x}'}^c(\tilde{\mathbf{x}}_i^{\mathcal{H}}). \tag{9}$$

This unit receives the sequential input h_v^T for a particular node v at different time steps from hyperbolic structure attention layer. The input representations are assumed to sufficiently capture local structural information at each time step. Once obtained the node representations for each time step snapshot, the next is to aggregate these node embeddings across a series of time snapshots. First, we capture the ordering information in the temporal attention module by using *position* embedding [6], $p^1, p^2, ..., p^3$, which embed the absolute temporal position of each snapshot. The position embeddings are combined with the output of the HSA module to obtain a sequence of input representations: $h_v^1 + p^1, h_v^2 + p^2, ..., h_v^T + p^T$ for node v across multiple time steps.

In contrast to HSA layer which operates on the representations of neighboring nodes, temporal attention layer takes all the temporal history of each node into account. To be specific, to compute the output representation of node v at time step t, we use scaled dot-product form of attention [22] where the queries, keys, and values are set as the input node representations. The (Q, K, V) are first transformed to a different space through linear projection matrices $W_q \in \mathbb{R}^{D' \times F'}$, $W_k \in \mathbb{R}^{D' \times F'}$ and $W_v \in \mathbb{R}^{D' \times F'}$ respectively. Then, we allow each time step t to attend over all time steps up to and including t, to preserve the auto-regressive property. The temporal self-attention function is defined as:

$$h_v^{ij} = \frac{((X_v W_q)(X_v W_k)^T)_{ij}}{\sqrt{F'}} + M_{ij}, \tag{10}$$

$$\beta_v^{ij} = \frac{\exp(h_v^{ij})}{\sum_{k=1}^T \exp(h_v^{ik})}, \tag{11}$$

$$Z_v = \beta_v(X_v W_v), \tag{12}$$

$$H^{\mathcal{H}} = \exp_{\mathbf{x}'}^c(Z_v) \tag{13}$$

where X_v denotes the $h_v^T + p^T$ which as the query to attend over its historical representations, $\beta_v \in \mathbb{R}^{T \times T}$ is the attention weight matrix obtained by multiplicative attention function and $M \in \mathbb{R}^{T \times T}$ is a mask matrix with each entry $M_{ij} \in \{-\infty, 0\}$ to enforce the auto-regressive property following the function [20]. To encode the temporal order, we define M as:

$$M_{ij} = \begin{cases} 0, & i \leq j \\ -\infty, & otherwise \end{cases} \tag{14}$$

When $M_{ij} = -\infty$, the softmax results in a zero attention weight, i.e., $\beta_v^{ij} = 0$, which switches off the attention from time-step i to j.

As the temporal attention is built in the Euclidean space, different with the structure attention unit, we need to feed the output embeddings back to the hyperbolic space (as given in Eqs. (13)).

4.4   Learning Objective

We formulate the learning objective to maximize the probability of linked nodes and minimize the probability of no interconnected nodes. In our model, we use the dynamic representation of a node v at time step t, h_v^t to preserve local proximity around v at time step t. The loss function $\mathcal{L}$ is based on binary cross-entropy which is defined as:

$$\mathcal{L} = \sum_{t=1}^{T} \sum_{v \in V} (\sum_{u \in \mathcal{N}_{walk(v)}^t} -\log(p(h_u^t, h_v^t)) - w_n \sum_{u' \in P_n^t(v)} \log(1 - p(h_{u'}^t, h_v^t))) \qquad (15)$$

where p is the probability which could be inferred by the Fermi-Dirac function [3], and $\mathcal{N}_{walk}^t(v)$ is the set of nodes that co-occur with v on fixed-length random walks at snapshot t. P_n^t is a negative sampling distribution for time step t, and w_n is the negative sampling ratio, a hyper-parameter to balance the positive and negative samples. Note that learning the representation of each node in hyperbolic space, the loss function $\mathcal{L}_t$ is only related to distance in the Poincare ball, and benefits to large-scale datasets.

5   Experiments and Analysis

In this section, we conduct extensive experiments with the aim of answering the following research questions:

- **RQ1** How does DynHAT perform?
- **RQ2** What does each component of DynHAT bring?

5.1   Datasets

To evaluate the effectiveness of our model, we conduct experiments on three datasets from real-world platforms. The datasets are summarized in Table 1.

- **Enron** [14] Enron dataset was collected and prepared by the CALO Project (A Cognitive Assistant that Learns and Organizes). It contains emails between employees of the company between January 1991 and July 2002.
- **UCI** [16] UCI dataset draws on longitudinal network data from an online community to examine patterns of users' behavior and social interaction, and infer the processes underpinning dynamics of system use. In this network, connections between users are made through online information.

- **MovieLens** [12] MovieLens contains rating data of multiple users for multiple movies, including movie metadata information and user attribute information. GroupLens Research collected data on movie ratings provided by MovieLens users from the late 1990s to the early 2000s. In this paper, we use a subset of MovieLens, ML-10M, consists of a user-tag interactions where the links connect users with the tags they applied on certain movies.

Table 1. Summary of the datasets

Dataset	Enron	UCI	ML-10M
Nodes	143	1,809	20,537
Edges[a]	2347	16,822	43,760
Time steps[b]	16	13	13

[a] Edge counts denotes the total edges across all time steps.
[b] The duration of each snapshot will affect the total number of snapshots. The proper granularity is more beneficial to capture evolving patterns.

5.2 Baselines

We present comparisons against several static graph embedding methods to analyze the gains of using temporal information for link prediction. To ensure a fair comparison, we provide access to the entire history of snapshots by constructing an aggregated graph up to time t, with link weights proportional to the cumulative weight till t agnostic to link occurrence time. More importantly, we also conduct experiments on several temporal graph embedding models to further demonstrate the superiority of the proposed DynHAT. These models are all in Euclidean space. As for hyperbolic model, HGCN, a recent model for static graphs, is used for one of baselines.

- **Node2vec** [9] Node2vec is a static embedding method to generate vector representations of nodes on a graph. It learns low-dimensional representations for nodes in a graph through the use of random walks.
- **GraphSAGE** [11] GraphSAGE is a framework for inductive representation learning on large graphs. It can be used to generate node embeddings for previously unseen nodes or entirely new input graphs, as long as these graphs have the same attribute schema as the training data.
- **GAT** [23] GAT leverages masked self-attentional layers to address the shortcomings of prior methods based on graph convolutions or their approximations. The self-attention mechanism is an advanced method which our model also takes advantage of.

- **HGCN** [3] HGCN is a static embedding method which leverages both the expressiveness of GCNs and hyperbolic geometry to learn node representations for hierarchical and scale-free graphs.
- **EvolveGCN** [17] EvolveGCN is a temporal model that extends GCN, which computes a seperate GCN model for each time step. The model is updated upon an input to the system every time, by using an RNN (e.g., GRU). There are two versions of the EvolveGCN: EvolveGCN-O and EvolveGCN-H. We test both and report the best result.
- **DynamicTriad** [28] DynamicTriad focuses on specific structure of triad to model how close triads are formed from open triads in dynamic networks.
- **DySAT** [20] Dynamic network employs GAT as a static layer and self-attention mechanism to capture the temporal graph evolution.

We use the same split as the previous works, i.e., 25% for the training set and 75% for the test set. The number of negative samples for each positive sample is 1. Besides, we fix the curvature as 1 in Hyperbolic structure attention layer.

5.3   Link Prediction Comparison (RQ 1)

We obtain node representations from DynHAT which can be applied to link prediction. In this paper, we conduct experiments on single-step and multi-step link prediction. Using the node representation trained on graph snapshots up to time step t, the single-step link prediction predicts the connections between nodes at time step $t+1$, while the multi-step link prediction predicts at multiple time steps start from $t+1$.

More specifically, given partially observed snapshots of a temporal graph $\mathbb{G} = \{\mathcal{G}_\infty, ..., \mathcal{G}_\mathcal{T}\}$, for single-step prediction, the latest embeddings h_v^t are used to predict the links at $\mathcal{G}^{t+1}$, classifying each node pair into links and non-links. For multi-step link prediction, the latest embeddings are used to predict the links at multiple future time steps $\{t+1, ..., t+\Delta\}$. In each dataset, we set $\Delta = 6$ for evaluation.

We use the Area Under the ROC Curve (AUC) [9] metric to evaluate link prediction performance. Note that we uniformly train both the baselines and DynHAT by using early stopping based on the performance of the training set.

Single-Step Link Prediction. The results of single-step link prediction are shown in Table 2. Our results indicate that the proposed model achieves gains of 3–4% AUC and AP, comparing to the best baseline across all datasets. On the one hand, the runners-up goes to the other temporal graph embedding model, which confirms the importance of temporal regularity in dynamic graph modeling. On the other hand, for hyperbolic model in static graph, our model consistently outperforms HGCN. In the following, we discuss the several insights from the comparative analysis of different methods.

First of all, the DySAT achieves the competitive performance to dynamic embedding methods across different datasets, underperforming DynHAT only by 3.88% and 2.67% in AUC and AP scores, respectively, despite of in Euclidean

Table 2. AUC (left) and AP (right) scores of single-step link prediction result.

Dataset	AUC			AP		
	Enron	UCI	ML-10M	Enron	UCI	ML-10M
Node2vec	82.81 ± 0.8	79.45 ± 0.7	85.57 ± 0.2	81.44 ± 1.1	78.22 ± 0.8	87.45 ± 0.3
GraphSAGE	84.3 ± 0.9	82.11 ± 0.6	87.3 ± 0.1	85.57 ± 1.2	83.67 ± 0.9	86.2 ± 0.1
GAT	83.8 ± 1.2	80.07 ± 0.9	85.4 ± 0.1	83.17 ± 1.9	79.93 ± 0.6	86.4 ± 0.3
HGCN	85.66 ± 0.8	82.71 ± 0.7	88.32 ± 0.2	82.45 ± 0.9	85.63 ± 0.3	86.17 ± 0.4
EvolveGCN	84.85 ± 0.9	84.16 ± 0.4	87.9 ± 0.2	86.23 ± 0.7	84.73 ± 1.1	86.72 ± 0.2
DynamicTriad	81.02 ± 0.6	84.51 ± 0.4	86.42 ± 0.1	85.83 ± 0.9	82.35 ± 0.5	86.59 ± 0.1
DySAT	88.50 ± 0.3	86.65 ± 0.2	89.73 ± 0.2	88.20 ± 0.4	86.7 ± 0.2	89.96 ± 0.1
DynHAT	**91.88 ± 1.2**	**88.78 ± 0.2**	**91.23 ± 0.3**	**90.87 ± 0.8**	**88.51 ± 1.2**	**93.16 ± 0.2**

space. One possible explanation is that joint structural and temporal modeling with expressive aggregators like multi-head attentions plays an important role for superior performance on link prediction. The performance gap between Dyn-HAT and DySAT suggests that the significantly benefit from hyperbolic geometry. Second, HGCN also has relatively good performance despite being agnostic to temporal information, which indicates further improvements to DynHAT on transforming the embeddings from Euclidean space to Hyperbolic space.

Multi-step Link Prediction. In this section, we select several relatively good performance models from difference aspect for comparison, then evaluate them on multi-step link prediction over $t + \Delta$ time steps, where Δ equals to 6. As is shown in Fig. 3, we observe a slight decay in performance overtime for all the models, which is expected. Specifically, we notice that the performance of each method except DySAT drops by different degrees, while our model and DySAT maintains a stable result overtime, that can attribute to the temporal attention module. For instance, the performance of the HGCN degrades dramatically on Enron from 85.54% to 82.88%, while DynHAT only declines about 1.3%. This demonstrates the capability of the temporal attention module to capture the most relevant historical context. Additionally, DynHAT maintains a consistent performance, comparing with DySAT which learns the node representation in Euclidean space. The superiority of hyperbolic space and the importance of modeling temporal context are supported in the experimental results.

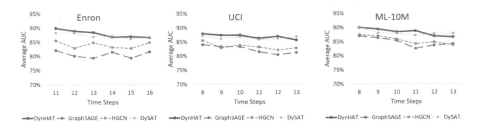

Fig. 3. AUC performance of DynHAT with different models on multi-step link prediction.

5.4   Ablation Study (RQ 2)

To investigate the superiority of the main components of our model, we compare DynHAT with different variants on Enron, UCI and Movielens datasets. We show the variant models as following and their result in Table 3. To validate the performance of temporal self-attention block for long-term prediction task, we set the finer granularity of snapshot, which means the shorter of duration.

- **DynHA** DynHAT removes the temporal attention block. Note that the variant model is different from static models since the embeddings are jointly optimized in Eqs. (15) to predict snapshot-specific neighborhoods, however without any explicit temporal evolution modeling.
- **DynAT** DyHAT without hyperbolic geometry where aggregating processes are built in Euclidean space.

Table 3. Ablation study on structural and temporal attention layer.

Dataset	AUC			AP		
	Enron	UCI	ML-10M	Enron	UCI	ML-10M
DynHA	88.93 ± 0.5	86.12 ± 0.5	86.76 ± 0.2	89.83 ± 0.8	85.71 ± 0.2	88.52 ± 0.2
DynAT	89.82 ± 0.4	87.35 ± 0.3	90.68 ± 0.5	89.62 ± 0.3	87.67 ± 0.3	91.73 ± 0.3
Original	**91.88 ± 1.2**	**88.78 ± 0.2**	**91.23 ± 0.3**	**90.87 ± 0.8**	**88.51 ± 1.2**	**93.16 ± 0.2**

As is shown in Table 3, we first make the wrap-up observation that removing any of the components will cause performance degradation. The effect of temporal self-attention layer is significant since the performance is decayed by removing the temporal block. Besides, we find that the finer granularity of snapshots, which means the shorter of the duration, would more fully utilized the historical representations especially in MovieLens dataset. This observation conforms to the nature of graph evolution since the rating behaviors in MovieLens correlated with time-efficient, while the communications in Enron and UCI span longer time intervals. We confirm that the proposed model leverage the temporal evolution embedding to better perform the final results. Additionally, we design the Euclidean variant of DynHAT, namely DynAT, proves that hyperbolic geometry enables the preservation of the hierarchical layout in the graph data naturally. DynHAT consistently outperforms the variants with almost 3% average gain in AUC and AP scores, validating our choice of joint structural in hyperbolic and temporal self-attention. Finally, the addition of both DynHA and DynAT improves performance even further, suggesting that both components are important in DynHAT.

6   Conclusions

In this work, we have presented a novel model DynHAT for dynamic graph representation learning in hyperbolic space. In DynHAT, we stack temporal attention layers on top of hyperbolic structural attention layers, considering distortions when representing real-world in Euclidean space. More specifically, our model computes dynamic node representations through joint two modules: hyperbolic structure attention (HSA) and Euclidean temporal attention (ETA). HSA leverages the superiority of hyperbolic mechanism and ETA captures the most relevant historical contexts through efficient self-attentions. To the best of our knowledge, this is the first work to address the temporal graph embedding via self-attention mechanism built-in hyperbolic space. Experimental results show the superiority of DynHAT for link prediction on several real-world datasets. For future work, we hope that our work will inspire the future development of dynamic graph embeddings in hyperbolic space.

References

1. Bacák, M.: Computing medians and means in hadamard spaces. SIAM J. Optim. **24**(3), 1542–1566 (2014)
2. Bronstein, M.M., Bruna, J., LeCun, Y., Szlam, A., Vandergheynst, P.: Geometric deep learning: going beyond euclidean data. IEEE Sig. Process. Mag. **34**(4), 18–42 (2017)
3. Chami, I., Ying, Z., Ré, C., Leskovec, J.: Hyperbolic graph convolutional neural networks. Adv. Neural. Inf. Process. Syst. **32**, 4868–4879 (2019)
4. Clauset, A., Moore, C., Newman, M.E.: Hierarchical structure and the prediction of missing links in networks. Nature **453**(7191), 98–101 (2008)
5. Ganea, O.E., Bécigneul, G., Hofmann, T.: Hyperbolic neural networks. arXiv preprint arXiv:1805.09112 (2018)
6. Gehring, J., Auli, M., Grangier, D., Yarats, D., Dauphin, Y.N.: Convolutional sequence to sequence learning. In: International Conference on Machine Learning, pp. 1243–1252. PMLR (2017)
7. Goyal, P., Chhetri, S.R., Canedo, A.: dyngraph2vec: capturing network dynamics using dynamic graph representation learning. Knowl. Based Syst. **187**, 104816 (2020)
8. Goyal, P., Kamra, N., He, X., Liu, Y.: DynGEM: deep embedding method for dynamic graphs. arXiv preprint arXiv:1805.11273 (2018)
9. Grover, A., Leskovec, J.: node2vec: scalable feature learning for networks. In: Proceedings of the 22nd ACM SIGKDD International Conference on Knowledge Discovery and Data Mining, pp. 855–864 (2016)
10. Gulcehre, C., et al.: Hyperbolic attention networks. arXiv preprint arXiv:1805.09786 (2018)
11. Hamilton, W.L., Ying, R., Leskovec, J.: Inductive representation learning on large graphs. In: Proceedings of the 31st International Conference on Neural Information Processing Systems, pp. 1025–1035 (2017)
12. Harper, F.M., Konstan, J.A.: The movielens datasets: history and context. ACM Trans. Interact. Intell. Syst. (TIIS) **5**(4), 1–19 (2015)

13. Kipf, T.N., Welling, M.: Semi-supervised classification with graph convolutional networks. arXiv preprint arXiv:1609.02907 (2016)
14. Klimt, B., Yang, Y.: The enron corpus: a new dataset for email classification research. In: Boulicaut, J.-F., Esposito, F., Giannotti, F., Pedreschi, D. (eds.) ECML 2004. LNCS (LNAI), vol. 3201, pp. 217–226. Springer, Heidelberg (2004). https://doi.org/10.1007/978-3-540-30115-8_22
15. Liu, Q., Nickel, M., Kiela, D.: Hyperbolic graph neural networks. arXiv preprint arXiv:1910.12892 (2019)
16. Panzarasa, P., Opsahl, T., Carley, K.M.: Patterns and dynamics of users' behavior and interaction: network analysis of an online community. J. Am. Soc. Inform. Sci. Technol. **60**(5), 911–932 (2009)
17. Pareja, A., et al.: EvolveGCN: evolving graph convolutional networks for dynamic graphs. In: Proceedings of the AAAI Conference on Artificial Intelligence, vol. 34, pp. 5363–5370 (2020)
18. Perozzi, B., Al-Rfou, R., Skiena, S.: DeepWalk: online learning of social representations. In: Proceedings of the 20th ACM SIGKDD International Conference on Knowledge Discovery and Data Mining, pp. 701–710 (2014)
19. Sala, F., De Sa, C., Gu, A., Ré, C.: Representation tradeoffs for hyperbolic embeddings. In: International Conference on Machine Learning, pp. 4460–4469. PMLR (2018)
20. Sankar, A., Wu, Y., Gou, L., Zhang, W., Yang, H.: DySAT: deep neural representation learning on dynamic graphs via self-attention networks. In: Proceedings of the 13th International Conference on Web Search and Data Mining, pp. 519–527 (2020)
21. Trivedi, R., Farajtabar, M., Biswal, P., Zha, H.: DyRep: learning representations over dynamic graphs. In: International Conference on Learning Representations (2019)
22. Vaswani, A., et al.: Attention is all you need. In: Advances in Neural Information Processing Systems, pp. 5998–6008 (2017)
23. Veličković, P., Cucurull, G., Casanova, A., Romero, A., Lio, P., Bengio, Y.: Graph attention networks. arXiv preprint arXiv:1710.10903 (2017)
24. Wei, C., Fang, W., Hu, G., Mahoney, M.W.: On the hyperbolicity of small-world and tree-like random graphs. In: International Symposium on Algorithms and Computation (2012)
25. Yang, M., Meng, Z., King, I.: FeatureNorm: L2 feature normalization for dynamic graph embedding. In: 2020 IEEE International Conference on Data Mining (ICDM), pp. 731–740. IEEE (2020)
26. Yang, M., Zhou, M., Kalander, M., Huang, Z., King, I.: Discrete-time temporal network embedding via implicit hierarchical learning in hyperbolic space. In: Proceedings of the 27th ACM SIGKDD Conference on Knowledge Discovery & Data Mining, pp. 1975–1985 (2021)
27. Zhang, Y., Wang, X., Shi, C., Jiang, X., Ye, Y.F.: Hyperbolic graph attention network. IEEE Trans. Big Data (2021)
28. Zhou, L., Yang, Y., Ren, X., Wu, F., Zhuang, Y.: Dynamic network embedding by modeling triadic closure process. In: Proceedings of the AAAI Conference on Artificial Intelligence, vol. 32 (2018)

Engineering Annotations to Support Analytical Provenance in Visual Exploration Processes

Maroua Tikat[ID], Aline Menin[ID], Michel Buffa[ID], and Marco Winckler[(✉)][ID]

University Côte d'Azur, SPARKS/wimmics team, Inria, CNRS, I3S, Nice, France
{maroua.tikat,aline.menin,michel.buffa,marco.winckler}@inria.fr

Abstract. This paper focuses on the fundamental role played by annotations to support provenance analysis in visual exploration processes of large datasets. Particularly, we investigate the use of annotations during the visual exploration of semantic datasets assisted by chained visualization techniques. In this paper, we identify three potential uses of annotations: (i) documenting findings (including errors in the dataset), (ii) supporting collaborative reasoning among teammates, and (iii) analysing provenance during the exploratory process. To demonstrate the feasibility of our approach, we implemented it as a tool support, while illustrating its usage and effectiveness through a series of use case scenarios. We identify the attributes and meta-data that describe the dependencies between annotations and visual representations, and we illustrate these dependencies through a domain-specific model.

Keywords: Annotations · Provenance analysis · Visual exploration · Information visualization · Data quality

1 Introduction

The amount and complexity of digital data has increased exponentially during the last decades. Nevertheless, the value of these data depends on the ability of decision makers to find relevant information that describes the phenomenon embedded in data. In this context, visual analytic tools, such as kibana [9] and Tableau [21], supports human reasoning through interactive tools that embed visual representations to highlight and reveal relationships (tendencies and patterns) within data [19]. Nonetheless, the visual exploration of large data sets is not a straightforward process. It is not unusual that, during the exploration process, a data analyst is confronted with many sorts of errors (e.g., missing, duplicated, inconsistent data) [11], which should be fixed in order to complete the analysis. In this context, it becomes part of the data analyst's duties the task of checking the integrity and validity of data. Moreover, data analysts must be able to interpret the findings found along the process in order to make decisions [13]. For this reason, some authors [4,13] suggests that "the expertise to

© Springer Nature Switzerland AG 2022
T. Di Noia et al. (Eds.): ICWE 2022, LNCS 13362, pp. 204–218, 2022.
https://doi.org/10.1007/978-3-031-09917-5_14

analyse and make informed decisions about these information-rich datasets is often best accomplished by a team".

Annotations are a suitable solution to record and process design decisions made by teams as they can compliment existing information with a rationale. Previous works [1,12,17] have shown that annotations are useful as a means to disclosure hidden relationships between data, to record the results of discussion and decisions made by team members, gather internal and external feedback on artefacts produced, to connect pieces of information such as results of usability evaluations and the design artefacts, to document and to justify design choices by describing them retrospectively. And yet, the ISO standard 9241-210 is very silent about how to record and process design decisions. To the best of our knowledge, there is no study investigating the use of annotations to record the visual exploration process of data.

Inspired by these previous works concerning the use of annotations to design user interfaces [7] we investigate in this paper the use of annotations to support decision-making processes through the visual exploration approach. We propose an approach where annotations are used to support analytical provenance studies by allowing data analysts to reason with various evidences collected during the exploration process and also trace back the results to the source of findings [15, 22]. Our approach is implemented by a plug-in embedded into a visualization tool called MGExplorer [15]. The usage of our tools are illustrated through a set of use case scenarios describing the exploration of the Wasabi dataset [2], a large dataset describing music data.

The remainder of this document is organized as follows. The Sect. 2 presents the concepts of annotation and provenance analysis. The Sect. 3 provides an overview of similar works highlighting the lack of studies investigating the use of annotations in visual exploratory processes. The Sect. 4 introduces the rational of our approach and presents a proposal for extending the W3C annotation model to support the idiosyncrasies of exploration process using visualization tools. The Sect. 5 describes a set of relevant use case scenarios (including annotation of multiple types of views and objects, and collaborative use of annotations) that demonstrate the utility of our approach. Finally, Sect. 6 presents our conclusions and future work.

2 Foundations

In this section we revise two key-concepts that support the understanding our approach: annotations and analytical provenance.

2.1 Annotations

The first studies on annotations were focused on paper textbooks and then transposed to electronic documents [14]. Annotating allows the interaction between distinct pieces of information to serve different purposes: description (placing data in a context, add sources of information, etc.), evaluation (reporting quality issues, questions or concerns, etc.) or a combination of both.

The W3C Recommendation defines an annotation is as a set of connected resources featuring a body and a target that are interrelated, so that an annotation can shared across different systems. The Fig. 1 shows the W3C's annotation model, where the target corresponds to the element we want to annotate, and the content of the body would usually is the target. The annotation might contain meta-data that contextualizes the body's contents. Annotations can assume many forms (ex. text, sketching, etc.) and be attached to different artefacts (ex. documents, images, etc.) [7]. However, annotation types are not described in W3C recommendation and must be created to every context of use.

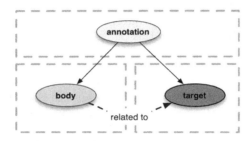

Fig. 1. The annotation model proposed by the W3C Recommendation.

2.2   Analytical Provenance

Analytical provenance is a means to understand users' reasoning processes while exploring data through visualization [18]. Users' interactions is used to identify patterns that can explain how users explore data visually. The outcomes of analytical provenance can assist the evaluation of systems and algorithms, building adaptive systems, model steering, replicating, reporting and storytelling [24].

We are interested in provenance data describing the history of graphical views and visualization states [20]; for that they can assist users on recreating analytical reasoning processes while supporting verification, replication, reapplication, and sharing of exploration paths. Such as data are often represented through history trees, as in VisTrails [3] which allows users to create visualizations during the exploration flow.

Typically, provenance data is visually encoded as a sequence of actions indicating users' interactions [24]. The data is then encoded as a graph where nodes are entities (or concepts) that change state during the exploration process connected through line segments that indicates their previous state. Graph encoding allows the user to navigate in the exploration path, while interacting directly with the history graph to generate a story of their analysis [6]. Tools such as MGExplorer [15] and GraphTrail [5] represent the workflow through segment lines connecting different views of data, allowing users to understand the actions performed from one view to another.

3   Related Work

Annotations are used for purposes as diverse as to provide an explanation by illustrating a drawing, to support the design process of interactive systems or to support decision-making processes by being used as decision cards [12]. As shown in [16], there are multiple tools available to annotate documents, images or textual data. In this work, we focus on annotating result sets from queries, expressed and explored through visualizations. Furthermore, we seek to record users' findings during an exploration process, as well as to share annotations with fellow data analysts to support collaborative data analysis. Hereafter, we present some of the existing annotation tools in the literature.

The SenseMap [17] tool supports browser-based online sensemaking through analytic provenance. The tool provide data curation to indicate relevance of nodes (views in the graph) through an interactive annotation process such as that: if a node is completely irrelevant, the user can remove it; if a node is not quite relevant but the user wants to keep it to have a look at some point, they can minimize it; and if a node is very relevant, the user can favor it.

The Glozz [23] environment for annotation and exploration of a corpus is based on a generic model that can conform (by instantiation) to any annotation paradigm. The tool allows the manual annotation of texts that may have been previously annotated, as well as the annotation and visualization of simple or complex structures (units, relations and patterns (or clusters)). It also allows the exploration of annotations.

The UAM corpus tool [12] is a software for corpus annotation and exploration that allows to annotate text and images.

The GATE (General Architecture for Text Engineering) [8] is an open-source infrastructure that provides a set of language engineering tools for collaborative corpus annotation.

The ANALEC [10] tool combines corpus annotation, visualization and query management. It allows ergonomic annotation via the concept of view and the use of elaborate filtering of the available information, frequency calculations, search for correlations, and generation of tables, figures and diagrams.

Our approach differs from previous works as we support the annotation of visualization techniques while linking it to the data represented in a view. Furthermore, our approach support collaborative data analysis through the sharing of annotated findings.

4   Our Approach

Our ultimate goal is to allow users to create annotations for recording decisions during the visual exploration process of data. We assume that annotations should formalize the relationship between the users' intentions (e.g., insights, questions, etc.) and actual artefacts of the visualization (i.e. the ones being annotated), such as a particular visual representation of the data. In order to accomplish this goal, we followed four steps:

1. **Create an annotation model** to describe the concepts covered by an annotation and the procedure to use the model together with visualization tools. Subsection 4.1 presents our proposed model.
2. **Define the dependencies** between the annotations and the visualizations being annotated (see Subsect. 4.2). The dependencies might refer to the scope and the diverse elements in the display (e.g., views, queries, set of itemsets, etc.).
3. **Identify the attributes of provenance data** that allows to store and restore annotations in the context (see Subsect. 4.3).
4. **Development of tool support** that implement annotations in the context of visualization. Our implementation of the annotation model is presented in Sect. 5 along with a set of use case scenarios to demonstrate the usage and feasibility of our tool.

4.1   Extending the Conceptual Model of Annotations

Visualization techniques can be generalized as complex artefacts comprising a **query**, which serve to fetch data from the data set, a **dashboard** that can host one or more **views** (each view featuring a visualization technique) that are composed of a subset of **objects** making reference to a particular itemset in the data set. This general definition can be applied to any visualization tool. It defines a scope where annotations created by the users can be connected to visual representation of data. The Sect. 5 shows different use case scenarios where annotations require a connection to views, objects, dashboard, and queries.

We also assume that an annotation might be a follow-up comment to a preexisting **annotation**, so that an annotation can be annotated. It might also be the case that an annotation is not connected to anything in particular, or be left over to be afterwards connected to a target.

In order to accommodate all these scenarios, we have extended the W3C annotation's model, as shown in Fig. 2. First of all, we create a new class called *Artefact* that is used to refine and explicitly describe any idiosyncrasies of what is annotated, i.e. an **information visualization**. This class allows to differentiate annotations created on other artefacts (e.g., documents, drawings, etc.). The remaining extensions refer to the type of **selector** that can be used to annotate the different elements and inherit from the class *Target*.

4.2   Dependencies Between Annotation and Visualizations

The annotation model described in the previous sections allows to describe annotations as singleton class *mge-annotation*, as shown in Fig. 3. The class *mge-annotation* is not connected to any other element, which grants independence of implementation of the approach from a particular visualization tool. The other

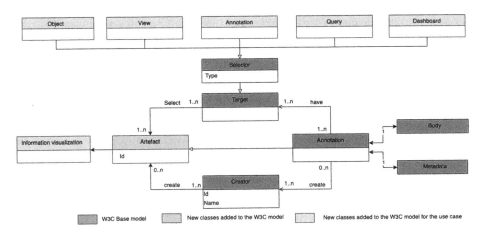

Fig. 2. Extended W3C annotation's model

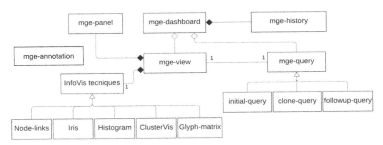

Fig. 3. MGExplorer model

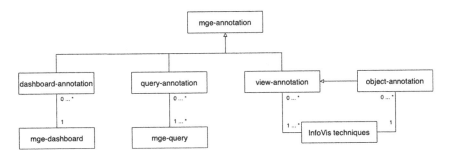

Fig. 4. Annotation targets available in MGExplorer

classes at Fig. 3 refer to the model used to describe the components of the tool MGExplorer that is used to illustrate the approach. Figure 4 shows the mapping between the singleton class *mge-annotation* and the other classes of MGExplorer.

It is worthy of note that the connections between the class *view-annotation* and the sub-set of data a view might contain, handled by the class *object-*

annotaiton, and the class *InfoVis technique* that refers to the actual visualization technique in the display. Further illustrations on how these connections are made at the tool level are illustrated in the Sect. 5. From a conceptual point of view, these classes also circumscribe the scope of annotations made on a quite specific (set of) object(s), a view displaying a visualization featuring relationships between data, a data source (query) providing the elements in the visualization, or a more loosely connected annotation that concerns the whole dashboard.

4.3   Attributes in Data Provenance

An annotation has a body and it also might have a meta-data. Whilst some of the body's contents is given by the users (ex. comments), other body attributes can be automatically collected by tools. Table 1 provides an exhaustive view of body attributes that can be captured when connecting different types of the target. These attributes are available through the classes in the mapping model shown (but not detailed) in Fig. 4. For example, when the user created a free annotation (i.e. target **None** in Table 1), we can only capture its *id*, *body* provided by the user, and the *timestamp*. However, when a user decides to connect the annotation to a target such as *Object*, it is possible to include other attributes automatically such as *views' title* (which describe the name of the window holding the data item), the *view's visualization technique* (which refers to the particular visualization being used to show data in the view), the *object* or the set of *views' subset* (corresponding to data items in the view). Such a combination of different attributes allows to determine the full context for data in the display and hence the data provenance.

Table 1. Annotation attributes

Body attributes	Targets				
	Object	View	Query	Dashboard	None
Id	x	x	x	x	x
View's title	x	x	x		
View's visualisation technique	x	x			
Object	x				
Object's type	x				
View's subset	x	x	x	x	
Body	x	x	x	x	x
Timestamp	x	x	x	x	x
Path sequence				x	

5   Use Case Scenarios and Tool Support

The use case scenarios presented hereafter, demonstrate the use of annotations when exploring the WASABI [2] data set, a SPARQL endpoint which consists of more than 2 million commercial songs retrieved from multiple sources on the web. In our scenarios we employ two queries. The first query retrieves data of a collaboration network of a particular artist described by type (producer, writer, performer) of collaboration. The second query retrieves data describing a network of artists by the genre of their productions.

The approach is implemented as a plugin for the tool MGExplorer [15]. This tool uses chained views to assist the exploration of multidimensional and multivariate graphs, which allows to depict analytical provenance via a sequence of views connected through line segments to represent their dependency, while supporting one or more visualization techniques applied to one or more datasets. Figure 5 depicts the exploration process as follows:

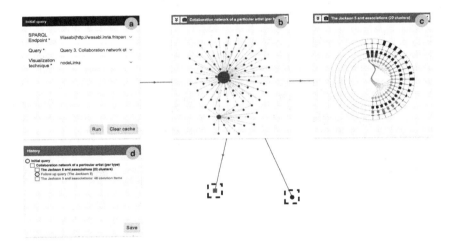

Fig. 5. Visualization tool

1. From a query panel, the user selects a SPARQL endpoint and executes a predefined query that retrieves a network data set describing a particular phenomena (co-authorship, co-occurrence, etc.) (Fig. 5a).
2. The resulting data set is visualized through a node-link diagram featuring a network (Fig. 5b). The nodes are interactive allowing to create new views (five techniques are available: network, clusters, pairwise relationships, temporal distribution, and listing of items) from data subsets (Fig. 5c). This subsetting operation is available in all visualization techniques, allowing the user to further explore the data set through different perspectives.

3. Upon each subsetting operation, a new view is created and linked to the previous view through a line segment. The provenance data regarding this operation is automatically included in a history panel (Fig. 5d).
4. The views can be moved around, allowing the user to rearrange the visualization space in meaningful ways. Further, users can hide any of the currently displayed views (Fig. 5e), which they may revisit later using the history panel, thus cleaning the display area in a way that helps them to focus on what is relevant to the task at hand.
5. The user can import new data by adding query panels, which resulting data can be explored seamlessly as the initial data set.

For the sake of coherence and to support analytical provenance, the annotation technique was implemented as a view that can be instantiated anytime and then connected to a view, an object, or the dashboard through line segments, or yet represented as a singleton when the annotation is free of context.

5.1 Overview of Annotations

While visually exploring the collaboration network of the artist *Michael Jackson* (Fig. 6a), we noticed a collaboration between him and *Justin Timberlake*. We decided then to further investigate it by displaying the list of songs that define this collaboration (Fig. 6b). We observe that the song on which these artists collaborated was released in 2014, which collaboration could not be possible since *Michael Jackson* died in 2009. To report this issue, we create a free annotation (Fig. 6c), where we indicate that *"Michael Jackson died in 2009"*.

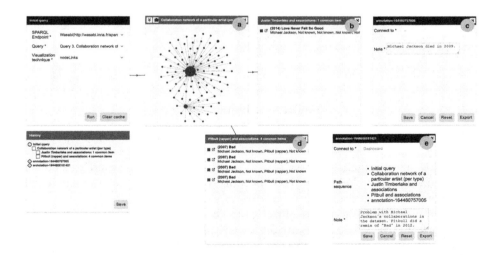

Fig. 6. Overview of annotations: choosing annotation's targets

We continue inspecting other collaborations of this same artist. We notice in the node-link diagram, a collaboration between Michael Jackson and Pitbull. The list of (Fig. 6d) shows that they worked together on the song "Bad" released in 2007. However, this cannot be true; Pitbull made a remix of the song "Bad" in 2012 but he never collaborated with Michael Jackson. To report the problem, we will annotate the whole exploration process by creating an annotation on the dashboard (Fig. 6e) indicating a *"Problem with Michael Jackson's collaborations in the dataset. Pitbull did a remix of "Bad" in 2012"*. This annotation is not linked to any particular element of the dashboard, but it rather retrieves the history (provenance data) of exploration.

5.2   Managing Multiple Annotations

When annotations are not connected to a particular item, we have to go through the whole data set to find the actual item causing issues. Alternatively, we can connect the annotation to the view causing the issue; as in Fig. 7a featuring a node-edge connected to the annotation *"Error: Pitbull didn't collaborate with Michael Jackson in 2007. He performed in a remix of the song "Bad" in 2012"*. This issue refers to two views in the display and we can connect both views to the annotation to reinforce our concerns. For that, by selecting those two views in the annotation window as shown at Fig. 7b, we create an annotation that connects to the two views through two line segments. Then we create a new annotation to report a duplicated song in the list of songs. Along the exploration process, the dashboard might become full of views. Thus, to reduce visual cluttering, we close this last annotation (Fig. 7e) which nonetheless remains in the history panel allowing us to retrace the exploration path and reopen the view if needed.

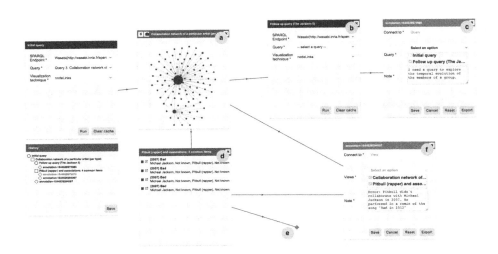

Fig. 7. Managing multiple annotations

To analyze the evolution of members in the group "The Jackson 5", we try a new query. We try to launch a new query from the node-link diagram (Fig. 7d) but we notice that query does not exist. Since this analysis is important for us, we create an annotation *"I need a query to explore the temporal evolution of the members of a group"* connecting the query view (Fig. 7e).

5.3   Annotating Objects in a View

Our approach also allows the user to annotate a specific item on a view. In this scenario, we demonstrate how to retrieve a data item causing issues with respect to the two collaborations of Michael Jackson seen in the previous scenarios. When exploring the node-link diagram, we first create an annotation and connect it to both links indicating the collaborations of Michael Jackson with Justin Timberlake and with the rapper Pitbull. As shown by Fig. 8a, the annotation view displays a description of the objects and it is linked to the view where the objects appear through a line segment. This approach works in every visualization technique. For instance, we further explore the collaboration between Michael Jackson and Pitbull using a different visualization technique, the ClusterViz. Here, we can create an annotation and link to the objects representing this collaboration (Fig. 8b).

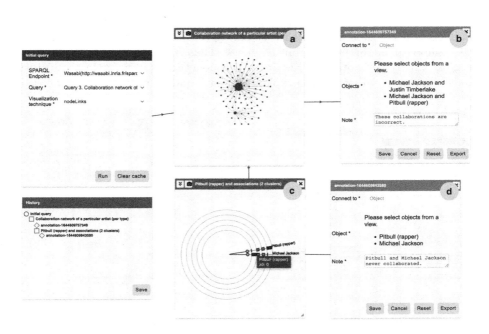

Fig. 8. Annotation of objects

5.4   Exporting Annotations

To export the data describing the annotations, we can use the button at the bottom of the annotation view (Fig. 9b). This action produces a *json* file (Fig. 9a), containing the attributes of the annotation, as shown in Table 1 and a link that allows the user to reopen the graphical annotation view.

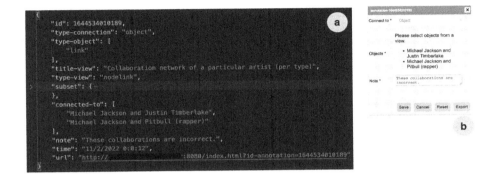

Fig. 9. Exporting annotations

5.5   Collaborative Use of Annotations

In this scenario, we demonstrate how annotations can be shared among teammates in order to support collaborative analysis of data sets. For that, we explore a data set describing the relationship network of artists based on the genre of their productions. We analyse the relationships using the node-link diagram (Fig. 10a), using the search bar under the visualization technique to locate the artist "Madonna" by. We found that Madonna produced songs of the same genre as other four artists. We use the visualization technique called IRIS (Fig. 10b) to identify what genres they have in common. The width of colored bars in IRIS represent the number of songs where Madonna have a genre in common with every other artist (in the periphery). By studying this chart, we notice an issue with the visualization: all bars have the same height and colors. However, as we hover over the bar between Madonna and one of the artists, the information box that appears shows that there is no song under the genre "dance" between those artists. We create an annotation on the dashboard to raise the issue (Fig. 10d) stating that *"Genres with no data shouldn't appear in the visualizations"*. Our colleague, *John Doe* could disambiguate or fix the issue. For that, our tool provides a shareable link of the dashboard, so that *John Doe* can open on their own browser and continue the exploration. When *John Doe* finds an answer to the issue, he replies by creating a new annotation *"It's a problem related to the system and not the dataset. It's fixed now."* which it connected to our the initial annotation raising the question (Fig. 10c).

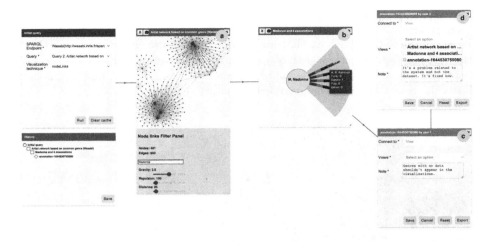

Fig. 10. Annotation sharing: collaborative use of annotations

5.6   Tracking Provenance Analysis

From the previous scenario, the user *John Doe* has an overview of the whole schema produced by us, including the data set, the query and the annotation created during the exploratory stages. This allows *John Doe* to track the path explored and retrieve the origin of the annotated data.

6   Discussion, Conclusions and Future Work

Annotation is a concept familiar on paper but it is often hard to implement and seldom fully exploited, beyond tools for annotating digital document. At the best of our knowledge, we could not find methods for annotating individual elements during the visual exploration of data sets. In this paper we discuss some of the problems for engineering annotations for supporting representation of provenance when exploring large data sets. On one hand, our approach allows to encode information about data provenance (i.e. sequence of data exploration) as part of the annotations, so when analyzing annotations it is possible to restore the full sequence of actions allowing users to go from queries to data in the display. On the other hand, annotations should help users to explain insights and decisions, which is necessary to perform provenance analysis on data. The validation of the approach is made by construction, which means that we demonstrate its feasibility by creating a tool and illustrating its use by a set of relevant scenarios.

Through the scenarios, we have shown how annotations can be used to provide information to complete the data set, point errors and mistakes, express user's needs, compare results, and share insights with other users. These examples are not exhaustive but yet representative for the use of annotations. We also have demonstrated how annotations can be extracted from the tools and yet include subsets of data and sequence of actions, thus become available to support analysis of provenance using other tools. It is interesting to notice that users might report issues with the data set using different combinations of annotations and views.

The originality of this paper concerns aspects for engineering annotation beyond digital document. As discussed here, we need to consider the specific context of the use of annotations (data sets and visualizations) for building the appropriate tools. We introduce a new topic and we want to level the discussion about the importance of having annotations to support the exploration process; for that we need innovative tools including the analysis of the provenance. Whilst the plug-in developed is specific to the visualization tool MGExplorer, we consider that the steps described in the approach are generic enough and can be adapted to support the development of other annotating tools.

We also demonstrated how to share annotations with other teammates to discuss findings. We want to advertise our tool to collect data from real users, not only for assessing the usability of the tool but also for collecting data enabling further investigations about analysis of provenance. In the future, we also consider to extend the possibility for including other annotation formats thus allowing to create annotations using highlighting of elements, support drawings, symbols, speech as replacement of text. Other improvements involve the synchronous edition and annotations.

References

1. Agosti, M., Ferro, N., Orio, N.: Annotations as a tool for disclosing hidden relationships between illuminated manuscripts. In: Basili, R., Pazienza, M.T. (eds.) AI*IA 2007. LNCS (LNAI), vol. 4733, pp. 662–673. Springer, Heidelberg (2007). https://doi.org/10.1007/978-3-540-74782-6_57
2. Buff, M., et al: The WASABI dataset: cultural, lyrics and audio analysis metadata about 2 million popular commercially released songs. In: The Semantic Web, ESWC 2021 (2021)
3. Callahan, S.P., Freire, J., Santos, E., Scheidegger, C.E., Silva, C.T., Vo, H.T.: Vistrails: visualization meets data management. In: Proceedings of the 2006 ACM SIGMOD International Conference on Management of Data, SIGMOD 2006, pp. 745–747. Association for Computing Machinery, New York (2006). https://doi.org/10.1145/1142473.1142574
4. Cernea, D.: User-Centered Collaborative Visualization. Ph.D. thesis, University of Kaiserslautern (2015). http://kluedo.ub.uni-kl.de/frontdoor/index/index/docId/4051
5. Dunne, C., Henry Riche, N., Lee, B., Metoyer, R., Robertson, G.: Graphtrail: analyzing large multivariate, heterogeneous networks while supporting exploration history. In: Proceedings of the SIGCHI Conference on Human Factors in Computing Ssystems, pp. 1663–1672 (2012)
6. Gratzl, S., Lex, A., Gehlenborg, N., Cosgrove, N., Streit, M.: From visual exploration to storytelling and back again. Comput. Graph. Forum **35**(3), 491–500 (2016)

7. Hak, J., Winckler, M., Navarre, D.: PANDA: prototyping using annotation and decision analysis. In: Luyten, K., Palanque, P.A. (eds.) Proceedings of EICS 2016 (2016)
8. Cunningham, H., Tablan, V., Bontcheva, K.: Language engineering tools for collaborative corpus annotation. In: Proceedings of Corpus Linguistics (2003)
9. Kibana (2022). https://www.elastic.co/kibana. Accessed Jan 2022
10. Landragin, F., Poibeau, T., Victorri, B.: ANALEC: a new tool for the dynamic annotation of textual data. In: International Conference on Language Resources and Evaluation, LREC 2012 (2012)
11. Laranjeiro, N., Soydemir, S.N., Bernardino, J.: A survey on data quality: classifying poor data. In: Proceedings of the 2015 IEEE 21st Pacific Rim International Symposium on Dependable Computing (2016)
12. Gutierrez Lopez, M., Rovelo, G., Haesen, M., Luyten, K., Coninx, K.: Capturing design decision rationale with decision cards. In: Bernhaupt, R., Dalvi, G., Joshi, A., Balkrishan, D.K., O'Neill, J., Winckler, M. (eds.) INTERACT 2017. LNCS, vol. 10513, pp. 463–482. Springer, Cham (2017). https://doi.org/10.1007/978-3-319-67744-6_29
13. Madanagopal, K., Ragan, E.D., Benjamin, P.: Analytic provenance in practice: The role of provenance in real-world visualization and data analysis environments. IEEE Comput. Graphics Appl. **39**(6), 30–45 (2019). https://doi.org/10.1109/MCG.2019.2933419
14. Marshall, C.C.: Annotation: from paper books to the digital library. In: Proceedings of the 2nd ACM International Conference on Digital Libraries, DL 1997, pp. 131–140. Association for Computing Machinery, New York (1997). https://doi.org/10.1145/263690.263806
15. Menin, A., Cava, R., Freitas, C.M.D.S., Corby, O., Winckler, M.: Towards a visual approach for representing analytical provenance in exploration processes. In: 25th International Conference Information Visualisation (2021)
16. Neves, M., Ševa, J.: An extensive review of tools for manual annotation of documents. Brief. Bioinf. **22**(1), 146–163 (2019)
17. Nguyen, P.H., Xu, K., Bardill, A., Salman, B., Herd, K., Wong, B.W.: Sensemap: supporting browser-based online sensemaking through analytic provenance. In: 2016 IEEE Conference on Visual Analytics Science and Technology (VAST), pp. 91–100 (2016). https://doi.org/10.1109/VAST.2016.7883515
18. North, C., et al.: Analytic provenance: process + interaction + insight. In: CHI Extended Abstracts Human Factors in Computing Systems, pp. 33–36 (2011)
19. Preim, B., Lawonn, K.: A survey of visual analytics for public health. In: Computer Graphics Forum, vol. 39, pp. 543–580. Wiley Online Library (2020)
20. Ragan, E.D., Endert, A., Sanyal, J., Chen, J.: Characterizing provenance in visualization and data analysis: an organizational framework of provenance types and purposes. IEEE Trans. Vis. Comput. Graph. **22**(1), 31–40 (2015)
21. Tableau (2022). https://www.public.tableau.com/s. Accessed Jan 2022
22. Toniolo, A., et al.: Supporting reasoning with different types of evidence in intelligence analysis. In: Proceedings of the 2015 International Conference on Autonomous Agents and Multiagent Systems, pp. 781–789 (2015)
23. Widlöcher, A., Mathet, Y.: The Glozz platform: a corpus annotation and mining tool. In: Proceedings of the 2012 ACM Symposium on Document Engineering, DocEng 2012 (2012)
24. Xu, K., Ottley, A., Walchshofer, C., Streit, M., Chang, R., Wenskovitch, J.: Survey on the analysis of user interactions and visualization provenance. Comput. Graph. Forum **39**(3), 757–783 (2020)

Lunatory: A Real-Time Distributed Trajectory Clustering Framework for Web Big Data

Yang Wu, Zhicheng Pan, Pingfu Chao, Junhua Fang[✉], Wei Chen, and Lei Zhao

Department of Computer Science and Technology, Soochow University, Suzhou, China
{20215227099,zcpan28}@stu.suda.edu.cn,
{pfchao,jhfang,robertchen,zhaol}@suda.edu.cn

Abstract. Web big data contains a wealth of valuable information, which can be extracted through web mining and knowledge extraction. Among them, the real-time location information of web can provide a richer calculation basis for existing applications, such as real-time monitoring systems and recommendation systems based on real-time trajectory clustering. However, as a trajectory is a sequence of user positions in the time dimension, the correlation calculation of the trajectories will inevitably incur a massive computational cost. In addition, such trajectory data is usually time-sensitive, that is, once the trajectory data has been generated and changed, the corresponding clustering results need to be output with low latency. Although the offline trajectory clustering has been well studied, extending such work to an online environment directly tends to incur (1) expensive network cost, (2) high processing latency, and (3) low accuracy results. To enable a real-time clustering on trajectory stream, we propose a distributed cLustering framework for hexagonal-based streaming trajectory (**Lunatory**). Lunatory covers three key components, that are: (1) *Simplifier*: to solve the problem of extensive network transmission in a distributed trajectory streaming system, a pivot trajectory data structure is introduced to simplify trajectories by reducing the number of samples and extracting key features; (2) *Partitioner*: to enhance the local computational efficiency of subsequent clustering, a hexagonal-based indexing strategy is proposed to index the pivot trajectories; (3) *Executor* extends DBSCAN to pivot trajectories and implements real-time trajectory clustering based on Flink. Empirical studies on real-world data validate the usefulness of our proposal and prove the huge advantage of our approach over available solutions in the literature.

Keywords: Spatio-temporal data · Real-time trajectory clustering · Distributed stream processing · Trajectory analysis

© Springer Nature Switzerland AG 2022
T. Di Noia et al. (Eds.): ICWE 2022, LNCS 13362, pp. 219–234, 2022.
https://doi.org/10.1007/978-3-031-09917-5_15

1   Introduction

With the proliferation of GPS-enable devices and mobile computing services [3], massive volume of trajectory data are collected to capture the mobility of vehicles. As one of the most fundamental problems in many trajectory analysis tasks [8,16,22], the trajectory clustering attempts to group a large number of trajectories into a few relatively homogeneous clusters to find representative paths or common moving trends, as exemplified in Fig. 1(a). Nowadays, since most applications that rely on trajectory clustering are time-sensitive, it is crucial to cluster the large-scale trajectory data in a real-time manner to maximize its value [23]. For instance, in the case of pandemic control during the COVID-19, a real-time monitoring and alerts of high-risk areas [22] can effectively reduce the chance of further transmission. Therefore, the real-time trajectory clustering, also termed as clustering on the trajectory stream, has been a hot topic in recent years.

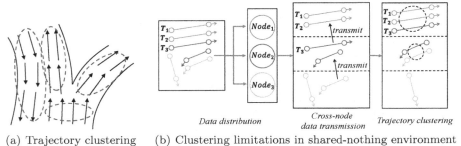

(a) Trajectory clustering   (b) Clustering limitations in shared-nothing environment

Fig. 1. An example of trajectory clustering and its limitations in DSPE processing.

However, most of the existing trajectory clustering methods are only for offline scenarios [1,10–12,14]. These methods perform clustering on entire trajectories, using specific similarity metric and designed clustering algorithms to cluster trajectories in a centralized environment. Despite their ideal clustering results, these methods are hardly applicable to the real-time environment. Nowadays there are some studies about trajectory clustering utilizing sliding window model in distributed environment [16,17], but the efficiency of these frameworks largely depends on the time span of the data set. Disatra [4] implements real-time trajectory clustering, but the accuracy of clustering result deteriorates due to its loose data structure Abstract Trajectory. Furthermore, a common problem that the computing state is generally split into different computing tasks under the distributed and parallel environment hinders our design of trajectory clustering. As shown in Fig. 1(b), the trajectories that belong to the same cluster(T_1, T_2 and T_3) are divided into different nodes($Node_1$ and $Node_2$). In summary, the challenges in designing real-time trajectory clustering can be summarized as:

- **Inadequate real-time guarantee**: Current clustering of trajectories often uses static offline trajectory datasets in an attempt to accomplish such operations through extensive offline computation. However, for a real-time pandemic aggregation alerting system, an offline situation or a system with insufficient real time can lead to many delayed judgments and unquantifiable losses. In such cases, we need to minimize the delay of data processing, which requires us to deeply integrate trajectory analysis with DSPE (Distributed Stream Processing Engine).
- **Accuracy Loss**: The accuracy loss is reflected in two aspects: (1) the trajectory as a whole will be broken up in different physical computing nodes by the distributed environment, which will either incur expensive costs when merging or cause performance bottlenecks in the aggregated computing nodes; (2) it is difficult to compress the real-time trajectory and design a reasonable data structure that represents the moving characteristics of real-time trajectory. The real-time abstract trajectory clustering proposed in [4] uses only one vector to represent the whole trajectory, which does not reflect the movement trend of the whole trajectory. Therefore, how to represent the trajectory is the one of the focus of our proposal.

To address the above challenges, we propose **Lunatory**, a real-time clustering framework for streaming trajectory. By integrating Lunatory into the existing mainstream DSPE [9], a real-time trajectory clustering framework is enabled, ensuring the accuracy of trajectory clustering results. Specifically, the major contributions of our paper include:

- We propose an online trajectory clustering framework Lunatory, which is compatible with accuracy and real-time.
- We characterize the feature information of the trajectory by simplifying the trajectory. At this stage, we propose an MDL-based trajectory simplification algorithm. Then we compress the simplified trajectory into a pivot trajectory.
- For efficient distributed trajectory clustering, we propose a complete pivot trajectory partitioning strategy based on hexagonal coordinates and extend DBSCAN to distributed line segment clustering.
- We implement all proposed methods on top of Flink [9]. Empirical studies on real-world data validate the usefulness of our proposal and prove the huge advantage of our approach over state-of-the-art solutions in the literature.

The rest of this paper is organized as follows. In Sect. 2, we divided the clustering methods into traditional and learning-based. We then present the preparatory knowledge for designing Lunatory in Sect. 3. We present the overall framework of Lunatory in its entirety in Sect. 4 and describe the details of each process in the framework. We analyse the experimental results in Sect. 5 and finally we conclude this article in brief in Sect. 6.

2   Related Work

2.1   Clustering Algorithms

There are currently many types of clustering algorithms, and here we choose the density-based clustering algorithm, which is the same as the one we used [4]. The high density data (within the region) belong to the same cluster is the basic idea of density-based clustering algorithm [23]. The typical ones include DBSCAN [7], OPTICS [2] and Mean-shift [5]. DBSCAN [7] finds the largest set of points of any shape that are density-connected by the radius Eps and the minimum number of points $MinPts$, but if the densities between clusters are different, the clustering results will significantly deteriorate. ST-DBSCAN [3] extends DBSCAN to be able to discover clusters on spatial-temporal data. In their work, they introduce a new density factor which represents the density of the cluster. It makes up for the disadvantage that DBSCAN cannot cluster points with different densities. However, these point-based algorithms do not consider the state information of a trajectory [23]. It makes them hard to be applied to trajectory clustering directly. In other words, if a trajectory is treated as a set of discrete points for clustering, a trajectory may be grouped into multiple clusters incorrectly. In addition, considering the spatial-temporal features of a trajectory, we need dedicated clustering algorithms for trajectories.

2.2   Trajectory Clustering

On top of point-based clustering algorithms, existing trajectory clustering methods can be roughly divided into two categories: partition-based [10,11] and density-based [1,12,14]. TRACLUS [12] first partitions trajectories into trajectory segments, and then perform a density-based clustering algorithm between trajectory segments. However, this algorithm cannot effectively handle incremental data in streaming environments. Based on TRACLUS, Li et al. [14] proposed an incremental clustering framework to allow new trajectories to be added to a database, and a new parameter is further introduced for a new step, i.e. generating micro-clusters before the final clusters. Other studies try to use sliding-window for trajectory clustering [16,18]. Mao et al. [16] address the problem of clustering streaming trajectories using the sliding-window model. They design two data structures to represent the spatial features of trajectories, and finally cluster streaming trajectories over a sliding window using OCluST. Since this framework incorporates the features of trajectories in a comprehensive manner, and also creates macro-clusters based on micro-clusters, it is expected to be time-consuming. Chen et al. [4] propose a real-time distributed trajectory clustering framework Disatra, in which an abstract data structure AT was introduced to describe the trajectory characteristics, and then use a density-based clustering algorithm on AT to generate clusters. Although Disatra extends trajectory clustering to the real-time environment, the accuracy of the clustering results is not satisfactory due to the huge information loss in the process of its radical trajectory compression, i.e. abstract trajectory.

2.3   Learning-Based Trajectory Clustering

The essential problem behind traditional clustering methods is that both the similarity definition and clustering processing are based on raw trajectory data [15], while the learning-based trajectory clustering framework aims to learn a deep trajectory representation, and then execute trajectory clustering analytics in the latent feature space [21]. The DETECT framework [22] selects the key parts of the trajectory and extracts their feature vectors to discover the context of travel activities, then the context-augmented trajectories are embedded into a latent space. Finally, it uses the loss function to refine the cluster assignment iteratively. Li et al. [13] propose a Seq2Seq-based method (t2vec) to learn trajectory representation for similarity calculation. This method is robust to trajectories of different length and sampling rate. Fang et al. [8] use t2vec and propose E^2DTC. According to the self-training mechanism, the framework iteratively optimizes the trajectory clustering assignment to make clusters more discriminative. Although the learning-based deep trajectory clustering framework has achieved excellent results in terms of clustering quality, this method has high requirements on the data used for training, making it hard to apply it in a distributed streaming environment. Hence, in this paper, we focus our research on traditional methods.

3   Preliminary

See (Table 1).

Table 1. Summary of notations

Notation	Description
$\mathcal{T} = \langle p_1, p_2, .., p_n \rangle$	Trajectory $\mathcal{T}$ consisting of n points
$p_i = \langle lon, lat, t \rangle$	A sampling point that forms the trajectory
$\mathcal{L}$	A set of trajectory segments
l_i	A trajectory segment in $\mathcal{L}$
ε	Distance threshold between pivot trajectories
ρ	Minimum number in ε-neighborhood
$\mathcal{N}_\varepsilon(l_i)$	The ε-neighborhood of trajectory segment l_i
$\mathcal{PT} = \{PT_1, PT_2, \ldots, PT_n\}$	A set of pivot trajectories
$PT = \{tc, \theta, bl, tr, t\}$	Pivot trajectory

Definition 1 (Trajectory). *A trajectory $\mathcal{T}$ is a series of chronologically ordered points $\mathcal{T} = \langle p_1, p_2, ..., p_n \rangle$, representing the trace of an moving object. Each point $p_i = \langle lon, lat, t \rangle$ denotes the object's location at timestamp t, and a line connecting two adjacent points is defined as a trajectory segment l_i.*

Although distance metrics like DTW and LCSS are widely used to measure the similarity between trajectories, since these methods are sensitive to trajectory length and sampling rate, we utilize the following trajectory distance to calculate the distance between two trajectories.

Definition 2 (Trajectory Distance). *Given two trajectory segments l_i and l_j, the start and end points of trajectory segment l_i are s_i and e_i. Similarly, the start and end points of trajectory segment l_j are s_j and e_j, respectively. Assuming that $|l_i| \geq |l_j|$, the trajectory distance between two trajectory segments is defined as $dist(l_i, l_j) = \omega_\perp \cdot d_\perp(l_i, l_j) + \omega_\| \cdot d_\|(l_i, l_j) + \omega_\theta \cdot d_\theta(l_i, l_j)$.*

Here, the weights $\omega_\perp$, $\omega_\|$, ω_θ can be adjusted as needed. We set these weights to 1 by default. An example of trajectory distance is given in Fig. 2.

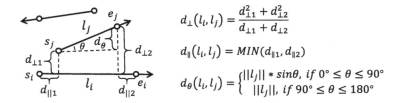

$$d_\perp(l_i, l_j) = \frac{d_{\perp 1}^2 + d_{\perp 2}^2}{d_{\perp 1} + d_{\perp 2}}$$

$$d_\|(l_i, l_j) = MIN(d_{\|1}, d_{\|2})$$

$$d_\theta(l_i, l_j) = \begin{cases} ||l_j|| * sin\theta, & if\ 0° \leq \theta \leq 90° \\ ||l_j||, & if\ 90° \leq \theta \leq 180° \end{cases}$$

Fig. 2. Trajectory distance

Definition 3 (Pivot Trajectory). *A compact synopsis data structure Pivot Trajectory $PT = \{tc, \theta, bl, tr, t\}$ is defined to describe the moving characteristics of a trajectory segment. Among them, tc represents the center point of a trajectory segment, θ denotes the deflection angle of the trajectory segment, bl and tr are the bottom left corner and top right corner of the MBR (Minimal Bounding Rectangle) enclosing the trajectory segment, respectively, and t represents the timestamp of the most recent trajectory segment.*

Definition 4 (Real-time Pivot Trajectory Clustering). *Given a set of PTs within a time window, called $\mathcal{PT}$, and a timestamp t, real-time pivot trajectory clustering performs trajectory clustering on the $\mathcal{PT}$ arrived before timestamp t to generate a cluster set $\mathcal{O} = \{c_1, c_2, \ldots, c_n\}$, which (1) $\forall PT_i \in \mathcal{PT}, \exists c_j \in \mathcal{O}$, so that $PT_i \in c_j$; (2) $\forall c_k \in \mathcal{O}, \forall PT_i, PT_j \in c_k$, PT_i and PT_j are densely connected; (3) $\forall c_i, c_j \in \mathcal{O}, c_i \neq \varnothing, c_j \neq \varnothing, and\ c_i \cap c_j \neq \varnothing$.*

Here, the concept of densely connected follows the same definition as in original DBSCAN [7], whose distance function is replaced by Definition 2.

4   Trajectory Clustering Framework

4.1   Framework Overview

Lunatory is a distributed clustering framework built on DSPE, which aims to achieve high-quality trajectory clustering in real-time. Overall, the Lunatory consists of three phases: pivot trajectory generation, hexagonal-based partitioning and clustering implementation, as shown in Fig. 3.

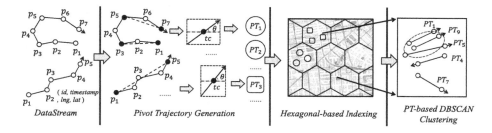

Fig. 3. Framework of Lunatory

- **Pivot Trajectory Generation.** First, we simplify the trajectory of a moving object. The purpose is to represent the trajectory with the least points while preserving the moving characteristics of the trajectory as much as possible. Ultimately, it can significantly reduce the computation cost while ensuring the accuracy of clustering results. The trajectory characteristics are extracted from the simplified trajectory segment to form PT_i. Since the PT_i contains a bounding box enclosing the simplified trajectory segment, partitioning the pivot trajectory ensures a trajectory segment will not cross multiple partitions. Therefore, it reduces the data redundancy and improves the utilization of node resources.
- **Hexagonal-based Indexing.** To avoid cross-node data transmission in a distributed environment, we adopt the hexagonal-based partitioning strategy to send PT with the same coding value to the same partition. At the same time, a overlap algorithm is designed to send pivot trajectories around the margin of a partition to its adjacent partitions, which improves the accuracy of clustering results while reducing the data transmission to the greatest extent.
- **Clustering Execution.** We perform PT-*based DBSCAN Clustering* on pivot trajectories in the same partition within a time window to obtain real-time clustering results. The aforementioned clustering process is performed in each distributed node. Finally, the clustering results in each node are collected to form final clusters.

4.2   Pivot Trajectory Generation

In the real-time environment, extracting more or less trajectory characteristics is a trade-off between high clustering accuracy and high efficiency. Therefore, we use the MDL (minimum description length) principle [19] to find the optimal division of trajectory.

Suppose that a trajectory $T = \langle p_1, p_2, .., p_n \rangle$ and a set of characteristic points $\{p_{c_1}, p_{c_2}, \ldots, p_{c_k}\}$. Every two adjacent characteristic points form a line segment $p_{c_j}p_{c_{j+1}}$. We use the two formulas mentioned in TRACLUS [12]: $L(H) = \sum_{j=1}^{k-1} \log_2(len(p_{c_j}p_{c_{j+1}}))$, which measures the degree of conciseness. $L(D|H) = \sum_{j=1}^{k-1} \sum_{i=c_j}^{c_{j+1}-1} \left\{ \log_2 \left(d_\perp \left(p_{c_j}p_{c_{j+1}}, p_ip_{i+1} \right) \right) + \log_2 \left(d_\theta \left(p_{c_j}p_{c_{j+1}}, p_ip_{i+1} \right) \right) \right\}$, which measures the degree of preciseness. Here, $len(p_{c_j}p_{c_{j+1}})$ denotes the Euclidean distance between p_{c_j} and $p_{c_{j+1}}$. Let $MDL_{par}(p_i, p_j) = L(H) + L(D|H)$ denote the MDL cost of a trajectory between p_i and p_j when assuming that p_ip_j is a simplified trajectory segment. Let $MDL_{nopar}(p_i, p_j) = L(H)$ denote the MDL cost when assuming that we don't need to simplify the trajectory $T = \langle p_i, .., p_j \rangle$, i.e., we preserve the original trajectory. Algorithm 1 shows the algorithm *MDL-based Trajectory Simplification*. We compute MDL_{par} and MDL_{nopar} for each point in a trajectory (line 5~6). If $MDL_{par} > MDLnopar$, we simplify the trajectory from p_{start} to p_{curr-1} to PT and add PT to set $\mathcal{PT}$ (line 8~11). Otherwise, we increase the length of a candidate trajectory segment (line 13).

Algorithm 1: MDL-based Trajectory Simplification

Input: Sampling points $\mathcal{P} = \{p_1, p_2, \ldots, p_n\}$
Output: A set of pivot trajectories $\mathcal{PT}$

1 Initialize PT by p_1;
2 start = 1, length = 1;
3 **while** *start + length $\leq$ n* **do**
4 $\quad$ curr = start + length;
5 $\quad$ $COST_{par} = MDL_{par}(p_{start}, p_{curr})$;
6 $\quad$ $COST_{nopar} = MDL_{nopar}(p_{start}, p_{curr})$;
7 $\quad$ **if** $COST_{par} > COST_{nopar}$ **then**
8 $\quad\quad$ Update PT by p_{start} and p_{curr-1};
9 $\quad\quad$ Add PT to set $\mathcal{PT}$;
10 $\quad\quad$ start = curr - 1, length = 1;
11 $\quad\quad$ Initialize PT by p_{start};
12 $\quad$ **else**
13 $\quad\quad$ length = length + 1;

14 Update PT by p_{start} and p_{end};
15 Add PT to set $\mathcal{PT}$;

Next, we calculate $PT_i = \{tc, \theta, bl, tr, t\}$ for each trajectory segment l_i. Since l_i consists of two sampling points, it is easy to calculate the trajectory segment center point tc, the deflection angle θ, the bottom left corner bl and the top right corner tr of the MBR enclosing l_i. We use the timestamp of the trajectory segment end point to represent the time t, which records the last timestamp of the current time window.

4.3   Hexagonal-Based Partitioning Strategy

The Grid system is essential for analyzing massive spatial data sets and dividing the earth's space into identifiable grid cells. In a grid-based spatial system, the more polygonal sides are used, the more a grid approximates a circle, and the more convenient it is to perform kNN query, etc. However, grid indexing requires the space to be filled with grids without gaps. It proves that the only shapes that can be used for grid spatial indexing are triangles, rectangles, and hexagons. Hexagons [6] have the most sides and are the closest to a circle, so in theory, they are the best choice in certain scenarios.

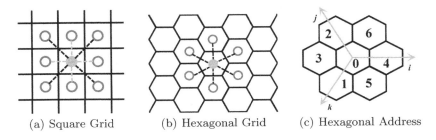

(a) Square Grid   (b) Hexagonal Grid   (c) Hexagonal Address

Fig. 4. Square grid and hexagonal grid (Color figure online)

We further elaborate on the difference between a square grid and a hexagonal grid. As shown in Fig. 4, hexagonal grid have only one type of distance between a hexagon center point and its neighbors, whereas there are two types of distance (marked as red and black) for a square grid. This property greatly simplifies the process of performing analysis and smoothing over gradients.

In general, for different levels of address generation, each hexagon contains the address of its parent hexagon. In this way, only the calculation method of the sub-grid address of each grid needs to be specified. For the sub-grid, it is only necessary to append the address of the sub-grid after the coordinates of its parent grid.

We encode tc from $PT_i \in \mathcal{PT}$ via H3 encoding and send PT_i to corresponding partition according to the encoding value of tc. Since we compress the simplified trajectory segment into a data structure PT with the midpoint tc of the trajectory segment, our index will not produce cross-partition data, so we can avoid the problem of cross-node data transmission in a distributed environment.

However, in the process of clustering, some extreme cases may occur. For example, the pivot trajectories in the same cluster are divided into different partitions, and these pivot trajectories are around the margin of the partition, which leads to the reduction of clustering accuracy. Therefore, we design a hexagon-based overlap mechanism. As shown in Fig. 5(a), we take the vertex of each hexagonal partition as the center of the circle, and draw an area with the radius of τ. For the PT_i whose tc falls within this range, we distribute it to two adjacent partitions and execute the clustering algorithm, respectively. The non-optimized cross-node data transmission will send the data to all other nodes, while our overlap mechanism only needs to send data to the two partitions participating the overlap, which minimize the data transmission and data redundancy while improving the algorithm efficiency. Figure 5(b) shows an example of the overlap. The red PT_i and black PT_j are expected to be in the same cluster. With the help of overlap mechanism, the red PT_i is sent to the partition containing PT_j, or vice versa, depending on which partition performs the clustering first.

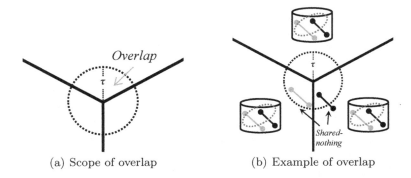

(a) Scope of overlap   (b) Example of overlap

Fig. 5. Overlap mechanism

4.4   Clustering Implementation

Since the pivot trajectories have both direction and length, which lead to arbitrary shapes of the clusters, we choose the density-based clustering method. Inspired by the idea of DBSCAN, Lee et al. [12] propose a line segment clustering algorithm. Similarly, we apply segment clustering to pivot trajectory within the current time window.

The trajectory distance is given in Sect. 3 Definition 2. Next, relevant concepts in *PT-based DBSCAN Clustering* are introduced:

– Core Trajectory Segment. Using the trajectory distance in Definition 2, we can calculate the number N of trajectory segments whose distance from l_i is less than or equal to the threshold ε. When N is greater than ρ, we call the trajectory segment l_i as the core trajectory segment, and define $\mathcal{N}_\varepsilon(l_i)$ as $\mathcal{N}_\varepsilon(l_j) = \{l_i \in \mathcal{L} \mid dist(l_i, l_j) \leq \varepsilon\}$.
– Directly Density-reachable. Given two trajectory segments $l_i, l_j \in \mathcal{L}$, if l_j is core segment and $l_i \in \mathcal{N}_\varepsilon(l_j)$, we call the trajectory segment l_i is directly density-reachable from the trajectory segment l_j.
– Density-reachable. Given a chain of trajectory segments $l_j, l_{j+1}, \ldots, l_{i-1}, l_i \in \mathcal{L}$, if l_k is directly density-reachable from l_{k+1}, we call the trajectory segment l_i is density-reachable to the trajectory segment l_j.
– Density-connected. Given two trajectory segments $l_i, l_j \in \mathcal{L}$, if there is a trajectory segment $l_k \in \mathcal{L}$ such that both l_i and l_j are density-reachable from l_k, we call the trajectory segment l_i is density-connected from the trajectory segment l_j.

Algorithm 2 shows the algorithm *PT-based DBSCAN Clustering*. Lines 1–6 and 16–18, the algorithm judge whether a *PT* is a core trajectory segment. If *PT* is determined as a core trajectory segment, the algorithm will continue to execute line 7–15. Otherwise, the *PT* is judged as a noise. Line 7–15, the algorithm computes the density-connected set of a core trajectory segment.

Algorithm 2: PT-based DBSCAN Clustering

Input: A set of pivot-trajectories $\mathcal{PT} = \{PT_1, PT_2, \ldots, PT_N\}$,
sliding window range $[ts_s, ts_e]$, two parameters ρ and ε
Output: A set of clusters $\mathcal{O} = \{c_1, c_2, \ldots, c_k\}$

1 Initialize cluster ID to be 1;
2 Mark pivot trajectories in $\mathcal{PT}$ as unclassified;
3 **for** $PT_i \in \mathcal{PT}$ *and* $PT_i.t \in [ts_s, ts_e]$ **do**
4   **if** PT_i *is unclassified* **then**
5   **if** $|\mathcal{N}_\varepsilon(PT_i)| \geq \rho$ **then**
6   Set cluster ID to $\forall PT_j \in \mathcal{N}_\varepsilon(PT_i)$;
7   Insert $\mathcal{N}_\varepsilon(PT_i)$ into a queue $\mathcal{Q}$;
8   **while** $\mathcal{Q} \neq \varnothing$ **do**
9   Get a $PT_k \in \mathcal{Q}$;
10   **if** $|\mathcal{N}_\varepsilon(PT_k)| \geq \rho$ **then**
11   **for** $S \in \mathcal{N}_\varepsilon(PT_k)$ **do**
12   **if** S *is unclassified or a noise* **then**
13   Set cluster ID to S;
14   Insert S to the queue $\mathcal{Q}$;
15   Remove PT_k *from* $\mathcal{Q}$;
16   cluster ID := cluster ID + 1;
17   **else**
18          $PT_i \leftarrow$ noise

We perform the real-time cluster to all pivot trajectories in the same time window. For $\mathcal{PT} = \{PT_1, PT_2, \ldots, PT_n\}$ in a partition, we randomly select an unclassified PT_i and judge whether PT_i is a core trajectory segment through trajectory distance and parameters, i.e., ε and ρ. If PT_i is the core trajectory segment, we continue to find all pivot trajectories density-connected with PT_i, and finally we set them as classified and assign the same cluster number to them. Otherwise, it is temporarily classified as noise. We repeat the above steps until all $PT_j \in \mathcal{PT}$ are classified.

5   Experimental Evaluation

5.1   Experimental Setup

Environment. We implement our proposal in Java and conduct all the experiments on top of Flink. The Flink system is deployed on a cluster which runs CentOS 7.4 operating system and is equipped with 128 processors (Intel(R) Xeon(R) CPU E7-8860 v3 @ 2.20 GHz). Overall, our cluster provides 120 computing nodes and a 512-core environment for the experiments.

DataSets. Experimental datasets are Chengdu and Beijing which are both real datasets with a certain uneven distribution, especially Beijing. Chengdu is around 900 GB publicly shared by DiDi Company's GAIA Open Dataset program, all from some district in Chengdu, Sichuan province, China; Beijing contains taxis' trajectories from Beijing, China. In general, the data structures of both is the same composed of vehicle ID, time stamp, latitude and longitude. In our experiments, these static datasets are released through Apache Kafka to simulate streaming scenario.

Baselines. Despite numerous trajectory clustering algorithms, there are few studies that are transferable to real-time scenario. Hence, we choose TRA-CLUS [12], ST-DBSCAN [3] and Disatra [4] as our baselines. TRACLUS is an offline partition-and-group framework, which can find common patterns in sub-trajectories. ST-DBSCAN is a classic algorithm for clustering spatio-temporal data. Disatra is a real-time trajectory clustering framework. Similar to us, the processing of trajectory is real-time. Nevertheless, it retains only one abstract data structure for a specific trajectory, which may reduce the clustering quality.

Metric. We study two performance metrics in our experiments: (1) *Latency*: the purposed Lunatory is to realize trajectory clustering under the condition of low latency. We measure latency by the running time of the entire framework. (2) *Accuracy*: we use the typical Silhouette Coefficient [20] as our metric for measuring clustering accuracy.

5.2 Efficiency Comparison

We evaluate the efficiency of our framework by comparing the execution time with ST-DBSCAN and Disatra. As shown in Fig. 6(a), with the increase of data volume, the execution time of ST-DBSCAN increases exponentially. In contrast, the latency of Lunatory is very low, and the increase of data volume has little impact on Lunatory. Figure 6(b) illustrates the latency between Lunatory and Disatra. Lunatory processes data slightly slower than Disatra. This is because Lunatory has an extra step of trajectory simplification than Disatra, and it spends some extra time to divide the current trajectory into simplified track segments.

Figure 7(a) shows the memory cost of ST-DBSCAN, Disatra and Lunatory. With the increase of data volume, the memory cost of ST-DBSCAN increases sharply. In contrast, the memory increase of Disatra and Lunatory is minor, and the memory cost of Lunatory is slightly more than that of Disatra. The reason is that Lunatory needs to store multiple simplified trajectory segments in memory. Figure 7(b) illustrates the throughput of ST-DBSCAN, TRACLUS, Disatra and Lunatory on different data sets. On both Beijing and Chengdu datasets, the throughput of Disatra and Lunatory is much higher than that of ST-DBSCAN and TRACLUS, which shows that our framework can be competent for trajectory clustering in real-time environment.

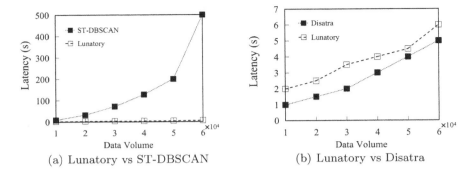

Fig. 6. Execution time comparison

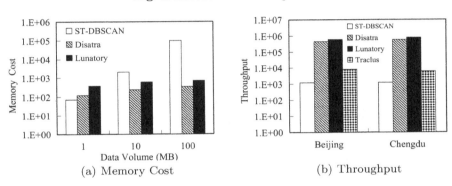

Fig. 7. Memory cost and throughput comparison

5.3 Accuracy Comparison

Silhouette Coefficient calculates the compactness of the same cluster and the interval between different clusters to judge whether the cluster is good or bad. The closer the silhouette coefficient is to 1, the better the clustering quality is. Figure 8 shows the silhouette coefficient values of Disatra and Lunatory in different data volumes and different time window sizes. We observe that when the window size is set to 720s and 7200s respectively, Lunatory's optimum silhouette coefficient is around 0.4. Although Disatra is on a par with Lunatory's silhouette coefficient, Lunatory always behaves better than Disatra. Combined with the experimental results in Sect. 5.2, our framework simplifies the whole trajectory, resulting in slightly higher execution time and memory cost than Disatra, but Lunatory's clustering quality is always better than Disatra, and has the same real-time performance as Disatra.

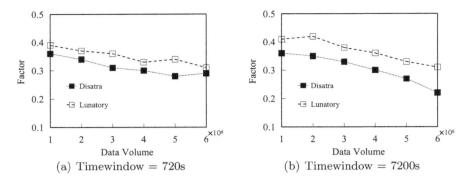

(a) Timewindow = 720s   (b) Timewindow = 7200s

Fig. 8. Clustering quality comparison

6 Conclusion

In this paper, we propose a distributed clustering framework for hexagonal-based streaming trajectory, called Lunatory. Each trajectory is simplified into a pivot trajectories with moving characteristics, then the pivot trajectories are partitioned by hexagonal-based indexing. In the end, pivot trajectories in a dense region are classified into a cluster. The main advantage of Lunatory is that it not only performs real-time trajectory clustering, but also has higher accuracy compared with other real-time trajectory clustering frameworks. With the involvement of a large number of real data sets and the analysis of the experimental results, it is proved that our framework has excellent timeliness and accuracy in real-time trajectory clustering over its counterparts.

Acknowledgements. This work was supported by National Natural Science Foundation of China under grant (No. 61802273, 62102277), Postdoctoral Science Foundation of China (No. 2020M681529), Natural Science Foundation of Jiangsu Province (BK20210703), China Science and Technology Plan Project of Suzhou (No. SYG202139), Postgraduate Research & Practice Innovation Program of Jiangsu Province (SJCX2_11342).

References

1. Agarwal, P.K., Fox, K., Munagala, K., Nath, A., Pan, J., Taylor, E.: Subtrajectory clustering: models and algorithms. In: Proceedings of the 37th ACM SIGMOD-SIGACT-SIGAI Symposium on Principles of Database Systems, pp. 75–87 (2018)
2. Ankerst, M., Breunig, M.M., Kriegel, H.P., Sander, J.: Optics: ordering points to identify the clustering structure. ACM SIGMOD Rec. **28**(2), 49–60 (1999)
3. Birant, D., Kut, A.: ST-DBScan: an algorithm for clustering spatial-temporal data. Data Knowl. Eng. **60**(1), 208–221 (2007)

4. Chen, L., Chao, P., Fang, J., Chen, W., Xu, J., Zhao, L.: Disatra: a real-time distributed abstract trajectory clustering. In: Zhang, W., Zou, L., Maamar, Z., Chen, L. (eds.) WISE 2021. LNCS, vol. 13080, pp. 619–635. Springer, Cham (2021). https://doi.org/10.1007/978-3-030-90888-1_47

5. Comaniciu, D., Meer, P.: Mean shift: a robust approach toward feature space analysis. IEEE Trans. Pattern Anal. Mach. Intell. **24**(5), 603–619 (2002)

6. Uber Engineering: H3: Uber's Hexagonal Hierarchical Spatial Index. https://eng.uber.com/h3/

7. Ester, M., Kriegel, H.P., Sander, J., Xu, X., et al.: A density-based algorithm for discovering clusters in large spatial databases with noise. In: KDD, vol. 96, pp. 226–231 (1996)

8. Fang, Z., Du, Y., Chen, L., Hu, Y., Gao, Y., Chen, G.: E 2 DTC: an end to end deep trajectory clustering framework via self-training. In: 2021 IEEE 37th International Conference on Data Engineering (ICDE), pp. 696–707. IEEE (2021)

9. Flink, A.: Apache Flink - Stateful Computations over Data Streams. https://flink.apache.org/

10. Gudmundsson, J., Valladares, N.: A GPU approach to subtrajectory clustering using the fréchet distance. IEEE Trans. Parallel Distrib. Syst. **26**(4), 924–937 (2014)

11. Hung, C.-C., Peng, W.-C., Lee, W.-C.: Clustering and aggregating clues of trajectories for mining trajectory patterns and routes. VLDB J. **24**(2), 169–192 (2011). https://doi.org/10.1007/s00778-011-0262-6

12. Lee, J.G., Han, J., Whang, K.Y.: Trajectory clustering: a partition-and-group framework. In: Proceedings of the 2007 ACM SIGMOD International Conference on Management of Data, pp. 593–604 (2007)

13. Li, X., Zhao, K., Cong, G., Jensen, C.S., Wei, W.: Deep representation learning for trajectory similarity computation. In: 2018 IEEE 34th International Conference on Data Engineering (ICDE), pp. 617–628. IEEE (2018)

14. Li, Z., Lee, J.-G., Li, X., Han, J.: Incremental clustering for trajectories. In: Kitagawa, H., Ishikawa, Y., Li, Q., Watanabe, C. (eds.) DASFAA 2010. LNCS, vol. 5982, pp. 32–46. Springer, Heidelberg (2010). https://doi.org/10.1007/978-3-642-12098-5_3

15. Liu, A., et al.: Representation learning with multi-level attention for activity trajectory similarity computation. IEEE Trans. Knowl. Data Eng. **34**(5), 2387–2400 (2020)

16. Mao, J., Song, Q., Jin, C., Zhang, Z., Zhou, A.: TSCluWin: trajectory stream clustering over sliding window. In: Navathe, S.B., Wu, W., Shekhar, S., Du, X., Wang, X.S., Xiong, H. (eds.) DASFAA 2016. LNCS, vol. 9643, pp. 133–148. Springer, Cham (2016). https://doi.org/10.1007/978-3-319-32049-6_9

17. Mao, J., Song, Q., Jin, C., Zhang, Z., Zhou, A.: Online clustering of streaming trajectories. Front. Comp. Sci. **12**(2), 245–263 (2018). https://doi.org/10.1007/s11704-017-6325-0

18. Mao, J., Wang, T., Jin, C., Zhou, A.: Feature grouping-based outlier detection upon streaming trajectories. IEEE Trans. Knowl. Data Eng. **29**(12), 2696–2709 (2017)

19. Myung, P.D., Myung, J.I., Pitt, M.A.: Advances in Minimum Description Length: Theory and Applications. MIT Press, Cambridge (2005)

20. Rousseeuw, P.J.: Silhouettes: a graphical aid to the interpretation and validation of cluster analysis. J. Comput. Appl. Math. **20**, 53–65 (1987)

21. Yao, D., Zhang, C., Zhu, Z., Huang, J., Bi, J.: Trajectory clustering via deep representation learning. In: 2017 International Joint Conference on Neural Networks (IJCNN), pp. 3880–3887. IEEE (2017)
22. Yue, M., Li, Y., Yang, H., Ahuja, R., Chiang, Y.Y., Shahabi, C.: Detect: deep trajectory clustering for mobility-behavior analysis. In: 2019 IEEE International Conference on Big Data (Big Data), pp. 988–997. IEEE (2019)
23. Zheng, Y.: Trajectory data mining: an overview. ACM Trans. Intell. Syst. Technol. (TIST) **6**(3), 1–41 (2015)

Web Mining and Knowledge Extraction

Building Knowledge Subgraphs in Question Answering over Knowledge Graphs

Sareh Aghaei[1]([✉])[ID], Kevin Angele[1][ID], and Anna Fensel[1,2][ID]

[1] Department of Computer Science, Semantic Technology Institute (STI), University of Innsbruck, Innsbruck, Austria
{sareh.aghaei,kevin.angele,anna.fensel}@sti2.at
[2] Wageningen Data Competence Center and Chair Group Consumption and Healthy Lifestyles, Wageningen University and Research, Wageningen, The Netherlands
anna.fensel@wur.nl

Abstract. Question answering over knowledge graphs targets to leverage facts in knowledge graphs to answer natural language questions. The presence of large number of facts, particularly in huge and well-known knowledge graphs such as DBpedia, makes it difficult to access the knowledge graph for each given question. This paper describes a generic solution based on Personal Page Rank for extracting a small subset from the knowledge graph as a knowledge subgraph which is likely to capture the answer of the question. Given a natural language question, relevant facts are determined by a bi-directed propagation process based on Personal Page Rank. Experiments are conducted over FreeBase, DBPedia and WikiMovie to demonstrate the effectiveness of the approach in terms of recall and size of the extracted knowledge subgraphs.

Keywords: Knowledge graphs · Question answering systems · Knowledge subgraph · Personal Page Rank

1 Introduction

With the growth of the data web, a massive amount of structured data has become available on the web in the form of knowledge graphs (KGs). To assist end users to access KGs, knowledge graph-based question answering systems (KGQASs) have emerged to answer natural language questions [2,5,10]. Although large KGs such as DBPedia with millions or billions of facts are ideal sources for answering questions, accessing these KGs for each given question has become an intricate challenge. To overcome this challenge, the recent KGQASs extract a subset from the KG namely a knowledge subgraph for the question posed over the KG as illustrated in Fig. 1.

A knowledge subgraph targets to prune irrelevant parts of the KG's search space and contains only a set of facts that is likely to capture the answer of a given question. Reducing the search space plays a key role in the efficiency of

© Springer Nature Switzerland AG 2022
T. Di Noia et al. (Eds.): ICWE 2022, LNCS 13362, pp. 237–251, 2022.
https://doi.org/10.1007/978-3-031-09917-5_16

different types of KGQASs including (1) rule-based, (2) information retrieval-based, and (3) semantic parsing-based systems (discussed in Sect. 2). Knowledge subgraphs lead to reducing manual works required for setting up the rule-based systems [1,24,27], pruning candidate entities and reducing training cost in the retrieval-based systems [20,22,23] and making improvements in the mapping stages of semantic-parsing systems due to preventing unnecessary computations [4].

Thus, the task of building knowledge subgraphs over huge KGs avoids exploring the whole KG for each question in KGQASs and narrows down the search space. Basically, a trade-off between answer presence and search space size [9] is required to build knowledge subgraphs. For example, the mean shortest path between entities in DBpedia is around 5-hops, so extracting relevant subgraphs only by navigating a predefined number of hops from a set of entities that represent the question's focus leads to a big part of the DBpedia however covers the answers, as an instance, given a simple question such as "Where is the capital of the US?", there is approximately 600K facts around 1-hop of the US's entity in DBPedia. In contrast, to further reduce the retrieved facts, commonly used techniques [12,14,23] even fail to capture answers of some simple questions that can be addressed through one fact (discussed later).

Therefore, the primary research question of this paper is *how to extract a knowledge subgraph for a posed natural language question that reduces the size of the KG significantly and covers the answer*. For example, given the question sentence "Give me all the companies with more than 1000 employees that were founded in the US from 1986 to 2000" over DBPedia, the extracted knowledge subgraph has to contain relevant facts around the entity of "the US" from millions facts stored in DBPedia which cover the foundation date and employee number of the companies located in the US. Note that the state-of-the-art KGQASs require to learn models for mapping the question to DBPedia facts to find the answer, where the extracted knowledge subgraph helps these systems to tackle with the huge search space size of DBPedia.

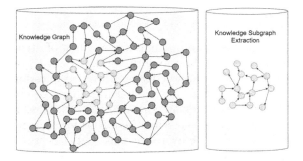

Fig. 1. Extraction a subset from the knowledge graph.

A general architecture to construct a knowledge subgraph for each question to avoid exploring the whole KG is shown in Fig. 2. The architecture consists of three main steps namely topic entity identification, neighborhood retrieval, and knowledge subgraph retrieval. The topic entity identification step employs entity linking (EL) to recognize named entities of questions which reflect the major focus of the questions and next map each entity mentioned in the questions to its corresponding entity in the KG (known as topic entity). Then, the neighbors around topic entities need to be retrieved through n-hop reasoning over the underlying KG. Finally, a knowledge subgraph which includes the topic entity as its first entity, is expanded based on various techniques such as heuristics, neural networks across the retrieved neighbors.

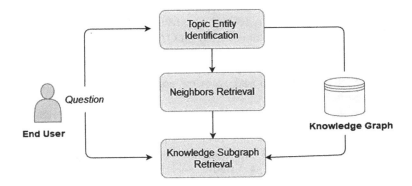

Fig. 2. General architecture of knowledge subgraph construction.

Personal Page Rank (PPR) [13] as a heuristic query-dependent technique is widely used in KGQASs to build a knowledge subgraph around the topic entity with respect to the natural language question posed by the end user [12,14,19,23]. This paper follows the research of [23] in using PPR and proposes a bi-directed propagation technique, called BiDPPR to compute relevance scores for nodes. The BiDPPR employs a bi-directed iterative process in which the scores are propagated through incoming and outgoing edges of nodes in each iteration. The major novelty of the proposed approach lies in detecting when there is no directed path from topic entities to answer entities, the PPR technique fails to build subgraphs covering the answer entities and then proposing a solution to deal with it. For example, given posed questions "Where does Piccadilly start?" and "Where was the author of the theory of relativity educated?" over WikiData and DBPedia, respectively, PPR technique fails to retrieve the knowledge subgraphs which cover the answers because there are no direct paths from topic entities ("Piccadilly" and "theory of relativity") to answer entities ("Dover street" and "ETH Zurich") over the underlying KGs as shown in Fig. 3. Note that although the question "Where does Piccadilly start?" only needs one fact to be answered, the PPR-generated knowledge subgraph does not include the answer.

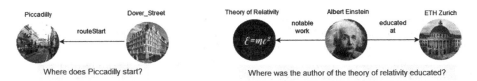

Fig. 3. The path between topic entity and answer entity

The main contributions of the paper can be summarized as follows:

1. An approach to build knowledge subgraphs over KGs for questions is proposed which follows the generic existing architecture shown in Fig. 2.
2. A new bi-directed propagation technique based on PPR is introduced to retrieve those entities from a KG which are more likely to answer questions.
3. Experimental results are demonstrated on QA datasets over FreeBase, DBPedia and WikiMovie and a comparison with available solutions to prove the effectiveness of the proposed approach in terms of recall. Furthermore, the results show how the proposed solution contributes to extracting smaller knowledge subgraphs.

The remind of the paper is organized as follows. Section 2 provides an overview on the related works. The proposed approach is discussed in Sect. 3, and Sect. 4 provides a detailed experimental evaluation including a comparison against state-of-the-art solutions. Finally, Sect. 5 concludes the paper and gives directions for future research.

2   Related Work

The research progress on building knowledge subgraphs in question answering (QA) over KGs can be divided into three categories including filtering-based techniques, heuristic-based techniques, and neural-based techniques.

1. **Filtering-based techniques** rely on predefined rules to filter the number of facts around topic entities. The definition of rules leads to limited scalability and researchers and developers require familiarity with the underlying scheme's KG. Moreover, these techniques are not able to significantly prune irrelevant entities. The introduced Graph Alignment Question Answering (GAQA) approach in [4], defines some query patterns and leverages users' interceptions through an interface to determine the number of required hops to retrieve the paths in the KG. Then, each given question is mapped into a query pattern according to the identified required hops. To prune unnecessary facts while avoid knowledge loss for answering the question, three filtering functions are inserted into the query patterns: (1) filtering out unnecessary predicates (e.g., predicates <http://dbpedia.org/ontology/wikiPageID>, <http://dbpedia.org/ontology/abstract> are assumed as unnecessary predicates in DBPedia KG), (2) filtering out unnecessary literal leaf nodes (e.g., the nodes with irrelevant

language tags have to be eliminated), and (3) filtering out unnecessary resource nodes (e.g., a set of unnecessary namespace URI is defined and resource nodes which belong to this set, are filtered). Finally, a SPARQL query is executed according to the mapped query pattern and the returned result is considered as the knowledge subgraph.

2. **Heuristic-based techniques** use heuristics to build a knowledge subgraph. The PPR [13] as a heuristic algorithm is widely applied in recent KGQASs to retrieve relevant facts around questions [12,14,19,23].

    The PageRank-Nibble (PRN) [3] is an approximate of PPR by applying a tolerance threshold (ϵ) which is used in [23]. Firstly, the topic entity is assumed as query node and all the paths with a maximum length starting at the topic entities are retrieved as a neighborhood graph. Then, the adjacency matrix of the neighborhood graph as a directed graph is generated based on the edge weights. The edge weight is calculated based on the similarity between the edge's surface form[1] and the question. To find the similarity between the question and the edge, GloVe[2] is applied to obtain vector representations and the cosine similarity between two vectors is calculated. Then, the initial PRN score of the topic entity is set to 1 and the other nodes are set to 0. Next, through an iterative process, the PRN score of nodes are computed. In each iteration t, the PRN score is propagated through the outgoing edges of the nodes. After T iterations, the k-top nodes with highest PRN scores (their scores are greater than ϵ) with edges among them are selected as the more relevant facts to the question. The main issue is that PRN fails to retrieve the answer entities once there is no directed path from topic entities to answer entities. The introduced approach in [14] follows the same idea in [23] and expands one hop for CVT[3] (Compound Value Type) entities in Freebase to obtain the extracted knowledge subgraphs (this expansion is applicable if the KG includes CVT nodes).

3. **Neural-based techniques** utilize neural networks to build a subgraph that contains facts relevant to a given question. The Pullnet [22] fulfills an iterative process to construct a subgraph. In each iteration, a graph convolutional network (graph CNN) is used to identify nodes that should be expanded using the pull operation. The pull operation retrieves the top facts from the KG around entity e which are constrained to have e as their subject or object. The retrieved facts are ranked based on the similarity between the fact's relation and the question using a classifier. Thus, the classifier predicts which retrieved facts are more relevant to the question. The major challenge of these techniques is the requirement for question-answer pairs as training data.

Current KGQASs can be classified as (1) rule-based, (2) information retrieval-based and (3) semantic parsing-based systems. In rule-based systems, much manual work is required in the preparation phase due to mappings from

---

[1] The surface form of an edge is the value of rdfs:label if the edge does not have a label, the variable part of its URI is adopted as the surface form.

[2] https://nlp.stanford.edu/projects/glove/.

[3] https://developers.google.com/freebase/guide/basic_concepts#cvts.

recognized entities to predefined queries or rules. Then, those queries or rules are evaluated over the underlying KG to retrieve the expected answer [1,24,27]. Extracting knowledge subgraphs reduces the manual work required for setting up a rule-based KGQAS. The information retrieval-based systems need to retrieve all candidate answers and then rank them to select the most pertinent answer. So, building a small knowledge subgraph can help pruning the candidate entities and improving the performance of the system [20,22,23]. KGQASs based on semantic parsing basically convert questions to executable queries. In these systems, the unstructured question is mapped to intermediate logical forms and then the intermediate forms are transformed into queries, such as SPARQL. Obviously, reducing the search space on KGs through constructing a pruned knowledge subgraph based on the input question makes improvements in mapping stages of semantic-parsing KGQASs [4].

Although the stream of research on QA over KGs has gained the solutions for building knowledge subgraphs, the recall and size of knowledge subgraphs still need to be improved. For example, filtering-based techniques are not effective in reducing size from a large KG such as DBPedia, PRN fails in building high-recall knowledge subgraphs once there are no directed paths from topic entities to answer entities, and neural-based techniques demand training question-answer pairs which are not available in many practical settings. This paper proposes a bi-directed propagation technique based on PPR (BiDPPR) to build high-recall knowledge subgraphs by considering incoming edges of nodes as well as outgoing edges while the size of the extracted subgraphs not being larger than those constructed by PRN.

3   The Approach

This section presents the proposed approach for constructing high-recall knowledge subgraphs according to the generic architecture shown in Fig. 2 that comprises three main stages including topic entity identification, neighborhood retrievals and knowledge subgraph retrieval.

3.1   Topic Entity Identification

The task of EL is to link an entity mentioned in a text corpus to the corresponding entity in a knowledge base [15]. Here, given a KG containing a set of entities and a set of questions, the goal of EL is to map each entity mentioned in questions to its corresponding entity in the KG [16,21]. The corresponding entities (known as topic entities) generally show the topic of the given question sentences. In this paper, the topic entities of questions are identified through existing EL tools including DBpedia Spotlight and S-MART. The DBpedia Spotlight system [17] automatically annotates questions' sentences with DBpedia URIs, and S-MART is applied for entity linking in FreeBase. This paper assumes that there is at least an entity mentioned in each question (known as topic mention), which shows the main focus of the question and EL identifies its mapping entity in the

KG. As an example, given the question "Give me all the companies with more than 1000 employees that were founded in the US from 1986 to 2000", the named entity "the US" is the topic mention which is mapped to <http://dbpedia.org/resource/United_States> as the topic entity.

3.2   Neighborhood Retrieval

Once the topic entity of the question is identified, all the entities in the underlying KG which have a distance (distance between two nodes is the number of edges in a shortest undirected path) smaller or equal n are extracted. The extracted entities along with relations among them are defined as neighborhood graph which consists of the n-hop neighbors around the topic entity (according to Definition 1). Generally, according to the number of required hops for reasoning over facts, questions can be grouped into two categories: simple questions and complex questions. A simple question, namely single-hop question, can be answered through only one fact whereas a complex question, called multi-hop question, requires reasoning over two or more facts of the KG [11,19]. Since, in real scenarios, the maximum length of path starting at topic entity do not exceed 3 in general [4], this paper considers $n = 3$.

Definition 1. *A neighborhood graph is defined as $G_N = (N_N, E_N)$ where N_N is a set of entities around the topic entity T_e with distance $d <= n$ from T_e (distance between two nodes is the number of edges in a shortest undirected path), E_N is a set of edges with distance $d < n$ from T_e and n is the depth (the longest undirected path) of the graph.*

To build neighborhood graphs with maximum depth n, SPARQL[4] patterns are defined according to n and T_e. Basically, the total number of possibilities to construct SPARQL patterns around the topic entity T_e with depth n is 2^n. Therefore, 2, 4 and 8 SPARQL patterns can be defined for depths 1, 2 and 3, respectively (the topic entities are shown in blue colour). Figure 4 illustrates all the possible states to construct SPARQL patterns with depth $n <= 3$ and Fig. 5 shows the SPARQL patterns when n is equal to 2.

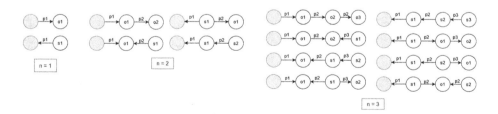

Fig. 4. Possible states to construct SPARQL patterns

---

[4] https://www.w3.org/TR/rdf-sparql-query/.

```
SELECT <T_e> ?p1 ?o1. ?o1 ?p2 ?o2          SELECT <T_e> ?p1 ?o1. ?s1 ?p2 ?o1
         WHERE {                                    WHERE {
         <T_e> ?p1 ?o1 .                            <T_e> ?p1 ?o1.
         ?o1 ?p2 ?o2                                ?s1 ?p2 ?o1
         }                                          }


SELECT ?s1 ?p1 <T_e>. ?s1 ?p2 ?o1          SELECT ?s1 ?p1 <T_e>. ?s2 ?p2 ?s1
         WHERE {                                    WHERE {
         ?s1 ?p1 <T_e>.                             ?s1 ?p1 <T_e>.
         ?s1 ?p2 ?o1                                ?s2 ?p2 ?s1
         }                                          }
```

Fig. 5. SPARQL patterns with depth 2

3.3   Knowledge Subgraph Retrieval

After creating a neighborhood graph for a given input question, a knowledge subgraph is retrieved around the topic entity across the neighborhood graph according to BiDPPR. The formal definition of a knowledge subgraph is provided in Definition 2.

Definition 2. *A knowledge subgraph is a subset of the neighborhood graph which can be defined as $G_K = (N_K, E_K)$ where $N_K \subset N_N$ and $E_K \subset E_N$ and N_K includes the entities which are more likely to be answer entities.*

The proposed technique, BiDPPR, tackles the issue of lacking a directed path from topic entity to answer entity in PRN through a bi-directed propagation process which is summarized as following:

– To consider the impact of incoming edges of a node during the propagation process as well as its outgoing edges, a linear combination of propagation along outgoing edges and incoming edges is utilized to find the BiDPPR score of nodes. If M denotes the adjacency matrix of the neighborhood G_N which presents the edge weights then the transpose of M can be considered as a matrix that includes the inverse relations between entities and let this matrix be M^T. Thus, the calculation of BiDPPR is formulated as:

$$pr_v^{(t)} = (1-\alpha)pr_v^{(t-1)} + \alpha\Big(\omega_1 \sum_r \sum_{<n,r,v>} w_r.pr_n^{(t-1)} + \omega_2 \sum_r \sum_{<v,r,n>} w_r^{(t)}.pr_n^{(t-1)}\Big) \tag{1}$$

Where w_r and w_r^t denote the weights of the edge r in both directions based on the adjacency matrix M and transpose of adjacency matrix M^T, respectively. Also, ω_1 and ω_2 are assumed as coefficient ratio for the incoming edges and outgoing edges, respectively.

– To compute the adjacency matrix, similar to [23], pretrained word embeddings GolVe is applied to generate the embedding of the question and the edges' surface forms. The cosine similarity between the embeddings of the given question and the edge is considered as the weight of that edge.

- To preserve the origin direction of edges, the impact of propagation along outgoing edges ω_1 should be greater than the impact of propagation along incoming edges ω_2.
- In the first initialization, BiDPPR scores are set to $\frac{1}{|N_N|}$ for all non-topic entities and the BiDPPR scores of topic entities are set to $1 + \frac{1}{|N_N|}$ (Eq. 2). Furthermore, the scores are normalized after each iteration to prevent any explosion.

$$pr_v^{(0)} = \begin{cases} \frac{1}{|N_N|} + 1 & topic\,entities \\ \frac{1}{|N_N|} & otherwise \end{cases} \tag{2}$$

Similar to PRN, the k-top nodes by BiDPPR score, along with edges among them are selected to make the knowledge subgraph after T iterations. It is noticeable that the sizes of extracted knowledge subgraphs do not increase in comparison to the extracted subgraphs by PRN. The size of the knowledge subgraph is dependant on K as well as ϵ. In Sect. 4 the coverage of PRN and BiDPPR for different values of K are compared.

Figure 6 illustrates the propagation process in PRN and BiDPPR in a sample neighborhood graph without any directed path from the topic entity A to the answer entity F. As shown in Fig. 6, in the first iteration $t = 1$, the PRN score will be 0 for all nodes except the topic entity A, and the propagation will only happen from node A (the edge are shown in blue colour). For $t = 2$, the PRN score will be non-zero for node A and its neighbors including B, C, D and E, and the propagation will happen from these nodes. For next iterations, the PRN score will be non-zero for the nodes A, B, C, D, E, G and H. Since H and G as dead nodes have no outgoing edges, their scores can not be propagated in the graph. Thus, the PRN score for the node F will stay at 0 by the end due to lack of a directed path from node A to node F. While in BiDPPR, the propagation does not start from a specific node (as the initial scores are not zero) however node A as the topic entity (with the initial score $\frac{1}{8} + 1$ according to 2) significantly impacts on its neighbors. Since the propagation spreads out in both directions in BiDPPR, the score of node F will increase remarkably in the next iteration $(t = 2)$ due to happening propagation along incoming edge of node B (note that the weight of the edge between F and B has to be high because its weight is computed based on cosine similarity between the embedding of the question sentence and the edge's label).

4   Experiments

In this section, the proposed approach is evaluated on Freebase, DBpedia and WikiMovies [18] with three QA-benchmarks separately. The code[5] is implemented in python and Stardog[6] is utilized to set up SPARQL endpoints. The PRN technique with $\epsilon = 1e - 6$ is performed.

---

[5] The GrafNet repository on the Github is reused according to the proposed approach.
[6] https://www.stardog.com/get-started/.

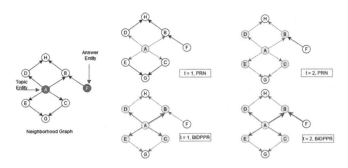

Fig. 6. Propagation process from the topic entity to the answer entity using PRN and BiDPPR

4.1 Knowledge Graphs

Freebase is a practical, scalable KG used to structure general human knowledge [8]. It was launched by Metaweb as an open, public and collaborative KG with schema templates for most kinds of possible entities such as persons, cities, movies, etc. in 2007.

DBPedia is extracted from structured data in Wikipedia through a crowd sourcing community that the main idea behind the extraction is using the key-value pairs in the Wikipedia infoboxes.

WikiMovies is the QA part of the Movie Dialog dataset and supports three different settings of knowledge including (1) using a traditional knowledge base (KB), (2) using Wikipedia as the source of knowledge, and (3) using information extraction over Wikipedia.

4.2 QA Datasets

WebQuestionsSP(WebQSP) dataset [26] includes 4737 natural language questions that were produced by crawling the Google suggest API [7] and are answered through Freebase entities. The questions need up to 2-hop reasoning from the KG. Moreover, the questions are more colloquial and biased towards topics that are frequently asked from Google [6,23].

QALD-6 [25] is the sixth installment of the QALD (Question Answering over Linked Data challenge) and focuses on questions which need up to 3-hop reasoning from the DBPedia. QALD-6 includes 350 training questions and 100 test questions which the test dataset is applied in this experiment.

MetaQA dataset [18] is a large-scale multi-hop dataset in the domain of movies. It includes more than 400k 1-hop, 2-hop and 3-hop questions, containing three individual datasets namely, MetaQA-1hop, MetaQA-2hop and MetaQA-3hop [20].

4.3 Metric

The number of entities in knowledge subgraphs is considered as a metric to compare sizes of knowledge subgraphs. Furthermore, recall as a classical metric to evaluate the effectiveness is adopted for showing the coverage of the constructed knowledge subgraphs. Here, recall is the fraction of the answers that are successfully retrieved by the subgraph as the following:

$$recall = \frac{retrieved\ entities \cap answer\ entities}{answer\ entities} \qquad (3)$$

4.4 Results

The experimental results for WebQSP, QLAD-6 and MetaQA datasets with 500 entities ($k = 500$) are shown in Table 1. On WebQSP dataset, the number for recall in PRN is 89.9%, this increased to 92.2% in BiDPPR. The BiDPPR is comparable to the PRN on QLAD-6, the recall improves by 22.1%. On MetaQA dataset, BiDPPR shows the recall improvement around 10% over 3-hop questions. In the case of MetaQA-1hop and MetaQA-2hop, both techniques achieve fully-coverage knowledge subgraphs.

Table 1. Results on WebQSP and MetaQA with 500 entities

Dataset	NPR	BiDPPR
WebQSP	89.9	92.2
QLAD-6	62.7	84.8
MetaQA-1hop	100	100
MetaQA-2hop	100	100
MetaQA-3hop	83.0	92.2

To illustrate that BiDPPR obtains higher recall knowledge subgraphs with fewer number of entities in comparison to NPR, WebQSP is selected as (1) WebQSP includes much more questions in compassion to QALD-6, and (2) Freebase is far larger than WikiMovies. Figure 7 presents the recalls of NPR and BiDPPR on WebQSP over the size of knowledge subgraphs. As the graph shows, the coverage of BiDPPR retrieval knowledge subgraphs is relatively quickly in comparison to NPR. For example, the number of entities to archive the recall 92.0% in NPR is $k = 1200$ while BiDPPR is able to achieve the same recall with $k = 500$.

One point to note is that BiDPPR uses the transpose of the adjacency matrices to consider the inverse direction of the relations. Since the transpose of a matrix can be done in $O(1)$ time (and space), BiDPPR does not affect the time complexity of NPR[7].

---

[7] Time complexity of NPR is O(m * n) [m = no. of iterations, n= no. of nodes].

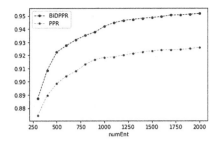

Fig. 7. Recall of BiDPPR and NPR on WebQSP with different number of entities.

4.5   Compared Approaches

BiDPPR is compared with NPR (used in [14,23]) according to Table 1. It is seen that BiDPPR finds higher coverage and smaller knowledge subgraphs for questions.

According to [14], the recall of NPR on WebQSP can increase to 94.9 with 2000 entities once the extracted subgraphs are expanded one hop for CVT entities in Freebase however BiDPPR gains the recall 95.2 with the same number of entities as shown in Table 2.

Table 2. Results on WebQSP with 2000 entities

Technique	NPR	NPR+CVT	BiDPPR
Coverage	92.6	94.9	95.2

The results reported by GAQA in [4] give the answer recall when answer entities are retrieved over the extracted knowledge subgraphs[8] and the coverage of the constructed knowledge subgraphs is not shown in its paper. Basically, GAQA can achieve full-coverage knowledge subgraphs if the query patterns are correctly identified due to it only filters the obvious unnecessary items (e.g., the predicates which are mainly used to link the KGs) however the knowledge graphs are significantly larger than those generated by BiDPPR. Since GAQA's source code is not publicly available, this research study re-implements GAQA's solution. In this re-implementation, 15 questions are randomly selected from each dataset (WebQSP and QLAD-6) and their query patterns are identified based on their SPARQL queries[9]. Figure 8 depicts the average size of the knowledge subgraphs (in terms of the number of entities) for the randomly selected questions and it is clearly shown that BiDPPR builds substantially smaller knowledge subgraphs.

---

[8] After constructing knowledge subgraphs, GAQA obtains answers of given questions over the extracted subgraphs based a graph-alignment method and then reports the results.

[9] The task of identifying query pattern needs end users' assistance in GAQA.

Furthermore, the recalls of the retrieved subgraphs by BiDPPR are 95.0% and 0.89 for the selected questions in WebSQP and QALD-6, respectively.

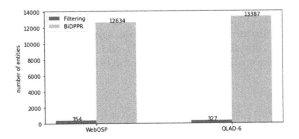

Fig. 8. Comparison of the knowledge subgraphs's size in BiDPPR and GAQA.

Compared to PullNet, BiDPPR needs no training data. PullNet has to train a classifier based on question-answer pairs to predict the relevant facts to questions. The results of PullNet are not directly comparable to the results of this paper due to PullNet's results show the recall after obtaining answers over the knowledge subgraphs and the source code is not available as well. However, according to [22], PullNet is able to retrieve far fewer entities with higher recall in comparison to NPR.

5   Conclusion

With the increasing growth of KGs, QA over KGs can be seen as the most promising approach to make the KGs easily accessible for end users. Since a KG is typically large and stores millions of facts, accessing the KG for each given question in KGQASs is difficult or even impossible. Extracting a small subset from the KG (known as knowledge subgraph) that is likely to contain the answer entity, defiantly reduce the search space and make the final answer extraction process easier. This paper proposes an approach including three major stages: topic entity identification, neighborhood retrieval and knowledge subgraph retrieval. The main focus of the approach is to introduce a new derivation of the PPR technique called BiDPPR to construct the knowledge subgraphs. Once there is no directed path from topic entities to answer entities, PPR technique fails to construct knowledge subgraphs which contain the answer entities. To address this problem, BiDPPR suggests propagating along the incoming edges as well as the outgoing edges. The proposed approach finds higher recall knowledge subgraphs with fewer entities than the ones created before. The effectiveness of the proposed approach in terms of recall and size is illustrated on WebQuestionsSP, QLAD-6 and MetaQA datasets which apply Freebase, DBPedia and WikiMovie as KGs to answer questions, respectively.

In the future, given a natural language question, a syntactic-semantic representation is created as question graph and the number of hops to retrieve the neighborhood graph is calculated based on the longest path in the question graph. Then, the task of QA over KGs is reduced to finding subgraph matches of the question graph over the knowledge subgraph.

Acknowledgement. This research has been supported by the project WordLiftNG within the Eureka, Eurostars Programme (grant agreement number 877857 with the Austrian Research Promotion Agency (FFG)) and the project KI-NET within the Interreg Osterreich-Bayern 2014–2020 programme (grant agreement number AB 292).

References

1. Abujabal, A., Yahya, M., Riedewald, M., Weikum, G.: Automated template generation for question answering over knowledge graphs. In: Proceedings of the 26th International Conference on World Wide Web, pp. 1191–1200 (2017)
2. Ait-Mlouk, A., Jiang, L.: Kbot: a knowledge graph based chatbot for natural language understanding over linked data. IEEE Access **8**, 149220–149230 (2020)
3. Andersen, R., Chung, F., Lang, K.: Using pagerank to locally partition a graph. Internet Math. **4**(1), 35–64 (2007)
4. Bakhshi, M., Nematbakhsh, M., Mohsenzadeh, M., Rahmani, A.M.: Data-driven construction of sparql queries by approximate question graph alignment in question answering over knowledge graphs. Exp. Syst. Appl. **146**, 113205 (2020)
5. Bao, J., Duan, N., Zhou, M., Zhao, T.: Knowledge-based question answering as machine translation. In: Proceedings of the 52nd Annual Meeting of the Association for Computational Linguistics (Volume 1: Long Papers), pp. 967–976 (2014)
6. Bast, H., Haussmann, E.: More accurate question answering on freebase. In: Proceedings of the 24th ACM International on Conference on Information and Knowledge Management, pp. 1431–1440 (2015)
7. Berant, J., Chou, A., Frostig, R., Liang, P.: Semantic parsing on freebase from question-answer pairs. In: Proceedings of the 2013 Conference on Empirical Methods in Natural Language Processing, pp. 1533–1544 (2013)
8. Bollacker, K., Evans, C., Paritosh, P., Sturge, T., Taylor, J.: Freebase: a collaboratively created graph database for structuring human knowledge. In: Proceedings of the 2008 ACM SIGMOD International Conference on Management of Data, pp. 1247–1250 (2008)
9. Christmann, P., Roy, R.S., Weikum, G.: Beyond ned: fast and effective search space reduction for complex question answering over knowledge bases. arXiv preprint arXiv:2108.08597 (2021)
10. Fensel, A., Toma, I., García, J.M., Stavrakantonakis, I., Fensel, D.: Enabling customers engagement and collaboration for small and medium-sized enterprises in ubiquitous multi-channel ecosystems. Comput. Ind. **65**(5), 891–904 (2014)
11. Fu, B., Qiu, Y., Tang, C., Li, Y., Yu, H., Sun, J.: A survey on complex question answering over knowledge base: recent advances and challenges. arXiv preprint arXiv:2007.13069 (2020)
12. Fu, K., et al.: Ts-extractor: large graph exploration via subgraph extraction based on topological and semantic information. J. Vis. **24**(1), 173–190 (2021)
13. Haveliwala, T.H.: Topic-sensitive pagerank. In: World Wide Web, pp. 517–526 (2002)

14. He, G., Lan, Y., Jiang, J., Zhao, W.X., Wen, J.R.: Improving multi-hop knowledge base question answering by learning intermediate supervision signals. In: Proceedings of the 14th ACM International Conference on Web Search and Data Mining, pp. 553–561 (2021)

15. Li, J., Sun, A., Han, J., Li, C.: A survey on deep learning for named entity recognition. IEEE Trans. Knowl. Data Eng. **34**, 50–70 (2020)

16. Ling, X., Singh, S., Weld, D.S.: Design challenges for entity linking. Trans. Assoc. Comput. Linguist. **3**, 315–328 (2015)

17. Mendes, P.N., Jakob, M., García-Silva, A., Bizer, C.: Dbpedia spotlight: shedding light on the web of documents. In: Proceedings of the 7th International Conference on Semantic Systems, pp. 1–8 (2011)

18. Miller, A., Fisch, A., Dodge, J., Karimi, A.H., Bordes, A., Weston, J.: Key-value memory networks for directly reading documents. arXiv preprint arXiv:1606.03126 (2016)

19. Qiu, Y., Wang, Y., Jin, X., Zhang, K.: Stepwise reasoning for multi-relation question answering over knowledge graph with weak supervision. In: Proceedings of the 13th International Conference on Web Search and Data Mining, pp. 474–482 (2020)

20. Saxena, A., Tripathi, A., Talukdar, P.: Improving multi-hop question answering over knowledge graphs using knowledge base embeddings. In: Proceedings of the 58th Annual Meeting of the Association for Computational Linguistics, pp. 4498–4507 (2020)

21. Shen, W., Wang, J., Han, J.: Entity linking with a knowledge base: issues, techniques, and solutions. IEEE Trans. Knowl. Data Eng. **27**(2), 443–460 (2014)

22. Sun, H., Bedrax-Weiss, T., Cohen, W.W.: Pullnet: open domain question answering with iterative retrieval on knowledge bases and text. arXiv preprint arXiv:1904.09537 (2019)

23. Sun, H., Dhingra, B., Zaheer, M., Mazaitis, K., Salakhutdinov, R., Cohen, W.W.: Open domain question answering using early fusion of knowledge bases and text. arXiv preprint arXiv:1809.00782 (2018)

24. Unger, C., Bühmann, L., Lehmann, J., Ngonga Ngomo, A.C., Gerber, D., Cimiano, P.: Template-based question answering over rdf data. In: Proceedings of the 21st International Conference on World Wide Web, pp. 639–648 (2012)

25. Unger, C., Ngomo, A.-C.N., Cabrio, E.: 6th open challenge on question answering over linked data (QALD-6). In: Sack, H., Dietze, S., Tordai, A., Lange, C. (eds.) SemWebEval 2016. CCIS, vol. 641, pp. 171–177. Springer, Cham (2016). https://doi.org/10.1007/978-3-319-46565-4_13

26. Yih, W., Richardson, M., Meek, C., Chang, M.W., Suh, J.: The value of semantic parse labeling for knowledge base question answering. In: Proceedings of the 54th Annual Meeting of the Association for Computational Linguistics (Volume 2: Short Papers), pp. 201–206 (2016)

27. Zheng, W., Yu, J.X., Zou, L., Cheng, H.: Question answering over knowledge graphs: question understanding via template decomposition. Proc. VLDB Endow. **11**(11), 1373–1386 (2018)

Dual-Attention Based Joint Aspect Sentiment Classification Model

Ping Gu and Zhipeng Zhang[(✉)]

Chongqing University, Chongqing, China
{guping2k,20191402011t}@cqu.edu.cn

Abstract. Aspect-Category based Sentiment Analysis (ACSA) aims to predict the aspect category and the sentiment polarity mentioned in a sentence. Most works treat it as two individual tasks: aspect category detection (ACD) and aspect category sentiment classification (ACSC), thus resulting in category missing and mismatch between sentiment words and aspect categories. This paper proposes a dual-attention based joint aspect sentiment classification model (AS-DATJM), which jointly predicts aspect category and sentiment polarity in one framework. Given a sentence, AS-DATJM firstly employs aspect aware attention in ACD to obtain the hidden aspect terms. With these terms as guidance, ACSC module aggregates relevant sentiment context over the Graph Convolutional Network. As a result, the inter-relations between aspect categories and sentiments can be captured and employed to predict both categories simultaneously. Extensive evaluations demonstrate the effctiveness of our model and results show that it outperforms the state-of-the-art methods on four benchmark datasets.

Keywords: Aspect-Category Sentiment Analysis · Multi-task learning · Dual-attention · Graph Convolutional Network

1 Introduction

Recently, the issue of sentiment analysis [1] has attracted great interest in the research field. Aspect-based Sentiment Analysis (ABSA) [2,3] task is an important fine-grained analysis task in the field of sentiment analysis. Since the main limitation of ABSA lies in the need of labeled aspect terms before sentiment classification, it is not suitable for practical application. Nowadays, many ABSA subtasks have been derived to handle this problem, for example, Aspect-Term based Sentiment Analysis (ATSA) [4,5], Aspect-Category based Sentiment Analysis (ACSA) [6–8] and others.

Compared with ATSA task, ACSA is more challenging and can classify the sentiment polarity of aspect categories without concerning the target aspect terms in the context. Therefore, we focus on Aspect-Category based Sentiment Analysis (ACSA) in this paper. Generally, ACSA can be divided into two subtasks: Aspect Category Detection (ACD) and Aspect Category Sentiment Classification (ACSC). Figure 1 presents an example to illustrate the two subtasks.

© Springer Nature Switzerland AG 2022
T. Di Noia et al. (Eds.): ICWE 2022, LNCS 13362, pp. 252–267, 2022.
https://doi.org/10.1007/978-3-031-09917-5_17

Specifically, ACD subtask detects the two aspect categories of ambience and service mentioned in the review sentence, and ACSC subtask predicts that the sentiment polarities of ambience and service are positive and negative, respectively.

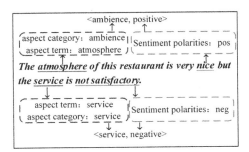

Fig. 1. The blue dashed box represents the ACD task, and the red dashed box represents the ACSC task. The underlined words are key examples, and the predicted results of the sentence are in angle brackets.

The state-of-the-art techniques for ACSA have been built on a variety of deep learning models. Zhou et al. [9] employed a semi-supervised word embedding method in most review sentences and generated mixed features to predict the aspect category. Wang et al. in 2016 [10], Tay et al. in 2018 [11] and Hu et al. in 2019 [12] labeled the aspect category and assigned appropriate sentiment words to the given aspect category. Xue and Li [13] applied the convolutional neural network to obtain the sentiment features in a sentence, and then through gating mechanism to sift the sentiment features related to the aspect category. Chi et al. [14] used aspect category to assist in constructing sentence features and transformed ACSA into sentence-pair classification. Cheng et al. [15] established a hierarchical attention network to obtain the classification of aspect category and aspect sentiment after manually labeling aspect terms. Li et al. [7] leveraged ACD as an auxiliary to find words that indicate the aspect category, and then judged the sentiment polarity of sentences according to the sentiment polarity of words. The above methods performed ACD and ACSC separately and ignored the interrelation of the two subtasks, which could lead to error propagation in ACSA.

In order to reflect the interrelation of ACSA's internal subtasks, Schmitt et al. [16] employed the end-to-end LSTM model to establish a joint model corresponding to the aspect category through extending sentiment labels, and once generate all aspect categories and aspect sentiment. Cai et al. [6] proposed to construct a hierarchical output model through the inner-relation between aspect category and sentiment polarity. However, these models were prone to missing some aspect categories and mismatching sentiments in case of multiple categories.

In this paper, we propose a dual-attention based joint aspect sentiment classification model (AS-DATJM), which performs ACD and ACSC tasks in an end-to-end manner and output the aspect category and category sentiment polarity simultaneously. Our model mainly consists of three modules. First, the aspect-specific representation module constructs the word vector representation with specific aspect information, and then employs Bi-LSTM to encode the contextual information of sentence under different aspect categories, which enables the model to obtain the feature representation of context in a sentence. On this basis, ACD module gets aspect term and sentence representation through aspect-specific attention mechanism. To model the relationship between aspect term and sentiment, ACSC module first adopts multi-layer GCN to encode each word by considering syntactic dependency relationship, and then employs self-attention mechanism to get sentiment words that have a modified relation to the aspect term. In this way, we can obtain the aspect-related sentiment feature more accurately, and alleviate the mismatch problem between aspect categories and sentiments. Finally, our model employs the prediction representations of aspect category and aspect sentiment obtained in the two modules to synchronously achieve the final prediction results. The AS-DATJM model code of this article has been open sourced[1].

In summary, our contribution is four-fold:

- We propose a novel joint model AS-DATJM for ACSA. This model adopts dual-attention mechanism to combine aspect category detection and aspect category sentiment classification tasks into a whole.
- Without labelling of aspect terms in the training set, the model can automatically discover the hidden aspect terms and employ them in detecting aspect categories to alleviate the missing problem of aspect categories.
- We use the multi-layer GCN to encode the syntactic dependency and through self-attention mechanism, it can focus on the description words that have a modified or sentiment relation with specific aspect terms to alleviate the mismatch between aspect categories and sentiment words.
- The experimental results demonstrate the effectiveness of AS-DATJM model in the four benchmark product review datasets from SemEval2015 and SemEval2016. Our model obviously improves performance especially in the case of more aspect categories.

2   Model Description

2.1   Problem Formulation

Given a review sentence with n words, $Text = \{w_1, w_2, w_3, \ldots, w_n\}$, the main task of ACSA is to detect the aspect categories mentioned in the sentence and identify the associated sentiment polarities. Formally, let $Aspect = \{v_1, v_2, \ldots, v_m\}$, be the set of m aspect categories and $Sentiment =$

---

[1] https://github.com/Codesleep/AS-DATJM.git.

$\{positive, negative, neutral\}$, be the set of sentiment polarity labels. For each review sentence, the goal of ACSA task is to generate a group of aspect category-sentiment polarity pairs, denoted as $\{\ldots, (y_i^a, y_i^s), \ldots\}$ where y_i^a represents the i-th aspect category in the input sentence and y_i^s represents the sentiment polarity corresponding to the i-th aspect category.

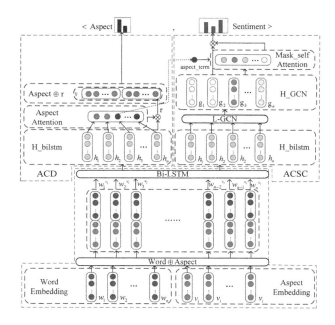

Fig. 2. The left is ACD module, the right is ACSC module, and the bottom is the aspect-specific representation module. $\oplus$ represents the concatenating operation between vectors. $\otimes$ represents the product operation between vectors.

For the ACSA task, we consider ACD and ACSC as a whole and detect aspect categories and corresponding sentiment polarities simultaneously. In the model, we firstly generate aspect-specific word representation and encode the contextual information of sentence with Bi-LSTM. Next in ACD module, we apply an attention mechanism to obtain the associated aspect terms and predict whether the sentence mentions the aspect category. Then employing the discovered aspect term as a query, we find out the aspect category-related sentiment words through multi-layer GCN and self-attention mechanism. Finally, we obtain the prediction of aspect category-sentiment polarity pairs. Figure 2 provides an overview of AS-DATJM.

2.2   Aspect-Specific Representation Module

Word Representation with Given Aspect: When considering different aspects in a review sentence, the importance of each word to that aspect determines its feature representation. Therefore, we will learn representation vectors for words with respect to each aspect. Suppose the vector of a sentence is $w \in R^{n \times d}$ where n is the number of words in the sentence and d is the dimension of the word vector. The i-th aspect category vector in a sentence is $v_i \in R^{1 \times d}$ Then, the word vector w^{v_i} with the i-th aspect category can be expressed as:

$$w^{v_i} = w \oplus [v_i]^{n \times d} \tag{1}$$

where $w^{v_i} \in R^{n \times 2d}$, $\oplus$ operator means to concatenate two vectors, $[v_i]^{n \times d}$ means to repeatedly expand the aspect category vector n times.

Contextual Encoding with Bi-LSTM: In order to obtain the long-term dependency of a review sentence, each aspect w^{v_i} is put into a Bi-LSTM network. We can obtain two hidden representations $\overrightarrow{H}$, $\overleftarrow{H}$ and then concatenate the forward hidden state and backward hidden state of each word:

$$\overrightarrow{H} = \overrightarrow{LSTM}(w^{v_i}) \quad \overleftarrow{H} = \overleftarrow{LSTM}(w^{v_i}) \tag{2}$$

$$H_{bi-lstm} = [\overrightarrow{H} : \overleftarrow{H}] \tag{3}$$

where $\overrightarrow{H} \in R^{n \times d}$ is the output of the forward LSTM hidden layer, $\overleftarrow{H} \in R^{n \times d}$ is the output of the afterward LSTM hidden layer and $H_{bi-lstm} \in R^{n \times 2d}$ is the output of the Bi-LSTM final hidden layer.

2.3   ACD Module

Given m aspects, we treat ACD task as a multi-label binary classification problem. For each aspect category, we learn different sentence representations with an attention mechanism, and obtain the specific aspect term which contributes most to the aspect.

Aspect Attention Mechanism: Here, we use the aspect's hidden states to supervise the generation of attention vector:

$$M = tanh(W_m H_{bi-lstm}) \tag{4}$$

$$\alpha_a = softmax(W_a M) \tag{5}$$

where $M \in R^{n \times 2d}$, $\alpha_a \in R^n$ is the aspect attention weight, W_m and W_a are the weight during training and $H_{bi-lstm}$ is the output of Bi-LSTM hidden layer.

Obtain the Aspect Term: To obtain the sentiment context words of a certain aspect, we first need to identify its relevant terms with respect to the aspect. It is well known that aspect terms contain the most aspect category information in the sentence, in other words, the words with the highest aspect attention weight. We can obtain the aspect terms as follows:

$$loc_{term} = Max_{loc}(\alpha_a) \tag{6}$$

where loc_{term} is the position of aspect terms in the sentence and the function Max_{loc} computes the position of term with the highest attention weight.

Sentence Representation for ACD: To enable our model to capture more aspect category features in the sentence, the aspect-specific sentence representation of the i-th aspect is generated by concatenating the aspect category vector v_i and the attention weighted representation of sentence:

$$r = \alpha_a H_{bi-lstm} \tag{7}$$

$$r_a = tanh(W_{ra}(r \oplus v_i)) \tag{8}$$

where r represents the attention-weighted representation of specific aspect in a sentence, $r_a \in R^{1 \times 3d}$ represents the aspect-specific sentence representation and W_{ra} represents the weight during training.

Aspect Category Classification: The sentence representation r_a is fed into a fully connected layer with sigmoid function to generate aspect category probability distribution p_i^a. Formally, for the i-th aspect category:

$$p_i^a = sigmoid(W_{pa}r_a + b_{pa}) \tag{9}$$

$$y_i^a = 1 \quad if(p_i^a > \delta) \tag{10}$$

where the weight W_{pa} and bias b_{pa} are training parameters during training, and δ is a threshold, which converts the probability into a binary output. If the i-th aspect category is mentioned in the sentence, $y_i^a = 1$, otherwise $y_i^a = 0$.

2.4   ACSC Module

When performing sentiment classification in a certain aspect of a review sentence, to avoid mismatching between aspect categories and sentiments, we employ multi-layer GCN network and self-attention mechanism to capture the contexts that have modified or sentiment relation to the aspect term. On this basis, we can obtain the sentence representation for sentiment classification.

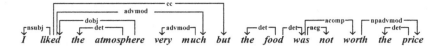

Fig. 3. An example of a dependency tree.

Multi-layer GCN Network: The syntactic dependency of a review sentence can facilitate to understand the modified or sentiment relation between words. In order to obtain the syntactic dependency of a given sentence, we first utilize spaCy[2] to establish the syntactic dependency tree of a review sentence (as shown in Fig. 3), and then construct the adjacency matrix $A \in R^{n \times n}$ with syntactic dependency according to the sentence dependency tree and the words in the sentence. Notably, dependency tree is diagraph. Although traditional GCN do not consider the direction problem, it can still be adjusted to accommodate the orientation perception. Therefore, we propose two variants of the AS-DATJM model, the AS-DATJM-DG model based on the undirected dependency graph and the AS-DATJM-DT model based on the directed dependency tree. The only difference between them is their adjacent matrix that of AS-DATJM-DT is much sparser than AS-DATJM-DG. In addition, based on the self-looping thought of GCN [17], we manually set each word to be adjacent to itself, that is, the diagonal value of the adjacency matrix A is 1. The details are as follows:

$$\tilde{H}_{gcn}^l = AW^l H_{gcn}^{l-1} \tag{11}$$

$$H_{gcn}^l = ReLU(\tilde{H}_{gcn}^l + b^l) \tag{12}$$

where H_{gcn}^l denotes the hidden feature matrix with syntactic dependency information, $H_{gcn}^l \in R^{n \times 2d}$, $\tilde{H}_{gcn}^l \in R^{n \times 2d}$, weight W^l and bias b^l are training parameters and H_{gcn}^{l-1} is the output of the upper level GCN network. When $l=1$, H_{gcn}^{l-1} is $H_{bi-lstm}$ the output of Bi-LSTM hidden layer.

Sentiment Attention Mechanism: We leverage the position of the aspect term obtained in the ACD module to determine the hidden feature vector of aspect terms in the multi-layer GCN as follows:

$$g_t^{l-gcn} = H_{gcn}^l[loc_{term}] \tag{13}$$

where $g_t^{l-gcn} \in R^{1 \times 2d}$ denotes the output vector of aspect terms in the hidden layer of L layer GCN.

Sentiment words usually have great correlation with aspect terms in a review sentence. Thus, we employ g_t^{l-gcn} as query and adopt self-attention to obtain the aspect related sentiment words. In order to avoid the problem that the aspect term attend to itself, we introduce a masking mechanism into self-attention:

---

[2] http://spacy.io/.

$$N = g_t^{l-gcn} H_{gcn}^{l \ T} \tag{14}$$

$$N_{mask} = mask(N[loc_{term}] = 0) \tag{15}$$

$$\alpha_s = softmax(N_{mask}) \tag{16}$$

where $N \in R^{1 \times n}$, $N_{mask} \in R^{1 \times n}$, $\alpha_s \in R^n$, N_{mask} represents that the relevance of aspect term is masked to 0. α_s represents the sentiment attention weight.

Sentence Representation for ACSC: The i-th aspect sentiment sentence can be expressed through sentiment attention weight and the hidden feature with syntactic dependency as follows:

$$r_s = tanh(W_{rs} \alpha_s H_{gcn}^l) \tag{17}$$

where r_s represents the sentence representation for sentiment prediction and W_{rs} is the weight during training.

Aspect Sentiment Classification: Sentence representation r_s is fed into fully connected layer with softmax function to generate the sentiment probability distribution of a specific aspect. Formally, for the sentiment category of the i-th aspect:

$$p_i^s = softmax(W_{ps} r_s + b_{ps}) \tag{18}$$

$$y_i^s = max(p_i^s) \tag{19}$$

where p_i^s is the classification probability of sentiment polarity. Weight W_{ps} and bias b_{ps} are parameters during training. Therefore, the final prediction aspect category-sentiment polarity of the i-th aspect in a sentence is denoted as $< y_i^a, y_i^s >$.

2.5   Joint Loss

According to the architecture we introduced above, the loss of ACSA originates from ACD and ACSC subtasks, respectively. Each prediction of ACD is a multi-label binary classification problem. Thus, the loss function of ACD subtask is defined as:

$$Loss_a = - \sum_{i=1}^{n} (\tilde{y}_i^a log(p_i^a) + (1 - \tilde{y}_i^a) log(1 - p_i^a)) \tag{20}$$

ACSC task is a single-label multi-classification problem. Thus, the loss function of ACSC subtask is defined as:

$$Loss_s = \sum_{i=1}^{n} \sum_{j \in C} (\tilde{y}_{i,j}^s log(p_{i,j}^s)) \tag{21}$$

where n is the number of samples. $\tilde{y}_i^a$, $\tilde{y}_{i,j}^s$ are the true labels, p_i^a represents the prediction probability of the i-th aspect and $p_{i,j}^s$ represents the sentiment polarity probability of the i-th aspect. C is the sentiment label set. So, the final loss function of ACSA task is defined as:

$$Loss = Loss_a + Loss_s + \lambda\|\theta\|_2 \tag{22}$$

where λ is the regulation factor of L2 and θ represents some parameters in our model.

3   Experiment Analysis

3.1   Data Set

We evaluate our model on benchmark datasets SemEval 2015 [3] and SemEval 2016 [2]. We randomly split the original training set into training set and validation set with a ratio of 9:1. To accurately and comprehensively find the aspect category-sentiment polarity pairs in customer reviews, we combine dataset's each sentence and their all-aspect categories into examples. If there exists an aspect category in the sentence, add the corresponding sentiment polarity, otherwise, the sentiment polarity is empty (denoted as N/A). Roth's work [16] proved the feasibility and correctness of our method extending sentiment dimension. The specific extended example of dataset is illustrated in Fig. 4.

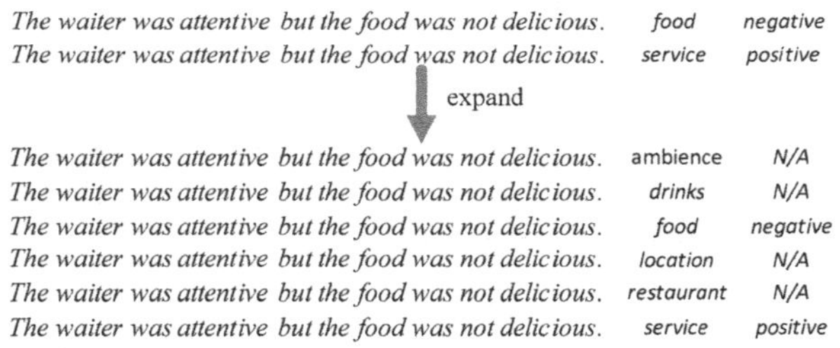

The waiter was attentive but the food was not delicious.	food	negative
The waiter was attentive but the food was not delicious.	service	positive

expand

The waiter was attentive but the food was not delicious.	ambience	N/A
The waiter was attentive but the food was not delicious.	drinks	N/A
The waiter was attentive but the food was not delicious.	food	negative
The waiter was attentive but the food was not delicious.	location	N/A
The waiter was attentive but the food was not delicious.	restaurant	N/A
The waiter was attentive but the food was not delicious.	service	positive

Fig. 4. The example of extended data sets.

3.2   Experimental Settings

The dataset statistics obtained after preprocessing are shown in Fig. 5. We calculate the Precision, Recall of the aspect category-sentiment polarity pairs, and Micro-F1 score as our final evaluation index, respectively. Notably, we only focus on the sentences with real sentiment and ignore the extended sentences without sentiment when calculating the evaluation index. We adopt the average scores of 5 runs as the final reported results to ensure the stability and reliability.

	Restaurant-15	Laptop-15	Restaurant-16	Laptop-16
Train	6702	30668	10200	44660
Test	3474	14102	3510	12584
Categories	30	198	30	198
Positive	1365	1295	1856	1702
Negative	609	941	773	1170
Neutral	93	129	135	174
N/A	8119	42405	10946	54198

Fig. 5. The statistics of the data set.

Method	Restaurant-15			Laptop-15			Restaurant-16			Laptop-16		
	P	R	F₁	P	R	F₁	P	R	F₁	P	R	F₁
Pipeline-BERT	38.12	70.00	49.35	36.91	51.62	43.02	43.62	79.06	56.21	31.92	51.56	39.42
Cartesian-BERT	72.02	49.15	58.42	73.06	21.18	32.83	74.96	63.84	68.94	64.99	27.40	39.54
AddOneDim-BERT	68.84	55.86	61.67	64.17	39.57	48.94	71.75	67.95	69.79	58.83	39.49	47.23
AddOneDim-LSTM	54.33	28.44	37.32	-	-	-	61.56	42.82	50.50	-	-	-
Hier-BERT	67.46	57.98	62.36	65.47	41.26	50.61	70.97	69.65	70.30	59.51	41.93	49.19
Hier-Transformer	70.22	59.96	64.67↑	65.63	51.95	57.79	73.72	73.21	73.45	58.06	48.29	52.72
Hier-GCN	71.93	58.03	64.23	71.90	54.73	62.13	76.37	72.83	74.55↑	61.43	48.42	54.15
S-AESC	71.01	58.30	64.03	64.15	61.05	62.56	76.83	71.39	74.01	62.49	49.39	55.17
AS-DATJM-DG	71.23	59.09	64.96↑↑	68.74	61.78	65.08↑↑	76.89	73.24	75.02↑↑	61.40	54.88	57.96↑↑
AS-DATJM-DT	69.36	58.52	63.48	68.97	58.59	63.35↑	76.27	69.65	72.81	56.53	56.04	56.29↑

Fig. 6. The results of model comparison (%). Select Micro-F1 as the evaluation index, and the two best results in each data set are indicated in bold (↑↑ indicates the best result, ↑ indicates the second-best result). The final result is the average of 5 runs' results of the models in different seeds.

We employ the 300-dimensional pretrained GloVe vector to initialize the word embedding. The conversion threshold of aspect category prediction probability δ is 0.5. Use the adam optimizer and set the learning rate to 0.0001. The batch size selects the optimal results according to the amount of data in each dataset, where we set the amount of two restaurant datasets to 72 and two laptop datasets to 256. 30 epochs per run. The hidden layer size is 300, the dropout rate of 0.3 is used and the L2-regularization is set to 0.00001.

3.3 Comparison Methods

In this section, we mainly summarize the previous ACSA joint models and consider them as benchmark methods for comparison.Fig. 6 shows the results of different methods on the dataset. All comparison methods are as follows:

- **Pipeline-BERT:** Establish pipelines for aspect category detection and sentiment polarity classification, respectively. Although this method can establish two subtask models well, it ignores the interrelation between the two subtasks.
- **Cartesian-BERT:** Adopt Cartesian product and BERT method as the sentence encoder.
- **AddOneDim-BERT** [16]: Add one dimension of sentiment polarity and adopt BERT method as the sentence encoder.

- **AddOneDim-LSTM** [16]: Add one dimension of sentiment polarity and adopt LSTM method as the sentence encoder.
- **Hier-BERT** [6]: Hierarchically process two subtasks and adopt the BERT method as the sentence encoder.
- **Hier-Transformer** [6]: On the basis of Hier-BERT, use Transformer method to establish the inner-relation between aspect category detection and sentiment polarity classification.
- **Hier-GCN** [6]: On the basis of Hier-BERT, use Hier-GCN method to establish the inner-relation between aspect category detection and sentiment polarity classification. To our knowledge, this method represents the latest research.
- **S-AESC** [18]: Aspect category detection and sentiment polarity classification each utilize a Bidirectional Gated Recurrent Unit (Bi-GRU) to extract sequence information, and then utilize an interaction layer to further consider the relation between the two tasks.
- **AS-DATJM-DG:** Our AS-DATJM method employs undirected dependency graph to construct syntactic dependency relation and leverages dual-attention mechanism to establish the interrelation between aspect category and aspect sentiment. On the basis of aspect term information automatically discovered, we can obtain the sentence representation of specific aspect and aspect sentiment.
- **AS-DATJM-DT:** A variant of our AS-DATJM method. The main difference lies in using the directed dependency tree as syntactic dependency.

3.4 Main Results

As shown from the comparative experiment results, Pipeline-BERT method ignores the interrelation between aspect category and sentiment detection, resulting in a very low precision and proving the effectiveness of the joint model. The recall of Cartesian-BERT is very low because of the class-parse problem when the number of aspect categories is too large, such as Laptop data. What is worse, AddOneDim-LSTM method also hardly obtain good performance in the Laptop data because the training algorithm cannot converge. In contrast, AddOneDim-BERT method can achieve better performance. For the four joint models (Hier-BERT, Hier-Transformer, Hier-Transformer, S-AESC), although they adopt different methods to establish the inner-relation between two subtasks to improve precision, they easily generate the missing of aspect category and the mismatch between aspect category and category sentiment, which leads to a relatively low recall in each dataset. This poor performance is especially obvious when the number of aspect categories is large.

In summary, among all the methods, our AS-DATJM method can provide higher F1 values and perform significantly better than the other benchmark methods. We can also observe that the AS-DATJM-DG method exhibits superior performance in comparison with the variant AS-DATJM-DT method. It is speculated that the adoption of directed dependency tree may lead to the loss of some important syntactic information.

3.5   Discussions on AS-DATJM

Ablation Study: We conduct ablation experiments to demonstrate the efficacy of each module in our model.

- **AS-DATJM-DG w/o Conca:** Remove the operation of concatenating aspect sentence vector and aspect category information.
- **AS-DATJM-DG w/o SAtt:** Remove the sentiment attention mechanism.
- **AS-DATJM-DG w/o GCN:** Remove the GCN network.
- **AS-DATJM-BiLSTM:** Replace multi-layer GCN network with multi-layer Bi-LSTM network.

Method	Restaurant-15 F_1	Laptop-15 F_1	Restaurant-16 F_1	Laptop-16 F_1
AS-DATJM-DG w/o Conca	63.82	64.11	73.03	57.17
AS-DATJM-DG w/o SAtt	61.18	62.04	72.03	54.36
AS-DATJM-DG w/o GCN	61.85	64.13	73.41	56.49
AS-DATJM-BiLSTM	63.67	64.49	74.32	57.03
AS-DATJM-DG	**64.96**	**65.08**	**75.02**	**57.96**

Fig. 7. The comparison results of ablation model (%).

As illustrated in Fig. 7, we can draw the following conclusions from the experimental results: First, concatenating the aspect category information enables the model to automatically discover the hidden aspect terms, thereby alleviating the missing problem of aspect categories. Second, compared with BiLSTM, GCN encodes the syntactic dependency to avoid the impact of context-free information. Finally, the sentiment attention mechanism can capture the words that have sentiment relation with specific aspect terms, and alleviate the mismatch between aspect categories and sentiment words, thus obviously improving model performance.

Impact of the Number of GCN Layers: In this section, we will explore the impact of the number of GCN layers on the model results. We gradually increase the number of GCN layers from 1 to 6. As can be seen in Fig. 8, when the number of GCN layers is 2, the F1 values reach the optimal performance. When layers more than 2, the F1 values exhibit the overall wave-like decrease trend. It is speculated that the nodes of the deep GCN network include too much cooccurrence information, which leads to the lack of difference between each node.

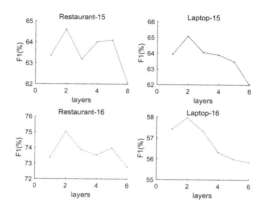

Fig. 8. Line graph of F1 value versus the number of GCN layers.

3.6 Quality Analysis

In this section, we will verify the advantage of our AS-DATJM model, analyze the causes of errors through some typical cases and then estimate its performance in correctly finding aspect category-sentiment polarity pairs.

Case Study: Figure 9 visualizes the attention weights and the final prediction results of 5 sentences. To verify the robustness of our model, we select sentences with positive category sentiment (a), sentences with negative category sentiment (b), and sentences with both (c). The results elaborate that our model can accurately find aspect categories in various sentences and assign the correct sentiment polarity to the corresponding aspect category. For example, in the sentence (c), our model first correctly finds the aspect term *"food"* of food aspect and the aspect term *"space "* of ambience aspect. Then, it accurately finds the sentiment description information *"great and tasty"* of food aspect and *"was too small"* of ambience aspect through syntactic dependency and aspect term. Finally, it generates category sentiment pairs *<food, positive>* and *<ambience, negative>*. In comparison with the previous models, our model can automatically discover aspect terms of specific aspect and find the description words that have sentiment relation with that aspect through attention mechanism to obtain the accurate aspect category-sentiment polarity pairs.

The sentences (d) and (e) are the final prediction results of the AS-DATJM-DG and AS-DATJM-DT models for the same sentence. Results indicate that both models correctly predict the aspect category and category sentiment of the sentence. It is worth noting that the restaurant aspect sentiment description information found by AS-DATJM-DG is *"highly overrated place"* while the sentiment description information found by AS-DATJM-DT is *"overrated place"*. Although they both find the most critical sentiment description word *"overrated"*, AS-DATJM-DT omits the sentiment-enhancing modal particle *"highly"*.

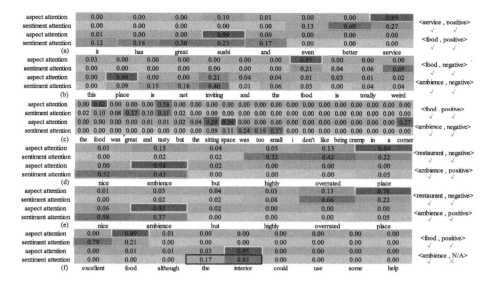

Fig. 9. The visualization of attention weight and word sentiment prediction results. The blue is the aspect attention weight while the red is the sentiment attention weight. The words in the yellow box are aspect terms, the green boxes are the correct category sentiment description information, and the black boxes are the wrong category sentiment description information.

It is analyzed that the directed dependency tree may lose some important syntactic information, which also evidently elaborates why AS-DATJM-DT obtains better performance than AS-DATJM-DG.

Error Analysis: Although our model correctly finds the ambience aspect term *"interior"* in the sentence (f), it also misjudges *"interior"* to ambience aspect sentiment description information. According to our analysis, we speculate that the sentiment attention mechanism is prone to look for words that have syntactic correlation with ambience aspect terms. Since there is no sentiment information related to ambience aspect in the sentence (f), the sentiment description information finally found is aspect term itself without any sentiment. Consequently, our model judges the sentiment of ambience aspect as non-existent. But looking through the entire short sentence, we can see that the ambience aspect sentiment polarity should be negative.

4 Conclusion

In this paper, we propose a dual-attention based joint aspect sentiment classification model. Our AS-DATJM model employs the aspect terms automatically discovered as an important basis of aspect category detection, and then uses the sentiment attention mechanism to obtain the sentiment description information that has syntactic relation with aspect terms. The experimental results prove the effectiveness of AS-DATJM, especially in the case of a large number of aspect categories. However, the sentiment in some sentences is expressed through a short sentence, Our future work will consider how to obtain more sentiment description information from short sentences.

References

1. Pang, B., Lee, L.: Opinion mining and sentiment analysis. Found. Trends® Inf. Retr. **2**, 1–135 (2008)
2. Pontiki, M., et al.: SemEval-2016 task 5: aspect based sentiment analysis, pp. 19–30 (January 2016)
3. Pontiki, M., Galanis, D., Papageorgiou, H., Manandhar, S., Androutsopoulos, I.: SemEval-2015 task 12: aspect based sentiment analysis. In: Proceedings of the 9th International Workshop on Semantic Evaluation, SemEval 2015, Denver, Colorado, June 2015, pp. 486–495. Association for Computational Linguistics (2015)
4. Yarowsky, D., Baldwin, T., Korhonen, A., Livescu, K., Bethard, S., (eds.): Proceedings of the 2013 Conference on Empirical Methods in Natural Language Processing, Seattle, Washington, USA, October 2013. Association for Computational Linguistics (2013)
5. Hu, M., Peng, Y., Huang, Z., Li, D., Lv, Y.: Open-domain targeted sentiment analysis via span-based extraction and classification. CoRR, vol. abs/1906.03820 (2019)
6. Cai, H., Tu, Y., Zhou, X., Yu, J., Xia, R.: Aspect-category based sentiment analysis with hierarchical graph convolutional network. In: Proceedings of the 28th International Conference on Computational Linguistics, Barcelona, Spain (Online), December 2020, pp. 833–843. International Committee on Computational Linguistics (2020)
7. Li, Y., Yin, C., Zhong, S.-H., Pan, X.: Multi-instance multi-label learning networks for aspect-category sentiment analysis. In: Proceedings of the 2020 Conference on Empirical Methods in Natural Language Processing (EMNLP), (Online), November 2020, pp. 3550–3560. Association for Computational Linguistics (2020)
8. A joint model for aspect-category sentiment analysis with contextualized aspect embedding. CoRR, vol. abs/1908.11017 (2019). Withdrawn
9. Zhou, X., Wan, X., Xiao, J.: Representation learning for aspect category detection in online reviews. In: AAAI (2015)
10. Wang, Y., Huang, M., Zhu, X., Zhao, L.: Attention-based LSTM for aspect-level sentiment classification. In: Proceedings of the 2016 Conference on Empirical Methods in Natural Language Processing, Austin, Texas, November 2016, pp. 606–615. Association for Computational Linguistics (2016)
11. Tay, Y., Luu, A.T., Hui, S.C.: Learning to attend via word-aspect associative fusion for aspect-based sentiment analysis. CoRR, vol. abs/1712.05403 (2017)
12. Hu, M., et al.: CAN: constrained attention networks for multi-aspect sentiment analysis. CoRR, vol. abs/1812.10735 (2018)
13. Xue, W., Li, T.: Aspect based sentiment analysis with gated convolutional networks. In: Proceedings of the 56th Annual Meeting of the Association for Computational Linguistics (Volume 1: Long Papers), Melbourne, Australia, pp. 2514–2523, July 2018. Association for Computational Linguistics (2018)

14. Chi, S., Huang, L., Qiu, X.: Utilizing bert for aspect-based sentiment analysis via constructing auxiliary sentence (March 2019)
15. Cheng, J., Zhao, S., Zhang, J., King, I., Zhang, X., Wang, H.: Aspect-level sentiment classification with HEAT (HiErarchical ATtention) network, pp. 97–106. Association for Computing Machinery, New York (2017)
16. Schmitt, M., Steinheber, S., Schreiber, K., Roth, B.: Joint aspect and polarity classification for aspect-based sentiment analysis with end-to-end neural networks. In: Proceedings of the 2018 Conference on Empirical Methods in Natural Language Processing, Brussels, Belgium, October–November 2018, pp. 1109–1114. Association for Computational Linguistics (2018)
17. Kipf, T.N., Welling, M.: Semi-supervised classification with graph convolutional networks. CoRR, vol. abs/1609.02907 (2016)
18. Lv, Y., Wei, F., Zheng, Y., et al.: A span-based model for aspect terms extraction and aspect sentiment classification. Neural Comput. Appl. **33**, 3769–3779 (2021). https://doi.org/10.1007/s00521-020-05221-x

Explaining a Deep Neural Model with Hierarchical Attention for Aspect-Based Sentiment Classification Using Diagnostic Classifiers

Kunal Geed[1], Flavius Frasincar[1], and Maria Mihaela Truşcă[2]

[1] Erasmus University Rotterdam, Burgemeester Oudlaan 50, 3062 PA Rotterdam,
The Netherlands
frasincar@ese.eur.nl
[2] Bucharest University of Economic Studies, 010374 Bucharest, Romania
maria.trusca@csie.ase.ro

Abstract. LCR-Rot-hop++ is a state-of-art model for Aspect-Based Sentiment Classification. However, it is also a black-box model where the information encoded in each layer is not understood by the user. This study uses diagnostic classifiers, single layer neural networks, to evaluate the information encoded in each layer of the LCR-Rot-hop++ model. This is done by using various hypotheses designed to test for information deemed useful for sentiment analysis. We conclude that the model did not focus on identifying the aspect mentions associated with a word and the structure of the sentence. However, the model excelled in encoding information to identify which words are related to the target. Lastly, the model was able to encode to some extent information about the word sentiment and sentiments of the words related to the target.

Keywords: Aspect-based sentiment classification · Neural rotatory attention model · Diagnostic classification

1 Introduction

The goal of Sentiment Analysis (SA) is to analyse a piece of text and identify the primary sentiment associated with a certain entity in the text [10]. According to [14] Aspect-Based Sentiment Analysis (ABSA) is a sub-task in SA and is generally divided into three different steps. The authors explain that the first step is to identify a sentiment-target pair, followed by classification of the sentiment-target pair, and, lastly, the aggregation of sentiment values to provide an overview. In this paper, we focus on neural networks designed for Aspect-Based Sentiment Classification (ABSC), which refers to the second step responsible for identifying the polarity associated with a specific target.

The application of ABSA is wide, and, although more complicated than SA, can lead to a much more comprehensive analysis. For this purpose, a state-of-the-art technique was developed in [17], which proposes a hybrid approach to

© Springer Nature Switzerland AG 2022
T. Di Noia et al. (Eds.): ICWE 2022, LNCS 13362, pp. 268–282, 2022.
https://doi.org/10.1007/978-3-031-09917-5_18

ABSA. Firstly, the authors make use of a domain ontology to identify aspects and sentiments towards these. Any inconclusive cases are then passed to a neural network that predicts the sentiments. Due to its high performance, we make use of this technique as the basis of our research.

Neural networks are considered to be black-box methods as the user is not able to explain the results based on the structure of the neural network, hence their inner-workings are not clear. Therefore, our research aims to improve the understanding of neural networks with a focus on the architecture presented in [17], which is part of the larger field of explainable AI (XAI). To solve this problem, we investigate if the model presented in [17] can capture specific information regarding the relationships between words and aspects. We further extend this by using the domain ontology to test if LCR-Rot-hop++ can encode the domain knowledge represented, in a sentiment analysis context, in the domain ontology. To investigate these questions, we use diagnostic classifiers as introduced in [7]. The major contributions of this work are as follows. While in [11] diagnostic classifiers are used to understand the inner-workings of the LCR-Rot-hop model, we focus on the more advanced LCR-Rot-hop++ model in this paper. Furthermore, in addition to diagnostic classifiers discussed in [11], we investigate if the aspects represented in the domain ontology are encoded in the neural network. To our knowledge, this is one of the first works that investigate the presence of a domain sentiment ontology signal in the representations produced by a neural attention model. All source data and code can be retrieved from https://github.com/KunalGeed/DC-LCR-Rot-hop_plus_plus.

The paper is structured as follows. In Sect. 2 we discuss the literature associated with ABSA and XAI. Section 3 explores the dataset used in this study and describes the pre-processing steps used to convert the dataset into the final dataset. In Sect. 4, we describe the methodology of the used aspect-based sentiment classifier and the methodology of diagnostic classifiers. Section 5 presents the results. Last, Sect. 6 draws conclusions from the results, states the limitations of our study, and suggests avenues for further research.

2 Related Works

This section discusses the relevant literature for this study. Section 2.1 provides a more in-depth analysis of Aspect-Based Sentiment Classification. Section 2.2 describes the related work of diagnostic classifiers.

2.1 Aspect-Based Sentiment Classification

ABSC usually relies on knowledge-based solutions, machine learning, or hybrid approaches. While classic machine learning models have modest performance rates, the more recent neural networks have managed to significantly increase the classification quality. Within neural networks, Long Short Term Memory (LSTM) [6] and its variants have shown great performance in ABSC. The Left-Center-Right (LCR) separated neural networks for ABSC is introduced in [16] based on a bi-directional LSTM to address two problems that were about the target representation and the connection between the target and its context.

Although knowledge-based and machine learning approaches had shown individual success, the hybrid techniques developed by combining them proved to be even more effective. The hybrid technique for ABSC introduced in [15] utilizes an ontology-based model to first find as many sentiment classifications as possible and then solves the inconclusive cases using the Bag-of-Words (BOW) model. The model is improved in [18] by changing the backup classifier to the LCR-Rot models proposed in [16]. The authors further extended and improved upon the LCR-Rot model by repeating the rotary mechanism n times (LCR-Rot-hop model). The LCR-Rot-hop model is further improved in [17] by introducing deep contextual word embeddings and hierarchical attention leading to the LCR-Rot-hop++ model.

2.2 Diagnostic Classifiers

With the increase in the use of black-box methods, such as neural networks, there is an increased need for techniques to investigate what happens inside these black-box methods part of XAI [5]. An approach similar to diagnostic classifiers was proposed in [1]. In their work, the authors outline a framework that facilitates the understanding of encoded representation using auxiliary prediction tasks. They score representations by training classifiers which take the representations as input to tackle the auxiliary prediction tasks. If the trained classifier is unable to predict the property being tested in the prediction task, then it is concluded that the representations have not encoded that information [1].

Another technique used to facilitate understanding of the models' innerworking is introduced in [2]. Using a generator model like Variational Auto-Encoder or Generative Adversarial Network, the proposed approach aims to generate artificial inputs that mimic the output produced by the analysed model. As the models are considered black-box methods with no access to their inner gradients, the optimization of the generator relies on an evolutionary strategy. In the end, the artificial inputs are analysed to provide insights into the model capabilities.

Considering that the visualization techniques were not sufficient to gain insight into the information encoded by the recurrent neural network, diagnostic classifiers are introduced in [7] to gain better insight into the information encoded by recurrent neural networks. This led to the development of diagnostic classifiers where the authors tested multiple hypotheses about the information processed by the network. If the diagnostic classifiers can accurately predict the information, then it is concluded that the information is encoded in the network [7].

[8] made use of diagnostic classifiers to link what is going on inside the neural network to linguistic theory. Specifically, they examine the ability of LSTM to process Negative Polarity Items (NPI). The results show that the model can determine a relationship between the licensing context and NPI. As explained

in [8], NPI are words that need to be licensed by a licensing context to form a valid sentence, for example, "He did not buy any books" where "any" is an NPI and "not" is a licensing context. The authors determine that a good language model must be able to encode this relationship. This study is able successfully to link linguistic theory to deep learning [8].

The work in [3] attempts to understand the inner-workings of neural networks and specifically what the neural networks learn about the target language. They determine that lower levels of a neural network are better at capturing morphology. Hence they also hypothesize that lower levels of the neural network capture word structure and the higher levels capture word semantics [3].

[11] makes use of diagnostic classifiers for ABSC. Specifically, the authors evaluate, in detail, the LCR-Rot-hop method developed in [18]. In [11] the LCR-Rot-hop method is analyzed to investigate if the internal layers can encode word information, such as Part-of-Speech (POS) tag, sentiment value, presence of aspect relation, and aspect related sentiment value of words. They conclude that the word structure (POS) is captured by the lower levels of the neural network, and the higher levels are able to encode information about aspect relation and aspect related sentiment value, which is in line with a hypothesis proposed in [3].

3   Specification of the Data

This study makes use of the SemEval 2016 Dataset, Task 5, Sub-task 1, which contains an annotated dataset for ABSA [13]. A review is divided at a sentence level and for each opinion in a sentence, the target, category, and polarity are stated. The polarity of the opinion is the sentiment (positive, negative, or neutral) that the opinion has towards the target. The target is the word in the opinion towards which the sentiment is directed. Last, the category is related to the target and shows which aspect the target belongs to. Table 1 shows the class frequencies for the training and test set used to evaluate LCR-Rot-hop++. In both the test and training set, the *Positive* class is in the majority with more than 70%, and the *Neutral* class is in the minority with less than 5%. This imbalance could make it more difficult for the neural network to learn the *Neutral* class.

Table 1. Polarity frequencies in Training and Test sets

Training data			Test data		
Polarity	Frequency	%	Polarity	Frequency	%
Negative	488	26.0	Negative	135	20.8
Neutral	72	3.8	Neutral	32	4.9
Positive	1319	70.2	Positive	483	74.3

Due to the fact that we use BERT word embeddings to represent words, we need to re-concatenate words that have been divided into word pieces in order to generate the dataset used to train and test the diagnostic classifiers. As any words that begin with "##" is a word piece belonging to the word preceding it, we can combine them into a single word. Due to each word also needing its own BERT word piece embedding and hidden states, when we combine the word pieces we also need to generate a single word embedding or hidden states for the newly formed word. The word embedding and hidden states represent the layer information that is output by each layer of the LCR-Rot-hop++ model, prior to the final MLP layer for sentiment classification. A proposed solution [19] was to use a recurrent neural network to combine word piece embeddings into a single word embedding, however, without a large dataset to train the neural network this would result in inadequate word embeddings. One of the methods to get a single embedding that captures the meaning of a larger piece of text, such as a phrase or a sentence, from the individual embedding is to average the word embeddings to get a single word embedding representing the entire phrase [9]. We use this approach to combine word pieces and their embedding and layer information into a single vector due to its simplicity.

4   Method

This section is dedicated to the proposed methodology. Section 4.1 presents the backup model of the the two-step approach HAABSA++, and Sect. 4.2 provides an overview of the diagnostic classifiers used to understand the inner-working of the LCR-Rot-hop++ model.

4.1   LCR-Rot-hop++

We aim to investigate if a layer of the backup model of the hybrid approach presented in [17] (more precisely the LCR-Rot-hop++ neural network) encodes certain information. We will begin by training the neural network proposed in [17] on the training data. After the training is complete, we extract the hidden layers from all the correctly predicted instances to generate the features for our training dataset. The accuracy of our methods will be evaluated on the SemEval 2016 test set. We make several diagnostic classifiers to test our various hypotheses. Furthermore, the diagnostic classifiers are trained only on the correctly predicted instances from the training data, as training on the incorrect instances can possibly lead to the diagnostic classifiers learning incorrect information.

The context representations for LCR-Rot-hop++ are calculated at the sentence level. However, to create our dataset we require these representations to be at the word level. We get the word-level representations by omitting the sum when calculating the context representations at the sentence level, hence the formula to get the word level layer information is given in Eq. 1.

$$r_i^l = \alpha_i^l \times h_i^l \tag{1}$$

Here, α_i^l is the attention score for the ith word in the left context. Similarly, h_i^l is the hidden state of the word. After this, we apply the hierarchical attention by multiplying the attention score calculated by the hierarchical attention process for the left context with r_i^l as shown in Eq. 2.

$$r_i^{l'} = \alpha^l \times r_i^l \tag{2}$$

Here, the α^l corresponds to the hierarchical attention score calculated for the left context. By making these changes we can extract hidden states of the various layers at the word level. In total five layers are extracted, $[e, h, r_1, r_2, r_3]$ which stand for the BERT embeddings, hidden states, hierarchical weighted representations 1, 2, and 3, respectively. The BERT embedding layer has a dimensionality of 768, while the rest of the layers have a dimensionality of 600. The dimensionality of 600 is due to the 300-dimensional hidden states of the bi-directional LSTM layer, which results in 600 neurons in total. The final layer is repeated three times (the hop part), hence resulting in five layers in total.

The newly extracted layer information is fed into a single layer MLP which is trained to predict the given hypothesis. A single layer MLP is used as we want a simple model, and the use of a simple model is also inspired by the works proposed in [3] and [11]. If a complicated model is required to extract the encoded information, then the information is not prominently present in the data. Due to the highly imbalanced nature of the dataset, we balance the dataset in the same manner as [11] by drawing $min(q_c, q_{mean})$ instances for each class, where q_c is the number of instances for class c, and q_{mean} is the average number of instances in a class, excluding the class with the highest number of instances.

4.2   Diagnostic Classifier

An overview of diagnostic classifiers is provided in Fig. 1. In this figure, we are evaluating the word "lousy" for the POS hypothesis. Knowing that each word is assigned a label that ranges between 0 and 4 for POS tags: Nouns, Adjectives, Adverbs, Verbs, or "Remaining" words, we notice that the adjective "lousy" is properly classified only by the first layers of the model.

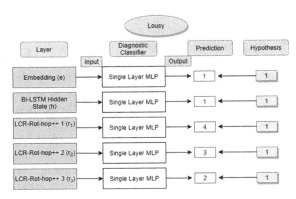

Fig. 1. Overview of the diagnostic classifier

In this paper, we test various hypotheses to analyze if the neural network encodes certain information. Below we list the various hypotheses being tested in this paper and how the corresponding tests are generated. Some of these have already been considered in [11], however, for the simpler LCR-Rot-hop model and not the advanced LCR-Rot-hop++ model.

POS tagging is the process of assigning tags to the words based on the POS and the grammatical categories such as tense, singular/plural, etc. Due to limited amounts of data available we omit predicting grammatical categories and limit ourselves to four Part-Of-Speech tags, already mentioned above. The words classified as anything other than these four are categorized under "Remaining". This process is done using the Stanford CoreNLP package. This hypothesis is designed to check if the neural network can understand the structure of a sentence and its various components. Figure 2a shows an example for POS classification.

Mention Tagging involves predicting the Aspect Mention related to the word. We use the ontology to identify the Aspect Mention a word is connected to. We match the word to a concept in the ontology and ensure maximum matches by checking all lexicalizations of a concept. If there is a match, we check what Aspect Mention this concept is a subclass of in order to identify the aspect the word is referring to. Due to the limited coverage of the ontology, the size of this dataset is much more limited than the others. This hypothesis helps to understand what part of the ontology the neural network can understand and is encoded in the neural network. We test this hypothesis by checking if the neural network can identify various aspects of the ontology. An example of mention tagging is given in Fig. 2b.

Aspect Relation Classification is the task of predicting the presence of a relation between the words in the context and the target/aspect. Hence, this is a binary classification problem. To generate the dataset, we make use of the Stanford Dependency Parser, which identifies the various grammatical relationships between words in a sentence. If any relationships exist between a context word and its target, we label that word as 1, and 0, otherwise. This hypothesis helps to check if the neural network is encoding information about the relationship between a context word and the target. Figure 2c shows an example of relation tagging. The dependencies are indicated by an arrow from the context word to the target word.

Word Sentiment Classification is the task of predicting the sentiment of a word as either *Positive, Neutral/No Sentiment*, or *Negative*. To identify word sentiment, we make use of a two-step procedure. First, we match the word to a concept in the ontology if it is possible. For this, we use the various lexical representations a concept has. After matching words to a concept, we check if the concept belongs to the *Positive* or *Negative* subclasses of the *Sentiment Value* class defined in the ontology and use that to identify the sentiment. If the word does not match any concept in the ontology or is related to a concept that does not belong to the Positive or Negative subclasses, we use as back-up the NLTK SentiWordNet library to identify the word sentiment. NLTK SentiWordNet identifies the sentiment based on its most frequently used context. It can also classify the word as *Neutral/No Sentiment*. Due to the limited coverage of the ontology, we have to use the NLTK SentiWordNet so that we have a larger dataset to be used to train and test. This hypothesis is designed to identify if the neural network can correctly detect the sentiment of the word. Figure 2d shows an example for Word Sentiment Classification.

Target-Related Sentiment Classification is a combination of the previous two tasks discussed, namely Word Sentiment Classification and Aspect Relation Classification. We generate another dataset which combines the information from the previous two datasets. If a word has a relation with the target (Aspect Relation Classification) we gather the sentiment of the word (Word Sentiment Classification) and assign that sentiment. If there is no relation or if the sentiment is Neutral, we identify it as "No sentiment". This hypothesis checks if the neural network can identify the words that have a relation to the target and what sentiment they hold. An example of this can be seen in Fig. 2e.

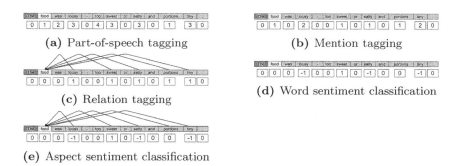

(a) Part-of-speech tagging

(b) Mention tagging

(c) Relation tagging

(d) Word sentiment classification

(e) Aspect sentiment classification

Fig. 2. Examples with part-of-speech tagging, mention tagging, relation tagging, word sentiment classification, and aspect sentiment classification

The diagnostic classifiers are implemented using the `scikit-learn` library in Python. We make use of the `MLPClassifier` function in the library for the diagnostic classifiers. `MLPClassifer` has the ReLU activation function and a constant learning rate of 0.001. Hyper-parameter optimization was performed using the `GridSearchCV` function provided in the `scikit-learn` library on the training data with three folds.

5   Evaluation

To analyze if the neural network can encode hypotheses, such as the structure of a sentence (POS tagging) or the sentiment of a word, we employ diagnostic classifiers to investigate if the layer information can encode the various information correctly. We make use of the accuracy and the weighted F1 score to measure the performance of the diagnostic classifier. We discuss individual hypotheses and compare them to the results reported in [11]. Last, we provide an overview of how the LCR-Rot-hop++ model encoded the various hypotheses and compare their performance.

POS Tagging. Table 2 shows the results for the diagnostic classifier trained to predict the POS tag of a word. Table 2 shows that the accuracy is highest for the embedding layer but falls as we move deeper into the neural network, although there is a slight increase at the end. A similar trend is shown by the F1 score, although there is an increase in the weighted F1 score in the second weighted hierarchical layer. This suggests that the deeper layers of the neural network encode less information about the POS tags. Overall, the embedding layer tends to best encode information about the structure of the sentence, while the information is lost or becomes less pronounced in the data as it moves deeper into the network. According to the results reported in [11], a steep fall in the accuracy is visible after the embedding layer, which continues in the hidden state layer. Last, the accuracy is stabilized for the weighted layers, although there is a slight increase in the third weighted layer, which is also observed in our results. However, our reported accuracies for POS tags are significantly lower compared to [11]. A possible reason for the relatively low accuracy and F1 scores could be the BERT embeddings used to represent words. This could confuse the diagnostic classifier as the same words have different representations, in different contexts, but could still have the same POS tag. As we move deeper into the neural network, we are losing information regarding the POS tags which suggest that the model is deeming it unnecessary for sentiment classification. The optimal number of neurons for each classifier is given in Table 2.

Table 2. Diagnostic classifier results for POS tagging

Layer	Accuracy (%)	F1 (%)	Number of neurons
Embedding	65.51%	69.96%	500
Hidden state	58.18%	63.58%	700
Hierarchical weighted state 1	55.57%	61.53%	500
Hierarchical weighted state 2	55.54%	61.62%	500
Hierarchical weighted state 3	56.50%	62.19%	700

Aspect Mention Tagging. The Aspect Mention tagging is a new task introduced in the current work to check if the various aspects in the domain are being encoded in the neural network. According to Table 3, the accuracy falls as we move deeper into the model. While the BERT embedding layer has the highest accuracy, the hierarchical weighted layers are the least effective. However, within the hierarchical weighted layers, the accuracy only decreases minutely and is relatively stable. It is to be noted that the Mention Tagging hypothesis has a highly imbalanced dataset, and after balancing the dataset we are left with a much smaller dataset which might adversely affect the classifier. Furthermore, due to the imbalance in the data, the weighted F1 is a better evaluation metric and also provides a slightly different result. According to F1, the performances of the embedding layer and the hidden state are extremely close to each other. The embedding layer is below the hidden layer by an extremely small margin. The trend for the weighted F1 scores is downwards, similar to the accuracy. From this information, we can see that the embedding layer is able to best encode information about the Aspect Mentions. Overall, our results suggest that as we move deeper into the neural network, information about the aspects is to some extent lost. It is to be noted that a word could be related to multiple aspects, and hence a multi-class diagnostic classifier could be replaced with a multi-label diagnostic classifier. The optimal number of neurons for each classifier is given in Table 3.

Table 3. Diagnostic classifier results for mention tagging

Layer	Accuracy (%)	F1 (%)	Number of neurons
Embedding	79.50%	61.91%	500
Hidden state	77.08%	61.99%	900
Hierarchical weighted state 1	73.49%	60.40%	700
Hierarchical weighted state 2	73.37%	59.68%	500
Hierarchical weighted state 3	73.15%	58.22%	500

Aspect Relation Classification. Table 4 shows the results of the diagnostic classifier for identifying Aspect Relations. This task checks if the neural network can identify words that are related to the target. Table 4 shows that the highest accuracy is present in the hidden state layer, while the lowest accuracy is in the embedding layer. As we go deeper into the neural network we see a huge spike in its ability to encode aspect relations at the hidden states layers, but after that, there is a small decline in accuracy for the next layer followed by small fluctuations in the remaining layers. A similar pattern is seen in the weighted F1 score, where the hidden state layer can encode the aspect relations best. This suggests that the model can identify words related to the target better as we move deeper into the neural network and although there is a small drop moving into the hierarchical layers, the model is able to identify words related to the target relatively well. This is logical as the neural network aims to identify words that are related to the target, towards which it is trying to classify the sentiment, and hence its ability to identify words related to the target should improve as we go deeper into the model. Out of all the layers, the hidden states appear to encode aspect relations the best. A possible reason for the hidden state performing better than the hierarchical layers could be that some words are related to the aspect but have no sentiment value, hence the model does not pay attention to those kinds of words deeper into the model, resulting in slightly lower accuracy. [11] showcases a similar pattern for aspect relations. There is a spike for the hidden state layer followed approximately the same values (or lower) for the weighted layers. The optimal number of neurons for each classifier is given in Table 4.

Word Sentiment Classification. Table 5 shows the performance of the diagnostic classifiers for identifying the sentiment of a word. The results prove that as we go deeper into the neural network, the accuracy and the weighted F1 score fall, although there is a spike for the third hierarchical weighted layer. A possible reason for the higher performance of the BERT embedding layer is probably due to the nature of word embeddings that can hold information about their context, alleviating the problem of sentiment detection. Overall, we see that information about the word sentiments is lost as we move deeper into the network. This could be justified due to Type-2 Sentiment Mentions [17] causing some words to not be important for determining the sentiment towards the target as they are not related to that aspect. [11] does find a similar downward trend initially, although at a much higher accuracy. [11] observes that following the downward trend, the accuracy stabilizes for the weighted layers, however, this is not the case for this study as we observe another increase in the final layer. The optimal number of neurons for each classifier is given in Table 5.

Table 4. Diagnostic classifier results for aspect relation

Layer	Accuracy (%)	F1 (%)	Number of neurons
Embedding	73.06%	78.03%	700
Hidden state	82.38%	84.04%	900
Hierarchical weighted state 1	80.85%	82.79%	500
Hierarchical weighted state 2	81.89%	83.53%	1100
Hierarchical weighted state 3	80.66%	82.58%	900

Table 5. Diagnostic classifier results for word sentiment

Layer	Accuracy (%)	F1 (%)	Number of neurons
Embedding	77.03%	80.81%	900
Hidden state	67.84%	73.69%	900
Hierarchical weighted state 1	66.82%	72.95%	700
Hierarchical weighted state 2	63.13%	70.27%	1100
Hierarchical weighted state 3	66.00%	72.01%	900

Target-Related Sentiment Classification. Table 6 shows the results for the diagnostic classification of the Target-Related Sentiment Classification task, which has to check if the neural network can predict the sentiment of the words specifically related to the target. Table 6 shows that the accuracy is highest in the hidden state layer and falls as we move deeper into the neural network, before rising again in the final layer. However, the accuracy never increases past the hidden state layer. The weighted F1 score follows a similar pattern, although it is much less pronounced for the spike in the final layer. As this hypothesis is a combination of two other hypotheses, its trend can be explained through them. We observe, that the Aspect Relation accuracy increases and then stabilizes but for the Word Sentiment hypothesis it decreases before a spike in accuracy at the end. The increase in accuracy for the hidden state layer is possibly due to the increase in the layers' ability to identify words related to the target being greater than the fall in its ability to identify the sentiment. Furthermore, as the accuracy for Aspect Relations stabilizes, but the accuracy for the word sentiment hypothesis continues to fall, we observe a downward trend for the layers following the hidden state. However, the final spike can be explained by the spike in accuracy for the Word Sentiment hypothesis, while the accuracy of the Aspect Relation hypothesis remains approximately the same. We observe that the neural network places more importance on identifying the sentiment of the words related to the aspect, as we observe a relatively good accuracy for Target-Related Sentiment Classification in the final layer, which is within expectations as that is an important task for ABSC. The optimal number of neurons for each classifier is given in Table 6.

Table 6. Diagnostic classifier results for target-related word sentiment

Layer	Accuracy (%)	F1 (%)	Number of neurons
Embedding	76.88%	85.27%	500
Hidden state	78.05%	87.22%	700
Hierarchical weighted state 1	76.05%	85.58%	700
Hierarchical weighted state 2	75.38%	85.10%	1100
Hierarchical weighted state 3	77.28%	85.61%	500

5.1 Overview

Figures 3a and 3b show the accuracy and F1 scores, respectively, for the different hypotheses in a single graph. We can see in Fig. 3b that the model is successful at learning about Aspect Relations, Word Sentiments, and the sentiment of the word if it is related to the target (Target-Related Word Sentiment). This is a good sign as these tasks are extremely important for ABSC. A major difference between Figs. 3b and 3a is that the Mention Tagging hypothesis is performing the worse when compared using the weighted F1 score but good when comparing based on the accuracy. A reason for this disparity in results could be due to the data imbalance and the fact that the Mention Tagging dataset is much smaller compared to the other hypotheses datasets due to the limited coverage of the ontology. The performance for POS tagging and Mention Tagging is low, based on the weighted F1 score, which suggests that the model is not able to encode information about the structure of the sentence and which Aspect Mention a word is related to. These results are to be expected as these tasks are not important for ABSC, as identifying the sentiment supersedes POS tagging and the Aspect Mentions are usually already identified.

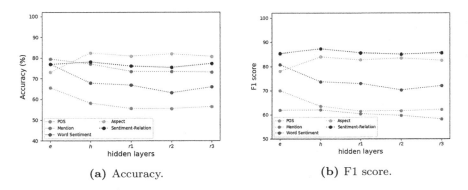

(a) Accuracy.   (b) F1 score.

Fig. 3. Overview of the Accuracy and F1 score for the different hypotheses.

From these results, we can conclude that while the LCR-Rot-hop++ model learns about the word sentiment and structure of the sentence in the starting layers, the more complex details such as which words are related to the target and the sentiment of those words are learnt deeper into the model.

6   Conclusion

In this study, we proposed the use of diagnostic classifiers to investigate if the hidden layers in the LCR-Rot-hop++ model can encode information regarding various hypotheses that are important for ABSC. These hypotheses are:

- POS tagging: We found that the BERT embeddings were the best in classifying POS tags, while the other layers had significantly lower accuracies and F1 scores. This implied that deeper into the model, information about the POS tags is not encoded. According to the weighted F1 score, the LCR-Rot-hop++ model does not capture information about the structure of the sentence.
- Mention Tagging: We found that the accuracy and weighted F1 score significantly fell deeper into the model. This implied that the neural network does not encode information about the Aspect Mention related to the word. The best accuracy for mention tagging was found in the embedding layer. This also suggested that the model did not find this information important as we lose this information as we proceed deeper into the network.

- Aspect Relation Classification: The neural network was able to encode information regarding which words are related to the target. We found relatively high accuracy and weighted F1 score. The weighted F1 score and the accuracy rose deeper into the network and stabilized at the hierarchical weighted layers. This means that the network was able to learn information about which words are related to the targets.
- Word Sentiment: The ability to identify the sentiment of a word fell as we went deeper into the neural network. The best accuracy and weighted F1 score were for the embedding layer. The relatively high accuracy and weighted F1 score for the embedding layer could be due to the contextualization. Overall, the LCR-Rot-hop++ showed moderate success in encoding information regarding the word sentiments.
- Target Related Word Sentiment: We found that the hidden state layer had the highest accuracy for the ability to identify words that are related to the target and then their sentiment. As we moved deeper to the network it fell for a bit before once again rising. Overall, we found that the neural network is able to encode information regarding the sentiments of the words related to the target the best, which is within expectations as this information is highly relevant for ABSC.

In the future, this research should be repeated for different neural networks designed for ABSC, as that might give insight into what kind of neural network works best for certain hypotheses. Furthermore, for the Mention Tagging hypothesis, a multi-class, multi-label diagnostic classifier could be trained to account for one word being related to multiple Aspect Mentions. In addition, as imbalanced datasets are present in the real world, we should look to combining the model with more advanced re-sampling techniques, such as Condensed Nearest Neighbor [12]. It is to be noted that this procedure must be done carefully, as certain oversampling techniques, such as SMOTE [4] and its variants, generate synthetic data and adding synthetic data is counter-intuitive as we want to investigate if the hypothesis is encoded in the layers originally. The final suggestion would be to explore how and where the neural network learns other concepts represented in the ontology besides the aspect mention (e.g., sentiment expressions).

References

1. Adi, Y., Kermany, E., Belinkov, Y., Lavi, O., Goldberg, Y.: Fine-grained analysis of sentence embeddings using auxiliary prediction tasks. In: 2017 International Conference on Learning Representations (ICLR 2017) (2016)
2. Barbalau, A., Cosma, A., Ionescu, R.T., Popescu, M.: A generic and model-agnostic exemplar synthetization framework for explainable AI. In: Hutter, F., Kersting, K., Lijffijt, J., Valera, I. (eds.) ECML PKDD 2020. LNCS (LNAI), vol. 12458, pp. 190–205. Springer, Cham (2021). https://doi.org/10.1007/978-3-030-67661-2_12
3. Belinkov, Y., Durrani, N., Dalvi, F., Sajjad, H., Glass, J.R.: What do neural machine translation models learn about morphology? In: 55th Annual Meeting of the Association for Computational Linguistics (ACL 2017), pp. 861–872. ACL (2017)

4. Chawla, N., Bowyer, K., Hall, L., Kegelmeyer, W.: SMOTE: synthetic minority over-sampling technique. J. Artif. Intell. Res. **16**, 321–357 (2002)
5. Chrupała, G., Alishahi, A.: Correlating neural and symbolic representations of language. In: 57th Annual Meeting of the Association for Computational Linguistics (ACL 2019), pp. 2952–2962. ACL (2019)
6. Hochreiter, S., Schmidhuber, J.: Long short-term memory. Neural Comput. **9**(8), 1735–1780 (1997)
7. Hupkes, D., Zuidema, W.: Visualisation and 'diagnostic classifiers' reveal how recurrent and recursive neural networks process hierarchical structure (extended abstract). In: 27th International Joint Conference on Artificial Intelligence (IJCAI 2018), pp. 5617–5621. International Joint Conferences on Artificial Intelligence Organization (2018)
8. Jumelet, J., Hupkes, D.: Do language models understand anything? On the ability of LSTMs to understand negative polarity items. In: 2018 EMNLP Workshop: Analyzing and Interpreting Neural Networks for NLP (BlackBox NLP 2019), pp. 222–231. ACL (2018)
9. Kenter, T., de Rijke, M.: Short text similarity with word embeddings. In: 24th ACM International on Conference on Information and Knowledge Management (CIKM 2015), pp. 1411–1420. ACM (2015)
10. Liu, B.: Sentiment Analysis: Mining Opinions, Sentiments, and Emotions, 2nd edn. Cambridge University Press (2020)
11. Meijer, L., Frasincar, F., Truşcă, M.M.: Explaining a neural attention model for aspect-based sentiment classification using diagnostic classification. In: 36th Annual ACM Symposium on Applied Computing (SAC 2021), pp. 821–827. ACM (2021)
12. More, A.: Survey of resampling techniques for improving classification performance in unbalanced datasets. arXiv preprint arXiv:1608.06048 (2016)
13. Pontiki, M., et al.: SemEval-2016 task 5: aspect based sentiment analysis. In: The 10th International Workshop on Semantic Evaluation (SemEval 2016), pp. 19–30. ACL (2016)
14. Schouten, K., Frasincar, F.: Survey on aspect-level sentiment analysis. IEEE Trans. Knowl. Data Eng. **28**(3), 813–830 (2016)
15. Schouten, K., Frasincar, F.: Ontology-driven sentiment analysis of product and service aspects. In: Gangemi, A., et al. (eds.) ESWC 2018. LNCS, vol. 10843, pp. 608–623. Springer, Cham (2018). https://doi.org/10.1007/978-3-319-93417-4_39
16. Shiliang, Z., Xia, R.: Left-center-right separated neural network for aspect-based sentiment analysis with rotatory attention. arXiv preprint arXiv:1802.00892 (2018)
17. Truşcă, M.M., Wassenberg, D., Frasincar, F., Dekker, R.: A hybrid approach for aspect-based sentiment analysis using deep contextual word embeddings and hierarchical attention. In: Bielikova, M., Mikkonen, T., Pautasso, C. (eds.) ICWE 2020. LNCS, vol. 12128, pp. 365–380. Springer, Cham (2020). https://doi.org/10.1007/978-3-030-50578-3_25
18. Wallaart, O., Frasincar, F.: A hybrid approach for aspect-based sentiment analysis using a lexicalized domain ontology and attentional neural models. In: Hitzler, P., et al. (eds.) ESWC 2019. LNCS, vol. 11503, pp. 363–378. Springer, Cham (2019). https://doi.org/10.1007/978-3-030-21348-0_24
19. Zhang, Z., et al.: Semantics-aware BERT for language understanding. In: 34th AAAI Conference on Artificial Intelligence (AAAI 2021), pp. 687–719. AAAI Press (2020)

A Model for Meteorological Knowledge Graphs: Application to Météo-France Data

Nadia Yacoubi Ayadi$^{(\boxtimes)}$, Catherine Faron , Franck Michel ,
Fabien Gandon , and Olivier Corby

University Côte d'Azur, Inria, CNRS, I3S (UMR 7271), Sophia-Antipolis, France
{nadia.yacoubi-ayadi,fabien.gandon,olivier.corby}@inria.fr,
{faron,fmichel}@i3s.unice.fr

Abstract. To study and predict meteorological phenomenons and to include them in broader studies, the ability to represent and exchange meteorological data is of paramount importance. A typical approach in integrating and publishing such data now is to formalize a knowledge graph relying on Linked Data and semantic Web standard models and practices. In this paper, we first discuss the semantic modelling issues related to spatio-temporal data such as meteorological observational data. We motivate the reuse of a network of existing ontologies to define a semantic model in which meteorological parameters are semantically defined, described and integrated. The model is generic enough to be adopted and extended by meteorological data providers to publish and integrate their sources while complying with Linked Data principles. Finally, we present a meteorological knowledge graph of weather observations based on our proposed model, published in the form of an RDF dataset, that we produced by transforming observation records made by Météo-France weather stations. It covers a large number of meteorological variables described through spatial and temporal dimensions and thus has the potential to serve several scientific case studies from different domains including agriculture, agronomy, environment, climate change and natural disasters.

Keywords: Knowledge graph · Semantic modelling · Observational data · Linked Data · Meteorology

1 Introduction

Meteorological data have attracted great interest in recent years since they are crucial for many application domains. Meteorological observations typically include measurements of several weather parameters such as wind direction and speed, air pressure, rainfall, humidity and temperature. However, these data are mostly collected and stored separately in different files using a tabular data format that lacks explicit semantics, which impedes their integration and sharing

© Springer Nature Switzerland AG 2022
T. Di Noia et al. (Eds.): ICWE 2022, LNCS 13362, pp. 283–299, 2022.
https://doi.org/10.1007/978-3-031-09917-5_19

to serve researchers from different domains such as agriculture, climate change studies or natural disaster monitoring. Publishing such data on the Web using Linked Data (LD) principles would make them more accessible, easier to discover and reuse. However, integrating and interpreting weather data requires rich metadata about studied features of interest such as the air, observed properties such as the temperature or the humidity, the utilized sampling strategy, the specific location of a weather station and the time (instant or interval) at which the property was measured, and a variety of other information. Getting insights into these heterogeneous data motivates the need of a semantic model in which domain-specific ontologies play a central role by providing a coherent view over it.

In this paper, we propose a semantic model that relies on a network of modular ontologies and domain vocabularies that capture common and specific characteristics of observational meteorological data at a fine grained level, including time, location, provenance, units of measurement, etc. We paid specific attention to propose a model that adheres to LD best practices and standards, thereby allowing for its re-use and extension by other meteorological data producers, and making it accommodated for multiple application domains. To deal with the complexity of the domain knowledge to be modelled, we adopt the SAMOD agile methodology [8] for ontology development, consisting of small steps within an iterative process that focuses on creating well-developed and documented models by using significant exemplar data so as to produce semantic models that are always ready-to-use and easily-understandable by humans. Based on the early work of Uschold & Gruninger [12] the SAMOD process is initiated by a motivating scenario that leads to a set of competency questions that, in turn, provide requirements on the knowledge graph model. We build a self-contained semantic model reusing and extending standard ontologies, among which the GeoSPARQL ontology for spatial features and relations [3], the Time ontology [4] for temporal entities and relations, the Sensor, Observation, Sample, and Actuator (SOSA) [6] and Semantic Sensor Network (SSN) ontologies [5] for sensors and observations, and the RDF Data Cube ontology [10] for aggregation and multidimensionality features.

Furthermore, we implement and make available a software pipeline that is reproducible to generate knowledge graphs compliant with the proposed semantic model. We use the pipeline to generate the first release of the WeKG-MF RDF knowledge graph constructed according to this model from open weather observations published by Météo-France. It includes weather observations from January 2019 till December 2021. To demonstrate the interest of WeKG-MF and the underlying semantic model, competency questions identified in our use case were translated into SPARQL queries to retrieve data from the WeKG-MF knowledge graph in order to meet expert requirements.

The paper is structured as follows. Section 2 describes a motivating scenario that allows us to identify a set of competency questions. Section 3 details our semantic model and highlights its design principles. Section 4 presents the RDF-based knowledge graph constructed from the observational weather data archives of Météo-France. Section 5 presents a validation of the proposed model and the constructed knowledge graph through a set of SPARQL queries implementing the competency questions identified in our motivating scenario. Section 6 presents the related work on lifting meteorological data into RDF datasets. Finally, we conclude and present perspectives of our work in Sect. 7.

2   Motivating Scenario and Competency Questions

In this section, we present a motivating scenario [8,12] inspired from requirements expressed by experts and collected in the context of the D2KAB French research project[1]. The primary objective of D2KAB is to create a framework to turn agriculture, agronomy and biodiversity data into semantically described, interoperable, actionable, and open knowledge. Experts in agronomy investigate the correlations between the development rate of plants and weather parameters. They are especially interested in comparing aggregated values of a weather parameter for the same period of time in the same geographic location across years, e.g. the Growing Daily Degrees (GDD) calculated from the daily average air temperature minus a certain threshold called base temperature. This motivating scenario already triggers competency questions that reflect the requirements on the knowledge that has to be represented in the proposed semantic model as well as the way of scoping and delimiting it [8,12]. We present some of them in the following:

CQ1. What is the measurement unit of a given weather parameter?
Several parameters such as atmospheric pressure, air temperature, wind speed, relative humidity, sea surface temperature are measured using different sensors and procedures, and the resulting numeric/qualitative values are included in weather reports. Measurement units and possible values for qualitative parameters are not included in these reports and are usually documented in external sources (e.g., WMO documentations).

CQ2. At what time of the day was the highest value of a weather parameter measured (observed)?
Temporal features are crucial for observational data. Indeed, within a 24-h time interval, sensors hosted by weather stations regularly produce different measurement values for the same weather parameter.

CQ3. What is the closest weather station to a specific spatial location?
This competency question points to the fact that the semantic model should encompass a spatial module to capture the geographic coordinates of stations by means of longitude and latitude values.

---

[1] https://www.d2kab.org/.

CQ4. For a specific location and given a calendar interval, provide time series of some aggregated (pre-computed) weather parameters.

Providing aggregated data over relevant time period and for a specific location/weather station is a recurrent need. For instance, daily minimum, maximum and mean temperature, cumulative rainfall during a period of time for each station are examples of significant aggregated parameters for different studies in agronomy or climate change studies.

According to *CQ1* and *CQ2*, weather parameters as well as their significance need to be clearly expressed and formalized. Metadata describing weather properties such as their possible lexical labels in different languages and their possible measurement units are required. *CQ4* is one example of competency questions that require the computation of aggregated values (sum of average temperatures, weekly average temperature). This motivated us to propose a semantic model presented in Sect. 3 that combines SSN/SOSA ontologies and RDF data cube vocabulary to represent inherent semantics of observations at different levels of semantic granularity.

3   Semantic Model

Our aim is to design a semantic model in which meteorological variables are semantically defined, described and integrated. The analysis of CQs presented in Sect. 2 led us to select a set of state-of-the art ontologies and thesauri to be re-used. It includes:

- the SOSA/SSN ontologies [5,6] designed for describing sensors and their observations, and that we extend with new classes to capture the semantics of meteorological observations and provide formal definitions of these new classes. The extension is motivated by the re-use of the Value Sets ontology design pattern;
- the Time Ontology [4] for describing the temporal properties of our data;
- the QUDT ontology and vocabulary [9] representing the various quantity and unit standards and supporting their processing such as conversion;
- the GeoSPARQL vocabulary [3] for representing spatial information in our data;
- the RDF data Cube Vocabulary [10] supporting the publication of multi-dimensional data, such as statistics. We use it to create spatio-temporal slices of meteorological observations by fixing time spans and geographic places as well as applying aggregation functions; SOSA/SSN ontologies only support the description of a single, atomic, observation.

The OWL formalization of our model as well as the related SKOS vocabulary are available in our Github repository[2]. The prefixes of ontologies and vocabularies reused or introduced in this paper are listed in the repository's README[3].

---

[2] https://github.com/Wimmics/d2kab/tree/main/meteo/ontology.
[3] https://github.com/Wimmics/d2kab/tree/main/meteo.

In the following we present in details our model according to four categories of features: features of interest, spatial features, temporal features, and aggregated features.

3.1 Features of Interest and Observable Properties: Describing Observations

In order to propose a self-contained model for representing and publishing meteorological data, we define three new classes. `weo:MeteorologicalObservation` is the core class of our model; it supports the description of a single, atomic observation. A meteorological observation is related to a particular feature of interest, instance of class `weo:MeteorologicalFeature`, and an observable property, instance of class `weo:WeatherProperty`. These three classes specialize classes from the SOSA/SSN ontologies as reflected by their formal definitions.

`weo:MeteorologicalFeature` is defined as a subclass of `sosa:Feature OfInterest` and serves to represent meteorological features of interest, that is phenomena or events such as precipitations, gusts or storms. Formally, the class is defined as follows:

$$weo : MeteorologicalFeature \equiv sosa : FeatureOfInterest \cap$$
$$\forall ssn : hasProperty.weo : WeatherProperty \cap \geq 1 \, ssn : hasProperty$$

`weo:WeatherProperty` is defined as a subclass of `sosa:ObservableProperty`. Its instances are observable properties of meteorological features. Precipitation amount, gust speed, air humidity are examples thereof. Formally, the class is defined as follows:

$$weo : WeatherProperty \equiv sosa : ObservableProperty \cap$$
$$\forall ssn : isPropertyOf.weo : MeteorologicalFeature \cap = 1 \, ssn : isPropertyOf$$

Instances of `weo:MeterologicalObservation` are observations of a weather property of a certain feature of interest. The definition of `weo:Meterological Observation` expresses that only one weather property and one meteorological feature is used for a given meteorological observation:

$$weo : MeteorologicalObservation \equiv sosa : Observation \cap$$
$$\forall sosa : observedProperty.weo : WeatherProperty \cap = 1 \, sosa : observedProperty \cap$$
$$\forall sosa : hasFeatureOfInterest.weo : MeteorologicalFeature \cap$$
$$= 1 \, sosa : hasFeatureOfInterest$$

Figure 1 depicts the RDF graph representing an example meteorological observation relative to the wind feature of interest and reporting the average wind speed observable property. Although SOSA/SSN ontologies are commonly used to represent knowledge about sensor data across domains, the definition of observable properties and features of interest, as well as their alignment with existing controlled vocabularies, are delegated to the community of interest. Thus, we have reused the Value Sets[4] (VS) ontology design pattern and we defined a SKOS[5] vocabulary whose concepts are instances of `weo:WeatherProperty` and `weo:MeteorologicalFeature` and represent the possible observable properties and features of interest. This SKOS vocabulary is available on our Github repository[6]. An excerpt of it is given in Listing 1.1. The SKOS concepts representing weather properties are aligned with both terms from the NERC Climate and Forecast Standard Names vocabulary and terms from the QUDT Quantity Kind vocabulary that includes general concepts about quantifiable quantities such as `quantity-kind:Speed` or `quantity-kind:Temperature`. For instance, `wevp:averageWindSpeed` and `wevp:gustSpeed` are declared as narrower than `qudt-kind:Speed` (and instances of class `qudt:Quantity Kind`). The vocabulary can be easily extended to include new observable properties and features as long as it is compliant with the proposed semantic model.

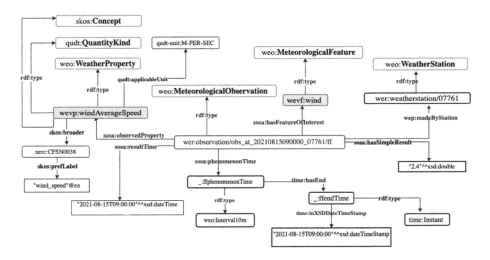

Fig. 1. Example meteorological observation of the `WindAverageSpeed` weather property

Observation results are literals and an observation is linked to its result by a property `sosa:hasSimpleResult`. Instead of repeating the measurement units within each observation, we denote it at the level of the SKOS concept representing the observable property in our vocabulary (Listing 1.1). Furthermore, some qualitative weather properties require the use of standard encoded values defined by the WMO. For instance, the ground state is a weather property whose possible values (dry, moist, etc.) are in a predefined set of values of the WMO 0901 code[7].

---

[4] https://www.w3.org/TR/swbp-specified-values/.

[5] https://www.w3.org/2004/02/skos/.

[6] https://github.com/Wimmics/d2kab/blob/main/meteo/ontology/features-properties-vocabulaire.ttl.

[7] https://epic.awi.de/id/eprint/29967/1/WMO2011i.pdf.

```
wevf:wind a weo:MeteorologicalFeature, skos:Concept ;
rdfs:label "wind"@en, "vent"@fr ;
ssn:hasProperty wevp:windAverageSpeed, wevp:windAverageDirection.

wevp:windAverageSpeed a weo:WeatherProperty, qudt:QuantityKind, skos:Concept ;
ssn:isPropertyOf wevf:wind ;
skos:broader nerc:CFSN0038, <http://qudt.org/2.1/vocab/quantitykind/Speed>;
qudt:applicableUnit <http://qudt.org/vocab/unit/M-PER-SEC> ;
skos:prefLabel "Vitesse moyenne du vent 10mn"@fr,"Average wind speed 10mn"@en;
wep:hasAbbreviation "ff".
```

Listing 1.1. SKOS representation of meteorological feature wind and related weather property windAverageSpeed.

```
@prefix : <http://ns.inria.fr/meteo/vocab/weatherproperty/wmocode/> .
:0901 a skos:Collection ;
  rdfs:label "State of ground without snow or ice cover"@en;
  skos:member :0901/0, :0901/1, ... ;

:0901/0 a skos:Concept; rdf:value 0 ;
  skos:definition "Surface of ground dry (without cracks and no appreciable
  amount of dust or loose sand)".

:0901/1 a skos:Concept; rdf:value 1;
  skos:definition "Surface of ground moist" .
```

Listing 1.2. SKOS collection representing the state of ground qualitative weather property (0901 WMO code).

For each qualitative weather properties, we created a skos:Collection whose members represent the possible values of the weather property as described in the WMO documentation. Listing 1.2 presents an excerpt of the skos:Collection of values for the *state of the ground* weather property.

3.2   Spatial Features: Locating the Weather Stations

A weather station typically hosts sensors and equipment for the purpose of measuring atmospheric conditions and providing information for weather forecasts. Whereas a description of sensors and equipment is not always made available by meteorological data providers, relevant metadata about weather stations generally include station identifier, name, latitude, longitude and altitude. Our model introduces the weo:WeatherStation class to represent any type of weather station. To capture stations' spatial location, weo:WeatherStation is introduced as a subclass of geosparql:Feature. Therefore, each instance of weo:WeatherStation has a geometry that is a point with specific coordinates. Following GeoSPARQL vocabulary, geo-coordinates of a weather station are defined as a Well-Known Text (WKT) literal (e.g., POINT(8.792667 41.918)). Our adoption of GeoSPARQL is motivated by the fact that it allows to efficiently query spatial data based on a set of spatial functions. It enables us to express spatial queries involving meteorological data, e.g. retrieving the closest station to a given location or the precipitations for a specific location. We also reused latitude, longitude, and altitude datatype properties from the WGS84 vocabulary since WKT literals do not integrate information about the altitude of a station.

3.3 Temporal Features: Defining Time Entities

In many cases, the observation of a given weather property is made over a period of time. The duration of a measurement varies depending on the property. For such cases, we reuse the `sosa:phenomenonTime` property to link an instance of `weo:MeteorologicalOb servation` to an instance of `time:Interval`. Since time durations are described in the documentation of weather observed properties, we defined different time interval classes by expressing an OWL restriction on their duration that may be declared in seconds, minutes or hours. The interest of doing this is that these time intervals are declared once in our model and are reused for all observations, and thus avoid substantial redundancy. For instance, in Fig. 1 the `wevp:windAverageSpeed` weather property is measured during a period of 10 min. This is denoted by property `sosa:phenomenonTime` whose value is an instance of class `weo:Interval10m`, while the end time of the interval is an instance of class `time:Instant`.

3.4 Aggregated Features: Defining Observation Slices

Observations produced by sensors can rapidly reach enormous volumes. The *CQ4* competency question (see Sect. 2) stresses the need to create focused and homogeneous sets of observations that share some dimension. In particular, creating times series of air temperatures or other weather parameters is a recurrent need. In this respect, we reuse the RDF Data Cube vocabulary (DCV)[8] to describe multi-dimensional data according to a 'data cube' model. Each data cube is an instance of class `qb:DataSet` and is linked to instances of class `qb:DataStructureDefinition` by property `qb:structure` (Fig. 2). A Data Structure Definition (DSD) defines the structure of a data cube and how observations are linked to the measures and dimensions of the data cube. Listing 1.3 presents an example of DSD `wes:annualTimeSeriesTemperature` that defines the structure of a data cube of air temperatures. According to this DSD, each observation contains three daily measures: the minimum, maximum and average temperatures. The `qb:Slice` class enables to represent a subset of observations that share the same dimensions. In our model, we declare spatio-temporal slices of observations by fixing the spatial and temporal dimensions: the spatial dimension may refer to the weather station, while the temporal dimension corresponds to a calendar interval. While the SOSA/SSN ontologies only support the description of a single, atomic, meteorological observation, an observation (instance of `qb:Observation`) in a spatio-temporal slice is represented by a set of measures (instances of `qb:MeasureProperty`) each linked to an observable

---

[8] https://www.w3.org/TR/vocab-data-cube/.

property (declared in our SKOS vocabulary) with property `qb:concept`. Furthermore, observations from the same `qb:Slice` have attributes such as the observation date that refers to a 24-h interval during which a certain value of a certain parameter is selected with respect to a specific condition or aggregation (e.g. maximum daily temperature).

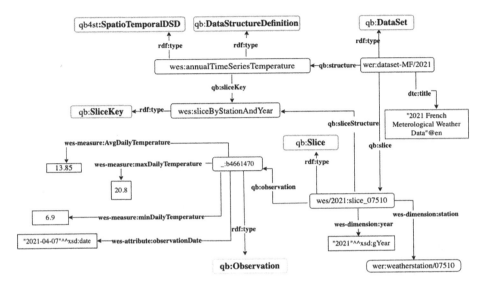

Fig. 2. Example of an RDF data Cube slice representing a TimeSeries of Air Temperatures

4   Météo-France Weather Observations RDF Dataset

This section presents the pipeline that we set up to lift the observation reports published by Météo-France into an RDF knowledge graph named *WeKG-MF* (Weather Knowledge Graph - Météo-France), that complies with the model presented in Sect. 3.

4.1   Météo-France Dataset

In France, the primary source of weather data and forecasting is the Météo-France[9] organisation. As a member of World Meteorological Organization (WMO)[10], Météo-France provides access to daily meteorological observations. These data are the result of measurements performed by 62 weather stations located in different regions in metropolitan France and overseas departments. Measurements are generated by different sensors/equipments hosted by weather

---

[9] https://www.meteofrance.com/.
[10] https://public.wmo.int/en/.

```
<http://ns.inria.fr/meteo/dataset-MF/2021> a qb:DataSet ;
qd:structure wes:annualTimeSeriesTemperature ;
dct:title "French Meterological Weather Data of 2021"@en ;
dct:description "Daily min/max/avg temperature in 2021"@en .

wes:annualTimeSeriesTemperature
a qb:DataStructureDefinition, qb4st:SpatioTemporalDSD ;
qb:component
[qb:dimension wes-dimension:year ; qb:componentAttachment qb:DataSet],
[qb:dimension wes-dimension:station ; qb:componentAttachment qb:Slice],
[qb:measure wes-measure:minDailyTemperature],
[qb:measure wes-measure:maxDailyTemperature],
[qb:measure wes-measure:avgDailyTemperature],
[qb:attribute wes-attribute:observationDate] ;
qb:sliceKey wes:SliceByStationAndYear.

wes-dimension:station a rdf:Property, qb:DimensionProperty ;
    rdfs:range weo:WeatherStation.

wes-dimension:year a rdf:Property, qb:DimensionProperty ;
    rdfs:range xsd:gYear.

wes-measure:minDailyTemp a  rdf:Property, qb:MeasureProperty ;
    rdfs:label "Daily Minimum Temperature"@en;
    rdfs:range xsd:decimal ;
    qb:concept wevp:minAirTemperature .
```

Listing 1.3. The `wes:annualTimeSeriesTemperature` Structure Definition.

stations, collected in daily tabular data files such as the table presented in Fig. 3. Each line corresponds to the values of meteorological parameters measured or observed at a given weather station (column 1) at a specific date and time (column 2). For instance, column u denotes the values of "relative air humidity" measured at different times of the day at different location. However, presented in a tabular-delimited structure and stored separately in different files, weather measurements are hardly exploitable.

numer_sta	date	pmer	tend	cod_tend	dd	ff	t	td	u	vv	ww	w1	w2	n	nbas	hbas	cl	cm	ch
07005	20210212030000	102710	-90	6	90	6.300000	269.350000	264.350000	68	20000	0	mq	mq	mq	mq	mq	mq	mq	mq
07015	20210212030000	102960	-10	6	50	3.000000	267.850000	265.150000	81	8940	0	mq	mq	mq	0	mq	mq	mq	mq
07020	20210212030000	102080	-20	6	100	13.100000	274.450000	267.950000	62	12000	2	2	mq	100	8	1250	35	mq	mq
07027	20210212030000	102300	-30	6	110	7.300000	271.350000	265.250000	63	41450	0	mq	mq	100	8	2580	mq	mq	mq

Fig. 3. Snapshot of a CSV file of meteorological parameters

4.2   Lifting Process

We downloaded from Météo-France's portal[11] the list of SYNOP[12] weather stations in GeoJSON format[13], and the monthly observation reports generated by

---

[11] https://donneespubliques.meteofrance.fr/?fond=produit&id_produit=90& id_rubrique=32.

[12] SYNOP: surface synoptic observations, a numerical code used for reporting observations made by weather stations.

[13] https://donneespubliques.meteofrance.fr/donnees_libres/Txt/Synop/postesSynop. json.

these stations as CSV files. Measurement are generated every 3 h and disseminated into the WMO network in less than 15 min. Then, we implemented a reproducible software pipeline to generate WeKG-MF in compliance with the proposed model. The core of the pipeline is the mapping task that is performed with Morph-xR2RML tool[14], an implementation of the xR2RML mapping language [7] for MongoDB databases. Pipeline scripts as well as xr2RML mapping triples are available in our github repository[15].

Additionally, we enriched the weather stations' descriptions by linking each station to the closest Wikidata entity, based on its geographic coordinates, using property dct:spatial. This allows us to get further information about the regions, departments and municipalities in which weather stations are located using simple SPARQL queries. Furthermore, leveraging Wikidata allows to benefit from its many links to other data sources, in particular the French national institute for statistics and economic studies (INSEE) which is highly used and trusted by French organisms.

WeKG-MF is published under an open licence, is assigned a DOI[16] and can be downloaded from Zenodo. In the short term, we intend to make it available through a public SPARQL endpoint. The current version of WeKG-MF covers the period from January 2019 to November 2021. Statistics about its content are provided in Table 1.

Table 1. Key statistics of the WeKG-MF dataset

Category	Resources
Total Nr. of triples	60.601.248
Nr. of classes	9
Nr. of weather stations	62
Nr. of Observations for 2019	2.788.528
Nr. of Observations for 2020	2.789.574
Nr. of Observations for 2021 (till November 2021)	2.528.467
Nr. of weather properties	22
Nr. of meteorological features	6
Nr. of Observations per observed property	≈ 405.328
Nr. of Air Temperatures slices	183
Nr. of links to Wikidata	92

---

[14] https://github.com/frmichel/morph-xr2rml/.

[15] https://github.com/Wimmics/d2kab/tree/main/meteo/Lifting-dataset.

[16] https://doi.org/10.5281/zenodo.5925413.

5   Validation: Implementing the Competency Questions

The validation process is intended to check the consistency of the model and its
ability to address requirements and cover the domain [8]. In Sect. 2, we have presented an example motivating scenario that pointed to a set of competency questions which reflect requirements that potential users may want to get answers
for. In this section, we evaluate the proposed semantic model by demonstrating
how CQs can be translated into SPARQL queries. Note that the model and the
WeKG-MF dataset were loaded in a Virtuoso triple store deployed as a Docker
image.

```
SELECT ?date ?hour ?station ?temp_max WHERE {
    {
    SELECT ?date   ?s   (MAX(?v) as   ?temp_max)
      WHERE {
        ?obs a   weo:MeteorologicalObservation;
          sosa:observedProperty wevp:airTemperature ;
          sosa:hasSimpleResult   ?v;
          wep:madeByStation ?s ;
          sosa:resultTime ?t .
        BIND(xsd:date("2020-08-01") as ?date)
        FILTER(xsd:date(?t) = ?date) }
      GROUP BY ?s ?date
    }
    ?obs a   weo:MeteorologicalObservation;
      sosa:observedProperty wevp:airTemperature ;
      sosa:hasSimpleResult   ?temp_max ;
      wep:madeByStation ?s ;
      sosa:resultTime ?t .
    ?s rdfs:label ?station   .
    FILTER(xsd:date(?t)= ?date)
    BIND(HOURS(?t) as ?hour) }
```

Listing 1.4. SPARQL query implementing CQ2

```
SELECT   ?label ?lat ?long ?coordinates WHERE {
        ?x rdfs:label ?label ;
          geosparql:hasGeometry [ geosparql:asWKT ?coordinates].
          geo:lat ?lat; geo:long ?long .
BIND("Point(0.1413499 45.1423348)"^^geosparql:wktLiteral as ?Currentposition)
BIND (geof:distance(?coordinates,?Currentposition , uom:metre) as ?distance)

}
ORDER BY ?distance
LIMIT 1
```

Listing 1.5. SPARQL query implementing CQ3

5.1   Querying Low-Level Observations

Let us first address *CQ2 "At what time was the highest value of a weather
parameter measured (observed)?"*. It points to the need to query the exact time
at which a given parameter reaches its peak. Our model captures the importance
of temporal features surrounding observational data by capturing the exact time

at which each and every observation is generated. The SPARQL query, presented in Listing 1.4, is a formal translation of CQ2 that allows us to retrieve, for each station available in the WeKG-MF dataset, at what time the maximum air temperature was reached on August 1st, 2021. It shows that *CQ2* can be successfully converted and executed as a SPARQL query over the dataset. Another set of SPARQL queries leveraging spatial GeoSPARQL functions demonstrate how end-users can query meteorological observations based on geospatial coordinates of weather stations. For instance, *CQ3* expresses the need to query the closest weather station given specific geospatial coordinates as formalized by the query of Listing 1.5.

5.2   Querying Observation Slices

Let us now address the *CQ4* "*For a specific location and given a calendar interval, provide time series of some aggregated weather parameters?*". This question motivates our adoption of the RDF Data Cube Vocabulary to represent pre-calculated time series of aggregated weather parameters. For example, in agronomy, experts are interested in calculating GDD values that are calculated based on the average daily temperature minus a base temperature which varies from a crop to another. Note that daily average temperature corresponds to the average of the minimum and maximum temperatures measured during a 24-h interval. Listing 1.6 shows the SPARQL query formalizing competency question CQ4 and shows it can easily calculate GDD values based on pre-calculated slices corresponding to a specific weather station and by selecting beginning date of a calendar interval. Note that the value of 10 in the query denotes an example of base temperature. Without pre-calculated slices, *CQ4* could be implemented by a SPARQL query that computes min/max/avg temperatures for a specific weather station on the fly. However, the complexity of the writing of the query as well as its execution time would be significantly higher. The generation of spatio-temporal slices is done once and they can be reused for the calculation of any new aggregated parameters and facilitates their implementation.

```
SELECT ?date ?station ?temp_avg ?GDD   WHERE {
    BIND(URI("http://ns.inria.fr/meteo/weatherstation/07510") as ?station)
    ?s   a qb:Slice ;
      wes-dimension:station ?station ;
      wes-dimension:year "2021"^^xsd:gYear ;
      qb:observation [
        a qb:Observation ;
        wes-attribute:observationDate ?date ;
        ?p ?temp_avg ] .
    ?p a qb:MeasureProperty ; qb:concept wevp:airTemperature .
    BIND((?temp_avg - 10) as ?GDD) }
ORDER BY ?date
```

Listing 1.6. SPARQL query implementing CQ4

5.3   Implemented Notebook and Visualizations

We developed a set of SPARQL queries available on the Github repository of our project[17], together with a Jupyter Notebook that demonstrate how the results of SPARQL queries can be used to generate visualizations from the WeKG-MF knowledge graph. As an example, Fig. 4 presents different types of data visualisations. The first plot (on the top-left) shows daily cumulative precipitations measured at the "Bordeaux-Merignac" station and the second one (on the top-right) shows the evolution of daily average temperature collected from weather stations located in the French region of "Nouvelle Aquitaine". Both plots show a comparison of aggregated values calculated based on two weather parameters (precipitation and air temperatures) available in the WeKG-MF knowledge graph. The third visualisation (on the bottom-center) shows the different weather stations located in Metropolitan France.

6   Related Work

In this section, we present existing research works on the publication of meteorological data as LOD datasets. First, the AEMET meteorological dataset [2] makes available some data sources from the Spanish Meteorological Office through a SPARQL endpoint. The dataset is based on the AEMET ontology network which follows a modular structure: a central ontology relates a set of ontologies that describe different sub-domains involved in the modeling of meteorological measurements. These sub-domains are: (meteorological) Measurements, Sensors, Time and Location. As an attempt to access to the dataset, we tried to quey the AEMET SPARQL endpoint[18], however, we noticed that the endpoint is no longer available[19]. The authors of [11] present an RDF dataset of meteorological measurements made by a weather station located at the Irstea experimental farm. Our proposition is in line with their work as we rely on most of the ontologies that they used (SOSA/SSN, GeoSPARQL, QUDT, OWL-Time ontology). Yet, we adopt somehow different design principles to propose a minimal yet extensible semantic model for meteorological data. Furthermore, we extend their work to support the description and dynamic generation of homogeneous slices of observations pre-calculated using aggregation functions over temporal and spatial dimensions. Thus, we are able to represent annual times series of daily min, max and average temperatures for each weather stations in our dataset.

The authors of [1] propose an ontological model to represent metadata and data schema of meteorological observation data from the Météo-France archives. The focus of this work is to enable access and understanding of the data sources (weather reports) with adherence to FAIR principles, yet without actually transforming the observational data included in weather reports into RDF data.

---

[17] https://github.com/Wimmics/d2kab/tree/main/meteo/sparql-examples.
[18] http://aemet.linkeddata.es/sparql.
[19] Last attempt on February, 7th 2022.

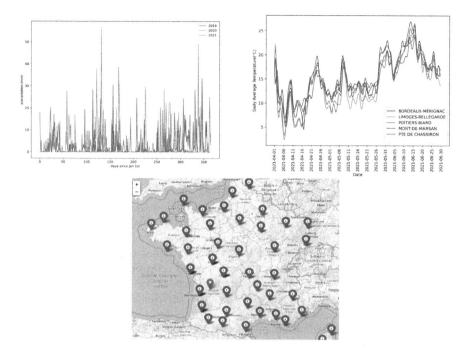

Fig. 4. Examples of Visualisation of Daily Precipitations, Average Temperature and Weather Stations Locations

In our work, we are interested not only in describing observational data but also in transforming them into semantically-enriched observations accessible via SPARQL queries in order to enable their integration in a wide range of applications from different domains such as agronomy or natural disaster monitoring.

7 Conclusion and Future Works

Meteorological observations refer to values of different weather observable properties measured across space and time by means of different sensors and equipment available in weather stations. Transforming these data into RDF knowledge graphs bridges the semantic gap between observational data and other resources also published on the Web as Linked Open Data, thus enabling their re-use in different domain applications. In terms of sustainability, we provide a fully automatic pipeline that enables us the update of the WeKG-MF graph over time with new weather data downloaded from Météo-France.

Towards this goal, in this paper we proposed a reusable and extensible model that semantically describes the multiple dimensions behind meteorological data. Our semantic model reuses the SOSA/SSN ontologies and extends it with new classes about specific feature of interest entities. These classes are rigorously defined and aligned with third-party vocabularies and ontologies. We rely on Time Ontology and GeoSPARQL to capture the spatio-temporal context surrounding observational data, as well as the QUDT schema and vocabulary to include metadata about measurement units of observed weather properties. We leverage the RDF Data Cube vocabulary to create slices of weather parameters that are the result of aggregation functions over spatial and temporal dimensions. This is typically needed to represent time series of min/max/average temperatures or precipitations in a given spatial area. We also propose a SKOS vocabulary of observable properties and features aligned with existing controlled vocabularies. In addition, we generated and published WeKG-MF, an RDF knowledge graph complying with this semantic model, from Météo-France meteorological data observations. To the best of our knowledge, our research work is the first that proposes a meteorological RDF-based knowledge graph.

This work was started in the context of the D2KAB French project[20]. Within this project, a use case concerns the design and development of a reading interface for the Plant Health Bulletins (PHB) that are meant to inform bio-vigilance stakeholders about the status of plant diseases and crop pests in French regions. This interface shall be able to augment reading experience by integrating related information likely to provide the reader with enriched context and insights into the data they are currently reading. Various related information may be involved, such as phenological stages of crops and pests, phenotyping information, taxonomic resources, geographic references and meteorological observations record history. In the latter, we typically expect the aggregated data (such as max/min/avg temperature or precipitation and the measure of Growing Daily Degrees) to be of utmost importance for experts to draw hypotheses about, e.g., the possible impact of weather conditions on the advent of crop pests at different periods or phenological stages.

Acknowledgements. This work was carried out within the project D2KAB "From Data to Knowledge in Agronomy and Biodiversity" financed by the French National Research Agency (ANR-18-CE23-0017).

References

1. Annane, A., Kamel, M., Aussenac-Gilles, N., Trojahn, C., Comparot, C., Baehr, C.: Un modèle sémantique en vue d'améliorer la fairisation des données météorologiques. In: Lefrançois, M. (ed.) IC 2021 : 32es Journées francophones d'Ingénierie des Connaissances (Proceedings of the 32nd French Knowledge Engineering Conference), Bordeaux, France, June 30–July 2, 2021, pp. 20–29 (2021). https://hal-emse.ccsd.cnrs.fr/emse-03260061
2. Atemezing, G.A., et al.: Transforming meteorological data into linked data. Semant. Web **4**(3), 285–290 (2013)
3. Battle, R., Kolas, D.: Enabling the geospatial semantic web with parliament and GeoSPARQL. Semant. Web **3**(4), 355–370 (2012)

---

[20] https://www.d2kab.org/.

4. Cox, S., Little, C.: Time ontology in OWL. W3C candidate recommendation 26 March 2020, W3C Organism (2020). https://www.w3.org/TR/owl-time/
5. Haller, A., et al.: The modular SSN ontology: a joint W3C and OGC standard specifying the semantics of sensors, observations, sampling, and actuation. Semant. Web **10**(1), 9–32 (2019)
6. Janowicz, K., Haller, A., Cox, S.J.D., Phuoc, D.L., Lefrançois, M.: SOSA: a lightweight ontology for sensors, observations, samples, and actuators. J. Web Semant. **56**, 1–10 (2019)
7. Michel, F., Djimenou, L., Faron-Zucker, C., Montagnat, J.: Translation of relational and non-relational databases into RDF with xR2RML. In: Monfort, V., Krempels, K., Majchrzak, T.A., Turk, Z. (eds.) WEBIST 2015 - Proceedings of the 11th International Conference on Web Information Systems and Technologies, Lisbon, Portugal, 20–22 May 2015, pp. 443–454. SciTePress (2015)
8. Peroni, S.: A simplified agile methodology for ontology development. In: Dragoni, M., Poveda-Villalón, M., Jimenez-Ruiz, E. (eds.) OWLED/ORE -2016. LNCS, vol. 10161, pp. 55–69. Springer, Cham (2017). https://doi.org/10.1007/978-3-319-54627-8_5
9. Hodgson, R., Keller, P.J., Spivak, J.H.: QUDT quantities, units, dimensions and data types ontologies. Tech. rep., NASA (2014). http://www.qudt.org/
10. Reynolds, D., Cyganiak, R.: The RDF data cube vocabulary. W3C recommendation. W3C (2014). https://www.w3.org/TR/2014/REC-vocab-data-cube-20140116/
11. Roussey, C., Bernard, S., André, G., Boffety, D.: Weather data publication on the LOD using SOSA/SSN ontology. Semant. Web **11**(4), 581–591 (2020)
12. Uschold, M., Gruninger, M.: Ontologies: principles, methods and applications. Knowl. Eng. Rev. **11**(2), 93–136 (1996)

An Ontological Approach for Recommending a Feature Selection Algorithm

Aparna Nayak$^{(\boxtimes)}$, Bojan Božić , and Luca Longo

SFI Centre for Research Training in Machine Learning, School of Computer Science,
Technological University Dublin, Dublin, Republic of Ireland
{aparna.nayak,bojan.bozic,luca.longo}@tudublin.ie

Abstract. Feature selection plays an important role in machine learning or data mining problems. Removing irrelevant features increases model accuracy and reduces the computational cost. However, selecting important features is not a simple task as one feature selection algorithm does not perform well on all the datasets that are of interest. This paper tries to address the recommendation of a feature selection algorithm based on dataset characteristics and quality. The research uses three types of dataset characteristics along with data quality metrics. The main contribution of the work is the utilization of Semantic Web techniques to develop a novel system that can aid in robust feature selection algorithm recommendations. The system's strength lies in assisting users of machine learning algorithms by providing more relevant feature selection algorithms for the dataset using an ontology called Feature Selection algorithm recommendation based on Data Characteristics and Quality (FSDCQ). Results are generated using six different feature selection algorithms and four types of classifiers on ten datasets from UCI repository. Recommendations take the form of "Feature selection algorithm X is recommended for dataset i, as it performed better on dataset j, similar to dataset i in terms of class overlap 0.3, label noise 0.2, completeness 0.9, conciseness 0.8 units". While the domain-specific ontology FSDCQ was created to aid in the task of algorithm recommendation for feature selection, it is easily applicable to other meta-learning scenarios.

Keywords: Feature selection algorithms · Meta-features · Ontology

1 Introduction

Feature selection is one of the core phases of any machine learning (ML) task, as it might significantly improve model building by removing irrelevant features. Several algorithms have been developed for such a phase and choosing one among the many is a costly decision, a trade-off between the time spent by automatic procedures and domain experts [4, 7]. Inappropriate feature selection algorithms might cause serious problems, such as compromising the quality of the patterns

© Springer Nature Switzerland AG 2022
T. Di Noia et al. (Eds.): ICWE 2022, LNCS 13362, pp. 300–314, 2022.
https://doi.org/10.1007/978-3-031-09917-5_20

to be learnt from data and, thus, model performance. A common approach is 'trial-and-error', which tends to be often effective [19]. Another approach is to choose a feature selection algorithm based on the characteristics of the dataset. Specifically, this can be implemented by using meta-learning concepts [36] and by utilizing dataset characteristics that are called "meta-features". Automating the algorithm selection process for feature selection is a challenge in data mining. However, if overcome, it has the potential to significantly increase data scientists and machine learning practitioners productivity [24]. There exists a relationship between the performance of a feature selection algorithm and the characteristics of the dataset [32].

To address this specific relationship, we propose a domain ontology along with the consideration of Dataset Characteristics and Quality (DCQ), respectively representing dataset characteristics and the quality of information. Feature Selection algorithm recommendation using DCQ (FSDCQ), is modeled by adding rules to the domain ontology DCQ, to enhance the expressivity which acts as a recommender. The benefits of using an ontology to deliver such a recommendation include interoperability, potential reuse, and sharing of knowledge [35]. The particular research question investigated in this research is: "To what extent can a domain ontology facilitate the recommendation of feature selection algorithms?". The work's main objective is the adoption of Semantic Web techniques to develop a novel system that can aid in robust feature selection algorithm recommendation. The use of rule languages enables a better understanding of the role of each meta-feature, thereby increasing the model's explainability [13,39,40].

The remainder of this article is structured as follows. Section 2 reviews related work on the existing approaches to automatically recommend feature selection algorithms, and existing ontologies to describe the dataset quality and its characteristics. Section 3 presents a novel domain ontology, followed by a description of an empirical experiment in Sect. 4. Results of such an experiment are presented and discussed in Sect. 5. Finally, Sect. 6 concludes the research work by providing directions for future work.

2 Related Work

This section briefly discusses the existing work on automatic feature selection recommendation methods and the application of ontologies related to data characteristics and its quality.

2.1 Feature Selection

The two primary feature selection methods identified include (i) the filter approach and (ii) the wrapper approach. While various feature selection algorithms have been proposed, some of these outperform others in terms of performance (for example, classification accuracy) for a given dataset [41]. This results in the emergence of a new research area devoted to establishing intrinsic relationships between dataset characteristics and feature selection algorithms. A literature review was carried out in order to identify techniques that recommend a feature selection algorithm based on meta-features. Meta-features, describe the properties of the dataset which are predictive for the performance of machine learning algorithms trained on them [29]. The description of a dataset in terms of its information/statistical properties can be referred to as dataset characteristics. Three distinct sets of measures are used to extract dataset characteristics: (i) simple, statistical, and information-theoretic features (ii) model-based features (iii) landmarking features [38]. Simple properties represent those taken from the attribute value table of the dataset. Statistical properties are used to determine the correlation and symmetry of attributes. Information-theoretical properties seek to characterise the nominal attributes and their relationship with the class attribute. Model-based properties adopt ML methods to represent datasets. Landmarking properties illustrate the performance achieved by simple classification algorithms.

Table 1 summarises the literature covering those approaches in which meta-features were used to build a recommendation model for automatically selecting algorithms in machine learning. In detail, an advisory function refers to a method that aims to recommend an algorithm from an existing knowledge base. The proposed work aims to use ontology as advisory function. Some of the applications that uses ontology as advisory methods/recommendation are, product recommendation based on text [31], health-care [5,6], higher education [17]. Therefore, it is a novel approach to solve recommendation of feature selection algorithm using ontology. To the best of our knowledge, no research has focused on considering data quality as a characteristic of a dataset. In this article, beside the aforementioned simple, statistical, information, and quality-based measures we propose an additional category to characterise datasets, which includes quality-based measures.

2.2   Ontology

A methodology to build an ontology from scratch is discussed in Methontology [8] where a set of activities conforming the ontology development process is presented. Following best practices in ontology development, the Data Characteristics and Quality (DCQ) ontology reuses appropriate classes from a set of ontologies that are designed for data quality and data mining applications. An extensive literature has been conducted to understand existing vocabularies to support meta-features, and a vocabulary of terms have been composed for DCQ.

Meta-features are usually described as a part of Data Mining (DM) ontologies. 'OntoDM' is a general data mining ontology designed to provide a unified framework for data mining research. It makes an attempt to encompass the entirety of the data mining cycle [20]. 'Expose' is an ontology for standardizing the description of machine learning experiments. This ontology is used to express and share meta-data about experiments [37].

Table 1. Literature review and comparison of advisory functions used for recommendations

Source	Advisory function	Number of datasets	Number of classification techniques	Number of feature selection algorithms	Evaluation metrics	Dataset characteristic			
						Simple, statistical	Information theoretical	Model based	Land marking
[11]	Ranking based on McNemar test	1082*	5	8	Accuracy	✓	✓	✗	✗
[14]	SVM	156	–	7	Accuracy	✓	✓	✗	✗
[15]	kNN	58	–	–	F1 score				
[19]	C5.0 decision tree	128	5	3	Accuracy, time complexity	✓	✓	✗	✗
[23]	Ranking based on MCPM	213	5	5	Learning time, Percentage of selected attributes, Error rate	✓	✓	✓	✓
[25]	kNN	47	–	10	Spearman's rank correlation	✓	✓	✗	✓
[26]	kNN	38	–	9	Accuracy	✓	✓	✗	✗
[27]	Regression	123	–	5	Correlation	✓	✓	✓	✗
[28]	Regression	54	–	9	Accuracy	✓	✓	✓	✓
[32]	J4.8 decision trees	26	4	3	Accuracy	✓	✗	✗	✗
[33]	kNN	84	–	–	Accuracy, Execution time	✓	✗	✗	✗
[41]	kNN	115	22	5	Recommendation hit ration based on accuracy	✓	✓	✗	✗
[43]	Variance, LIBSVM	84	–	3	Accuracy	✓	✓	✓	✓

* includes artificial dataset

To represent the relationship between data mining tasks and dataset characteristics, multiple ontologies have been designed. 'OntoDM-KDD' [21], 'OntoDT' [22], 'CRISP-DM' [34] are some of the additional ontologies that are based on data mining-related concepts. 'DMOP' is a data mining optimization ontology that supports various stages of the data mining process [12]. A class hierarchy that relates datasets and their features that were established in DMOP is reused in DCQ.

Data quality is one of the essential component while describing a dataset. Data Quality Management (DQM) is an ontology that refers to the conceptualization of the data quality domain, the establishment of cleaning standards, and the reporting of data quality problems [9]. Data Cleaning Ontology (DCO) refines and extends data cleaning operations which directly assesses data quality [2]. Reasoning Violations Ontology (RVO) describes the reasoning errors of RDF and OWL [3]. Another matured ontology is recommended by the World Wide Web Consortium (W3C)[1] which covers most of the aspects of data quality [1].

3   A Novel Ontological Model

In order to recommend feature selection algorithms intelligently by extracting meta-features from a dataset, reuse of classes from existing ontologies is proposed. Specifically, the proposed ontology is developed by considering and

---
[1] https://www.w3.org/TR/vocab-dqv/.

reusing classes from the 'OntoDT', 'OntoDM-KDD', 'CRISP-DM' ontologies along with the 'DCO', 'DQM', 'RVO', and 'DQV' ontologies. The W3C recommendation ontology language, OWL (Web Ontology Language), is adopted to develop such an ontology with Protégé editor.

3.1 Feature Selection Algorithm Recommendation Using Dataset Characteristics and Quality (FSDCQ) Ontology

Over the last several decades, researchers in meta-learning have actively investigated data characteristics that may aid in the development of models. The DQV ontology proposes categories, dimensions, and metrics for data quality, and a similar approach is used in DCQ, where data characteristics are viewed as metrics. These metrics are classified into five dimensions, which fall under the dataset characteristics and quality category as shown in Tables 4 and 5. The class hierarchy of the FSDCQ ontology is shown in Fig. 1. Table 2 depicts ontology metrics of FSDCQ before adding individuals.

The data characteristics and quality vocabulary requirements are specified with a set of competency questions. Competency questions also help users evaluate an ontology. To develop competency questions, we must first define our domain of interest, for which our ontology will serve as a representation. Information gathering is a critical component to accomplishing this goal, especially if we do not fully understand the subject matter for which we are developing an ontology. FSDCQ is primarily concerned with conceptualizing the relationship between meta-features and a feature selection algorithm.

Table 2. FSDCQ metrics

Property	Count
Axioms	396
Classes	39
Logical axioms	326

Fig. 1. Class hierarchy of FSDCQ

Competency questions are directed at users and help us define the scope of an ontology. In other words, these are the queries for which users search an ontology and its associated knowledge base for solutions. The following are the main competence questions linked with proposed FSDCQ:

- **CQ:** Given a machine learning classification task/dataset, which feature selection algorithm will yield optimal results? This competency question is decomposed into many sub-questions. Coarse-grained questions include
    - **CQa:** Given only a set of pieces of data quality information, which feature selection algorithm performs the best?
    - **CQb:** Given only a set of pieces of data characteristics information, which feature selection algorithm performs the best?

The competency questions, at a more granular level, are listed in Table 3. These questions can be queried on the FSDCQ ontology using SPARQL to understand whether the modeled ontology meets the user requirements.

4   Proposed Methodology

This section presents a recommendation model for feature selection algorithm, as depicted in Fig. 2. The implementation process is divided into three main steps, as detailed below:

Table 3. Competency questions of Feature Selection algorithm recommendation using Dataset Characteristics and Quality ontology

CQ2: What characteristics belong to a dataset?
CQ3: What are the different measures to compute data quality for classification tasks?
CQ4: Which feature selection algorithm is suitable for reaching the data quality level X?
CQ5: What are the dataset characteristics that a feature selection method X requires?

- extraction of dataset characteristics and quality information;
- formation of a rule base using feature selection algorithms;
- populating ontology for the recommendations

These steps are described in details in the following sections.

4.1   Extraction of Dataset Characteristics and Quality

The dataset repository contains multiple datasets from which meta-features are extracted. Flat files are used in the experiment, which contain lines of text extracted from a collection of uniform records, each of which contains multiple attributes separated by a comma, semicolon, space, or tab.

1. Preprocessing: This is the first phase in which raw dataset is considered as input. Headers in the original dataset are not considered for analysis. Missing values are treated and categorical string values are encoded to integer values as presence of these of feature values prevents the extraction of certain characterization measures.

2. Feature extraction: In this step, the meta-features listed in Tables 4 and 5 are extracted both from the preprocessed data and the original dataset. Table 5 lists the data quality metrics that are proposed by this research for meta-learning. A supporting document is made available in the git repository that explains the formulas/algorithms used to compute all the meta-features.

Dataset characteristics are broadly classified into three dimensions as described in Sect. 2.1. The proposed research takes into account the characteristics of the dataset identified as significant by [23]. Table 4 gives an overview of the direct measures that are considered to model FSDCQ. Meta-features related to data quality are classified into two dimensions. The classification dimension represents the important metrics for machine learning classification tasks.

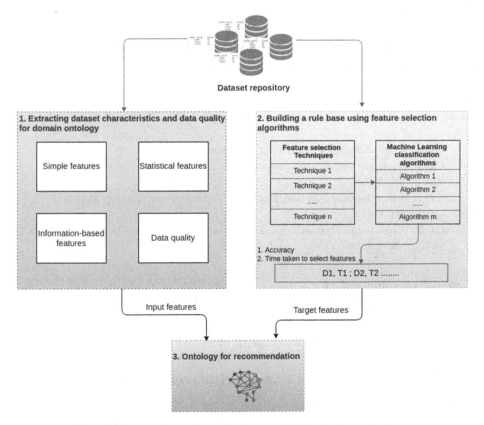

Fig. 2. Proposed recommendation model for feature selection

Intrinsic dimension represents the metrics that are independent of user's context [42]. Table 5 gives a list of data quality metrics that are extracted to model the ontology FSDCQ. The extracted meta-features are populated in the proposed ontology, which is described in Sect. 4.3.

4.2 Building a Rule Base

A rule base is an external knowledge that is added to the ontology to enhance the expressivity of the ontology. This rule base helps to identify the relationship between the feature selection algorithm and the database. Feature selection algorithms are grouped into two broad categories: filter and wrapper. The filter method is based on the dataset characteristics, while the wrapper approach measures the feature subset using the learning algorithm's error rate as the evaluation function. Due to the complex nature of wrapper methods, the proposed research focuses on the filter method for experiments. The proposed study considers a range of feature selection algorithms characterized by their filter classes and evaluation criteria (refer Fig. 3). Feature selection algorithms are evaluated by considering different types of classifiers such as instance (kNN), symbolic (C4.5), statistical (Naive bayes), and connectionist (SVM) approaches. To implement machine learning models, one algorithm is chosen from each type of classifier. Feature selection algorithms for recommendations are ranked based on two performance metrics, 1. Accuracy of the model 2. Time required for the feature selection algorithm to select features. As a result, for each dataset, we have a ranking of the feature selection methods. This ranking is used to determine the optimal feature selection methods, which serve as the target features.

Table 4. Characteristics selected to describe the dataset

Dataset characteristic	Metrics	Description
Simple	Number of classes	Represents the properties taken from the flat file.
	Number of features	
	Number of instances	
Statistical	Average correlation of the feature attributes	Calculates the degree of linear relation degree between all attribute pairs.
	Average asymmetry of the features	Describes the distribution of data from the symmetry condition.
Information	Class entropy	Indicates the probability distribution of observations in a set of data that correspond to a certain class.
	Signal/noise ratio	Indicates the amount of inadequate data in the dataset.
	Equivalent number of attributes	Represents minimum number of attributes required to represent the class

Table 5. Proposed metrics to measure data quality

Dimension	Metrics	Description
Classification	Class overlap	When a region in the data space contains data points from multiple classes.
	Outlier detection	Identifies an unusual data item.
	Class imbalance	Indicates difference in the number of examples in each class. It can be calculated with the entropy of class proportions, imbalance ratio.
Intrinsic	Completeness	Refers to the comprehensiveness or wholeness of the data.
	Conciseness	Refers to uniqueness of the data points.
	Accuracy	Refers to whether the data values stored for an object are the correct values

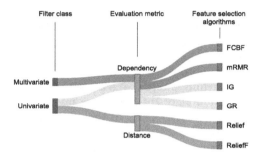

Fig. 3. Feature selection algorithms considered in FSDCQ

4.3 Populating Ontology for the Recommendations

Meta-features that are described in Sect. 4.1 are populated as individuals in the ontology along with highly ranked feature selection algorithms that are calculated in Sect. 4.2. It acts as historical data for recommendations. These meta-features are uplifted using mapping languages. Some of the existing mapping languages are R2RML [16,30], JUMA [10], MappingMaster [18]. Semantic Web Rule Language (SWRL) rules are formulated to recommend feature selection algorithms that are based on historical data. Meta-features will be antecedent of the SWRL rule where as feature selection algorithm will be consequent. Listing 4.1 shows sample of SWRL rule where ?d1 and ?d2 are variables to unify dataset instances, ?mf1 for meta-feature 1, ?fsa for feature selection algorithm. Axiom 'differentFrom' is important to avoid same dataset instances getting binded for variables d1 and d2. SWRL selects feature selection algorithm for dataset d2, if all the attributes of d1 and d2 are same.

```
dcat:dataset(?d1)  ^  dcat:dataset(?d2)  ^  FSDCQ:hasMF1(?d1, ?mf1)
^  FSDCQ:hasMF1(?d2, ?mf1)  ^  FSDCQ:hasFSA(?d1, ?fsa)
^  differentFrom(?d1,?d2) -> sqwrl:select(?d2, ?fsa)
```

Listing 4.1. SWRL rule format for recommendations

5 Experimental Results and Discussion

The overall goal of the FSDCQ is to provide assistance with decision-making phases that affect the result of the knowledge discovery process. It concentrates on two stages of the CRISP-DM process (data understanding and data preparation), which need a significant search for alternative approaches. One such approach is feature selection. Data mining practitioners can consult the FSDCQ ontology to describe meta-features of the dataset. Another application of FSDCQ is meta-learning, which involves the analysis of meta-features to recommend the feature selection algorithm. Thus, the novel objective is to support meta-analysis of machine learning experiments to automatically identify feature selection algorithms that are predictive of good or bad performance. Experiments are conducted on a laptop running Linux Mint 19.3 Cinnamon and powered by an Intel(R) Core(TM) i7-9750H CPU running at 2.60GHz with 16GB of RAM. The experiment is publicly accessible through a git repository[2] and makes use of ten datasets from the UCI repository. Dataset characteristics and quality information are extracted as mentioned in Sect. 4.1. Basic dataset characteristics of the considered dataset are tabulated in Table 6. Datasets are considered to have a small to a large number of features, a small to a large number of attributes, and be a binary or multiclass. Datasets are preprocessed to extract their characteristics and quality information.

Table 6. Basic dataset characteristics

Dataset	Features	Attributes	Classes
Wholesale customer	8	440	2
Caesarian	6	79	2
Bank	17	45211	2
Bank note	5	1371	2
Heart failure	13	299	2
Wine	14	177	3
HCV energy	29	1385	4
Las vegas trip	20	504	7
Iris	5	149	3
Glass	11	213	6

---

[2] https://github.com/aparnanayakn/onto-DCQ-FS.git.

The classification accuracy of the model and the time required to select features by each feature selection algorithm are used to rank feature selection algorithms for each dataset. However, classification algorithms exhibit varying degrees of bias. In order to overcome this limitation, four representative classification algorithms are considered in the proposed research. Highlighted algorithms in each type are considered for evaluating feature selection techniques.

The extracted characteristics and quality features are mapped to the proposed ontology FSDCQ using MappingMaster [18]. MappingMaster is a domain-specific language for defining spreadsheet-to-OWL ontology mappings. It allows to map individuals to the ontology by mapping classes, object properties, and data properties. The Fig. 4 depicts the screenshot the Protégé after it has been populated with individuals. We can observe that file 'test1.csv' has no feature selection algorithms in property assertions.

Relationships between individuals have to be inferred to recommend a feature selection algorithm. SWRL is a rule-based language that extends the ontology axioms with rules in antecedent-consequent form. These rules are based on OWL classes and properties, which work on the concept of unification. Object properties that describe meta-features will be antecedent of the rules. Corresponding feature selection algorithms will be the consequent of the rules.

Fig. 4. Individuals and their properties

The proposed work has two key components. First, domain ontology, FSDCQ which can be evaluated using competency questions. Competency questions are answered with the help of SPARQL queries. This helps users understand the domain represented in the ontology. Another key component is the rule-based recommendation model, which can be evaluated using the recommendation hit ratio. This metric is evaluated by comparing the time taken to select features by the recommended feature selection algorithm and accuracy of the classifiers by incorporating the recommended feature selection algorithm with the accuracy of classifiers with non-recommended feature selection algorithms. However, in the current experiment, ten samples are considered, along with an additional two samples for testing. Recommendations for two testing samples is as shown in Fig. 5. These testing samples have same features to that of testing samples, which can be seen in Fig. 6.

dataset	co	outlierDe	instances	attributes	uniqu	entropy	snr	ena	symmetr	fsa1	fsa2
Wholesale cus	0	0.00057	440	8	2	0.90732	50.71	2.44432	0	MI	GR
Caesarian.csv	0	0.00211	79	6	2	0.98038	1.36378	0.18146	0	mrmr	fcbf
bank-full.csv	0	1.43E-05	45211	17	2	0.52063	5.38246	0.02144	0	fcbf	GR
data_banknot	0	0.00292	1371	5	2	0.99123	161.965	0.1288	0.75	fcbf	GR
heart_failure_o	0	0.00103	299	13	2	0.90554	4.23422	0.0598	0.2	MI	MI
wine.data	0	0.00323	177	14	3	0.98843	12.0104	0.14553	0.53846	relieff	GR
HCV-Egy-Data	0	0	1385	29	4	0.99952	2.72289	0.03517	0.73333	GR	GR
LasVegasTripA	0	0.00377	504	20	7	0.96622	0.04546	0.04299	0	GR	GR
iris.data	0	0	149	5	3	0.99996	8.38172	0.18377	0.5	relieff	GR
glass.data	0	0.00171	213	11	6	0.84301	6.97003	0.05771	0.5	MI	GR
test1.csv	0	0.00103	299	13	2	0.90554	4.23422	0.0598	0.2		
test2.csv	0	0.00211	79	6	2	0.98038	1.36378	0.18146	0		

Fig. 5. Recommendations using SQWRL

Fig. 6. FSDCQ individuals in flat file format

6   Conclusion and Future Works

We introduced the FSDCQ ontology in this research study. It establishes a conceptual framework for meta-learning and the links between meta-features in order to facilitate algorithm recommendation. The methodology proposed for recommending feature selection algorithms establishes relationships between ontology individuals and unifies them to recommend feature selection algorithms.

In a future study, we will strengthen the FSDCQ ontology by enhancing the expressivity of SWRL rules. In the proposed research, the unification property is utilized for the recommendation. However, in the real-world, we may have many situations where multiple features of the dataset are similar but not the same values. Unification fails to recommend feature selection algorithms in such cases. Identifying the most frequently occurring pattern as a recommendation rule will be other future work of the study. Another interesting extension would be clustering the datasets based on their domain, and feature selection algorithm recommendation can be based on the domain. Additionally, FSDCQ can be upgraded to identify the root causes of data quality problems.

Acknowledgements. This publication has emanated from research supported in part by a grant from Science Foundation Ireland under Grant number 18/CRT/6183. For the purpose of Open Access, the author has applied a CC BY public copyright licence to any Author Accepted Manuscript version arising from this submission.

References

1. Albertoni, R., Isaac, A.: Introducing the data quality vocabulary (DQV). Semantic Web **12**(1), 81–97 (2021)
2. Almeida, R., Maio, P., Oliveira, P., Barroso, J.: An ontology-based methodology for reusing data cleaning knowledge. In: Proceedings of the International Conference on Knowledge Engineering and Ontology Development (KEOD 2015), pp. 202–211. SciTePress (2015)

3. Bozic, B., Brennan, R., Feeney, K., Mendel-Gleason, G.: Describing reasoning results with RVO, the reasoning violations ontology. In: MEPDaW and LDQ Co-located with ESWC, CEUR Workshop Proceedings, vol. 1585, pp. 62–69 (2016)
4. Chandrashekar, G., Sahin, F.: A survey on feature selection methods. Comput. Electr. Eng. **40**(1), 16–28 (2014)
5. Chen, J., Li, K., Rong, H., Bilal, K., Yang, N., Li, K.: A disease diagnosis and treatment recommendation system based on big data mining and cloud computing. Inf. Sci. **435**, 124–149 (2018)
6. Chen, R.C., Huang, Y.H., Bau, C.T., Chen, S.M.: A recommendation system based on domain ontology and SWRL for anti-diabetic drugs selection. Expert Syst. Appl. **39**(4), 3995–4006 (2012)
7. Dash, M., Liu, H.: Feature selection for classification. Intell. Data Anal. **1**(1–4), 131–156 (1997)
8. Fernández-López, M., Gómez-Pérez, A., Juristo, N.: Methontology: from ontological art towards ontological engineering (1997)
9. Fürber, C., Hepp, M.: Towards a vocabulary for data quality management in semantic web architectures. In: Proceedings of the 2011 EDBT/ICDT Workshop on Linked Web Data Management, pp. 1–8. ACM (2011)
10. Junior, A.C., Debruyne, C., Longo, L., O'Sullivan, D.: On the mental workload assessment of uplift mapping representations in linked data. In: Longo, L., Leva, M.C. (eds.) H-WORKLOAD 2018. CCIS, vol. 1012, pp. 160–179. Springer, Cham (2019). https://doi.org/10.1007/978-3-030-14273-5_10
11. Kalousis, A., Hilario, M.: Feature selection for meta-learning. In: Cheung, D., Williams, G.J., Li, Q. (eds.) PAKDD 2001. LNCS (LNAI), vol. 2035, pp. 222–233. Springer, Heidelberg (2001). https://doi.org/10.1007/3-540-45357-1_26
12. Keet, C.M., Lawrynowicz, A., d'Amato, C., Kalousis, A., Nguyen, P., Palma, R., Stevens, R., Hilario, M.: The data mining optimization ontology. J. Web Semant. **32**, 43–53 (2015)
13. Longo, L., Goebel, R., Lecue, F., Kieseberg, P., Holzinger, A.: Explainable artificial intelligence: concepts, applications, research challenges and visions. In: Holzinger, A., Kieseberg, P., Tjoa, A.M., Weippl, E. (eds.) CD-MAKE 2020. LNCS, vol. 12279, pp. 1–16. Springer, Cham (2020). https://doi.org/10.1007/978-3-030-57321-8_1
14. Mantovani, R.G., Rossi, A.L.D., Alcobaça, E., Vanschoren, J., de Carvalho, A.C.P.L.F.: A meta-learning recommender system for hyperparameter tuning: predicting when tuning improves SVM classifiers. Inf. Sci. **501**, 193–221 (2019)
15. Nakamura, M., Otsuka, A., Kimura, H.: Automatic selection of classification algorithms for non-experts using meta-features. China-USA Bus. Rev. **13**(3) (2014)
16. Nayak, A., Bozic, B., Longo, L.: Extending r2rml-f to support dynamic datatype and language tags. Proc. Comput. Sci. **192**, 709–716 (2021). Knowledge-Based and Intelligent Information & Engineering Systems: Proceedings of the 25th International Conference KES2021
17. Obeid, C., Lahoud, I., El Khoury, H., Champin, P.A.: Ontology-based recommender system in higher education. In: Companion Proceedings of the The Web Conference 2018, pp. 1031–1034 (2018)
18. O'Connor, M.J., Halaschek-Wiener, C., Musen, M.A.: Mapping master: a flexible approach for mapping spreadsheets to OWL. In: Patel-Schneider, P.F., et al. (eds.) ISWC 2010. LNCS, vol. 6497, pp. 194–208. Springer, Heidelberg (2010). https://doi.org/10.1007/978-3-642-17749-1_13
19. Oreski, D., Oreski, S., Klicek, B.: Effects of dataset characteristics on the performance of feature selection techniques. Appl. Soft Comput. **52**, 109–119 (2017)

20. Panov, P., Dzeroski, S., Soldatova, L.N.: Ontodm: An ontology of data mining. In: Workshops Proceedings of the 8th IEEE International Conference on Data Mining, pp. 752–760. IEEE Computer Society (2008)
21. Panov, P., Soldatova, L., Džeroski, S.: OntoDM-KDD: ontology for representing the knowledge discovery process. In: Fürnkranz, J., Hüllermeier, E., Higuchi, T. (eds.) DS 2013. LNCS (LNAI), vol. 8140, pp. 126–140. Springer, Heidelberg (2013). https://doi.org/10.1007/978-3-642-40897-7_9
22. Panov, P., Soldatova, L.N., Dzeroski, S.: Generic ontology of datatypes. Inf. Sci. **329**, 900–920 (2016)
23. Parmezan, A.R.S., Lee, H.D., Spolaôr, N., Wu, F.C.: Automatic recommendation of feature selection algorithms based on dataset characteristics. Expert Syst. Appl. **185**, 115589 (2021)
24. Parmezan, A.R.S., Lee, H.D., Wu, F.C.: Metalearning for choosing feature selection algorithms in data mining: proposal of a new framework. Expert Syst. Appl. **75**, 1–24 (2017)
25. Peng, Y., Flach, P.A., Soares, C., Brazdil, P.: Improved dataset characterisation for meta-learning. In: Lange, S., Satoh, K., Smith, C.H. (eds.) DS 2002. LNCS, vol. 2534, pp. 141–152. Springer, Heidelberg (2002). https://doi.org/10.1007/3-540-36182-0_14
26. Pise, N., Kulkarni, P.: Algorithm selection for classification problems. In: SAI Computing Conference (SAI), pp. 203–211. IEEE (2016)
27. Reif, M., Shafait, F., Dengel, A.: Prediction of classifier training time including parameter optimization. In: Bach, J., Edelkamp, S. (eds.) KI 2011. LNCS (LNAI), vol. 7006, pp. 260–271. Springer, Heidelberg (2011). https://doi.org/10.1007/978-3-642-24455-1_25
28. Reif, M., Shafait, F., Goldstein, M., Breuel, T., Dengel, A.: Automatic classifier selection for non-experts. Pattern Anal. Appl. **17**(1), 83–96 (2012). https://doi.org/10.1007/s10044-012-0280-z
29. Rivolli, A., Garcia, L.P., Soares, C., Vanschoren, J., de Carvalho, A.C.: Meta-features for meta-learning. Knowl. Based Syst. **240**, 108101 (2022)
30. Rodriguez-Muro, M., Rezk, M.: Efficient sparql-to-sql with r2rml mappings. J. Web Semant. **33**, 141–169 (2015)
31. Rosa, R.L., Schwartz, G.M., Ruggiero, W.V., Rodríguez, D.Z.: A knowledge-based recommendation system that includes sentiment analysis and deep learning. IEEE Trans. Indust. Inf. **15**(4), 2124–2135 (2018)
32. Shilbayeh, S., Vadera, S.: Feature selection in meta learning framework. In: Science and Information Conference, pp. 269–275. IEEE (2014)
33. Song, Q., Wang, G., Wang, C.: Automatic recommendation of classification algorithms based on dataset characteristics. Pattern Recogn. **45**(7), 2672–2689 (2012)
34. Tianxing, M., Myint, M., Guan, W., Zhukova, N., Mustafin, N.: A hierarchical data mining process ontology. In: 28th Conference of Open Innovations Association (FRUCT), pp. 465–471. IEEE (2021)
35. Uschold, M., Gruninger, M.: Ontologies: principles, methods and applications. Knowl. Eng. Rev. **11**(2), 93–136 (1996)
36. Vanschoren, J.: Meta-learning: A Survey. arXiv preprint arXiv:1810.03548 (2018)
37. Vanschoren, J., Soldatova, L.: Exposé: an ontology for data mining experiments. In: International Workshop on Third Generation Data Mining: Towards Service-Oriented Knowledge Discovery (SoKD-2010), pp. 31–46 (2010)
38. Vilalta, R., Giraud-Carrier, C.G., Brazdil, P., Soares, C.: Using meta-learning to support data mining. Int. J. Comput. Sci. Appl. **1**(1), 31–45 (2004)

39. Vilone, G., Longo, L.: Classification of explainable artificial intelligence methods through their output formats. Mach. Learn. Knowl. Extract. **3**(3), 615–661 (2021)
40. Vilone, G., Longo, L.: Notions of explainability and evaluation approaches for explainable artificial intelligence. Inf. Fusion **76**, 89–106 (2021)
41. Wang, G., Song, Q., Sun, H., Zhang, X., Xu, B., Zhou, Y.: A feature subset selection algorithm automatic recommendation method. J. Artif. Intell. Res. **47**, 1–34 (2013)
42. Zaveri, A., Rula, A., Maurino, A., Pietrobon, R., Lehmann, J., Auer, S.: Quality assessment for linked data: a survey. Semantic Web **7**(1), 63–93 (2016)
43. Zhongguo, Y., Hongqi, L., Ali, S., Yile, A.: Choosing classification algorithms and its optimum parameters based on data set characteristics. J. Comput. **28**(5), 26–38 (2017)

Towards Bridging the Gap Between Knowledge Graphs and Chatbots

Annemarie Wittig[1], Aleksandr Perevalov[1,2], and Andreas Both[2,3(✉)]

[1] Anhalt University of Applied Sciences, Köthen, Germany
[2] Leipzig University of Applied Sciences, Leipzig, Germany
andreas.both@htwk-leipzig.de
[3] DATEV eG, Nuremberg, Germany

Abstract. Chatbots are nowadays being applied widely in different life domains. One major reason for this trend is the mature development process that is supported by large companies and sophisticated conversational platforms. However, the required development steps are mostly done manually while transforming existing knowledge bases into interaction configurations, s.t., algorithms integrated into the conversational platforms are enabled to learn the intended interaction patterns. However, already existing domain knowledge may get vanished while transforming a structured knowledge base into a "flat" text representation without references backwards. In this paper, we aim for an automatic process dedicated to generating interaction configurations for a conversational platform (Google Dialogflow) from an existing domain-specific knowledge base. Our ultimate goal is to generate chatbot configurations automatically, s.t., the quality and efficiency are increased.

Keywords: Dialog systems · Chatbots · Knowledge graphs · Synthetic data generation · Natural-language interfaces · Software generator · Human-computer interactions

1 Introduction

Chatbots and other natural-language user interfaces have become a major driver for interactive systems. It is not hard to predict a very important role of such systems for user interaction in the future. The technology for creating chatbots is becoming more powerful and robust (e.g., [1,7]). Platforms like Amazon Alexa[1], Google Dialogflow[2], and Microsoft Bot Framework[3] as well as powerful open-source frameworks (like Rasa[4]) provide a rich set of features to build (novel) Web-based dialog systems without strong technical skills.

---

[1] cf., https://developer.amazon.com/alexa/.
[2] cf., https://cloud.google.com/dialogflow.
[3] cf., https://dev.botframework.com/.
[4] cf., https://rasa.com/ and https://github.com/RasaHQ/rasa.

© Springer Nature Switzerland AG 2022
T. Di Noia et al. (Eds.): ICWE 2022, LNCS 13362, pp. 315–322, 2022.
https://doi.org/10.1007/978-3-031-09917-5_21

However, creating a chatbot using one of the well-known conversational plat-forms might become time-consuming while doing the configuration process man-ually. This process demands the alignment of a domain-specific knowledge base with the possible user-chatbot interaction patterns (or intents). Typically, this process is done manually and cannot take advantage of pre-existing knowledge. A few research initiatives have recently addressed this automation challenge and are therefore considered as related work. For example, in [8] BPMN models are used as input for a chatbot generator. Another approach uses HTML pages, annotated with specific information, to create a specific chatbot automatically, as described in [3].

To the best of our knowledge, a pre-existing knowledge graph (KG) [6] cannot be directly used for configuring chatbot platforms, although it might already perfectly define the domain knowledge in a machine-readable format. From this observation, we conclude the demand for a process that will enable usage of the domain-specific knowledge bases for creating the configurations, s.t., a chatbot can be generated automatically while preserving the modeled domain knowledge. This approach follows the same goal as Question Answering over KGs [4]: to make structured domain-specific data accessible by natural-language input.

Our long-term goal is to establish a generalized, robust engineering app-roach to create a chatbot configuration based solely on an existing standardized domain-specific knowledge base. In this paper, we consider a special type of knowledge bases – knowledge graphs (KGs). We hypothesize that from a KG, the training data for interaction patterns of a chatbot (typically: questions and its intents; in this paper, we generally use the term *questions*) can be generated. Typically, for a KG, *natural language verbalizations* of triples as a whole are not available. Therefore, in this paper, we manually established *fragment templates* for such verbalizations. We have done so, by defining templates that can be combined with actual questions. Additionally, replacing and combining abstract concepts (e.g., Employee) and relations (e.g., hasEmail) in the KG leads to usable questions. While doing so, a question fragment such as *"What's the <hasEmail> of <Employee>?"* pointing to the concept Email can be transformed to the real question *"What's the mail of Andreas Both?"* or *"What's the email address of the employee, who teaches Question Answering and Chatbots lecture?"* etc.

Given this scenario, we derived the following research questions: *Research question 1 (RQ_1):* "Is it possible to automatically generate a chatbot configura-tion from a given knowledge graph, s.t., the chatbot answer quality is comparable to a manually generated system?"; *Research question 2 (RQ_1):* "Is the quality of such an automatic process sufficient for real user interaction?".

To start the discussion with the scientific community regarding the research questions and to preliminarily validate our approach, we used an exemplary KG describing a department of a university including: timetable of the offered courses, courses (and their instances), appointments, lectures, and the employees of the university considering their general information. For executing the exper-iments, we use Google Dialogflow as a platform for creating a chatbot from the configuration. Hence, the whole setting can only be influenced by the data pro-vided to the Google Dialogflow, especially since the exact processing of the data

Fig. 1. Big picture of KG-based chatbot generation process

by it is encapsulated. The experimental results show overall good results for the training and testing with the generated data.

Although the approach is not yet generalized, our experimental analyses show great potential. Hence, we propose to the research community the future directions of generating Web-based natural-language user interfaces from domain-specific knowledge bases.

The paper is structured as follows. In the next section, we will describe our approach. Our experiments are described in Sect. 3. In Sect. 4, we will discuss our findings and sketch a future end-to-end process for generating chatbots automatically from a KG. The paper is concluded in Sect. 5.

2 Approach

Our process is driven by the domain knowledge represented as a knowledge graph and will create the data required for configuring a chatbot using the Dialogflow platform (cf., Fig. 1). The main idea is driven by the observation that an available information modeling of a domain is already providing well-suited knowledge representation (as it is already done in many companies/industries[5]). Typically, RDF-based knowledge graphs are used for technical implementation (cf., [5]). Hence, it is also used here. Consequently, our *approach is aiming to automatically generate the textual training data (natural-language questions) for a conversational platform from a given knowledge graph.* In the following, we will describe the requirements for the two main tasks of the training data generator. A chatbot is based on the interaction patterns or, more precisely – intents. They are the essential part of a dialogue and are activated depending on the input of a user. On activation, the answer, predefined in the configuration, is provided by the system. The input questions might contain specific parts which are reflecting a particular intention and therefore are used by the underlying intent-detection algorithm to compute the correct response. All this information needs to be provided to the conversational platform.

In this work, the domain-specific knowledge base is represented as an RDF-based[6] knowledge graph. Hence, the data has a common-sense knowledge (e.g., a lecturer is teaching courses) and the concrete instances are also represented within the KG (e.g., the instance with the label "Andreas Both" is a lecturer, "Andreas Both" is teaching the course "Web Engineering"). Given this information, we assume that for each intent at least one textual representation of a

---

[5] cf., https://iirds.org/, https://blog.cambridgesemantics.com/merck-kgaa-bosch-and-deloitte-share-their-knowledge-graph-stories, http://internationaldataspaces.org.

[6] cf., https://www.w3.org/TR/rdf11-primer/.

E₁ contains *simple questions*, e.g., *"With which* [academic title] *do I address the* [employee] [Andreas Both]*?"* that can be derived from a KG like:

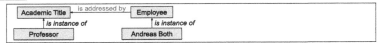

E₂ contains *mid-size questions*, e.g., *"With which* [academic title] *do I address the* [employee] *who is responsible for the* [course] [Web Engineering]*?"* that can be derived from a KG like:

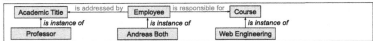

E₃ contains *long questions*, e.g., *"With which* [academic title] *do I address the* [employee] *who is responsible for the* [course] *that is part of the* [study program] [computer science]*?"* that can be derived from a KG like:

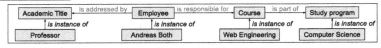

Fig. 2. Knowledge evaluation patterns.

question can be generated. For example, the question *"Who teaches courses?"* can be generated from the described common-sense knowledge, and the question *"Is Andreas Both teaching Web Engineering?"* from the described instance. There are several options available to mix terminology and instances, e.g., *"Who teaches Web Engineering?"*. Obviously, substrings like "Andreas Both" or "Web Engineering" reflect the required parameters of the user's input and can be used to compute the expected chatbot response. For a completely automated process, we assume that such textual questions are generated automatically from the KG and the instances are highlighted within the questions using framework-specific markup. Figure 2 shows the examples of how training data can be generated. There, E₁ contains verbalizations that are generated using a simple pattern that is based on a predicate. Correspondingly, E₂ uses 2 edges of the given KG and E₃ uses 3 edges to generate verbalizations.

3 Experiment

To validate the approach, an ad hoc ontology of the Anhalt University using the domain knowledge of the authors was used. For the evaluation, 3 experiments (Exp₁, Exp₂, and Exp₃) regarding different verbalization types were designed. For each experiment, we create three types of input based on the complexity of the question (E₁, E₂, E₃). The complexity depends on how many triples are integrated into the question. Considering the KG, these facts are directly correlating with the KG edges that would be used to compute an answer (cf., Fig. 2).

In all experiments, the Google Dialogflow conversational platform was used. The experiments were performed using the API to ensure uniformity of execution. We trained a model for each verbalization type (Exp₁, Exp₂, and Exp₃)

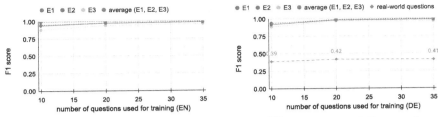

(a) Exp_1^{EN}: Evaluation of English dataset   (b) Exp_1^{DE}: Evaluation of German dataset

Fig. 3. Exp_1: Evaluation of label-based generation of verbalizations of training data

and evaluated the quality for E_1 (simple), E_2 (medium), and E_3 (long) questions (and also the average quality) separately for English and German. Additionally, we used a randomly selected subset of *503 real-world German questions*[7] to evaluate the German model. These questions were collected through an integration of the chatbot into the live learning management system (LMS) of the Anhalt University. The users, Anhalt University's bachelor students of different years, were provided with a general description of the supported topics and instructed to create related questions that are used as a dataset. However, the underlying ontology was *not* changed relating to the collected real-world input from actual users. All models were evaluated using a 5-fold cross-validation where N randomly selected questions are used for the training with $N \in \{10, 20, 35, 50, 100, 150, 200, 250, 500\}$ and the quality evaluation was concluded by using F1 scores. Hence, the knowledge representation needs to be considered static. In the following, we will evaluate three different training data generations (the data is available in our online appendix) and their quality regarding the real-world questions.

Exp$_1$: Verbalization Using Only Concept and Entity Labels. In this experiment, we used only the labels of concepts and entities to generate the training data for the chatbot (cf., Fig. 3). A simple verbalization could be *"academic title Andreas Both ?"* (cf., the example in Fig. 2). The structure of such data can only roughly be described as a natural language. Due to the usage of only labels, only test sets of 10, 20, and 35 questions per intent were generated and evaluated for E_1, E_2, and E_3 questions (cf., Fig. 3a and 3b). However, even this comparatively low number of training data is sufficient. As Fig. 3 demonstrates, the F1 score is increasing w.r.t. the number of the provided training data. In general, the quality of the chatbot model is acceptable (leading to the assumption that the named entities and concepts are dominating features of the Dialogflow's intent detection model). Surprisingly, even the evaluation of the real-world questions (cf., Fig. 3b) is reasonable (between 0.39 and 0.42).

Exp$_2$: Verbalization Using Predefined Patterns. In our second evaluation, we used predefined templates to simulate the creation of natural-language questions. They use all defined labels (cf., Fig. 2), vastly increasing the number

---

[7] The data is available in our online appendix at https://doi.org/hnb3.

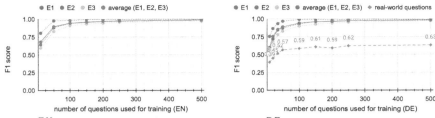

(a) Exp_2^{EN}: Evaluation of English dataset (b) Exp_2^{DE}: Evaluation of German dataset

Fig. 4. Exp_2: Evaluation of sentence-based generation of verbalizations of training data

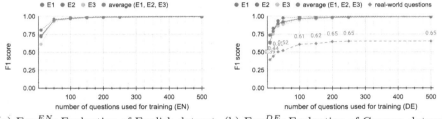

(a) Exp_3^{EN}: Evaluation of English dataset (b) Exp_3^{DE}: Evaluation of German dataset

Fig. 5. Exp_3: Evaluation of clause-based generation of verbalizations of training data

of questions generated to up to 500. The generated E_1 verbalizations can be considered to reflect well-formed natural language (e.g., *"With which academic title address the employee Andreas Both?"*). For E_2 and E_3 questions, we simply replaced the addressed entity or concept with a question that is pointing to it. For example, the entity *"Andreas Both"*, contained in the previously mentioned E_1 question, could be addressed using questions aiming for an answer of type Employee, e.g., *"Who is responsible for Web Engineering?"*. Combining both questions results in a E_2 question such as *"With which academic title address the employee Who is responsible for Web Engineering?"*. Obviously, the natural-language quality of the mid-size (E_2) and long (E_3) questions will not always be high. Nevertheless, the Exp_2's evaluation quality is increased in comparison to Exp_1 (cf., Fig. 4). In particular, the generated German model shows improved quality regarding the real-world questions (cf., Fig. 4b).

Exp$_3$: Verbalization Using Subordinate Clause. The final evaluation was done with additional templates. The generation mechanism is the same as in Exp_2. However, the templates were improved, s.t., the combinability of templates is increased. As the simple questions (E_1) are not created by combining question templates, they are equal to the ones of Exp_2. However, we intentionally created additional templates to extend questions with subordinate clauses. They lead to more natural sentences, e.g., *"With which academic degree do I address employee, who is responsible for Web Engineering?"*. The results of the evaluation are shown in Fig. 5. It shows a very similar model quality as Exp_2

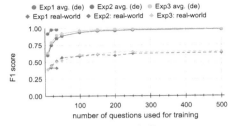

Evaluation	Correlation
Exp_1	0.971
Exp_2	0.984
Exp_3	0.936

(a) Comparison of trained German models' quality vs. real-world questions.

(b) Correlation of German model quality and German real-world questions

Fig. 6. Comparison of results.

for both languages. However, the evaluation of the German real-world questions shows a significant improvement in comparison to Exp_2, which is also achieved with smaller training sets (with 200 questions Exp_2: 0.59 vs. Exp_3: 0.65). Hence, we can assume that a better natural-language representation of the generated training data is leading to an improved chatbot quality.

4   Discussion

Our experiments show that the approach for automatic training data generation along with the Google Dialogflow intent detection module demonstrates decent results. Despite the approach having significant limitations, as only pre-defined templates were used in the experiments, the Dialogflow's models were still capable of providing reasonable quality, as summarized in Fig. 6a.

Even while using such an unideal process, we are capable to highlight the potential advantages of our approach by the conducted experiments: (1) An automatic process is capable of generating more training data than a manual process, which might improve the quality towards a very high level; (2) Our approach is also able to create multilingual conversational interfaces, leading to higher chatbot generation efficiency and better maintainability of web applications, as they are often built for multilingual environments.

Given our results, the automatic generation of chatbots is possible (i.e., our research question RQ_1 is answered). The obvious advantage is complete coverage of the modeled knowledge domain in the training data for the intents of the chatbot. In addition, our approach enables the efficient provision of significantly larger training data than a human chatbot maintainer would like to generate manually. The correlations of the real-world questions and the average model quality is also very high (cf., Fig. 6b). Hence, the RQ_2 is answered too.

We identified the automatic training data generation as a crucial but missing component for actually achieving the end-to-end automation for creating chatbots based on a given KG. Consequently, our research results point to the fact that scientific investment into establishing robust methods to automatically generate natural-language questions from a KG is required (cf., [2,9]). Hence, we would propose to the research community to develop such a component.

5   Conclusions and Future Work

In this paper, we proposed an end-to-end process for automatically configuring a chatbot by generating training data. The proposed process is based on a domain-specific knowledge base, represented by a knowledge graph, which is a common approach for representing semantic data and is providing terminology (concepts and predicates) as well as concrete data instances. The process was implemented and evaluated while simulating the intent detection task. The experimental results show that it is possible to achieve reasonable quality for real-world questions. Nevertheless, fine-tuning the results and iterative extension of the verbalization templates is required.

However, such an automated process might have a very positive impact on the time and costs (i.e., *efficiency*) for establishing chatbots. Additionally, indicated by our experiments, we assume that *higher quality* can be achieved as more training data can be generated automatically with much higher efficiency in comparison to a manual process. This would foster the generation of future NL-driven Web applications, as the domain-specific knowledge model is typically available (because it is also used for other applications).

References

1. Abdellatif, A., Badran, K., Costa, D., Shihab, E.: A comparison of natural language understanding platforms for chatbots in software engineering. IEEE Transactions on Software Engineering (2021)
2. Bouayad-Agha, N., Casamayor, G., Wanner, L.: Natural language generation in the context of the semantic web. Semantic Web **5**, 493–513 (2014)
3. Chittò, P., Baez, M., Daniel, F., Benatallah, B.: Automatic generation of chatbots for conversational web browsing. In: Dobbie, G., Frank, U., Kappel, G., Liddle, S.W., Mayr, H.C. (eds.) ER 2020. LNCS, vol. 12400, pp. 239–249. Springer, Cham (2020). https://doi.org/10.1007/978-3-030-62522-1_17
4. Diefenbach, D., Both, A., Singh, K.D., Maret, P.: Towards a question answering system over the semantic web. Semantic Web **11**, 421–439 (2020)
5. Galkin, M., Auer, S., Scerri, S.: Enterprise knowledge graphs: a backbone of linked enterprise data. In: 2016 IEEE/WIC/ACM International Conference on Web Intelligence (WI), pp. 497–502. IEEE (2016)
6. Hogan, A., et al.: Knowledge graphs. Synthesis Lectures on Data. Semant. Knowl. **12**(2), 1–257 (2021)
7. Janarthanam, S.: Hands-on chatbots and conversational UI development: build chatbots and voice user interfaces with Chatfuel, Dialogflow. Twilio, and Alexa Skills. Packt Publishing Ltd., Microsoft Bot Framework (2017)
8. López, A., Sànchez-Ferreres, J., Carmona, J., Padró, L.: From process models to chatbots. In: Giorgini, P., Weber, B. (eds.) CAiSE 2019. LNCS, vol. 11483, pp. 383–398. Springer, Cham (2019). https://doi.org/10.1007/978-3-030-21290-2_24
9. Seyler, D., Yahya, M., Berberich, K.: Generating quiz questions from knowledge graphs. In: Proceedings of the 24th International Conference on World Wide Web (2015)

Web Security and Privacy

Configurable Per-Query Data Minimization for Privacy-Compliant Web APIs

Frank Pallas[(✉)][ID], David Hartmann[ID], Paul Heinrich[ID], Josefine Kipke[ID], and Elias Grünewald[ID]

Information Systems Engineering, TU Berlin, Berlin, Germany
{fp,dh,ph,jk,eg}@ise.tu-berlin.de

Abstract. The purpose of regulatory data minimization obligations is to limit personal data to the absolute minimum necessary for a given context. Beyond the initial data collection, storage, and processing, data minimization is also required for subsequent data releases, as it is the case when data are provided using query-capable Web APIs. Data-providing Web APIs, however, typically lack sophisticated data minimization features, leaving the task open to manual and all too often missing implementations. In this paper, we address the problem of data minimization for data-providing, query-capable Web APIs. Based on a careful analysis of functional and non-functional requirements, we introduce JANUS, an easy-to-use, highly configurable solution for implementing legally compliant data minimization in GraphQL Web APIs. JANUS provides a rich set of information reduction functionalities that can be configured for different client roles accessing the API. We present a technical proof-of-concept along with experimental measurements that indicate reasonable overheads. JANUS is thus a practical solution for implementing GraphQL APIs in line with the regulatory principle of data minimization.

Keywords: Privacy · Data protection · Data minimization · Anonymization · Web APIs · GraphQL · Privacy Engineering

1 Introduction

Data minimization is one of the core principles of privacy regulations such as the GDPR. Basically, it requires to limit personal data to the absolute minimum necessary in a given context. Beyond collection, storage and processing of personal data, this minimization obligation also applies to subsequent data releases. Any such release of personal data – between different departments of an organization or to external parties – must thus also be confined to the absolute minimum required by the particular recipient. Depending on the usecase and the client role, this can require to pseudonymize data, to strip off certain sensitive attributes, or to apply information reduction methods such as generalization or noising to avoid re-identification.

© Springer Nature Switzerland AG 2022
T. Di Noia et al. (Eds.): ICWE 2022, LNCS 13362, pp. 325–340, 2022.
https://doi.org/10.1007/978-3-031-09917-5_22

Real-world usecases involving such releases of personal data today typically employ query-capable Web APIs following paradigms such as REST [7] or GraphQL [3]. Existing technology stacks broadly used in industry to implement such APIs do, however, so far not provide the means necessary for implementing above-mentioned data minimization techniques in a developer-friendly, coherent, and reliable fashion easily adoptable to the different minimization requirements applicable for different usecases and data-requesting parties (or roles). Beyond fundamental mechanisms for access control, data controllers providing personal data via Web APIs are thus currently left without proper technical support for meeting regulatory requirements. The only alternative currently lies in individually implemented external wrapper components, which raise significant efforts and are error-prone.

We herein close this gap by introducing the concept of per-query role-based data minimization for data-providing Web APIs. We identify a set of functional and non-functional requirements that must be met by a technical mechanism in order to fulfill regulatory requirements and be practically applicable. On this basis, we present JANUS, a ready-to-use extension to one of the most widely used software stacks for building GraphQL APIs – Apollo – that facilitates low-effort integration of a broad variety of data reduction techniques. All components are provided under an open source license in publicly available repositories.

The remainder of this paper is structured as follows: Sect. 2 provides relevant preliminaries on legal requirements for data minimization and on respective technical measures for implementing it in practice. A motivating and illustrative scenario is also provided here. On this basis, we distill functional and non-functional requirements in Sect. 3 and elaborate on the integration approach, architecture, provided functionality, and performance assessment of our prototypical implementation in Sect. 4. Limitations of our approach, pathways for future work and a conclusion are provided in Sect. 5.

2   Preliminaries

In the following, we set out the necessary preliminaries to contextualize our approach in the light of legal and technical givens and provide an illustrative scenario motivating and guiding our subsequent considerations.

2.1   Regulatory Background

As briefly touched above, data minimization is a core concept of modern privacy regulations. The GDPR [6] can be taken as a representative for comparably structured legislations such as California's CCPA or China's PIPL here: In Art. 5 (1c), it requires that "personal data shall be [...] limited to what is necessary in relation to the purposes for which they are processed". Noteworthily, data minimization must not only be applied to the collection of personal data but also for their processing and for providing access to them [5,6].

In practice, this can be done in two different veins: First, the amount of data can be minimized. As the European Data Protection Board points out [5], this refers to the "quantitative and qualitative" amount, thus including "the volume of personal data, as well as the types, categories and level of detail". Insofar, the data minimization principle requires to remove as many attributes of the data as possible and to limit the level of detail for the remaining ones to the absolute minimum required in a given context.

Second, the minimization principle does not require to minimize the amount of data in general but only that of *personal* data. Another viable approach is thus to anonymize ("de-personalize") initially personal data. In so doing, the mere removal of explicit identifiers such as names is, however, typically not sufficient due to re-identification risks. Different information reduction techniques (see Sect. 2.2) can reduce these risks and ultimately render data non-personal.

For both approaches, the required level of information reduction and de-personalization cannot be determined universally but must be assessed on a per-case basis, taking into account factors such as the nature and scope of the data, the context it is to be processed in, etc. [8]. This particularly also includes the distinction between different data recipients: releasing data to an academic research group will, for instance, typically require less strict minimization than providing it to an international insurance company or even the general public.

2.2   Information Reduction and Anonymization

From the technical perspective, information reduction and anonymization can take place in different forms [10,16,17]: *Attribute suppression* means to completely remove certain attributes (such as an explicit identifier or a particular characteristic) from a data point. *Generalization*, in turn, reduces the level of detail at which an attribute is included. Typical examples here comprise the replacement of detailed dates-of-birth with more general year-of-birth ranges, blinding digits from a ZIP code (sometimes considered as a separate technique of *character replacement*), and so forth. *Hashing* herein refers to substituting a value with the result of a (basically) non-revertible hash-function, retaining uniqueness and validatability without revealing the underlying plain-text data.[1]

Beyond these mechanisms, anonymity measures such as k-anonymity [20], ℓ-diversity [15], or t-closeness [14] were introduced to guarantee certain levels of non-identifiability within a dataset. However, these measures as well as the techniques and algorithms for implementing them are targeted at (rather) static datasets that are to be released only once or on rather infrequent occasions. In the context of query-capable APIs delivering continuously changing data, such anonymization schemes cannot be reasonably applied.

For such contexts, different forms of *noising* (sometimes also referred to as *perturbation*) are thus proposed. Advanced approaches of "differential privacy"

---

[1] Hashing is thus often considered as a particular form of pseudonymization when applied to identifiers. A substantial reversion risk may, however, still exist – for a detailed discussion, see [8].

[4] here provide statistical guarantees but can only be applied to aggregating queries such as sum, count, etc. and are thus limited to a particular class of use-cases. When data are needed in non-aggregated form, in turn, noising is typically done in a way that makes individual values "less accurate whilst retaining the overall distribution" [2], e.g. through in-/decreasing numerical values according to typical probability distributions with the level of noise depending on "the level of information [detail] required and the impact on individuals' privacy" [2].

2.3 Data-Providing Web APIs and Data Minimization

The broad reception of these and further techniques and their importance for achieving regulatory compliance notwithstanding, established and easily reusable technical implementations are currently missing. Where available at all, respective programming libraries so far only provide the mathematical or algorithmical core functionality while lacking coherent and low-effort integration into current application architectures and, in particular, programming stacks for building data-providing Web APIs.

Such APIs today mostly follow one of the two paradigmatic approaches of REST and GraphQL. Of these, GraphQL provides significant benefits over REST in matters such as request-response-latencies or the amount of data to be transferred in real-world usecases [22,23]. Together with its capabilities for client-specified queries [3], this increasingly makes GraphQL the paradigm of choice for implementing data-providing Web APIs, especially when relevant data structures become more complex and when different parties only need certain subsets of the data. We therefore focus on GraphQL herein.

In service-oriented architectures, such APIs are used by external parties (such as the users of a given app or third parties) as well as by internal ones. As soon as this involves personal data, the minimization principle comes into play, requiring the provided data to be limited to the amount absolutely necessary for the respective party and/or role. However, technical tools for doing so in established GraphQL programming stacks are rare. Existing approaches such as *GraphQL Shield* [25] or *GraphQL RBAC* [24] only implement simple permission layers and do not support the implementation of further information reduction and anonymization functionalities.

Altogether, we thus know a broad variety of fundamental information reduction and anonymization techniques aimed at the data minimization principle. When used in proper combination, they may, depending on the type of data, the context, and the party receiving the data, even allow to render data non-personal from the regulatory perspective. At the same time, the practical application of these techniques in real-world Web APIs is – like for other privacy/data protection principles and technologies [12,18] – hindered by a lack of easily adoptable technical solutions that smoothly integrate into established technology stacks and development practices [13].

2.4   Illustrative Scenario

To guide and illustrate our subsequent considerations, we assume the exemplary scenario of a period tracking app implementing a common architecture with a smartphone- or web-application sending and retrieving data to/from a Web API, which, in turn, stores and retrieves data in/from a backend database.

Basically, such period tracking apps provide valuable insights for their users regarding estimated pain, contraception and ovulation. At the same time, however, the web API may also be used for sharing menstrual data with other parties to generate additional benefits: With sufficiently minimized and/or de-personalized menstrual data being queryable from the API, a scientific research group would, for instance, be able to gain new insights on the relationship between health and periods. Public health programs, in turn, would be able to better recognize and counteract existing challenges related to menstrual hygiene (including, e.g., a lack of infrastructure available) based on such data [19]. Internal processes of app development might also benefit from appropriately minimized usage data and, last but not least, even users themselves could profit from queries like "how severe is my pain compared to other users of the same age cohort" being facilitated by the API and therefore available in the app.

In all these and many further usecases, the sharing of – sufficiently minimized – period data with parties beyond the data subjects themselves proposes noteworthy societal or individual benefits. On the other hand, given the sensitive nature of such data, the technical mechanisms for doing so must also be reliable and ideally not implemented individually in an ad-hoc fashion, motivating the development of a re-usable component that can be easily integrated into existing Web API frameworks. Any such component must fulfill several functional and non-functional requirements which shall be laid out below.

3   Requirements

In line with other endeavors of practical privacy engineering (such as [11,12,18]), we formulate a set of functional and non-functional requirements that need to be fulfilled. Functional requirements here refer to the core functionality that needs to be provided while non-functional requirements address the practical applicability in real-world technology stacks and architectures.

3.1   Functional Requirements

Attribute-Level Role-Based Access Control (FR1): The first step towards data minimization depending on different parties or roles accessing a GraphQL API is to restrict access to single attributes of data items depending on the accessing party. In our illustrative scenario, an external academic research team might, for instance, be allowed to access detailed menstrual data but only without identifiers such as names etc., while internal account management might access these identifiers but not the sensitive attributes like menstrual cycles or pain.

Any solution must therefore implement access control on a per-attribute level. To integrate well with broadly established practices in access management and control in general, doing so on the basis of roles appears most appropriate.

Attribute-Level Role-Based Information Reduction (FR2): Besides the mere blocking of access to single attributes, it must be possible to implement data minimization through applying different forms of information reduction to different attributes, again according to different roles performing data access. In the just-mentioned example, the detailed data provided to an academic research team might have to be subject to generalization of age cohorts to meet regulatory requirements while an internal product improvement team may only see noised usage patterns.

Rich and Extendible Set of Information Reduction Methods (FR3): As effective data minimization is subject to highly case-specific requirements that must be met for achieving regulatory compliance, a diversity of different information reduction techniques can be necessary, ranging from numerical categorization over character replacements to different approaches of statistical noising. This calls for a rich set of such functionalities – covering numerical and non-numerical values – to be built upon when defining case- and role-specific information reduction schemes. Ideally, this set should be easily extensible in onward development to accommodate additionally identified information reduction needs.

Configurability (FR4): In addition, any technical solution must be highly configurable and allow for adjustable levels of information reduction to satisfy different regulatory requirements while meeting certain accuracy constraints [9].

3.2 Nonfunctional Requirements

Low Integration Overhead (NFR1): Smooth and low-effort integration into at least one software stack widely used in practice for implementing data-providing Web APIs fosters practical applicability and viability. At the same time, the connection to an externally maintained role-definition and authentication subsystem – e.g., via widely-used JSON Web Tokens (JWTs) – is a necessary precondition for being interoperable with already existing system architectures.

Reusability (NFR2): Reusability in a broad variety of application architectures, thorough documentation, and public availability foster software artifacts' practical adoption. This also comprises the availability under an open source licence for commercial use via common code repositories and distribution via package managers. The latter, eventually, introduce quality assurance, e.g., through code linting, automatic update mechanisms, and security alerts.

Reasonable Performance Overhead (NFR3): Article 25 of the GDPR states that technical measures for materializing privacy principles must be applied "depending on the cost of implementation". Any solution must thus not introduce disproportional performance overheads. The overheads must, in turn, be experimentally determined in realistic settings and with different configurations to demonstrate the practical viability.

4   Approach and Implementation

To fulfill these requirements, we introduce the concept of per-query role-based data minimization in Web APIs and provide a ready-to-use implementation for Apollo, one of the most-widely used software stacks for implementing GraphQL APIs. Given its broad adoption in practice, building upon Apollo is a promising starting point for keeping integration overhead low for practitioners (see *NFR1*). Besides mere adoption, Apollo also provides a mature framework for implementing custom extensions (for details, see below) and thus allows to integrate our intended functionality in a modular and low-effort fashion, supporting the fulfillment of *NFR1* even further.

Following this fundamental choice of Apollo as our target platform, the integration approach, implementation details, practical usage, and experimentally determined overheads of our prototypical implementation JANUS shall be laid out below.

4.1   Architecture Integration

As delineated in *FR1 and FR2*, JANUS must provide functionalities for attribute-level access control and information reduction. Basically, these can be implemented in GraphQL using either a middleware- or a schema-directive-driven approach. Both can extend Apollo's integrated resolver functionality to first query a data field and then subject it to further processing, thus smoothly integrating into Apollo's general design and processing flow (see *NFR1*). However, they function in a significantly different manner: In the middleware-driven approach, the resolver can be provided with middleware functions that execute any logic before and after the resolution of the field. Furthermore, middleware functions can call subsequent ones when passing the execution and modify the request and response object at any time, thus possibly creating an onion-like resolving flow.

GraphQL schema directives, in turn, define post-processing steps to be executed on already resolved data fields before returning them through the API. Configured directly in the schema by adding the directive behind the targeted data field, directives can be used on specified fields or types of schemas. It is also possible to define a directive pipeline with subsequent directives. Compared with the middleware approach, integrating additional functionality via schema directives is simpler and provides more clarity (expectably leading to less integration overhead for developers, see *NFR1*) while still allowing to implement a sufficient level of logical complexity through combining multiple schema directives. We thus chose the approach of schema directives for integrating our functionality into the Apollo stack at runtime, employing the `SchemaDirectiveVisitor` class provided by the *graphql-tools*[2] library.

Both, access control and information reduction are to be implemented on the basis of roles (see *FR1 and FR2*). We thus need a mechanism for managing users, assigning them to roles, letting them log in and then make requests on the basis of these roles. On the server side, in turn, above-mentioned schema directives must be defined depending on these roles and requests must be processed accordingly. To ensure integratability with a wide variety of pre-existing systems and architectures here (*NFR1*), we opted to keep role management, authentication, etc. external to our solution and to base our functionality on externally maintained roles provided via JSON Web Tokens. JANUS simply needs the role parameter to be passed for mapping the role to a set of schema directives to be applied. Figure 1 depicts the resulting general architecture.

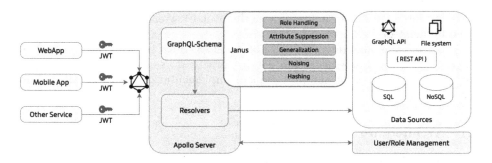

Fig. 1. Apollo server architecture and JANUS integration.

4.2 Implementation

Given this general architecture and integration approach, JANUS' functionality is implemented in two separate modules with well-distinguished scopes: First, a module is needed that provides a rich set of information reduction methods for various data types (*FR3*). These are provided in the package *janus-value-anonymizer*, which is publicly available under an open source license on Github as well as in the npm package managing system (thus meeting *NFR2*).[3] Possible extensions with additional information reduction methods (as required in *FR3*) can easily be introduced in this module. In addition, this module can also be used in other contexts than JANUS-enabled Apollo/GraphQL APIs, thus providing additional benefits in matters of reusability (*NFR2*).

Second, a module is needed that specifically wraps the access control and information reduction functionality for an Apollo GraphQL server via custom

---

[2] https://github.com/ardatan/graphql-tools.
[3] https://github.com/PrivacyEngineering/janus-value-anonymizer.

directives. This is done in a separate package comprising a collection of respective directives called *janus-graphql-anonym-directives* which is also available under an open source license and provided via Github and npm.[4]

Given this natural two-way split, the flow of a request for a single data object – including the authentication and role-specific token provision exemplarily implemented in Apollo – and the corresponding processing steps are depicted in Fig. 2: After a http(s) request (including a previously generated role-token) is sent by the client, the respective data is fetched from the database by the resolver and returned to the server. Directives added to the corresponding data fields in the schema are called by the Apollo server directly after the resolver has fetched the data. The directives, in turn, use the JWT tokens to extract the provided role of the current requester. Depending on that role, the directive requests the role-dependent parameters from the developer's implementation of the directives (see Sect. 4.3). Based on these parameters, the directive then executes the information reduction function(s) and hands over the processed object back to the Apollo Server which finally returns it back to the requester.

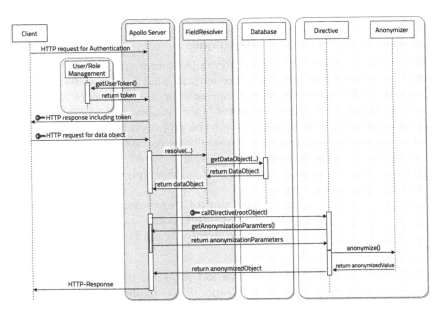

Fig. 2. General sequence of operations triggered by a http request containing an exemplary data object.

4.3   Usage and Configuration Mechanism

After installing JANUS and integrating it into a given Apollo deployment, multiple custom directives for simple attribute suppression (implementing basic

---

[4] https://github.com/PrivacyEngineering/janus-graphql-anonym-directives.

per-attribute access control, *FR1*) and the three more advanced information reduction techniques generalization, noise, and hashing (*FR2*) can be easily specified and parameterized. Noteworthily, the specification mechanism allows for role-dependent behavior as well as for the integration of components external to JANUS itself. Besides flexible configurability (*FR4*), this may also help lowering the integration overhead (cf. *NFR1*), especially in complex enterprise environments.[5] A so-specified custom directive can then be added to a GraphQL schema by appending its name at the end of the definition for the data field it shall be applied to, using the common, decorator-style syntax (e.g., @noise) as depicted in Listing 1.1.

Listing 1.1. Adding the directive to the schema.

```
directive @noise on FIELD_DEFINITION
...
type Symptom {
    pain: Float @noise
    ...
}
```

4.4   Information Reduction Techniques

Having laid out the general architecture, implementation, and usage of JANUS, the provided information reduction mechanisms shall be elaborated on in some more detail. The most fundamental approach for information reduction is the complete suppression of single attributes (such as names, identifiers, etc.). This functionality can be implemented through the suppression directive, which effectively implements per-attribute role based access control and can be applied to fields of any data type. In case the requester does not hold a role allowed to access a data field the directive is attached to, it simply suppresses that field's data and returns null instead.

Besides this basic role-based access control, JANUS comprises three advanced information reduction methods – generalization, noise, and hashing – which function on different data types and can be selectively applied, independent of each other.[6]

Generalization: The generalization method supports the data types number, string, and date. Since a schema in GraphQL has explicitly typed fields, it is, however, not possible to turn a number value (integer or float) into another data type that represents a range of numbers without contradicting the schema definition. For the generalization of number values, we thus let single numbers represent a range. If, for example, a generalization step size of 10 is used, delimiter-based generalization results would be 0 (representing 0–9), 10 (for 10–19), 20 (for

---

[5] Details on the necessary steps for installation, integration, and directive specification are provided at https://github.com/PrivacyEngineering/janus-graphql-anonym-directives.

[6] Details on available parameters etc. are again provided at https://github.com/PrivacyEngineering/janus-value-anonymizer.

20–29), and so forth. This ensures that exactly one number represents one range. Because generalization is a core method for implementing data minimization, it is also implemented for dates and strings. For dates, natural generalization boundaries are given by the different units (second, minute, etc.). For strings, in turn, it is possible to specify how many letters should appear in plain text and at what point they should be hidden with asterisks (∗).

Noise: The noise function can be used on the data types number and date. When using noise, one has to define the mathematical probability distribution to be used for sampling the noise value that is added to the original value. Every distribution available in the *probability-distributions* package[7] (such as Laplacian, Normal, etc.) can be used here. Together with a map of configuration parameters corresponding to the distribution, developers have a broad flexibility in implementing the noise behavior. Since noise is mainly useful on numeric values, it is implemented for integers, floats and dates.

Hashing: Hash-based data minimization is implemented using the (so far) secure hashing function SHA3 with output lengths as available in the *crypto-js*[8] library (224, 256, 384, or 512 bits). Other hashing algorithms more resistant to brute-forcing [8] as well as capabilities for including salt are not implemented at the moment but might be easily added in the future.

4.5 Preliminary Performance Evaluation

To experimentally determine the performance overhead caused by the integration of JANUS and, thus, to validate the fulfillment of *NFR3*, we prototypically implemented a GraphQL API backend for the period tracking scenario envisioned in Sect. 2.4 and ran several performance tests against this API with and without JANUS being active. This exemplary backend mainly consists of a GraphQL web server based on Apollo and a PostgreSQL database holding the data to be provided. The data model comprises a realistic composition of *1:1*, *1:n*, and *n:m* relationships between entities. The data minimization directives are included as described above.[9]

For the experiments, we applied established principles of security-/privacy-related performance benchmarking [18], using realistic datasets and state-of-the-art public cloud instances on Microsoft Azure in the same region. We measured two metrics by running respective experiments against the API instances without ("Baseline") and with JANUS installed: 1) the latency added by our information reduction directives and 2) the imposed reduction in matters of throughput. For covering aspects like general directive invocation overhead etc. separately, we also included a "no-operation" directive. In this case, requested data traversed

---

[7] https://www.npmjs.com/package/probability-distributions.

[8] https://www.npmjs.com/package/crypto-js.

[9] The exemplary implementation can be found here: https://github.com/PrivacyEngineering/janus-period-tracking-app.

through the directive loop before being delivered, albeit without applying any information reduction.[10]

Latency: Figure 3 depicts the latencies observed for the different directives with 1000 data objects being requested. Noteworthily, the no-op directive does not significantly differ from the baseline, validating the efficiency of our general, directive-based integration approach. When JANUS is used with the generalization, noise and hashing information reduction methods, latencies increase at different rates: Generalization and noise lead to 3–4.5-fold latencies while hashing results in a factor of 8.5. These results are substantial, but given the comparably time-consuming operations JANUS introduces compared to simply handing over the data from the resolver to the API endpoint, they fall within expectable and justified ranges. Interestingly, the relative overhead decreases significantly with more objects being requested and processed. For instance, moving from 1.000 to 10.000 objects results in a 8.5-fold latency for the baseline but only a 2.6-fold one with hashing being performed. We assume either some sort of static delay factor introduced by *crypto-js* or a general, JANUS-independent side-effect of Apollo when serializing larger responses. In any case, this aspect clearly deserves further examination in the future.

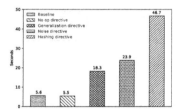

Fig. 3. Mean latency (seconds) with generalization, noise, and hash information reduction for 1000 data objects.

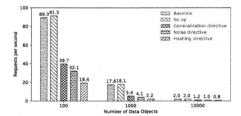

Fig. 4. Mean throughput (in requests per second) for different object frequencies for no operation, baseline, generalization, noise and hash information reduction methods.

Throughput: Figure 4 shows the measured throughput for 100, 1.000 and 10.000 data objects comparing all information reduction methods with non-operational directives and the baseline. Again, baseline and no-op do not differ significantly (with no-op in fact being slightly more performant). Of the remaining ones, generalization has the lowest impact, followed by noise and hashing. Like for the latency experiments, overheads are substantial compared to simply delivering results without any further processing, but stay within expectable and justified

---

[10] More details on the experiment setting are left out here due to space constraints but can be provided upon request. Employed scripts are available at https://github.com/PrivacyEngineering/janus-performance-evaluation.

ranges given the computational efforts required by information reduction. The relative loss factor again decreases with larger responses containing 10.000 data elements for all information reduction methods. This speaks in favor of above-mentioned assumption of a serialization-related side-effect.

Given the computational overheads necessarily induced by the implemented information reduction methods compared to simply delivering data without further processing, these overheads are far from being unexpected. Especially for cases where data minimization is an indispensable precondition for implementing legally compliant API-based data provision to different parties at all, however, the observed overheads will presumably be considered reasonable (see *NFR3*). In addition, JANUS' concept of *per-query and role-based* data minimization allows to selectively apply information reduction techniques where actually required, facilitating fine-tuned and differentiated adjustments.

Last but not least, the relative overhead of JANUS will expectably decline in more complex application architectures involving a multitude of further factors such as data preprocessing, additional database calls, mobile data transfers, etc. (for a vivid example on the effect of such factors, see [18]).

5   Limitations, Future Work and Conclusion

Introducing the concept of per-query role-based access control and information reduction to the domain of data-providing, query-capable Web APIs, identifying respective requirements, and providing a first practically usable prototype for an established GraphQL stack were the definite foci of the work presented herein. Given the rather initial state, several limitations naturally remain and various aspects had to be left open for future work.

First of all, we refrained from adding overall complexity by complementing our approach with consent management mechanisms. Clearly, policy languages such as the extensive XACML [1] or the lightweight YaPPL [21] would have provided more detailed and individually adjustable control over data releases. However, they would also require a significantly more extensive user management and custom vocabulary definitions and also introduce extra performance overhead. Moreover, client-side complexity would drastically increase as well, which impedes the low-effort integration of our component.

Additionally, the provision of further well-known anonymization and information reduction techniques would clearly advance JANUS' scope of application. In particular, the integration of ε-differential privacy with custom additive noise mechanisms is an obvious candidate here and would allow for aggregating queries with clearly specified guarantees. Similarly, the existing information reduction methods could also be advanced with more complex functionalities like string ranges etc. Based on the general architecture provided herein, we expect such extensions to be straightforward implementation tasks based on available ready-to-use packages, which we invite the community for doing so.

Finally, more in-depth examinations of the so far only preliminarily assessed performance impacts are a clear subject for future work. For instance, the effects observed for larger responses in Sect. 4.5 deserve closer inspection, the overall impact of JANUS in more complex end-to-end settings is so far unvalidated, the effect of combining different information reduction methods should be illuminated, etc. All this should, of course, go hand in hand with dedicated performance optimizations of the initial, unoptimized prototype implementation presented and provided herein.

These open issues notwithstanding, we herein presented the first-of-its-kind re-usable component that combines role-based access control with per-query data minimization for modern Web and in particular GraphQL APIs. The application scenarios for JANUS in the course of practical privacy engineering are manifold and were illustrated with a period-tracking application example without limiting its generality for other real-world scenarios. The performance impacts were shown to be non-negligible but still appear to be acceptable, especially for use-cases that would not be implementable in a legally compliant way without solid information reduction being applied before the release of initially personal data.

We emphasize the particular importance of both legal and technical requirements that guided the design of JANUS' general architecture and its implementation. Under these practice-oriented guidelines, we are convinced of the possible low-effort integratability of our open source component into many real-world systems for effectively heightening the level of privacy. Noteworthily, JANUS does not, per se, provide any guarantees in matters of regulatory compliance, given the multitude of factors influencing what needs to be implemented in a particular case. It does, however, equip developers of data-providing GraphQL APIs with the technical capabilities for fulfilling case-dependent legal data minimization obligations in a handy, highly configurable, and easy to use manner.

References

1. Anderson, A., et al.: Extensible Access Control Markup Language (XACML) Version 1.0. OASIS (2003)
2. Art. 29 Data Protection Working Party: Opinion 05/2014 on anonymisation techniques - wp216 (2014). https://ec.europa.eu/justice/article-29/documentation/opinion-recommendation/files/2014/wp216_en.pdf
3. Brito, G., Mombach, T., Valente, M.T.: Migrating to GraphQL: a practical assessment. In: 2019 IEEE 26th International Conference on Software Analysis, Evolution and Reengineering (SANER), pp. 140–150 (2019). https://doi.org/10.1109/SANER.2019.8667986
4. Dwork, C.: Differential privacy: a survey of results. In: Agrawal, M., Du, D., Duan, Z., Li, A. (eds.) TAMC 2008. LNCS, vol. 4978, pp. 1–19. Springer, Heidelberg (2008). https://doi.org/10.1007/978-3-540-79228-4_1
5. European Data Protection Board: Guidelines 4/2019 on article 25 - data protection by design and by default (2019). https://edpb.europa.eu/sites/default/files/consultation/edpb_Guideline4/2019_201904_dataprotection_by_design_and_by_default.pdf
6. European Parliament and Council of the European Union: Regulation (EU) 2016/679 of 27 April 2016. General Data Protection Regulation (2018)

7. Fielding, R.: Representative state transfer. Architectural Styles and the Design of Network-based Software Architecture, pp. 76–85 (2000)
8. Finck, M., Pallas, F.: They who must not be identified-distinguishing personal from non-personal data under the GDPR. Int. Data Privacy Law **10**(1), 11–36 (2020). https://doi.org/10.1093/idpl/ipz026
9. Ghinita, G., Karras, P., Kalnis, P., Mamoulis, N.: A framework for efficient data anonymization under privacy and accuracy constraints. ACM Trans. Database Syst. (TODS) **34**(2), 1–47 (2009)
10. Gruschka, N., Mavroeidis, V., Vishi, K., Jensen, M.: Privacy issues and data protection in big data: a case study analysis under GDPR. In: 2018 IEEE International Conference on Big Data (Big Data), pp. 5027–5033. IEEE (2018)
11. Grünewald, E., Pallas, F.: TILT: A GDPR-aligned transparency information language and toolkit for practical privacy engineering. In: Proceedings of the 2021 Conference on Fairness, Accountability, and Transparency. ACM, New York (2021). https://doi.org/10.1145/3442188.3445925
12. Grünewald, E., Wille, P., Pallas, F., Borges, M.C., Ulbricht, M.R.: TIRA: an OpenAPI extension and toolbox for GDPR transparency in RESTful architectures. In: 2021 International Workshop on Privacy Engineering. IEEE (2021)
13. Kostova, B., Gürses, S., Troncoso, C.: Privacy engineering meets software engineering. On the challenges of engineering privacy by design. arXiv:2007.08613 (2020)
14. Li, N., Li, T., Venkatasubramanian, S.: t-closeness: privacy beyond k-anonymity and l-diversity. In: 23rd International Conference on Data Engineering, pp. 106–115. IEEE (2007). https://doi.org/10.1109/ICDE.2007.367856
15. Machanavajjhala, A., Kifer, D., Gehrke, J., Venkitasubramaniam, M.: l-diversity: privacy beyond k-anonymity. ACM Trans. Knowl. Discov. Data **1**(1), 3 (2007). https://doi.org/10.1145/1217299.1217302
16. Majeed, A., Lee, S.: Anonymization techniques for privacy preserving data publishing: a comprehensive survey. IEEE Access **9**, 8512–8545 (2021). https://doi.org/10.1109/ACCESS.2020.3045700
17. Marques., J., Bernardino., J.: Analysis of data anonymization techniques. In: Proceedings of the 12th International Joint Conference on Knowledge Discovery, Knowledge Engineering and Knowledge Management - KEOD, pp. 235–241. SciTePress (2020). https://doi.org/10.5220/0010142302350241
18. Pallas, F., et al.: Towards application-layer purpose-based access control. In: 35th Symposium on Applied Computing, pp. 1288–1296. ACM (2020). https://doi.org/10.1145/3341105.3375764
19. Smith, A.D., Muli, A., Schwab, K.J., Hennegan, J.: National monitoring for menstrual health and hygiene: is the type of menstrual material used indicative of needs across 10 countries? Int. J. Environ. Res. Public Health **17**(8), 2633 (2020)
20. Sweeney, L.: k-anonymity: a model for protecting privacy. Int. J. Uncertain. Fuzziness Knowl.-Based Syst. **10**(05), 557–570 (2002). https://doi.org/10.1142/S0218488502001648
21. Ulbricht, M.-R., Pallas, F.: YaPPL - a lightweight privacy preference language for legally sufficient and automated consent provision in IoT scenarios. In: Garcia-Alfaro, J., Herrera-Joancomartí, J., Livraga, G., Rios, R. (eds.) DPM/CBT -2018. LNCS, vol. 11025, pp. 329–344. Springer, Cham (2018). https://doi.org/10.1007/978-3-030-00305-0_23
22. Vogel, M., Weber, S., Zirpins, C.: Experiences on migrating RESTful web services to GraphQL. In: Braubach, L., et al. (eds.) ICSOC 2017. LNCS, vol. 10797, pp. 283–295. Springer, Cham (2018). https://doi.org/10.1007/978-3-319-91764-1_23

23. Wittern, E., Cha, A., Davis, J.C., Baudart, G., Mandel, L.: An empirical study of GraphQL schemas. In: Yangui, S., Bouassida Rodriguez, I., Drira, K., Tari, Z. (eds.) ICSOC 2019. LNCS, vol. 11895, pp. 3–19. Springer, Cham (2019). https://doi.org/10.1007/978-3-030-33702-5_1
24. Yang, F.: GraphQL role-based access control (RBAC) middleware (2018). https://github.com/Canner/graphql-rbac
25. Zavadlal, M.: GraphQL-Shield: a GraphQL tool to ease the creation of permission layer (2021). https://github.com/maticzav/graphql-shield

Effective Malicious URL Detection by Using Generative Adversarial Networks

Jinbu Geng[1,2], Shuhao Li[1,2(✉)], Zhicheng Liu[1,3], Zhenyu Cheng[1], and Li Fan[1]

[1] Institute of Information Engineering, Chinese Academy of Sciences, Beijing, China
{gengjinbu,lishuhao,chengzhenyu,fanli}@iie.ac.cn, liuzhicheng@cert.org.cn
[2] School of Cyber Security, University of Chinese Academy of Sciences, Beijing, China
[3] National Computer Network Emergency Response Technical Team/Coordination Center of China, Beijing, China

Abstract. Malicious URL, a.k.a. malicious website, pose a great threat to Web security. In particular, concept drift caused by variants of malicious URL degrades the performance of existing detection methods based on the available attack patterns. In this paper, We conduct an extensive measurement study of the realistic URL and find that the hierarchical semantics feature is suitable for identifying malicious URL. Therefore, we propose URLGAN, a deep neural network model equipped with the hierarchical semantics features, to detect distinguish between malicious and normal URL. Firstly, we embed the entire URL into a hierarchical semantics structure. Secondly, hierarchical semantics features are extracted from the hierarchical semantics structure through BERT. Then, the extracted features are combined with features generated by the generator, similar but slightly different, to enable the condition discriminator to extract the essential difference between normal and malicious URL. Notably, with the features generated by the generator, we enhance the robustness of the system to detect malicious URL variants. Extensive experiments on the public dataset and our data collected from specific targets demonstrate that our method achieves superior performance to other methods and protects specific targets from the susceptibility of malicious URL.

Keywords: Web security · Deep learning · Malicious URL Detection · Hierarchical semantics features · Concept drift

1 Introduction

URL, short for Uniform Resource Locator, is the global address for documents and other resources on the World Wide Web. Malicious URL is widely abused by

This work is supported by the National Key Research and Development Program of China (Grant No. 2018YFB0804704), and the National Natural Science Foundation of China (Grant No. U1736218).

ⓒ Springer Nature Switzerland AG 2022
T. Di Noia et al. (Eds.): ICWE 2022, LNCS 13362, pp. 341–356, 2022.
https://doi.org/10.1007/978-3-031-09917-5_23

attackers for cyber attacks, causing serious losses to companies and individuals. Popular types of attacks using malicious URLs include: Malware Download, Phishing, and Spam [13]. According to the 2021 Webroot BrightCloud Threat Report [1], phishing attacks increased by 510% from January to February of 2020, in the early months of the pandemic, and then leveled off in the summer. Therefore, it is crucial to effectively detect malicious URL.

Existing attack traffic detection methods for malicious URL are classified into: (i) Blacklisting, and (ii) Machine Learning. Blacklist methods typically maintain a list of known malicious URL for detection. Whenever a new URL is accessed, a database lookup is performed. A warning is generated if the URL is blacklisted and considered malicious. Due to their simplicity and efficiency, blacklist methods are one of the most commonly used techniques in many antivirus systems today. However, the blacklist cannot exhaustively list all possible malicious URL, especially since new malicious URL variants are easily generated every day. Attackers can easily bypass all blacklists by generating new URL algorithmically.

In contrast, machine learning methods attempt to analyze URL and their corresponding website or webpage information by extracting good feature representations of URL and training predictive models on training data of malicious and benign URL. Most importantly, machine learning methods can detect malicious URL variants. The basic assumption of machine learning methods is that the distribution of features for malicious and benign URL is different. However, the use of obfuscation techniques [7,11,14,16] makes it more difficult to detect the malicious URL variants. Besides, how to mine more effective features is a crucial topic for malicious URL detection. Consequently, concept drift is an inevitable challenge to the robustness and tolerance of model.

To address the above issues, we propose a model based on hierarchical semantics features using deep learning to detect malicious URL effectively. Our insight is built on the facts: (1) The parameter information of normal URL is different from that of malicious URL. For instance, phishing URL often contain additional parameters in order to induce victims to enter important information. (2) The attack patterns initiated by malicious URL of the same family are similar, and the attack patterns initiated by malicious URL of different families are different. (3) Deep learning can learn appropriate features directly from (usually unstructured) data, so as to help us reduce the pain of feature engineering and build models without any domain expertise. (4) Aversarially generated samples can well simulate the variants of malicious URL, so as to improve the robustness and tolerance of the model.

We first transform the URL into a hierarchical semantics structure, and then extract the hierarchical semantics features. In order to effectively mitigate adversarial sample attacks and combat zero day malicious URL, we use generative adversarial networks (GAN) to generate similar hierarchical semantics features with different noise for each category of samples. The generated features can be used to simulate attack patterns triggered by malicious URL variants. It is worth mentioning that we use deeper and more essential variants of hierarchical semantic features to replace the original variants of URL. As a result, the generated feature samples automatically discover the dependency and sequence patterns of malicious URL in hierarchical semantics, which is of great significance for malicious URL detection as well as for the defense against obfuscation attacks. Finally, the condition discriminator is used to classify the hierarchical semantics features in addition to constraining and optimizing the generator. The optimized generator will produce features that are more essential and similar for each category.

In summary, we make the following contributions.

- We transform URL classification into semantics classification, which can not only visually observe different attack patterns, but also use advanced semantic classification techniques irrespective of field and character obfuscation.
- We simulate the attack patterns of malicious URL variants through URLGAN to increase the diversity and variability of data, which are used to detect zero day malicious URL attacks.
- We explore the problem of concept drift on publicly available datasets ISCX-URL2016 [11] and improve the classification performance of malicious URL detection by introducing URLGAN model.
- We implement a prototype of URLGAN and achieve competitive results in comparative experiments. At the same time, we apply URLGAN to specific target and detect a number of malicious URLs.

The rest of this paper is outlined as follows. Section 2 reviews related work of malicious URL detection. Section 3 presents our system scheme and details its different components. Section 4 elaborates the experimental results. Finally, we draw a conclusion in Sect. 5.

2   Related Work

The work in this paper is based on hierarchical semantics features of URL, using a method based on GAN for malicious URL detection. Hence, Therefore, we briefly discuss the work related to the feature representation of malicious URL and GAN networks.

URL contains a variety of useful information, and the efficient feature representation that can be extracted from it includes lexical features, host features, content features, and even context and popularity features [16]. Among them, lexical features are most widely used because of their simple acquisition and good performance. Lexical features are lexical properties that are obtained by processing URL strings. The motivation is that, based on the "appearance" of a URL, it should be possible to identify the malicious nature of a web address. Kolari *et al.* [6] is one of the first people to extract word features from URL strings through the bag-of-words model. In order to solve the loss of order information, Ma *et al.* [10] preserves the order information of some words in the URL by providing a separate dictionary for each component of the URL. Marchal *et al.* [12] focuses on measuring the internal URL correlation between the registered domain and the rest of the URL to detect malicious URL. Although efficient feature representation can improve the prediction model, the selection of optimal features is often impractical. With the development of deep learning, more and more researchers try to use deep learning to deal with feature representation. Le et al. [8] uses CNN to extract lexical features from characters and words to detect malicious URLs. Afzal et al. [2] uses the lexical and semantic features of URL extracted by an LSTM network to distinguish malicious URL from benign URL. Although the above methods have made great achievements in detecting known malicious URL, they are helpless in the face of malicious URL variants and the resulting concept drift.

To deal with malicious URL variants, exploring the possible evolution direction based on the existing malicious URL is the most effective solution. Prakash et al. [15] proposes five heuristic methods to enumerate simple combinations of known phishing websites to find new phishing URLs. The URL is decomposed into multiple components through an approximate matching algorithm to match with the entries in the blacklist. However, this heuristic method relies heavily on the prior knowledge of researchers. In addition, the heuristic strategy is interpretable to the attacker, the attacker can implement confusion and confrontation attacks. Generative adversarial network [5] uses deep network to generate similar cases of input cases, which is an important method to defend confrontation attacks in network security. Yun et al. [17] combines GAN with the learning arrangements of n-grams from real domain names to form a new domain name. Liu et al. [9] uses the GAN network to explore the HTTP behavior patterns of malware variants. Anand et al. [3] solves the problem of URL detection deviation under a few categories by training text to generate antagonistic networks (text-GANs).

To the best of our knowledge, the existing methods only use GAN to generate the original case, rather than generating its corresponding more essential and accurate features. In addition, how to use the generated sample to improve the accuracy of the model and weaken the impact of concept drift can not be ignored. Therefore, we propose URLGAN to solve the above problems.

3   System Scheme

In this section, we build a hybrid structure neural network model, called URL-GAN. The architecture of the model is shown in Fig. 1, which is composed of hierarchical semantics structure, GAN_BERT and classifier. The hierarchical semantics structure is to transform the URL into a semantics problem through hierarchical encoding. GAN_BERT extracts hierarchical semantics features from the hierarchical semantics structure and generate similar features with different noise for each category of samples. The classifier follows GANBERT and is used to optimize the generator and classify the hierarchical semantics features. These parts are detailed in the following sections.

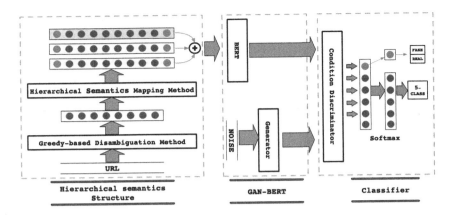

Fig. 1. The Architecture of URLGAN.

3.1   Hierarchical Semantics Structure

URL defines the global address of documents and other resources on the World Wide Web. The protocol identifier and the resource name form the URL. Protocol identifier and resource name, such as Fig. 2. The protocol identifier indicates which protocol is used, and the resource name specifies the IP address or domain name of the resource. Hence, we propose the URLGAN model based on these two fields. The resource name consists of fields such as "Userinfo", "Host", "Path", etc. Thus, URL can provide not only lexical but also specific order features, i.e. hierarchical semantics features. As shown in Fig. 3, the hierarchical semantics feature consist of 2 parts: (i) Lexical Feature, as one of semantic features; (ii) Order Feature, as another one of semantic features. In order to extract the lexical features of the URL and further order features, we need to split the original URL by the greedy algorithm. The process is as follows.

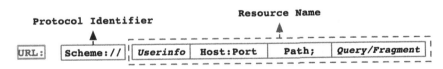

Fig. 2. Example of a URL. The protocol identifier and the resource name are separated by a colon and two forward slashes.

Step 1. Create a fixed-size vocabulary containing individual characters, regular words, and sub-words that best fit the structure of the resource search.

Step 2. Each field is first divided into combinations of regular words and sub-fields by means of the greedy algorithm.

Step 3. Each sub-field continues to be divided into combinations of sub-words and remaining-fields by means of a greedy algorithm.

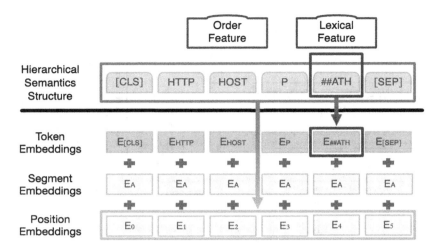

Fig. 3. Hierarchical semantics mapping.

Step 4. Each remaining-field continues to be divided into combinations of individual characters by a greedy algorithm (punctuation marks are considered as individual characters).

Step 5. Precede each sub-words and individual characters with a "##" mark.

Hierarchical Semantics Mapping Method. After splitting, the URL is divided into a hierarchical semantic structure S of length n. Hierarchical semantics mapping method is used to map S to a vector V. As shown in Fig. 3, hierarchical semantics mapping method is based on embedding operations. The position embedding layer deals with the position of S, maintaining the order vector p. The token embedding layer deals with the word of S, maintaining the word vector t. The segment embedding operations is not required.

S of length n thus obtains two different vector representations, given as:

Token Embedding t: $(1, n + 3, 768)$, a vector representation of each word. Note that two special nodes are inserted at the beginning ([CLS]) of S and at the end ([SEP]) of S.

Position Embedding p: $(1, n + 3, 768)$, a vector representation of the positions.

These representations are summed by element to obtain a synthetic representation:

$$X = t + p \tag{1}$$

where $X(1, n+3, 768)$ is the vectorized representation of S.

3.2   GAN_BERT

In order to replace the original variant of the URL with a deeper and more essential variant of the hierarchical semantic features, we extract the real hierarchical semantic features rf of the vector X. Besides, we use generator to generate similar hierarchical semantics features gf with different noise for each category of samples. GAN_BERT is used to deal with rf and gf.

Real Semantics Feature Extraction. Real semantics features are extracted by the BERT network, which is composed of l hidden layers. There are two sub-layers in each hidden layers, a multi-head attention function and a feed-forward function.

The multi-head attention function is used to spatially fuse the information of different nodes for each word of input X. It is composed of h (the number of "attention heads") different self-attention results.

$$M = \text{Concat} (\text{head}_1, \ldots, \text{head}_h)W^O \tag{2}$$

$$\text{head}_i = \text{Attention} \left(XW_i^Q, XW_i^K, XW_i^V \right) \tag{3}$$

$$\text{Attention} (Q, K, V) = \text{SoftMax} \left(\frac{QK^T}{\sqrt{d_k}} \right) V \tag{4}$$

where h is the number of "attention heads". Each head maintains an independent weight matrix (W_i^Q, W_i^K, W_i^V), which is multiplied by the input X to produce a different matrix (Q, K, V) for "attention".

The feed-forward function mainly provides a non-linear transformation and consolidates each word with its own "unique" representation, increasing the variability between words, expressed as:

$$\text{FFN}(X) = \max (0, XW_1 + b_1) W_2 + b_2 \tag{5}$$

Each sub-layer is accompanied by a residual connection. Therefore, the output of the sub-layer is represented as:

$$X^{i+1} = f_{ln}(X^i + (f_{sn}(X^i))) \tag{6}$$

where X^i is the input vector, X^{i+1} is the output vector, f_{ln} is the layer normalization function for normalization along with the word embedding dimension, and f_{sn} is M or FFN (the current layer's operation function).

The semantics feature is obtained by the following equation:

$$rf = X^{2l+1} \tag{7}$$

where rf is the real semantics feature, X^{2l+1} is the output vector of the l th hidden layer.

Similar Semantics Feature Generation. Generative adversarial networks is a deep learning model that is one of the most promising approaches for unsupervised learning on complex distributions in recent years. The model generates fairly good outputs by playing each other's learning with two modules in the framework: the generator $\mathcal{G}$ and the discriminator $\mathcal{D}$. The purpose of $\mathcal{G}$ is to map the random noise into similar instances, that is, the hierarchical semantics features of different categories of malicious URLs in this paper. More specifically, as shown in Fig. 4(a), the generator is: $N * \{Dense \Rightarrow BatchNorm \Rightarrow LeakyRelu\}$. For the Gaussian noise n_vec, the output of $\mathcal{G}$ is represented as:

$$gf = \mathcal{G}(n\_vec) \tag{8}$$

where gf is the similar semantics feature generated by $\mathcal{G}$, and n_vec is the Gaussian noise vector. In contrast to the original GAN, GAN_BERT generate the hierarchical semantic features directly instead of the original URLs.

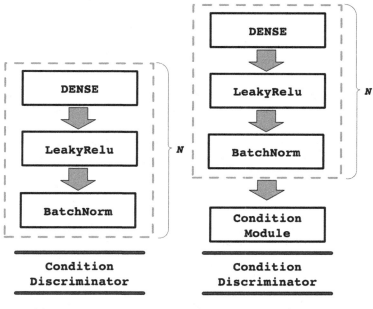

(a) Generator Module.   (b) Condition Discriminator Module.

Fig. 4. Specific modules of Generator and Condition Discriminator. Condition Discriminator layer includes $N * \{Dense \Rightarrow LeakyRelu \Rightarrow BatchNorm\}$ and a subsequent conditional module.

3.3   Classifier

There are two purposes of classifier. One is to optimize the whole model through the loss function in the training process, and the other is to classify the real input in the testing process. As shown in Fig. 1, the classifier is mainly contains two parts: condition discriminator and classification layer ($Dense \Rightarrow Softmax$). Following is the specific description of the condition discriminator.

Condition Discriminator. We propose a condition discriminator based on the traditional discriminator by adding a conditional judgment module, in order to make maximum use of the generated semantics features. The generated semantics features are used not only to calculate the difference with the real features, but also to make category judgments when the conditions are satisfied. As shown in Fig. 4(b), the condition discriminator layer is consists of: $N*$ $\{Dense \Rightarrow LeakyRelu \Rightarrow BatchNorm\}$ ($\mathcal{D}$) and a subsequent conditional module ($\mathcal{CM}$). For gf, $\mathcal{CM}$ makes a judgment on its result vector (R) after $\mathcal{G}$. The formula is as follows.

$$F_{\mathcal{CM}} = \begin{cases} 1, & \text{if } t < R_{max} \\ 0, & \text{otherwise.} \end{cases} \tag{9}$$

where t is the preset threshold (in this paper, 0.7) and R_{max} is the largest element value in R.

Hence, URLGAN is trained over a $(k+1)$-category objective: $(1, ..., k)$ denotes the probability that the input belongs to each category, and $k + 1$ denotes the probability that the input is gf. More formally, let rfs and gfs denote the real features distribution and the generated features, respectively. Three loss functions are donated to cooperate with the condition judge: $L_{\mathcal{D}}$ loss of $\mathcal{D}$, $L_{\mathcal{G}}$ loss of $\mathcal{G}$ and $L_{\mathcal{CM}}$ loss of $\mathcal{CM}$.

$L_{\mathcal{D}}$ is defined as:

$$L_{\mathcal{D}} = L_{\mathcal{D}_{\text{sup}}} + L_{\mathcal{D}_{\text{unsup}}} \tag{10}$$

$$L_{\mathcal{D}_{\text{sup}}} = -\mathbb{E}_{x,y \sim rfs} \log [p_{\text{m}}(\hat{y} = y \mid x, y \in (1, \ldots, k))] \tag{11}$$

$$L_{\mathcal{D}_{\text{unsup}}} = -\mathbb{E}_{x \sim rfs} \log [1 - p_{\text{m}}(\hat{y} = y \mid x, y = k+1)] \tag{12}$$
$$- \mathbb{E}_{x \sim gfs} \log [p'_{\text{m}}(\hat{y} = y \mid x, y = k+1)]$$

where $p_{\text{m}}(\hat{y} = y \mid x, y \in (1, \ldots, k))$ is the probability provided by the URLGAN that rf is belonging to one of the target categories, $p_{\text{m}}(\hat{y} = y \mid x, y = k+1)$ is the probability that rf is belonging to the fake category and $p'_{\text{m}}(\hat{y} = y \mid x, y = k+1)$ is the probability that gf is belonging to the fake category. $L_{\mathcal{D}_{\text{sup}}}$ measures the error in assigning the wrong category to a rf among the original k categories. $L_{\mathcal{D}_{\text{unsup}}}$ measures the error in assigning the wrong category to a gf. $L_{\mathcal{CM}}$ is defined as:

$$L_{\mathcal{CM}} = -\mathbb{E}_{x \sim gfs} \log [p'_{\text{m}}(\hat{y} = y \mid x, y \in (1, \ldots, k))] \cdot F_{\mathcal{CM}} \tag{13}$$

where $p'_{\mathrm{m}}(\hat{y} = y \mid x, y \in (1, \ldots, k))$ is the probability provided by the URLGAN that $x(gf)$ is belonging to one of the target categories. $L_{\mathcal{CM}}$ measures the error in assigning the wrong category to a gf among the original k categories under condition $F_{\mathcal{CM}}$.

$L_{\mathcal{G}}$ is defined as:

$$L_{\mathcal{G}} = L_{\mathcal{G}_{\mathrm{fm}}} + L_{\mathcal{G}_{\mathrm{unsup}}} \tag{14}$$

$$L_{\mathcal{G}_{\mathrm{fm}}} = \| \mathbb{E}_{x \sim rfs} f(x) - \mathbb{E}_{x \sim gfs} f(x) \|_2^2 \tag{15}$$

$$L_{\mathcal{G}_{\mathrm{unsup}}} = -\mathbb{E}_{x \sim gfs} \log \left[1 - p_m(\hat{y} = y \mid x, y = k+1) \right] \tag{16}$$

where $f(x)$ is the activation on an intermediate layer of $\mathcal{D}$. $L_{\mathcal{G}_{\mathrm{fm}}}$ means the error between the intermediate representations of gf and rf. $L_{\mathcal{G}_{\mathrm{unsup}}}$ means the error induced by gf correctly identified by $L_{\mathcal{D}}$.

After training with the above three loss functions, we actually deploy and utilize URLGAN to detect malicious URLs and their variants. In the actual detection deployment, the generator is not used. Other structures of the model are the same as those during training, and share parameters.

4   Evaluation

In this section, we perform various experiments on ISCX-URL2016 and expound how some malicious attackers deploy malicious URLs in practice. In particular, the experiments are intended to satisfy the following demands:

– Analyze the concept drift on ISCX-URL2016 and demonstrate the diversity of hierarchical semantic features generated by URLGAN in fitting malicious URL variants.
– Verify the effectiveness of URLGAN against concept drift on ISCX-URL2016.
– Explore actual malicious URL to further understand the intent of malicious attackers in realistic scenarios.

4.1   Data Sets

Table 1. The distribution of the ISCX-URL2016.

Categories	All		Train		Test
	Count	PCT(%)	Count₁	Count₂	Count
Benign	35300	30.90	25000	10000	10300
Spam	12000	10.50	8000	10000	4000
Phishing	10000	8.75	6600	10000	3400
Malware	11500	10.07	8000	10000	3500
Defacement	45450	39.78	30000	10000	15450

[a] $Count_1$ is the sample before data sampling.
[b] $Count_2$ is the result after data sampling.

We build sample collections from the public data set ISCX-URL2016 (1 category of benign, 4 categories of malicious). The distribution of ISCX-URL2016 is shown in Table 1. The data set is divided into training set and testing set according to time in order to analyze the concept drift of the data. We further sample each category in the training set to maintain the same number (10000), so as to avoid the deviation of model training in deep learning.

In addition, we find malicious URLs in traffic tracking collected from specific information sensitive targets (such as educational websites, governments and other important security portals) from June 11 to July 11, 2018. URLGAN is implemented in Python3.6 based on the libraries of PyTorch and trained on 2 NVIDIA TITAN XP GPUs.

4.2   Concept Drift on ISCX-URL2016

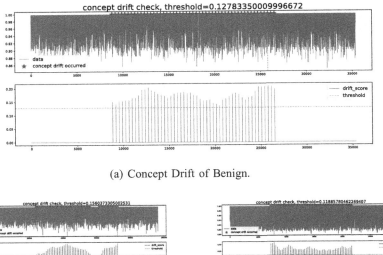

(a) Concept Drift of Benign.

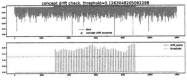

(b) Concept Drift of Spam.

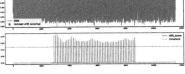

(c) Concept Drift of Phishing.

(d) Concept Drift of Malware.

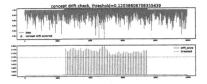

(e) Concept Drift of Defacement.

Fig. 5. The Analysis of Concept Drift. Where the drift_score is over the threshold, we determine that a concept drift has occurred.

Concept drift is an important data phenomenon in AI learning, which shows that the data distribution in the test stage (real-time distribution) is inconsistent with that in the training stage (historical distribution). We use a concept drift detection method based on time-windows [4] to compare whether the characteristics of the new window data deviate enough from the characteristics of historical window. Let $\hat{\mu}_W$ denote the characteristics of window W. $\hat{\mu}_W$ is the average of $\hat{\mu}_t$ for $t \in W$. $\hat{\mu}_t$ is an evaluation metric for the hierarchical semantics features of URLs:

$$\hat{\mu}_t = COSSIM_{t,0} = \frac{f_t \cdot f_0}{\|f_t\| \|f_0\|} = \frac{\sum_{i=1}^{n}(f_{ti} \times f_{0i})}{\sqrt{\sum_{i=1}^{n}(f_{ti})^2} \times \sqrt{\sum_{i=1}^{n}(f_{0i})^2}} \quad (17)$$

where f_t and f_0 is the hierarchical semantics features of URL U_t and U_0. $COSSIM_{t,0}$ indicates the cosine similarity of f_t and f_0.

W undergoes concept drift, if the difference ($drift\_score$) between the average ($\hat{\mu}_{W_0}, \hat{\mu}_{W_1}$) of the two sub-windows (W_0, W_1) is greater than threshold ϵ_{cut} computed as:

$$\epsilon_{cut} = \sqrt{\frac{1}{2\,m} \times \ln \frac{4\,|W|}{\delta}} \quad (18)$$

$$m = \frac{2}{1/|W_0| + 1/|W_1|} \quad (19)$$

where $|W|$ to denotes the length of W, m is the harmonic mean of $|W_0|$ and $|W_1|$.

The concept drift on ISCX-URL2016 is shown as Fig. 5, and we determine that a concept drift occurs when the $drift\_score$ exceeds the threshold. We use $\star$ to mark the position where the concept drift occurs in the data, and the red dotted line (vertical direction) to indicate the most obvious position where the concept drift occurs. It can be seen that Fig. 5(a), Fig. 5(b), Fig. 5(d) and Fig. 5(e) have significant concept drift at 2/3 of the data, with Fig. 5(c) at 1/3. Therefore, dividing the data set according to the ratio of 2:1 (training: testing) will be more conducive to analyze the model's resistance to concept drift.

4.3   Diversity of Generated Data

To illustrate the capability of our approach to detect malicious URL variants, in-class diversity and extra-class discriminability of the generated samples are first evaluated by $COSSIM$. $COSSIM_{x_0,x_1} \in 0, 1$ indicates the cosine similarity of f_{x_0} and f_{x_1}. The larger the $COSSIM_{x_0,x_1}$, the higher the similarity of f_{x_0} and f_{x_1}. We randomly select 1000 generated feature pairs from each given category and calculate their $COSSIM$ scores. For comparison, we do the same for real feature pairs.

As shown in Fig. 6(a), the distribution of $COSSIM$ scores for each category proves that the generated features are highly diverse. By introducing noise into the generator, we get a wider range of $COSSIM$ scores than the real features.

That is to say, malicious URL variants can be well modeled by the generator, and the URLGAN not only is able to detect the known malicious URL, but also further mitigate the serious threat of malicious URL variants. Notably, the minimum $COSSIM$ scores generated features remain above 0.4 indicating that the generated features are extra-class classifiable. The $COSSIM$ distributions of URLGAN and BERT on the testing set (Fig. 6(b)) further indicate that the generated features are extra-class classifiable and can help URLGAN to extract more accurate and essential features.

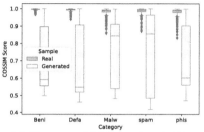
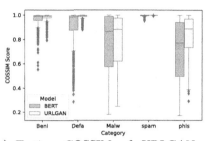

(a) Training COSSIM of URLGAN.　(b) Testing COSSIM of URLGAN and BERT.

Fig. 6. The distribution of $COSSIM$ scores for each category.

4.4 Detection Performance

URLGAN is a comprehensive model based on generator. In order to prove its detection performance, we compare it with the BERT model without generator. In addition, we also compare the results of our model with other published models. To better describe the detection performance of models, there are three commonly used metrics: $Precision(P) = \frac{TP}{TP+FP}$, $Recall(R) = \frac{TP}{TP+FN}$, and $F1 = \frac{2*Precision*Recall}{Precision+Recall}$. Since the ISCX-URL2016 contains multiple categories, we use three averages ($micro, macro, weighted$) to adequately measure the performance of the model.

Table 2 shows the comparison of experimental results for the dataset ISCX-URL2016. It is evident from the table that our system achieves better results in all three averages ($micro, macro, weighted$). Especially, in the case of extremely imbalanced data, URLGAN still achieves more than 94% for $microP, microR$, and $microF1$. The results compared with BERT sharing the same structure show that the fault tolerance of the model is improved due to the increased diversity of data, which is consistent with our expectation of detecting malicious URL variants. Meanwhile, the results further show that the data generated by our model can reduce the influence of concept drift, that is, improve the model's resistance to concept drift.

Table 2. Comparison of detection performance over URLGAN, BERT, LSTM and CNN on ISCX-URL2016 (%).

Method	macroP	macroR	macroF1	weightedP	weightedR	weightedF1	microP	microR	microF1
URLGAN	**91.61**	**86.80**	**89.11**	**94.88**	**94.98**	**94.82**	**94.98**	**94.98**	**94.98**
BERT	88.63	84.45	86.04	90.93	90.51	90.340	90.51	90.51	90.51
LSTM [2]	82.15	80.89	82.98	90.91	90.04	90.38	90.04	90.04	90.04
CNN [8]	73.92	72.52	73.24	84.81	84.78	84.78	84.78	84.78	84.78

[a] $microF1$ shows the performance of the model under extremely imbalanced data.
[b] $macroF1$ and $weightedF1$ show performance of the model under highly recognizable categories.

We apply URLGAN to protect specific targets and detect malicious URL. It is used to analyze the detection ability of the designed model for malicious URL variants and analyze the attacker's attack intention, so as to provide a theoretical basis for subsequent protection.

Table 3. List of potential malicious URL threats and corresponding categories.

	URL	Category
1	http://35732.camdvr.org/update?id=08f92e10	Malware
2	http://bcash-ddt.net/?223a06=2243078&id=38579623604	Malware
3	http://pzrk.ru/img/logo4.gif?288858f8=680024312&id=54531249931	Malware
4	http://www.report-download.com/advplatform/CnetInstaller.exe?appid=75012479	Malware
5	http://00.000h4s.tk/Panel/bot.php	Malware
6	http://www.zghhrl.com/wp-login.php	Phishing

Table 3 presents the malicious URL find in realistic environments. As can be seen, URL $1, 2, 3, 4$ are malware URL with the same order semantics. Although 5 is also a malware URL, its order semantics is completely different from $1, 2, 3, 4$. The comparison between $1, 2, 3, 4$ and 5 shows that our model can deal with the URL variants caused by changing the order semantics in the real environment and the further pattern drift caused by them. Even though 5 and 6 have the same order semantics, they can still be identified as different categories by our model through the lexical features. This shows that hierarchical semantic features are categorical. In conclusion, the generation and use of hierarchical semantic features can not only improve the performance of URLGAN in detecting malicious URL and their variants, but also mitigate the effect of pattern drift.

5   Conclusion

In this paper, we propose a malicious URL detection model (URLGAN) that extracts the hierarchical semantics features from URL. The analysis of public data set ISCX-URL2016 shows that concept drift exists objectively. We extract hierarchical semantics features from the original URL and combine the similar features generated by the generator to ensure that the condition discriminator obtains the essential difference between normal URL and malicious URL. The distribution experiment of $COSSIM$ shows that the generated similar features are diverse and categorical. Comparative experiments on public datasets with existing state-of-the-art work show that URLGAN is superior in detecting malicious URLs and their variants, and can effectively reduce the impact caused by concept drift. Additionally, the performance in realistic environment further proves that our model can improve the protection of specific targets. In short, we present key insights on how to detect concept drift caused by malicious URL variants, which will shed lights on understanding web attack and employing proactive defenses.

References

1. Survey shows phishing attacks are up and few are spared. https://mypage. webroot.com/rs/557-FSI-195/images/IDG_Report_Increased_Phising_Attacks. pdf. Accessed 11 Feb 2022
2. Afzal, S., Asim, M., Javed, A.R., Beg, M.O., Baker, T.: URLdeepDetect: a deep learning approach for detecting malicious URLs using semantic vector models. J. Netw. Syst. Manage. **29**(3), 1–27 (2021). https://doi.org/10.1007/s10922-021-09587-8
3. Anand, A., Gorde, K., Moniz, J.R.A., Park, N., Chakraborty, T., Chu, B.T.: Phishing URL detection with oversampling based on text generative adversarial networks. In: 2018 IEEE International Conference on Big Data (Big Data), pp. 1168–1177. IEEE (2018)
4. Gama, J., Žliobaitė, I., Bifet, A., Pechenizkiy, M., Bouchachia, A.: A survey on concept drift adaptation. ACM Comput. Surv. (CSUR) **46**(4), 1–37 (2014)
5. Goodfellow, I., et al.: Generative adversarial nets. In: Advances in Neural Information Processing Systems, vol. 27 (2014)
6. Kolari, P., Finin, T., Joshi, A., et al.: SVMs for the blogosphere: blog identification and splog detection. In: AAAI Spring Symposium on Computational Approaches to Analysing Weblogs (2006)
7. Le, A., Markopoulou, A., Faloutsos, M.: PhishDef: URL names say it all. In: 2011 Proceedings IEEE INFOCOM, pp. 191–195. IEEE (2011)
8. Le, H., Pham, Q., Sahoo, D., Hoi, S.C.: URLNet: learning a URL representation with deep learning for malicious URL detection. arXiv preprint arXiv:1802.03162 (2018)
9. Liu, Z., Li, S., Zhang, Y., Yun, X., Cheng, Z.: Efficient malware originated traffic classification by using generative adversarial networks. In: 2020 IEEE Symposium on Computers and Communications (ISCC), pp. 1–7. IEEE (2020)
10. Ma, J., Saul, L.K., Savage, S., Voelker, G.M.: Identifying suspicious URLs: an application of large-scale online learning. In: Proceedings of the 26th Annual International Conference on Machine Learning, pp. 681–688 (2009)
11. Mamun, M.S.I., Rathore, M.A., Lashkari, A.H., Stakhanova, N., Ghorbani, A.A.: Detecting malicious URLs using lexical analysis. In: Chen, J., Piuri, V., Su, C., Yung, M. (eds.) NSS 2016. LNCS, vol. 9955, pp. 467–482. Springer, Cham (2016). https://doi.org/10.1007/978-3-319-46298-1_30
12. Marchal, S., François, J., State, R., Engel, T.: PhishStorm: detecting phishing with streaming analytics. IEEE Trans. Netw. Serv. Manage. **11**(4), 458–471 (2014)

13. Patil, D.R., Patil, J.: Survey on malicious web pages detection techniques. Int. J. u- e-Serv. Sci. Technol. **8**(5), 195–206 (2015)
14. Patil, P., Rane, R., Bhalekar, M.: Detecting spam and phishing mails using SVM and obfuscation URL detection algorithm. In: 2017 International Conference on Inventive Systems and Control (ICISC), pp. 1–4. IEEE (2017)
15. Prakash, P., Kumar, M., Kompella, R.R., Gupta, M.: PhishNet: predictive blacklisting to detect phishing attacks. In: 2010 Proceedings IEEE INFOCOM, pp. 1–5. IEEE (2010)
16. Sahoo, D., Liu, C., Hoi, S.C.: Malicious URL detection using machine learning: a survey. arXiv preprint arXiv:1701.07179 (2017)
17. Yun, X., Huang, J., Wang, Y., Zang, T., Zhou, Y., Zhang, Y.: Khaos: an adversarial neural network DGA with high anti-detection ability. IEEE Trans. Inf. Forensics Secur. **15**, 2225–2240 (2019)

MEMTD: Encrypted Malware Traffic Detection Using Multimodal Deep Learning

Xiaotian Zhang, Jintian Lu, Jiakun Sun, Ruizhi Xiao, and Shuyuan Jin[✉]

School of Computer Science and Engineering, Sun Yat-sen University,
Guangzhou, China
{zhangxt73,lujd6,sunjk3,xiaorzh3}@mail2.sysu.edu.cn,
jinshuyuan@mail.sysu.edu.cn

Abstract. Malware that generates encrypted traffic presents a great threat to Internet security. The existing state-of-the-art malware traffic detection techniques based on deep learning (DL) ignore the heterogeneity of encrypted traffic, resulting in their inability to further improve detection performance. This paper applies multimodal DL to detect encrypted malware traffic, proposing a multimodal encrypted malware traffic detection (MEMTD) approach. MEMTD extracts features from three types of modal data—the transport layer security (TLS) handshake payload bytes (encryption behavior modal data), packet length sequence (spatial modal data), and packet arrival-time interval sequence (time modal data) of encrypted traffic. Moreover, an intermediate fusion mechanism is adopted in the MEMTD approach to mine the dependencies among modalities and fuse the discriminative traffic features, improving detection performance. The experimental results on datasets containing 8 malware families and normal traffic show that the MEMTD approach achieves 0.9996 macro-F1 and outperforms other single-modal DL detection methods.

Keywords: Malware traffic detection · Encrypted traffic · Multimodal deep learning · Intermediate fusion mechanism

1 Introduction

Encrypted malware traffic detection is a challenge in cyberspace security. Software what intentionally executes malicious payloads on victim computers is considered malware [1]. There are different types of malware families or malicious software, including viruses, botnets, Trojan horses, etc., which have caused great damage to the property and privacy of Internet users. Due to the wide usage of encryption techniques, malware adopts transport layer security (TLS) to hide its malicious attempts, which makes the detection of malware traffic more difficult.

To detect encrypted malware traffic, some researchers have utilized machine learning (ML) and deep learning (DL) algorithms. ML-based detection combines artificially designing statistical features (e.g., maximum packet length) and

© Springer Nature Switzerland AG 2022
T. Di Noia et al. (Eds.): ICWE 2022, LNCS 13362, pp. 357–372, 2022.
https://doi.org/10.1007/978-3-031-09917-5_24

selecting the ML model (e.g., logistic regression) to classify encrypted traffic into different malware families [2–5]. This kind of detection decomposes the encrypted traffic classification problem into two subproblems, i.e., feature engineering and model training driven by domain experts. The result of each subproblem directly affect final classification performance [6], resulting in that ML-based detection cannot guarantee the best classification performance. Moreover, ML-based detection requires expert experience. In recent years, DL has emerged, allowing for the combination of feature design and model training in an end-to-end model and the automatic learning of complex feature representations [6–12]. Generally, encrypted malware traffic detection methods based on DL employ only one modal type of encrypted traffic, such as packet payload bytes or header fields, to classify encrypted traffic. These single-modal detection methods based on DL have focused on designing complex deep neural networks instead of considering other modalities of encrypted traffic to improve detection performance.

The above researchers employing DL-based detection have ignored the heterogeneity of traffic data, which allows for the conversion of network traffic into multimodal data. As multimodal data, the payload of packets exchanged during the handshake phase, the packet length sequence (PLS), and the packet arrival-time interval sequence (PAIS) can contribute to the detection of encrypted malware traffic. First, TLS handshake payload bytes (HPBs) can be employed to extract traffic information about the encryption suite and security degree, i.e., encryption behavior modal information. Second, the PLS can be utilized to extract the information of the packet length changes in traffic flow, i.e., spatial modal information. Finally, the PAIS can represent the information of the arrival time changes in the flow, i.e., time modal information. In this context, the multimodal DL method is suitable for extracting features and classifying encrypted network traffic since can exploit all the available modal information of network traffic jointly to obtain a hierarchical representation.

This paper proposes a multimodal encrypted malware traffic detection approach, namely MEMTD, which jointly extracts features from the TLS HPBs, PLS, and PAIS of encrypted traffic. Moreover, the different modal feature extraction networks in MEMTD—ConvNet, GruNet-1, and GruNet-2—are designed to learn the representation of different modal information. While maintaining high-precision performance, MEMTD has better robustness because feature representation is enhanced by multiple modal inputs. MEMTD further adopts an intermediate fusion mechanism to avoid overfitting and any possible learning failures in representing the associations between modalities.

Our contributions can be briefly summarized as follows:

- We propose an MEMTD approach to detect encrypted malware traffic. This approach extracts three types of modal information—encryption behavior, spatial, and time modal information—from the encrypted traffic, improving detection performance with enhanced feature representation.
- We adopt the intermediate fusion mechanism to improve the utilization of multimodal features. The intermediate fusion mechanism has the capability of learning the dependencies between modalities, which employs two fusion networks to fuse multimodal features gradually.

– The experimental results demonstrate that the MEMTD approach achieves high performance with 99.94% accuracy (ACC) and 99.96% macro-F1 indicators.

2   Related Works

2.1   ML-Based Detection

With the advent of ML technology, researchers have tried to classify encrypted traffic without decryption. Anderson et al. proposed for the first time that unencrypted TLS headers can be used together with packet statistics as features of encrypted traffic to identify malware families, with 11-multinomial logistic regression [2]. Shekhawat et al. leveraged TLS handshake and statistical features to represent encrypted traffic and used random forest algorithms to design a two-layer detection framework for fast benign traffic filtering and malware traffic classification [3]. A feature set that included a modified NIST testing suite to represent the randomness of the content was proposed to identify the traffic protocol [4]. Moreover, [5] was based on random forest algorithms and designed the features of packet information, time, transmission control protocol (TCP) flag field, and application layer load information for identifying malicious encrypted traffic. The above ML-based method required the manual design of traffic features and could not solve the encrypted traffic classification in an end-to-end manner. However, various research views concerning the analysis of encrypted traffic have been proposed in these works, contributing to the understanding of the heterogeneity of encrypted traffic.

2.2   DL-Based Detection

To avoid the limitation of manually designing encrypted traffic features, the researchers used DL technology to design the end-to-end detection model for encrypted traffic classification. FS-Net with multilayer encoder-decoder structure built by Liu et al. can input the PLSs of raw flows to achieve excellent encrypted traffic classification performance [6]. In another work, Bi-gated recurrent unit (GRU) was also used to implement feature extraction, but unlike FS-Net with a reconstruction mechanism, the method proposed in [7] added an attention mechanism to learn the local flow information. Dong et al. proposed the CETAnalytics framework, which adopts packet payload bytes as input to classify encrypted traffic and implemented the framework through a 1-dimensional convolutional neural network (1D-CNN) with residual structure and the Bi-GRU with an attention mechanism [8]. A traffic classification method that integrates long short-term memory (LSTM) and a CNN to identify traffic via three packet payloads at any position of the encrypted flow was proposed by [9]. Moreover, [10,11] adopted a CNN to build an end-to-end encrypted traffic classification neural network. For training with fewer samples or speeding up traffic recognition, many improvements were made to the network architecture.

In the abovementioned single-modal detection based on DL, many complex neural network structures have been adopted by researchers, but the improvement of distinction performance is limited. An alternative idea is multimodal DL, which extracts complementary information from the modalities and yields a richer representation since this method can produce much-improved performance compared to using a single modality [13]. Although multimodal DL has been widely used in computer vision [14], emotion recognition [15], and other fields, it is difficult to find research based on multimodal DL in the field of encrypted malicious traffic detection. The only application of multimodal DL methods in the field of traffic classification is the MIMETIC approach proposed by Giuseppe et al. [16]. However, the MIMETIC framework is designed for mobile network traffic classification and adopts only two modalities from traffic bytes as input, which does not verify its effectiveness in terms of malicious traffic detection tasks. To detect encrypted malware traffic, this paper proposes a multimodal DL method that can use the three different modalities jointly to represent features and adopt the intermediate fusion mechanism to enhance the ability to learn the dependencies between modalities.

3 Multimodal Encrypted Malware Traffic Detection

3.1 Overview

As shown in Fig. 1, the MEMTD approach contains three steps, namely, multimodal data preprocessing, different modal feature extraction, and intermediate fusion and detection.

In the first step, MEMTD converts the raw traffic into multimodal data, TLS HPBs, PLS, and PAIS. In the second step, ConvNet, GruNet-1, and GruNet-2 are employed to extract the different modal feature vectors. In the last step, MEMTD adopts an intermediate fusion mechanism to gradually fuse the three feature vectors and classify the encrypted traffic. Moreover, to improve the different modal feature representation ability, the MEMTD approach adopts a pretraining and fine-tuning training process.

3.2 Multimodal Data Preprocessing

The first step of the MEMTD approach is the multimodal data preprocessing of the traffic flow. A flow is a set of packets sharing 5 tuples (i.e., the IP of the source, IP of the destination, port of the source, port of the destination, and transport-level protocol), taking no account of their sending directions. To analyze flow in multiple modalities, we extract TLS HPBs, PLS, and PAIS from a flow as MEMTD input.

For notational convenience, an input flow to MEMTD is defined as follows:

$$F = [p_1, p_2, \ldots, p_{|F|}] \tag{1}$$

$$p_i = \{t_i, l_i, b_i, d_i\}, i \in \{1, 2, \ldots, |F|\}, t_1 < t_2 < \ldots < t_{|F|} \tag{2}$$

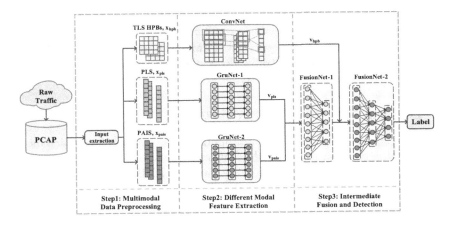

Fig. 1. Overview of the MEMTD approach.

where p_i stands for the i-th data packet in the flow, including the packet arrival-time $t_i \in [0, \infty]$ in seconds, the packet length $l_i \in \{1, 2, \ldots, 1500\}$ in bytes, the packet payload bytes $b_i = [b_i^1, b_i^2, \ldots, b_i^{l_i}], b_i^j \in \{0, 1, \ldots, 225\}, j = 1, 2, \ldots, l_i$, and the sending direction of the packet $d_i \in \{1, -1\}$ (1 and -1 indicate whether the sender is the client).

Unlike benign users, malware leverages TLS encryption technology for con-fusion rather than security, so malware developers tend to use older cipher suites than those utilized by enterprises when adopting TLS [2]. In addition, the unen-crypted fields in the data packet sent during the TLS handshake phase, such as the protocol version of the TLS, the list of optional cipher suites provided by the client, and extension items, all can be considered discriminative information used to classify malware families. Therefore, the MEMTD approach introduces the HPBs, defined as $x_{hpb} = (b_{ch}, b_{sh})$, to obtain prominent features in the dimen-sion of encryption behavior, where $b_{ch}, b_{sh} \in b_i, i \in [1, 2, \ldots, |F|]$ are the packets that carry client hello and server hello messages in the TLS handshake phase.

After the TLS handshake, the flow enters the data transmission stage, con-taining significant application layer information. However, the packet payload in the data transmission stage is encrypted and is thus not suitable to be directly input into the deep neural network. Although some researchers have employed encrypted packet payload bytes as the input of the CNN, it has been demonstrated that the network learns only the lengths of encrypted packets as features [12]. Therefore, PLS and PAIS are designed to record the flow infor-mation of all positions, including those in the data transmission stage. PLS is defined as a sequence with $|F|$ elements, $x_{pls} = [d_1 l_1, d_2 l_2, \ldots, d_{|F|} l_{|F|}]$ and $d_i, l_i \in p_i$. While x_{pls} includes the behavior information of a flow in the con-tent dimension, PAIS describes a flow from the perspective of time, denoted as $x_{pais} = [a_1, a_2, \ldots, a_{|F|-1}]$, where the element a_i $(i = 1, 2, \ldots, |F| - 1)$ is calculated by the following:

$$a_i = d_{i+1}(t_{i+1} - t_i) \tag{3}$$

where $t_i \in p_i$ and $d_{i+1}, t_{i+1} \in p_{i+1}$. To format the inputs of the DL network, all the x_{hpb}, x_{pls}, and x_{pais} of traffic flows perform zero-padded and truncated operations in the input extraction step.

3.3 Different Modal Feature Extraction

The second step of MEMTD is different modal feature extraction, which includes three neural networks to develop the features of different modalities.

To capture the local information on the TLS HPBs, we design a ConvNet constructed with the translation-invariant 1D-CNN structure to accept x_{hpb}, as shown in Figure Fig. 2(a). Its first layer accepts a 256-dimensional vector, x_{hpb}, and embeds each element of x_{hpb} into a 60-dimensional vector to enrich the representation of information preserved in each byte. Then, the embedded vector is passed to the Conv Block composed of two 1D convolution layers with three convolution kernel lengths (i.e., 2, 4, and 6). In addition, the output of the first convolution operation is normalized and passed to a rectified linear unit (ReLU) function. Subsequently, after the processing of the maximum pooling layer connected to the Conv Block, the output vector with fewer dimensions becomes the feature vector of HPBs, v_{hpb}. Finally, v_{hpb} is sent to a classification layer to obtain the distribution over different malware families and benign users during pretraining, and the traffic category with the maximum probability is adopted as the output label. A multilayer perceptron with a softmax layer implements the classification layer. During fine-tuning, the v_{hpb} is sent to the FusionNet of MEMTD.

Different from extracting the field information in the packet payload by 1D-CNN, x_{pls} and x_{pais} are more appropriate for utilizing GRU to obtain the feature vector representing the entire flow. GRU and LSTM have long-term memory for the sequence, but GRU has fewer parameters than LSTM. Specifically, x_{pls} and x_{pais} utilize GruNet-1 and GruNet-2 to extract different modal features, respectively, and these two networks have the same structure, GruNet, but different parameters, as shown in Fig. 2(b). First, the embedding layer of GruNet accepts sequence data and selects x_{pls} or x_{pais} as input according to the different usages of traffic modalities. Moreover, three Bi-GRU layers are responsible for extracting the feature vector of sequence data, and their hidden state dimension is 80. The output of the embedding layer is defined as $s = [s_1, s_2, \ldots, s_L]$, where $L = 20$ represents the number of Bi-GRU units per layer. Each layer of the three-layer Bi-GRU has a forward $\overrightarrow{GRU}_i$ network and a backward $\overleftarrow{GRU}_i$ network, where $i \in \{1, 2, 3\}$ represents the network level. The calculation process of Bi-GRU relies on the hidden state to accumulate and transfer the information of sequence elements from two directions, as follows:

$$\overrightarrow{h}_t^i = \overrightarrow{GRU}_i(\overrightarrow{h}_{t-1}^i, (\overrightarrow{h}_t^{i-1}, \overleftarrow{h}_t^{i-1})), t \in \{1, 2, \ldots, L\}, i \in \{1, 2, 3\} \tag{4}$$

$$\overleftarrow{h}_t^i = \overleftarrow{GRU}_i(\overleftarrow{h}_{t-1}^i, (\overrightarrow{h}_t^{i-1}, \overleftarrow{h}_t^{i-1})), t \in \{1, 2, \ldots, L\}, i \in \{1, 2, 3\} \tag{5}$$

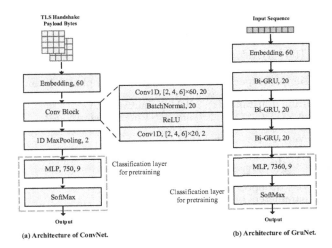

Fig. 2. Network structure used in the different modal feature extraction stage of MEMTD. Figure 2(a) shows the architecture of ConvNet, and Fig. 2(b) shows that of GruNet-1 and GruNet-2. The classification layer used for pretraining in the figure is removed in the fine-tuning stage of MEMTD.

where $\overrightarrow{h}_t^i$ and $\overleftarrow{h}_t^i$ represent the hidden states of $\overrightarrow{GRU}_i$ and $\overleftarrow{GRU}_i$ at time step t, respectively. States $\overrightarrow{h}_0^i, \overleftarrow{h}_{L+1}^i, i \in \{0, 1, 2\}$ are both zero vectors, and $\overrightarrow{h}_t^0 = s_t, \overleftarrow{h}_t^0 = s_t, t \in \{1, 2, \ldots, L\}$.

The feature vector extracted by Bi-GRU, $v_{seq} = [\overrightarrow{h}_1^3, \overleftarrow{h}_1^3, \ldots, \overrightarrow{h}_L^3, \overleftarrow{h}_L^3, \overrightarrow{h}_L^1, \overleftarrow{h}_1^1, \overrightarrow{h}_L^2, \overleftarrow{h}_1^2]$, is designed as v_{pls} or v_{pais} according to the different instances, GruNet-1 or GruNet-2, respectively. Similar to ConvNet processing HPBs modal feature vectors, v_{pls} and v_{pais} are input to the multilayer perceptron with soft-max during pretraining and then sent to the FusionNet of MEMTD during fine-tuning.

3.4   Intermediate Fusion and Detection

Through intramodal learning, ConvNet, GruNet-1, and GruNet-2 output the feature vectors of different modalities, v_{hpb}, v_{pls}, and v_{pais}, respectively, employed as the input of the third step of MEMTD. In this step, MEMTD processes feature fusion, and the shared presentation layers (i.e., FusionNet-1 and FushionNet-2) learn the dependencies of the modalities and classify the traffic as belonging to a benign or malware family.

MEMTD provides an intermediate fusion mechanism to combine modal feature vectors from different sources because simple splicing may lead to the insufficient usage of the extracted information [13]. First, the output vectors of GruNet-1 and GruNet-2, v_{pls} and v_{pais}, are fused by FusionNet-1 constructed with a multilayer perceptron. Then, the output vector of FusionNet-1 and the output vector of CovnNet, v_{hpb}, are sent to FusionNet-2, a multilayer perceptron

---

Algorithm 1: Training MEMTD

Input: Sample sets

$S^i = \{(s_1^i, y_1), (s_2^i, y_2), \ldots, (s_N^i, y_N)\}, i \in \{1, 2, 3\}, y_n \in \{1, 2, \ldots, K\}$

where s_n^1, s_n^2, s_n^3 and y_n represent the $x_{hpb}, x_{pls}, x_{pais}$ and label of the n-th sample respectively. The number of samples is N, and the number of traffic categories is K.

Output: A trained instantiated MEMTD network, Net.

Require: $ConvNet, GruNet, FusionNet$-1 and $FusionNet$-2.

1 $Net_1 \leftarrow ConvNet$
2 $Net_2 \leftarrow GruNet$ // i.e., GruNet-1
3 $Net_3 \leftarrow GruNet$ // i.e., GruNet-2
4 **for** i *in* $\{1, 2, 3\}$ **do**
5 | Train(Net_i, S^i) // pretraining stage
6 | $Net_i \leftarrow Net_i$ dropped MLP layer and softmax
7 | Freezing parameters of Net_i
8 **end**
9 $Net \leftarrow$ Combine($Net_{1,2,3}, FusionNet$-1, 2)
10 Train($Net, S^{1,2,3}$) // fine-tuning stage

---

with a softmax layer added to the tail. Finally, the softmax layer outputs a vector representing the probability of the traffic category, from which the predicted label can be obtained. This label is the result of detecting encrypted malware traffic.

3.5   MEMTD Training Process

The training process of multimodal DL methods has two crucial stages: learning the features within each modality and representing the associations between modalities automatically. As displayed in Algorithm 1, the training process of the MEMTD approach includes pretraining and fine-tuning, which correspond to the aforementioned two stages.

First, three neural networks, Net_1, Net_2, and Net_3, are instantiated and correspond to three modal feature extraction networks, ConvNet, GruNet-1, and GruNet-2, respectively. Second, these networks are trained with HPBs, PLS, and PAIS sample sets to classify traffic families in the pretraining phase. Step 5 in Algorithm 1, Train(Net_i, S^i), represents the network training with the corresponding modal data and labels of the sample set. The trained ConvNet, GruNet-1, and GruNet-2 can be employed as single-modal classifiers to detect encrypted malicious traffic and be used to demonstrate the effectiveness of modalities in experiments. Finally, ConvNet, GruNet-1, and GruNet-2 remove the multilayer perceptron and are combined with FusionNet-1 and FusionNet-2 to form a multimodal DL network. MEMTD needs only to adopt the previous layers of the trained single-modal networks to represent the feature vectors because the lower layers of a network can extract the more general features, which can be transferred to other tasks [17]. In the fine-tuning stage, the MEMTD network needs only to train the parameters of the fusion layer and learn the fusion of multimodal feature vectors and final classification. Moreover, the loss function adopted in pretraining and fine-tuning is the cross-entropy function.

4 Evaluation

4.1 Dataset

To evaluate the performance of the MEMTD approach, we employ the Stratosphere Research Laboratory dataset from the cybersecurity group of the Artificial Intelligence Centre at the Czech Technical University in Prague as raw traffic [18]. This dataset was collected through a project responsible for long-term malware capture and provides malicious and benign traffic to the Stratosphere Intrusion Prevention System.

In the experiment, 47 pcap files were adopted, including 17 pcap files with benign traffic and 30 pcap files generated by 8 different malware families. Table 1 shows the number of secure sockets layer (SSL)/TLS flows in each family. We deliberately do not balance the number of flows between different families to imitate the actual network situation.

Table 1. Detailed dataset description

ID	Families	Pcaps	Flows
1	Bunitu	4	5,259
2	Caphaw	1	2,057
3	Dridex	3	111
4	HTBot	6	18,813
5	Miuref	3	2,499
6	Neris	3	4,365
7	TrickBot	4	522
8	Zbot	6	7,398
9	Normal	17	24,885
Total		47	65,909

4.2 Experiment Settlement

For a complete analysis, this paper includes the following methods as baselines:

- FS-Net [6] inputs the PLS into a DL model with a reconstruction mechanism for encrypted traffic classification, which is implemented by Bi-GRU.
- [9] proposed the building of a convolutional LSTM (CLSTM) neural network to classify encrypted traffic, utilizing the payload bytes of three consecutive packets in a flow. For convenience, CLSTM is used to represent [9].
- The three single-modal feature extraction networks in the MEMTD method, i.e., ConvNet, GruNet-1, and GruNet-2, are employed as independent single-modality DL networks to detect malware traffic.

– Different variants of the MEMTD approach, MEMTD-T and MEMTD-L, utilize v_{hpb} as the input of Fusion-1 and input v_{pls} and v_{pais} into Fusion-2, respectively. Furthermore, MEMTD without the intermediate fusion mechanism is instantiated as MEMTD-S.

We evaluate all methods based on ACC and macro-F1 indicators. The reason for using macro-F1 indicator is that it can evaluate the detection performance of the method in imbalanced data. The definitions are as follows:

$$ACC = \frac{\sum_{i=1}^{C}(TP_i + TN_i)}{\sum_{i=1}^{C}(TP_i + TN_i + FP_i + FN_i)} \tag{6}$$

$$precision_i = \frac{TP_i}{TP_i + FP_i}, recall_i = \frac{TP_i}{TP_i + FN_i} \tag{7}$$

$$macro\text{-}F1 = \frac{1}{C}\sum_{i=1}^{C} F1_i, F1_i = 2 \times \frac{recall_i \times precision_i}{recall_i + precision_i} \tag{8}$$

where TP_i, TN_i, FP_i, FN_i, respectively, represent the number of true positive, true negative, false positive and false negative entries in the $i\text{-}th$ family. Moreover, the number of traffic families is $C = 9$.

4.3   Experimental Results and Analysis

To evaluate the performance of MEMTD, we compare the proposed approach with other DL detection methods in the comparison experiments section. Then, we analyze several properties of MEMTD, which contribute to improving detection performance:

– **The three input modalities** contain distinguishing information, which is conducive for encrypted malware traffic detection. To demonstrate the validity of the adopted modalities, pretrained ConvNet, GruNet-1, and GruNet-2 are utilized to detect malicious traffic in the ablation experiments section.
– **The intermediate fusion mechanism** can enhance the presentation of intermodal dependence and relieve the difficulty of fusing features from heterogeneous data. For comparison, the variants of the MEMTD approach are utilized to research the effect of different fusion orders in the feature fusion experiments section. They are implemented as MEMTD-T, MEMTD-L, and MEMTD-S as displayed in Table 3.
– **Imbalanced malicious traffic detection** is more relevant to the needs of actual cyberspace security, and the MEMTD approach can accomplish this task. Learning a robust and comprehensive representation of encrypted traffic is key to traffic classification, and the imbalanced distribution of malicious traffic emphasizes this requirement. We discuss further in the imbalance detection analysis section.

Table 2. Experimental results

ID	Families	CLSTM		FS-Net		**MEMTD**	
		Precision	Recall	Precision	Recall	Precision	Recall
1	Bunitu	0.8932	0.8970	0.9480	**1.0000**	**1.000**	0.9994
2	Caphaw	0.5397	0.4873	0.9842	0.9780	**0.9982**	**0.9973**
3	Dridex	0.7177	0.6696	**1.0000**	0.8666	**1.0000**	**1.0000**
4	HTBot	0.7164	0.7617	**1.0000**	**1.0000**	0.9884	0.9995
5	Miuref	0.9252	0.9432	0.9280	0.7813	**1.0000**	**1.0000**
6	Neris	0.8960	0.8581	0.9826	0.9817	**1.0000**	**1.0000**
7	TrickBot	0.9268	0.9344	0.9832	**1.0000**	**1.0000**	**1.0000**
8	Zbot	0.8061	0.7690	**1.0000**	0.9978	**1.0000**	**1.0000**
9	Normal	0.7858	0.5789	0.9592	0.9825	**1.0000**	**1.0000**
ACC		0.8118		0.9936		**0.9994**	
macro-F1		0.7815		0.9638		**0.9996**	

Comparison Experiments. Table 2 illustrates the performance comparison between the MEMTD approach and other DL methods in terms of encryption malware traffic detection. The conclusions obtained are presented below.

a. The MEMTD approach obtains the best performance compared to other methods and can effectively identify each malware family. According to Table 2, the macro-F1 indicator of MEMTD reached 99.96%, which means that even if a certain malware family has much less traffic than those other families (e.g., Dridex or TrickBot), MEMTD can also identify them with high performance.

b. The introduction of other modal inputs can improve the performance of end-to-end DL models. The MEMTD approach inputs the same PLS as the input of FS-Net and adds the other two modalities, HPBs and PAIS. The MEMTD improved macro-F1 by 3.58% without the reconstruction mechanism of FS-Net. This result demonstrates that the introduction of multimodal learning can break the performance bottleneck of complex neural networks in a single modality.

c. The MEMTD approach can extract comprehensive traffic information without introducing a complex neural network structure. In the different modal feature extraction step, MEMTD does not combine a CNN and a recurrent neural network (RNN) to form a complex feature representation layer. However, the performance of the MEMTD approach is much better than that of the CLSTM method that combines CNN and LSTM.

Ablation Experiments. The classification performance of the MEMTD approach and its three pretrained single-modal deep networks are illustrated in Fig. 3(a). The following conclusions can be drawn.

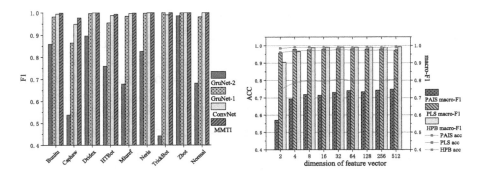

(a) Experimental results of the single-   (b) Experimental results of networks with
modal deep neural networks in MEMTD.   different feature vector dimensions.

Fig. 3. Analysis of three modalities and their corresponding feature vector dimensions.

Table 3. Experimental results of different fusion strategies

Methods	Fusion-1 inputs	Fusion-2 inputs	macro-F1	ACC
MEMTD	v_{pls} and v_{pais}	v_{fus1} and v_{hpb}	**99.96%**	**99.94%**
MEMTD-T	v_{hpb} and v_{pls}	v_{fus1} and v_{pais}	99.41%	99.91%
MEMTD-L	v_{hpb} and v_{pais}	v_{fus1} and v_{pls}	99.89%	99.87%
MEMTD-S	–	v_{hpb}, v_{pls}, and v_{pais}	99.55%	99.80%

a. The experimental results show that ConvNet, GruNet-1, and GruNet-2 can identify encrypted malware family traffic, demonstrating that HPBs, PLS, and PAIS include distinguished classification information. The most distinguishable information is that on the distribution of packet payload bytes in the SSL/TLS handshake phase. In addition, the traffic generated by different malicious behaviors differs more greatly in terms of packet length than in terms of packet arrival time.

b. The combined usage of modalities complements the feature representation of encrypted traffic. In each malware family detection task, the F1 indicator of MEMTD exceeds the three single-modal classifiers. This result indicates that the classification information extracted by ConvNet, GruNet-1, and GruNet-2 is not lost in the feature fusion step of the MEMTD approach. Moreover, the association and dependence between modalities are learned by fusion layers in the fine-tuning stage to supplement traffic features and improve detection performance.

c. The selection of the packets employed to input CNN affects performance. As shown in Fig. 3(a), ConvNet adopting $x_hpb = (p_ch, p_sh)$ as input has an F1 indicator of more than 0.94 in each family. The macro-F1 indicator of the CLSTM method utilizing three random consecutive packet payloads as input is only 0.7815, although the structure of CLSTM is more complicated than that in ConvNet. Therefore, the distinctive features of encrypted malicious traffic are in the TLS handshake phase, specifically, in client hello and server hello messages, not in other locations.

Feature Fusion Experiments. The dimensions of the feature vectors, v_{hpb}, v_{pls}, and v_{pais}, determine the richness of the corresponding modal information. Their impact on detection is evaluated through experiments, as shown in Fig. 3(b). Table 3 shows the experimental results of the variants of the MEMTD approach, where v_{fus1} represents the output vector of FusionNet-1. The classification performance of these networks with different dimensions of feature vectors and different variants of MEMTD indicates the following conclusions.

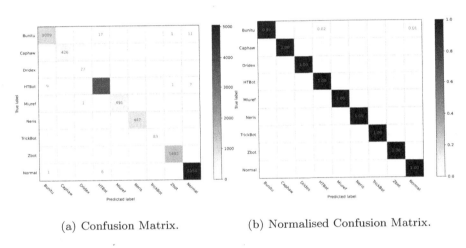

(a) Confusion Matrix.   (b) Normalised Confusion Matrix.

Fig. 4. Confusion matrix of MEMTD.

a. As the dimensions of the feature vectors, v_{hpb}, v_{pls}, and v_{pais}, increase in Fig. 3(b), the F1 indicator and ACC rise. Nonetheless, the improvement tends to be gentle with the exponential growth of the dimension of vectors. After the dimensions exceed 32, the three feature vectors no longer significantly enhance detection performance. Considering the balance of performance and training time, the MEMTD approach adopts 32 as the dimension of v_{hpb}, v_{pls}, and v_{pais}.

b. The proposed MEMTD intermediate fusion mechanism enhances detection performance and outperforms all other variants. After fusing the vectors representing the features of the full flow, v_{pls} and v_{pais}, by FusionNet-1, FusionNet-2 combines v_{fus1} and v_{hpb} to classify the flow. This strategy allows the MEMTD approach to fuse feature vectors from different sources effectively.

c. The fusion order of the feature vectors, v_{hpb}, v_{pls}, and v_{pais}, affects the detection performance. In particular, the experimental results in Table 3 elaborate that the input of the last feature fusion layer has a more significant effect. The modality validity experiments in Fig. 3(a) demonstrate that the discriminative information in HPBs, PLS, and PAIS decreases in order. The macro-F1 indicator of MEMTD-L, which inputs PLS to FusionNet-2, is lower than that of MEMTD. In addition, the performance of MEMTD-T, which applies PAIS as the input of FusionNet-2, is poorer than that of MEMTD-S, which utilizes the simple concatenation of feature vectors. Therefore, this paper proposes to placing the feature vector of the most discriminative modality into the final fusion layer in the multimodal DL method.

Imbalanced Detection Analysis. The confusion matrix of MEMTD performance is displayed in Fig. 4. Figure 4(a) shows the MEMTD classification result for imbalanced malware traffic detection. Interestingly, MEMTD has excellent identification performance against malware families with few samples, Dridex and TrickBot. In contrast, the malware with the third-largest number of samples in the dataset, Bunitu, has the worst identification result, as shown in Fig. 4(b). This experimental results indicate that malicious traffic detection differs from general imbalanced classification tasks. The number of traffic samples of a particular malware does not directly determine its traffic detection ability. Therefore, the MEMTD approach does not utilize cost-sensitive learning methods to alleviate the impact of imbalanced datasets but instead focuses on capturing intra- and intermodal dependencies to enhance the representation of encrypted traffic.

5   Conclusion

This paper proposes a multimodal DL method named MEMTD to detect encrypted malware traffic. The MEMTD approach extracts three modal features from the raw network traffic, where intra- and intermodality dependencies can be captured by learning. In addition, the MEMTD approach employs the translation-invariant 1D-CNN structure to build ConvNet, which extracts feature vectors from packets in a flow containing client hello and server hello messages. For PLS and PAIS, the MEMTD approach adopts a modal feature extraction network, GruNet, constructed by Bi-GRU, to learn feature representation. After pretraining, the three modal inputs can be abstracted into feature vectors containing information within the modalities. To thoroughly learn the dependencies between modalities, the MEMTD approach adopts an intermediate fusion mechanism to fuse feature vectors and classify malware traffic. We demonstrate the effectiveness of the MEMTD approach on an imbalanced dataset that mimics actual network states, the experimental results of which show that the MEMTD approach outperforms other single-modal DL methods and is also effective for imbalanced malware traffic.

Acknowledgment. This work was supported by the National key research and development program of China (Grant No. 2018YFB1800705).

References

1. Aslan, Ö.A., Samet, R.: A comprehensive review on malware detection approaches. IEEE Access **8**, 6249–6271 (2020)
2. Anderson, B., Paul, S., McGrew, D.: Deciphering malware's use of TLS (without decryption). J. Comput. Virol. Hacking Tech. **14**(3), 195–211 (2018). https://doi.org/10.1007/s11416-017-0306-6
3. Shekhawat, A.S., Di Troia, F., Stamp, M.: Feature analysis of encrypted malicious traffic. Expert Syst. Appl. **125**, 130–141 (2019)
4. Niu, W., Zhuo, Z., Zhang, X., Xiaojiang, D., Yang, G., Guizani, M.: A heuristic statistical testing based approach for encrypted network traffic identification. IEEE Trans. Veh. Technol. **68**(4), 3843–3853 (2019)
5. Fang, Y., Xu, Y., Huang, C., Liu, L., Zhang, L.: Against malicious SSL/TLS encryption: identify malicious traffic based on random forest. In: Yang, X.-S., Sherratt, S., Dey, N., Joshi, A. (eds.) Fourth International Congress on Information and Communication Technology. AISC, vol. 1027, pp. 99–115. Springer, Singapore (2020). https://doi.org/10.1007/978-981-32-9343-4_10
6. Liu, C., He, L., Xiong, G., Cao, Z., Li, Z.: FS-Net: a flow sequence network for encrypted traffic classification. In: IEEE INFOCOM 2019-IEEE Conference on Computer Communications, pp. 1171–1179. IEEE (2019)
7. Liu, X., et al.: Attention-based bidirectional GRU networks for efficient https traffic classification. Inf. Sci. **541**, 297–315 (2020)
8. Dong, C., Zhang, C., Zhigang, L., Liu, B., Jiang, B.: CETAnalytics: comprehensive effective traffic information analytics for encrypted traffic classification. Comput. Netw. **176**, 107258 (2020)
9. Zou, Z., Ge, J., Zheng, H., Wu, Y., Han, C., Yao, Z.: Encrypted traffic classification with a convolutional long short-term memory neural network. In: 2018 IEEE 20th International Conference on High Performance Computing and Communications; IEEE 16th International Conference on Smart City; IEEE 4th International Conference on Data Science and Systems (HPCC/SmartCity/DSS), pp. 329–334. IEEE (2018)
10. Huang, H., Deng, H., Chen, J., Han, L., Wang, W.: Automatic multi-task learning system for abnormal network traffic detection. Int. J. Emerging Technol. Learn. **13**(4), 4–20 (2018). https://doi.org/10.3991/ijet.v13i04.8466 https://online-journals.org/index.php/i-jet/article/view/8466
11. Congyuan, X., Shen, J., Xin, D.: A method of few-shot network intrusion detection based on meta-learning framework. IEEE Trans. Inf. Forensics Secur. **15**, 3540–3552 (2020)
12. Tong, X., Tan, X., Chen, L., Yang, J., Zheng, Q.: BFSN: a novel method of encrypted traffic classification based on bidirectional flow sequence network. In: 2020 3rd International Conference on Hot Information-Centric Networking (HotICN), pp. 160–165. IEEE (2020)
13. Ramachandram, D., Taylor, G.W.: Deep multimodal learning: a survey on recent advances and trends. IEEE Signal Process. Mag. **34**(6), 96–108 (2017)
14. Eitel, A., Springenberg, J.T., Spinello, L., Riedmiller, M., Burgard, W.: Multimodal deep learning for robust RGB-D object recognition. In: 2015 IEEE/RSJ International Conference on Intelligent Robots and Systems (IROS), pp. 681–687. IEEE (2015)
15. Ebrahimi Kahou, S., Michalski, V., Konda, K., Memisevic, R., Pal, C.: Recurrent neural networks for emotion recognition in video. In: Proceedings of the 2015 ACM on International Conference on Multimodal Interaction, pp. 467–474 (2015)

16. Aceto, G., Ciuonzo, D., Montieri, A., Pescapè, A.: MIMETIC: mobile encrypted traffic classification using multimodal deep learning. Comput. Netw. **165**, 106944 (2019)
17. Kaya, A., Keceli, A.S., Catal, C., Yalic, H.Y., Temucin, H., Tekinerdogan, B.: Analysis of transfer learning for deep neural network based plant classification models. Comput. Electron. Agric. **158**, 20–29 (2019)
18. Stratosphere: Stratosphere laboratory datasets (2015). https://www.stratosphereips.org/datasets-overview. Accessed 13 Mar 2020

Web User Interfaces

A Web Crowdsourcing Platform for Territorial Control in Smart Cities

Andrea Pazienza[1]([✉])(iD), Domenico Lofù[1,2](iD), Giampaolo Flace[1](iD),
Marco Salzedo[1](iD), Pietro Noviello[1](iD), Eugenio Di Sciascio[2](iD),
and Felice Vitulano[1](iD)

[1] Innovation Lab, Exprivia S.p.A., Via A. Olivetti 11, 70056 Molfetta, Italy
{andrea.pazienza,domenico.lofu,giampaolo.flace,marco.salzedo,
pietro.noviello,felice.vitulano}@exprivia.com
[2] Polytechnic University of Bari, Via E. Orabona 4, 70125 Bari, Italy
{domenico.lofu,eugenio.disciascio}@poliba.it

Abstract. Nowadays citizens engage with smart city ecosystems in several ways using smartphones, mobile devices, connected cars, and drones. Pairing devices and data with a city's infrastructure and services can improve sustainability and achieve an improvement in awareness and territorial control. Communities can improve energy distribution and decrease traffic congestion with the help of IoT technologies. To support and streamline such a process, in this paper we introduce a Web crowdsourcing platform as a Common Operational Picture dashboard to interoperate with smart devices, collect urban data from them, and monitor the city in real-time. Its application to the Metropolitan City of Bari is presented and discussed.

Keywords: Web crowdsourcing · COP · Smart city

1 Introduction

Crowdsourcing is based on the concept of involving the participation of a large number of individuals to solve certain problems together. Web crowdsourcing provides a new model for solving problems by gathering data also from interactive objects. The Internet of Things (IoT) offers services in almost all daily fields through advanced connectivity of devices, systems, and services, particularly smart applications. Hence, the idea of exploiting the Web crowdsourcing concept to smart city projects may help in fostering the activity of territorial control and monitoring by collecting data from citizens, including feedback and evaluation about urban services, city functioning, quality of life, as well as improvement suggestions. In particular, taking into consideration also autonomous devices, in particular Unmanned Aerial Vehicles (UAVs) such as drones, and self-driving vehicles, their IoT characteristics can be exploited to collect data from a limited urban area while achieving territorial control and obtaining an improved urban situational awareness.

© Springer Nature Switzerland AG 2022
T. Di Noia et al. (Eds.): ICWE 2022, LNCS 13362, pp. 375–382, 2022.
https://doi.org/10.1007/978-3-031-09917-5_25

In this context, a Common Operational Picture (COP) is defined as a shared representation of widespread and general knowledge concerning operation. Situational Awareness (SA) is at the basis of decision processes to maintain and understand what is happening in a certain situation and leverage this information to avoid or mitigate risks. SA can thus be considered as a purposeful act of an entity of a comprehensive system. This act directs interest to the relative combination of circumstances and entities that have aims and goals in common contexts at a certain moment.

In this work, we present a smart city crowdsourcing Web platform capable of monitoring the territory in near real-time, involving the creation of COP-based dashboards, able to collect data from a number of heterogeneous sources. Such data can be processed and analyzed to show geo-located information on a dedicated interactive map. In particular, we are interested in the geo-tracking of moving objects, and the real-time consultation of the data received and their trend over time. Furthermore, from a SA perspective, this solution may help to understand the perception of events, especially in critical ones. For example, exceeding the maximum speed of a vehicle inside the city or their presence in forbidden areas, will have to activate appropriate alarms or signaling mechanisms that will be managed by city authorities.

The remainder of the paper is structured as follows. Section 2 provides an overview of related work and technologies which were investigated as background knowledge. The next section presents our proposal, i.e. a Web crowdsourcing platform, including its functional architecture and the employed technological stack. Section 4 describes a possible scenario of territorial control by monitoring a smart city by means of our Web crowdsourcing platform. Finally, Sect. 5 concludes the paper, with an outline of future work.

2   Related Work

One of the steps towards SA is to make a transition into Smart Cities. Here, IoT play an important role to gather relevant information from the city, citizens, and the corresponding communication networks that transfer the information in real-time. In this respect, the works in [7,10] proposed solution for a smart city mobility monitoring platform based on crowdsourcing mobile solutions to gather and provide open traffic data, supporting an ecosystem for collaborative development of new Intelligent Transportation Systems applications.

Other works, such as in [3,6,8], investigated the role of IoT in smart city projects, analysing the evolution of research in the field of the smart city and related technologies, including crowdsourcing.

Since the popularity of the crowdsourcing for performing various tasks online increased significantly in the past few years, several frameworks and Web-based solutions have been provided, witnessing the need for tools to develop and run subjective quality assessment experiments [4,9]. Authors in [5] proposed a framework to enable a worldwide crowdsourcing approach to the generation of OBD-II data, similarly to OpenStreetMap for cartography.

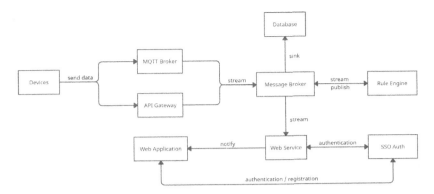

Fig. 1. Architectural diagram of the Web crowdsourcing platform.

In this landscape, COP-based solutions aiming at achieving situational awareness scenarios have been proposed, devoted to maintaining an understanding of what's going on around people at every moment and using that information to mitigate risks [1,2].

3   Crowdsourcing Data from Smart Autonomous Devices

This section presents the functional architecture of the Web crowdsourcing platfom, paying attention to the flow of data, ranging from the collection in the field to the persistence and use of them on the system. In Fig. 1 the architectural diagram is shown.

The intelligent devices for data collection in the field are enabled to transmit data, after authentication, using the protocols in two ways, namely MQTT (Message Queuing Telemetry Transport) and REST (REpresentational State Transfer). The devices that support the transmission of data via MQTT, convey them into an MQTT broker on specific topics for each type of device. If the devices do not support the MQTT communication protocol, the transmission of data is allowed by making requests to specific REST API endpoints. In this case, a massive transmission of data is also allowed. The internal data management of the system is mediated by a *Message Broker (MB)*, which acts as a communication bus common to all system components. In the MB the data are merged into two streams based on the type of information, called *tracking* and *events* respectively. The tracking messages correspond to those sent by smart devices, generally made up of information such as: instant time of detection, values detected by sensors and the current geographical position. The *API Gateway* component, once received, publishes them on the topic *tracking* of the MB. Instead, the messages arriving on the MQTT broker are consumed and inserted in the MB in the same way. Notifications and alerts are generated by the *Rule Engine* component, which has the task of applying user-defined rules and controls to the data it receives in streaming from the MB topic *tracking*.

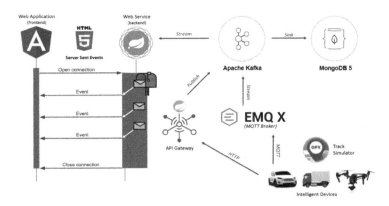

Fig. 2. Data Flow of the Crowdsourcing Architecture

Examples of rules may concern the exceeding of threshold values, access to forbidden areas, exit from geofence areas, and so on. Any data in transit on the topics of the MB is persistent on a time-series database within tables or collections. The choice of the type of database is dictated by the need for efficient reading queries over time intervals. A *Single Sign-On (SSO)* solution is used for managing user roles and data, system authentication, and for the use of services such as password registration and recovery. The *Web Service* component has back-end functionality and exposes all the services necessary for the Web application that the end-user will use. The main services concern the fetch of context information for initialization purposes by querying the database, and the presentation of the data in near real-time from the MB. A *Web Application* allows the end-user to access all the tools of the COP such as the geo-localized display of information and events in order to be able to reconstruct in any moment the SA of the monitored territory.

3.1   Technological Stack

As shown in Fig. 2, moving objects send data to the platform via MQTT or HTTP protocol. In the first case, the messages are published on specific topics present in the MQTT broker, implemented with *EMQ-X*[1]. Subsequently, the MB, represented by *Apache Kafka*[2], uses a special connector to consume them by collecting them in more generic topics (e.g., *tracks*). In the second case, instead, the intelligent devices send data by making HTTP requests to specific REST API implemented in the *API Gateway*. The latter, once the data has been received, in sequence or in batches, publishes them directly on specific Kafka topics. At this point, once the messages arrive on the Kafka topics, they are persisted on the *MongoDB 5* database[3], storing their content in the form of documents within

---

[1] EMQ-X: https://www.emqx.io/.

[2] Apache Kafka: https://kafka.apache.org/.

[3] MongoDB: https://www.mongodb.com/.

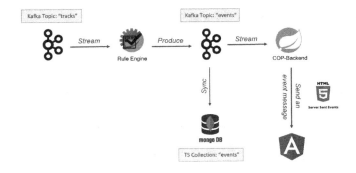

Fig. 3. Rule Engine diagram for the management of alarm and notification events.

specific timeseries collections. At the same time, the *Web Service* assumes the role of consumer of the messages present in the Kafka topics, in order to serialize them and transmit them in near real-time through notifications to the *Web Application*, using the *Server Sent Event* (SSE) protocol.

The generation of notifications (e.g., alarms), as shown in Fig. 3, is taken over by the *Rule Engine*, which consumes the tracking messages present on Kafka in order to subject them to certain rules hand-coded, such as simple conditions on threshold values or violation of constraints on geofence areas. In the latter case, a GIS library is used which is part of the Mapbox SDK and is able to verify whether or not a geographical point (i.e., the actual position of the device) belongs to a geographical area delimited by a polygon. In particular, keeping track in memory of the last known positions for each monitored device, it is possible to trace the input and output of devices within these areas. If a rule is triggered, an event message is generated which can be of the type alarm or information, and finally published on the Kafka topic *events*. At this point, through a Kafka connector of type *MongoDB SinkConnector*, once the messages in the topic are received, they are synchronized on the database in the time series collection *events*. Finally, the Web Service component subscribes to the topic *events* consuming the messages and then sending them to the front-end via the SSE protocol. More precisely, the *SseEmitter* component of *Spring*[4] is used to create an SSE channel dedicated to events, accessible after authentication. Finally, the *Web Application* implemented with *Angular 12*[5], subscribes to this channel. User authentication is managed through SSO using *Keycloak*[6], which is also entrusted with saving user data, and registering and managing accounts for them. The interaction between the Web Application user and the SSO is mediated by a back-end service called *COP-Auth* which acts as middleware. This component exposes REST APIs that allow the front-end to register and authenticate the user at a higher level. After the user successfully logs into

---

[4] Spring: https://spring.io/.
[5] Angular: https://angular.io/.
[6] Keycloak: https://www.keycloak.org/.

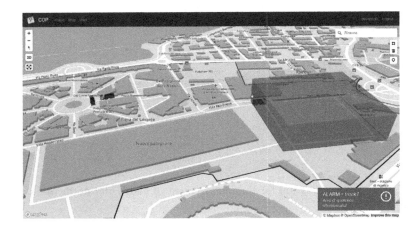

Fig. 4. Dynamic display of 3D objects and notifications.

the system, she receives an auth-token used for invoking the secure back-end resources provided by the micro-services. The latter, before allowing any request to the resources, interact with SSO and evaluate the validity of the authentication token provided in input. To render the map of the territory and display on it the objects dynamically monitored on the Web application, $MapboxGLJS$[7] is used, a Javascript library that exploits the $WebGL$ 2 hardware acceleration. In particular, the $Deck.GL$ library[8] is used to render the layers in 3D.

4 The Case of Metropolitan Area of Bari

The proposed solution has been applied in the context of the Italian national project called *Casa delle Tecnologie Emergenti*, in the Metropolitan Area of Bari, to allow near real-time monitoring of the exhibition districts, nameley a limited area representing a small-scale model of a smart city in which the tracking data of self-driving vehicles, traditional vehicles and drones, related to telemetry and environmental information, allow the monitoring staff to visually identify any dangers in a promptly and interactive fashion, through notifications or alarms generated autonomously by the system. In particular, the alarms are generated through the rule engine of the Web crowdsourcing platform through the analysis of time windows and the streaming of the captured incoming data.

In the presence of events inside the "Fiera del Levante", a large complex that has been selected as an experimental site, a large influx of people is expected, whose security and privacy must be guaranteed. Thanks to our Web crowdsourcing platform it is indeed possible to define geofence areas for which drones cannot fly and areas forbidden to the circulation of both self-driving and traditional vehicles. Furthermore, since there are moving vehicles, it is also necessary

---

[7] MapboxGLJS: https://www.mapbox.com/mapbox-gljs.
[8] Deck.GL: https://deck.gl/.

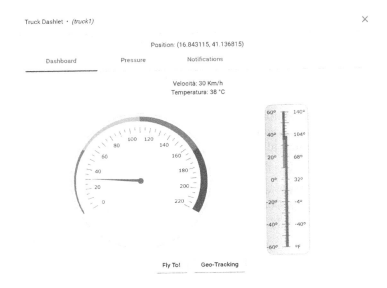

Truck Dashlet · *(truck1)*   ✕

Position: (16.843115, 41.136815)

Dashboard   Pressure   Notifications

Velocità: 30 Km/h
Temperatura: 38 °C

Fig. 5. Telemetry Dashlet.

to monitor the speed of each vehicle in order to efficiently manage traffic control. The Web crowdsourcing platform allows the monitoring of moving objects, such as self-driving vans and drones, and also the management of the definition and control of access to unauthorized areas by each of them.

Therefore, as shown in Fig. 4, the monitoring operator can interact with the devices tracked by the system, having access not only to information related to their position, but also to a whole series of telemetry data that can be viewed in real time in dashlets containing animated widgets, graphs or tables. It is worth noting that in the early stages of the project, we simulated classes of smart objects in order to generate realistic telemetry values. In particular, once authenticated, the operator chooses the *Map* item in the menu, then a map implemented with *Mapbox* is rendered. Here, the boundaries of the monitored place are delimited by a polygon, outlined in black. Trucks and drones are rendered on the map using the *Deck.GL* 3D library, automatically resized according to the zoom set by the operator.

Interestingly, by clicking on any device, a dashlet appears where, as can be seen in Fig. 5, it is possible to view the speed and temperature detected in real time of the vehicle through dynamic widgets, as well as graphs relating to the trend of the detections. Finally, the *notifications* tab shows the history of all the alarm and information events recorded in a tabular and paginated form. Events are notified in near real-time at the bottom right, with a event type colored box showing the type of event, the identifier of the concerned vehicle, and information content.

5   Conclusion

In this work, a Web crowdsourcing platform has been presented as a COP solution aimed at geolocalizing and monitoring drones in flight, self-driving electric vehicles, traditional vehicles, pedestrians, and IoT devices installed in urban areas, as well as crowdsourced information, gathered for territorial control in the framework of the monitoring of Bari city.

In future works, such a solution can take advantage of the recent introduction of the 5G network which allows intelligent devices to transmit data extremely fast, reducing the problem of latency.

Acknowledgements. This work was partially funded by the Italian MISE FSC 2014/20 Asse I project 'CASA delle TECNOLOGIE EMERGENTI', and by the Italian P.O. Puglia FESR 2014/20 project 6ESURE5 'SECURE SAFE APULIA'.

References

1. Ardito, C., et al.: Towards a situation awareness for ehealth in ageing society. In: Proceedings of AIxAS 2020, pp. 40–55 (2020)
2. Ardito, C., et al.: Management at the edge of situation awareness during patient telemonitoring. In: Baldoni, M., Bandini, S. (eds.) AIxIA 2020. LNCS (LNAI), vol. 12414, pp. 372–387. Springer, Cham (2021). https://doi.org/10.1007/978-3-030-77091-4_23
3. Boccadoro, P., Daniele, V., Di Gennaro, P., Lofù, D., Tedeschi, P.: Water quality prediction on a sigfox-compliant IOT device: The road ahead of waters. Ad Hoc Netw. **126**, 102749 (2022)
4. Hoßfeld, T., et al.: Survey of web-based crowdsourcing frameworks for subjective quality assessment. In: 2014 IEEE 16th International Workshop on Multimedia Signal Processing, MMSP, pp. 1–6. IEEE (2014)
5. Loseto, G., Gramegna, F., Pinto, A., Ruta, M., Scioscia, F.: A mobile and web platform for crowdsourcing obd-ii vehicle data. OJIOT **7**(1), 43–58 (2021)
6. Pazienza, A., et al.: A novel integrated industrial approach with cobots in the age of industry 4.0 through conversational interaction and computer vision. In: Proceedings of the Italian Conference on Computational Linguistics, CLiC-it 2019 (2019)
7. Pazienza, A., Polimeno, G., Vitulano, F., Maruccia, Y.: Towards a digital future: an innovative semantic IoT integrated platform for industry 4.0, healthcare, and territorial control. In: 2019 IEEE International Conference on Systems, Man and Cybernetics, SMC, pp. 587–592. IEEE (2019)
8. Shahrour, I., Xie, X.: Role of internet of things (IOT) and crowdsourcing in smart city projects. Smart Cities **4**(4), 1276–1292 (2021)
9. Staletić, N., Labus, A., Bogdanović, Z., Despotović-Zrakić, M., Radenković, B.: Citizens' readiness to crowdsource smart city services: a developing country perspective. Cities **107**, 102883 (2020)
10. Suciu, G., Butca, C., Dobre, C., Popescu, C.: Smart city mobility simulation and monitoring platform. In: 2017 21st International Conference on Control Systems and Computer Science, CSCS (2017)

Supporting Natural Language Interaction with the Web

Marcos Baez[ID], Cinzia Cappiello[ID], Claudia M. Cutrupi[ID],
Maristella Matera[(✉)] [ID], Isabella Possaghi[ID], Emanuele Pucci[ID],
Gianluca Spadone[ID], and Antonella Pasquale[ID]

Politecnico di Milano, Piazza L. Da Vinci 32, 20133 Milano, Italy
{marcos.baez,cinzia.cappiello,claudiam.cutrupi,maristella.matera,
isabella.possaghi,emanuele.pucci,gianluca.spadone,
antonella.pasquale}@polimi.it

Abstract. Conversational AI is disrupting the way information is accessed. However, there is still a lack of conversational technologies leveraging the Web. This paper introduces an approach to support the notion of Conversational Web Browsing. It illustrates design patterns for navigating websites through conversation and shows how such patterns are sustained by a Web architecture that integrates NLP technologies.

Keywords: Conversational AI · Conversational Web · Conversational design patterns

1 Introduction

Conversational agents (CAs) are pervading a broad range of activities, as their natural language (NL) paradigm simplifies the interaction with digital systems. They offer benefits in different situations where users may take advantage of voice-based interaction for accomplishing their tasks [3,8]. Recent works are capitalising on this technology, for example to design voice-based CAs for searching the Web [2], to automatically generate CAs out of a website content [9], or to enable end users to customize their CAs for the Web [5]. This interest shows the feasibility and potential of NL interaction for making the Web truly for everyone. However, very often the CA development and deployment is detached from Web architectures: CAs are seen as tools that complement the Web access experience by providing additional content, not granting access to the website content itself. There can be situations, instead, where some forms of disabilities (whether permanent, temporary, situational) demand for a voice-based access to the website. Despite this need, there is still a lack of proposals for a full-fledged integration of Conversational AI within Web architectures.

This paper tries to fill this gap by illustrating the conceptual architecture of *ConWeb*, a framework for *Conversational Web Browsing*. The idea is to enable users to navigate content and services accessible on the Web by "talking to websites" instead of browsing them visually, by expressing their goals in natural

© Springer Nature Switzerland AG 2022
T. Di Noia et al. (Eds.): ICWE 2022, LNCS 13362, pp. 383–390, 2022.
https://doi.org/10.1007/978-3-031-09917-5_26

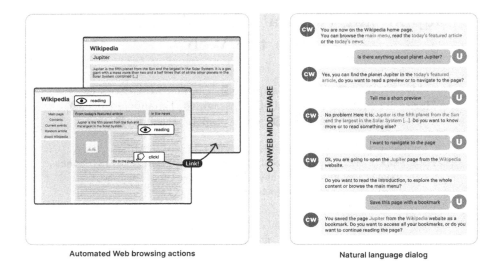

Fig. 1. An example of a Conversational Web Browsing on Wikipedia. The reported conversation recalls the conversational patterns resulting from the user research [1].

language and accessing the websites through a dialog mediated by a conversational agent (e.g., a voice-based browser plugin). ConWeb tries to respond to some requirements that we identified through an extensive human-centred process. With the help of 26 blind and visually impaired (BVI) users, along different sessions of interviews and co-design workshops, we were able to identify and validate some prominent challenges and some related interaction-design patterns sustaining the notion of Conversational Web Browsing [1].

After illustrating the notion of Conversational Web Browsing and highlighting the main challenges behind the provision of this new paradigm (Sect. 2), in Sect. 3 this paper outlines the main results of the conducted user research. Section 4 illustrates the design of *ConWeb*, a software platform for the Conversational Web that integrates information models, NLP models and other components of a Web architecture to manage a voice-based dialogue organized around the identified patterns for conversational Web browsing. Section 5 finally draws our conclusions and outlines our future work.

2 Conversational Web Browsing

To explain the main idea behind Conversational Web Browsing, we illustrate a scenario of a user browsing the Wikipedia Home Page[1] by dialoguing with a conversational agent (e.g., a smart speaker or a voice-based browser plugin). As represented in Fig. 1, starting from the home page the user can be introduced with a short description along with the main organisation of the website. The

---
[1] https://en.wikipedia.org/wiki/Main_Page.

user could also at any point get oriented by inquiring about the content available in a given context, e.g., by uttering *"Is there anything about planet Jupiter?"*. The user can then *navigate* the website by following up on one of the available options (e.g., *"I want to navigate to [...]"*). These requests can trigger navigation within or across pages in the website (e.g., from the Home to an article page). Ultimately, the user can browse the structure of the content or directly read the available content. To enable such interaction, a middleware sitting between the user and the website should be able to identify the offerings and content of the website that can be accessed through the conversational medium, interpret user *intents* and associated *entities* from user utterances, and automatically perform related *actions* on the website (e.g., click, extract information).

This paradigm is one of the few emerging approaches exploring the integration of conversational capabilities into the Web [2,5,9]. Previous work explored basic issues posed by a tight integration of Conversational AI with the Web, related to automating Web browsing actions to respond to NL user commands [4], with a focus on technical feasibility. This paper tries to give a further contribution by discussing how to support more articulated *design patterns* for conversational Web browsing that were identified through an extensive user research [1]. Incorporating conversational patterns is fundamental to support recurrent sequences of human-bot interactions [7] serving expected browsing tasks. The following sections illustrate the user requirements and the technical aspects that pattern integration implies.

3   User Requirements

In the time period from April to September 2021 we conducted a user research that involved 26 BVI users by means of online structured interviews and in-presence focus groups and co-design sessions. We first asked them to describe their experience with current voice-based assistive technologies. By using online tools for CA rapid prototyping (e.g., DialogFlow), we then solicited them to express their desiderata on the design of novel CAs for accessing websites. A complete description of the study is reported in [1]. In the following we illustrate some of the identified conversation *patterns*, which mainly refer to the structure of conversation for Web browsing. These patterns guided us in extending a preliminary version of the ConWeb prototype [4] to: *i)* support an incremental, dialog-based exploration of the Website, and *ii)* grant flexibility in the dialog organization, to fulfil the need of personalized browsing experiences.

Shaping-Up the Map of the Navigable Space. Users claimed that learning the structure of the website is a crucial initial step when they access a website for the first time. For this reason, they asked for strategies to identify *high-level navigation mechanisms* to support them in understanding the website structure, and fluidly move along the main areas (e.g., in Fig. 1: "You can browse the main menu, [...]"). To identify how to move along different information nodes, they highlighted mechanisms for *link predictability* (e.g.: "Do you want to read a preview, or [...]") and for *keeping track of the navigational context* (e.g.: "You are now in the Wikipedia Home Page.").

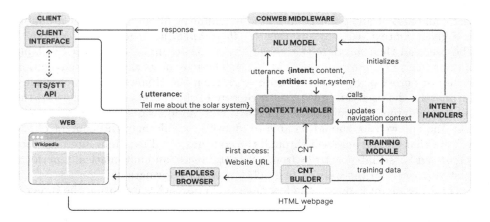

Fig. 2. Conceptual architecture of the ConWeb platform.

Navigating Through Intelligible and Quick Mechanisms. Depending on their tasks and preferences, participants demanded for different navigation strategies. They described *in-depth explorations* to narrow down navigation options along the hierarchy of nodes, but especially *punctual, fast-served requests* were discussed as a means to locate a desired content (e.g.: "Is there anything about [...]"), along with the capability of *bookmarking information nodes* (e.g.: "Save this page as a bookmark") for a direct access to content of interest.

Summarizing and Segmenting the Page Content. The research conversational paradigms should *prevent unwanted and unneeded explorations* resulting in poor user experiences. *Segmenting contents and highlighting characterizing keywords* could help localize the content of interest (e.g.: "Jupiter is [*<short content preview>*]. Do you want to know more or reading something else?").

Providing Access to Conversation-Scaffolding Intents. Users frequently expressed the need for *scaffolding intents* to help them identify possible actions at different navigation levels and for the provision of *feedback on the system status*, such as the use of landmark cues.

4   The ConWeb Platform

Translating the identified interaction patterns into architectural choices for the design of the ConWeb platform has required focusing on the following aspects:

- A conversational-browsing model must be built when the website is first accessed, to index and present to the users the available conversation nodes and the navigation structures that can sustain conversational browsing.
- A conversation node does not necessarily correspond to an entire Web page; it can be a content paragraph, a navigation menu, a link, or any other element in the Web page that can be presented independently from the others and has a role in the progressive exploration of the website content.

- A context representation characterising the navigation status must be handled to let the users to move easily backward, i.e., along previous conversation nodes, and forward, i.e., to identify and explore new reachable nodes.
- To extract browsing-relevant intents and entities from the user utterances, an NLP engine must be adequately trained starting from the website content.
- Recognized intents and entities must be matched with navigation- and content-reading actions as deriving from the conversational-browsing model.
- The resulting CA must recognise website-specific intents as well as scaffolding intents related to auxiliary commands for the user to control the conversation.

Figure 2 illustrates the resulting conceptual architecture. The current version of the framework has been implemented by embedding the conversational capabilities into a traditional browser. In particular, it serves its logic via a client that uses external APIs (Google APIs in the current prototype version) for Text-To-Speech and Speech-To-Text translation. It gathers the NL user utterance and builds a request that embeds additional user session parameters needed to control and handle the user navigation context. At the server-side, an NLP engine (RASA in the current implementation) parses the user utterance to extract browsing intents and entities. Also considering the navigational context, the framework identifies and performs the necessary navigation actions. For example, for the user's request "Tell me about the solar system", the intent is a content request, and solar and system are the entities extracted. It is thus possible to identify the conversation node where those entities can be found, and to navigate automatically towards that node. The automatic navigation is performed through a headless browser (Selenium in the current prototype), which starts a browser session every time a new page is accessed. As a fundamental step to manage navigation, a context handler parses the page HTML to create a model that can help map the interpreted intents and entities onto contextual navigation actions. By invoking proper intent handlers, this module also builds the responses that the client renders in form of conversation. This mapping is the most challenging aspect. As described in the following, it requires integrating the NLP pipeline with the execution of browsing actions contextualised for the accessed website.

4.1   Conversation-Oriented Navigation Tree (CNT)

When a website is accessed for the first time, a conversational-browsing model is built to index the available content segments and the navigational structures that can sustain conversational browsing. This is needed for providing the user with an overview of the available content, for allowing her to move within the available content space based on the tracked navigational context, and for enacting a direct navigation towards a content responding to a search key.

As reported in Fig. 3, for each accessed Web page a Conversation-oriented Navigation Tree (CNT) is built to represent the hierarchical nesting of different page elements, the *conversation nodes*. Conversation nodes represent content segments (e.g., the leaf nodes in Fig. 3, representing the available articles), or

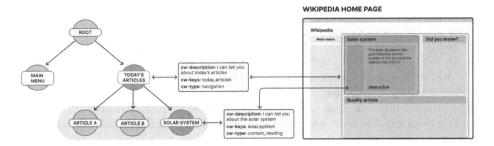

Fig. 3. Conversation-oriented Navigation Tree

navigational indices providing access to content segments (e.g., the *Today's arti-cles* index). Their granularity serves the purpose of building a dialog for the incremental exploration of the website content. Each CNT node also specifies attributes and descriptions extracted from the Web page, which can help ren-der the node content through conversation. The CNT traversal then supports both the progressive visit or the direct access (i.e., by means of search keys) to the specified conversation nodes. Pertinent conversation nodes are identified by matching the intent and entities extracted from the user's utterances with the descriptions and keys summarizing the content of a node.

4.2   Building the CNT

The specific content and the descriptive attributes stored in each CNT node are extracted from the HTML code of the accessed Web page. Based on the user request, a headless browser simulates navigation actions and downloads the HTML code of a page. The extraction of many of the CNT elements can be per-formed automatically, by parsing the HTML code. However, to make the process more effective, specific annotations can augment the page HTML to tag and spec-ify the elements useful for building the tree. For example, content-oriented tags can be used to add short summaries of content segments (`<cw-description>`), and representative keys (`<cw-keys>`). A type tag (`<cw-type>`) then character-izes page segments as *content* or *navigation* elements, with the latter providing navigational structures for indexing content nodes. These annotations can guide the page interpretation process and the extraction of relevant CNT elements.

4.3   Training the NLP Model

The NLP model for intent classification and entity extraction has to be trained for each website. While the recognition of some intents and entities (e.g., those for scaffolding commands) is content-agnostic and can be handled in the same way for any Web site, i.e., it does not need specific training, for some others (e.g., content-access requests) the NLP outcome depends on the knowledge on the specific Web site content. For this reason, in addition to representing the hierarchy of conversation nodes, the CNT also specifies the "domain knowledge" that can be used for the automatic generation of a website-specific training data set. Starting from the keys indexing each conversation node, a list of training sentences for each content-access intent is automatically generated and used to train the NLU model for intent classification and entity extraction.

4.4   Handling the Classified Intents

To perform proper navigation actions and build conversational responses to the user's requests, ConWeb includes a library of *Intent Handlers* that are invoked depending on the outcome of the intent classification and entity extraction. For example, a *Navigation handler* enables moving along the entire CNT to localize a conversation node when a content-access intent is recognized, whereas a *Link handler* and a *Content Reading handler* build the conversation for presenting nodes of type navigation and content, respectively: if the user request is for accessing a content node, after localizing the node in the tree the Content Reading handler build the dialog for rendering the node description; if instead the request refers to a link traversal, then an automatic navigation to the corresponding page is enacted together with the provision of feedback messages to inform the user of the content of the target node. A *Scaffolding Intents* handler serves commands available at any conversation node, such as those for getting information on the current page, help, back and forth commands, access to the bookmark list.

Intent handlers enforce separation of concerns and grant flexibility: they make it easy introducing additional conversational patterns, for example to manage Web page components not yet covered by our current prototype (e.g., forms or image-reading intents). Other extensions of the intent-handler library can also be conceived to accommodate specific users preferences, for example related to varying text-reading styles. This last feature responds to the need for personalization recurrently remarked during the conducted user research [1].

5   Conclusion

This paper has discussed interaction and architectural patterns that can make the Web accessible through an NL interaction. It has shown how Conversational AI can be integrated within Web architectures, to provide an additional channel for accessing websites. So far, our work has mainly focused on content-oriented websites. Even if further elements are needed to cover the requirements posed by other website categories, we are confident the flexibility offered by the ConWeb architecture can favour the extensions needed for handling other types of intents. There are however some limits that will be investigated in our future work.

The performance for training on the fly the NLU model has to be improved. When a website is accessed for the first time, the current prototype requires up to 10 s to generate the training data set and update the model. Our future work will focus on identifying lightweight techniques to reduce the response time.

The current ConWeb prototype requires augmenting the website HTML with the CNT annotations. We are now designing proper authoring environments and also want to capitalize on standardization activities[2] that are proposing HTML extensions for accessibility. For granting conversational access to any website, even those not properly augmented, we are working on deriving CNT elements through the automatic extraction/summarization of the website content.

Our future work will be devoted to user studies that will also address sighted users, to understand if the assumptions derived with and for BVI people can be extended to other classes of users. Involving BVI users has allowed us to identify the most stringent requirements for a conversational browsing detached from the visual channel. However, in line with recent initiatives [6], we are confident the resulting approach can benefit people universally, and has a potential that will impact Web Engineering in the coming years.

Acknowledgments. We are grateful to the associations UICI, ADV, Real Eyes Sport for their help in the user research. This paper is dedicated to Prof. Florian Daniel, who suddenly passed away in April 2020. He first had identified the value of this research.

References

1. Baez, M., et al.: Exploring challenges for conversational web browsing with blind and visually impaired users. In: CHI 2022 Extended Abstracts. ACM (2022)
2. Cambre, J., et al.: Firefox voice: an open and extensible voice assistant built upon the web. In: CHI 2021, pp. 1–18 (2021)
3. Chang, Y., et al.: Tourgether: exploring tourists' real-time sharing of experiences as a means of encouraging point-of-interest exploration. ACM Interact. Mob. Wearable Ubiquitous Technol. **3**(4), 128:1–128:25 (2019)
4. Chittò, P., Baez, M., Daniel, F., Benatallah, B.: Automatic generation of chatbots for conversational web browsing. In: Dobbie, G., Frank, U., Kappel, G., Liddle, S.W., Mayr, H.C. (eds.) ER 2020. LNCS, vol. 12400, pp. 239–249. Springer, Cham (2020). https://doi.org/10.1007/978-3-030-62522-1_17
5. Fischer, M.H., Campagna, G., Choi, E., Lam, M.S.: DIY assistant: a multi-modal end-user programmable virtual assistant. In: PLDI 2021, pp. 312–327. ACM (2021)
6. Microsoft: Inclusive design (2022). https://www.microsoft.com/design/inclusive/
7. Moore, R.J., Arar, R.: Conversational UX Design: A Practitioner's Guide to the Natural Conversation Framework. Morgan & Claypool (2019)
8. Pradhan, A., Mehta, K., Findlater, L.: Accessibility came by accident. Use of voice-controlled intelligent personal assistants by people with disabilities. In: CHI 2018, pp. 1–13 (2018)
9. Ripa, G., Torre, M., Firmenich, S., Rossi, G.: End-user development of voice user interfaces based on web content. In: Malizia, A., Valtolina, S., Morch, A., Serrano, A., Stratton, A. (eds.) IS-EUD 2019. LNCS, vol. 11553, pp. 34–50. Springer, Cham (2019). https://doi.org/10.1007/978-3-030-24781-2_3

---

[2] See https://schema.org/SpeakableSpecification.

User Acceptance of Modified Web Page Loading Based on Progressive Streaming

Lucas Vogel$^{(\boxtimes)}$ and Thomas Springer

TU Dresden, 01069 Dresden, Germany
`lucas.vogel2@tu-dresden.de`

Abstract. In times of the pandemic, it becomes more evident that our modern society relies heavily on the internet for most areas of life. As websites become more complex and their size increases, the amount of code slows down their loading speed, especially on mobile devices with poor network connectivity. Various improvements exist to optimize the code before and after delivering a web page to a client. However, the delivery and rendering itself was rarely examined. In this paper, we evaluate two new methods of loading and displaying websites faster, namely Text-First and Layout-First. Layout-First reduced the time until first contentful paint (FCP) on average from 281.75 s down to 6.43 s at 32 KB/s, a difference of more than 4.5 min. Text-First reached the FCP on average in 2.15 s at the same network speed. However, our user study revealed that not every technological improvement is well accepted by users. Results showed that users will wait longer if the layout is stable while loading the page. More than 85% of participants preferred the Layout-First method introduced in this paper.

Keywords: Progressive page loading · Initial page load · Page streaming · User experience · User acceptance

1 Introduction

Web response times always matter for users. But is it still a matter of concern with vastly increasing network speed and device resources? Yes, it is, since every network speed improvement is responded with more complex web applications with richer content and logic[1]. As described in the paper by Nah et al., a user expects a response from a web page in 2 s, or a majority of users will leave [4]. This fact stands in contrast to a recent publication by Google in 2018, which states that access to pages on mobile devices takes on average 15 s to load [1]. The problem becomes even more apparent in situations where the user is confronted with a slow network, in rural regions, in a train, or if the network access is downgraded to less than EDGE speed once the flat rate of the data plan is used up. Even in countries like Germany, the coverage of

---

[1] https://httparchive.org/reports/state-of-the-web.

© Springer Nature Switzerland AG 2022
T. Di Noia et al. (Eds.): ICWE 2022, LNCS 13362, pp. 391–405, 2022.
https://doi.org/10.1007/978-3-031-09917-5_27

cellular networks leaves significant gaps, especially in rural areas[2]. The results are partially absurd loading times far beyond any acceptable limit. For instance, facebook.com loads nearly 3 min (best-measured case) before the first content-ful paint, retrieved at 32 KB/s. From a set of the 20 most popular loadable web pages (from the Alexa Top List, October 27, 2020) for 19 pages, the user gets a timeout due to too slow loading when the pages are retrieved at 8 KB/s (all tested websites except google.com). This is also true for small web pages if they are not optimized correctly, resulting in longer loading times and increased energy consumption. A multitude of approaches exists targeting performance improvements for the initial page load. Nevertheless, the problem is still present since the above-presented performance values result from measurements based on modern web browsers that incorporate well-accepted approaches to speed up page loading. This paper explores an approach to speed up the initial page load both from technical feasibility and user acceptance by modifying the loading behavior. The concept is based on streaming server-side pre-processed content and layout information for progressively enhanced web page rendering at the client that allows faster first contentful paint.

The contribution of the paper is twofold: Firstly, we introduce two novel page loading mechanisms based on the concepts of progressive enhancement and streaming, namely Text-First and Layout-First. While Text-First primarily accelerates the transmission of text and content, Layout-First pre-renders the HTML with CSS beforehand and maintains a stable layout presented to the user. Secondly, we provide insights into performance improvements and user acceptance of the two introduced mechanisms based on performance measurements and a user study. The rest of the paper is organized as follows. In Sect. 2 we introduce key terms and concepts related to initial page load. In Sect. 3 related work is discussed, followed by results of a preliminary user study presented in Sect. 4. The two novel page loading methods are explained in Sect. 5. Evaluation results with respect to performance and user acceptance for the two new methods are discussed in Sect. 6. Finally, conclusions and future work are described in Sect. 7.

2   Background

This section describes major elements that form the basics for the technique developed in this paper. **A typical fetch- and render pipeline for a web page:** To render a web page, a browser starts by sending a request to the dedicated server to fetch the main HTML file of the page. For the render process, a parser is used to iterate over every HTML document statement after the main HTML file download is completed. This file might refer to multiple external resources, which are not embedded in the HTML file itself but linked synchronously or asynchronously. By default, the link is synchronous and, as a result, render-blocking. This aspect is described in-depth in the following sections. The process between the first received data of the main HTML file and the first render of a page is called `critical rendering path`. It describes the

---

[2] https://www.breitband-monitor.de/funkloch/karte.

fetching and processing of all render-blocking files. This includes the creation of the DOM and the CSSOM, intercepted by render-blocking JavaScript parsing. With speculative parsing this step can be optimized, the parser "looks ahead" and fetches resources needed later to parallelize a portion of the required network requests[3]. However, all external files need to be downloaded before parsing the main HTML file can be completed with speculative parsing.

Measuring the Loading Time of a Web Page: The time frame between the point in time a user requests a web page and the point in time the page is loaded entirely in the browser is an important performance metric for web pages. Technically, a web page can be considered as "loaded" in several stages. A key metric is `first contentful paint` (or FCP for short) which determines the speed at which the user can access information on a page. It marks the point at which any kind of content (media or text) is displayed to the user. At this stage, the content of a page could be displayed, as it is in a render-acceptable form. Therefore, if shown at this stage, enables first information retrieval and navigation on a page by the user.

Render-Blocking Resources: As described above, web pages can have external resources that are loaded synchronously and therefore block the rendering of the page. Fetching a resource, the currently used versions of HTTP (2 & 3) do not require a full TCP handshake for every request. However, this was not always the case. Still, an overhead for fetching and rendering an external file is present. Therefore, multiple large, externally loaded, render-blocking files or a large main HTML file will slow down the loading and display time. Optimizations like speculative parsing can only reduce this issue, but it still will not solve the core problem. A current solution is to bundle all external resources together in one or a small number of files to be loaded together, like `webpack`[4]. However, the base problem still exists. If the bundled file is large, devices with a slow network connection will have to wait for the entire file to be fetched, even if they might only use a section of the code that exists in the bundle. If, for example, the CSS is bundled and loaded asynchronously, it may be missing by the time the browser displays the HTML, and thus, the page will not display correctly until the whole CSS bundle is fetched and parsed. Until now, no data existed on the user acceptance of this behavior. Another possible technique is to bundle all external data by inlining all external resources directly in the main HTML file, providing only a single file for the whole page. This process highlights the same problem for devices with a slow network connection, as it still has to load all code, but now in a single file, independent of if the code is needed at this stage of displaying a page or not. As a result, the whole page becomes render-blocking. The best way, in theory, is to pre-process all resources, remove all unused code, and deliver only what is needed. As the convenience of a readily available full CSS- or JavaScript-Framework can easily outweigh the amount of work necessary for every component to be checked every time a web page is deployed, this

---

[3] https://developer.mozilla.org/en-US/docs/Glossary/speculative_parsing.
[4] https://webpack.js.org.

might not be done in practice. Furthermore, the main HTML page can still be too large even with said optimizations for very slow network speeds.

3   Related Work

Numerous techniques exist to improve the loading speed of web pages. In the following section, the most suitable methods are described in detail, followed by a discussion.

Google Pagespeed was published in 2015 and is a module for Apache and Nginx based servers. The core idea consists of automatically improving initial page loading speeds by enforcing best practices [6]. These include structural changes, like combining resource files of the same type, removal of comments and unnecessary elements, and content optimization like conversion of images to compressed modern web formats. Pagespeed is therefore different to AMP[5], as it optimizes existing code and does not provide a framework for creating a web application. The result is a smaller, optimized web page that loads in the traditional way. No optimization is made for the actual loading phase of a web page. Also, no content loading is postponed, only non-essential resources. Depending on the type of web page, this can still result in long loading times at slow network speeds if the main page is significantly large.

Hotwired is a group of frameworks that use the idea of transmitting HTML "over the wire". The idea is hereby that instead of pure JSON data that has to be converted to HTML at the client-side, the server sends the final HTML instead. Turbo is one of those developed frameworks[6]. The web page is split into frames for this to work. If a change is made in the frame, only the HTML of the frame is updated. The changes will be transmitted over WebSocket. This changes the speed and fluidity of handling the web page. However, the initial transmission of the web page will still be handled the traditional way of loading the page as a block.

In [3] the authors describe a technique of rendering CSS above the fold, using PhantomJS to find all matching CSS declarations of an element. If the element is inside a predefined viewport (above-the-fold), it is marked as critical and will be part of the CSS included in the modified web page. The way this "inlining" works is by collecting all critical CSS declarations and inserting them in a style-element in the header of a page. All remaining CSS is then asynchronously loaded with JavaScript once the page finished loading. This has pros and cons. By inlining the code in a style-element, pseudo-elements and classes can be addressed. The style attribute of individual elements is not capable of doing so. However, this increases the initial page size, and a overhead is induced by asynchronously linking the original CSS. Even if the time to first render is reduced, it might slow down render time at lower network speeds because the main page has a larger initial download size. Also, the technique is only used above-the-fold.

---

[5] https://amp.dev.

[6] https://turbo.hotwired.dev/.

All related methods will enhance the loading speed of web pages in different ways. However, all of them pursue the goal that the web page will look identical to the original while rendering, and achieve this as fast as possible. Moreover, various shortcomings were found in all further investigated techniques.

Polaris [5] as well as VROOM [8] only optimize the loading order of dependencies, not the content of the dependency itself. In paper [2], the structure and implementation of the developed software were not described in necessary detail and is missing specific data on how the software was tested [2]. The techniques [9] and react[7] cannot be generally applied to a universal web page. The developed software of paper [9] has the issue that often the original DOM in the correct order is required by JavaScript [9]. Method [9] only works with `reactjs`, and no other framework. Puffin OS[8] will render all web pages entirely on the server. For this to work correctly, it needs all data, including plain text passwords, sent to the server to work. Method [10] uses a Proxy system, which will not work with modern `https` or alternatively, has to break the encryption. Both techniques are not viable options. Finally, `Critical` [7] renders the HTML and CSS which is used above-the-fold. This technique will increase render time. However, if web pages could use this approach for the whole page efficiently, render times could be decreased even more. In general, not a single investigated technique or framework provides a complete solution ranging from server to client. Also, no method modifies the loading- and render-process itself. We hypothesize that this is mainly due to a lack of available data regarding user loading behavior acceptance. Therefore, a preliminary study was needed to collect said information. From the related work analysis, we found that a multitude of approaches exists that address performance improvements for initial page loading. While they fix partial problems related to the loading and rendering pipeline, fundamental issues of web page loading are not addressed comprehensively. A significant problem is the organization of content and layout in separate files that need to be completely downloaded before rendering and displaying are possible. Even worse, since modern web pages are responsive and built with a CMS, alternative content for different form factors and JavaScript frameworks blows up the number of files, individual file size, and render-blocking dependencies.

4 Preliminary Study

This preliminary study aimed to gather data about the acceptance of loading mechanisms based on progressive enhancement. The pre-study consisted of an anonymous online questionnaire regarding the acceptance of a web page loading behavior. The participants were shown animations[9] side-by-side of a mock-up web page loaded in two different ways with a slow network speed. The first version displayed the slower, all-or-nothing method of the current way a browser displays a web page. The second version showed a web page that loads the

---

[7] https://reactjs.org.
[8] https://puffin.com/os.
[9] https://imgur.com/a/2wXs3jX.

resources separately: first the HTML+Text of a page, followed by the CSS. As a result, users get the first content (HTML+Text) much earlier than the second version but have to accept layout changes due to the separate load of CSS. Therefore, users had to choose a trade-off in the study. We hypothesized that users would overwhelmingly choose the second version, as it delivers information faster, shown in the animation in footnote 9. Users could only answer by choosing one of the two options provided as radio buttons below the animation. As an optional field, participants could tell their age. The provided questionnaire was answered by 228 people. The users are expected to mainly consist of computer science students and faculty members, as it was spread by a faculty email newsletter, which might have induced a bias due to expert knowledge. The participants ranged from 15 to 72 years of age. Regarding loading preference, 59.21% of users chose the faster version with the progressively displayed content. However, this also concludes that 40.79% would rather wait longer for the web page to render with the correct layout. From this observation, we created two loading mechanisms to further investigate the trade-off between progressively enhanced initial page loading with faster first contentful paint and the degree of progressively enhanced web page content and layout accepted by a majority of the users.

5   Concept of Progressively Streamed Web Pages

The core idea of the developed concept is to control the render process by continuously adding content to the page. For it to work, server-side and client-side components are introduced. The server-side component pre-processes the page data and sent it via a stream to the client-side component, where it is progressively rendered and displayed. The pre-processing extracts the content, layout and code data minimally required to render the page, eliminate render-blocking links to external files and their dependencies and convert the resulting page data to a streamable representation. For pre-processing HTML, JavaScript, and CSS are deconstructed into individual characters. This allows the prioritization of content and styling by changing the order of delivery on a per-character level. After pre-processing, the web page is ready to be delivered. Initially, a minimal page with the client-side code is transferred, which will establish the stream connection. After a successful connection, the server-side component starts to transfer page data as a stream while the client-side component continuously re-adds the content to the page in order to be rendered. Guided by the results of the preliminary study in Sect. 4 we designed two methods for prioritizing and ordering page data, namely Text-First and Layout-First.

5.1   Loading Methods

The **Text-First method** prioritizes fast content display over a correct and stable page layout. This method aims to deliver the core information as fast as possible and delay all other code. For this, the three main components of modern web pages (HTML+Text, CSS, and JavaScript) are split and re-ordered for fast text loading, with all three parts separated. The pre-processing on the server-side component allows the separation of text and HTML. This is achieved by extracting all text and replacing most of the intermediate HTML with minimal placeholder tags. This extraction excludes links and headlines, as they provide semantic information or functionality to a page. The inserted placeholder tags are invisible in the browser window. The sending order is structured in the following way: First, the text with placeholders will be transmitted and rendered. At this stage, the user can already access the content of a page, similar to a text-only browser. After that, the HTML is loaded, and placeholders are filled with content. The HTML itself includes more markers for CSS and JS. After another render of the page, the CSS and JavaScript are loaded and inserted via placeholders in the same way. This ensures a minimal time until the first content can be displayed at the cost of significant layout shift during progressive page loading. In contrast, the **layout-first method** prioritizes correct and stable page layout over a fast content display. This technique allows the reduction or elimination of the significant layout shift that appears by inserting HTML/Text, CSS, and JavaScript after each other. However, integrating these components for a streaming-based transfer results in an overhead per text element sent to the client. In theory, the transfer of page content should be slower than Text-First but might result in a better balance between transfer speed and user experience, as shown in the preliminary study. This proposed method uses a self-implemented universal server-side-rendering framework to place the CSS at the correct location in the HTML of a page. Furthermore, sending unused CSS is delayed, as the currently unused classes might be necessary for elements that are inserted by JavaScript at a later point. Therefore, page data is ordered in the following way: first, HTML with Text and integrated render-critical CSS will be streamed and rendered in sections. These sections only end with text or a closing tag, and care is taken not to render the content if it ends with a half-transmitted tag element, which can affect the layout. Following the correct transmission, the delayed CSS is loaded and inserted, followed by JavaScript and a page refresh for the JavaScript-Hooks to fire.

5.2 Pre-processing at the Server-Side Component

As visible in Fig. 5 at marker 'A', the server-side component pre-processes the web page before delivering it to the client. This optimization is different from the techniques which were theorized by the pre-study. Both described technologies share most of the code needed to provide a progressively loaded and streamed web page, as it is illustrated in Fig. 1, where the differences in code are highlighted in violet. Both share a common filter and modifier but differ in the preparation of the sending order. As a first step, the received raw web page data is filtered for CSS and JavaScript (part **A1** in the figure). If external links for CSS or JavaScript are found, the external content is fetched first, and a placeholder replaces the link in the saved HTML. If internal CSS or JavaScript is found, it will be replaced the same way. All CSS and JavaScript will be used later in the sending order, part **A3**. After filtering all JavaScript and CSS, the page is modified if necessary. This is the case if the pre-processed web page runs on a different domain or subdomain. Also, requests like form data that requires backend logic can be forwarded to the correct address. To prepare the sending order with the Text-First method, the HEAD and BODY of the HTML document are split and handled separately, as seen in part **A3(1)**. The HEAD-elements (for example meta-tags) are separated into individual packages, with placeholders for externally linked JavaScript and CSS. In the BODY, certain elements are protected and won't be separated. Those elements are headline tags and links, as they provide semantic structure and functionality to navigate the web. Next, all other elements are extracted and replaced by placeholder tags. These placeholders are HTML tags, starting with a text character, followed by an ascending number. With this setup, no placeholders are rendered on the final page. Even though it is not required in the specification[10], browsers like Firefox will not recognize tags that start with a number and display them as text. Therefore, the described structure has to be used. The sending order starts with the BODY-text containing said placeholders, followed by the BODY-HTML-parts that match the marker. Afterwards, all HTML of the HEAD is inserted. Finally, CSS and JavaScript are added to the sending order. Therefore, when loading the page, a full separation of components is possible, with a focus on sending the content of a page first. The splitting of HEAD and BODY-parts as well as the handling of HEAD-Elements is similar for layout- and Text-First as shown in part **A3(1)** and **A3(2)**. For the BODY, a headless browser is used for Layout-First (see **A3(2)**) to pre-render the page and determine targets of all CSS classes. Then, all CSS for a specific element or section is inserted into the respective positions. In this case, the sending order begins with the attributes of the BODY-Element, like styles. Especially if the BODY-Element has a layout-critical property like a border, margin padding, width, or height specifications, this will move the visible content if applied later, so it has to come first. Afterward, the rendered HTML of the BODY is inserted, followed by the HEAD, and the original CSS and JavaScript. The original CSS is inserted again, as it may be necessary for certain JavaScript-applications at a later point.

5.3   Streaming-Based Delivery Process

Without the rendering step, the delivered HTML structure is the same as loading the page without the proposed optimization. The rendering uses a browser to load the final HTML of a website, which includes elements added by JavaScript, to ensure visual similarity necessary in the user evaluation. However, it is possible for dynamic applications that rely on JavaScript for rendering elements to fetch the raw HTML directly. The pre-rendering will still work, but dynamically added elements will only appear after loading and executing the JavaScript of the page. As a result, JavaScript-based web applications are not affected as the HTML structure stays the same. This also includes additional web elements like

---

[10] https://html.spec.whatwg.org/multipage/syntax.html.

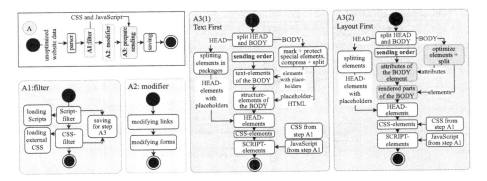

Fig. 1. Server-side pre-processing procedures: overview (top), filtering (A1), modification (A2), and prepare sending for Text-First (A3(1)) and Layout-First (A3(2)).

embedded advertisements. The current approach with a headless browser does not optimize the page in real time. Performance improvements regarding the preparation of websites are part of our future work. As part of the developed technique, the targeted web page is fetched and processed before it is requested by the client, similar to a CDN, as shown in Fig. 2. However, hosting on the original server is also possible. The element labeled with 'A' in Fig. 2 is described in detail in the following section. During this stage, all linked external resources of a page are fetched and processed. Afterwards, the processed sequence of data is saved until it is needed. If a client requests the modified page, a request will be sent to the server-side pre-processing component. There, a minimal web page is prepared with a UUID to identify a client and delivered to the browser. After the client has received and parsed the minimal page, the included JavaScript will establish a WebSocket connection, using the UUID as a second parameter. Moreover, the current index of the last received data is sent for continuing the sending process if the connection fails. After all data is transferred, the server will send a final package to indicate a successful and complete transmission. To further reduce client-side code, the data is sent as strings, with a predefined maximum length.

5.4 Rendering at the Client-Side Component

When the client receives data from the server via WebSocket, the type of package is examined. If it is the "finished" package, the connection is closed. If it contains JavaScript, the code will be inserted and executed. Otherwise, if it contains HTML, it is appended at the respective location. As the minimal web page already contains a basic HTML structure with the `head` and `body`-Element, a `location`-attribute of the data package includes the target of the content. This is possible by utilizing the `insertAdjacentHTML`-function to insert HTML as it will not interfere with user input. In this prototype, if a section of data is split into multiple parts due to a large size, it will be cached and then followed by a

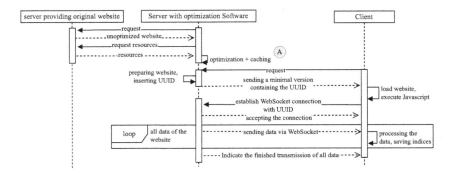

Fig. 2. Program sequence of the pre-processing and delivery of a pre-processed web page via WebSocket

"render" package. The rendering process then adds the contents of the cache to the target element.

5.5   Technical Implementation

Two options have been considered for the implementation of the stream-based transmission of page data, namely HTTP/3 and WebSockets. While HTTP/3 already uses streams internally, WebSockets need additional effort to upgrade a HTTP connection to streaming. Particularly, to upgrade to a WebSocket connection a minimal HTML-Page (file size of 2.5 KB) with custom JavaScript that can establish a WebSocket-Connection back to the Server needs to be delivered to the browser. Streaming via WebSocket has several advantages over the traditional loading method. Mainly, it allows to send and render web pages in parts as well as reconnect and resume sending after connection loss by saving the index of the last sent character. WebSockets are supported by most browsers natively without any extra framework. According to https://caniuse.com WebSockets are supported by 98.37% of browsers (all browsers except Opera Mini), as of August 2021[11]. Therefore, the developed software will be supported by every browser that can establish such a connection. However, upgrading the connection to WebSocket will result in an overhead visible in the evaluation, especially at higher network speeds. The developed server-side software consists of a Node.JS application, that uses **puppeteer** to fetch data, HTML and generate CSS usage maps, and **htmlparser2** for the parsing of HTML, in order to detect external links. For WebSocket, the **websocket**-package is used, as it provides a plain WebSocket interface without the need for further client-side code like **socket.io**. The Website is hosted via **ExpressJS**.

---

[11] caniuse.com/websockets.

6   Evaluation

The goal of our evaluation was to answer two major questions: 1. Is streaming-based progressive page loading significantly decreasing time for initial page load? and 2. Are progressive page loading methods, i.e., text- and Layout-First, affecting user satisfaction?

6.1   Experiment on User Satisfaction

A user study was conducted to test the user satisfaction of progressive page load. A web-based questionnaire allowed for evaluating a larger, unsupervised group of people and in multiple languages (German and English were provided). For the test, a video displayed three different loading behaviors (reference, Text-First and Layout-First) on a device with reduced network speed in direct comparison. A video was chosen as it ensures that every participant sees the same timing of items appearing on the screen. Users were then asked to name their favorite loading behavior and the reasons for their choice. This was done by using a Likert-scale (5 steps - "very bad" to "very good") for ranking the three loading behaviors. Pre-defined answers were given for naming the reasons with additional text input fields if the shown answers were insufficient. The three shown versions in the video consisted of the Text-First method, the Layout-First method, and a control displaying the unmodified loading behavior. The displayed websites were selected by multiple factors: if the website is actually shown and renders correctly (in contrast to only displaying a consent message when visiting or not rendering correctly with one of the techniques) and if the website has enough content to differentiate the three loading methods. For example, `google.com` mainly consists of white space, and therefore the modification is less visible. To ensure a wide representation of websites, the `similarweb.com`-platform was used by selecting the following websites from the Top 50-pages of these categories: `amazon.com` from `E-commerce And Shopping`, `netflix.com` from `TV Movies and Streaming`, `qq.com` from `News and Media` as well as `medium.com` from `Social Networks And Online Communities`.

6.2   Results of the User Evaluation

The survey was accessible online from November 10th to 23rd, 2020. All questions were answered in full by 138 people. The users are expected to mainly consist of computer science students and faculty members, as it was spread by a faculty email newsletter, which might have induced a bias due to expert knowledge. 85.29% of users preferred Layout-First over Text-First (8.09%) and unmodified loading (6.62%). Users preferring Layout-First described as their main reason: "they liked the way the web page changes visually while loading" (selected by 35% of users), and "that the contents stayed on the correct location while doing so". This is visible in Fig. 3a. The speed of accessing the information of a web page was the most important aspect for 31% and the speed of displaying the information for 28% of users. Most importantly, those users also mainly disliked the Text-First method and the unmodified version because both change the web page visually while loading (43%) and for the speed, in which both versions display the whole page (35%). Both distributions are shown in Fig. 3b (these describe choices from users that chose the other technology as their favorite in Fig. 3a). With 8.09%, Text-First is still chosen more often than unmodified version. Users who preferred Text-First mainly answered that they chose this version because of the speed at which the content can be accessed (82%). The main reasons the other two techniques were disliked are the speed at which the web page is displayed (46%) and the speed at which the content can be accessed (27%). 6.62% of users selected the reference loading method as their preferred loading method. The main reason chosen was the way the web page changes while loading (45%). One user answered by individual text, answering that it is a "habit" (translated from German). These users disliked both developed methods, mainly because of the way the web page changes while loading (45%) and the visibility of the loading progress (33%).

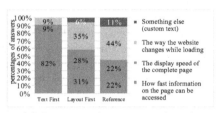

(a) Reasons why users preferred a specific technique

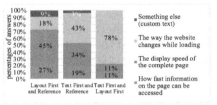

(b) Reasons why users disliked techniques

Fig. 3. Reasons why users prefer or dislike techniques

6.3   Experiment on Performance

For the technical tests, a filtered Alexa Top-List from 2020 was used. This data set includes the top 20 websites worldwide from 2020, and each website was loaded twice to account for errors without caching. Then all data were averaged for each collected measurement. The number of websites that could be tested per data point was constrained by time and network limits. At 128 KB/s and slower, at least one page of the set cloud not be loaded fully with the standard reference loading behavior. For example, `office.com` took more than 72 h to load once before aborting. Furthermore, the reference loading behavior could not be tested at speeds below 32 KB/s. `Google.com` was the only website that loaded at 8 KB/s without a timeout with the standard loading method. Therefore, the web pages are not compared for their full loading time, as browsers prevent the complete loading of a page at the slowest tested speeds. Instead, displaying the entire page is the last compared data point. However, this is sufficient for comparison as the loading process until the described point is the crucial tested factor. The three main data points that could be evaluated are the FCP, the time until all text of a page is loaded (the content), and the time it takes until all text and layout are fully loaded. A FCP marks the point when a user first sees a section of the content displayed in the browser. For Text-First, this means when the first section of text is displayed. The FCP of Layout-First measures the first block of rendered HTML. The time until the text finished loading was chosen as it marks the time a user can access all written information on a page. This includes links. At this point, the user can generally decide what to do next (stay on the page, go back or navigate a link). Therefore, this data point is chosen. Loading the text and layout is the last comparable marker, restricted by the reference loading method not loading all scripts at lower network speeds without aborting. Ideally, the collected information would include JavaScript as well. To maximize the comparability of the measured data, every fetched web page is only measured from the `responseStart`-Event onward to reduce the influence of network delays. The test setup consisted of a headless Chromium browser driven by the puppeteer framework. The network speed was limited with the `NetworkLinkConditioner`-system extension, which was used on all tests. The tested speeds were 8 kb/s, 32 kb/s, 128 kb/s, 512 kb/s, and 2048 kb/s without additional package loss and measured with the `performance timing`-API provided by chromium and custom marker for the developed techniques. The server was hosted on a VM with two cores of an Intel Haswell CPU at 2.00 GHz, 16 GB RAM, and a 10 Gbit/s NIC. It runs Debian 4.19.37-5. A network speed of 900 MBit/s download and 700 MBit/s upload was determined by the `speedtest-cli` from `speedtest.net`.

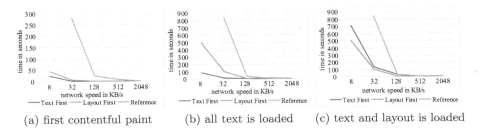

(a) first contentful paint   (b) all text is loaded   (c) text and layout is loaded

Fig. 4. Measured times needed until a specific event on a page is detected

6.4   Results of the Technical Evaluation

While loading until the FCP, the Text-First and Layout-First methods were always faster than the reference loading method, as shown in Fig. 4a. The difference between progressive loading methods and the reference increases significantly with a decrease in network speed. As described in the paper by Nah et al., a user expects a response from a web page in 2 s, or a majority of users will leave [4]. FCP can be one possible indicator if this mark is reached. The Text-First-method ensures a near 2-s response even at 32 KB/s and is up to 280 s faster than the reference at the same speed (4.7 min). The two-second-mark is not reached with the Layout-First method at this speed, however, with only a 4-s difference to Text-First and is still 275 s faster than the reference. As seen in the Fig. 4b, a near 2-s response is reached by the reference only at 2048 KB/s, at which point the FCP of the Text-First method only takes 0.2 s, even with the WebSocket-overhead. The next comparable point in time is when the text of a web page is fully loaded. As shown in Fig. 4b, the time differences are more visible than at the FCP. At 32 KB/s, Text-First loaded 829 s faster than the reference loading method (13.8 min), and it took less than 14 s to transfer and display all text. With Layout-First, this transfer took about 97 s, as the rendered HTML was included as part of the data that was sent to the client. At all measured speeds, Text-First was the fastest, like at the FCP. For 512 KB/s and 2048 KB/s, Text-First transferred all the content in less than 2 s. However, at the same speeds, Layout-First was slower than the reference loading method. The last compared data point is the completed transfer of all text, HTML, and CSS, as shown in Fig. 4c. In contrast to the previous tests, Layout-First was faster than Text-First at slower speeds. At 32 KB/s, Layout-First loaded 743.57 s (12.4 min) faster than the reference and took 99.7 s to transfer all HTML, text, and CSS of a page. While loading the page, the user could already use the partially loaded page with Text-First and Layout-First, which distinguishes both versions to reference. We argue that separating Text and HTML and also introducing placeholders in combination with frequent redraws of the complete page slowed down the display speed for Text-First. This overhead is evened out at 512 KB/s and higher, at which point Text-First overtakes Layout-First again. Layout-First bottoms out at around 10 s of transfer speed. We speculate that the overhead is caused by all the included rendered CSS and sending data via WebSockets. In summary, Text-First was the fastest at sending all page content to the client. However, as seen in Sect. 6.2, users prefer Layout-First by 85%, even if it was often slower. Still, Layout-First was significantly faster than the reference.

6.5   Discussion Regarding Data Comparability

The surveys for the pre-study and the user evaluation were carried out online and were sent mainly to computer science students and faculty members. This might skew the data as there is a possible bias towards new methods and the acceptance of modified UI behaviors due to a more profound knowledge of underlying technologies. Also, the data collected is missing the reference data for 8 KB/s. It was not possible to collect this data without consistent timeouts by the Chromium browser. It might be possible to load all pages repeatedly until they finish the entire transfer. This would, however, make the data not comparable, as it only includes "best cases". In contrast, Text-First and Layout-First loaded all test pages without a single error or timeout and might even be able to load at even slower speeds.

7   Conclusion

This paper presented two new methods to improve initial page loading behavior by loading them progressively as a stream. A pre-study concluded that users prefer speed, but only if the layout of the final page stays fixed as close as possible. Therefore, two new techniques were developed. The first method, called "Text-First", transferred the text of a web page as fast as possible, followed by HTML, CSS, and JavaScript. The second technique, "Layout-First", renders the web page including the text with the necessary CSS and embeds it into the HTML. This rendered HTML is then transferred in a stream via WebSockets. A user study with 138 people revealed that 85% of users prefer Layout-First over Text-First and the reference loading version. Furthermore, both developed methods significantly improve transfer times at slow network speeds as loading times typically increase exponentially with a decrease in network speed. Future Work will include development of techniques reducing page layout shift and evaluating even more methods of streaming web pages.

References

1. An, D.: Find out how you stack up to new industry benchmarks for mobile page speed. Think with Google-Mobile, Data & Measurement (2018)
2. Iskandar, T.F., Lubis, M., Kusumasari, T.F., Lubis, A.R.: Comparison between client-side and server-side rendering in the web development. In: IOP Conference Series: Materials Science and Engineering, vol. 801. IOP Publishing (2020)
3. Jovanovski, G., Zaytsev, V.: Critical css rules–decreasing time to first render by inlining css rules for over-the-fold elements. In: Postproceedings of 2016 Seminar on Advanced Techniques and Tools for Software Evolution (SATToSE), pp. 353–356 (2016)
4. Nah, F.F.H.: A study on tolerable waiting time: how long are web users willing to wait? Behav. Inf. Technol. **23**(3), 153–163 (2004)
5. Netravali, R., Goyal, A., Mickens, J., Balakrishnan, H.: Polaris: faster page loads using fine-grained dependency tracking. In: 13th {USENIX} Symposium on Networked Systems Design and Implementation, {NSDI} 2016 (2016)
6. PageSpeed, G.: Pagespeed documentation (2020). modpagespeed.com/doc/
7. Podjarny, G., Dumoulin, C.R.: Progressive consolidation of web page resources, US Patent 9,785,621 (10 October 2017)
8. Ruamviboonsuk, V., Netravali, R., Uluyol, M., Madhyastha, H.V.: Vroom: accelerating the mobile web with server-aided dependency resolution. In: Proceedings of the Conference of the ACM Special Interest Group on Data Communication, pp. 390–403 (2017)
9. Naveen Kumar, S.G., Madugundu, P.K., Bose, J., Mogali, S.C.S.: A hybrid web rendering framework on cloud. In: 2016 IEEE International Conference on Web Services (ICWS), pp. 602–608. IEEE (2016)
10. Shalunov, S., Hazel, G., Benoliel, M.: System and method for improving webpage loading speeds, US Patent App. 14/758,961 (12 January 2017)

We Don't Need No Real Users?! Surveying the Adoption of User-less Automation Tools by UI Design Practitioners

Maxim Bakaev[1]([✉])(iD), Maximilian Speicher[2](iD), Johanna Jagow[2],
Sebastian Heil[3](iD), and Martin Gaedke[3](iD)

[1] Novosibirsk State Technical University, Novosibirsk, Russia
`bakaev@corp.nstu.ru`
[2] Jagow Speicher, Barcelona, Spain
`icwe@maxspeicher.com`
[3] Technische Universität Chemnitz, Chemnitz, Germany
`{sebastian.heil,martin.gaedke}@informatik.tu-chemnitz.de`

Abstract. The main principles for designing successful UIs in a perfect world have long been known—considering many possible solutions for a problem and involving representative users in the process. In practice, however, reasons for violating those principles can be plentiful: the infamous tight budgets and schedules, lack of management buy-in, restrictions for face-to-face meetings, etc. Yet, design tools that do not require real users, such as AI-/ML-powered solutions, which could mitigate these issues seem to experience a rather low adoption rate in industry. In this paper, we present a survey with 34 professional digital designers and user researchers intended to investigate the above hypotheses. We inquire into awareness and usage of 61 such tools and platforms, as well as participants' design and research processes and general design tool adoption in industry. From the results we identify three particular challenges and three opportunities. Finding and recruiting relevant participants for user studies seems to be indeed problematic, and professional designers and researchers often lack the time and resources to follow a textbook process. They are, however, open to novel tools addressing these shortcomings— particular for ideation and evaluation—but at the same time seem to be largely unfamiliar with AI-/ML-based approaches or do not (yet) see added value in them. With these findings as a starting point, the Web Engineering community can work towards a deeper understanding of designers' and researchers' needs that could be met with AI-/ML-based support tools.

Keywords: AI/ML · Design tools · Online survey · Ui design · User interfaces

M. Bakaev and M. Speicher—Contributed equally to this work.

© Springer Nature Switzerland AG 2022
T. Di Noia et al. (Eds.): ICWE 2022, LNCS 13362, pp. 406–414, 2022.
https://doi.org/10.1007/978-3-031-09917-5_28

1   Introduction

Today, Human-Centered Design (HCD) [12] is one of the most widely used and taught methodologies in digital product design. In an optimal world, when following an HCD approach, designers and user researchers conduct a wide variety of generative and evaluative research and build and iterate on a multitude of wireframes, mockups, and prototypes, so that all relevant groups of users are fully understood. Yet, in reality, such a thorough execution of the HCD methodology is rarely the case, often due to tight schedules and budgets. Particularly user research, though naturally best done with real users, is often perceived as costly and time-consuming and reduced to only the bare necessities [8,11,14].

A potential remedy are advances in *machine learning* (ML) and *artificial intelligence* (AI), which could make it possible to automate parts of the HCD process. This would support two main target groups: *digital designers* and *user researchers* working with tight deadlines and budgets. Platforms or tools leveraging AI/ML have aimed at generating (prototypes of) interfaces (e.g., [3,4]), evaluating usability (e.g., [9,14]), providing interface-related metrics (e.g., [1,13]), and much more. Yet, even though some of those systems are available as readily usable software or web apps, they are—to the best of our knowledge—not widely used in industry. Many of the academic projects seem to have trouble gaining traction in professional circles and therefore do not become well known beyond the academic HCI community. This may be due to a lack of resources for marketing, and therefore awareness, or potentially may have its basis in more intrinsic reasons. In this paper, we intend to take a first step towards getting to the bottom of this. In the related secondary research that came to our attention, most authors perform systematic mapping [2,7], without much concern about the actual usage of the tools. Some notable recent exceptions with the focus on industry [10,15] consider relatively narrow applications and are not exploratory.

By conducting a **survey with 34 professional digital designers and user researchers**, we investigate the above hypotheses: Practitioners often lack the time and resources for a textbook process and they do mostly not leverage AI-/ML-based tools, many of which stem from academic projects, to mitigate that. Specifically, we inquire into *(1)* challenges with participants' design and research processes; *(2)* the usage of platforms and tools in industry in general; and *(3)* awareness and usage of AI-/ML-based systems in particular. Based on this, we identify *three challenges* and *three opportunities*. Our results suggest that finding real users can be problematic, and that digital designers and researchers in industry do indeed struggle with tight resources, which leads to shortcuts in their processes. They would particularly appreciate support in ideation and evaluation stages. At the same time, they seem to be largely unaware of existing AI-/ML-based tools that could support them. Therefore, new and better products particularly aimed at designers and researchers might have a good chance to gain traction.

These challenges and opportunities shall serve as a starting point for a larger research project concerned with designers' and researchers' needs towards AI-/ML-based support tools and how those needs can be met.

2   The Survey Description

2.1   Material

For the survey, we assembled a structured list of tools for designers that require no real users (i.e., they are *"user-less"*), focus on UI design, and enable at least some degree of automation (e.g., a simple wireframing tool requires no real users, but also provides no automation). Accordingly, we did not include software for user behavior or interaction tracking, web analytics (remote) user testing, security vulnerabilities assessment, load testing, WYSIWYG editors, etc. The collection was performed in March 2021 and our strategy was threefold, based on three different *data sources*:

1. Tools extracted from academic publications known to us beforehand (e.g., [3–5, 9, 13]) or found through Google Scholar. The employed queries were aimed towards either existing literature reviews (e.g., *"review of UI design tools"*) or specific applications and categories (*"automated usability testing"*, *"model-driven engineering"*, etc.). It is hard to judge these tools' viability from their user base (often non-existent) since usually that is not the authors' primary motivation. Instead, we relied on research interest and recency—we would only consider the developments with a latest publication no more than 5 years old.
2. Tools from the relevant lists available in Wikipedia, e.g., *"List of GUI testing tools"*, *"Comparison of GUI testing tools"*, *"GUI software testing"*, etc.
3. Tools manually selected from the results returned by major search engines (Google, Bing, Yahoo!, Yandex) as the most relevant ones. By this time we would already have categories emerged from the first two data sources that were used as the input keywords: *"UI Prototyping automation"*, *"HTML/CSS validators"*, *"UI metrics tools"*, *"tools for design guidelines"*, *"user behavior models based software tools"*, *"automated usability evaluation"*, etc.

Based on this, we found 61 relevant "user-less" tools and platforms (the full list of the tools, as well as the survey questions and answers are presented in the papers' Online Appendix[1]).

2.2   Design and Procedure

The survey consisted of 28 questions distributed over four parts: *(1)* participants' research and design processes and their challenges and obstacles; *(2)* familiarity with and usage of common classes of design/research tools; *(3)* familiarity with and usage of the 61 tools and platforms identified above; and *(4)* demographic information and open-ended feedback. Most questions from the second part on were optional, in case participants did not know any of the mentioned tools.

The survey was implemented and conducted in UserZoom, and we estimated the completion time to be 20–40 min, depending on the amount of detail in the open-ended feedback.

---

[1] https://github.com/heseba/UserlessDesignSurvey.

2.3   Recruitment

Participants were recruited through personal contacts and postings in professional groups on LinkedIn, since the relatively complex survey and nature of our questions required input from digital design and user research professionals with multiple years of experience in industry. The survey was piloted with 3 designers/researchers who helped us fix minor issues with wording, and was online from April thru August 2021.

3   Survey Results

3.1   The Participants

In total, 34 practicing digital designers and user researchers participated in our survey, with a median completion time of 35 min. Of all the participants, 62% indicated their gender as female, 36% as male and 6% preferred not to say. The age ranged from 24 to 57 ($\mu = 34.2$, $\sigma = 5.21$). Most of the participants indicated their country of residence as Germany (52%) or the U.S. (23%); the rest was distributed between Austria, Bulgaria, France, Romania, Spain, Sweden, South Korea and Switzerland.

The majority of participants had a university degree: either Bachelor's (24%), Master's (47%), or a doctorate (21%). Their experience in the field ranged from 1.5 to "over 30" years ($\mu = 8.4$, $\sigma = 4.82$), which implies a considerable level of professional maturity, and several reported working for major companies. 48% of their job titles involved design while 29% related to user research. "Software" was the most-mentioned industry (38%).

Regarding platforms (multiple answers possible), 100% of the participants reported that they specialize in web. The two major mobile platforms, iOS (59%) and Android (56%), were nearly equally popular with the participants. Finally, Windows and macOS were mentioned by 35% and 29%, respectively.

3.2   What Do Participants' Research and Design Processes Look Like?

With respect to the descriptions of their design and research process, participants' replies (Q1, open-ended) yielded nothing that would have rejected our initial hypotheses about how those processes look like in industry. A selection of representative quotes reads:

- *"We take 6 steps: 1 Plan 2 Research 3 Design 4 Develop 5 Test 6 Launch & Learn"*
- *"- research users - define problem space - generate ideas - prioritize ideas - develop MVP prototypes - test with users - evaluate if the problem was addressed - iterate"*

– *"That is very project-dependent. When it comes to the entire development of a new product, I like to use the principle of the double diamond. That means I start with broad research (trends, interviews, competition) and the identification of the problem and then move on to focusing the insights. After that the first solutions and ideas are developed, which are implemented in the final step."*
– One participant replied simply *"9241-210..."*, referring to ISO standard 9241-210:2019 – *Ergonomics of human-system interaction.*

Our intentions here were to *(1)* inquire into participants' baselines regarding their design and research routines, and *(2)* possibly discover first hints at the use of "user-less", or even AI-/ML-based tools, which we did not.

3.3   What are Obstacles and Limitations?

The most notable problem pronounced by the participants was *finding and recruiting real users, especially specialized ones*, in time frames that are often limited by stakeholders and corporate/agile processes. This was explicitly mentioned by 11 out of 32 participants who provided meaningful answers. Another 4 participants complained about corporate priorities and processes that conflict with fulfilling user needs. Notable quotes highlighting these issues include:

– *"The low amount of researchers on the team and the lack of specialized users is often a limitation."*
– *"The biggest obstacle would be access to actual users. Our users are a fairly specific, so I cannot just ask anyone to test the majority of our designs. The busy schedules of our users also conflict with the agile system in which my team tries to operate so it is rarely feasible that we have the time to sync up with users."*
– *"In a B2B context in a very specialized domains it is nearly impossible to recruit user in the timeframes given by the agile process."*
– *"Discrepancy between customers needs and corporate benefits. Historically determined barriers such as the willingness to change the product."*
– *"Decisions are made based on hierarchy or personal taste."*

3.4   Which Platforms and Tools are Used?

In the open-ended process question (Q1), 4 of the participants already mentioned Figma, which was the only tool mentioned by more than one participant. Regarding common classes of design and research tools (Q4), *heuristics /guidelines /design patterns* (91%) were best known, closely followed by *user testing platforms* (88%). Averaged per category, the overall awareness was 72.4%, which confirms our hypothesis that most digital designers know about the most common tools in their field. Of all the categories, tools for *automated UX/UI analysis*, such as EyeQuant or Feng-GUI, however, lie considerably below the average (32%).

Answers to a range of more specialized questions (Q5–Q17) confirm this. Particularly *design guidelines organization/validation tools* (e.g., material.io, Test.ai) are widely known (69.4% on average) and relatively intensively used (21.5%). The highest actual usage (48.2% on average) was found for *HTML/CSS and accessibility validators* (e.g., W3C validator, WAVE Web Accessibility Evaluation Tool). Quantitative tools dealing with *UI-/UX-related metrics and KPIs* (e.g., Aalto Interface Metrics [13], Zyro) were, on average, known by 52.0% of the participants and used by 17.7%. *GOMS/KLM tools* (e.g., CogTool, Cogulator), also quantitative in nature, were known on average by 17.6% of the participants, but used only by 3.9%.

At the same time, the tools that support *automated ("user-less") usability validation/evaluation* (e.g., Kobold [9], Qualidator) were known to only 8.8% of the participants and actively used by none. In the related open-ended questions (Q6 and Q8), participants falsely named Tobii, UserZoom, QXscore, etc. as examples of tools based on AI/ML. This suggests little familiarity with that class of tools and hints at existing misconceptions about what denotes AI/ML. Selected quotes from the open-ended questions read as follows:

- *"Heuristics - we often run Nielsen Norman heuristics on our products. Best Practices - Our product design language provides best practice guidelines for creating/using components and incorporating language into experiences."*
- *"We don't use any ML/AI based products to my knowledge."*
- in Q6, regarding AI-/ML-based tools: *"Tobii (not sure)"*

As a side note, we did an additional analysis of Q7, which was answered by all 34 participants. In this question, we asked about knowing and using 11 prototyping tools that have some degree of automation (e.g., Figma, InVision, Adobe XD). The Pearson correlation between "know" and "use" scores turned out to be highly significant and **negative** ($r_{11} = -0.834$, p = 0.001). This underpins that digital designers and user researchers are generally aware of many of the more popular tools, but seem to be sticking to one or two of those. Additionally, usage reported by our participants roughly matches the numbers reported in the *2020 Design Tools Survey*, with moderate deviations [6].

3.5   What are Reasons for Not Using AI-/ML-Based Tools?

When explicitly asked (Q19) about the reasons for not using the tools from the preceding questions of the survey, the leading answer by far was *"never heard of those"* (91%). The next reasons in popularity were *"required usage fees"* (24%) and *"I don't see the added value"* (21%). The reason *"too cumbersome"* was selected by no-one, probably due to the fact that the tools were not actively used by our selection of participants.

4   Findings and Discussion

From the above results, we derive *(1)* three particularly salient challenges with practitioners' design and research processes and the current knowledge and usage of AI-/ML-based systems, and *(2)* three corresponding opportunities to be seized by developers of (future) AI-/ML-based systems aimed at digital designers and user researchers.

- CHALLENGE 1. **Availability of users.** Finding and recruiting relevant participants for user studies, especially for specialized products.
- CHALLENGE 2. **Lack of time and resources.** Tight deadlines and timeframes limited by stakeholders and processes, and a lack of user research resources.
- CHALLENGE 3. **Designers' unfamiliarity with ML/AI.** There seems to be little awareness of what exactly ML-/AI-based systems constitute and in which ways they can support design processes.
- OPPORTUNITY 1. **Openness to new things.** In principle, digital designers and user researchers welcome tools that support their processes and they do follow the topic (e.g., *"Not a part of our current process, but open to trying them if they can mitigate our issues finding qualified users."*).
- OPPORTUNITY 2. **Open playing field.** New AI-/ML-based tools do have a chance to gain traction as currently, there seem to be no established players.
- OPPORTUNITY 3. **Support for ideation & evaluation.** Specifically ideation (in the sense of creating wireframes, mockups, and prototypes) and evaluation (of design artifacts) are mentioned as the activities in which practitioners would appreciate support.

In conclusion, regarding limitations of this work and prospects for further research, we would like to note the following:

- Our sample size was relatively small and not representative, particularly when looking at the distribution of countries of residence. Therefore, the results of this survey only scratch the surface of the topic. For more in-depth analysis, we shall consider interviews with professional users of particular commercial tools and platforms.
- Still, our results confirm two hypothesis about the current state of UI design in practice, i.e., *(1)* practitioners are often restricted in how thoroughly they can follow a proper design process; and *(2)* many designers/researchers are not yet aware of the possibilities of "user-less" and AI-/ML-based platforms and tools, and/or lack access.
- Our results suggest massive opportunities for the engineering of AI-/ML-based systems that can support digital designers and user researchers in industry. We are confident that our findings can inspire further research in practical "user-less" UI design.
- However, we need more research in the form of: *(1)* creating a proper taxonomy from the selection of 61 tools and platforms; *(2)* gaining more in-depth qualitative insights into practitioners experiences with "user-less" and AI-/ML-based tools; and *(3)* conducting proper requirements engineering to reliably determine digital designers' and researchers' needs.

Acknowledgement. The study was funded by RFBR according to the research project No. 19-29-01017. The research was partially funded by the Deutsche Forschu ngsgemeinschaft (DFG, German Research Foundation) – Project-ID 416228727–SFB 1410.

References

1. Bakaev, M., Heil, S., Khvorostov, V., Gaedke, M.: Auto-extraction and integration of metrics for web user interfaces. J. Web Eng. 17(6–7), 561–590 (2019). https://doi.org/10.13052/jwe1540-9589.17676
2. Banerjee, I., Nguyen, B., Garousi, V., Memon, A.: Graphical user interface (GUI) testing: systematic mapping and repository. Inf. Softw. Technol. **55**(10), 1679–1694 (2013). https://doi.org/10.1016/j.infsof.2013.03.004
3. Buschek, D., Anlauff, C., Lachner, F.: Paper2Wire: a case study of user-centred development of machine learning tools for UX designers. In: Proceedings of the Conference on Mensch und Computer, MuC 2020, pp. 33–41. ACM, New York (2020). https://doi.org/10.1145/3404983.3405506
4. Chen, C., Su, T., Meng, G., Xing, Z., Liu, Y.: From UI design image to GUI skeleton: a neural machine translator to bootstrap mobile GUI implementation. In: Proceedings of the 40th International Conference on Software Engineering, ICSE 2018, pp. 665–676. ACM (2018). https://doi.org/10.1145/3180155.3180240
5. Dayama, N.R., Todi, K., Saarelainen, T., Oulasvirta, A.: GRIDS: interactive layout design with integer programming. In: Proceedings of the 2020 CHI Conference on Human Factors in Computing Systems, vol. 20, pp. 1–13. ACM, New York (2020). https://doi.org/10.1145/3313831.3376553
6. Dexter, S.: The rise and fall of InVision, January 2021. https://uxdesign.cc/the-rise-and-fall-of-invision-dc2d58c65534, ISSN: 2766–5267
7. Frich, J., MacDonald Vermeulen, L., Remy, C., Biskjaer, M.M., Dalsgaard, P.: Mapping the landscape of creativity support tools in HCI. In: Proceedings of the 2019 CHI Conference on Human Factors in Computing Systems, pp. 1–18 (2019)
8. Frick, T.: Designing for sustainability: a guide to building greener digital products and services. O'Reilly Media, Inc. (2016)
9. Grigera, J., Garrido, A., Rivero, J.M., Rossi, G.: Automatic detection of usability smells in web applications. Int. J. Human-Comput. Stud. **97**, 129–148 (2017). https://doi.org/10.1016/j.ijhcs.2016.09.009
10. Junior, N., Costa, H., Karita, L., Machado, I., Soares, L.: Experiences and practices in GUI functional testing: A software practitioners' view. In: Brazilian Symposium on Software Engineering, pp. 195–204 (2021)
11. Nebeling, M., Speicher, M., Norrie, M.C.: Crowdstudy: general toolkit for crowd-sourced evaluation of web interfaces. In: Proceedings of the 5th ACM SIGCHI Symposium on Engineering Interactive Computing Systems, EICS 2013, pp. 255–264. ACM, New York (2013). https://doi.org/10.1145/2494603.2480303
12. Norman, D.: The design of everyday things: Revised and expanded edition. Basic books (2013)
13. Oulasvirta, A., et al.: Aalto Interface Metrics (AIM): a service and codebase for computational GUI evaluation. In: The 31st Annual ACM Symposium on User Interface Software and Technology Adjunct Proceedings, UIST 2018 Adjunct, pp. 16–19. ACM, New York (2018). https://doi.org/10.1145/3266037.3266087

14. Speicher, M., Both, A., Gaedke, M.: Ensuring web interface quality through usability-based split testing. In: Casteleyn, S., Rossi, G., Winckler, M. (eds.) ICWE 2014. LNCS, vol. 8541, pp. 93–110. Springer, Cham (2014). https://doi.org/10.1007/978-3-319-08245-5_6

15. Wang, W., et al.: An empirical study of Android test generation tools in industrial cases. In: 2018 33rd IEEE/ACM International Conference on Automated Software Engineering, ASE, pp. 738–748. IEEE (2018)

Ph.D. Symposium

Achieving Corruption-Transparency in Service Governance Processes with Blockchain-Technology Based e-Participation

Mohammad Mustafa Ibrahimy[1]([✉]) [iD], Alex Norta[2] [iD], and Peeter Normak[1]

[1] School of Digital Technologies, Tallinn University, Tallinn, Estonia
{ibrahimy,pnormak}@tlu.ee
[2] Dymaxion, Tallinn, Estonia
alex.norta.phd@ieee.org

Abstract. Corruption takes place in public procurement by public servants through intermediaries due to the use of centralized systems and complicated processes. Blockchain and Web3 has the potential to remove these intermediaries, instead allowing institutions to build trust among public servants and citizens through a decentralized web. It is feasible to positively reinforce the transparency in tackling corruption in public procurement by establishing an e-participatory governance infrastructure using token economics from smart-contract blockchain technology. The overall success of public procurement in terms of service delivery to citizens is associated with citizen e-participation. Thus, increased e-participation through automated processes makes the government accountable and transparent in the provision of services that lead to the progress and economic growth of a country. In this paper, we investigate the potential of blockchain and smart-contracts to improve the efficiency, trust, and transparency of public procurement in the case of Afghanistan. Moreover, we identify the existing barriers namely lack of trust, transparency, the complexity of procurement documents, and inappropriate record-keeping system. To address these issues, we propose a blockchain-based e-participatory infrastructure to boost transparency by curbing public procurement corruption.

Keywords: Corruption · Transparency · Blockchain · Smart-contract · Token economy · e-Participation

1 Introduction and Motivation

Adopting information- and communication technologies (ICTs) and Web 3.0 helps governments to transform public administrations allowing them to deliver excellent services to citizens [1]. The Web3 is a novel concept of the web evolution from Web1 and Web2. The term Web3 (also called Web 3.0) was coined by Gavin Wood, the co-founder of Ethereum in 2014. The concept of Web3 is

© Springer Nature Switzerland AG 2022
T. Di Noia et al. (Eds.): ICWE 2022, LNCS 13362, pp. 417–425, 2022.
https://doi.org/10.1007/978-3-031-09917-5_29

based on blockchain and other related technologies that are cryptographic, distributed and permissionless [2,3]. Web3 and its application allow to automate the bureaucratic processes in the institutions and formalize their rules by writing the code that is the result of public discussion and collaborative actions of all network participants. Moreover, Web3 is represented as the backbone of a series of blockchain networks, distributed ledger, or a set of protocols. These blockchain networks are simply the processor for blockchain distributed applications (DApps) that run on top of the Web3. The Web2 is considered as a front-end revolution, whereas the Web3 forms the backend revolution [4]. Thus, Web3 is a combination of virtual/augmented reality with artificial intelligence (AI) and blockchain technologies.

Corruption is one of the main reasons that Afghanistan has remained as a developing country, whereas after two decades this phenomenon has not faded, but rather grown [5]. This country suffers from diverse conflicts such as corruption, lack of transparency, lack of e-participation in the organizational processes, which is mainly reflected in the public procurement, and administration system [6]. International donors and partners (e.g., USAID, European Union, The World Bank, and so on) have supported Afghanistan in various fields, especially in building infrastructure and implementing and funding projects. Moreover, Ahmad [7] argues that the legacy systems of public procurement in Afghanistan restrict the ability of the government's overall supply chain and thus, the current centralized procurement system could not process procurement requisitions quickly enough to meet the requirements. These legacy systems exclude all stakeholders in that they are not able to track, audit, and monitor the ongoing projects, thereby yielding large-scale corruption due to a lack of interoperability of systems, and a lack of transparency and trust in the procurement processes. In the mean time, government usually allocates funds for projects and there is no information about how these funds are being utilized, however, a major portion of these funds remain unused and rarely used for the actual project due to corruption. Therefore, utilizing blockchain technology in the public sector has a great impact on a country's economic growth, particularly in case of developing countries to track public funds and minimize corruption [8].

The term blockchain refers to a virtual chain of blocks, which is a sequence of blocks of data that are cryptographically connected together [9], is an immutable digital ledger, and a cyber security technology that uses mathematical hash values to identify changes in digital data, and stores transaction of any type [10]. In contrast, smart contracts are computer programs [4], and are stored on a blockchain that run automatically when predetermined conditions are met [11]. Smart contracts are created and viewed on the web using a decentralized application (dApp) [12]. Moreover, blockchain technology is a decentralized, tamper-proof, and peer-to-peer network that facilitates transparency, trust, efficiency, and accountability in the public sector. In particular, blockchain-based smart contracts promise the automatic execution of transactions without involving a third-party. Adopting such technology has the potential to provide a great solution in public e-procurement [13]. Thus, blockchain technology has a potential role in delivering better public services as well as boosting public trust and political involvement [14].

The state of the art shows that transparency in corruption can be achieved by establishing a degree of e-participation [15]. Correspondingly, a framework has been developed by Mærøe et al. [15] for e-participatory budgeting with varying degrees for citizen participation in the governance process, while a gap exists pertaining to how to establish and intensify e-participation with means of smart-contract blockchain technology. Therefore, this study aims to evaluate the existing blockchain-based models and describe the best-governance models, and develop a blockchain-based e-participatory infrastructure to achieve transparency, combat corruption as well as increase citizen participation in service governance processes in the public sector.

2   Related Work

Blockchain as an element of distributed ledger technology (DLT) provides the following advantages in relation to achieving transparency and tackling corruption [16]:

1. **Transparency:** A DLT-based platform records important changes to stored data allowing each connected node to verify the transactions. Thus, transactions can be made more transparent.
2. **Immutability:** Stored data cannot be changed, and thus, is safe from manipulation.
3. **Security:** Given the distributed nature of ledgers, data is protected against fraud and attack on a single server.
4. **Inclusiveness:** Everyone can access public blockchain, thus opportunities are opened for the citizen participation.
5. **Disintermediation:** DLT systems operate without intermediary, or central administrator and protect participants against risks of fraud and corruption. This reduces the cost of transactions.

Blockchain is a decentralized ledger that may function as a trustworthy third party without being controlled, or supervised by any single institution. This distinguishing feature of the technology makes it appropriate for resolving a variety of challenges encountered by e-procurement platforms [17].

Several studies propose various blockchain-based architectures and models for solving different issues. Elabdallaoui et al. [18] present a blockchain-based infrastructure to improve the public procurement procedure. The application of smart contracts reduces the number of middlemen in the conclusion of public contracts. Pertaining to e-participation, Schere et al. [19] investigate evaluation criteria based on the usefulness, usage, and acceptability of the e-participation model (i.e., VoiceE as a regional eParticipation model in the European Union) from a socio-technical perspective with respect to users and processes. Moreover,

Karkin [20] highlights three broad barrier categories for the e-participation process such as technological, legal/ethical, and administrative/structural. Therefore, these obstacles before establishing an e-participatory governance infrastructure should be addressed.

Shaikh and Goldsmith [21] design a blockchain-based architecture for e-participation to enhance citizen engagement, improve transparency, reduce costs as well as increase the level of trust among government organizations and citizens in Oman. Similarly, Benítez-Martínez et al. [22] design a novel governance model that uses a federated permissioned model based on neural blockchain technology and smart contracts that avoid corruption in the area of public procurement. The focus rests particularly on Government-to-Business (G2B) interactions, and includes procurement-associated activities such as tender design and publication, bidding, requests to participate, bid evaluation, as well as contracting. The proposed governance model involves stakeholders of all public sector in order to eliminate any possible corrupt activities that take place in the administrative process while also addressing security and transparency issues. This governance model also promotes procurement procedures and combats corruption. The participation aspect is not addressed in this study, as well as the context being general and not country-specific. Meanwhile, the study does not address the application of token economics with smart-contract blockchain technology for supporting citizen e-participation and thus, constitutes the gap for our study.

In the context of the public sector, there are areas of administrative action where the use of blockchain is not permitted due to a lack of legal coverage. Thus, an in-depth analysis and review of the administrative procedures in use is required before introducing blockchain-technology based e-participation. Moreover, the infrastructure on which blockchains are implemented also needs to be addressed [23]. Employing an e-participatory architecture should address several challenges such as lack of trust and transparency and the impact on decision making, complex processes, corrupt practices in service process, inappropriate record keeping systems and documentation practices in the public sector [13–20]. On the other hand, technical, social and political factors as well as a better understanding of citizens and other associated stakeholders with different needs and preferences should be considered when implementing the e-participatory architecture [24].

3 Objectives

The main objectives of this Ph.D. thesis are:

- To evaluate the existing blockchain based e-participation models.
- To discover the best-practice governance models for enhancing transparency and tackling corruption in the public sector.
- To develop an e-procurement reference model for blockchain based e-participation.

This Ph.D. project fills the gap in the current state of the art by posing the main research question: How to establish an e-participatory governance infrastructure in which the token economics from smart-contract blockchain technology positively reinforces the transparency in tackling public-sector corruption? From the main question we deduce three other sub questions. How to adopt the best-practice governance models for enhancing public-sector corruption transparency? How to integrate a suitable e-participation model that encourages and enables the public to observe and investigate transparently public-sector corruption attempts and -cases? How to integrate a smart-contract blockchain-based token economy into the public-sector governance that positively reinforces the conflict management arising from public-sector corruption investigations?

4 Methodology

This research uses the design-science research (DSR) methodology. Design science in information systems (IS) research is concerned with the development of artifacts to solve real-world issues, which is inherently a problem-solving process [25,26]. Design science also intends to solve problems associated with organizations through creating and evaluating IT artifacts designed to meet the identified business need. The DSR paradigm "seeks to extend the boundaries of human and organizational capabilities by creating new and innovative artifacts" [[25], p. 75]. According to Hevner et al. [25] artifacts are defined as constructs represented by a vocabulary, or symbols, models referred to abstraction and representation, methods that represents algorithms and practices and finally, instantiations could be an implementation, or a prototype system. As a result, this study follows DSR in the areas of IS as a research methodology and we follow the guidelines proposed by [25] in our research.

- **Design as an Artifact:** DSR must develop a feasible artifact in the form of a construct, a model, a method, or an instantiation. Our work results in developing an e-participatory governance infrastructure based on the following theories: associated anti-corruption theories, blockchain theory, stakeholder, and e-democracy theory. Moreover, we use the UTAUT model (Unified Theory of Acceptance and Use of Technology) to understand how this e-participation infrastructure is valued by the users.
- **Problem Relevance:** DSR must produce technical solutions using blockchain technologies and smart contracts to the relevant and important public-sector problems. Our work pertains to the issues of middlemen and intermediaries using smart contracts that address the corruption issues through automatic transaction execution.

- **Design Evaluation:** Our architecture in its design evaluation phase follows the scalable socio-technical method designed by Saay and Norta [27]. With the help of this method, an architecture designer can share a project with several expert groups that facilitates negotiation with the user and expert groups in different steps of the design and evaluation process.
- **Research Contribution:** Our contribution is to develop a blockchain-based e-participatory governance infrastructure, that enables the public to observe and investigate corruption attempts and cases in the public procurement.
- **Research Rigor:** For better producing quality decentralized applications (dApp) design, we use the decentralized agent-oriented method (DAOM) proposed by Udokwu, C., Brandtner, P., Norta, A. et al. [28] that provides a realistic and proper representation of phases that are required in developing decentralized applications (dApps). We use a support tool for the DAOM method that requires less modelling effort and offers more usability in developing DAOM-diagram models, so that we can design our architecture accurately.
- **Design as a Search Process:** We analyze the available various e-participation models to establish the e-Participatory governance infrastructures that satisfy the laws on the problem environment.
- **Communication of Research:** We present the results effectively both to the technology-oriented and management-oriented audiences. We also present this work to the conferences, journals, workshops and Ph.D. symposia.

Based on the above guidelines, a research plan is deduced, which is presented in the next section.

5   Research Plan

In this section, we present the time line for this Ph.D. project as shown in the Table 1. At the moment, we express the problem relevance, main- and sub-research questions, and the methodology. Finally, our main contributions to web engineering are: (1) designing a blockchain-based e-participatory architecture to fill the gap in the area of system design. Since blockchain is an important part of Web 3.0 and constitutes the future of e-governance and web engineering, we focus in (2) on defining Web 3.0 concepts and their relevance with decentralized ledger- and blockchain technology in the context of web engineering.

Table 1. Time frame for Ph.D. research.

Activity	2021–2022	2022–2023	2023–2024	2024–2025
	Sep-Aug	Sep-Aug	Sep-Aug	Sep-Aug
Problem Relevance: Identifying and analysing challenges in blockchain technologies, smart contract, token economy, and e-Participation	✓			
Research Contribution: Analyzing various governance models, and Identifying the best-practice models out of them to be adopted for enhancing public-sector corruption transparency	✓	✓		
Research Contribution: Designing a suitable blockchain-based e-Participation model		✓	✓	
Research Contribution: Integrating a smart-contract blockchain-based token economy into the public sector			✓	
Design as an artifact/Design evaluation/Design as a search process: Composition of the thesis and preliminary defense			✓	✓
Research Communication: The defense of the Ph.D. thesis				✓

6 Conclusion

The complex processes and the use of centralized systems in the public sector lead to a set of challenges that includes inappropriate record-keeping systems, a lack of trust, and a lack of transparency. To address these issues, this Ph.D. project proposes a blockchain-based e-participatory governance infrastructure using token economics with smart-contract blockchain technologies with the goal of supporting citizen e-participation to minimize corruption and improve transparency.

Acknowledgements. This PhD project is financed from the state budget of the Republic of Estonia and co-financed by Tallinn University.

References

1. Terzi, S., et al.: Blockchain 3.0 smart contracts in E-government 3.0 applications. arXiv preprint https://doi.org/10.48550/arXiv.1910.06092 (2019)
2. Ducrée, J., et al.: Blockchain for organizing effective grass-roots actions on a global commons: saving the planet. Front. Blockchain **3**(33) (2020). https://doi.org/10.3389/fbloc.2020.00033
3. Chohan, U.W.: Web 3.0: The Future Architecture of the Internet? Available at SSRN (2022)
4. Voshmgir, S.: Token Economy- How the Web3 Reinvents the Internet, 2nd edn. Token Kitchen, Berlin (2020)
5. Yusufzada, S., Zhiqiang X.: Public Administration in Afghanistan: Challenges and Way Forward. Open J. Soc. Sci. **7**(6) (2019). https://doi.org/10.4236/jss.2019.76012
6. Mujtaba, B.G.: Ethnic diversity, distrust and corruption in Afghanistan: reflections on the creation of an inclusive culture. Equality, diversity and inclusion. Int. J. (2013). https://doi.org/10.1108/EDI-12-2012-0113
7. Ahmed, N.: Challenges of Public Procurement in Afghanistan: A Case Study of Finance and Administrative Directorate in Kunar. Brac University, Diss (2020)
8. Mohite, A., Ajay, A.: Blockchain for government fund tracking using hyperledger. In: 2018 International Conference on Computational Techniques, Electronics and Mechanical Systems (CTEMS). IEEE (2018). https://doi.org/10.1109/CTEMS.2018.8769200
9. Guarda, T., Augusto, M.F., Haz, L., Díaz-Nafría, J.M.: Blockchain and government transformation. In: Rocha, Á., Ferrás, C., López-López, P.C., Guarda, T. (eds.) ICITS 2021. AISC, vol. 1330, pp. 88–95. Springer, Cham (2021). https://doi.org/10.1007/978-3-030-68285-9_9
10. Joshi, P., et al.: A blockchain based framework for fraud detection. In: 2019 Conference on Next Generation Computing Applications (NextComp). IEEE (2019). https://doi.org/10.1109/NEXTCOMP.2019.8883647
11. IBM. https://www.ibm.com/topics/smart-contracts. Accessed 6 Feb 2022
12. Dixit, A., Deval, V., Dwivedi, V., Norta, A., Draheim, D.: Towards user-centered and legally relevant smart-contract development: a systematic literature review. J. Indust. Inf. Integrat. **26** (2022), https://doi.org/10.1016/j.jii.2021.100314
13. Akaba, T.I., Norta, A., Udokwu, C., Draheim, D.: A framework for the adoption of blockchain-based e-procurement systems in the public sector. In: Hattingh, M., Matthee, M., Smuts, H., Pappas, I., Dwivedi, Y.K., Mäntymäki, M. (eds.) I3E 2020. LNCS, vol. 12066, pp. 3–14. Springer, Cham (2020). https://doi.org/10.1007/978-3-030-44999-5_1
14. Anastasiadou, M., Santos, V., Montargil, F.: Which technology to which challenge in democratic governance? An approach using design science research. Transform. Gov. People Process Policy **15**(4), 512–531 (2021). https://doi.org/10.1108/TG-03-2020-0045
15. Mærøe, A.R., Norta, A., Tsap, V., Pappel, I.: Increasing citizen participation in e-participatory budgeting processes. J. Inf. Technol. Polit. **18**(2), 125–147 (2021)
16. Transparency International. knowledgehub.transparency.org. Accessed 25 Mar 2022

17. Nodehi, T., Zutshi, A., Grilo, A.: A blockchain based architecture for fulfilling the needs of an E-procurement platform. In: 5th North American International Conference on Industrial Engineering and Operations Management-IEOM, pp. 234–245. IEOM Society International, Michigan (2020)

18. Elalaoui Elabdallaoui, H., Elfazziki, A., Sadgal, M.: A blockchain-based platform for the e-procurement management in the public sector. In: Attiogbé, C., Ben Yahia, S. (eds.) MEDI 2021. LNCS, vol. 12732, pp. 213–223. Springer, Cham (2021). https://doi.org/10.1007/978-3-030-78428-7_17

19. Scherer, S., Wimmer, M.A.: A regional model for E-participation in the EU: evaluation and lessons learned from VoicE. In: Tambouris, E., Macintosh, A., Glassey, O. (eds.) ePart 2010. LNCS, vol. 6229, pp. 162–173. Springer, Heidelberg (2010). https://doi.org/10.1007/978-3-642-15158-3_14

20. Karkin, N.: Barriers for sustainable e-participation process: the case of Turkey. In: Anthopoulos, L., Reddick, C. (eds) Government e-Strategic Planning and Management. Public Administration and Information Technology, vol. 3. Springer, New York (2014). https://doi.org/10.1007/978-1-4614-8462-2_12

21. Shaikh, A.K., Goldsmith, L.T.: A conceptual model for E-participation by Omani citizens using blockchain technology. WAS Sci. Nat. 4(1) (2021). ISSN:2766–7715

22. Benítez-Martínez, F.L., Romero-Frías, E., Hurtado-Torres, M.V.: Neural blockchain technology for a new anticorruption token: towards a novel governance model. J. Inf. Technol. Politics 00(00), 1–18 (2022). https://doi.org/10.1080/19331681.2022.2027317

23. Triana Casallas, J.A., Cueva-Lovelle, J.M., Rodr'ıguez Molano, J.I.: Smart contracts with blockchain in the public sector. Int. J. Interact. Multim. Artif. Intell. 6(3), 63 (2020). https://doi.org/10.9781/ijimai.2020.07.005

24. Karamagioli, E., Koulolias, V.: Challenges and barriers in implementing e-participation tools. One year of experience from implementing Gov2demoss in 64 municipalities in Spain. Int. J. Electron. Gov. 1(4)(2008). https://doi.org/10.1504/IJEG.2008.022070

25. Hevner, A.R., March, S.T., Park, J., Ram, S.: Design science in information systems research. MIS Quart. 28(1), 75–105 (2004). https://doi.org/10.2307/25148625

26. Prat, N., Comyn-Wattiau, I., Akoka, J.: Artifact Evaluation in Information Systems Design-Science Research-A Holistic View, vol. 23, pp. 1–16. PACIS, France (2014)

27. Saay, S., Norta, A.: Designing a scalable socio-technical method for evaluating large e-governance systems. In: Bhattacharyya, S., Gandhi, T., Sharma, K., Dutta, P. (eds.) Advanced Computational and Communication Paradigms. LNEE, vol. 475, pp. 571–580. Springer, Singapore (2018). https://doi.org/10.1007/978-981-10-8240-5_64

28. Udokwu, C., Brandtner, P., Norta, A., Kormiltsyn, A., Matulevičius, R.: Implementation and evaluation of the DAOM framework and support tool for designing blockchain decentralized applications. Int. J. Inf. Technol. 13(6), 2245–2263 (2021). https://doi.org/10.1007/s41870-021-00816-6

Applying a Healthcare Web of Things Framework for Infertility Treatments

Anastasiia Gorelova[✉] and Santiago Meliá

Department of Computer Languages and Systems, Universidad de Alicante, Carretera de San Vicente s/n, 03690 San Vicente del Raspeig, Alicante, Spain
ag153@alu.ua.es, santi@ua.es

Abstract. According to doctors and researchers, fertility problems are becoming epidemic proportions. Meanwhile, the demand for infertility treatment is increasing by 5–10% per year. To support the growing demand, physicians need to define personalized remote monitoring treatments supported by devices that send real-time information on hormones levels, heart-rate, temperature, etc. To this end, Healthcare Monitoring Systems (HMS) have recently appeared, based on increasingly advanced devices that help to manage this task. However, current solutions are expensive and not very customizable by physicians themselves. In this paper, we propose a framework called MoSTHealth, based on digital twins and Model-Driven Engineering (MDE), allows healthcare experts to model a personalized Web of Things (WoT) HMS scenario per treatment and per patient. Thanks to MDE, the simulated scenario allows us to generate a Service-Oriented enterprise cloud architecture that integrates a prediction module based on machine learning and data analysis. In this paper, a WoT HMS scenario for infertility treatment is presented as a case study. In this scenario, a specific care plan is defined, associated with a set of devices, including the use of a biosensing device that sends hormones levels in real-time.

Keywords: Infertility treatment · Web of Things (WoT) · Internet of Things (IoT) devices · Healthcare Monitoring System (HMS) · Simulator · Digital twin

1 Introduction

According to researchers, fertility problems are becoming epidemic proportions [1]. One in four couples in a developed country has trouble conceiving, and about 48.5 million couples suffer from infertility worldwide [2]. And unfortunately, infertility is increasing. Meanwhile, the demand for infertility treatment is increasing by 5–10% per year [1]. To support the growing demand and increase the probability of successful results, physicians need to define personalized remote monitoring treatments supported by devices that send real-time information on: hormones levels, heart rate, temperature, activity etc.

The democratization of Internet of Things (IoT) devices has facilitated the proliferation of Healthcare Monitoring Systems (HMSs) that are capable of supporting any type of treatment or condition remotely. However, to achieve their full potential, these

© Springer Nature Switzerland AG 2022
T. Di Noia et al. (Eds.): ICWE 2022, LNCS 13362, pp. 426–431, 2022.
https://doi.org/10.1007/978-3-031-09917-5_30

devices must efficiently address the customization demanded by different WoT HMS scenarios. In this sense, it is recognized by the scientific community [3, 4], the need for WoT HMS simulators, which perform a virtual representation of complex scenarios that allow a qualitative and quantitative prediction based on machine learning and data analysis, ensuring that the WoT HMS achieves the desired requirements before its implementation.

Recently, a novel paradigm called Digital Twin [5] has emerged with great potential, which enables the representation of virtual entities that are not only limited to the devices of an WoT system, but allow the complete representation of the real objects that make up the scenario, e.g., people, processes, tasks and devices. Specifically, Digital Twin is considered by several authors [6] a disruptive technology for use in WoT healthcare domain, as it would allow to represent not only patient monitoring scenarios, but also more complex systems such as smart hospitals, thus providing a complete view of patient care.

We propose a framework called MoSTHealth that uses the Digital Twin paradigm to perform both modelling and simulation of WoT HMS scenarios. The use is not only reduced to patient care in a remote way, but also involves a complex environment with integration with other sources of information such as smart hospitals that allows capturing all patient information within a medical institution.

Precisely, MoSTHealth has the ability to model a scenario thanks to the integration of several disciplines such as MDE for modelling and defining transformations to code, Digital Twin as a paradigm to fully represent WoT HMS scenarios, and the application of artificial intelligence techniques such as fine-grain and coarse-grain machine learning to provide the solution with a prediction mechanism.

2   Background

Some authors [7] point out that the application of Digital Twin in the Healthcare domain is absolutely revolutionary, as its use would allow predicting and simulating scenarios in many contexts. On the one hand, it allows us to define at a micro level a scenario of a care plan for a patient whose vital signs are collected by means of biosensors and where predictive algorithms are applied to detect possible risks. On the other hand, using Digital Twin we can also represent a macro-level scenario with a smart hospital in which healthcare experts, patients and healthcare equipment are represented. In this context, there are several proposals that apply Digital Twin to the Healthcare domain. For example, [8] applies the digital twin representation of a human body, where its organs and internal processes are represented. [9] introduced an approach for managing the knowledge of artificial intelligence-based, learning eHealth systems via digital twins, which are subdivided into subtypes of twins, such as personal, group and system. Furthermore, [10] presents a digital twin approach of a WoT eHealth framework for supporting home hospitalization of users with chronic diseases. The platform includes communication with several sensors to monitor the progress of the patient and contains a decision support system, which analyzes the health data and creates different rules related to care. Unlike our proposal, it is not adapted for people with disabilities nor presents a friendly environment for health experts.

3   Objectives

1. Improved integration of WoT HMS into the workflow of healthcare systems, allowing health experts to take a part in the definition and maintenance of the monitoring system.
2. Significant reduction of WoT HMS development costs by applying MDE techniques.
3. Improvement of infertility treatments thanks to a better personalized follow-up of each patient.
4. The scientific validation of the proposal through a family of empirical studies and use cases to study the user experience (UX), satisfaction and intention of use of the final solution from patients and health experts.

4   MoSTHealth: A MDE Framework for Modeling and Simulating WoT HMS Based on Digital Twins

This project proposes the implementation of a framework called Modelling Scenarios of Digital Twins for Health (MoSTHealth) that is based on the MDE paradigm, that allows the modelling of the virtual entities or digital twins that are necessary to simulate and deploy different healthcare scenarios with IoT devices. The framework will have a multi-device user interface that provides a satisfactory user experience for medical experts to define and manage the scenario of different patients. A mobile user interface for patients so that they can enter and receive all their treatment information. Using the MDE paradigm, we start from a previous MoSIoT [11] core, which is extended for MoSTHealth by redefining the reference model and the metamodel, especially with the ability and capacity to introduce concepts from both HMS and health entities. From this point, then we will make a definition of a new domain model and thus obtain a new scenario model that allows to reproduce any type of WoT HMS scenario. In order to define a standard and interoperable solution based on WoT paradigm, our reference model has adopted standard ontologies provided by W3C and HL7. Thus, MoSTHealth takes for the definition of the devices ontology of the Web of Things architecture [12]. For the definition of care plans we rely on the HL7 FHIR standard and the EU-GDPR 2 that will allow us to interact with medical entities. For the definition of patients, we rely on ontologies for users such as FOAF [13], and for people with disabilities such as the W3C Web Accessibility Initiative (WAI) [14]. Furthermore, to manage and store the digital twins of each of the scenarios we will establish an enterprise cloud architecture with a set of secure web services that have been generated with an MDE approach such as OOH4RIA [15]. Based on the domain and scenario models, this provides a scalable and reliable enterprise solution. To provide a storage mechanism for the history of the Digital Twin generated in the scenarios will be used standard repositories such as Digital Twin Domain Language (DTDL) [16]. It is important to emphasize that the digital twins must represent the concepts coming from the medical entities in order to be considered in a complete HMS scenario. To simulate the behavior of the virtual entities that make up the WoT HMS scenario we will implement a prediction module that is integrated within the framework itself. To offer a complete simulation, the module combines two approaches: it will work with a coarse-grain machine learning approach, analyzing the historical datasets of the Digital Twins that are generated during a certain period of time, and that are sent by the framework to the defined DTDL resources, this will allow locating patterns in these scenarios. Once the patterns are detected, the simulator will apply a fine-grained machine learning approach inspired by the approach [17], where the machine learning algorithms are already integrated into the properties of the digital twins by means of micro-learning units called learned attributes. To obtain and send data through a REST API we will integrate the MoSTHealth with one or more IoT Hubs.

4.1 The IoT HMS Solution for Infertility Treatment: A Case Study

In this case study, the simulator allows the physician by an app to define infertility treatment technique and indicating the devices to be used. A patient is provided with three devices (see Fig. 1): two wearable sensors and a smartphone with a downloaded application.

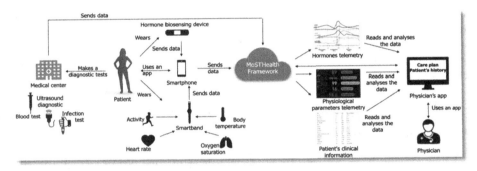

Fig. 1. Schematic structure of pregnancy planning system

One of the wearable devices is a smart band that reads physiological parameters such as heart rate, body temperature, oxygen saturation and daily activities. Another device is a wearable biosensor which performs real-time monitoring of ovulation hormones [18]. All the data from the wearable devices is transferred to the smartphone. In turn, the smartphone sends the data to a MoSTHealth Framework. With the help of the system, a physician can have an access to patient's health data: results of the clinical test made in a medical center, physiological parameters and hormones levels changing in real-time. Moreover, the system can suggest a care plan based on the data stored in MoSTHealth Framework.

5 Work Done

To create a truly relevant, useful and successful product it is essential to have done user experience (UX) research. One of the widely used UX research methodologies is a usability testing. So, we created a bunch of tasks and questions in a usability testing tool - Loop11 [19]. The test performs on an application prototype that we made for the medical expert's part of the MoSTHealth, using a prototyping tool for Web and mobile apps called Justinmind [20]. After processing the results, we will be able to determine the requirements of physicians to the application and estimate the level of usability. Finally, we defined the reference model, and implemented a first version of the MoSTHealth framework and mobile user interfaces of the domain and medical experts. The work flow conforms to established timeline and corresponds to 6-th month of Anastasiia Gorelova's PhD.

6   Plan for Future Work

To complete the definition of user requirements, we will create a patient's application prototype and perform the usability test. The next step will be to complete the construction of the MoSTHealth framework, which consists of: development of service-oriented backend of the domain model, Web application development for a domain expert, transformations to obtain backend of scenario model, transformations to obtain persistence of scenario model, integration of scenario business logic with IoT Hub, development of multi-device application for patients. The next stage will be an empirical evaluation of artefacts which incorporates: empirical experiments (EE) of MoSTHealth UX and EE of MoSTHealth of patient's and clinical's intention of adoption. And final phase will be a dissemination of project results.

Contributions. This project makes a contribution to followings topics related to Web Engineering: Web application modelling and engineering, Web of things, Mobile Web applications and Web services.

Funding. This work has been funded by SkoPS project EU (Ref 2020-1-DE01-KA226HE-005772), co-funded by by the Spanish Ministry of Science and Innovation under contract PID2019-111196RB-I00 (Access@IoT), and by the Generalitat Valenciana (GVA) through the AICO/2020/143 project.

References

1. SingleCare Team. Infertility statistics 2021: How many couples are affected by infertility? https://www.singlecare.com/blog/news/infertilitystatistics/#:~:text=One%20in%204%20couples%20in,million%20couples%20experience%20infertility%20worldwide
2. Elhussein, O.G., Ahmed, M.A., Suliman, S.O., Yahya, L.I., Adam, I.: Epidemiology of infertility and characteristics of infertile couples requesting assisted reproduction in a low-resource setting in Africa. Sudan. 5, 7 (2019). https://doi.org/10.1186/s40738-019-0060-1. . SingleCareTeam
3. D'Angelo, G., Ferretti, S., Ghini, V.: Simulation of the Internet of Things. In: 2016 International Conference on High Performance Computing & Simulation (HPCS) (2016)
4. Ojie, E., Pereira, E.: Simulation tools in internet of things: a review. In: Proceedings of the 1st International Conference on Internet of Things and Machine Learning, pp. 1–7 (2017)
5. He, Y., Guo, J., Zheng, X.: From surveillance to digital twin: challenges and recent advances of signal processing for industrial Internet of Things. IEEE Signal Process. Mag. 35(5), 120–129 (2018)

6. Fuller, A., et al.: Digital twin: enabling technologies, challenges and open research. IEEE Access **8**, 108952–108971 (2020)
7. Benson, M.: Digital twins will revolutionize healthcare. Eng. Technol. **16**(2), 50–53 (2021)
8. Barnabas, J., Raj, P.: The human body: a digital twin of the cyber physical systems. In: Advances in Computers, pp. 219–246. Elsevier (2020)
9. Lutze, R.: Digital twins in eHealth: prospects and challenges focussing on information management. In: 2019 IEEEICE/ITMC, pp. 1–9. https://doi.org/10.1109/ICE.2019.8792622
10. Velasco, C.A., Yehya, M., Philip, A.: Architecture of a web of things eHealth framework for the support of users with chronic diseases. In: DSAI 2016, pp. 47–53. Association for Computing Machinery, New York (2016)
11. Meliá, S., et al.: MoSIoT: modeling and simulating IoT healthcare-monitoring systems for people with disabilities. Int. J. Environ. Res. Publ. Health **18**(12), 6357 (2021)
12. Web of Things (WoT) Architecture 1.1. W3C. https://www.w3.org/TR/2020/WD-wot-archit ecture11-20201124/
13. The Friend of a Friend (FOAF) Project. http://www.foaf-project.org/
14. Diverse Abilities and Barriers. W3C Web Accessibility Initiative (2017). https://www.w3. org/WAI/people-use-web/abilities-barriers/
15. Meliá, S., Gómez, J., Pérez, S., Díaz, O.: Architectural and technological variability in rich internet applications. IEEE Internet Comput. **14**(3), 24–32 (2010)
16. Mateev, M.: Industry 4.0 and the digital twin for building industry. Industry 4.0 **5**(1), 29–32 (2020)
17. Hartmann, T., Moawad, A., Fouquet, F., Le Traon, Y.: The next evolution of MDE: a seamless integration of machine learning into domain modeling. Softw. Syst. Model. **18**(2), 1285–1304 (2017)
18. Estrogen, Progesterone, LH, FSH & Getting Pregnant. Fertility2family. 3 July 2021. https:// fertility2family.com.au/2021/07/what-is-estrogen-progesterone-lh-and-fsh/
19. Infertility treatment application prototype. Loop11. https://www.loop11.com/ui/?l11_uid= 87103
20. Infertility treatment application prototype. Justinmind. https://www.justinmind.com/use rnote/tests/69038898/69252645/69258235/index.html

Blockchain and AI to Build an Alzheimer's Risk Calculator

Paolo Sorino$^{(\boxtimes)}$ (iD)

Politecnico di Bari, Bari, Italy
`paolo.sorino@poliba.it`

Abstract. The problems affecting healthcare databases and medical records are numerous, although the potential of the data stored in them is high. However, medical records are hidden across hospitals, and data sharing processes fail to provide accountable data control. Blockchain technology has been successfully applied in various fields to support distributed data management and data quality. This article evidences how Blockchain is expected to be leveraged to better organize and sharing of healthcare's big data with mixed EHR (Electronic Health Records) and imaging (CAT, RX, etc.) sources. The aim is to exploit these data through Artificial Intelligence methods in order to build an Alzheimer's risk calculator based on neuro-images.

Keywords: Blockchain · Artificial Intelligence · Recommander system · Alzheimer's disease · E-Health

1 Introduction

Nowadays, we are inundated with tons of data coming from every aspect of our lives, such as social activities, science, work, health, etc. Advances in technology have helped us generate more and more data, up to a level where it has become unmanageable with currently available technologies. This has led to the creation of "big data", term that describes big, unmanageable data. To meet our current and future social needs, we must develop new strategies to organize this data and derive meaningful information [1]. This problem is particular crucial in the health domain. In this field, in addition to the above mentioned problems, each hospital collects data in a "independent" way, and this leads to having large amounts of data, inhomogeneous and often inconsistent with a waste of hardware resources that are exploited in the centralized data servers. In fact, healthcare providers routinely enter clinical and laboratory data [2] into healthcare databases. One of the most commonly used forms of healthcare databases is electronic health records (EHRs). Physicians enter routine clinical and laboratory data into EHRs as a record of patient care [3]. All of this data is collected

Student's Ph.D. Supervisor: Tommaso Di Noia, Rodolfo Sardone and Fedelucio Narducci.

© Springer Nature Switzerland AG 2022
T. Di Noia et al. (Eds.): ICWE 2022, LNCS 13362, pp. 432–436, 2022.
https://doi.org/10.1007/978-3-031-09917-5_31

in a proprietary manner, thus to share and reuse it in hospitals other than those collecting it is difficult. Therefore, it is necessary to find solutions that allow transparency and, at the same time, ensure privacy as the use of the Blockchain, considered a cryptographically secure, reliable, and fast digital technology. It creates a decentralized database for which there is a copy for each center that participates in its creation. Each time a center enters a new piece of data, it appears in all copies of the registry itself. On the one hand, it allows doctors and researchers at the different centers to access all new data and stay up-to-date, and on the other hand, it allows for early intervention if a database is breached: only the database that is no longer secure can be closed, and the others kept operational. This process would facilitate data retrieval and exchange for research use. In addition, such data could be used to develop web applications based on artificial intelligence that the National Health System could use for diagnosis, screening, or research studies.

2 Proposed Work

2.1 Aims and Objectives

The aim of this project is twofold: i) to create a platform based on blockchain technology in the healthcare system [4], ii) to design and implement a E-Health Recommender System [5,6]. The first part will deal with the storage of medical records in Blockchain, patients will be allowed to upload their clinical data through a specific app in order to create a network that can facilitate data for diagnostic and research purposes. Privacy is guaranteed upstream by the Blockchain. The platform will need to ensure sharing of healthcare's big data with mixed EHR (Electronic Health Records) and imaging (CAT, RX, etc.) sources [7]. This technology is helpful to medical institutions to gain insight and enhance the analysis of medical records. It can help avoid the fear of data manipulation in healthcare and supports a unique data storage pattern at the highest level of security. It provides versatility, interconnection, accountability, and authentication for data acces. The Blockchain platform will be used for health data sharing, electronic health record keeping to provide easy access to data for research and screening. The second aim is to use artificial intelligence techniques [8] for developing AI-based diagnostic tools [9] using data collected by the Blockchain platform. A personalized risk calculator(E-Health Recommender System) [5,6] will be developed for Alzheimer's disease [10] in order to detect the onset of diseases at an earlier stage and intervene with specific treatment to retard cognitive decline. The population to be used in the project is the population of Puglia (Bari), between 40 and 60 years old [11].

2.2 Methods

For development of the E-Health Recommender System, it will be necessary to focus on the procedures to be implemented in the two parts of the project. In the development of the first part of the project, a preliminary investigation will be carried out to identify all the problems in the healthcare database. A shared Blockchain platform will be developed that can provide a high level of security and privacy. Afterwards, a Blockchain-based computer network will be generated to interconnect the various hospitals to facilitate the sharing of patient data. The data that will be collected within the Blockchain will be in addition to textual data and images of instrumental examinations. This data will be used to develop an Alzheimer's risk calculator using federated learning techniques [12] in Python [13]. For the development of the second part of the project, we will proceed initially with the research of the optimal parameters to insert in the algorithm to obtain best performance. An algorithm capable of calculating the risk of Alzheimer's will then be trained. The algorithm will be provided with a database of neuro-images, collected in the Radiological Informative Systems of a network of hospitals. These images will first be preprocessed and then used to train and test the algorithm [14]. The performance of the developed system will be verified by comparing the values of the metrics during the training and testing phases [15,16]. An Explainability [17] analysis will be performed to understand the final diagnosis. The last part of the project will instead focus on the development of a web platform for predicting Alzheimer's risk in order to employ it as a E-Health Recommender System in epidemiological studies or screening. Connection to this online platform will be restricted to employees only and allowed after entering a username and password.

Fig. 1. Shown the project steps for the development of the E-Health recommender system

2.3 Risk Prediction Model for Alzheimer's Disease

The application to be developed allows the doctor to upload the CT or MRI brain image and receives as output the estimated patient's risk of developing Alzheimer's [18]. In addition, throw the different functions of the web app, the doctor can export the prediction, add notes, check the patient's medical history (medical records, laboratory tests, previous CT/MRI scans, medications taken), enter new patient data (update clinical tests, medications taken) or make a new prediction for a new patient. Each patient is identified with a unique ID.n Fig. 2 a mockup of the Web App for Alzheimer's prediction is proposed. Several studies have proposed the use of AI in clinical practices to predict conditions such as heart disease, non-alcoholic fatty liver disease (NAFLD), or cancer [9,19,20]. The proposed application might be used for epidemiological studies or screening.

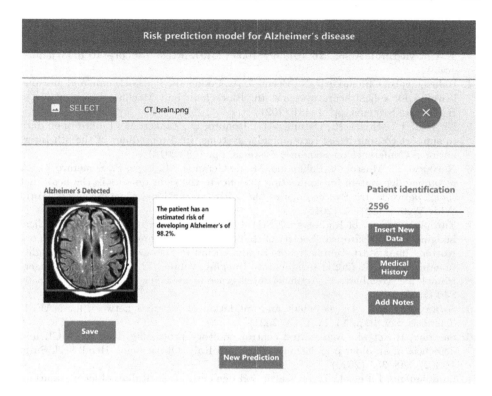

Fig. 2. Mockup of the Web App for Alzheimer's prediction

3   Contribution to Web Engineering

The proposed work provides an innovative contribution to web engineering as it involves the development of a Blockchain platform to improve data storage across hospitals and develop an image-based Alzheimer's risk calculator employing artificial intelligence techniques that are Web-Based in a way that makes it accessible and usable to the entire national healthcare system. The system receives MRI or CT images as input, analyses them and provides the risk of Alzheimer's disease and the accuracy with which the diagnosis was generated.

References

1. Dash, S., Shakyawar, S.K., Sharma, M., Kaushik, S.: Big data in healthcare: management, analysis and future prospects. J. Big Data **6**(1), 1–25 (2019)
2. Lohr, K.N., Donaldson, M.S., et al.: Health Data in the Information Age: Use, Disclosure, and Privacy. National Academies Press (1994)

3. Yuan, N., Dudley, R.A., Boscardin, W.J., Lin, G.A.: Electronic health records systems and hospital clinical performance: a study of nationwide hospital data. J. Am. Med. Inf. Assoc. **26**(10), 999–1009 (2019). https://doi.org/10.1093/jamia/ocz092

4. Balusamy, B., Chilamkurti, N., Beena, L.A., Poongodi, T.: Blockchain and machine learning for e-healthcare systems. In: Blockchain and Machine Learning for e-Healthcare Systems, pp. 1–481 (2021)

5. Di Noia, T., Mirizzi, R., Ostuni, V.C., Romito, D., Zanker, M.: Linked open data to support content-based recommender systems. In: Proceedings of the 8th International Conference on Semantic Systems, pp. 1–8 (2012)

6. Narducci, F., Musto, C., Polignano, M., de Gemmis, M., Lops, P., Semeraro, G.: A recommender system for connecting patients to the right doctors in the healthnet social network. In: Proceedings of the 24th International Conference on World Wide Web, pp. 81–82 (2015)

7. European Society of Radiology (ESR). ESR white paper: blockchain and medical imaging, author European Society of Radiology (ESR) communications@myesr. org Kotter Elmar Marti-Bonmati Luis Brady Adrian P. Desouza Nandita M. Insights Imaging **12**(1), 82 (2021) Insights into Imaging, volume 12, 1, 82, 2021, Springer

8. Hamet, P., Tremblay, J.: Artificial intelligence in medicine. Metabolism **69**, S36–S40 (2017)

9. Sorino, P.; et al.: Development and validation of a neural network for NAFLD diagnosis. Sci. Rep. **11**(1), 1–13 (2021)

10. Sardone, R., et al.: Age-related central auditory processing disorder, MCI, and dementia in an older population of Southern Italy. Otolaryngol. Head Neck Surg. **163**(2), 348–355 (2020)

11. Lampignano, L., et al.: Liver health and dementia in an Italian older population: findings from the Salus in Apulia Study. Front. Aging Neurosci. **13** (2021)

12. Xu, J., et al.: Federated learning for healthcare informatics. J. Healthc. Inf. Res. **5**(1), 1–19 (2021)

13. Van Rossum, G., Drake, F.L.: Python 3 Reference Manual. 1441412697. CreateSpace, Scotts Valley (2009)

14. Uçar, M.K., Nour, M., Sindi, H., Polat, K.: The effect of training and testing process on machine learning in biomedical datasets. Math. Prob. Eng. **2020** (2020)

15. Sokolova, M., Japkowicz, N., Szpakowicz, S.: Beyond accuracy, F-score and ROC: a family of discriminant measures for performance evaluation. Austral. Joint Conf. Artif. Intell. 1015–1021 (2006)

16. Susmaga, R.: Confusion matrix visualization. Intell. Inf. Process. Web Min. 107–116 (2004)

17. Amann, J., Blasimme, A., Vayena, E., Frey, D., Madai, V.I.: Explainability for artificial intelligence in healthcare: a multidisciplinary perspective. BMC Med. Inf. Decis. Making **20**(1), 1–9 (2020)

18. El-Sappagh, S., Alonso, J.M., Islam, S.M., Sultan, A.M., Kwak, K.S.: A multilayer multimodal detection and prediction model based on explainable artificial intelligence for Alzheimer' disease. Sci. Rep. **11**(1), 1–26 (2021)

19. Mohan, S., Thirumalai, C., Srivastava, G.: Effective heart disease prediction using hybrid machine learning techniques. IEEE Access **7**, 81542–81554 (2019)

20. Cruz, J.A., Wishart, D.S.: Applications of machine learning in cancer prediction and prognosis. Cancer Inf. **2**, 117693510600200030 (2006)

Bridging Static Site Generation
with the Dynamic Web

Juho Vepsäläinen and Petri Vuorimaa[✉]

Aalto University, Espoo, Finland
petri.vuorimaa@aalto.fi
https://www.aalto.fi/en/department-of-computer-science

Abstract. Historically web sites have been developed using HTML for their markup either by authoring it directly or through abstraction to generate it. The currently available tools exist in a continuum of static, developer-oriented tools and dynamic services that cater to non-technical users. In this paper, we propose an approach that sits in the middle by using JSON for site definitions. The definition is leveraged on the client-side for editing, bridging the continuum's ends.

Keywords: Static site generation · JSON · Software architecture

1 Brief Introduction to Static Site Generation

Static Site Generators (SSG) have become a hot topic in the developer community as they provide a set of benefits over more traditional server-based dynamic approaches:

- Fast page load time: As there's less processing to do, also pages tend to load faster [1,2]
- Efficient scalability: By definition, it's easy to scale static sites across multiple servers on a CDN [1]
- Availability and security: Since there's no dynamic server portion, also attack surface is largely reduced and the server logic required is a magnitude simpler in terms of logic [1,2]
- Versioning: As static sites are versioned automatically, it is easy to track changes using systems such as Git or GitHub [2]

As a side effect, static sites consume fewer resources and therefore consume fewer natural resources than their dynamic brethren [1].

Supported by Aalto University.

T. Di Noia et al. (Eds.): ICWE 2022, LNCS 13362, pp. 437–442, 2022.
https://doi.org/10.1007/978-3-031-09917-5_32

1.1   Challenges of SSG

The main drawback of SSG has to do with the need to **write** and to alter data as that's the sweet spot for dynamic sites. In the worst case for SSG, an update to the content will force you to regenerate and deploy the entire site. In a dynamic solution generating a page using a database, the problem is close to non-existent.

The main challenge for SSG is to retain the benefits while addressing the cost of updates and allowing easy edits for the editors of a site. It is good to note that although the developer and the site's editor can be the same person, it's not always so, and that's when different expectations for User Experience (UX) might arise. Something suitable for developers isn't necessarily good for editors and vice versa.

1.2   SSG with a Headless Content Server

When site content is coupled with its markup, the site editors have to worry about both when editing. For this reason, so-called headless content servers have appeared on the market [3].

They are a step forward, but they still require developer attention and have limitations in terms of flexibility. Anything that should be modifiable has to show up in the data model.

2   SSG Using JSON as an Intermediate Target

In this paper, we propose using JSON as an intermediate target to define aspects, such as site markup, styling, state management, content binding, and routing. As a side effect of doing this, developing an editor that runs on top of the deployed site itself becomes possible.

2.1   Why JSON?

JSON is the universal data format of the web, and handling is built right into JavaScript. You could replace it with any other format, but it has proven to be a good fit for demonstrating the ideas due to its relative simplicity. According to Nurseitov et al. [4], JSON is more performant than its XML counterpart, making the choice even more lucrative.

2.2   Constraints

For the approach to work, it is paramount that the definitions capture it all. Due to this constraint, commonly used techniques, such as using separate CSS files for styling, become restricted and are limited only for special cases such as highlighting code. The same goes for aspects like state management, as ideally, they should be handled within the HTML markup.

2.3   Aspects of the Architecture

Given the constraints, several technical decisions must be made for the system to exist. I've listed my choices and related options below[1]:

- Routing: custom JSON definition to describe data sources, possible data transforms, routes, route expansions, metadata, which layouts to use for rendering pages, rendering target (HTML, XML)
- Layouting and components: custom JSON definition that's mapped to HTML or XML depending on the target
- Data binding: custom `__bind` property to bind data to the current scope
- State management: Sidewind,[2] a state manager that comes with a small runtime and allows state management within HTML
- Styling: Twind, a derivative of Tailwind, a popular utility CSS solution that allows authoring styling within HTML

2.4   Routing

Each site has a routing scheme that defines the available pages. In dynamic sites, the routes can be created on-demand, but in SSG they need to be predefined on some level, although mixing the approaches is possible. In other words, dynamic functionality can be overlaid on top of a static site, but that's another discussion.

For a static site, page structure can be either defined implicitly through file structure and a convention or configuration. In the former approach, routing information is encoded to file naming and the way they are laid out.

In the latter approach, a mapping between routes and files is defined using a separate configuration file. After realizing it gives an additional degree of flexibility while being explicit and declarative by nature, we chose this approach.

A good routing approach should fulfill at least the following criteria:

1. It should be easy to understand the existing routes and add new ones
2. It should be possible to define how routes are connected to data and which layout is used for rendering them
3. It should be possible to attach metadata per route for Search Engine Optimization (SEO) purposes
4. It should be possible to map arbitrary input data to a page or multiple pages, assuming it's a collection

To fulfill the first three criteria, we ended up with the following JSON definition where the object key defines the route name, and then within the value properties, the route is declared in detail.

---

[1] The selection has been explored in a personal project called Gustwind (https://gustwind.js.org/).

[2] https://sidewind.js.org/.

In the example below, project README.md file is mapped to the site's index while pushing it through a Markdown transform that's converting it to HTML. Then it's rendered using a layout, and the layout also has access to meta-information related to it.

```
{
  "/": {
    "meta": { "title": "Gustwind", ... },
    "layout": "siteIndex",
    "dataSources": [
      {
        "id": "readme",
        "operation": "file",
        "input": "./README.md",
        "transformWith": ["markdown"]
      }
    ]
  }
}
```

The root route ("/") of the site is a particular case, and for any other route, a simple name can be used (i.e., "blog"). The routes can also be nested arbitrarily by using a "routes" field inside which you can use the same definition.

Handling the fourth criteria of mapping data to multiple pages is more complex, and we ended up implementing expansion syntax for this purpose as follows:

```
{
  "blog": {
    ...
    "expand": {
      "dataSources": [ { ... } ],
      "matchBy": {
        "dataSource": "blogPosts",
        "collection": "content",
        "slug": "data.slug"
      },
      "layout": "blogPage",
      "meta": { "__title": "match.name", ... }
    }
  }
}
```

The trick was to allow matching against processed data to generate pages. The use case is typical, especially when you have a group of files you wish to map to a website, so it made sense to support it.

2.5 Components

Components are a useful abstraction in web development as they allow you to capture meaningful entities for reuse. They allow you to capture repetition within a single interface, and the advent of front-end frameworks and Web Components [5] has made them a popular approach.

We've ended up with the following component definition:

```
{
  "element": "nav",
  "class": "sticky top−0",
  "children": [ ... ]
  "attributes": {
    "title": "Navigation"
  }
}
```

Above would map as HTML like this:

```
<nav class="sticky top−0" title="Navigation">...</nav>
```

2.6 Layouts and Data Binding

For layouts, we consider the following criteria important:

1. It should be possible to connect to data from a layout
2. It should be possible to compose layouts and components for reuse
3. It should be possible to perform nested data binding to allow passing specific data to components

The following example illustrates a whole layout with head and body sections inside which components are then bound to data using the __bind property. In addition, __ prefix is used to bind data to children for iteration, and the same convention can be used for binding to attributes as well:

```
{
  "head": [ { "element": "MetaFields" } ],
  "body": [
    { "element": "MainNavigation" },
    {
      "element": "div",
      "class": "md:mx−auto my−8 px−4 md:px−0 w−full",
      "__bind": "readme",
      "__children": "content"
    },
    { "element": "MainFooter" }
  ]
}
```

To capture a subset of data for a component, `__bind` can be applied anywhere within the component tree. The scheme could be expanded to support React.js style props and concrete component examples to document it.

3   Discussion

Due to space constraints, we didn't cover styling and state management in detail. However, they fit the same scheme well and allow development of full-fledged web sites and applications. We believe the approach yields the following benefits that are to be proven and give a starting point for further research:

1. Given the system uses JSON as an intermediate format, is it possible to develop client-side editors on top of it by providing a JSON definition next to an HTML page rendered by the system?
2. Given it's possible to mix the generated pages with dynamic content by using upcoming web technologies, such as edge computing, can the approach be used to mix the techniques?
3. The usage of JSON yields further value in knowledge sharing. Could, for example component registries be implemented on top of the approach?
4. Does the architecture scale to using legacy technologies within it, for example using the islands or widget architectures?
5. Which different techniques can be leveraged on top of the approach to improve it further? What benefits do they provide?
6. How does the approach compare with established SSGs?

Completing the work would have the potential to provide a new approach for developing websites and applications. Due to the nature of the specification, it could become a standard for different technical implementations besides the reference one allowing usage across multiple platforms, and the ideas might scale beyond the web.

References

1. Petersen, H.: From Static and Dynamic Websites to Static Site Generators. University of TARTU, Institute of Computer Science (2016)
2. Camden, R., Rinaldi, B.: Working with Static Sites: Bringing the Power of Simplicity to Modern Sites. O'Reilly Media Inc., Newton (2017)
3. Öfverstedt, L.: Why go headless-a comparative study between traditional CMS and the emerging headless trend. Department of Information Technology, Uppsala University (2018)
4. Nurseitov, N., et al.: Comparison of JSON and XML data interchange formats: a case study. In: 22nd International Conference on Computer Applications in Industry and Engineering 2009, CAINE 2009, pp. 157–162 (2009)
5. Pelkonen, H.: Web components as application building blocks. MS thesis, School of Science, Aalto University (2014)

Enhance Web-Components in Order to Increase Security and Maintainability

Tobias Münch$^{(\boxtimes)}$ and Rainer Roosmann

University of Applied Sciences Osnabrück, Albrechtstraße 30,
49076 Osnabrück, Germany
{t.muench,r.roosmann}@hs-osnabrueck.de

Abstract. Today's development of client-side web applications is based on one of the JavaScript-frameworks, such as Angular or React. The excessive dependencies that arise in the ecosystem from the Node-Package-Manager increase the security risk and the dependency of your own web application on third-party packages. Moreover, the framework-less approach proposes a renaissance of classic web development, because it strives to avoid external dependencies as far as possible and to fall back on the standards. Whether the implementation achieves maintainability and security of frameworks is questionable. Therefore, it makes sense to research which core concepts of the frameworks meet the requirements for maintainability and security and how these are implemented. The novelty is that the concepts to be explored are moved to a standard in order to ensure the developer efficiency, security, performance and maintainability in the long term. This allows existing approaches to focus on other essential features.

Keywords: Web application modelling and engineering · Developer efficiency · Concepts and patterns · Standards

1 Introduction

The component-based-software-development (CBSD) has encouraged software developers to reuse code to achieve multiple benefits. It has been proven by previous work, that the reuse of code fragments can be used to improve software quality, decrease the time-to-market period and boost overall developer efficiency [1–3]. The CBSD approach does not only has advantages, but can also lead to the so-called dependency hell if used excessively [4,5]. Using the example of the Node-Package-Manager (NPM) ecosystem, it can be shown that the dependencies increase super-linear due to their transitivity [6,7]. From this approach it can be deduced that the probability of a security-critical incident such as supply chain attacks increases with the number of external dependencies used. Zimmermann and Staicu have mentioned NPM as "a smallworld with high risks" [8]. This security issue can be proven by past as well as current incidents [9,13]. This leads to the question: Do we need these numerous dependencies when developing web applications?

© Springer Nature Switzerland AG 2022
T. Di Noia et al. (Eds.): ICWE 2022, LNCS 13362, pp. 443–449, 2022.
https://doi.org/10.1007/978-3-031-09917-5_33

Francesco Strazzullo proposed the frameworkless development approach, which represents a kind of renaissance of classic web development based on standards [14], that structures web applications by using web components based on the W3C standards such as Shadow-DOM, Custom-Elements, HTML-Templates and ES-modules [15,16]. This allows web applications to be developed without CBSD dependencies, but there are limitations in benefits such as time-to-market period and developer efficiency compared to using frameworks or libraries. As a disadvantage, concepts such as a virtual DOM must be implemented by the developer himself [14]. Whether the implementation achieves maintainability and security of frameworks is questionable. Since all components have to be developed in-house with the frameworkless approach, this circumstance has a negative effect on the maintainability of growing and long-lasting software. However, it must be taken into account that breaking changes occur much less frequently with standards than with frameworks. These quite different concepts are leading to the following research questions:

RQ1 What are the main concepts and patterns to increase security and maintainability in web-applications while using frameworks or libraries?

RQ2 How can these concepts be evaluated against the non-functional requirements of performance, resource-efficiency, security and maintainability?

RQ3 How can the concepts on hand be composed into a standardization proposal in order to increase developer efficiency in the long term while complying with the non-functional requirements?

2   Related Works

In this section we discuss the closest related work contained mainly in three distinct research areas: Software Reusability, client-side web-applications and developer effectiveness.

Software Reusability with it's dependencies have been widely discussed. Ahmaro et al. described different principles, taxonomies, approaches, advantages, factors and adaptations of reusability. It describes reusability in the levels of code, design, specification and application system. He concludes that reusability at all levels of frameworks, libraries and others brings significant benefits to industrial software development. It includes advantages like increased productivity and effectiveness, accelerated development and reduction of operational costs [18]. These can be seen in common frameworks such as Angular, React or Vue.JS. According to a study by Stackoverflow [17], these three are the most common. In addition, they impressively show how the concepts from the CBSD have been transferred to frameworks and client-side software architecture of web applications. Model-View-*, Boilerplates client-side code and asynchronous programming [19] should be mentioned here. However, there are currently few scientific articles on the concepts behind client-side web app architectures. The fact that the reuse of source code not only brings advantages bur also brings disadvantages which can be seen in the Javascript ecosystem NPM [8,9].

The extension of web components is discussed for **client-side web appli-cations**. Krug and Gaedke propose an extension "SmartComposition: Bring-ing Component-Based SoftwareEngineering to the Web" in 2015 [20]. They have shown how to extend web-components, to create complex distributed web-applications by extending the W3C-Web-Components. They see further research in creating hassle-free composition of web-components. As part of his doctorate, Herzberg evaluated the formal conditions and created a concept for creating secure web components [21]. Strazzullo describes a practical approach how web components can be used to carry out a frameworkless development [14].

Developer effectiveness was examined by Forsgren et al. more closely and set up the SPACE-framework [10]. Productivity is divided into the facets of (s)atisfaction, (p)erformance, (a)ctivity, (c)ommunication and (e)fficiency, but there is no single metric to measure. Satisfaction relates to a developer's envi-ronment so that he can identify with the team and the tools used [10, 11]. The performance describes how quickly a developer can implement a functionality [10]. However, Forsgren acknowledges: "The performance of software develop-ers is hard to quantify". There is also a two-way relationship between software quality and performance. Activity is described by a number of actions and out-puts that occur as part of the work. Communication and colloboration measures how people communicate and work with each other. Developer efficiency and flow measures the extent to which development work is accomplished without external disruption from people or systems [10, 12].

3   Research Approach, Objectives, Methodology

3.1   Approach

The approach we propose is a sequence of chapters that aim at answering con-tiguous aforementioned research questions. In the beginning, the scope of the investigation is determined. For this purpose, the distribution of frameworks or libraries like Angular, React and Vue.JS on Github and scientific papers should be examined. The three most popular frameworks are selected for the further procedure. The frameworkless approach is chosen for these approaches, too. At the end of this step, the technologies to be examined have been selected and understood.

Second, it is examined how security and maintainability can be measured in client-side web-applications, which are using web-frameworks or libraries.

Third, concepts and patterns in the state-of-the-art web-frameworks identi-fied and reviewed (RQ1). Then it is examined how the concrete implementation takes place in the specified technologies and how the usage of the implementation can be found automatically.

According to the state of the art, it should be examined how the non-functional requirements performance, resource efficiency, security and maintain-ability can be applied and automatically evaluated for the concepts on hand (RQ2). This should make the selected non-functional requirements comparable.

The result of this is that an automated evaluation can take place and it was evaluated which framework best implements the respective concept.

Based on the evaluated implementations from the previous work, a concept with the aim to increase security and maintainability is to be developed (RQ3). As a result there is a concept based on W3C web-components created, to increase developer productivity through security and maintainability.

At last a proof-of-concept of the developed concept should take place. First, a selection is made which open-source web browser should be extended in the form of Chromium or Firefox. The browser engine is then supplemented with the concepts developed previously. The implementation will be evaluated and compared with the previous implementations. At the end, it should have turned out that the concept created is resilient and meets the non-functional requirements.

3.2   Methodology

Identify Popular Frameworks. A systematic review of papers is carried out in order to select the relevant frameworks and libraries. For this purpose, publications are first classified according to the keywords web frameworks and web libraries. This is followed by further filtering according to client-side concepts, which are executed in the web browser. The results are categorized according to the examined aspects. It can then be quantitatively determined which framework has been examined and how. In addition, surveys such as those from Stackoverflow are used [17].

Measure Security and Maintainability. In order to measure the security and maintainability requirements in frameworks and libraries, the state of the art is worked out [20,21]. Based on these requirements, the essential concepts and patterns from the frameworks are examined and evaluated. In addition, it is discovered how to verify which concepts are used in a web application.

Examination and Distribution of Concepts and Patterns. In order to examine the distribution of concepts and patterns, a self-implemented crawler is used to automatically review existing Github repositories to determine which software projects have used these concepts. In addition, it is worked out how and to what extend these patterns are used in open source projects on Github.

Evaluation of Non-functional Requirements. The state of the art for measuring the non-functional requirements (NFR) of performance, resource efficiency, security and maintainability is developed and, if necessary, transferred to web applications [10,21]. It is then ensured that the measurement of concepts and patterns of the web applications can be carried out automatically.

Concepts of Web-Technologies. The concept wills consist of the aspects 1) standard interface for developers, 2) documentation of this interface and 3) description of the internal functioning, so that implementation in web browsers or libraries is possible. The documentation will be based on the specifications and the form of the organizations WHATWG and ECMA-International.

Modern Web-Browsers. The browsers like Chrome and Edge are based on Chromium's open-source engine. A JavaScript engine is used within a browser, which implements the ECMAScript standard. The V8 engine is an example. The guidelines and requirements of a web-browser must be followed to create a transferable proof-of-concept as a JavaScript-library. The library is evaluated against the specified NFRs.

4   Current State and Roadmap

As part of the EFRE-project Vet:ProVieh, the frameworkless approach was successfully applied and a progressive web app was developed, which implements various business cases from the veterinary industry. On the one hand disadvantages of frameworkless development could be confirmed from the project, as basic patterns such as listings, virtual DOM or two-way binding had to be implemented independently. Furthermore it can be confirmed that complex compositions of web components limit maintainability [20]. On the other hand, the application is very performant and resource-efficient.

Familiarization with Angular and Frameworkless Development has taken place. Currently, the systematic review of web frameworks is being carried out. Significant papers have been identified and will be examined in more depth.

The Proposal should be achieved within four years. The induction phase will be completed in three months. 12 months are planned for the identification of the concepts. The current technology is then evaluated over a period of nine months. The concept will then be maintained a period of 12 months. The proof-of-concept will be carried out over the next six months. Six months are planned for submissions, discussions and defense.

5   Conclusion and Future Work

With the approach described, a concept can be developed that improves the W3C web components in terms of security and maintainability. The procedure described can contribute to the research field of web engineering: a) client-side web applications can be better examined systematically with regard to the non-functional requirements of performance, resource efficiency, security and maintainability, b) comparability and evaluation of frameworks and libraries can be improved, c) insights into client-side web architectures and patterns are gained and d) a viable concept for the extension of W3C web-components and the frameworkless development is created.

The result is a evaluated concept to create secure and maintainable web components. The proof-of-concept met the WHATWG and ECMA specifications and can be transferred. This is the foundation for long-term, intercompatibility and stable client-side web applications and could be adopted into the standard to support a large number of applications.

References

1. Basili, V.R., Briand, L.C., Melo, W.L.: How reuse influences productivity in object-oriented systems. Commun. ACM **39**(10), 104–116 (1996)
2. Mohagheghi, P., et al.: An empirical study of software reuse vs. defect-density and stability. In: Proceedings. 26th International Conference on Software Engineering. IEEE (2004)
3. Abdalkareem, R., et al.: Why do developers use trivial packages? An empirical case study on npm. In: Proceedings of the 2017 11th Joint Meeting on Foundations of Software Engineering (2017)
4. Bogart, C., et al.: When and how to make breaking changes: policies and practices in 18 open source software ecosystems. ACM Trans. Softw. Eng. Methodol. (TOSEM) **30**(4), 1–56 (2021)
5. Abate, P., et al.: Dependency solving: a separate concern in component evolution management. J. Syst. Softw. **85**(10), 2228–2240 (2012)
6. Bavota, G., et al.: How the apache community upgrades dependencies: an evolutionary study. Empir. Softw. Eng. **20**(5), 1275–1317 (2015). https://doi.org/10.1007/s10664-014-9325-9
7. Decan, A., et al.: On the topology of package dependency networks: a comparison of three programming language ecosystems. In: Proceedings of the 10th European Conference on Software Architecture Workshops (2016)
8. Zimmermann, M., et al.: Small world with high risks: a study of security threats in the npm ecosystem. In: 28th USENIX Security Symposium (USENIX Security 19) (2019)
9. Haraine Rayne: 'Critical Severity' Warning: Malware Found in Widely Deployed npm Packages, Security-Week (Web), November 2021
10. Forsgren, N., et al.: The SPACE of developer productivity: there's more to it than you think. Queue **19**(1), 20–48 (2021)
11. Storey, M.A., Zimmermann, T., et al.: Towards a theory of software developer job satisfaction and perceived productivity. IEEE Trans. Softw. Eng. **47**, 2125–2142 (2019)
12. Brumby, D.P., Janssen, C.P., Mark, G.: How do interruptions affect productivity? In: Sadowski, C., Zimmermann, T. (eds.) Rethinking Productivity in Software Engineering, pp. 85–107. Apress, Berkeley, CA (2019). https://doi.org/10.1007/978-1-4842-4221-6_9
13. Macdonald, F.: A programmer almost broke the Internet last week by deleting 11 lines of code (2016). http://www.sciencealert.com/how-a-programmer-almost-broke-the-internet-by-deleting-11-lines-of-code
14. Strazzullo, F.: Frameworkless Front-End Development - Do You Control Your Dependencies or Are They Controlling You? Apress (2019). https://doi.org/10.1007/978-1-4842-4967-3
15. W3C: HTML-Templates (2014). https://www.w3.org/TR/html-templates/
16. WHATWG: HTML Standard (2022). https://html.spec.whatwg.org/multipage/custom-elements.html#custom-elements. Updated 21.01.22

17. Stack Overflow: Stack Overflow Developer Survey 2021 (2021). https://insights. stackoverflow.com/survey/2021. Accessed 29 Jan 22

18. Ahmaro, I., Abualkishik, A.M., Yusoff, M.Z.M.: Taxonomy, definition, approaches, benefits, reusability levels, factors and adaption of software reusability: a review of the research literature. J. Appl. Sci. **14**(20), 2396–2421 (2014)

19. Kulesza, R., de Sousa, M.F., de Araújo, M.L.M., de Araújo, C.P., Filho, A.M.: Evolution of web systems architectures: a roadmap. In: Roesler, V., Barrére, E., Willrich, R. (eds.) Special Topics in Multimedia, IoT and Web Technologies, pp. 3–21. Springer, Cham (2020). https://doi.org/10.1007/978-3-030-35102-1_1

20. Krug, M., Gaedke, M.: SmartComposition: bringing component-based software engineering to the web. In: Proceedings of the 17th International Conference on Information Integration and Web-based Applications & Services (2015)

21. Herzberg, M.: Formal Foundations for Provably Safe Web Components. Dissertation, University of Sheffield (2019)

FAIRification of Citizen Science Data

Reynaldo Alvarez Luna[1]([⊠]) [iD], José Zubcoff[2] [iD], Irene Garrigós[2] [iD],
and Hector Gonz[1] [iD]

[1] University of Informatics Sciences, Havana, Cuba
{rluna,hglez}@uci.cu
[2] Department of Languages and Computing Systems, University of Alicante,
Alicante, Spain
{jose.zubcoff,igarrigos}@ua.es

Abstract. Citizen Science (CS) initiatives encourage citizens to collect local data, contributing to knowledge creation and scientific development. However, these CS initiatives do not follow metadata nor data-sharing standards, which hampers their discoverability and reusability out of the scope of them. To improve this scenario in CS is crucial to consider Findable, Accessible, Interoperable and Reusable (FAIR) guidelines for research data sharing. This work proposes a FAIRification process (i.e. making CS initiatives more FAIR compliant), enhancing data sharing capacities in the CS context. It will be considered the adoption of Web standards, Web application programming interfaces (APIs) and Web augmentation. This approach contributes to the production of FAIR data in CS for data consumers. As preliminary results this paper explains the FAIRification process. The research objectives and plan are also presented.

Keywords: Citizen science · Data sharing · FAIR guidelines · Open data

1 Introduction

Citizen Science (CS) has different definitions depending on the scope, but it is mainly considered as a collaborative process to generate knowledge [10]. As stated in [5], CS is crucial in the production of relevant data to analyse and monitor certain natural, economic or social processes. Therefore, CS initiatives support the growth of research data, with millions of volunteers generating data from observations and sensors [2].

One of the Ten Principles of CS [13] refers to data sharing, aiming that "Citizen science project data and metadata are made publicly available and where possible, results are published in an open-access format". From its inception CS aims to open data and contribute to science. However, in practice even if the data is available, it is difficult to discover it outside the project's environment. Further on this issue, some reviews works identify the need for standards adoption by the platforms and infrastructures supporting CS initiatives [6,11]. In

© Springer Nature Switzerland AG 2022
T. Di Noia et al. (Eds.): ICWE 2022, LNCS 13362, pp. 450–454, 2022.
https://doi.org/10.1007/978-3-031-09917-5_34

[3,14] difficulties in accessing data and metadata are highlighted. These works reveal challenges in ensuring interoperability through data standards, or building robust and sustainable infrastructures. At this point, the main problems identified which hampers data sharing in CS projects are: (i) the lack of open access to data and metadata, (ii) the indiscriminate use of metadata without using widely adopted standards, and (iii) the unavailable services solutions to facilitate the reuse of data. These problems are hindering the discovery of data generated by CS initiatives. It consequently limits the access of data scientists and data consumers in generating value through applications or data analytics. The investment of time for improving the replicability and scalability of CS projects is claimed by the COST Action report [12].

In [16] there were defined the FAIR (Findable, Accessible, Interoperable and Reusable) guidelines to tackle the data problems explained before. The development of solutions that aim to comply with the FAIR guidelines are fundamentally based on the adoption of recognised Web standards. There are several proposals [1,7,15] based on the adoption of Data Catalogue Vocabulary (DCAT[1]) to improve the data compliance with the FAIR guidelines. If DCAT is properly implemented, it facilitates the interoperability and findability of dataset metadata and its consumption by using different applications [7]. In addition to adopting the DCAT standard, more efforts are required to achieve FAIR data by allowing also the data reuse and access. For this purpose, in this thesis we are going to consider the automatic generation of Web APIs [9] in order to improve reusability of the available data. Moreover, since citizens are generally not experts in the field, the accessibility of data is crucial. Thus, in this work, Web augmentation solutions [8] will be developed to enrich the user interaction with data.

Therefore, we aim to define a FAIRification process - i.e. making CS data FAIR - fulfilling the following objectives:

- reviewing existing CS platforms regarding FAIR guidelines' compliance
- mapping metadata from CS platforms and from DCAT
- providing access to CS data through Web APIs
- developing of Web augmenters to improve the user interaction with data
- evaluating our FAIRification approach

This paper is structured as follows. In Sect. 2, the current work and preliminary results are detailed. The Sect. 3 describes the methodology and the main research steps.

2 Current Work and Preliminary Results

This thesis development is now in the first research year. So far, a process has been defined for improving the CS data compliance with FAIR guidelines (i.e. FAIRification process) which is explained in the next section. This process has

---

[1] https://www.w3.org/TR/vocab-dcat-3/.

to be improved based on the evaluation experiments performed. Moreover, a review of existing CS platforms regarding FAIR guidelines compliance has been carried out.

2.1   FAIRification of Citizen Science Platforms

The analysis of data repositories of CS platforms shows the lack of metadata and sharing standards adoption, hampering the fulfilment of FAIR guidelines. In this section we define our FAIRification process which aim is to (i) enrich CS platforms by means of mapping elements from the PPSR-Core metadata[2] (profusely used in CS projects) to their counterparts from the W3C standard DCAT metadata, as well as (ii) generate Web APIs to facilitate the access to the corresponding CS data. The whole process is represented by the schema in Fig. 1.

The process begins when a data publisher or a platform manager retrieves

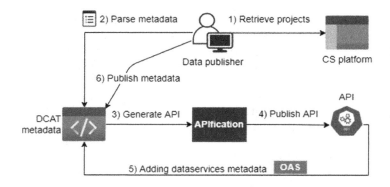

Fig. 1. General process for improving FAIR

the metadata of the catalogue. Then, the second step consists of parsing the relevant metadata fields to the DCAT vocabulary. Once the DCAT specification is generated, a dataset is accessible through the project metadata specification. In this step we increase data interoperability by adopting standards. Regarding reusability, the process continues with the step 3 from Fig. 1, which consists of an APIfication process [9] to facilitate the data sharing improving the accessibility and reusability. When the Web API is published (step 4), the specification of data services is thus added to the DCAT metadata (step 5). Finally, the process ends with the publication of the complete metadata catalogue defined as step 6.

The generated DCAT file within the process is validated with a SHACL online validator,[3] using the generic profile of DCAT. The validation report returns a positive conformance result for the tested RDF files. This implies that the implemented parser generates DCAT complaint outputs ready to be shared as a data catalogue.

---

[2] https://core.citizenscience.org/.
[3] https://data.vlaanderen.be/shacl-validator/.

3   Methodology and Research Plan

The methodology for the research is Action Research [4]. Its core activities consists on identifying a problem, finding a solution and demonstrating that the solution is feasible. Following this methodology, the research was planned in an incremental way. The FAIR guidelines qualities are approached in different research phases as will be detailed below.

During the current first year of the research, the main related work is being analysed identifying issues for improving CS data sharing. Moreover, the FAIRification process defined in previous section has been developed. This work entitled "FAIRification of Citizen Science data through metadata-driven Web API development" has been submitted for the main conference of the International Conference on Web Engineering (ICWE 2022). This process includes the adoption of DCAT and the automatic generation of Web APIs regarding findability, interoperability and reusability (F, I and R from FAIR).

In the second year of the research, as seen in Fig. 2, we will complete the FAIRification process considering data accessibility (A from FAIR). This will be carried out through the definition and development of Web augmenters for improving user interaction with CS projects data.

Finally, in the third and last year, the FAIRification process will be further improved based on its empirical evaluation with several case studies. Furthermore, in each year the research progress will be published in different international conferences and journals within the research scope.

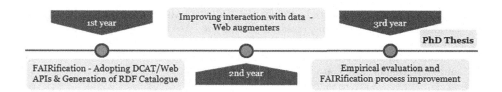

Fig. 2. Research timeline

Acknowledgements. This research work has been partially funded by the Proyecto Habana 2021.

References

1. Albertoni, R., et al.: Data catalog vocabulary (DCAT)-version 2. World Wide Web Consortium (2020)
2. Baker, B.: Frontiers of citizen science: explosive growth in low-cost technologies engage the public in research. Bioscience **66**(11), 921–927 (2016)
3. Bowser, A., et al.: Still in need of norms: the state of the data in citizen science. Citizen Sci. Theory Pract. **5**(1) (2020)

4. Clark, J.S., Porath, S., Thiele, J., Jobe, M.: Action Research. New Prairie Press, New York (2020)

5. Cooper, C.B., Rasmussen, L.M., Jones, E.D.: Perspective: the power (dynamics) of open data in citizen science. Front. Clim. **3**, 57 (2021)

6. De Pourcq, K., Ceccaroni, L.: On the importance of data standards in citizen science— COST action CA15212. Citizen Science Cost Action (2018)

7. Färber, M., Lamprecht, D.: The data set knowledge graph: creating a linked open data source for data sets. Quant. Sci. Stud., 1–30 (2021)

8. González-Mora, C., Garrigós, I., Casteleyn, S., Firmenich, S.: A web augmentation framework for accessibility based on voice interaction. In: Bielikova, M., Mikkonen, T., Pautasso, C. (eds.) ICWE 2020. LNCS, vol. 12128, pp. 547–550. Springer, Cham (2020). https://doi.org/10.1007/978-3-030-50578-3_42

9. González-Mora, C., Garrigós, I., Zubcoff, J., Mazón, J.N.: Model-based generation of web application programming interfaces to access open data. J. Web Eng. **19**, 194–217 (2020)

10. Haklay, M.M., Dörler, D., Heigl, F., Manzoni, M., Hecker, S., Vohland, K.: What is citizen science? The challenges of definition. In: The Science of Citizen Science, p. 13 (2021)

11. Liu, H.Y., Dörler, D., Heigl, F., Grossberndt, S.: Citizen science platforms. In: The Science of Citizen Science, p. 439 (2021)

12. Perelló, J., et al.: The recent past and possible futures of citizen science: final remarks. In: The Science of Citizen Science, p. 517 (2021)

13. Robinson, L.D., Cawthray, J.L., West, S.E., Bonn, A., Ansine, J.: Ten principles of citizen science. In: Citizen Science: Innovation in Open Science, Society and Policy, pp. 27–40 (2018)

14. Shwe, K.M.: Study on the data management of citizen science: from the data life cycle perspective. Data Inf. Manage. **4**(4), 279–296 (2020)

15. Tompkins, V.T., Honick, B.J., Polley, K.L., Qin, J.: MetaFAIR: a metadata application profile for managing research data. Proc. Assoc. Inf. Sci. Technol. **58**(1), 337–345 (2021)

16. Wilkinson, M.D., et al.: The fair guiding principles for scientific data management and stewardship. Sci. Data **3**(1), 1–9 (2016)

Towards Differentially Private Machine Learning Models and Their Robustness to Adversaries

Alberto Carlo Maria Mancino[✉] and Tommaso Di Noia

Politecnico di Bari, Bari, Italy
{alberto.mancino,tommaso.dinoia}@poliba.it

Abstract. The pervasiveness of modern machine learning algorithms exposes users to new vulnerabilities: violation of sensitive information stored in the training data and wrong model behaviors caused by adversaries. State-of-the-art approaches to prevent such behaviors are usually based on Differential Privacy (DP) and Adversarial Training (AT). DP is a rigorous formulation of privacy in probabilist terms to prevent information leakages that could reveal private information about the users, while AT algorithms empirically increase the system's robustness, injecting adversarial examples during the training process. Both techniques involve achieving their goal by modeling noise introduced into the system. We propose analyzing the relationship between these two techniques, studying how one affects the other. Our objective is to design a mechanism that guarantees DP and robustness against adversarial attacks, injecting modeled noise into the system. We propose Recommender Systems as an application scenario because of the severe risks to user privacy and system sensitivity to adversaries.

Keywords: Differential privacy · Adversarial training · Recommender systems · Privacy preservation · System robustness

1 Introduction

In the Big Data era, machine learning (ML) models are widely used in heterogeneous scenarios, enhancing most of the massive data available on the Web. Their exceptional performance on many learning tasks has enabled the emergence of several new services that users can benefit from in their everyday digital lives. However, to provide personalized services, they need access to a sizeable fine-grained collection of user data, critically raising the risks concerning their privacy.

Despite the benefits of legitimate ML applications, the potential risk of infringing user privacy must not be underestimated, and nowadays, people are increasingly aware of the risks they run by sharing their data. This common feeling of insecurity led the governments to legislate to regulate the usage and manipulation of users' sensible data. Some examples are the GDPR by the European Union [8], the CCPA in California [5], and the Cybersecurity Law in China [20].

© Springer Nature Switzerland AG 2022
T. Di Noia et al. (Eds.): ICWE 2022, LNCS 13362, pp. 455–461, 2022.
https://doi.org/10.1007/978-3-031-09917-5_35

Among the most widely used ML models on the Web, **Recommender Systems** (RSs) play a central role due to their ability to intercept and imitate user preferences. Online platforms benefit from the ability of these systems to exploit side information [4] and extrapolate behavioral patterns from historical users' interactions and assist them in facing the overwhelming quantity of products, with lists of personalized recommendations. However, everything has two sides, so do RSs.

RSs require users to provide their personal preferences for different items to compute tailored recommendations. The primary efforts of industry and academia have focused on improving recommendation accuracy while finding a suitable tradeoff between privacy and personalization is still an open question. Numerous privacy-preserving recommenders have been proposed in recent years, including **differential privacy** (DP) [7].

DP is a rigorous and provable formulation of privacy in probabilistic terms. The output of a model that respects the DP paradigm is insensitive to adding or removing a particular record. DP injects noise into sensitive data or the computation to achieve its goal. The strength of DP is the ability to quantify the privacy budget ϵ and the lower computational effort required concerning other classic privacy-preserving techniques.

Admitting protecting the users' privacy is a critical concern for Recommender Systems, their exposure to adversaries able to exploit their vulnerabilities must also be taken into account. RSs are affected by two main risks: integrity and availability. Compromising the integrity means inducing the system to produce an output different from the original one. While compromising the availability means reducing the recommendation performance.

Adversarial Training (AT) [11] is receiving considerable attention from the research community as a proven method against adversarial attacks [16]. The basic idea behind AT is to inject adversarial examples, slightly perturbated data aiming to fool the system, during the training loops. A system trained as just mentioned can face adversaries attacks without sensibly changing its behavior.

Recent works have shown the fragility of recommenders, like BPR, to adversarial perturbations [12], i.e., small perturbation added to the recommender model parameters. *He et al.* [12] proposed a defence strategy named *adversarial regularizer*, a solution based on the adversarial training procedure. Their work showed that it is possible to build a recommender system robust to adversarial noise and paved the way for different novel models that improved the robustness of recommender systems.

Given the vulnerabilities of recommender systems, concerning both privacy preservation, and adversarial robustness, and see the diversity of the different solutions proposed in the literature, my research aims to investigate the following open question: **is there a rigorous way to implement a recommender system able to protect users' privacy under the DP paradigm and be robust against adversarial perturbation?**

Recent papers like [14] demonstrate a connection between differential privacy and robustness against adversarial examples. Nevertheless, it is still an under-investigated field despite the fundamental role of the two aspects in our daily life. Furthermore, to the best of my knowledge, very few works have focused on the specific field of RSs.

However, an initial study [10] underlines the risk of applying DP techniques when facing adversarial attacks: the noise introduced in the system could help the attacker remain undetected, potentially facilitating him/her ability to degrade the system performances. Thus, a further research question arises: **could differential privacy impact the robustness of a ML system? Which is the interplay between DP and AT?**

In addition, studies on DP and AT indicate that the separate application of both techniques weakens recommender systems' accuracy. So, it is crucial to consider the following question: **how much does DP and AT impact separately the accuracy of the RSs? How do the performances vary when applied both?**

2 Research Overview

This section briefly summarizes the latest research contributions about differential privacy and adversarial training in machine learning, particularly in recommender systems. Then describes the earliest solutions proposed in the literature that combine both techniques and analyze the consequences.

2.1 Privacy Preservation with Differential Privacy (DP)

Differential Privacy (DP) [7] is a mathematical definition of privacy related to the quantity of information of an individual an attacker could disclose. Given a generic computation over the data we want to protect, DP proves that the structured injection of noise can hide the characteristics of the individuals of the system.

Consider a randomized mechanism $\mathcal{M}$ that takes as input a dataset d and returns a value in a space $\mathcal{O}$. $\mathcal{M}$ is said to satisfy DP if given any two adjacent datasets d_1 and d_2, that differ by only one record, and for any subset of possible outputs $\mathcal{S} \subseteq \mathcal{O}$, we have

$$P(\mathcal{M}(d_1) \in \mathcal{S}) < e^{\epsilon} P(\mathcal{M}(d_2) \in \mathcal{S}) + \delta \tag{1}$$

where $e > 0$ and $\delta \in [0, 1]$ are parameters that define the privacy strength of the randomized mechanism. Concretely DP is a rigorous and quantifiable guarantee for removing or adding a record in the dataset without sensibly altering the algorithm's outcome. Consequentially, a malicious attacker can not distinguish the presence or absence of an individual in the dataset.

In recommender systems (RS), a formal application of DP was introduced by McSherry et al. [17] with a collaborative filtering model. They propose randomizing the users' ratings before sharing them with the system and factor the learning algorithm into two phases, aggregation/learning and individual recommendation. Then they analyze the impact of privacy adaptations on the accuracy performance. Other works [13,22] propose to inject noise, usually laplacian, directly into the objective function, satisfying the differential privacy. At the same time, Friedman et al. [9] studied an approach with noisy ratings and a strategy that exploits a perturbed version of the stochastic gradient descent. De Montjove [19] also proposed to perturb the input of the recommender, but in the specific area of point-of-interest recommendation.

2.2 Robustness to Adversaries with Adversarial Training (AT)

Researchers have shown that ML models are susceptible to small perturbations [3,21]. Adversaries could exploit this behavior to compromise the system's proper functioning with imperceptible perturbations. Figure 1 of [11] is a classic example of how it is possible to lead a system to a misclassification. Goodfellow et al. [11] proposed *adversarial training*, a defense based on the minimax learning strategy to address this drawback, defined as in Eq. 2.

$$\min_{\Theta}[\mathcal{L}(f(\mathbf{x};\Theta),y) + \lambda \underbrace{\max_{\delta:\|\delta\|\leq\epsilon} \mathcal{L}(f(\mathbf{x}+\delta;\Theta),y)}_{\text{Adversarial Regularizer}}] \tag{2}$$

$$\underbrace{\phantom{\min_{\Theta}[\mathcal{L}(f(\mathbf{x};\Theta),y) + \lambda \max_{\delta:\|\delta\|\leq\epsilon} \mathcal{L}(f(\mathbf{x}+\delta;\Theta),y)]}}_{\text{Adversarial Regularized Loss}}$$

The *adversarial regularizer* mitigates the attack surface considering an adversary's behavior who aims to maximize the system's loss.

The same behavior also applies to Recommender Systems, where a malicious can destroy the accuracy of the systems with injected noise [6,12,15,18].

A recommender's three main components could be principally perturbed by an adversary: the interactions (e.g., injecting fake records), the side-information data, and the model parameters. The adversarial training techniques have also been applied to recommenders to improve their *robustness to adversaries*, i.e., their capacity to not significantly change the output when adversary noise is instilled into the system.

2.3 The Interplay Between DP and AT

Sections 2.1 and 2.2 underlined the growing need to consider the vulnerabilities of ML models, particularly with RSs. Differential privacy is necessary to guarantee the protection of user data while adversarial training robustifies the system against malicious attacks.

Although it is fair that a system should guarantee both the cited aspects, the literature still lacks studies that clarify how to design such a model. Lecuyer et al. [14] proved the existence of a connection between DP and AT. Their study provides a formal definition of adversarial robustness in mathematical terms. Then applying DP to the input, they derived stability bounds for the expected output and combined them with their definition of robustness. In this way, they derived a certified defense and proved its efficacy against adversarial attacks.

Another research direction studied how an attacker could leverage the DP noise to compromise the system's integrity, acting undetected. Giraldo et al. showed that an attacker could fool the adversarial classifier when DP noise is injected into the system, with the possibility of biasing the model more than he/she could do without the application of DP. They evaluate their hypothesis over a traffic congestion problem

These works demonstrate that a connection between DP and AT exists, but it is not obvious that it could benefit the privacy and robustness performance. Furthermore, both impacts on the system's accuracy must be taken into account. These aspects, and the open possibilities and needs in Recommender Systems, motivate my research in studying the interplay between these two crucial techniques. It is still under-discussed the relationship of both techniques with a privacy-by-design technique as Federated Learning [2].

3   Research Direction

Here I summarize the direction of my research proposal being in the first year of my Ph.D., given the potentialities and the limits briefly described in Sect. 2 about modeling a recommender that grants differential privacy (DP) and robustness to adversaries, with adversarial training (AT).

Different studies highlighted how much both DP and AT could degrade the accuracy performances [1,17]. Consequently, I propose first analyzing the trade-off between **utility**, **privacy** and **security** in RSs. The study aims to evaluate how applying differential privacy simultaneously with adversarial training on the same recommender affects its accuracy and beyond-accuracy metrics. The performance could be evaluated varying the nature of the recommender system (such as latent factor, neural, graph-based), the DP and AT algorithms, and the privacy/perturbation budget.

Then it is necessary to deepen when and how differential privacy and adversarial training influence the performances of each other. The nature of the relationship between these two methods is still undisclosed.

Finally, the findings could be formalized to propose a rigorous formulation on modeling a secure and private recommender system quantifying the amount of sacrificed accuracy.

References

1. Anelli, V.W., Bellogín, A., Deldjoo, Y., Di Noia, T., Merra, F.A.: MSAP: multi-step adversarial perturbations on recommender systems embeddings. In: FLAIRS Conference (2021)
2. Anelli, V.W., Deldjoo, Y., Di Noia, T., Ferrara, A., Narducci, F.: How to put users in control of their data in federated top-n recommendation with learning to rank. In: SAC, pp. 1359–1362. ACM (2021)
3. Anelli, V.W., Di Noia, T., Malitesta, D., Merra, F.A.: Assessing perceptual and recommendation mutation of adversarially-poisoned visual recommenders (short paper). In: DP@AI*IA. CEUR Workshop Proceedings, vol. 2776, pp. 49–56. CEUR-WS.org (2020)
4. Anelli, V.W., Di Noia, T., Di Sciascio, E., Ferrara, A., Mancino, A.C.M.: Sparse feature factorization for recommender systems with knowledge graphs. In: RecSys, pp. 154–165. ACM (2021)
5. California State Legislature: The California consumer privacy act of 2018 (2018). https://leginfo.legislature.ca.gov/faces/billTextClient.xhtml?bill_id=201720180A B375
6. Deldjoo, Y., Di Noia, T., Di Sciascio, E., Merra, F.A.: How dataset characteristics affect the robustness of collaborative recommendation models. In: SIGIR, pp. 951–960. ACM (2020)
7. Dwork, C.: Differential privacy. In: Bugliesi, M., Preneel, B., Sassone, V., Wegener, I. (eds.) ICALP 2006. LNCS, vol. 4052, pp. 1–12. Springer, Heidelberg (2006). https://doi.org/10.1007/11787006_1
8. European Commission: 2018 reform of EU data protection rules (2018). https://ec. europa.eu/info/priorities/justice-and-fundamental-rights/data-protection/2018-reform-eu-data-protection-rules/eu-data-protection-rules_en
9. Friedman, A., Berkovsky, S., Kaafar, M.A.: A differential privacy framework for matrix factorization recommender systems. User Model. User-Adapt. Interact. **26**(5), 425–458 (2016). https://doi.org/10.1007/s11257-016-9177-7
10. Giraldo, J., Cárdenas, A.A., Kantarcioglu, M., Katz, J.: Adversarial classification under differential privacy. In: NDSS. The Internet Society (2020)
11. Goodfellow, I.J., Shlens, J., Szegedy, C.: Explaining and harnessing adversarial examples. In: ICLR (Poster) (2015)
12. He, X., He, Z., Du, X., Chua, T.: Adversarial personalized ranking for recommendation. In: SIGIR, pp. 355–364. ACM (2018)
13. Hua, J., Xia, C., Zhong, S.: Differentially private matrix factorization. In: IJCAI, pp. 1763–1770. AAAI Press (2015)
14. Lécuyer, M., Atlidakis, V., Geambasu, R., Hsu, D., Jana, S.: Certified robustness to adversarial examples with differential privacy. In: IEEE Symposium on Security and Privacy, pp. 656–672. IEEE (2019)
15. Li, B., Wang, Y., Singh, A., Vorobeychik, Y.: Data poisoning attacks on factorization-based collaborative filtering. In: NIPS, pp. 1885–1893 (2016)
16. Maini, P., Wong, E., Kolter, J.Z.: Adversarial robustness against the union of multiple perturbation models. In: ICML. Proceedings of Machine Learning Research, vol. 119, pp. 6640–6650. PMLR (2020)
17. McSherry, F., Mironov, I.: Differentially private recommender systems: building privacy into the Netflix prize contenders. In: KDD, pp. 627–636. ACM (2009)
18. O'Mahony, M.P., Hurley, N.J., Silvestre, G.C.M.: Recommender systems: attack types and strategies. In: AAAI, pp. 334–339. AAAI Press/The MIT Press (2005)

19. Song, Y., Dahlmeier, D., Bressan, S.: Not so unique in the crowd: a simple and effective algorithm for anonymizing location data. In: PIR@SIGIR. CEUR Workshop Proceedings, vol. 1225, pp. 19–24. CEUR-WS.org (2014)
20. Standing Committee of the National People's Congress of Popular Republic of China: China internet security law (2017). http://www.npc.gov.cn/npc/c1481/201507/82ce4cb5549c4f56be8a6744cf2b3273.shtml
21. Szegedy, C., et al.: Intriguing properties of neural networks. In: ICLR (Poster) (2014)
22. Zhang, F., Lee, V.E., Choo, K.R.: JO-DPMF: differentially private matrix factorization learning through joint optimization. Inf. Sci. **467**, 271–281 (2018)

Posters and Demonstrations

A Metadata-Driven Tool for FAIR Data Production in Citizen Science Platforms

Reynaldo Alvarez[1]([✉])(iD), César González-Mora[2](iD), Irene Garrigós[2](iD), and Jose Zubcoff[2](iD)

[1] University of Informatics Sciences, Havana, Cuba
rluna@uci.cu
[2] Department of Languages and Computing Systems, University of Alicante, Alicante, Spain
{cgmora,igarrigos,jose.zubcoff}@ua.es

Abstract. Citizen Science (CS) platforms include a large number of projects that manage data from citizen observations. However, data and metadata are not easily available and do not generally comply with standards. This makes it difficult to share data through the mechanisms commonly used in the scientific community, affecting the reuse of data outside the context of CS platforms. The adoption of Web standards could improve the FAIR (Findable, Accessible, Interoperable and Reusable) quality of shared data. Adopting standards is not enough; it is also important to provide the technologies that make it possible to find the data, access it, share it and be able to interoperate with the data. For this purpose, this paper presents a tool for the production of FAIR data from PPSR (Public Participation in Scientific Research) Core metadata model based platforms. The tool allows (i) transforming metadata from CS platforms to the DCAT (Data Catalogue Vocabulary) standard, (ii) generating Web APIs from the available data, and (iii) building a DCAT-validated data catalogue. This approach improves the FAIR compliance of CS data, empowering data consumers and developers.

Keywords: Citizen Science · DCAT · FAIR · Web APIs

1 Introduction

Citizen Science (CS) is as a collaborative research process, from the citizens, in order to generate knowledge [4]. Due to the growth of data generated by such initiatives, several Web platforms have been developed that host multiple projects. These platforms aim to make CS initiatives visible and accessible. Including their activities, observations, guidelines, examples and relevant outcomes [5]. However, CS data and metadata are poorly accessible or, at best, CS initiatives do not use recognised standards for data sharing. This situation makes it difficult data findability and reusability outside the platforms where they are hosted.

© Springer Nature Switzerland AG 2022
T. Di Noia et al. (Eds.): ICWE 2022, LNCS 13362, pp. 465–468, 2022.
https://doi.org/10.1007/978-3-031-09917-5_36

SciStarter[1] is a CS platform that hosts a representative number (currently 1587) of CS projects [2]. Given the variety of projects SciStarter will be used as an example for the development of this work. Regarding metadata, Scistarter implements the Public Participation Scientific Research (PPSR-Core[2]) metadata model. Although, PPSR-Core is a good step to standardise CS platforms metadata, is a model in development not recognised as standard out of the scope of CS. Therefore, solutions to enrich CS platforms based on the FAIR (Findable, Accessible, Interoperable and Reusable) guidelines [6] ameliorates data sharing. Additionally, FAIR adoption also emphasises discoverability for the integration and reuse of data by the scientific community adopting recognised Web standards like Data Catalogue Vocabulary (DCAT[3]) [1].

In this sense, this paper presents a metadata-driven tool for the production of FAIR data in CS. This approach improves the interoperability ("I" from FAIR) of the platform through the generation of DCAT serialised data. Also, to enforce reusability quality ("R" from FAIR), our proposal includes Web API generation [3] to easily access and reuse CS data. Therefore, data is made findable and accessible ("F&A" from FAIR) out of the scope of CS field to allow better integration of data and its consequent knowledge creation.

2   Enriching CS Platforms Following the FAIR Guidelines

The tool enriches CS platforms through metadata mapping and Web API generation following the FAIR guidelines. The features implemented are represented by the components diagram shown in Fig. 1, and the corresponding programming code is publicly available online in a GitHub repository[4]. The intended users of this tool could be data owners, data consumers and developers.

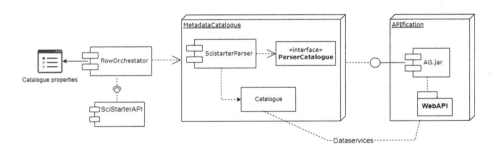

Fig. 1. Components' diagram of the solution

The implemented tool has a functionality for setting up the catalogue metadata input in a *Catalogue properties* file. This properties file contains a descrip-

---

[1] https://scistarter.org/.
[2] https://core.citizenscience.org/docs/.
[3] https://www.w3.org/TR/vocab-dcat-2/.
[4] https://github.com/ralvarezluna/csdatalab-apigen.

tion, the catalogue URL and the source of projects' metadata, as shown in Fig. 2 (a). After the configuration phase, another function retrieves the list of projects from the source specified in the properties file, which could be a local file or a remote endpoint such as *SciStarterAPI*. Once metadata is gathered, the class *ScistarterParser* (implementation of the *ParserCatalogue* interface) maps the metadata fields from Scistarter format to DCAT. This mapped metadata is added to the *Catalogue* object.

Regarding data reuse, the tool has a feature that calls to the *APIfication* block from Fig. 1, which starts the generation of a *Web API* for the corresponding data [3]. Once Web APIs are generated and published, the specification of data services is thus added to the DCAT metadata *Catalogue*. Finally, this *Catalogue* could be exported or persisted to share as serialised linked data. In this sense, an extract of the corresponding serialised output of the catalogue is shown in the Fig. 2 (b).

```
{
    "id": 6285,
    "legacy_id": 100006285,
    "name": "Project Sidewalk",
    "created": 1618958134763.884,
    "updated": 1641593998925.274,
    "guid": "50e842ba-2e17-5def-8532-6a508580ea34",
    "presenter": "The Makeability Lab at the University of Washington",
    "description": "Despite comprehensive civil rights legislation...",
    "url": "https://sidewalk-sea.cs.washington.edu",
    "search_terms": "accessibility,virtual,sidewalk...",
    "regions": null,
    "metadata_publication_url": "https://sidewalk-sea.cs.washington.edu/api",
    "data_publication_url": "https://sidewalk-sea.cs.washington.edu",
    "data_license": "MIT License",
    "sustainable_development_goals": "SDG_11"
}
```

```
@prefix dcat: <http://www.w3.org/ns/dcat#> .
@prefix xsd: <http://www.w3.org/2001/XMLSchema#> .
...
<https://scistarter.org/catalogue/> a dcat:Catalog ;
    dct:description "DCAT catalogue of SciStarter"@en ;
    dct:publisher <https://scistarter.org> ;
    dct:title "SciStarter FAIR catalogue"@en ;
    dcat:dataset <https://scistarter.org/50e842ba-2e17...> ;
<https://scistarter.org/50e842ba-2e17...> a
    dcat:Dataset, dcat:DataService, dcat:Distribution ;
    dct:conformsTo <https://www.w3.org/TR/vocab-dcat-2/> ;
    dcat:description "Despite comprehensive civil rights..."@en ;
    dcat:distribution <https://sidewalk-sea.cs.washington.edu/> ;
    dcat:keyword "accessibility,virtual,sidewalk..."@en ;
    dcat:theme <http://metadata.un.org/sdg/11> .
    dcat:accessURL <https://sidewalk-sea.cs.washington.edu/> ;
    dcat:endpointURL <https://sidewalk-sea.cs.washington.edu/api> ;
    dcat:mediaType <text/csv> .
```

(a)   (b)

Fig. 2. Extracts of the JSON input (a) and the serialised catalogue output (b)

Finally, the generated DCAT RDF file within the process is validated through an implementation of the W3C Shapes Constraint Language (SHACL[5]) online validator[6], using the generic profile of DCAT. The validation report results positive for the output RDF files. The conformity of the validated files, implies that the implemented parser generates DCAT complaints outputs ready to share as data catalogues.

For supporting the catalogue creation as RDF, an open source library called **datacatalogtordf**[7] is used. It supports DCAT specification classes and metadata conversion to RDF using as basis the RDFLib[8], which is a W3C recommended library for Python[9].

---

[5] https://www.w3.org/TR/shacl/.
[6] https://data.vlaanderen.be/shacl-validator/.
[7] https://github.com/Informasjonsforvaltning/datacatalogtordf.
[8] https://rdflib.readthedocs.io/en/stable/#.
[9] https://www.w3.org/2001/sw/wiki/RDFLib.

The developed tool has been tested on more than 300 CS projects from SciStarter using random queries. The tool can be applicable to all JSON accessible data catalogues that follow PPSR-Core or at least contain the mandatory attributes required by DCAT. In addition, the tool can be used for creating customized data catalogues.

3   Conclusions

In this paper we present a metadata-driven tool that enriches CS platforms by conforming them to standards and improving their FAIR quality for data sharing. FAIR compliant data production is achieved by (i) mapping and enriching metadata to DCAT, (ii) generating Web APIs, and (iii) validating the DCAT metadata catalogue using a SHACL validator. The generated DCAT metadata and Web APIs improve CS platforms' compliance with FAIR guidelines, making data available in a standard way to data consumers and developers.

The tool features have been presented using SciStarter as example of CS platform. However, it is designed for working with similar PPSR-Core catalogues with minimal development efforts. Therefore, the proposal serves as a driver to follow the path of the FAIR data production in the field of CS. Consequently, as future work, the parser will be extended to support other CS platforms. Moreover, although, the output of the process has been validated, more experimentation tasks will be conducted involving users and performance tests.

References

1. Albertoni, R., et al.: Data catalog vocabulary (DCAT)-version 2. World Wide Web Consortium (2020)
2. Ben Zaken, D., Gal, K., Shani, G., Segal, A., Cavalier, D.: Intelligent recommendations for citizen science. Proc. AAAI Conf. Artif. Intell. **35**(17), 14693–14701 (2021)
3. González-Mora, C., Garrigós, I., Zubcoff, J., Mazón, J.N.: Model-based generation of web application programming interfaces to access open data. J. Web Eng. **19**, 194–217 (2020)
4. Haklay, M.M., Dörler, D., Heigl, F., Manzoni, M., Hecker, S., Vohland, K.: What is citizen science? The challenges of definition. In: Vohland, K., et al. (eds.) The Science of Citizen Science, pp. 13–33. Springer, Cham (2021). https://doi.org/10.1007/978-3-030-58278-4_2
5. Liu, H.-Y., Dörler, D., Heigl, F., Grossberndt, S.: Citizen science platforms. In: Vohland, K., et al. (eds.) The Science of Citizen Science, pp. 439–459. Springer, Cham (2021). https://doi.org/10.1007/978-3-030-58278-4_22
6. Wilkinson, M.D., et al.: The fair guiding principles for scientific data management and stewardship. Sci. Data **3**(1), 1–9 (2016)

A New Compatibility Measure
for Harmonic EDM Mixing

Gabriel Bibbó Frau(✉) and Angel Faraldo⊙

Universitat Pompeu Fabra, Barcelona 08018, Spain
gabobibbo@gmail.com, angel.faraldo@upf.edu

Abstract. DJ track selection can benefit from software-generated recommendations that optimise harmonic transitions. Emerging techniques (such as Tonal Interval Vectors) enable the definition of new metrics for harmonic compatibility (HC) estimation that improve the performance of existing applications. Thus, the aim of this study is to provide the DJ with a new tool to improve his/her musical selections. We present a software package that can estimate the HC between digital music recordings, with a particular focus on modern dance music and the workflow of the DJ. The user must define a target track for which the calculation is to be made, and obtains the HC values expressed as a percentage with respect to each track in the music collection. The system also calculates a pitch transposition interval for each candidate track that, if applied, maximizes the HC with respect to the target track. Its graphical user interface allows the user to easily run it simultaneously with the DJ software of choice during live performances. The system, tested with musically experienced users, generates pitch transposition suggestions that improve mixes in 73.7% of cases.

Keywords: DJ · Harmonic compatibility · Harmonic mixing · Tonal Interval Vector (TIV) · Pitch transposition · Interface

1 Introduction

The primary challenge in music mixing is to make two or more pieces fit together both in tempo and harmony (aligning their temporal and spectral dimensions) [1].

While aligning the tracks in tempo has been explored quite extensively, the automatic harmonic alignment has proved to be a more challenging computational task [1]. Professional DJs use a technique for *harmonic mixing* based on key notation, where successive songs of the DJ set have the same or a related key. That ensures that they fit together harmonically and reduces dissonance when playing two songs at the same time. This technique is by far the most widely used in EDM (Electronic Dance Music), although recent work [1] questions its use in specific cases (e.g. for music outside the major/minor scale framework).

The primary issue is that the key estimation itself might be error-prone. Then, it is not clear how listeners might perceive the mix of two tracks since

© Springer Nature Switzerland AG 2022
T. Di Noia et al. (Eds.): ICWE 2022, LNCS 13362, pp. 469–472, 2022.
https://doi.org/10.1007/978-3-031-09917-5_37

a global property like the key does not provide lower-level information about other elements of the musical composition [2]. Furthermore, this method makes it impossible to determine harmonic compatibility between different tracks sharing the same key, thus motivating a metric below the key level. In addition, key detection algorithms usually return the most prevalent key throughout the track's duration without giving the user the chance to identify the best points in time for mixing. Finally, if the pitch-shifting functionality is used to transpose the musical key, it is essential to consider the quantization effect of only comparing whole semitone shifts. Not considering fine-scale tuning between songs that have the same key could lead to highly dissonant mistuned mixes [2].

To address this lack of analyses, new methods based on perceptual relatedness and consonance have shown to give promising results [3]. The perceptually-motivated Tonal Interval Vector (TIV) feature computes the small- and large-scale HC between pairs of audio tracks in a collection. Another study [4] evaluates the advantages and drawbacks of existing HC measuring algorithms using a database of EDM loops of 32 beats, finding that the TIVs implementations are usually preferred by most listeners [4].

2   Implementation

The entire software is open source and can be downloaded from the project's Github repository.[1] Users can review this web guide to better understand its usage.[2] It was conceived to be used by DJs in live performances, where they have a main track playing and want to find another track that allows them to create a harmonic transition.

For this purpose, we provide information regarding the HC, with a one-to-many mapping, similar to other existing mixing software. This implementation saves the information on disc to optimise the computational cost of analysing the audio tracks, providing a smooth real-time operation.

The main module of the programme deals with the analysis of audio tracks using Music Information Retrieval techniques. They are first source-separated to remove the percussive elements, which do not convey melodic information. A single chroma vector is computed as the mean of the NNLSChroma from each frame, which is then is converted into a Tonal Interval Vector (TIV). The HC is calculated as the *small-scale* measure score between the TIV pairs of candidate and target track.

The optimisation of the system parameters was based on the responses obtained in an experiment with musically trained users. Taking into account their ratings, we re-calibrated the system parameters until we maximised the similarity between the users' responses and our system's suggestions.

---

[1] Project repository https://github.com/gbibbo/harmonic_mix.
[2] Presentation poster: http://hcs.cactuslatam.com/.

3   Evaluation

3.1   Experiment Design

We verified whether users' preferences, in favour of one of two options, coincided with the suggestions of our system by means of an online survey in which 15 people participated.[3] Users were presented with 10 examples, each composed of two 32 beats (16 s) audio fragments, which we call "Clips". Each Clip is the resulting mix from an excerpt of the target track overlapped with an excerpt from the candidate track. One of the two Clips contains the mix of the two tracks in their original version. The other contains the same mix with the original target track, whereas the pitch of the candidate track has been made higher or lower by means of transposition. After each user listened to the clip, they are asked to score the harmonic result of each mix on a scale of 1 to 5.

Summarising, participants were presented with two practically identical Clips, the only difference being that one of them was subject to pitch transposition and, consequently, a different HC value. In this way, we aim to eliminate the variables that can generate pleasure when listening to a mix, so that the user focuses his or her attention on the modification introduced by the pitch alteration.

3.2   Metrics

True Positive Rate (TPR). We did not consider the HC measures in absolute terms, but in relative terms, as the difference in HC values between Clip 1 and Clip 2 (for both the user scores and the HC values suggested by our system). That representation allows to analyse on a case-by-case basis whether the user agreed with the system's suggestions (ref. to as "true positives"). This can be seen in the Fig. 1 by studying the sign of the variables, defining two regions. Samples located in the top right quadrant or the bottom left quadrant (with green background) are "true positives". But samples in the top left quadrant or the bottom right (with red background) correspond to system suggestions that did not match user preferences. Considering the number of scores in the green area, and the total of answers N, we can define the True Positive Rate (TPR), Eq. 1.

$$TPR = \frac{\sum_u \sum_e [c_{e,u} > 0][d_e > 0] + \sum_u \sum_e [c_{e,u} < 0][d_e < 0]}{N - \sum_u \sum_e [c_{e,u} = 0]} \qquad (1)$$

where $c_{e,u}$ is the difference of scores given by user u between Clip 1 and 2 for example e, and d_e is the difference in scores returned by the system. The resulting TPR of our experiment is 73.7%.

Chi-Squared Test. The χ^2 test is the standard way of assessing whether variables c and d are related and dependent. Assuming an $\alpha = 0.05$, which represents a 5% risk in our estimation, results in $\chi^2 = 36,67 > p_{value} = 3,84$. We thus reject the null hypothesis and conclude that our variables are related: to each other: the system's suggestions are not random, but instead match user's preferences.

---

[3] Online survey https://forms.gle/1VaerdHwhvxehuz77.

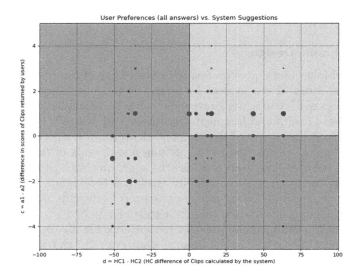

Fig. 1. All user responses in the experiment, plotted against the system suggestions. Bigger dots mean accumulation of equal responses in the same place.

4 Conclusions

Recently, several studies have been published using new techniques based on TIVs, but so far this knowledge has not been made available to the final user. Our comprehensive work includes an extensive analysis of the current techniques used to calculate HC and defines future lines of work to improve the system's performance. The system we propose generates pitch transposition suggestions that improve mixes in 73.7% of the cases. Measuring HC is a very subjective task of which there is little previous experience. In this paper we propose a new method of analysing the results. Finally, by making the system available online, we aim to provide the DJ with more information for successful pitch transpositions.

References

1. Gebhardt, R.B., Margraf, J.: Applying psychoacoustics to key detection and root note extraction in EDM. In: Proceedings of the 13th International Symposium on CMMR, pp. 482–492 (2017)
2. Gebhardt, R., Davies, M., Seeber, B.: Harmonic mixing based on roughness and pitch commonality (2015)
3. Bernardes, G., Cocharro, D., Caetano, M., Guedes, C., Davies, M.E.: A multi-level tonal interval space for modelling pitch relatedness and musical consonance. J. New Music Res. **45**(4), 281–294 (2016)
4. Fernández, M.P.: Harmonic compatibility for loops in electronic music (Doctoral dissertation, Master's thesis. Universitat Pompeu Fabra) (2020)

Compaz: Exploring the Potentials of Shared Dictionary Compression on the Web

Benjamin Wollmer[1,3]([✉]) [ID], Wolfram Wingerath[2,3] [ID], Sophie Ferrlein[3] [ID], Felix Gessert[3] [ID], and Norbert Ritter[1]

[1] University of Hamburg, Hamburg, Germany
{benjamin.wollmer,dbis-research.inf}@uni-hamburg.de
[2] University of Oldenburg, Oldenburg, Germany
data-science@uni-oldenburg.de
[3] Baqend, Hamburg, Germany
research@baqend.com

Abstract. In this demonstration, we present Compaz, an extensible benchmarking tool for web compression that enables evaluating approach-es before they have been fully implemented and deployed. Compaz makes this possible by collecting all relevant data from user journeys on live websites first and then performing the benchmark analysis as a subsequent step with global knowledge of all transmitted resources. In our demonstration scenario, the audience can witness how current websites could improve their compression ratio and save bandwidth. They can choose from standard and widespread approaches such as *Brotli* or *gzip* and advanced approaches like *shared dictionary compression* that are currently not even supported by any browser.

Keywords: Delta encoding · Caching · Dictionary compression

1 Introduction and State of the Art

Compression is one of the critical components to tune the performance of websites. However, we have not seen much movement in browser support of different compression algorithms over the last decades [10]. Since then, *gzip* has been the most widely used format for text-based compression, with *Brotli* as the only noteworthy contender [4]. Nevertheless, advanced approaches like *delta encoding* [6] or *shared dictionary compression* [3,5,7] could achieve better compression ratios using cached data as dictionaries. Since some of these advanced approaches are extremely complex, assessing their true potential for practical use cases remains challenging (especially for approaches that have not been implemented, yet). This paper introduces Compaz, an extensible compression analyzer that can benchmark context-reliant compression approaches without deploying them to an actual website [9]. Similar to tools like WebPageTest, it evaluates an existing website, but with a focus on possible payload improvements instead of the current performance.

© Springer Nature Switzerland AG 2022
T. Di Noia et al. (Eds.): ICWE 2022, LNCS 13362, pp. 473–476, 2022.
https://doi.org/10.1007/978-3-031-09917-5_38

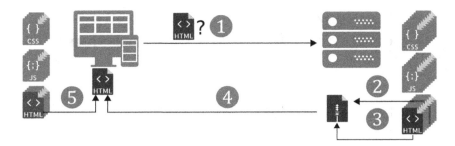

Fig. 1. Sharing the client's context while requesting a file (1) and choosing the best dictionary (2) for compression (3) is a core challenge of shared dictionary approaches.

Motivating Example: Shared Dictionary Compression. We are particularly interested in the potential benefits of advanced shared dictionary compression as illustrated in Fig. 1. A client request (1) shares its context, like the cache state, while requesting a file. The server could choose one of those files to be the dictionary (2) used for compressing the requested file (3) and send the compressed file to the client (4). The client uses its cached files (5) along the compressed file to compute the initially requested file. This has some implications: First, the client needs to describe its cache state to the server. Since the cache can easily hold hundreds of files, sharing a list of every file in the cache is not feasible. Furthermore, the server would need to have every file of the client cache at hand, which can work for static content, but is especially difficult for dynamically rendered HTML. Moreover, the server would have to know which cache entry would be the best dictionary for this request. Still, this is a simplification of the problem, and for the best performance, this would need support for other advanced caching techniques [8] and CDNS. Since the compression result depends on the client cache, the results differ for each user, and therefore, the cache hit rate on the CDN level could drastically suffer from such an approach. This indicates that an implementation would be some approximation but not the optimal solution for data saving. Nevertheless, testing actual implementations is currently not easily done. While we had browser support for shared dictionary compression over HTTP (SDCH), it was removed due to a lack of traction [1], and as a result, browser support for custom dictionaries is currently nonexistent, and we have to fall back to a synthetic environment. Unlike static dictionary approaches like Brotli [2], user data is necessary to evaluate the impact of (dynamic) shared dictionary compression, since the compression result depends on the available dictionaries (e.g., previously visited HTML files) in the current client context and cannot be tested with a static set of files.

2   Compaz in a Nutshell

Generally, Compaz can be split into three parts: The collection of input data, the benchmarking of compression algorithms, and the data access.

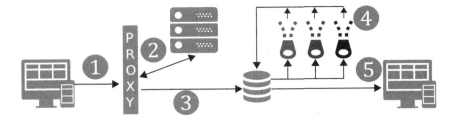

Fig. 2. Compaz utilizes a proxy to capture user journeys (1–2) and persists them in a database (3), so that the journey data can be used by different compressors (4) to compare the approaches (5).

Collecting Data. Compaz utilizes Selenium[1] to navigate through user-defined journeys. Compaz currently supports three ways to define a journey. First, it can be defined as a static list of URLs, where Compaz will call the URLs one by one. Similarly, a list of regular expressions can be defined. These will be used to find links within the HTML so that Compaz will click them and proceed with the navigation. Compaz can also start a browser session that a user will manually handle as a third option. As Fig. 2 shows, the browser connects through a proxy, from which we can copy each request and persist it in Compaz's database. This makes sure that we see every request, but even more importantly, we only consider requests that were not served by the client's cache. Additionally, we keep the chronological order and therefore can reconstruct which assets were available at which point in time for a shared dictionary approach.

Compressing Data. After a journey has been completed, it can be used by the compressors. For a shared dictionary approach, Compaz replays the requests and uses the decompressed assets to compress them with different approaches. Compaz provides the compressor instance with every asset for a shared dictionary approach, which could potentially be used as a dictionary to decompress (and therefore compress at the server side) the asset. It calculates every combination and keeps the best result. As mentioned in Sect. 1, this approach would not be feasible in practice but shows us the best potential of each compressor. The considered assets can be configured to, e.g., only consider those of the same MIME type or only those from a specific page in the journey. Furthermore, different compressors can be chained so that the output of one compressor is the input of another, which brings a significant improvement for some approaches. While we only persist the metrics for the compression results, we keep the original raw journey. This ensures that we can compare new approaches later against the same dataset, even if the approach did not exist while the journey was collected.

Comparing Data. The results are available via the API. We also created a frontend, which visualizes the results. Since the results are as low as on asset level, finding the best solution per asset is possible. This also shows which pages contain assets that could serve as dictionaries for shared dictionary approaches.

---

[1] https://www.selenium.dev/.

Prototyping New Compression Algorithms. Compaz was designed to be easily extendable, so new compression approaches can be benchmarked quickly without deploying them on live servers. As of now, Compaz has support for *gzip*, *open-vcdiff*, *Brotli*, and *zstandard*. Except for *gzip*, all other compressors can make use of a dictionary. To implement a new compressor, one must implement a configuration class with all necessary configuration parameters (e.g., compression level or window size) and the compressor itself. The compressor only needs two methods to be implemented: *compress* and *decompress*. While only the former is required for the calculation, the latter is to ensure integrity. Our unit test suite will automatically pick up each compressor without the need to write new tests. The logic to provide available dictionaries and chain different compressions is handled by Compaz and does not need any implementation considerations.

Similarly, new navigators can be implemented. We already provide an abstract class, which acts as a wrapper for Selenium. Each navigator can access the currently rendered DOM to decide the next action to be taken.

3   Conclusion

This paper has shown how Compaz can create repeatable compression evaluations using user journeys instead of arbitrary single files. Combined with Compaz's extensibility, this ensures comparability of old results to new compression techniques. Compaz can be used to guide further research by evaluating a gold standard for currently not supported compression techniques, like delta encoding, before investing work in browser support or performance optimizations.

References

1. Intent to Unship: SDCH (2016). https://groups.google.com/a/chromium.org/d/msg/blink-dev/nQl0ORHy7sw/HNpR96sqAgAJ. Accessed 20 Feb 2022
2. Alakuijala, J., et al.: Brotli: a general-purpose data compressor. ACM Trans. Inf. Syst. **37**(1), 1–30 (2019)
3. Chan, M.C., Woo, T.: Cache-based compaction: a new technique for optimizing web transfer. In: Conference on Computer Communications, IEEE INFOCOM 1999 (1999)
4. Fischbacher, T., Kliuchnikov, E., Comsa, I.: Web Almanac: Compression. https://almanac.httparchive.org/en/2021/compression. Accessed 25 Feb 2022
5. McQuade, B., Mixter, K., Lee, W.H., Butler, J.: A proposal for shared dictionary compression over http (2016)
6. Mogul, J.C., Douglis, F., Feldmann, A., Krishnamurthy, B.: Potential benefits of delta encoding and data compression for HTTP. ACM SIGCOMM Comput. Commun. Rev. **27**(4), 181–194 (1997)
7. Shapira, O.: Shared Dictionary Compression for HTTP at LinkedIn. https://engineering.linkedin.com/shared-dictionary-compression-http-linkedin
8. Wingerath, W., et al.: Speed Kit: a polyglot gdpr-compliant approach for caching personalized content. In: 36th ICDE 2020, Dallas, Texas, 20–24 April 2020 (2020)
9. Wollmer, B., Wingerath, W., Ferrlein, S., Panse, F., Gessert, F., Ritter, N.: The case for cross-entity delta encoding in web compression. In: 22th ICWE (2022)
10. Wollmer, B., Wingerath, W., Ritter, N.: Context-aware encoding & delivery in the web. In: 20th ICWE 2020, Helsinki, Finland, 9–12 June 2020 (2020)

Social Events Analyzer (SEA): A Toolkit for Mining Social Workflows by Means of Federated Process Mining

Javier Rojo[1]([⊠]) [iD], José García-Alonso[1] [iD], Javier Berrocal[1] [iD],
Juan Hernández[1] [iD], Juan M. Murillo[1] [iD], and Carlos Canal[2] [iD]

[1] University of Extremadura, Caceres, Spain
{javirojo,jgaralo,jberolm,juanher,juanmamu}@unex.es
[2] Universidad de Málaga, Málaga, Spain
canal@lcc.uma.es

Abstract. Users' smartphones collect information about the different interactions they perform in their daily life, including web interactions. Mining this information to discover user's processes provides information about them as individuals and as part of a social group. However, analyzing events produced by human behavior, where indeterminism and variability prevail, is a complex task. Techniques such as process mining focus on analyzing customary event logs produced by a system where all the possible interactions are predefined. The analysis become even harder when it involves a group of people whose joint activity is considered part of a Social Workflow. In this demo we present Social Events Analyzer (SEA), a toolkit for easy Social Workflow analysis using a technique called Federated Process Mining. The tool offers models more faithful to the behavior of the users that make up a Social Workflow and opens the door to the use of process mining as a basis for the creation of new automatic procedures adapted to the user behavior.

Keywords: Process mining · Pattern discovery · Social workflows · Federated process mining

1 Introduction

Smartphones constantly collect information about their user's daily actions [7], including the interactions users perform with web pages [6]. These actions can be considered as the events of a process modeling the user's behaviour. This allows techniques such as process mining to analyze this process at the individual level, but also considering the users as part of a group with similar behaviour's processes or Social Workflows (SOW) [3].

However, current process mining techniques are designed to mine information obtained from well-defined processes. Human behavior represented in Social Workflows is usually not deterministic, but highly variable [3]. So, analyzing this kind of information becomes a problem for process mining. Even more at the

T. Di Noia et al. (Eds.): ICWE 2022, LNCS 13362, pp. 477–480, 2022.
https://doi.org/10.1007/978-3-031-09917-5_39

societal level, where indeterminism from different users is aggregated—obtaining processes that do not provide real knowledge about any of the users or about the group itself.

Current techniques such as clustering [4] try to solve this problem, grouping users in not previously-known clusters according their behaviour. Nevertheless, they do not focus on mining a concrete Social Workflow, but on mining all users data, not knowing *a priori* behavioural patterns of interest to be met by users that are going to be analyzed.

In order to offer an alternative in these situations, Social Events Analyzer (SEA) has been developed. This tool allows to perform a first phase of individual mining in each user's smartphone to filter those users and traces that meet a concrete, looked for, behaviour. In this way, only users with common behavioural patterns are considered part of the social group to be analyzed later. The premise on which this tool is based is that human behaviour is not erratic per se [2]. So, individually analyzing each user's behaviour before integrating it improve the representation of each user in the Social Workflow and the one of the users' group consequently.

Thanks to this tool, processes that could not be analyzed otherwise due to heterogeneity in users interactions, can now be analyzed. As well, some additional benefits come from filtering data on smartphones: reduction of the amount of data sent to server —reducing the energy footprint [1]—, and reduction of the computational load on server.

Moreover, SEA allows the development of automatic systems using processes' information to make recommendations or personalize processes itself. Complementing this manuscript, the use of SEA on a WoT/IoT use case is shown[1].

2   Social Events Analyzer (SEA)

Social Events Analyzer (SEA) is based on the novel Federated Process Mining concept. It offers the necessary tools to carry out process mining on Social Workflows by means of Federated Process Mining, where process mining is performed on two phases: an individual first one on users' smartphones, generating an individual model in order to filter users that are going to belong to a concrete Social Workflow; and a second one on a server, generating social processes with data resulting from filtering in the first phase. Since the interesting behaviour's pattern —or patterns— to be meet by users is known a priori, filtering is performed by means of a query where this behaviour is represented. For example, the query may ask for users who have ended up watching economic news videos on YouTube when they started watching videos about the COVID-19 pandemic. For users meeting the pattern sought in their individual models, traces are checked one by one, sending to the server only those that contains the pattern. In this way, traces are only checked when the behaviour is enclosed in the model and it is known that the user meet the searched behavior —this results in greater

---

[1] https://youtu.be/d2tOYWWhYC0.

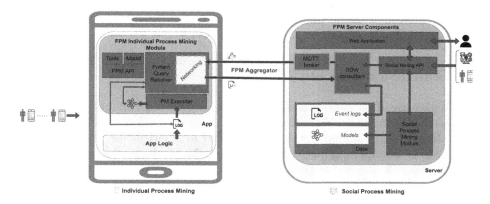

Fig. 1. SEA's architecture.

efficiency when many queries are made or when the amount of traces to be stored is very large.

Social Events Analyzer —Fig. 1— offers a concrete implementation of Federated Process Mining in the way of a series of components that must be included in the application that generates the data and a complete Federated Process Mining server. The three main components, that are divided into a number of sub-components, are:

Individual Process Mining component[2]. This component is the one deployed on smartphones. At the moment it is only available on Android devices. Specifically, SEA offers the *FPM Individual Process Mining module*, which must be included in the mobile application that generates the event log —in .XES format— to be mined. The generation of this event log must be addressed by developers of the application—using information collected in the app logic.

Social Process Mining Component[3]. This component is the one that is deployed on the server. It is actually a set of web services—implemented in Python—and a web application—in Typescript—that work together. Each of them is in charge of part of the functions to be performed by the Social Process Mining component, highlighting the Social Mining API. It is a REST API that works as an access point to the Social Workflows information, offering data and operations to manage it to the Web Application, to third-parties or even to the users' smartphones themselves when these are the ones interested in accessing the data of a given Social Workflow.

FPM Aggregator. This component has been implemented as part of the previous ones —mark in green color in Fig. 1—, using previous works on the deployment of APIs in mobile devices [5]. It is employed to enable communication between individual and social parties—being used to send queries from *Social*

---

[2] https://bitbucket.org/spilab/individualpmmodule.

[3] https://bitbucket.org/spilab/fpmserver.

Mining component to the smartphones in Linear Temporal Logic (LTL) format and to send traces from these as response to queries.

3 Conclusion and Future Work

SEA makes use of the concept of Federated Process Mining to enable the usage of process mining on Social Workflows. For this purpose, it offers a complete toolkit with the necessary components to be included in smartphones and the server where social mining is going to be performed. As result, models more faithful to the members of a social group and the optimization of resources needed to perform process mining are achieved. In addition, SEA brings the arrival of a new generation of automatic systems based on user process information.

Acknowledgments. This work was supported by the projects 0499_4IE_PLUS_4_E (Interreg V-A España-Portugal 2014–2020), RTI2018-094591-B-I00 (MCIU/AEI/ FEDER, UE), and UMA18-FEDERJA-180 (Junta de Andalucía/ATech/FEDER), by the Department of Economy and Infrastructure of the Government of Extremadura (GR18112, IB18030), by the FPU19/03965 grant and by the European Regional Development Fund.

References

1. Berrocal, J., et al.: Early evaluation of mobile applications' resource consumption and operating costs. IEEE Access **8**, 146648–146665 (2020). https://doi.org/10. 1109/ACCESS.2020.3015082
2. Gonzalez, M.C., Hidalgo, C.A., Barabasi, A.L.: Understanding individual human mobility patterns. Nature **453**(7196), 779–782 (2008). https://doi.org/10.1038/ nature06958
3. Görg, S., Bergmann, R.: Social workflows - vision and potential study. Inf. Syst. **50**, 1–19 (2015). https://doi.org/10.1016/j.is.2014.12.007
4. Jablonski, S., Röglinger, M., Schönig, S., Wyrtki, K.M.: Multi-perspective clustering of process execution traces. EMISAJ Int. J. Concept. Model. **14**(2), 1–22 (2019). https://doi.org/10.18417/emisa.14.2
5. Laso, S., Linaje, M., Garcia-Alonso, J., Murillo, J.M., Berrocal, J.: Artifact abstract: deployment of apis on android mobile devices and microcontrollers. In: 2020 IEEE International Conference on Pervasive Computing and Communications (PerCom), pp. 1–2 (2020). https://doi.org/10.1109/PerCom45495.2020.9127353
6. Poggi, N., Muthusamy, V., Carrera, D., Khalaf, R.: Business process mining from e-commerce web logs. In: Daniel, F., Wang, J., Weber, B. (eds.) BPM 2013. LNCS, vol. 8094, pp. 65–80. Springer, Heidelberg (2013). https://doi.org/10.1007/978-3-642-40176-3_7
7. Rojo, J., Flores-Martin, D., Garcia-Alonso, J., Murillo, J.M., Berrocal, J.: Automating the interactions among iot devices using neural networks. In: 2020 IEEE International Conference on Pervasive Computing and Communications Workshops (PerCom Workshops), pp. 1–6 (2020). https://doi.org/10.1109/ PerComWorkshops48775.2020.9156111

Solid Web Monetization

Merlijn Sebrechts[(✉)] [ID], Tom Goethals [ID], Thomas Dupont [ID],
Wannes Kerckhove, Ruben Taelman [ID], Filip De Turck [ID],
and Bruno Volckaert [ID]

IDLab, Department of Information Technology (intec), Ghent University - imec,
Ghent, Belgium
merlijn.sebrechts@ugent.be

Abstract. The Solid decentralization effort decouples data from services, so that users are in full control over their personal data. In this light, Web Monetization has been proposed as an alternative business model for web services that does not depend on data collection anymore. Integrating Web Monetization with Solid, however, remains difficult because of the heterogeneity of Interledger wallet implementations, lack of mechanisms for securely paying on behalf of a user, and an inherent issue of trusting content providers to handle payments. We propose the Web Monetization Provider as a solution to these challenges. The WMP acts as a third party, hiding the underlying complexity of transactions and acting as a source of trust in Web Monetization interactions. This demo shows a working end-to-end example including a website providing monetized content, a WMP, and a dashboard for configuring WMP into a Solid identity.

Keywords: Web Monetization · Solid · Micropayments · Payment processing · Interledger · Open payments

1 Introduction

Solid is a research project initiated in 2016 by Prof. Tim Berners-Lee, which aims to overcome issues with the current internet which sees data harvesting firms (e.g. Facebook, Google) capitalize on data originating from their users. The Solid decentralization effort decouples data from services, so that users are in full control over their personal data [1,2]. This decoupling means services cannot depend on data collection as a primary business model anymore. As a result, alternative forms of monetization, such as micropayments via Web Monetization are essential for incentivizing application development. With Web Monetization, paying for content is seamlessly integrated into the browser. While a user is consuming content, they stream micropayments to the content creator using the browser. This makes it easy to create pay-per-view business models for web content.

The goal of this research is to integrate Web Monetization with Solid applications. This will enable users to consume monetized content from Solid enabled

© Springer Nature Switzerland AG 2022
T. Di Noia et al. (Eds.): ICWE 2022, LNCS 13362, pp. 481–486, 2022.
https://doi.org/10.1007/978-3-031-09917-5_40

applications without needing to rely on browser extensions. Although commercial products like Coil [3] already offer Web Monetization, they do not integrate with the Solid ecosystem and rely on non-standard browser extensions. The Interledger protocol (ILP) seems like a natural fit in order to achieve this objective: it is an open protocol for secure payments across disparate payment networks [4,5]. The ILP STREAM protocol [6], specifically, makes it possible to reliably stream payments from one payment provider to another. However, implementing extension-less Web Monetization on top of ILP is not an easy task because of a number of challenges.

1. The heterogeneity of Interledger (ILP) wallet implementations makes it difficult to encapsulate the logic required for streaming payments between wallets because they use different protocols and different authentication schemes.
2. There is a lack of mechanisms for reliably and securely performing these payments on behalf of the user.
3. There is an inherent issue of trust, by requiring the client to orchestrate the payment setup and thus determining the rate and the amount of the payment stream.

To solve these challenges, we introduce a *Web Monetization Provider (WMP)*. This is a third party between the content consumer and the content creator that hides the underlying complexity of ILP wallets and acts as an independent source of trust. In this demo, we present a full end-to-end implementation of extension-less Web Monetization using a WMP.

2   Solid Web Monetization Provider (WMP)

A Web Monetization Provider (WMP) is a standardized third party between the content consumer and the content creator. The WMP acts as an authority, sending micropayments to the content creator in name of the content consumer. Adding this third party into the transaction makes it easy for content creators to receive micro-payments in a generic way and avoids vendor lock-in by allowing content consumers to freely choose which WMP to use. Specifically, the WMP solves the challenges described in Sect. 1 in the following way.

1. The complexity of dealing with the heterogeneity of Interledger wallet implementations is handled by the WMP. This makes it easier for client developers to create Web Monetization enabled applications without having to write code for every single possible wallet implementation.
2. The WMP handles streaming payments for monetized sessions. In exchange, the user subscribes to the WMP by paying a monthly fee, or funds the WMP for a predetermined amount using transaction-based charges like debit card payments. The WMP is free to choose its revenue model and spending strategy. This loose coupling adds a lot of flexibility to the Web Monetization model and again helps to reduce client-side complexity.

3. The WMP API is an open specification, enabling different parties to compete in providing WMP services. This benefits the users as they can now choose which WMP to trust as their Web Monetization agent, and can easily switch providers at any time while still being able to consume the monetized content in the same way. This model perfectly aligns with the Solid philosophy where you as a user are in full control of your data, including sharing and using.

Figure 1 shows an overview of how the WMP interacts with other actors in the context of Web Monetization. A consumer registers with the WMP in order to set up a subscription payment from the consumer's wallet to the WMP Wallet. When the consumer uses a Monetized Solid App, it reads the WMP reference from the consumer's pod. The app uses this reference to contact the WMP to start a monetization session. Using this session, the app streams consumer interactions with the content. The WMP uses this information to stream micropayments from the WMP Wallet to the Content Provider's wallet. With the goal of furthering the discussion around Solid Web Monetization, the Solid Web Monetization Provider W3C Editor's Draft [7] was created.

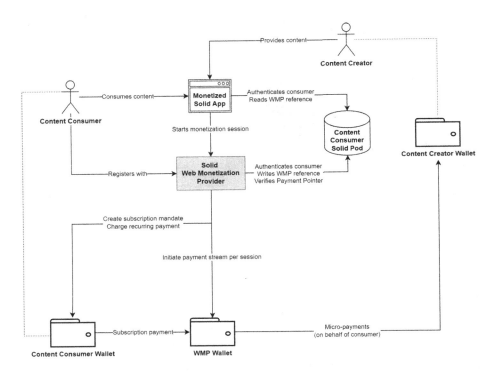

Fig. 1. Overview of interactions in a Web Monetization use case.

3   Demonstration

The demo[1] shows a complete end-to-end working example of a Solid Web Monetization app. A content-creator hosts web monetized content that visiting users pay for through micropayments. These micropayments are sent over the interledger network from the visiting user's wallet to the content creator's wallet, using the WMP. Aligning with Solid's vision, all required data is stored in the visiting user's Solid pod. The demo consists of three applications shown in Fig. 2:

- The Solid Accountant allows to configure a Web Monetization wallet into a Solid identity. This is a browser application written in Angular 13 and TypeScript.
- The Solid MicroStore is an example Web Monetized Solid application. This is a browser application written in Angular 13 and TypeScript.
- The Solid WMP is a Web Monetization Provider with a fake currency. It performs micropayments to payment pointers on behalf of a user. That user

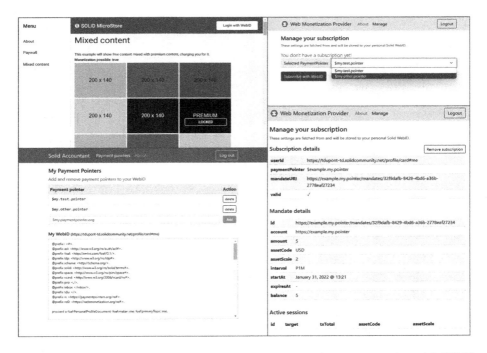

Fig. 2. Demonstration of a proof of concept monetized web-app interacting with WMP and Solid. Clockwise: The Solid MicroStore hosts Web Monetized content. The Web Monetization Provider is used to create and manage a subscription. The Solid Accountant is used to configure the WMP in a user's Solid Pod.

---

[1] https://knowledgeonwebscale.github.io/solid-web-monetization/demo/intro/.

trusts the WMP and has an active subscription with it. This is a server application written in Kotlin 1.6.10 on top of JDK 16. The Vert.x toolkit is used as a Web/Micro-service framework.

This demo allows a user to log in to their personal Solid pod and register a personal payment pointer. Afterwards they can subscribe to the Web Monetization Provider that will manage micropayments on their behalf. The user can then visit the MicroStore component to showcase how the registered WMP can be requested from a Solid WebID and instructed to pay micropayments to the content provider's payment pointer embedded in the web page.

4 Conclusions and Future Work

The Web Monetization Provider makes it possible for content providers to implement a seamless and extension-less Web Monetization experience. The WMP also allows content consumers to easily set up micropayments in order to access and seamlessly pay for content. The WMP addresses a number of challenges; specifically, the heterogeneity of the Interledger wallet implementations, the lack of mechanisms to perform payments on behalf of users, and the issue of trust in Web Monetization micropayments. This demo shows a working end-to-end example including a website providing monetized content, a WMP, and a dashboard for configuring WMP into a Solid identity. With the goal of furthering the discussion around Solid Web Monetization, we created the Solid Web Monetization Provider W3C Editor's Draft [7].

Important future work in this area includes working with the Web Monetization and Interledger ecosystems to align these standards to enable standards-compliant Solid Web Monetization. Moreover, investigating a plugin-based approach to support different Wallet providers will make it easier to implement Solid Web Monetization and WMPs.

Acknowledgments. – This research was partially funded by Grant for the Web, a fund to boost open, fair, and inclusive standards and innovation in Web Monetization.

– Ruben Taelman is a postdoctoral fellow of the Research Foundation - Flanders (FWO) (1274521N).

References

1. Mansour, E., et al.: A demonstration of the solid platform for social web applications. In: Proceedings of the 25th International Conference Companion on World Wide Web, ser. WWW 2016 Companion. Republic and Canton of Geneva, CHE: International World Wide Web Conferences Steering Committee, April 2016, pp. 223–226 (2016). https://doi.org/10.1145/2872518.2890529
2. Solid Project, "Solid: Your data, your choice. Advancing Web standards to empower people" (2022). https://solidproject.org/
3. Coil Technologies, "Coil - A new way to enjoy content" (2022). https://coil.com/
4. Thomas, S., Schwartz, E.: A Protocol for Interledger Payments, p. 25 (2015)

5. Hope-Bailie, A., Thomas, S.: Interledger: creating a standard for payments. In: Proceedings of the 25th International Conference Companion on World Wide Web, ser. WWW 2016 Companion. Republic and Canton of Geneva, CHE: International World Wide Web Conferences Steering Committee, April 2016, pp. 281–282 (2016). https://doi.org/10.1145/2872518.2889307
6. Interledger Foundation, "STREAM: A Multiplexed Money and Data Transport for ILP" (2020). https://interledger.org/rfcs/0029-stream/
7. Dupont, T., Kerckhove, W.: Solid Web Monetization Provider W3C Editor's Draft, February 2022. https://knowledgeonwebscale.github.io/solid-web-monetization/spec.html

Web Push Notifications from Solid Pods

Christoph H.-J. Braun$^{(\boxtimes)}$ and Tobias Käfer

Institute AIFB, Karlsruhe Institute of Technology (KIT), Karlsruhe, Germany
braun@kit.edu, tobias.kaefer@kit.edu

Abstract. Our demo showcases how a Solid Pod, i.e. a web server that adheres to the Solid Protocol, can be extended to support Web Push Notifications for Progressive Web Applications (PWAs). For a user's perspective, we present a PWA where a user can choose to receive Web Push Notifications when a message is posted to her Solid Pod's inbox.

1 Introduction

The Solid Project[1], Tim Berners-Lee's endeavor to re-decentralise the Web, aims to decouple data from consuming applications while ensuring data privacy. The Solid Protocol [2] connects mature Web technologies like the Resource Description Framework (RDF) and RESTful HTTPS APIs and an adaptation of Open ID Connect: Users store data in personal online data storages (Pods) and define access control on their resources as desired.

The Solid Protocol focuses on establishing server-side technologies while relying on generic client-side libraries (for HTTP and RDF) to create Web applications. For example, if developers need to react on updates of resources, they currently need to rely on polling, which is battery-draining on mobile, or WebSocket-based subscriptions, which are not standardised. Yet, nowadays live updates and notifications are a commonly expected feature of an application.

To live up to user expectations, Progressive Web Applications (PWAs) offer a rich feature set including Web Push Notifications, i.e. a notification scheme where push messages are delivered to Web applications via the browsers' messaging service. Such notifications can even be received when the Web application is closed. We thus ask: What if the Solid Protocol supported Web Push Notifications from Solid Pods to help developers create modern Web applications easily? To this end, we showcase:

- A notification scheme for Web Push Notifications from Solid Pods.
- A data model for Solid Web Push subscriptions using RDF.

---

[1] https://solidproject.org.

Website http://uvdsl.solid.aifb.kit.edu/conf/2022/icwe/demo
Demo https://km.aifb.kit.edu/services/solid-web-pwa/
Code https://github.com/uvdsl/solid-web-push.

T. Di Noia et al. (Eds.): ICWE 2022, LNCS 13362, pp. 487–490, 2022.
https://doi.org/10.1007/978-3-031-09917-5_41

– An extension module for Solid Pods to support the notification scheme.
– A PWA that uses these Solid Web Push Notifications.

This paper is structured as follows: First, we give a short overview on related work. Next, outline the system architecture. Then, we touch on our data model. Hereafter, we provide a walkthrough of our demo.

2   Related Work

We briefly survey related work in the realm of the Solid Protocol [2] and its notification schemes. An early description about Solid is provided in [3].

The current state of notification schemes in Solid are comprised of two alternatives: Either the client relies on polling to detect updates on a resource independent of the Pod's implementation, or the client uses a WebSocket Subscription as defined in version v0.7.0 of the Solid Protocol[2]. As the WebSocket notification scheme is currently supported by the most used Pod implementations we rely on this scheme in our demo as a fallback when the user chooses not to receive push notifications.

Recently, the Solid Community Notification Panel started reworking Solid's notification protocol. Four notification schemes are currently proposed[3]: (1) The WebSocket Subscription defines a notification scheme for bi-directional communication between client and Pod using WebSockets. (2) The EventSource Subscription defines a notification for uni-directional server-sent events from Pod to client using HTTP/2. (3) The Linked Data Notification Subscription defines a notification scheme relying on the Solid Protocol itself for sending Pod-to-Pod notifications. (4) The WebHook Subscription defines a notification scheme for pod-to-server callbacks using HTTP.

Web Push Notifications have been proposed in an IETF Draft for Generic Event Delivery using HTTP Push [6] and have been picked up by the W3C in the Push API [1]. With this demo, we propose an additional notification scheme of Solid Web Push Notifications in Pod-to-PWA fashion.

3   System Architecture

With Solid, each user is identified by a WebID, a URI which derefenced yields the user's Solid profile document. This profile document is stored on the user's personal online data storage (Pod) where the user can store any data under self-defined access control. On the Pod, there exists an inbox where messages to the user can be posted to. Using some app, the user can access this data after logging in to the app with her WebID.

To receive notifications even when the app is closed, we extend the Solid Pod with an additional module to support Web Push Notifications for Pod-stored resources. We implement the corresponding client-side functionality in our PWA.

---

[2] https://github.com/solid/solid-spec/blob/master/api-websockets.md.
[3] https://solid.github.io/notifications/protocol.

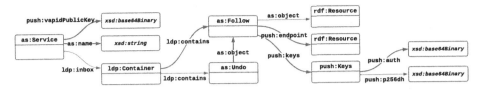

Fig. 1. The RDF datamodel underlying our Solid Web Push Notification scheme. We use CURIEs, abbreviated URIs, with prefixes from http://prefix.cc/. We use *push* as prefix that is short for https://purl.org/solid-web-push/vocab#.

The current state of Solid Notification schemes allows us to demonstrate Web Push Notifications for resources stored on any Solid Pod. However, considering security and scope of Web Push Notifications from Solid Pods, we envision a service that is able to send Web Push Notifications only for resources stored in that particular Pod, a Pod-scoped notification service.

An application developer can use the Pod-provided Web Push service and does not need to implement it herself as a server-side component of the application. Instead, the developer may specify an app-specific inbox on the user's Solid Pod where his server posts messages to which in turn can then be forwarded by the Pod's Web Push service. This way, the developer is still in control of the user experience when sending Push Notifications to the user. That said, developers are still free to implement their own Push Notification service.

4 Modeling Solid Web Push Subscriptions

We model a Web Push subscriptions and the corresponding service on the Solid Pod in RDF, as illustrated in Fig. 1: To describe Web Push subscriptions, we defined an ontology based on existing definitions from [6]. Next to typical elements of a Web Push subscription such as *endpoint, auth* key and *p256dh* key, our subscription model includes the resource which the client requests notifications about. We use terms from ActivityStreams [4] to model the Solid Web Push service and subscription requests from clients, and terms from the Linked Data Platform [5] to model the service inbox which clients post subscriptions to.

5 Demonstrator Walkthrough

To demonstrate Solid Web Push Notifications, we provide a PWA where a user can choose to receive Push Notifications whenever her Pod inbox is updated. Following the Solid Protocol, a user logs in to our demo PWA with her Solid WebID. By default, the PWA relies on Solid's WebSocket Notifications to receive updates on the user's Pod inbox. If the user decides to receive Push Notifications, the user simply clicks the bell icon in the top right corner. This substitutes the WebSocket Notifications for Web Push Notifications from our Solid Web Push service. These notifications will be received even when the PWA is closed.

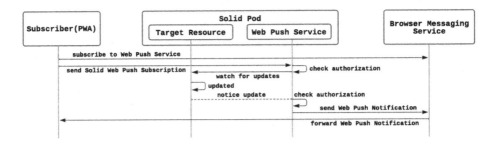

Fig. 2. An excerpt from the Solid Web Push Notification sequence diagram.

Under the hood, the PWA follows the Solid Web Push Notification scheme: A Solid Web Push subscription is sent the Solid Web Push service. The service then acts as a proxy forwarding any Pod-issued update notifications on the resource to the PWA using Web Push as illustrated by Fig. 2. When the user chooses not to receive Push Notifications anymore, an undo request for the subscription is sent to the service canceling the Solid Web Push subscription. For an extensive sequence diagram of the Solid Web Push Notification scheme, we recommend the interested reader to take a look at our website which is linked on the first page.

6   Conclusion

In this demo, we showcased an extension to Solid Pods to support Web Push Notifications. We modeled the corresponding Solid Web Push service information and associated subscriptions using RDF. We propose our approach for discussion in the growing Solid ecosystem as Push Notifications are a common feature of today's apps, especially on mobile. Natively supporting Web Push Notifications from Solid Pods could facilitate developing application that live up to user expectations and thus contribute to the wider acceptance of the Solid Protocol.

References

1. Beverloo, P., Thomson, M.: Push API. W3C Working Draft, W3C (2021). https://www.w3.org/TR/push-api/
2. Capadisli, S., Berners-Lee, T., Verborgh, R., Kjernsmo, K.: Solid Protocol. Version 0.9.0, W3C Solid CG (2021). https://solidproject.org/TR/protocol
3. Mansour, E., et al.: A demonstration of the solid platform for social web applications. In: Proceedings of the 25th WWW. ACM (2016)
4. Snell, J.M., Prodromou, E.: Activity Streams 2.0. W3C Recommendation, W3C (2017). https://www.w3.org/TR/activitystreams-core/
5. Speicher, S., Arwe, J., Malhotra, A.: Linked Data Platform 1.0. W3C Recommendation, W3C (2015). https://www.w3.org/TR/ldp/
6. Thomson, M., Damaggio, E., Raymor, B.: Generic Event Delivery Using HTTP Push. RFC 8030, IETF (2016). http://ietf.org/rfc/rfc8030.txt

Tutorials

A Guide for Quantum Web Services Deployment

Jaime Alvarado-Valiente(✉) 🆔, Javier Romero-Álvarez 🆔,
Jose Garcia-Alonso 🆔, and Juan M. Murillo 🆔

Escuela Politécnica, Quercus Software Engineering Group, University of
Extremadura, Av. de la Universidad, S/N, 10003 Cáceres, Spain
{jaimeav,jromero,jgaralo,juanmamu}@unex.es

Abstract. Quantum computing is a new paradigm for solving problems
that classical computers cannot reach. To the point that it is already generating interest in the scientific and industrial communities. Currently,
quantum computers and technology are being developed to support the
execution of quantum software. Several large computer companies have
already built functional quantum computers, and developed several programming languages and quantum simulators that can be used by the
general public. All this infrastructure for quantum computing is offered
to quantum developers through the cloud, following a model similar to
the familiar Infrastructure as a Service. However, due to the early stages
of quantum computing taking advantage of the capabilities of these computers requires a very in depth knowledge of quantum programming and
quantum hardware that is far from what cloud developers are used to in
classical cloud offerings. Although the future of quantum computing is
still unknown, it is highly certain that there must be a time when quantum computing coexists with classical computing. At the same time, one
of the most well-known and tested solutions for the communication of
heterogeneous computing systems are web services. In this tutorial we
will offer an introductory view on how quantum algorithms can be converted into web services, how this web services can be deployed, using the
Amazon Braket platform for quantum computing, and invoked through
classical web services endpoints. Finally, we will propose a way in which
a disadvantage of current quantum computers in terms of web services
can be transformed into an advantage for web services through the use
of a Quantum API Gateway.

Keywords: Quantum software development · Quantum web services ·
Quantum programming

1 Introduction

The emergence of quantum computing has brought a new paradigm in computing
and software engineering, leading to new horizons in the field of problem-solving
applications of computation [1]. Thus, this new technology is useful for tasks

© Springer Nature Switzerland AG 2022
T. Di Noia et al. (Eds.): ICWE 2022, LNCS 13362, pp. 493–496, 2022.
https://doi.org/10.1007/978-3-031-09917-5_42

that the most powerful classical computers cannot do in a reasonable time, such as the discovery of new materials or drugs, big data analysis or even for military applications [2,3].

Several large computer companies have already built functional quantum computers, and developed dozens of programming languages and quantum simulators that can be used by the general public. This new paradigm is changing both the world of computing and the areas in which it can be applied [4]. However, at the current time, and for the foreseeable future, quantum computing must coexists with classical computing (in which has been called hybrid classical-quantum architectures). The principles of service-oriented computing present a good guideline to be followed for these hybrid architectures due to the long history of classical service engineering [5]. Nevertheless, the development and deployment of quantum services is limited by the current lack of tools and techniques on this domain.

From a service-oriented computing point of view, quantum software integration should not be very different from classical services [6]. However, today the lack of Software Engineering techniques for quantum services is affecting almost every aspect of quantum services. To address this situations, alternatives are beginning to emerge that translate classical processes to quantum computing [7,8].

Therefore, the aim of this tutorial is to show how quantum web services could be implemented and deployed for hybrid classical-quantum architectures. Specifically, examples of solving real-world problems using quantum computing in Amazon Braket will be presented. Also, we will propose a way in which a disadvantage of current quantum computers in terms of web services can be transformed into an advantage for web services through the use of a Quantum API Gateway [9].

2   Intended Audience

The tutorial is aimed for both academic and industrial attendees interested in service-oriented quantum computing. The desirable technical background is the following: basic knowledge of quantum software development is nice to have but not a requirement to follow the tutorial. Basic knowledge of web services, JSON files and Python programming language are required to follow the practical part of the tutorial but not to understand the underlying concepts. Both source code of all the used examples and an introduction to the basics of quantum computing will be provided during the tutorial.

To participate in the practical part of the tutorial, a laptop with a text editor, a Python installation and also an Amazon Web Services account would be necessary.

Detailed instructions for the preparation of the environment before attending the tutorial are provided. These instructions include the first steps to run quantum code using the developer machine as a local simulator and also using the Amazon Braket SDK. Also, advanced steps are included for those people who really want to use Amazon Braket to exploit the full potential of real quantum machines, although it will not be necessary for the tutorial.

The tutorial slides along with the above-mentioned instructions for setting up the environment and additional resources are available online.[1]

3   Outline of the Tutorial

In this section, we provide a provisional outline of the tutorial. The proposed duration of the tutorial is half-day (three hours) including both lectures and practical activities:

1. **Introduction**
   - First, a short lecture focused on the servitization of quantum software, or how to convert an existing quantum algorithm into a traditional web service.
   - This will be followed by an exemplification of how these services can be deployed and executed using Python libraries for classical web services and Postman for testing the deployed web services.
   - Quantum algorithms will be used as an example, which will be adapted to the Amazon Braket platform and programming language, although adaptation to a different quantum platform should be straightforward.
2. **Practical session**
   - A practical session will be run in which attendees can deploy and invoke their first quantum web service.
   - Shor's algorithm for factoring large numbers and a solution to the Travelling Salesman Problem will be used, as a representation of gate-based quantum computing and annealing-based quantum computing respectively.
   - The implementation of these quantum algorithms, adapted to Amazon Braket, will be provided and attendants will focus on deploying and using them as traditional web services.
3. **Quantum Software as a Service**
   - Some of the current limitations of quantum computers will be discussed, such as that quantum algorithms cannot be deployed once and run multiple times as we are used to with classical services. Each run of a quantum service involves a new deployment of the quantum algorithm.
   - Attendees will be introduced to Quantum API Gateway as a tool to address this disadvantage, thanks to the fact that it can be used to the benefit of the quantum service developer. This tool improves the efficiency of quantum services by deploying the service to the most appropriate quantum computer available for each execution taking into account execution times, costs, availability and other aspects.
   - An example of its use will be performed with the previously developed quantum web services.

---

[1] https://drive.google.com/drive/folders/1rejfd4mcyryEH5SzlBeyOfNSzH-OJOye?usp=sharing.

4   Learning Objectives and Outcomes

At the end of the tutorial, attendees will obtain knowledge on:

- The servitisation of quantum algorithms.
- How to invoke quantum services from classical software, along with possible options for deploying quantum services.
- Quantum Web Services in the real world with Amazon Braket.
- Thinking in terms of hybrid classical-quantum web services architectures.

Acknowledgements. This work was supported by the projects 0499_4IE_PLUS_4_E (Interreg V-A España-Portugal 2014–2020), RTI2018-094591-B-I00 (MCIU/AEI/ FEDER, UE), Junta de Extremadura, Regional Ministry of Economy, Science and Digital Agenda (GR21133), and the European Regional Development Fund.

References

1. Zhao, J.: Quantum software engineering: landscapes and horizons. arXiv:2007.07047 (2020)
2. MacQuarrie, E.R., Simon, C., Simmons, S., Maine, E.: The emerging commercial landscape of quantum computing. Nat. Rev. Phys. **2**(11), 596–598 (2020)
3. Neumann, N.M., van Heesch, M.P., Phillipson, F., Smallegange, A.A.: Quantum computing for military applications. In: 2021 International Conference on Military Communication and Information Systems (ICMCIS), pp. 1–8. IEEE (2021)
4. Piattini, M., Peterssen, G., Pérez-Castillo, R.: Quantum computing: a new software engineering golden age. SIGSOFT Softw. Eng. Notes **45**(3), pp. 12–14, July 2020. https://doi.org/10.1145/3402127.3402131
5. Moguel, E., Berrocal, J., García-Alonso, J., Murillo, J.M.: A roadmap for quantum software engineering: applying the lessons learned from the classics. In: Q-SET@ QCE, pp. 5–13 (2020)
6. Pérez-Delgado, C.A., Perez-Gonzalez, H.G.: Towards a quantum software modeling language. In: Proceedings of the IEEE/ACM 42nd International Conference on Software Engineering Workshops, pp. 442–444 (2020)
7. McCaskey, A., Dumitrescu, E., Liakh, D., Humble, T.: Hybrid programming for near-term quantum computing systems. In: 2018 IEEE International Conference on Rebooting Computing (ICRC), pp. 1–12. IEEE (2018)
8. Moguel, E., Rojo, J., Valencia, D., Berrocal, J., Garcia-Alonso, J., Murillo, J.M.: Quantum service-oriented computing: current landscape and challenges. Softw. Qual. J., 1–20 (2022). https://doi.org/10.1007/s11219-022-09589-y
9. Garcia-Alonso, J.M., Rojo, J., Valencia, D., Moguel, E., Berrocal, J., Murillo, J.M.: Quantum software as a service through a quantum API gateway. IEEE Internet Comput. **26**(1), 34–41 (2021)

About Lightweight Code Generation

Andreas Schmidt[1,2]([⊠]) [ID]

[1] Karlsruhe Institute of Technology, Karlsruhe, Germany
andreas.schmidt@kit.edu
[2] University of Applied Sciences, Karlsruhe, Germany

Abstract. There is often something mystical about code generation [1]. This is partly due to tools, that are able to achieve a high degree of generation thanks to their flexibility and universality, but this also makes the tools extremely complex and restricts their use to suitably trained persons. This also applies to the OMG's "Model Driven Architecture" approach, which has tried to establish a standard in this field and to enable the exchange between different tools through additional technologies. A "code generation light" approach, which would often be sufficient in many cases, is difficult to implement with these tools.

In principle, however, getting started with code generation is actually quite simple. Only two things are needed: (1) a model that describes the application to be realized, and (2) a template, which transforms the model into code.

In the simplest case, the model can consist of a series of statements in an ASCII file, or of an object graph over which the template iterates. This provides a clear separation between the semantic aspects (model) and the technical aspects (template).

This tutorial will introduce lightweight generator technologies that can easily integrated into your own software development process and delegate tedious, monotonous programming tasks to the code-generator, so that you can concentrate on the more demanding and interesting programming tasks. For this reason, a number of different software generator technologies and their functional principles will be presented and how they can be realized with minimal effort. The tutorial also includes practical parts in which the participants perform a series of concrete tasks in the sphere of software code-generation.

Keywords: Code generator · Lightweight-code-generation-approach · Software-development process

1 Introduction

The general functionality of a generator is shown in Fig. 1. The generator receives as input an abstract model of the application to be realized as well as transformation rules describing the transformation of the abstract model into the target source-code. In simple cases, the transformation rules can also be hardcoded and integrated into the generator, or in more complex cases, also several transformation steps can be performed up to the final generation of the source-code. The input model is formal and abstracts from the implementation details of the target platform. Depending on the target platform,

T. Di Noia et al. (Eds.): ICWE 2022, LNCS 13362, pp. 497–500, 2022.
https://doi.org/10.1007/978-3-031-09917-5_43

the generated code is then interpreted or in a further transformation step compiled and afterwards executed.

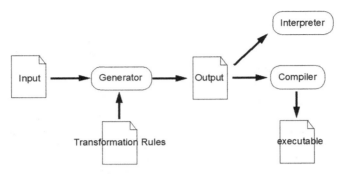

Fig. 1. Generator principle.

2   Model and Transformation Rules

This is the part where our lightweight approach deviates most from the OMG's Model Driven Architecture approach. Instead of relying on additional and complex technologies like UML, XMI, and MOF [2], the approach followed here uses a simple template mechanism and a model representation "suited" to the problem. So for example, our model can be represented by a piece of programing code, simple text which is easily parsable with regular expressions or an object-net, generated by a number of API calls. Figure 2 shows two possible representations of the same model, representing the entities "Film" and "Person" with a 1:n relationship, representing the director of a film, in between. Of course, if needed, more complex mechanisms like an own domain specific language (DSL) parsed by an own parser like a combination of lex, & yacc [3] or antlr [4] can be used. But this is outside the scope of this tutorial.

```php
<?php

    include 'MetaModel.class.php';

    $mod = MetaModel::createModel('FilmDB');

    $film = $mod->addClass('Film');
    $film->addAttribute('title','String');
    $film->addAttribute('year', 'Integer');
    $film->addRelation('director', 1,
                       $person, 'is_director');

    $person = $mod->addClass('Person');
    $person->addAttribute('name','String');
    $person->addAttribute('birthdate','Date');
    $person->addRelation('directed_films', MANY,
                       $film, 'is_director');
```

```
<Film(title:String,
      year:Integer,
      actors:array(Person),
      director:Person)>

<Person(name:String,
        birthdate:date,
        films:array(Film),
        directed_films:array(Film))>
```

(a) API-based   (b) Text-based

Fig. 2. Different representation forms of the same model.

3   Structure of the Tutorial

As starting point, a so-called scaffolding process is used, as it is offered by a number of web development frameworks. Scaffolding refers to the automatic generation of software artifacts around access to databases, such as database access layer, REST API, user interfaces, etc. Within this context, the underlying concepts of the model-driven software development process such as models, meta-models, transformation rules, templates, etc. are introduced and exemplified in the context of the implementation of a simple, but generally valid scaffolding approach. For this purpose, an existing application is analyzed and its underlying source code is broken down into its components according to the approach of Stahl and Völter [5]. In Fig. 3 the code is partitioned into the generic part, the schematic part, and the individual part. While the generic and the individual part, representing the application logic, is not of interest for us, we focus on the schematic part of the code. For this part, we have to extract an appropriate model, containing all the information necessary to be able to formulate transformation rules for the generation of this code. Additionally, the transformation rules (the templates), have to be implemented.

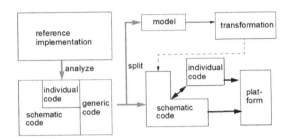

Fig. 3. General concept of model driven software development (from [2]).

The tutorial also includes a series of practical exercises where participants can practically intensify what they have learned. See Sect. 4 and 6 for a description of the necessary software.

4   Utilized Tools

Instead of using a specialized tool like EMF [6], our lightweight approach uses a scripting language in interaction with Regular Expressions [7] and additional shell commands. We start from scratch, and write our own generator tool with minimal effort, but maximum fit to our problem. We use PHP [8] as the language of choice in this tutorial, because of its integrated template engine, which can easily be used for the formulation of our transformation rules without the need of supplementary libraries. Additionally, Regular Expression play an important rule for parsing the provided model information.

5   Learning Objectives

The aim of the tutorial is to familiarize the participants with the principle concepts of code generation and how easily these concepts can used in many software development projects. After the tutorial, the participants will be able to recognize automation potential in their software development process and develop their own generators based on scripting languages. By building a generator "from scratch", the focus is on the important components and how they interact, so that a deeper understanding of the functionality is gained than if only a concrete tool with a specific GUI will been presented.

6   Software Requirements for the Hands-On Part

- PHP Interpreter (download and install from [9]).
- BASH-Shell:

  - Unix and Mac users: none, the needed tools are already part of your distribution
  - Windows users: Please download and install cygwin [10] on your computer.

7   Intended Audience

Software developers and programmers. Knowledge of regular expressions and PHP are helpful but not essential.

References

1. Schmidt, A., Kimmig, D., Bittner K., Dickerhof, M.: Teaching model-driven software development: revealing the great miracle of code generation to students. In: Whalley, J. (eds.) Proceedings of the Sixteenth Australasian Computing Education Conference Auckland 2016, pp. 97–104, ACM (2014)
2. Franke, D.S.: Model Driven Architecture (OMG): Applying MDA to Enterprise Computing. Wiley, Hoboken (2010)
3. Levine, J.R., Mason, T., Brown, D.: Lex & Yacc. O'Reilly, Sebastopol (1992)
4. Terence, P.: The Definitive ANTLR 4 Reference, 2nd edn. Pragmatic Bookshelf, Raleigh (2013)
5. Stahl, T., Völter, M.: Model-Driven Software Development: Technology, Engineering, Management. Wiley, Chichester (2006)
6. Steinberg, D., Budinsky, F., Paternostro, M., Merks, E.: EMF: Eclipse Modeling Framework, 2nd edn. Addison-Wesley, Boston (2008)
7. Friedl, J.: Mastering Regular Expressions: Understand Your Data and Be More Productive. O'Reilly Inc., UK (2006)
8. Sklar, D.: Learning PHP. O'Reilly Inc., UK (2016)
9. PHP Download page. https://www.php.net/downloads.php. Accessed 3 May 2022
10. Cygwin Homepage. https://www.cygwin.com/. Accessed 3 May 2022

SPARQL Endpoints and Web API (SWApi)

Pasquale Lisena[1][(✉)][iD] and Albert Meroño-Peñuela[2]

[1] EURECOM, Sophia Antipolis, France
`pasquale.lisena@eurecom.fr`
[2] King's College London, London, UK
`albert.merono@kcl.ac.uk`

Abstract. The success of Semantic Web technology has boosted the publication of Knowledge Graphs in the Web of Data, and several technologies to access them have become available covering different spots in the spectrum of expressivity: from the highly expressive SPARQL to the controlled access of Linked Data APIs, with GraphQL in between. Many of these technologies have reached industry-grade maturity. Finding the trade-offs between them is often difficult in the daily work of developers, interested in quick API deployment and easy data ingestion. This tutorial covers this in-between technology space, with the main goal of providing strategies and tools for publishing Web APIs that ensure the easy consumption of data coming from SPARQL endpoints. Together with an overview of state-of-the-art technologies, the tutorial focuses on two novel technologies: SPARQL Transformer, which allows to get a more compact JSON structure for SPARQL results, decreasing the effort required by developers in interfacing JavaScript and Python applications; and grlc, an automatic way of building APIs on top of SPARQL endpoints by sharing queries on collaborative platforms. Moreover, recent developments are presented to combine the two, offering a complete resource for developers and researchers. Hands-on sessions are proposed to internalise those concepts with practical exercises.

Keywords: API · Semantic Web · Web Development

1 Introduction

A crucial factor in the adoption of the Web of Data consists in the possibility of obtaining access to the published resources. However, this access is not always simple, constrained by languages and templates that are sub-optimal for application development. As a consequence, recent ongoing initiatives such as EasierRDF and LDFlex are strongly pushing the proposal of new solutions for making the Web of Data developer-friendly [2,5].

In order to bridge the gap between research and real-world applications, this tutorial intends to face two crucial problems in using data from the Semantic Web and Knowledge Graphs. First, going beyond the standard output of

© Springer Nature Switzerland AG 2022
T. Di Noia et al. (Eds.): ICWE 2022, LNCS 13362, pp. 501–504, 2022.
https://doi.org/10.1007/978-3-031-09917-5_44

SPARQL triple-stores, we show solutions for aggregating data, parsing, and give to the output a ready-to-use JSON structure. Second, we discuss how to detach SPARQL queries from the application logic, wrapping them in convenient Web APIs automatically.

The goal of this tutorial is to give participants sufficient knowledge for:

1. understanding the landscape of mature, production-ready and industry-grade technological solutions for publishing Web APIs on top of RDF datasets;
2. republishing RDF data through Web APIs, to increase the use and adoption of RDF datasets, even outside the Semantic Web community;
3. retrieving data from SPARQL endpoints in a more practical format to be used in small proofs-of-concept, living software or interactive notebooks (i.e. Jupyter), minimising the effort for accessing data.

2   Detailed Description

This half-day tutorial is decomposed into two parts, consisting each of slides and hands-on exercises:

- The first part focuses on data reshaping and merging. After summarising the main issues related to RDF data consumption by developers, we introduce different solutions coming from the literature, such as RDFJS [1], LDflex [11], GraphQL-based strategies [10] and others. We then explain the fundamentals of SPARQL Transformer [6,7] and present in-depth details about its querying and templating features, its parsing capabilities, and its merging strategy, giving to the audience a complete picture of the library. Examples of usage in JavaScript and Python are shown. Some hands-on exercises are proposed in order to make the public play with the application, making use of the SPARQL Transformer playground.
- The second part covers the publication of Web APIs on top of SPARQL endpoints. Different specifications - e.g. smartAPI [4], Linked Data API specification, OpenAPI - and services - e.g. BASIL [3] - for describing RESTful APIs are introduced to the audience. Then, we show the grlc application [8] and explain the different parts of the framework: the GitHub repository, the self-generated UI and the automatically exposed API. The attendees are then guided to publish their own API in the second hands-on session. Finally, we introduce the integration of SPARQL Transformer in grlc and we conclude the tutorial with a summary of the covered topics.

3   Intended Audience and Level

This tutorial is directed to anyone who works with RDF data and SPARQL, and in particular is interested in providing quick access to the data and/or Web APIs on top of them. We assume that most participants are familiar with basic Semantic Web technologies (RDF, SPARQL), have some developer experience (e.g. JSON), and have some notions of HTTP and REST APIs. The tutorial aims to provide them a general know-how and practical information for developing Web APIs on top of SPARQL endpoints.

For the hands-on session, the participants are expected to use a personal computer with a web browser installed; and to have a personal GitHub account (free).

4   Tutorial Material

The tutorial material consists of slides and pointers to online application, which is permanently available at https://api4kg.github.io/swapi-tutorial/, with the main pointers summarised in Table 1.

Table 1. List of resources used for the Tutorial

Resource	Web Address
Tutorial Website	https://api4kg.github.io/swapi-tutorial
SPARQL Transformer	https://github.com/D2KLab/sparql-transformer
Playground	https://d2klab.github.io/sparql-transformer/
grlc	https://github.com/CLARIAH/grlc
Demo	http://grlc.io/

An extended presentation of the topics introduced in the tutorial can be found in [9].

5   Biography of Presenters

Pasquale Lisena (http://pasqlisena.github.io/) is a researcher in the Data Science department at EURECOM, Sophia Antipolis (France), working on Knowledge Graphs and information extraction in the domain of digital humanities. He obtained his PhD in Computer Science from Sorbonne University of Paris in 2019, with a thesis on music representation and recommendation under the supervision of Raphaël Troncy. He was part of several national and international project, such as DOREMUS, SILKNOW and Odeuropa, actively contributing in developing domain-specific knowledge graphs and realising knowledge-driven AI technologies. His experiences include tutorials in conferences of the field (K-CAP 2017, ESWC 2018 and 2021, ISWC 2020, TheWebConf 2021). He is teaching in the Engineering program at EURECOM as assistant teaching in the Web Interaction course and as main lecturer in the Introduction to Data Bases course.

Albert Meroño Peñuela (https://www.albertmeronyo.org/) is an Assistant Professor in Computer Science at King's College London, and works on Knowledge Graph construction, access, and use in digital humanities workflows, where he has built large (>10 billion triples) Knowledge Graphs for history and musicology. Previously he has been a postdoctoral researcher at the Knowledge Representation & Reasoning group of the Vrije Universiteit Amsterdam; the lead engineer for structured data in CLARIAH (https://clariah.nl/), a 32M EUR Dutch project for integrating Digital Humanities data; and has served in CLARIAH's Technical Board as coordinator of the LOD Interest Group. His automated Linked Data API construction methods (http://grlc.io) are today used in Elsevier, TNO, the eScience Center, and 3200 other users. He has been teaching BSc and MSc courses at the VU since 2013 on Knowledge Representation, AI, and Digital Humanities; and has supervised the BSc/MSc theses of 33 students.

References

1. Bergwinkl, T., Luggen, M., elf Pavlik, Regalia, B., Savastano, P., Verborgh, R.: Interface Specification: RDF Representation, Draft Report. Tech. rep. W3C (2017)
2. Booth, D., Chute, C.G., Glaser, H., Solbrig, H.: Toward Easier RDF. In: W3C Workshop on Web Standardization for Graph Data, Berlin (2019)
3. Daga, E., Panziera, L., Pedrinaci, C.: A basilar approach for building web APIS on top of SPARQL endpoints. In: Maleshkova, M., Verborgh, R., Stadtmüller, S. (eds.) Proceedings of the Third Workshop on Services and Applications over Linked APIs and Data, vol. 1359, pp. 22–32 (2015), http://oro.open.ac.uk/44026/, Co-located with the 12th Extended Semantic Web Conference (ESWC 2015)
4. Dumontier, M., et al.: smartAPI: towards a more intelligent network of Web APIs. In: Proceedings of the 25th conference on Intelligent Systems for Molecular Biology and the 16th European Conference on Computational Biology (2017)
5. Gandon, F., et al.: Graph data on the web: extend the pivot don't reinvent the wheel. In: W3C Workshop on Web Standardization for Graph Data, Berlin (2019)
6. Lisena, P., Meroño-Peñuela, A., Kuhn, T., Troncy, R.: Easy web API development with SPARQL transformer. In: 18th International Semantic Web Conference (ISWC), in-use Track, Auckland, pp. 454–470 (2019). https://doi.org/10.1007/978-3-030-30796-7_28
7. Lisena, P., Troncy, R.: Transforming the JSON output of SPARQL queries for linked data clients. In: WWW'18 Companion: The 2018 Web Conference Companion. ACM, Lyon (2018). https://doi.org/10.1145/3184558.3188739
8. Meroño-Peñuela, A., Hoekstra, R.: grlc makes GitHub taste like linked data APIs. In: Sack, H., Rizzo, G., Steinmetz, N., Mladenić, D., Auer, S., Lange, C. (eds.) ESWC 2016. LNCS, vol. 9989, pp. 342–353. Springer, Cham (2016). https://doi.org/10.1007/978-3-319-47602-5_48
9. Meroñ-Peñuela, A., Lisena, P., MartÂnez-Ortiz, C.: Web data APIS for knowledge graphs: easing access to semantic data for application developers. Synth. Lect. Data Semant. Knowl. **12**(1), 1–118 (2021). https://doi.org/10.2200/S01114ED1V01Y202107DSK021
10. Taelman, R., Vander Sande, M., Verborgh, R.: Bridges between GraphQL and RDF. In: W3C Workshop on Web Standardization for Graph Data, Berlin (2019)
11. Verborgh, R., Taelman, R.: LDflex: a read/write linked data abstraction for front-end web developers. In: Pan, J.Z., et al. (eds.) ISWC 2020. LNCS, vol. 12507, pp. 193–211. Springer, Cham (2020). https://doi.org/10.1007/978-3-030-62466-8_13

Web Engineering
with Human-in-the-Loop

Dmitry Ustalov⬛, Nikita Pavlichenko⬛, Boris Tseytlin[(✉)]⬛,
Daria Baidakova, and Alexey Drutsa

Toloka, Lucerne, Switzerland
{dustalov,pavlichenko,btseytlin,dbaidakova,adrutsa}@toloka.ai

Abstract. Modern Web applications employ sophisticated Machine Learning models to rank news, posts, products, and other items presented to the users or contributed by them. To keep these models useful, one has to constantly train, evaluate, and monitor these models using freshly annotated data, which can be done using crowdsourcing. In this tutorial we will present a portion of our six-year experience in solving real-world tasks with human-in-the-loop pipelines that combine efforts made by humans and machines. We will introduce data labeling via public crowdsourcing marketplaces and present the critical components of efficient data labeling. Then, we will run a practical session, where participants address a challenging real-world Information Retrieval for e-Commerce task, experiment with selecting settings for the labeling process, and launch their label collection project on real crowds within the tutorial session. We will present useful quality control techniques and provide the attendees with an opportunity to discuss their annotation ideas. Methods and techniques described in this tutorial can be applied to any crowdsourced data and are not bound to any specific crowdsourcing platform.

1 Introduction

Web engineers have to carefully improve and productionize Machine Learning models by gathering and annotation large amounts of data, which can be achieved using crowdsourcing. The goal of our tutorial is to bridge the gap between Web Engineering and Human-in-the-Loop by demonstrating how one can successfully improve a Web application or Web service by obtaining high-quality relevance judgements from a crowdsourcing marketplace.

2 Definition of Intended Audience

We expect that the audience has a minimal understanding of how ranking on the Web works, so our tutorial will address an audience with various backgrounds and interests. We do not require specific prerequisite knowledge or skills, and we will provide all the necessary icebreakers during the introduction.

© Springer Nature Switzerland AG 2022
T. Di Noia et al. (Eds.): ICWE 2022, LNCS 13362, pp. 505–508, 2022.
https://doi.org/10.1007/978-3-031-09917-5_45

Beginners will benefit from our introductory materials and step-by-step instructions on what to do to annotate the data and use the obtained labels in their Web application. Software Engineers will find helpful ready-to-go solutions and code examples to achieve their engineering goals. Researchers will dive deep into our presentation of computational methods for quality control. Practitioners will refine their experience of shipping large-scale data collection pipelines while we highlight the best practices and pitfalls. This should make our topic highly interesting for anyone who develops a Web service or software product based on machine learning. As a result, each attendee will learn how to construct a label collection pipeline, obtain high-quality labels under a limited budget, and avoid common pitfalls.

3   Overview of the Tutorial Structure

Since we have a practical part involving running data annotation tasks on one of the largest public crowdsourcing marketplaces that consumes a significant amount of time, we would like to organize our full-day tutorial according to the following schedule: Introduction to Crowdsourcing, Key Components for Efficient Data Collection, Hands-On Practice Session, Computational Quality Control, Final Remarks and Conclusion.

3.1   Introduction to Crowdsourcing

We will start with an introduction that includes crowdsourcing terminology and examples of tasks on crowdsourcing marketplaces. We will also demonstrate why crowdsourcing is becoming more popular in working with data on a large scale, showing successful crowdsourcing applications for Information Retrieval and e-Commerce, and describing current industry trends of crowdsourcing use.

3.2   Key Components for Efficient Data Collection

We will discuss quality control techniques that include approaches before task performance (selection of workers, education, and exam tasks), the ones during task performance (golden sets, motivation of workers, tricks to remove bots and cheaters), and approaches after task performance (post verification/acceptance, consensus between workers). We will share best practices, including critical aspects and pitfalls when designing instructions and interfaces for workers, vital settings in different types of templates, training and examination for workers selection, pipelines for evaluating the labeling process.

3.3   Hands-On Practice Session

We will conduct *a hands-on practice session*, which is the vital and the longest part of our tutorial. We will encourage the attendees to apply the techniques, and best practices learned during the first part of the tutorial. For this purpose, we let the attendees run their own crowdsourced Web Search Ranking Quality Evaluation for the e-Commerce pipeline on real crowd workers. As the *input* the attendees have snapshots of crawled documents from the Web and the corresponding search query formulations, as the *output* they should provide rankings of these documents w.r.t. the query using pairwise comparisons. The attendees will brainstorm the suitable Human-in-the-Loop pipeline for the given task and set up and launch the relevance judgement gathering project online on the real crowd. Since creating a project from scratch might be time-consuming, we propose that our attendees choose from the most popular pre-defined templates (e.g., text or picture input). We will also provide the attendees with pre-allocated accounts and datasets for annotation. By the end of the practice session, the attendees will learn to construct a functional pipeline for data collection and labeling, become familiar with one of the largest crowdsourcing marketplaces, and launch projects on their own.

3.4   Computational Quality Control

We will describe how to process the raw labels obtained from the crowdsourcing marketplace and transform these data into knowledge suitable for downstream applications. We will discuss the popular answer aggregation models in crowdsourcing, including methods for aggregating categorical responses (Dawid-Skene, GLAD, etc.) and pairwise comparisons (Bradley-Terry, NoisyBT, etc.). We will present Crowd-Kit, an open-source Python library implementing all these methods, and describe the end-to-end process to evaluate the Web ranking and search using the described Human-in-the-Loop technology. Also, we will show the useful datasets, software, and references for further studies and experiments.

3.5   Final Remarks and Conclusion

Finally, we will finish with analyzing obtained results from the launched projects. This step demonstrates the process of verification of collected rankings. Together with the attendees, we will analyze outcome label distribution, check worker quality and contribution, elaborate on budget control, detect possible anomalies and problems. We will then share practical advice, discuss pitfalls and possible solutions, ask the attendees for feedback on the learning progress, and answer final questions.

4   Conclusion

We believe that, by the end of the tutorial, attendees will be familiar with

- modern approaches to Web-scale ranking evaluation, including online and offline approaches
- practice of creating, configuring, and running data collection projects on real workers on one of the largest global crowdsourcing platforms

– advanced methods that allow to balance out between the quality and costs
– state-of-the-art techniques to control the annotation quality and to aggregate
  the annotation results.

References

1. Daniel, F., Kucherbaev, P., Cappiello, C., Benatallah, B., Allahbakhsh, M.: Quality
   control in crowdsourcing: a survey of quality attributes, assessment techniques, and
   assurance actions. ACM Comput. Surv. **51**(1), 7:1–7:40 (2018)
2. Ustalov, D., Pavlichenko, N., Losev, V., Giliazev, I., Tulin, E.: A general-purpose
   crowdsourcing computational quality control toolkit for python. In: The Ninth AAAI
   Conference on Human Computation and Crowdsourcing: Works-in-Progress and
   Demonstration Track (HCOMP 2021) (2021)
3. Zheng, Y., Li, G., Li, Y., Shan, C., Cheng, R.: Truth inference in crowdsourcing: is
   the problem solved? Proc. VLDB Endowm. **10**(5), 541–552 (2017)

Author Index

Aghaei, Sareh 237
Alvarado-Valiente, Jaime 493
Alvarez, Reynaldo 162, 465
Angele, Kevin 237
Auer, Sören 148

Baez, Marcos 383
Baidakova, Daria 505
Bakaev, Maxim 406
Banks, Vanessa 49
Berrocal, Javier 477
Bibbó Frau, Gabriel 469
Bossu, Remy 49
Both, Andreas 315
Božić, Bojan 300
Braun, Christoph H.-J. 487
Buffa, Michel 204

Canal, Carlos 477
Cappiello, Cinzia 383
Chang, Chia-Hui 117
Chao, Pingfu 66, 219
Chen, Lifu 66
Chen, Wei 219
Cheng, Zhenyu 341
Corby, Olivier 283
Cutrupi, Claudia M. 383

De Turck, Filip 481
Di Noia, Tommaso 455
Di Sciascio, Eugenio 375
Ding, Tianyu 31
Dong, Ruihai 3
Drutsa, Alexey 505
Duan, Dingyang 189
Duan, Liang 82
Dupont, Thomas 481

Fan, Li 341
Fang, Junhua 66, 219
Faraldo, Angel 469
Faron, Catherine 283
Fensel, Anna 237
Ferrlein, Sophie 177, 473

Flace, Giampaolo 375
Frasincar, Flavius 268

Gaedke, Martin 406
Gandon, Fabien 283
García-Alonso, José 477, 493
Garrigós, Irene 162, 450, 465
Geed, Kunal 268
Geng, Jinbu 341
Gessert, Felix 177, 473
Goethals, Tom 481
Gonz, Hector 450
González Diez, Hector Raúl 162
González-Mora, César 162, 465
Gorelova, Anastasiia 426
Grünewald, Elias 325
Gu, Ping 252

Han, Tianshuo 31
Haris, Muhammad 148
Hartmann, David 325
He, Ming 31
Heil, Sebastian 406
Heinrich, Paul 325
Hernández, Juan 477
Hurley, Neil 3

Ibrahimy, Mohammad Mustafa 417
Imran, Muhammad 49

Jagow, Johanna 406
Jin, Shuyuan 357

Käfer, Tobias 487
Kerckhove, Wannes 481
Kim, Jae-Yun 132
Kipke, Josefine 325

Lawlor, Aonghus 3
Li, Shuhao 341
Liang, Zhihong 82
Lin, Tzu-Ping 117
Lisena, Pasquale 501
Liu, An 66

Liu, Wei   16
Liu, Zhicheng   341
Lofù, Domenico   375
Longo, Luca   300
Lu, Jintian   357
Luna, Reynaldo Alvarez   450

Mancino, Alberto Carlo Maria   455
Matera, Maristella   383
Mazón, Jose-Norberto   162
Meliá, Santiago   426
Menin, Aline   204
Meroño-Peñuela, Albert   501
Michel, Franck   283
Moon, Soo-Mook   132
Mu, Nan   189
Muhammad, Khalil   3
Münch, Tobias   443
Murillo, Juan M.   477, 493

Nayak, Aparna   300
Normak, Peeter   417
Norta, Alex   417
Noviello, Pietro   375

Ofli, Ferda   49

Pallas, Frank   325
Pan, Zhicheng   219
Pan, Zhou   16
Panse, Fabian   177
Pasquale, Antonella   383
Pavlichenko, Nikita   505
Pazienza, Andrea   375
Pennington, Catherine   49
Perevalov, Aleksandr   315
Possaghi, Isabella   383
Pucci, Emanuele   383

Qazi, Umair   49
Qi, Zhiwei   82

Reilly-Morgan, Diarmuid O'   3
Ritter, Norbert   177, 473
Roch, Julien   49
Rojo, Javier   477
Romero-Álvarez, Javier   493
Roosmann, Rainer   443

Salzedo, Marco   375
Schmidt, Andreas   497
Sebrechts, Merlijn   481
Shen, Jiahui   189
Smyth, Barry   3
Sorino, Paolo   432
Spadone, Gianluca   383
Speicher, Maximilian   406
Springer, Thomas   101, 391
Stocker, Markus   148
Sun, Jiakun   357

Taelman, Ruben   481
Tikat, Maroua   204
Tragos, Elias   3
Truşcă, Maria Mihaela   268
Tseytlin, Boris   505

Ustalov, Dmitry   505

Vepsäläinen, Juho   437
Vitulano, Felice   375
Vogel, Lucas   101, 391
Volckaert, Bruno   481
Vuorimaa, Petri   437

Wang, Qinqin   3
Winckler, Marco   204
Wingerath, Wolfram   177, 473
Wittig, Annemarie   315
Wollmer, Benjamin   177, 473
Wu, Cheng-Ju   117
Wu, Yang   219

Xiao, Ruizhi   357

Yacoubi Ayadi, Nadia   283
Yang, Xiao   189
Yin, Jian   16
Yue, Kun   82

Zha, Daren   189
Zhang, Xiaotian   357
Zhang, Zhipeng   252
Zhao, Lei   219
Zhao, Pengpeng   66
Zubcoff, José   162, 450, 465